REDUCING GLOBAL POVERTY
PATTERNS OF POTENTIAL HUMAN PROGRESS
VOLUME 1

Copyright © 2009 Frederick S. Pardee Center for
International Futures, University of Denver

Published by Paradigm Publishers,
3360 Mitchell Lane, Suite E, Boulder, CO 80301, USA.
Paradigm Publishers is the trade name of
Birkenkamp & Company, LLC, Dean Birkenkamp,
President and Publisher.

Published on the Indian Subcontinent by Oxford
University Press India, 1 Jai Singh Road, Post Box 43,
New Delhi 110001 India.

Library of Congress Cataloging-in-Publication Data

Reducing global poverty / Barry B. Hughes ... [et al.].

p. cm.—(Patterns of potential human progress)

Includes bibliographical references and index.

ISBN 978-1-59451-639-9 (hardcover : alk. paper)
1. Poverty—Government policy.
2. Income distribution.
3. Globalization. I. Hughes, Barry, 1945–

HC79.P6R43 2008

339.4'6—dc22

2008023698

Cover design by Bounford.com
Designed and typeset by Bounford.com
Printed by Progress Press Co. Ltd., Malta

13 12 11 10 09   1 2 3 4 5

Picture credits

(Photos are from left to right):

Chapter 1	Chapter 5	Chapter 9
Roxolana Wynar	Lindsay McNicholas	Marc Sydnor
Anna Russo	Nicole Salamader	Joy Woelhart
Kirsten Benites	Anna Russo	Megan McGee

Chapter 2	Chapter 6	Chapter 10
Marc Sydnor	Joel Pruce	Marc Sydnor
Amy Watson	Laura Doss	Heather Adkinson
Roberto Fierro	Marc Sydnor	Shannon Duffy

Chapter 3	Chapter 7	
Sarah McCune	Marc Sydnor	
Shelley Siman	Leah Berry	
Marc Sydnor	Marc Sydnor	

Chapter 4	Chapter 8	
Marc Sydnor	Eric Reiff	
Megan McGee	Marc Sydnor	
Mohammad Holil	Pilipino Navarro	

Cover Art

The cover art, an oil painting by Margaret Lawless, represents a
world populated by individuals with very different incomes and life
situations, most of whom are poor and very large numbers of whom
suffer great poverty. Its images represent differing segments of the
world's population, the dynamism of movement within and between
them, the disruptive character of transition, and the uncertainty of
the future even for those who attain economic well-being.

Although poverty brings degradation and even death, the painting
captures our fundamental belief that all humans deserve treatment
that draws attention to their basic dignity and beauty. That belief
has influenced also our choice of pictures throughout this volume,
even though we could have chosen very painful images of the
affects of poverty.

The S-curve of the hillside behind the three abstract figures suggests
the character of multiple and interacting global human transitions,
of which the movement from poverty to well-being is only one.
The transformation of the global human condition to long-term,
sustainable well-being encompasses many such transitions, which
are therefore a pervasive theme and image of work from the
Frederick S. Pardee Center for International Futures.

REDUCING GLOBAL POVERTY
PATTERNS OF POTENTIAL HUMAN PROGRESS

VOLUME 1

Barry B. Hughes • Mohammod T. Irfan • Haider Khan
Krishna B. Kumar • Dale S. Rothman • José R. Solórzano

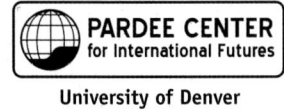

PARDEE CENTER
for International Futures

University of Denver

Paradigm Publishers
Boulder • London

OXFORD
UNIVERSITY PRESS

Oxford University Press India
New Delhi

Preface

This is the first in a series of volumes that explore prospects for human development— how development appears to be unfolding globally and locally, how we would like it to evolve, and how better to ensure that we move it in desired directions. The UN Development Programme's (UNDP) annual Human Development Report (HDR) heavily influenced this series. Although our volumes are totally independent from the HDRs, they share the UNDP's attention to different specific issues each year. In our case, however, the analyses are forward looking with a time horizon of fifty years further into the century, making the series something of an HDR plus fifty. The country-specific tables accompanying the volumes constitute the most extensive available set of long-term forecasts across multiple issues of human development.

Each volume will be global, long-term, and integrated in perspective across a wide range of human development systems (namely systems such as population growth, the spread of education, the advance of health, the growth of economies, and changes in governance patterns). This first volume focuses on poverty reduction, recognized in the Millennium Development Goals to be the foundational human development goal. The next will look at the future of global education, and the third will turn to prospects for global health.

The volumes emerge from the Frederick S. Pardee Center for International Futures at the University of Denver's Josef Korbel School of International Studies. The International Futures (IFs) modeling project has been dedicated for three decades to developing and using the strongest possible global, long-term, multiple issue capability for exploring the future of key global issues. At the core of the project is the IFs computer system, with an extensive database, forecasting capability, and scenario analysis assistance. IFs facilitates such analysis for 182 countries individually or in groupings, across demographic, economic, energy, agricultural, environmental, and sociopolitical issues.

The IFs system has been used in support of many forecasting projects, including those of the European Commission, the U.S. National Intelligence Council, and the UN Environment Programme. The partners of the IFs team in such projects have been numerous, as they are in this set of volumes. For example, cooperation with the RAND Corporation has been very important in developing this first volume.

Among the philosophical underpinnings of the IFs project are the beliefs that (1) prediction is impossible, but forecasting is necessary for understanding change and to support policy making; (2) analysis should always be built around alternative possible futures; and (3) the tools for forecasting should be fully open and transparent (IFs with Pardee is freely available to all users).

The long-term, global, and integrated multiple-issue characteristics of this series make the effort both unique and highly ambitious. A number of assumptions underlie our belief that it is time for such a set of volumes focused on a variety of human development systems.

First, human development systems are growing in scope and scale. Human numbers and incomes continue to rise, causing the extent of our interactions with each other and with our broader environment to grow rapidly. This does not mean that issues are necessarily becoming more fundamentally insurmountable than in past eras. It does mean, however, that attention to the issues must have a global perspective, as well as local and regional ones, and that the issues require an integrated perspective.

Second, change in human systems has accelerated. Although demographic growth is slowing, global economic growth has gradually risen, and sociopolitical change is extraordinarily rapid. One important ramification of the pace of change is that it has become more important to look further ahead and to anticipate where that change may be or could be taking us. A long-term perspective, as well as an integrated and global one, is required.

Third, goals and priorities for human systems are becoming clearer and are more frequently and consistently enunciated. For instance, the UN Millennium Summit and the 2002 conference in Johannesburg set specific goals for 2015, including many that focus on the human condition. Such goals are increasingly guiding a sense of collective human opportunity and responsibility.

Fourth, understanding of human systems has grown rapidly more sophisticated. With respect to data, the second half of the twentieth century was a period of explosion in human assessment of all the elements of sustainable development. It is remarkable to recall that at the middle of the twentieth century, the gross national product (GNP) was a relatively new measure and that the human database concerning worldwide individual life conditions, economic well-being, and social capacity was skimpy at best. Large-scale and consistent data collection has now characterized most of the world since about 1960 and has continued to improve. In addition, new concepts and measures linked to such data, such as the human development index, have emerged to tell us much about ourselves.

With respect to understanding the dynamics of our systems, progress has been equally rapid. Although it may sometimes be discouraging that debates about the drivers of economic growth, poverty reduction, and other change are so extensive and intense, any survey of the unfolding of development theory will quickly show the accumulation of insights. Windows into understanding the world condition have opened.

Fifth, and derivatively, the domain of human choice and action is broadening. Constructive action depends on being able to set goals, on being able to assess the condition of our environment, and on being able to anticipate the dynamics that might unfold with and without our action. As we have argued, each of these foundations of human action has strengthened.

Sixth, human development itself has increasingly given us new levers for action, should we choose to use them. These include the vast benefits of human development to date: the advance in the life conditions and individual capacity of so many, the growing wealth of humanity, the growth of our social capacity, and the expansion of a broad knowledge base. For instance, the recent emergence of new information and communication technologies has dramatically enriched the human ability to access existing knowledge, to develop and use networks for its application, and to accelerate creation of still more knowledge.

Seventh and finally, discussions and debates concerning the appropriateness of goals, the quality of measures, and the patterns of likely and possible development have emerged globally. There will probably always be metadebates around the need for conscious social choice and action to manage transitions (versus letting self-correcting systems function), as well as minidebates concerning the most appropriate tactics for accomplishing goals that have already been set. In the turmoil of those debates, we should not lose sight of the importance of their occurring at all.

Will humanity grasp its opportunities to build on these foundations and substantially enhance the global human condition in this century? Will we build a transition to sustainable development broadly defined to include human capacity development, social justice, and environmental sustainability? Our success in reducing poverty and in eliminating altogether the most egregious manifestations of it will be one key test. It is to that collective effort that we dedicate this volume.

Our success in reducing poverty is foundational to sustainable development.

Acknowledgments

The authors give special thanks to Frederick S. Pardee, who not only funded the development of this report but helped conceptualize the series that this volume initiates. In addition, he has generated a constant flow of ideas with respect to the subjects and structure of this volume, with special attention to the supporting data tables in the volume and online. It is often asserted that a volume would not exist without the contributions of a particular individual. In this instance, the contributions of Frederick Pardee were, in fact, absolutely essential.

The authors of the volume take both credit and responsibility for its ultimate content. We built, however, on tremendous foundations of work directed toward understanding and reducing global poverty. The hope that motivated our work was that this study would contribute something to that ongoing stream of effort.

The IFs simulation model, the core tool of this volume, has been developed over a great many years under the direction of Barry Hughes at the University of Denver. Thanks to the support of the University of Denver and the Frederick S. Pardee Center for International Futures, the complete system, including both a downloadable version and an online version, is available for all users at www.ifs.du.edu.

IFs, developed originally as an educational tool, owes much to the large number of students, instructors, and analysts who have used or reacted to the system over many years and provided much-appreciated advice for enhancement. It is impossible to name all those who have provided feedback and ideas, but they include John Agard, James Allan, Alan AtKisson, Robert Ayres, Steven Bankes, Gerald Barney, Christian Berg, Donald Borock, Mark Boyer, Peter Brecke, Stuart Bremer, Matthew Burrows, Jonathan Cave, Richard Chadwick, Claudio Cioffi-Revilla, Sam Cole, Tom Coyne, Mark Crescenzi, Thomas Cusack, Jim Dator, Paul Desanker, Pol Descamps, Karl Deutsch, Bert de Vries, James Dewar, William Dixon, Faye Duchin, Joan Eamer, Rich Engel, Thomas Ferelman, Martina Floerke, Miriam Galt, Siwa Msangi, Jay Gary, Ted Gordon, Paolo Guerrieri, Harold Guetzkow, Elizabeth Hanson, Jim Harris, Paul Herman, Henk Hilderink, Evan Hillebrand, Dennis Hodgson, Ronald Inglehart, Patrick James, Peter Johnston, Jari Kaivo-oja, Eric Kemp-Benedict, Ronald Kickert, Douglas Lemke, Paul Lucas, Jyrki Luukkanen, Pentti Malaska, Edward Mansfield, Mihajlo Mesarovic, Sergei Parinov, Robert Pestel, Dennis Pirages, Brian Pollins, Aromar Revi, Peter Rindfuss, Phil Schrodt, Paul Senese, Thomas Shook, Dale Smith, Harvey Starr, Jeff Staats, Douglas Stuart, Donald Sylvan, Thomas Tesch, William Thompson, Ildiko Tulbure, Matti Vainio, Eric Vardac, Bart Verspagen, Benjamin Warr, Ochola Washington, Brian Weatherford, Markku Wilenius, Paul Williamson, and Jonathan Wilkenfeld.

IFs team members who made special contributions to this volume include Jonathan Chesebro (data), Anwar Hossain (long-term data leadership), Julius Gatune (feedback and ideas), Jonathan Moyer (documentation and web support), and Marc Sydnor (project management on volume production). IFs team members who provided more general support include Kazi Imran Ahmed, Debasis Bhattacharya, Janet Dickson, Bethany Fisher, Sheila Flynn, Kia Tamaki Harrold, George Horton, Jaime Melendez, Edinson Oquendo, Cecilia Peterson, and Jay Thompson. Important earlier colleagues in the IFs project include Shannon Brady, Warren Cristopher, James Chung, Kay Drucker, Michael Ferrier, Richard Fuchs, Michael Niemann, Padma Padula, Terrance Peet-Lukes, and Jamal Waheed. Current and former personnel at the University of Denver who assisted in many varied ways include Chad Burnham, Cindy Crouch, Chris Grubb, Steve Hick, Mat Nau, Kenneth Stafford, Robert Stocker, and Phil Tripp.

Most recent funding for IFs comes from Frederick S. Pardee, the United Nations Environment Programme (as part of its Global Environment Outlook 4), and the U.S. National Intelligence Center (as part of its Project 2020: Mapping the Global Future and the emerging Project 2025). Other recent developments within International Futures have been funded in part by the TERRA project of the European

Commission, by the Strategic Assessments Group of the U.S. Central Intelligence Agency, and by the RAND Frederick S. Pardee Center for Longer-Range Global Policy and the Future of the Human Condition. In addition, the European Union Center at the University of Michigan provided support for enhancing the user interface and ease of use of the IFs system. Thanks also to the National Science Foundation, the Cleveland Foundation, the Exxon Education Foundation, the Kettering Family Foundation, the Pacific Cultural Foundation, the United States Institute of Peace, and General Motors for funding that contributed to earlier generations of IFs.

James Dewar, William Overholt, Howard Shatz, Brook Stearns, and Gregory Treverton of the RAND Corporation provided useful feedback specific to drafts of this volume, including some full manuscript reviews. At Paradigm Publishers, Jennifer Knerr, long-term editor and friend of the IFs project, was as always wonderfully helpful and supportive. And, once again, Melanie Stafford greatly helped bring things together.

Other than the authors, none of the named individuals or institutions bears any responsibility for the current status of the model or for the analysis presented here. Their support is nonetheless greatly appreciated—it takes a world to write such a volume.

Barry B. Hughes

Contents

List of Boxes

List of Figures

List of Maps

List of Tables

Abbreviations

ACC	Ahluwalia, Carter, and Chenery	MA	Millennium Ecosystem Assessment
AIDS	acquired immune deficiency syndrome	MDG	Millennium Development Goal(s)
BRICs	Brazil, Russia, India, and China	MER	market exchange rates
DOE	U.S. Department of Energy	MFP	multifactor productivity
DRC	Democratic Republic of the Congo	NAS	national account statistics
EIA	Energy Information Agency (of the US DOE)	NEPAD	New Partnership for Africa's Development
FDI	foreign direct investment	NGO	nongovernmental organization
FGT	Foster, Greer, and Thorbecke	OECD	Organization for Economic Cooperation and Development
G-7	Group of 7 (Canada, France, Germany, Italy, Japan, United Kingdom, United States)	PEI	Poverty and Environment Initiative
		PEP	Poverty-Environment Partnership
GDP	gross domestic product	PPP	purchasing power parity
GEO	Global Environment Outlook	R&D	research and development
GNI	gross national income	SAM	social accounting matrix
GSG	Global Scenario Group	SRES	Special Report on Emissions Scenarios
GTAP	Global Trade and Analysis Project	SSA	sub-Saharan Africa
GWP	gross world product	TI	Transparency International
HDI	human development index	UN	United Nations
HDR	Human Development Report	UNDP	United Nations Development Programme
HELI	Health and Environment Linkages Initiative	UNEP	United Nations Environment Programme
HIV	human immunodeficiency virus		
HPI	human poverty index	WCED	World Commission on Environment and Development
IBRD	International Bank for Reconstruction and Development (World Bank)	WDI	World Development Indicators
ICP	International Comparison Project	WEC	World Energy Council
IDA	International Development Association (World Bank)	WHO	World Health Organization
IEA	International Energy Agency		
IFI	international financial institution		
IFs	International Futures (modeling system)		
IIASA	International Institute for Applied Systems Analysis		
IMF	International Monetary Fund		
IISD	International Institute for Sustainable Development		
IPCC	Intergovernmental Panel on Climate Change		

Introduction

Global Poverty

Poverty, the inability to attain a "minimum" level of well-being, is the most fundamental economic and social problem facing humanity. In the extreme case, poverty actually kills people. Even when it does not kill, poverty is a basic deprivation that stunts the very possibility of human development. It is therefore stating the obvious to declare that the reduction and ultimately the eradication of poverty must be a central goal for the people on this planet.

Even before the widespread publicity associated with the Millennium Development Goals (MDGs) by the United Nations, global poverty was understood to be a somewhat intractable problem. World Bank documents in the 1970s and 1980s illustrate the many efforts to analyze the state of global poverty and many proposals to reduce global poverty. However, with the increased emphasis given to the goal of poverty reduction in the MDGs, the measurement of poverty and its speedy amelioration have now become central to the efforts of the entire global development community.

There are deep moral motivations for a commitment to poverty reduction. To take one well-known approach, the Rawlsian principle of justice as fairness leads directly to the consideration of the state of the poor and a commitment to improve their lives. More recently, the Nobel laureate Amartya Sen advanced an even broader concept. According to Sen's capabilities approach, a liberal society is committed to the equalization of capabilities that roughly correspond to one's ability to lead a human life with reasonable longevity, nutrition, health, and social functionings. The upshot of Sen's approach is also that we must seriously try to improve the conditions of the poor in this world.

The Character and Extent of Poverty

Poverty is not a single phenomenon with a simple foundation, invariant across geographic location and social condition. Poverty has many

There are deep moral motivations for a commitment to poverty reduction.

faces. Important aspects of the global poverty profile include its global distribution, the rural-urban divide, its gender aspect, and features specific to particular countries or regions such as the caste system in India.

The spatial nature of poverty

Using two standard measures of poverty, namely living on less than $1 or $2 per day, Table 1.1 shows World Bank data and forecasts across the economically less developed part of our world.

South Asia and sub-Saharan Africa have two of the largest concentrations of the poor. In the more than sixty years since the end of World War II, East Asia has undergone the greatest progress in reducing poverty. In the last thirty years, the People's Republic of China (PRC) has shown a remarkable reduction in poverty also, although in absolute numbers China still has a large number of poor people.

More specifically, approximately 1 billion people globally lived on less than $1 per day

Table 1.1 World Bank data and forecasts of poverty

| | Millions of persons living on | | | | | |
| | Less than $1 per day | | | Less than $2 per day | | |
Region or country	1990	2004	2015	1990	2004	2015
East Asia and the Pacific	476	169	40	1,113	684	296
China	374	128	29	819	452	186
Rest of East Asia and the Pacific	102	41	11	294	232	110
South Asia	479	446	256	954	1,116	997
India	376	371	217	734	868	772
Rest of South Asia	103	76	39	220	248	226
Europe and Central Asia	2	4	2	20	46	16
Middle East and North Africa	5	4	2	49	59	38
Sub-Saharan Africa	240	298	290	396	522	567
Latin America and the Caribbean	45	47	34	115	121	102
Total	*1,247*	*970*	*624*	*2,647*	*2,548*	*2,017*
Excluding China	*873*	*841*	*595*	*1,828*	*2,096*	*1,831*

| | Percentage of the population living on | | | | | |
| | Less than $1 per day | | | Less than $2 per day | | |
Region or country	1990	2004	2015	1990	2004	2015
East Asia and the Pacific	29.8	9.1	2.0	69.7	36.6	14.5
China	33.0	9.9	2.1	72.2	34.9	13.4
Rest of East Asia and the Pacific	22.1	7.1	1.6	63.7	40.4	16.9
South Asia	43.0	30.8	15.1	85.7	77.1	59.0
India	44.3	34.3	17.6	86.4	80.4	62.7
Rest of South Asia	38.9	20.6	8.5	83.4	67.6	49.2
Europe and Central Asia	0.5	0.9	0.3	4.3	9.8	3.4
Middle East and North Africa	2.3	1.5	0.7	21.7	19.7	10.3
Sub-Saharan Africa	46.7	41.1	31.4	77.1	72.0	61.5
Latin America and the Caribbean	10.2	8.6	5.5	26.3	22.2	16.3
Total	*28.7*	*18.1*	*10.2*	*60.8*	*47.6*	*32.9*
Excluding China	*27.1*	*20.7*	*12.6*	*56.8*	*51.6*	*38.7*

Source: World Bank 2008: 46 (Table 1.5).

in 2004, and more than 2.5 billion or half of all those in low- and middle-income countries lived on less than $2 per day. Although there has been limited reduction in those numbers since 1990 (none at all at $2 per day), the percentages have declined significantly, and the World Bank anticipates substantial further decline by 2015. In fact, the Bank expects the percentage of those living on less than $1 per day to have been cut by almost two-thirds between 1990 and 2015. Clearly, the extremely rapid reduction of poverty in China greatly influences broader trends. In India the numbers of the poorest fell little in the 1990s, but Thailand and Vietnam (not shown) achieved significant reductions.[1] And sub-Saharan Africa has experienced much smaller reductions since 1990 in the percentage living on less than $1 or $2 and, in fact, has seen substantial growth in the numbers of people living at those levels.

In addition to region of the world, urban/rural location affects the likelihood of living in poverty. The UN calculated that the urban share of global population reached 50 percent in 2007. In developing countries, however, the portion of the population in urban areas is closer to 40 percent, with the 50 percent number to be reached in about 2020.[2] Poverty is, however, disproportionately a rural phenomenon, and only about 30 percent of the world's poor live in urban areas (Ravallion 2001b: 2). Poverty will likely become predominantly an urban phenomenon as urban population growth outpaces that in rural areas. Martin Ravallion forecast that the urban share of poverty will reach 40 percent in 2020 and 50 percent about 2035 (when the urban population share reaches 61 percent).

The social nature of poverty

Subpopulations within societies differ significantly in their poverty levels. Both case studies (Agarwal, Humphries and Robeyns 2005; Nussbaum and Glover 1995) and empirical analyses (UN ECLAC 2005: 44–45) indicate that being female makes one more vulnerable to poverty.

One of the distressing manifestations of poverty and gender inequality is the phenomenon of excess mortality and artificially lower survival rates of women in many parts of the world. This phenomenon is known as "missing women" (Sen 1992b). In the United States and Europe, there tend to be more women than men in the total population, with a female-male ratio of 1.05. One reason is that women are biologically "hardier" than men and, given equal care, survive better. The situations in the developed West and in less developed nations reveal a sharp contrast. The contrast is especially grim in parts of Asia and North Africa, where the female-male ratio can be as low as 0.95. Using the Western ratio as the benchmark, approximately 100 million women worldwide appear to be "missing." Even adjusted measures with other benchmarks suggest that the number is roughly 60 million.[3]

The effects of income poverty and various dimensions of social exclusion upon the lives of individuals and subpopulations overlap and interact. A further element of vulnerability comes from being in the wrong segment of a status-hierarchical society. One example of this is the caste system in India. Particularly in rural areas, the intersection of gender and caste can make a woman very vulnerable, as the following example so movingly illustrates:

"I may die, but I still cannot go out. If there's something in the house, we eat. Otherwise, we go to sleep." So Metha Bai, a young widow with two young children in Rajasthan, India, described her plight as a member of a caste whose women are traditionally prohibited from working outside the home—even when, as here, survival itself is at issue. If she stays at home, she and her children may die shortly. If she attempts to go out, her in-laws will beat her and abuse her children (Nussbaum and Glover 1995: 1).

Like gender, age often shapes poverty rates, with the young and old suffering disproportionately. Ethnic differences within countries also commonly coincide with considerable differences in poverty levels. For instance, indigenous populations typically have rates of poverty that are multiples of the rates in European settler populations, as do the descendents of imported slaves. An extreme example is Paraguay, where the rate is nearly 8 to 1 (UN ECLAC 2005: 49).

This report will not be able to forecast poverty specifically for social subgroups, and its differentiation of poverty will be overwhelmingly structured by the borders of

Subpopulations within societies differ significantly in their poverty levels.

countries. Moreover, it will focus heavily upon the income bases of poverty. It is important, nonetheless, to recognize the complex social character of poverty around the world.

Why This Report?

The phenomenon of global poverty is the fundamental issue of global development, and a web search on "poverty" brings up over 50 million cyber addresses. One might therefore reasonably conclude that enough has been and is being done by others. Yet there are several remarkably large deficiencies in the huge body of studies and policy analyses on poverty. First, partly because of the time horizon of 2015 identified by the Millennium Development Goals, and in spite of the very long horizon of many interventions to reduce poverty, little analysis explores the longer-term human future on this critical issue. Second, global analyses of poverty typically do not cover regions of continents, much less individual countries. It is critical, however, to be able to explore the spatial dimension of poverty broadly. Third, there is a natural tendency for analysts and institutions to focus on specific, targeted interventions for several reasons: (1) sometimes because they are seen as "silver bullets"; (2) sometimes because of scholars' knowledge of or familiarity with the research terrain; and, more fundamentally, (3) because it is critical that we understand the different implications of various interventions. A much smaller portion of analysis explores a wide range of interventions, however, both singly and in comparison and in combination.

The need for a long horizon

Poverty will not disappear by 2015, even when defined with a bar as low as an income of just $1 per day for each individual. If the MDG of reducing the rate of poverty in the developing world by half between 1990 and 2015 were met but not exceeded, there would still be nearly 890 million people living on less than that amount. And although there is substantial consensus that the goal will likely be met and even exceeded globally, it will almost certainly not be met in sub-Saharan Africa.

We thus need to think beyond 2015, as well as maintaining and strengthening our efforts through that year. As humans, we understandably tend to be impatient. We want

to see change in our lifetime so that we and our families and communities can benefit from it. Yet much sociopolitical change is slow. Payoffs for investment often accrue to successor generations, sometimes the children of those who act, but often their grandchildren and even great-grandchildren. In addition, changes often require sequencing. Thus shorter-term and longer-term horizons are essential.

It is also important to understand that, as critical as the reduction of poverty may be, it is not the only high-priority human goal. When historians of the future look back on the twenty-first century, hopefully they will be able to look at it in terms of a long, broad sustainability transition. That transition is likely to be defined, much as it already is today, in terms of individual human development (including poverty reduction and the development and exercise of human capabilities), social development (including the expansion of human participation in governance and social decision making on the basis of justice and fairness), and a sustainable relationship between humanity and its broader environment. The positioning of poverty as one aspect of this larger transition is another reason that both longer-term and near-term perspectives are needed.

The importance of maintaining global and country-specific perspectives

The global assault on poverty requires simultaneous attention to multiple levels of analysis. Global and continental perspectives help us to grasp the magnitude of the problem, to understand trends, and to begin to speculate about the appropriate interventions. Although some action against poverty is clearly being undertaken at the global level, most of it remains at and within individual countries.

This study crosses levels of analysis. Earlier chapters devote more attention to the global and continental level. Chapter 7 begins to explore regions within continents, and Chapter 8 dives into such regions, individual countries, and even subregions of countries. Most important, for those who have specific country interests, the forecast tables at the end of the volume provide an extensive set of variables for mapping poverty and human well-being more generally.

It is unique to analyze poverty in the long term and at global and country-specific levels, with attention to multiple possible interventions.

The value of a deep and integrated look at poverty drivers

The transitions that have essentially eliminated the most extreme poverty in the rich countries of the world were broad and complex. The long and very substantial rise of incomes was clearly the key proximate driver of success, but stating that gives us little real insight.

Perhaps it was the introduction of widespread use of soap and other sanitation measures that set off the demographic transition and ultimately brought about the development of that portion of the world situated primarily around the North Atlantic. Perhaps it was the adoption of legal systems and the protection of property that triggered economic growth. Perhaps it was the invention of the stirrup or oxen harnesses, allowing the plowing of heavy soils. Perhaps it was the interaction of European peoples with others on the same latitudes, facilitating the diffusion of agricultural technology (a là Diamond 1997).

Perhaps, and actually most likely, it was a combination of many factors. Analysis of the prospects for global poverty reduction similarly requires attention to a broad range of forces, not simply the increase in income or changes in its distribution, but the deep drivers that give rise to both of those and also to demographic change that obviously helps immediately frame the number and characteristics of the poor.

Integrated methodology

There are many possible and useful ways of studying complex, integrated change over a long time horizon, including historical analysis and immersion in particular cultural environments. In this volume we have looked to the accumulated theoretical and empirical knowledge about the drivers of change and turned to an integrated computer simulation of global change as a principal tool for analysis.

The International Futures (IFs) simulation is a computer system that represents the structures of global demographic, economic, and sociopolitical systems and their interaction, with additional detail on agricultural, energy, education, health and (to a more limited extent), environmental systems. It provides detail for 182 countries. An extensive database supports the model. IFs is available for web-based use or for download,

so that the analyses in this volume can be replicated, amended, or extended.

Computer models have great limitations, which the next section will elaborate. At the same time, however, they have substantial strengths. They explicitly and formally represent assumptions about relationships. In the case of IFs, users of the system can quite flexibly change such assumptions. Such changes allow policy analysts to simulate interventions or experiments and explore their primary and secondary consequences. Using IFs, such explorations can extend to midcentury, well beyond the meaningful range of simple extrapolative analysis or regression models.

The IFs system makes it possible to explore not just the obvious linkages between poverty and its proximate drivers of economic and population growth and distribution. It is also possible to drill down into the deep drivers, including the development of human capital (education and health), the character and effectiveness of governance, and knowledge extension and diffusion.

Caveats and Cautions

There are, of course, limitations to our study. Caution needs to be exercised in interpreting poverty forecasts for several reasons.

Conflicts over poverty conceptualization

As Chapter 2 will discuss in greater detail, there is no universally accepted definition of poverty. Although income- or consumption-based measures are the most commonly used, many would prefer the broader "capabilities"-based approach of Sen (1984, 1999). The World Bank (1980, p. 32) defined extreme poverty even more broadly as a "condition of life so characterized by malnutrition, illiteracy, and disease as to be beneath any reasonable definition of human decency."

Within the income- and consumption-based measures, poverty can be measured in an absolute sense (for instance, those earning less than $1 per day) or a relative sense (for example, those earning less than a third of the average for the country). In each case, the poverty lines can be drawn at very different levels. Even though the absolute $1-per-day poverty measure has gained widespread usage, including extensive attention in this report, it

A methodology combining historical analysis and computer simulation of change supports this volume.

Conceptual, data, and model limitations reduce confidence in forecasting.

is by no means the best possible or universally accepted measure.

Despite limitations, the $1-per-day measure is easily quantifiable and calculable and allows ready comparison with estimates from other sources. We therefore use it as our benchmark measure but also selectively present absolute poverty measures with $2, $5, and $10 per day as the poverty line, look sometimes at the poverty gap (a measure capturing distribution more fully), and provide some information on other measures of human condition, such as life expectancy and education.

Data and measurement limitations

Chapter 2 also discusses the controversies surrounding the data. Household surveys on expenditure and income across a sample of the population form the basis for poverty data. However, in very poor countries, average consumption levels determined by national surveys are in general lower than average consumption estimated from aggregate national accounts (country-level statistics that include total household consumption). As better-designed surveys and better data collection methods come into use, we hope that the discrepancy between the two will diminish. In the meantime, IFs uses survey data to set the initialize conditions and national income data to compute changes in poverty rates.

Over and beyond that, we have highly incomplete data concerning poverty on a more disaggregated basis—for instance, by gender, rural versus urban status, skilled versus unskilled, or chronic versus transient poverty. Our general knowledge of the preponderance of poverty within specific groups, such as the rural, the unskilled, women, and indigenous populations, somewhat mitigates this limitation. Yet availability of disaggregated data (and structural representations in the model based on them) would have allowed us to study specific policies to alleviate poverty for subpopulations.

Model limitations

To the best of our knowledge, IFs is the only large-scale integrated global modeling system of its kind that can be used as a thinking tool for the analysis of near-term through long-term country-specific, regional, and global futures across multiple, interacting policy areas. Its economic, political, demographic, social, and environmental modules can handle a wide variety of inputs and capture various interactions.

Despite these strengths, there is a limit to the number of interactions it can capture in detail. For instance, through governmental budget constraints it can capture the decreased availability of resources for health expenditures if more is spent on education. However, it cannot capture the improved political empowerment that the disadvantaged can get from education, allowing them to demand policies that are conducive to poverty reduction.

Limitations on interpretation

Perhaps the greatest caution needs to be exercised in the interpretation of the poverty reduction outcomes we present in tables and figures throughout this volume. Our preferred interpretation of these numbers is the following.

IFs is a model of the economic, social, political, and other forces that can affect the evolution of income, poverty, and similar variables. It is extensive but incomplete. Indeed, no model can be complete. For reasons of simplicity, tractability, and concern with larger issues, many aspects of the world and interactions among them have to be left out. In short, IFs is a thinking tool, not a predicting tool.

Therefore, the reader should view IFs results as providing *tendencies*—simulated outcomes that can give us an idea of how certain strategic interventions fare under the assumptions of the model—rather than *predictions* of how the world will really be. It would have been very difficult in the late 1970s, for example, for any person or model to predict the sudden takeoff in the Chinese and Indian economies in the 1980s and 1990s. These are noncontinuous changes that arise from a confluence of complex political, economic, and social factors. One can conduct a scenario exercise with IFs to study what poverty outcomes would be when one or more countries embark on such economic "miracles," but IFs cannot confidently anticipate such miracles in the first place.

The larger contextual process finds methodological resonance in the "calibration" and "simulation" strategy followed by the modern macroeconomic literature since the

1980s; for instance, see Edward C. Prescott (2006). In this approach, model builders calibrate parameters so that the model outcomes broadly match key observed data. They then test the model by comparing a few ancillary outcomes or time paths of variables with data not used in the original calibration of the model. A match here increases the confidence that the model indeed captures aspects of reality. A model is never truly validated but does accrue increasing credibility from the process (see Hughes 2006 with respect to IFs). Analysts then use the model to simulate the future of an economy or other systems. Often, they conduct "counterfactual" policy exercises, asking how the simulated outcome might look under policies different from the current ones. They often use simulated outcomes for comparing policy alternatives and for getting an idea of the order of magnitude of responsiveness. Again, the search is for tendencies rather than predictions.

Why do this exercise?

A natural question is why the exercise we conduct is useful despite the described limitations in conceptualization, data, model, and result interpretation. In brief, poverty reduction is an overarching imperative facing the world today. Poverty is such a complex and multifaceted problem that any study of it will necessarily fall short. However, given the seriousness of the problem, it is important to take the small but bold steps needed to tackle it. Our model and simulation-based approach is one such step, useful in exploring the evolution of poverty under alternate strategies and scenarios.

The errors of the analysis are unlikely to be so large as to render meaningless all mappings of poverty reduction strategies into likely futures. For instance, fifty years from now the number of poor people in sub-Saharan Africa will almost certainly be lower or higher than the estimate the model generates, but history is highly likely to vindicate its expectation that most of the poor people in the world will live in that region.

Research on poverty, like the extent of poverty itself, is continuously evolving and improving. New concepts, measurements, and research methodologies appear in the study of poverty on an ongoing basis, and studies such as

ours and the debates surrounding them can only aid this process.

Most importantly, there is an urgent need to explore the efficacy of the many poverty reduction strategies that have been proposed. Given the time it takes for these strategies to work and for results to become visible in the form of lower poverty figures, it is critical to take a long-term, future-oriented perspective in such an assessment. Our model and simulation approach allows us to look far enough into the future to be a useful step in this direction.

Road Map for This Volume

Simply put, we want in this volume to understand what poverty is and to be able to describe its character and magnitude. We want to understand what the range of possible human futures is with respect to poverty, given reasonable assumptions about changes in its key or proximate drivers. We want to identify strategies for its reduction and for the elimination of poverty in its most severe and life-threatening manifestations. And we want to explore the possible leverage that various individual interventions and more complex strategies might give us with respect to accelerating the reduction of poverty. Figure 1.1 portrays these desires and helps to structure the volume around them.

Chapter 2 discusses poverty in conceptual terms and considers how to measure it. Conceptually, important distinctions exist

In spite of its limitations, all policy action requires forecasting.

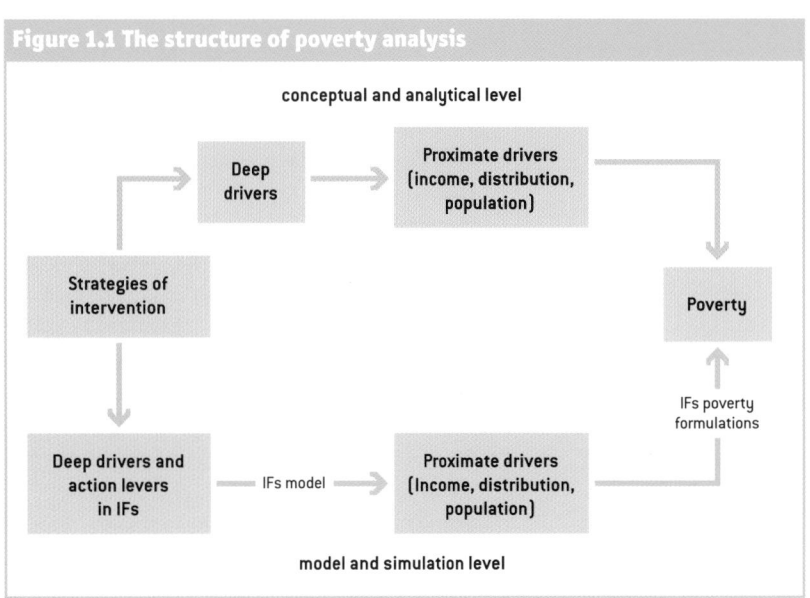

Figure 1.1 The structure of poverty analysis

conceptual and analytical level

Deep drivers → Proximate drivers (income, distribution, population) → Poverty

Strategies of intervention

Deep drivers and action levers in IFs — IFs model → Proximate drivers (Income, distribution, population) → IFs poverty formulations → Poverty

model and simulation level

between poverty as an absolute and as a relative phenomenon, poverty as a chronic and as a transitory condition, and poverty in income terms and as an expression of capabilities deprivation. At the interface between conceptualization and measurement, especially when one attempts to construct summary measures or indexes for countries, there are important issues regarding the number or portion of a population falling below a poverty line versus poverty measures that also capture the severity of poverty relative to such a line. When one turns to collecting information and data, issues arise with regard to the operationalization of understandings of income and consumption and the relationship between data from the micro or survey level and that from the macro or national accounts level. In short, poverty may seem to be a simple concept, but in spite of much continuing progress, defining and measuring it is far from simple.

Chapter 3 turns to the critical task of understanding the foundations of poverty. To set the stage for assessing interventions that are likely to reduce poverty, the chapter discusses factors that drive poverty, both at a proximal and at a deep level. Economic growth, income inequality, and population are the proximate drivers of poverty; by knowing them, we can calculate the extent of poverty. The chapter then identifies and surveys deep drivers of poverty—factors that affect one or more proximate drivers. Different types of capital (physical, human, social, and knowledge capital) and fertility are examples of such deep drivers.

Next, Chapter 3 surveys policy levers believed to be useful in reducing poverty. We cannot just will accelerated economic growth; we must help bring it about. The chapter therefore explores the levers for intervention that have been identified in the development literature and via policy analysis. A key purpose of the chapter is to create an extensive inventory of such measures to explore throughout the volume. Decreasing import duties, increasing public expenditure on health and education, and increasing the foreign aid flowing from developed to developing countries are examples of policy levers that would address one or more of the deep drivers, which in turn drive the proximate drivers of growth and inequality. We rely heavily on policies

suggested by a wide variety of development organizations and researchers. Since a given policy is rarely implemented in isolation, from this survey we tease out strategic packages and conceptual and philosophical orientations toward poverty reduction. We identify three major strategic orientations—inward (self-reliant), outward (open), and foreign assistance (aid)—and the strategic components that are part of these orientations.

Chapters 2 and 3 thus collectively treat the top layer of Figure 1.1, the conceptualization and analysis of poverty and the forces that determine its extent. Chapter 4 moves to the bottom layer and shifts attention to exploring the future of poverty and the extent of human leverage upon it. The chapter first reviews efforts that have been made to forecast the likely extent of poverty and the methods by which they have done so. It then sketches briefly the tools and approaches that might be considered ideal for analyzing the future course of poverty. The chapter concludes with an introduction of the International Futures system as the primary tool used in this volume, identifying where it falls short of the ideal, as well as indicating the capabilities that it does offer.

Chapters 5 and 6 move further along the bottom layer of Figure 1.1 by considering possible futures for the proximate drivers of poverty and using IFs to explore the poverty futures that might be associated with those. Chapter 5 introduces and explores the base case forecast of IFs, because most subsequent analysis builds on the base case. Insofar as this volume is concerned with the impact that specific interventions might have relative to a baseline, the specification of the baseline itself may not be so important. But insofar as it is also concerned with the possible absolute levels and rates of future poverty, the elaboration of the base case of IFs in Chapter 5 is essential.

Chapter 6 looks at a likely range of futures for the proximate drivers and how those futures might frame the likely futures of poverty relative to the base case. In short, this analysis provides some understanding of the scope for human action. How much might be we able to accelerate the reduction of global poverty? Although Chapter 5 supports the conclusion that we are already well on course to dramatically reduce human poverty

The volume explores interventions and combinations of them, using a base case forecast.

before midcentury, Chapter 6 suggests that the scope for incremental human action remains very substantial.

Chapter 7 reaches back to Chapter 3's analysis of the specific levers and strategies for accelerating growth and otherwise reducing poverty, exploring them individually and in combination. It also begins to consider regional differences in the situations underlying poverty and therefore in the interventions with respect to deeper drivers that might be most effective. It concludes that there are no silver bullets in terms of individual interventions that capture most of the potential gains in poverty reduction. It argues instead that large numbers of small actions contribute to poverty reduction and that, very importantly, those contributions have a substantially additive (as opposed to overlapping or mutually exclusive) character.

Chapters 8 and 9 extend the analysis of poverty futures and strategies that Chapter 7 begins. Chapter 8 further explores regional variations in the specifics of poverty and identifies selected countries for closer attention. Countries, even within regions, vary considerably in their prospects regardless of their policy choices. The chapter therefore builds a stronger base for extended analysis of strategies for poverty reduction. The tables that accompany this volume extend the analysis of Chapter 8.

Chapter 9 widens the analysis by stepping back and looking at additional relationships of importance when considering poverty. For instance, poverty is strongly linked to environmental quality, and the linkages run in both directions, setting up feedback loops: the environment can fail to provide resources to reduce poverty, and poverty can exacerbate various kinds of environmental damage. Similarly, quality of governance and the presence or absence of domestic conflict shape the ability of societies to break free of poverty. Again, relationships run in both directions.

Conclusion

All major social philosophies and religions direct attention to the existence of poverty and call on us to address the problem. In relative terms, it may be correct to assert that the poor are and always will be with us, if only because relative poverty levels float upward with average incomes. Yet we have much reason to believe that extreme global poverty—poverty that strips individuals of the ability to develop and manifest their personal capabilities and that through malnutrition, inadequate health care, and other deficiencies can literally kill—need not persist.

---

1 ADB (2004b) examines poverty experiences in Asia over this period. Wang (2005) and Srivastava (2005) provide information on China and India, respectively.

2 See http://esa.un.org/unup for the 2005 Population Revision numbers.

3 Sen believes that Europe and the United States are not the proper benchmark for a variety of reasons,

including longer overall life expectancies, the history of wartime deaths of males in the West, and higher South Asian fertility rates with associated maternal mortality. In sub-Saharan Africa, there is little female disadvantage in terms of relative mortality rates, and continental life expectancy is no higher and fertility rates are no lower than in South Asia. Using sub-Saharan Africa as the benchmark still leaves a total of more than 100

million "missing women." Sen points out that another way of "dealing with this problem is to calculate what the expected number of females would be had there been no female disadvantage in survival, given the actual life expectancy and the actual fertility rates in these respective countries." Even with this type of calculation, the number of "missing women" is still roughly 60 million.

Concepts and Measurement

In September 2000, the Millennium Summit of UN members issued the Millennium Declaration. That declaration defined eight Millennium Development Goals (MDGs), an integrated global commitment to significantly reduce human poverty and underdevelopment by 2015. The 2002 World Summit on Sustainable Development in Johannesburg slightly extended but primarily reaffirmed those goals. The MDGs include eighteen elaborated targets and forty-eight mostly quantifiable indicators.

The first goal, reduction of poverty and hunger, calls for the dual targets of halving by 2015 the proportion of people around the world who live on less than $1 per day and the proportion who suffer from hunger. The three more specific indicators that accompany the poverty target and broaden attention to poverty are as follows:

1. The proportion of the population below $1 per day at purchasing power parity (PPP).

2. The poverty gap ratio, $1 per day.
3. The share of the poorest quintile in national income or consumption.

The very specific conceptualization and measurement of poverty embedded in the first MDG is extremely useful, and this report relies heavily upon it for much the same reason as do the UN, the World Bank, and others who pursue poverty reduction, namely that the definition is clear and the indicators are available. However, debate continues about how more generally and ideally to define and measure poverty, and this chapter reports on that debate in two parts.

The first part begins with fundamental conceptual issues related to the meaning and measurement of poverty. We discuss issues related to the conceptualization of poverty in income terms, beginning with the presentation of two groups of poverty measures (headcount/ headcount ratio and poverty gap). The discussion then presents the ideas of relative poverty and proceeds further to explore the notion of capabilities as a broader foundation for understanding poverty.

The rest of the chapter addresses some of the many complications confronting practical efforts to apply measures and to forecast poverty futures. Our critical focus in the second part is on the most influential approach to poverty measurement, that of the World Bank.

The Concept and Measurement of Poverty

There is a vast literature on the definition and measurement of poverty. Caterina Ruggeri Laderchi, Ruhi Saith, and Frances Stewart (2006: 11) compare four approaches to poverty definition—monetary, capability, social exclusion, and participatory:

> The considerable lack of overlaps between the different approaches means that targeting according to one type of poverty will involve serious targeting errors in relation to other types. Moreover, definitions also have implications for policy. While a monetary approach suggests a focus on increasing money incomes (by economic growth, or redistribution), a capability approach tends to lead to more emphasis on the provision of public goods. Social exclusion draws attention to the need to break down exclusionary factors, for example, by redistribution and antidiscrimination policies.

Ruggeri Laderchi and her colleagues make a good point about conceptualization affecting policy. A largely monetary approach has steered this volume toward domestic and international policy levers (see Chapters 7 and 8) that mainly seek to increase money incomes. Antidiscrimination policies do not figure prominently in the list of interventions for the simple reason that they do not directly influence an aggregate income-based poverty measure; indeed, there is no structure in our model to assess such policies.

A focus primarily on income and interventions to enhance it is important because it is difficult to envision a poverty assessment methodology in which an increase in money incomes would be *bad* for poverty reduction. Nonetheless, attention to human capability

is also critical, and this chapter will explore Amartya Sen's approach to defining and using capabilities, related in part to health and education. It will direct much more limited attention to social exclusion and participation.

Income Poverty: Absolute Measures

The common general intuition is that **poverty** exists when a group of people cannot attain a "minimum" level of well-being. The minimum could be at least partly dependent upon the prevailing standards of society and therefore measure **relative poverty**, an issue to which the discussion will return. However, there are dimensions of well-being, such as biological minimums in nutrition, that might actually define **absolute poverty** in a manner that can allow comparison of people across societies.

Many complications can arise in setting income-based poverty levels in either absolute or relative terms. Gary Fields (2001) identified four questions:

1. Is the basis income or consumption, and how comprehensively will either one be measured?
2. What is the income-receiving unit: individual, family, per capita, or adult equivalent?
3. Will there be a single poverty line or will there be separate ones for urban and rural areas or different regions of the country?
4. Is the poverty line income determined scientifically, politically, subjectively, or as a matter of convenience?

In the following sections we discuss two groups of absolute income poverty measures: (1) the poverty headcount and headcount ratio and (2) the poverty gap within the general class of measures that are more sensitive to the deprivation of poorer people.

The poverty headcount and headcount ratio

Poverty headcount is defined as the number of people in a population who fall below a specified poverty line, such as $1 per day. From that we can derive the poverty **headcount ratio**, the fraction (normally percentage) of the total population that is poor.

These two measures have features that make them very attractive and widely used. First, they are simple in both concept and measurement.

■ *Although the MDGs include very specific targets and indicators for poverty, conceptualization and measurement of poverty require broader perspectives.* ■

■ *Both monetary and capabilities approaches help in understanding poverty.* ■

When we are told that 1 billion persons in the world are poor using a poverty line of U.S.$1 per person per day, the extent of poverty seems obvious. Second, they are universal, in that they potentially allow direct comparison of people anywhere in the world. Third, the data for use of the measures have been widely gathered via surveys around the world—they are available.

The measures also have many weaknesses. The headcount's most significant blind spot is that the measure is insensitive to the depth of deprivation among the poor. For example, a person well below the poverty line, earning only a few cents per day, may be said to be suffering much more than a person with daily income just below a dollar. Therefore the headcount does not satisfy a desired measurement property called **strong monotonicity**, which states that a poverty index must show less poverty in response to any increase in a poor person's income. Unfortunately, if large numbers of people moved from an income of 50¢ per day to 75¢ per day, a poverty headcount based on $1 per day would show no change.

Nor does headcount satisfy **distributional sensitivity**, which requires that any transfer from a poor person to a less poor person must also show an increase in poverty because the less poor person has a lower level of need. Ironically, if a poor person transferred enough money to a less poor person to lift the recipient above the poverty line, the poverty headcount would fall, contrary to commonsense notions of poverty reduction. A related problem with headcount is that if a poor person were to die from poverty-related deprivation and disease,

poverty as measured by this index would show a decrease. That certainly seems perverse.[1]

The poverty gap and the FGT family of measures

The poverty gap, another widely used measure, is the average (normalized) income shortfall among the poor, expressed as the average shortfall as a fraction of the poverty line. The IFs model calculates the poverty gap and its various power functions, as well as the headcount and headcount ratio.

The poverty gap measure is responsive to the distance of people below the poverty line and therefore does exhibit strong monotonicity. Still, problems persist. If an individual just below the poverty line were to receive a large enough income gain to escape poverty, the average income among the remaining poor would fall, and therefore poverty would rise. And if one individual moved from 50¢ to 30¢ per day, whereas another moved from 70¢ to 90¢ per day, they would offset each other. Our commonsense notions of poverty would say that the loss of 20¢ per day at a lower level is more significant than the gain of 20¢ at a higher level (the property of distributional sensitivity).

A variation of the measure can reduce the impact of the first weakness and eliminate the second weakness. The poverty shortfall of poor individuals can be used as a weighting scheme to give more weight to the poorer individuals. For instance, the gap of individuals below the poverty line can be squared. A popular family of such indexes is the one developed by James Foster,

---

Box 2.1 The Foster, Greer, and Thorbecke family of poverty measures

The FGT index, which has been used with increasing frequency in macroeconomic models incorporating poverty analysis, has many desirable properties. In addition to having the monotonicity and distributional sensitivity properties, it also has the property of being **additively subgroup decomposable**. That means that the index is decomposable by subgroups (according to region, income class etc.) among the poor. It can also be used to measure specific types of poverty. Thus, for instance, this index can take into account the intensity of food poverty for different groups of poor people, which is done by looking at the deprivation of

calories. The poverty measure is given by:

$$p = 1/n \sum (Gj/z)^a$$

where
- n = total population
- q = the number of poor
- z = the poverty line
- Gj = food expenditure shortfall of the jth individual ($j = 1,2,...,q$)

In many studies, a value of "$a = 2$" is used, which satisfies both the monotonicity and transfer axioms of Amartya Sen.

Source: Khan and Weiss (2006).

Joel Greer, and Erik Thorbecke (FGT). Box 2.1 gives further technical details.

There are other weaknesses of all standard absolute poverty measures. For instance, public goods and negative externalities do not often enter into the calculations of poverty indexes, but arguably they should.[2] Haider Khan (1994a, 1997a) shows theoretically that under even an egalitarian distribution of bads, proper use of environmental accounting would show rather more poverty under most circumstances than do our standard measurements.

Setting absolute poverty levels

The establishment of useful absolute poverty levels is also complicated. The widespread use of $1 per day at purchasing power parity, often referred to as the level of **extreme poverty**, is closely related to the rough correspondence between that level and the ability to acquire enough food to avoid calorie-related malnutrition.[3] It is not a coincidence that global counts of those suffering extreme poverty and those suffering malnutrition are similar. Box 2.2 explains purchasing power parities.

Montek S. Ahluwalia, Nicholas Carter, and Hollis Chenery (1979) first identified an absolute international poverty measure for comparison across countries. In doing so they used the International Comparison Project's (ICP's) earliest version of purchasing power parity data to explore global levels (see Kravis, Heston, and Summers 1978a, 1978b).[4] They set the poverty line based primarily on data from India. The level chosen was $200 per capita, the forty-fifth percentile of income in India in 1970 ICP dollars, which in 1985 dollars is quite close to the more contemporary $1-per-day level. That initial specification of poverty level also corresponded roughly with access to 2,250 calories per day.

Since 1990 the World Bank (see Ravallion, Datt, and van de Walle 1991) has relied upon a head-count measure of poverty based on a perception that extreme poverty exists with incomes of less than $1 per day at 1985 PPP. One dollar per day was subsequently converted to $1.08 per day at 1993 prices measured at PPP, but the shorthand, casual reference to $1 per day remains common and will be the practice in this study also.[5]

Unfortunately, the adjusted value is very controversial. Critics such as Thomas W. Pogge and Sanjay G. Reddy (2003) have argued that

Box 2.2 Purchasing power parity

Economic measures such as gross domestic product, income, or household consumption are often compared across countries by converting values to a common unit such as dollars using official market exchange rates (MER). Doing so is useful but ignores the very different purchasing power that a dollar has in different countries. Economic measures can also be converted into common units by computing purchasing power parity (PPP) between countries. To do so, a standard market basket of goods is identified, priced in local currencies, and used to compute the PPP exchange rate.

Typically, poorer countries have higher income and consumption levels when PPP rates are used. For China, for instance, the income levels are about 2.5 times as high (recently revised downward), partly because the official MER is maintained at a low rate, but even developing countries that allow currencies to float freely typically have a PPP rate that is substantially higher than the MER.

In order to make the $1-per-day poverty rate truly comparable across countries, the PPP rate is used.

the basket of goods used for PPP calculation does not reflect consumption by the poor and that changing the base year for the $1-per-day poverty definition from 1985 to 1993 is not innocuous (since they potentially yield different poverty numbers; there is no easy way to convert one line to the other).

A common argument is that the adjustment to 1993 was far below the inflation rate of the dollar over those eight years and that the adjusted level should therefore actually be much higher. For instance, Nanak Kakwani (2004a) converted poverty lines constructed in the late 1990s for ten low-income countries into 1993 PPP dollars using the relevant consumer price indices (CPIs) and PPP exchange rates. He found that the poverty lines diverged from the $1.08 per day World Bank's standard. For Gambia, the line was the highest, at $2.52 per day.

Martin Ravallion (2002a: 4) offered a spirited reply to criticism around inflation-based adjustment:

The naive approach of simply adjusting the old line upwards for inflation in the US would ignore the fact that there has been (in effect), a PPP devaluation of poor countries relative to the US over the period. For example, China's and Indonesia's poverty lines at 1985 PPP are almost identical to their poverty line at 1993 PPP; India's poverty line at 1993 PPP is only 17 percent higher than its poverty line at 1985 PPP. Yet adjusting the 1985 $1/day line for US inflation would entail an upward increase of roughly 50 percent. In other words, if we had simply

Setting absolute poverty levels for comparison across countries and adjusting them for inflation are far from trivial tasks.

adjusted the $1/day line for inflation in the US between 1985 and 1993 we would have obtained a poverty line which is well above the median of the 10 lowest poverty lines at 1993 PPP, and so could no longer claim to be the poverty line that is typical of poor countries. That would certainly entail a recalibration of the ruler.

In spite of the ongoing debates, the analysis of this report accepts the World Bank's numbers from recent surveys using the $1.08 standard as the best calculations available of extreme poverty headcount and rates. Because our base forecasting year is 2000 and because most economic data are now presented in constant 2000 dollars, our preference would have been to convert the $1.08 level from 1993 dollars into 2000 dollars; but the difficulty that even the World Bank has in adjusting the level across base years argues strongly against doing so.

Nonetheless, this report looks fifty years into the future. It would be unreasonable to expect the most common measure of absolute poverty to be unchanged during this period. Moreover, for selected regions of interest to us, including the transition economies of Eastern Europe, $1 per day is already not a very useful benchmark. We therefore frequently use the $2 per day standard (actually $2.15 at 1993 PPP), sometimes referred to as **moderate poverty**.

More generally, our use of lognormal representations of income distributions (see Chapters 3 and 4), allows the estimation of poverty headcount and rate at essentially any level of interest, for instance, $10 per day. The same foundations allow the estimation of a percentile level (such as the poorest quintile) and the inverted calculation of the income level that separates that quintile from the rest of the population (see again the third indicator for the first MDG target at the beginning of this chapter).

Income Poverty, Relatively Speaking

Is poverty in the eye of the beholder? Some people have thought so. Indeed, there is little doubt that people in different parts of the world feel subjectively different senses of deprivation relative to reference groups in their own societies. Thus, a $1 per day poverty line,

even for all "developing" countries, seems quite arbitrary and is usually justified by underlining the need for a uniform comparison of the success or failure of poverty reduction strategies followed by different developing countries. In contrast, a relative poverty measure may be attractive in assessing a subjective sense of well-being within a particular country.[6]

"Relative poverty" really embodies two separate ideas and sets of measures. On the one hand, there is poverty relative to some group within a population. For instance, a group that is relatively the poorest (e.g., the poorest 10, 20, or 40 percent) is identified, and the poverty measure is taken to be the average real income at a certain time of this "poorest" group.

On the other hand, there is poverty relative to average national incomes. For example, Martin Ravallion, Gaurav Datt, and Dominique van de Walle (1991) show empirically that the poverty lines used in countries tend to increase with their consumption levels. Abdel Gadir Ali (1997) quite forthrightly defends raising the poverty line as the mean increases. He claims that this is "obvious to us, Africans living amidst poverty." Although there are different ways of adjusting the poverty line as a function of the mean income or consumption, the easiest such adjustment is to raise the former in proportion to any increase in the latter. This will clearly lead to a continuously redefined relative poverty measure.[7]

The Capabilities Approach to Poverty
Some basic issues

Income allows comparison across individuals. The use of income-based poverty measures implicitly builds on an assumption that some degree of income equality, either the collective surpassing of an absolute poverty line or of a line relative to others in society, is desirable. But is income the right metric?

In his preface to *Inequality Reexamined*, Sen suggests it is not:

The central question in the analysis and assessment of equality is, I argue here, "equality of what?" I also argue that a common characteristic of virtually all the approaches to the ethics of social arrangements that have stood the test of

We need to use monetary measures of absolute poverty that supplement that of extreme poverty.

Relative poverty measures should supplement those for absolute poverty, particularly as incomes rise.

time is to want equality of *something*—something that has an important place in that particular theory. Not only do the income egalitarians ... demand equal incomes, and welfare-egalitarians ask for equal welfare levels, but also classical utilitarians insist on equal weights on the utilities of all, and pure libertarians demand equality with respect to an entire class of rights and liberties. (Sen 1992a: ix; italics in the original)

Sen argues that what we need to equalize is not income or utility but human capabilities. A crucial distinction is between **functionings** and **capabilities**: "'functioning' is an achievement such as a level of nourishment or general state of health, and a 'capability' is the ability to achieve" (Kakwani 2006). Capabilities so defined do not lend themselves to easy measurement. In an essay discussing the empirical issues in making the capability approach operational, Sebastian Silva Leander (2005: 4) notes:

The question of how best to capture capabilities when measuring poverty has yet to be resolved at the conceptual level and hence, there is no consensus on how to proceed with this at the empirical level. The hard fact is that it is extremely difficult (arguably impossible) to observe capabilities in practice. And while it may be possible to approximate a very crude version of this concept by estimating vectors of achievable functionings, this will not take into account the concerns relating to agency and autonomy (i.e., why a person chooses or not to execute his attainable functionings), which are an important component of Sen's critique of neoclassical theory.

Underlying the capabilities perspective is thus a respect for individual diversity. One may choose the best possible functionings for oneself from all available ones. Poverty or deprivation in general is thereby redefined as not just inadequate income, but as more fundamental inadequacies of capabilities.

At the same time, the principle of equalizing capabilities in Sen's analysis of development leads to a policy of redistributing resources toward certain socially and economically disadvantaged groups (thereby linking the capabilities approach to those of social exclusion and participation). It is useful to underline the *social* nature of capabilities. Khan (1998) pointed out that without a concrete set of social, political, and economic institutions in the background, the concept of capabilities remains intractable and suggests the use of the term "social capabilities."

Since 1990, the United Nations, through its *Human Development Reports (HDRs)*, has supported the use of measures of human development and human capabilities.[8] Among other things, that has resulted in the formulation of the human development index (HDI). In addition to national income per capita, the HDI includes other capabilities-based functionings such as life expectancy and literacy rates (see Box 2.3 for more details). One does not have to accept the specific form of the United Nations' human development index to see the usefulness of moving beyond consumption- and income-based measures.

More recently, the UNDP has developed the human poverty index (HPI). It is a composite index measuring deprivations, as opposed to achievements, in the same three basic dimensions captured by the HDI (see, again, Box 2.3). Sakiko Fukuda-Parr (2006) reported that the correlation between the HPI and the $1-per-day poverty measure is weak.[9] Countries such as Pakistan and Yemen, which have lower levels of income poverty, have higher levels of HPI, whereas the situation is reversed in a country such as Tanzania. Similar reversals are seen in the rankings of per capita gross domestic

A capabilities-based approach to assessing poverty has much merit, and the HDI can help.

Box 2.3 The United Nations Human Development Index (HDI)

The UN HDI is a composite measure of several human development factors such as income, literacy, education, and life expectancy. Many consider it the standard measure of human development or well-being for countries. The United Nations Development Programme (UNDP) developed the HDI in 1990 under the guidance of Mahbub ul Haq. The UNDP provides it annually in its *Human Development Reports*.

The HDI aggregates measures of three basic dimensions of human development: standard of living, basic knowledge acquisition, and the expected length of life. Knowledge is measured by adult literacy rate (given two-thirds weight) and the combined primary, secondary, and tertiary school enrollment rate (one-third weight). Standard of living is measured by a log of gross domestic product (GDP) per capita at purchasing power parity (PPP), capped with a maximum that can rise over time. Finally, length of the average life is measured by life expectancy at birth.

Source: UN 2007.

product (GDP) and HDI. Therefore, higher incomes do not automatically translate into lower poverty in this framework.

The relationship between income poverty and capability poverty

In spite of imperfect correlations, there is a direct relationship between the two primary approaches to understanding poverty. As income grows, other things being equal, realization of capabilities also increases. In addition, improvement of basic education or health care confers greater ability to generate income so as to escape income poverty.

Antipoverty policy should not concentrate solely on reducing income poverty, although that should be an important component. The fundamental issues associated with poverty and deprivation should be understood in terms of the freedoms people have and the lives they can actually lead; capabilities are themselves essential.

This contrast can be seen in several different areas connected to human well-being. As Sen illustrates, in the United States African Americans are poorer in terms of income than American whites; when compared to the rest of the world, however, African Americans are far richer, thus softening this inequality. But when other measurements of capability, such as the basic capability to live to a mature age, are considered, the situation looks very different. As a racial group, African Americans have a higher mortality rate than American whites. Furthermore, in some parts of the United States, the average life expectancy of an African American male is lower than that in some developing countries, which constitutes a very significant deprivation of capabilities. In the same light, focusing in Europe on the ability to be employed and the negative effects of unemployment, despite income support, paints a troubling picture.

Box 2.4 Chronic versus transient poverty: Where the poor are and why they are poor

It is important to understand that identifying poverty is not a simple problem because poverty has many different aspects and several dimensions. Two of the most important types of poverty uncovered by recent research are known as chronic and transient poverty.

Chronic poverty persists in spite of economic growth and interventions such as temporary transfers of income. The chronically poor are almost always poor throughout their lives and often pass this condition to future generations. In general, they benefit the least from economic growth and standard development projects. If and when the chronically poor have employment, it is insecure and often at very low wages. Many live in rural areas, urban slums, and conflict zones and often suffer mild to extreme health problems. Children, the elderly, and people with disabilities are particularly affected by chronic poverty. The chronically poor are the "invisible" poor; development projects often have little or no positive effects on their situations. Barriers to accessing resources and pursuing opportunities are the main reasons for the persistence of chronic poverty.

Those suffering **transient poverty** are not *always* in an economic and social situation that could be called "poor." They are the "sometimes poor." They are at risk of becoming chronically poor. They suffer many of the same risks and lack of opportunities to gain access to productive assets and lack basic capabilities. Transient poverty is particularly common in economies that are undergoing some type of transition, such as the Russian economy.

It has been estimated that in the world today there are between 300 and 420 million people trapped in chronic poverty. The chronically poor live in all regions of the world, with the largest numbers residing in South Asia. Additionally, the nations with the highest levels of chronic poverty, roughly 40 percent, are in sub-Saharan Africa. In terms of actual numbers of chronically poor individuals in the various regions of the world, 121.3 million reside in sub-Saharan Africa, 84.9 million in East Asia and the Pacific, and 187.5 million in South Asia, 28 million individuals are chronically poor and residing throughout the rest of the world.

Why are they poor? Although the picture differs slightly from country to country, both financial and physical asset holdings are among the major determining factors as to which households will suffer either of these aspects of poverty. For example, in China the lack of physical capital is a significant determining factor for both chronic and transient poverty; however, large household size and low level of education for the head of household determine chronic but not transient poverty. Isolation in remote rural areas is often associated with chronic poverty as well.

Events such as natural disasters, internal and external wars, and disease can promote the continuance of chronic poverty and transform transient poverty into chronic poverty. There could also be social and economic barriers arising from a caste system, as in India, or from belonging to groups that are generally discriminated against, such as the Indios in Latin America, the Burakumin in Japan, or women almost everywhere.

In the *Chronic Poverty Report*, the Chronic Poverty Research Center of the University of Manchester offers several suggestions for a framework of action for handling the problems presented by chronic poverty. Many of these suggestions also apply to transient poverty. Promoting livelihood security is a key step in helping the world's poor. This is especially pertinent when considering the effects of disease, war, and disasters on the chronically and transient poor. Also, ensuring access to opportunities and providing the means to access resources and capabilities are important in preventing both aspects of poverty. Additionally, there is a pressing need for empowering the chronically and transient poor to overcome the discriminatory factors that they face. In this light, basic education turns out to be an important part of a general antipoverty strategy. Finally, national and international efforts should focus on providing the needed resources to the geographical areas where the (chronically) poor are located. Thus the spatial dimension of poverty must be recognized as an important strategic variable in thinking about poverty reduction strategies (more on this in Chapter 3).

Source: Chronic Poverty Research Center 2005; World Bank, Attacking Poverty, World Development Report 2000–2001.

To summarize, there are at least three critical areas in which the capabilities approach can help us understand the dimensions of deprivation, and hence poverty and its effects, better than income-based measures can. One is the specificities of deprivation in concrete, nonincome dimensions such as health or literacy. The second is the variability in people's ability to convert income to concrete functionings and capabilities. Finally, the *social* capabilities approach helps focus attention directly on the institutions that help or hinder individuals to various degrees in realizing concrete achievements. Gender discrimination is an obvious but not the only illustration of this point. Similarly, the capabilities approach could be helpful on the important issue of chronic versus transient poverty (see Box 2.4).

The measurement of poverty in this book

In considering measures tied to capabilities and functionings, a few common themes emerge.

- Except for the HDI and HPI, most of the measures tied to capabilities and functionings have been applied to small groups of countries. Measures that attempt to more completely capture the nonincome facets of poverty are hard to generalize across countries, and data to support them are less readily available than those for the income-based measures.
- The application of capability-based measures appears very limited and when implemented captures functionings (achievements) such as nourishment rather than true capabilities (the ability to achieve). The HPI, though available for a broad cross-section of countries, is ultimately based on functionings.

It is important not to lose track of the reality that poverty is much more than an income-based phenomenon. Expansion of human capabilities and the freedom of action to which they give rise lie at the heart of human development.[10] Our forecasts in this report will, nonetheless, use mainly income- or consumption-based measures of poverty. We will supplement attention to income by some measures of education and health and by the

HDI and HPI, all of which are considerably more difficult to forecast. Except for these supplements, the current state of the art appears to offer no alternate measure to income that can be broadly and consistently applied to study global poverty across countries and time.

The Consequences of Conceptualization and Measurement Perspectives

The strengths and weaknesses of poverty concepts and measurements are not abstract. Very often, those who are closest to the poor, for instance field representatives of nongovernmental organizations (NGOs), see a variety of problems that may not always be apparent from more conceptual perspectives. They may begin with the nature of headcount ratio indexes widely used, but the problems go well beyond a critique of this special class of poverty measures.[11] In particular, there are problems that merit discussion related to the balance between the extent of poverty and the resources directed at addressing it, aggregation of poverty into single numbers, policy time horizons for even helpful interventions, and market and nonmarket aspects of poverty.

Poverty incidence and resource availability

People involved in ground-level operations experience increasing pressure on their ability to provide services to the poor when their absolute number increases, even though the national or even regional statistics may show a decline in the percentage of poverty. If there is a limited amount of food to be distributed to the poor or a limited amount of shelter for them, it is their absolute number that really matters for the adequate provision of these services. With budget constraints that often cannot be relaxed as the absolute number of poor increases, the per capita service provision has to decline.

Improvements in measurement might indicate a poverty decline even when nothing has changed. That is what apparently happened in Ghana in the 1990s (Kanbur 2004). Since the 1980s, the household income expenditure surveys have improved a great deal. Previously omitted elements, such as production for home consumption, regional price variations, and

This study, although heavily focused on income poverty, also looks to capabilities.

imputation of use value to dwellings, are now routinely taken into account.

Disconnects between measurement and reality can work in the opposite direction as well. Information on public services provision is still not well integrated into these surveys. Although surveys sometimes contain separate modules on health, education, and infrastructure, these measures are rarely integrated fully into the income- or consumption-based measures of poverty estimates for households.

The problem of aggregation

Regional or group disaggregations may also pull in different directions, leading to different perceptions regarding trends in poverty at different levels of aggregation, a "poverty decomposition problem." For example, Ravi Kanbur (2004) cites the case of Ghana, where during 1987–1991 national poverty declined, as did rural poverty, but urban poverty actually rose. In Mexico in 1994, exactly the opposite regional trends were observed along with a decrease in national poverty.

Until disaggregation in analysis becomes routinely possible, we can begin with the basic understanding that different people who may be equally well informed may nevertheless look at different levels of analysis and assess them differently. As Kanbur (2004) and many practitioners, particularly NGO staff at the local level, have underlined, the more nuanced distribution and character of poverty (including the chronic/transient distinction) may be of as much relevance as percentage reductions in headcounts.

Thinking across time

Another set of issues in poverty reduction analysis flows from varying time horizons of different analysts considering the impact of poverty reduction policies. For example, economic theorists considering growth-oriented policies often think in equilibrium economics terms. That is, they focus on the results of policies after an economy has had the time to adjust to a policy intervention, perhaps five to ten years in the future.

Practitioners on the ground may shake their collective heads in disbelief at such perspectives, pointing out that the short run—even today or tomorrow—may be what really matters for the poor, especially the poorest.

The discussion in Chapter 7 of the impact of increased savings and investment rates on poverty in the short and long run illustrates this issue. Although increased saving may ultimately help drive economic growth and reduce poverty, its immediate and shorter-run impact on consumption levels can be significant, especially in the poorest countries and populations. The key question here has to be how to ensure the protection of the more vulnerable among the poor. More disaggregated policy-oriented models are really needed to address these issues.

Markets are not the only institutions

The assumption of most economists is that the perfectly competitive market structure is a reasonable approximation of the context for analysis of poverty, and there is no question that income levels and distributions are essential foundations. Approaches to poverty analysis rooted in an understanding of capabilities and social exclusion look, however, to a wider context. Embeddedness of the poor refers to their connections, or lack thereof, with all the economic, social, and political institutions that affect their lives (Khan 2003). Both (often imperfect) market and nonmarket institutions shape poverty. For instance, the existence or nonexistence of unions in the formal sector and the absence of bargaining power in the informal sector are features of particular socioeconomic structures in which the poor are embedded. Although it is very difficult to represent such features of societies in models, the analysis should not ignore them.

Controversies Related to Measurement and Data

Concepts should translate into measurement and data. Yet even measurement of the simplest concept of poverty, namely income poverty headcount, is plagued with some significant problems.

National income accounts versus household survey data

The core of the World Bank's empirical approach to determining how many people earn less than $1 per day (as in Table 1.1) is the use of country-based surveys. The number of surveys has steadily expanded, reaching 454 across ninety-seven developing countries in the analysis by Shaohua Chen and Martin Ravallion (2004) that provided much of the poverty data used by the Millennium Project (2005) in its elaboration of proposals for meeting the MDGs. Such surveys allow an understanding of distributions of income or consumption levels across national populations and the specifications of shares associated with deciles or quintiles of population (or even the manipulation of data at the individual respondent level). The data have gradually become more freely available and easy to use.

Unfortunately, the country-level values obtained for household consumption from surveys are not the same as the values provided by aggregate national account statistics (NAS) and tend to be lower, especially for poorer countries. Moreover, the ratio between the values based on survey and national account statistics has been decreasing over time, thereby increasing the discrepancy between the two measurement approaches.

The two approaches thus give very different estimates for the levels of poverty and for its pattern of change. Both are imperfect approaches to poverty measurement. The great advantage of the survey approach is that it allows more rigorous checks on the quality and consistency of the underlying data, and it still remains the first choice for most of those working in the field. However, there are reasons to believe that household surveys may underreport the total value of household consumption (for example, the value that must be imputed for public services like schooling and health care) and that some of what the surveys miss will affect the poor. Hence the underlying data from the World Bank (see, again, Table 1.1) may significantly overestimate global poverty[12] and understate the degree of actual poverty reduction.[13] It has also been argued that national accounts statistics overstate consumption and its growth.

The choice of analysts between data based on surveys and data based on national accounts statistics would not be so problematic if the calculations of the ratios of mean societal consumption of the two were fundamentally constant over time. Then the estimates of

poverty might vary across methodologies, but the patterns of change over time would be fundamentally the same. The problem is exacerbated because there has been a strong tendency for the discrepancy to grow over time. Angus Deaton (2004:12) notes that the rate of consumption growth in surveys is about half that in national accounts. The low ratio in India is especially striking.

Surjit S.Bhalla (2002, 2003) argued in favor of national account statistics and used them to estimate changes in poverty in the 1990s. He calculated a much more rapid decline than has been found in the World Bank surveys. Xavier Sala-i-Martin (2002a, 2002b) and others have also used national accounts and have similarly reported rates of decrease in global poverty (and/or declines in global inequality) that exceed the assessments of the World Bank.

Deaton (2004) is among those who have attempted to analyze the strengths and weaknesses of the two data types. Although he did not fully resolve the issue, he provided insights relevant to doing so. With respect to national accounts, he notes the following:

- A number of expert observers have suggested that growth rates in China have been overreported in recent years; assuming overreporting by about 2 percent per year eliminates the difference in the pattern of change between national accounts and surveys (Deaton 2004: 14).
- Consumption in national account data is fundamentally a residual, calculated by measuring production and adjusting it for exports, imports, and other items. Moreover, other values often are rooted in physical volumes, converted to monetary terms with prices that are not always easy to determine, thereby complicating that residual computation (Deaton 2004: 28).
- National accounts can pick up some double counting of consumption, for instance, vegetable oil attributed both to household use and restaurants (Deaton 2004: 33).

With respect to surveys, Deaton suggests the following:

- Surveys may be subject to underreporting of income/consumption by the richest. If so,

The controversy over the use of national account statistics versus the use of surveys is significant.

it would explain why survey means tend to be lower than those of national accounts, and also suggest that surveys still capture relatively accurately the situation of those living in poverty.

- Surveys appear sensitive to a variety of selection and structural issues. For instance, recall of consumption expenditures over the previous thirty days (the traditional survey horizon) was shown in an Indian study to be 17 percent less than that over seven days (Deaton 2004: 34–35).
- Rapid urbanization could affect surveys over time because urban dwellers may have greater noncompliance with surveys (Deaton 2004: 27).
- Surveys are less likely than national accounts to pick up consumption on behalf of households provided by nonprofit institutions (Deaton 2004: 31).
- Surveys have incomplete coverage, leaving out groups such as students and the military (Deaton 2004: 34).

Recognizing the strengths and weaknesses in both approaches, Deaton concluded:

> The downward bias in survey measures of consumption almost certainly biases upwards the World Banks' global poverty estimates, and since it is unlikely that all of the growth discrepancy between surveys and the NAS is due to faults in the latter, the rate of poverty decline is likely downward biased. We need an international initiative to provide a set of consistent international protocols for survey design, as well as deeper study into the effects of nonsampling errors, particularly noncompliance. (2004: 41)

The PPP basket and base year changes

There are other issues that complicate the count of those living in poverty because international comparisons require a standard international poverty line. One is the appropriate calculation of the purchasing power parity exchange rate. The rates are based on prices of general bundles of consumer goods, not on bundles consumed specifically by the poor. And what is consumed by the poor varies over time. Yet changes in PPP

exchange rates have significant effects on poverty estimates. In one dramatic instance, a recalculation of the PPP exchange rate removed poverty completely from a country.[14]

A second issue is the treatment of inflation in the context of PPP. Resetting the original poverty line from a base of 1985 to one of 1993 caused complications and became a minor part of the disagreement on the accuracy of the World Bank poverty estimates for the 1990s.

How should we proceed?

Debates in the poverty measurement literature are far from academic when it comes to exploring the possible futures of poverty and analysis of strategies for alleviating it. Given that the most significant debate is that between the use of surveys and national accounts, how should IFs use the two data levels in shaping its forecasting?

The short answer is simple: specification of initial conditions for the base year of the forecast should use survey data because they are the best source for judging contemporary poverty levels; forecasting of consumption levels, however, will inevitably be done at the macro level of national accounts, because it is impossible to forecast at the micro level of the households upon which surveys are based.

If we anticipate a continued divergence in the measurements of poverty from surveys and those from natural accounts, this inevitable link of simulation to national accounts could cause the results to build in a faster reduction of poverty rates than would an approach that in some fashion anticipates survey results. It is really not sensible, however, to expect that the ratio of poverty based on surveys to that based on national accounts can continue to decline significantly. This analysis does not anticipate that result.[15]

A somewhat longer answer, to be elaborated on further in subsequent chapters, is this:

- The analysis in this book begins in 2000 and uses estimates of poverty in that year or years close to it from World Bank sources, thereby essentially accepting the higher estimates for initial poverty levels from the survey data, rather than (1) computing poverty levels directly from national accounts or (2) creating values for 2000 from surveys based on 1990 data and using national account forecasting thereafter (as Bhalla does). Thus the study must recognize some possible upward bias in its initial conditions and be a little cautious in comparison of results with 1990.

- Analysis after 2000 in this book uses national accounts to drive poverty computations. To the degree that historical national accounts have biased economic growth rates upward, there may be some upward bias in our results as well. Our book depends on scenario analysis to explore the implications of substantially different patterns of economic growth.

- It does not appear reasonable to expect that the ratio of means from surveys and national accounts can continue to decline indefinitely and therefore simply to extrapolate future historical declines in that ratio. Nonetheless, the IFs modeling system allows an exogenous specification of change in the ratio for those who want to hypothesize continued decline in it.

Conclusion

This chapter has attempted two important stage-setting tasks for the rest of the book. The first set of fundamental issues addressed relates to the analytical task of pinpointing the meaning of poverty and the various conceptual issues associated with measurement. A survey of the literature shows both the richness of various approaches and the challenges each of them poses. The second set of issues relates to the actual empirical task of estimating poverty for policy purposes. Here the foundational approach of the World Bank naturally gains prominence. Yet in reviewing that approach, a number of conceptual, statistical, and policy issues arise.

Consideration of these conceptual issues, with a view to investigating the processes and policies for poverty reduction, logically leads us to consider what the drivers of poverty reduction are and what various poverty reduction strategies might be. They are the subjects of the next chapter.

1 Khan (2004) has introduced an axiom of biological stress and derived a new adjusted index to prevent such perverse results.

2 Public goods are characterized by nonexcludability and nonrivalry. Negative externalities are negative effects on other agents that are generated in production or consumption by agents engaging in market activities. In both cases there are important market failures.

3 Banerjee and Duflo (2006) documented the use of income by those living on less than one dollar a day and found that food expenditures were lower than expected, at 54–78 percent of the total.

4 The data on purchasing power parities has evolved over time with the use of Penn World Tables (PWT), which grew out of the ICP. In 2002 the PWT 6.1 replaced PWT 5.6. The PPP conversion factors were not created for analysis of poverty, however, and the use of them is therefore itself subject to some criticism and uncertainty (Kasrshenas 2004).

5 Bhalla (2002) questions whether a price differential of only 8 percent between 1985 and 1993 is reasonable.

6 The emerging literature on "subjective well-being approach to poverty" does not yet include a well-established poverty measure. See Kingdon and Knight (2004).

7 There are many examples of relative poverty lines, including half the median income (Fuchs 1969); two-thirds of the median income, as is done by the Luxembourg Income Study (Atkinson, Rainwater, and Smeeding 1995); and half the mean income, as is done by the European Union (Atkinson 1998;

O'Higgins and Jenkins 1990). On some occasions, the World Bank uses two-thirds of the median income as a relative poverty measure.

8 The late Pakistani economist Mahbub ul-Haq initiated the HDRs. Key ideas came from Sen. Foster and Sen (1997, chap. A.7) and Sen (1992a, 1999) summarize Sen's work.

9 Our calculation of the R-square is about 0.4.

10 The interested reader can see the tables associated with this volume for extended forecasts of additional variables related to human development in all its dimensions. Future volumes will focus specifically on capabilities-based human development indicators, notably education and health.

11 See Khan (1997 a, 1997b, 1998, 2005a) for a more detailed discussion of the limitations of the headcount measure.

12 This debate was originally stimulated by alternative estimates for India based on national accounts statistics and was widened to include global figures in Bhalla (2002). A highly combative technical debate ensued; see Ravallion (2002a, 2002b) and Bhalla (2003). The dramatic claim in Bhalla (2002, 2003) was that because of the underestimate of poverty reduction in the World Bank data, the Millennium Development Goal of halving poverty between 1990 and 2015 had already been achieved by 2000. Probably few development professionals accept this proposition.

13 Deaton (2001) has an authoritative survey of the key issues. He rejects the approach in Bhalla (2002) of assuming that survey data are wrong in their

average but correct in their distribution, stating "the last condition is a real stretch" (Deaton 2001: 135). Hence there is considerable doubt about the accuracy of the rapid fall in poverty found in Bhalla (2002).

14 Deaton (2001: 128) recounts how for the mid-1990s, Thailand was shown "as having only 0.1 percent of its population living on less than $1/day at PPP. This virtual elimination of poverty was cited in the *New York Times* by then Chief Economist [sic] of the World Bank Joseph Stiglitz as one of the consequences of the Asian economic miracle ... but it is much more likely a tribute to inappropriate PPP conversion." Ravallion (2002a) summarizes the approach for international comparisons; see also Ravallion (2001).

15 It is possible that the two forecasting problems are in fact linked. The World Bank continues to assume that real GDP growth at market exchange rates (MER) and PPP are identical. The IFs system (see Chapter 5) posits that GDP growth for developing countries at PPP is slower that that at MER. The recent downward revision of PPP values for China and other countries provides support for the IFs approach. Deaton (2004: 14) has noted that a 2 percent downward revision of Chinese growth would reconcile poverty change using NAS and survey-based approaches. The difference in IFs forecasts between the two rates is actually 3 percent, more than enough to accomplish that reconciliation. The difference in growth rates of Chinese GDP at MER and PPP is, however, negligible in historical data series, suggesting either that the IFs presumption is false or that the two data series have been incorrectly aligned over time.

3

Drivers and Strategies for Poverty Reduction

● *Economic growth, income distribution, and population growth proximately determine poverty, but deep drivers and policy levers more fundamentally shape it.* ●

The previous chapters presented poverty reduction as an overarching global imperative of current times. In this chapter, we discuss factors that drive poverty, both at a proximal and at a deeper level. We also survey some promising strategies that have been proposed to reduce poverty.

We first discuss the **proximate drivers** of income poverty—economic growth, inequality, and population and its growth—with which we can calculate poverty measures. We next identify and survey the **deep drivers** of poverty, the factors that drive one or more of the proximate drivers. Different types of capital (physical, human, social, and knowledge capital), labor, and fertility are examples of such drivers. Without an understanding of these deep drivers, it will not be possible to have a meaningful discussion of the mechanisms through which various strategies tackle poverty.

We then survey **policy levers**, the policies and interventions that have been proposed to reduce poverty. Decreasing import duties,

increasing public expenditure on health and education, and increasing the foreign aid flowing from developed to developing countries are examples of policy levers that could move one or more of the deep drivers, which in turn drive the proximate drivers of growth and inequality.

It is it useful conceptually to separate the action-oriented policy levers from the theoretical, model-driven deep factors that drive poverty. Doing so allows us to address policies that tackle multiple drivers at once, as well as multiple policies that could affect a given driver. For instance, human capital is one of the deep drivers of economic growth. Education subsidy is a policy lever that influences the accumulation of human capital. But it could also influence social capital, another driver of economic growth, by imparting knowledge of institutions to students, inculcating civic behavior in them, and allowing the formation of social networks. Such a subsidy could also affect inequality, another proximate driver, by improving the access of the poor to productive opportunities. Similarly, multiple policies can address a given deep driver. For instance, in addition to education subsidy, greater openness to trade, which increases the influx of new technologies, can raise the return on acquisition of human capital.

A given policy is rarely implemented in isolation but is usually part of a larger **strategic package**, a combination of individual policies. Although IFs can be used to study the effects of individual interventions, it can be better used to study the outcomes of implementing strategic packages; this is the approach we pursue in Chapter 7. There are several reasons for studying policies bundled into such packages.

- As Ravi Kanbur and Lyn Squire (1999: 2) note, "poverty reducing strategies must recognize the interactions among the policies—the impact of appropriately designed combinations will be greater than the sum of the individual parts." For example, they point out that improved health increases earning potential, increased education leads to better health, and increased provision of safety nets for the poor allows them to undertake riskier, high-return activities that can increase their own and their countries' income. One cannot simply add up the effects of individual interventions to assess a strategic package.

- On a related note, resource constraints and other trade-offs that arise when multiple policies are implemented should be taken into account when one studies the effect of a combination of policies. As the World Bank (1980: 83) states, "In the past the severity of the trade-off between poverty reduction and growth has sometimes been exaggerated. ... It would be wrong, however, to suggest there are no trade-offs." For example, increases in spending in one facet of poverty reduction, say health, necessarily come at the expense of another, say R&D subsidies to increase growth.

- Strategic packages of policies can capture conceptual and philosophical orientations toward poverty reduction. Field experience, progress in research, and global change lead to ever-evolving conceptualizations of poverty reduction strategies. Prior to the

1980s, the World Bank focused primarily on economic growth. Then, the *World Development Report 1980* (World Bank 1980) extensively discussed "human development" as an important strategic orientation. The Bank solidified this stance in the *World Development Report 1990*, asserting that the challenge of development is to improve the quality of life. These and other conceptualizations, such as "pro-poor" and "external orientation," represent the evolution of the policy community's approach to tackling poverty.

The Proximate Drivers of Poverty

In this section, we discuss how growth, inequality, and population are the proximate drivers of poverty. We devote very limited attention to population, because growth and inequality determine the rate of poverty; population then determines the number in poverty.

The connections among growth, inequality, and poverty

Inequality (the distribution of income or consumption), growth, and poverty form the three vertices of a "triangle," arithmetically connected in a fairly straightforward way (Bourguignon 2003). In order to understand this connection, we first discuss the representation and characterization of inequality.

The Lorenz curve is the most widely used method for representing inequality in earnings, income, or wealth (see Figure 3.1). It portrays the *cumulative* share of income (or any other quantity distributed across a population) held by increasingly well-to-do *cumulative* shares of population. The more equally distributed a factor is, the closer the Lorenz curve will be to the hypotenuse of the right triangle, sometimes called the line of equality. The **Gini coefficient** is the "area of inequality" immediately below the hypotenuse (A) divided by the area of the triangle (A+B); thus larger Gini coefficients indicate greater inequality.

The Lorenz curve is "nonparametric" in that it is an empirical distribution that accurately represents survey data on income or consumption for a society. Although the Lorenz curve is useful conceptually to capture the dynamically evolving distribution of income or consumption, it is more convenient

Figure 3.1 The Lorenz curve and the Gini coefficient

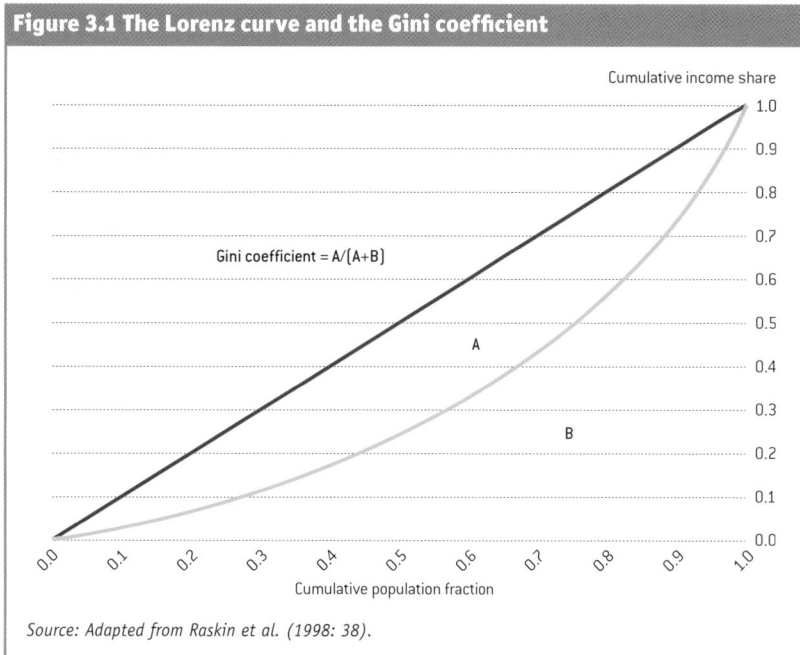

Gini coefficient = A/(A+B)

A

B

Cumulative income share

Cumulative population fraction

Source: Adapted from Raskin et al. (1998: 38).

population that earns or consumes up to a given amount). Although income and consumption are not exactly distributed in a lognormal form for every country, it is a very good approximation to observed empirical distributions. As François Bourguignon (2003: 7) notes, a **lognormal distribution** is "a standard approximation of empirical distributions in the applied literature." A variable is lognormally distributed if the natural logarithm of that variable is normally distributed, as in the well-known bell curve. Figure 3.2 shows a lognormal density curve.

One advantage of using a lognormal density to capture the distribution of income in a society is that it can be fully specified with only two parameters, average income and the standard deviation of it. More useful for our purposes, and as elaborated in Box 3.1, the Gini coefficient can be used in lieu of the standard deviation (Appendix 2 to this volume provides an extended discussion).

Figure 3.2 provides an illustration of how to obtain the poverty headcount from a lognormal density curve. For a specified poverty line—for example, the one corresponding to $1 per day—the area to the left of the line gives the poverty headcount ratio. The first vertical line in Figure 3.2 shows the poverty line, and hatched lines show the area corresponding to the headcount ratio. The poverty headcount *number* is the headcount *ratio* times population. Box 3.1 shows the formal relationships among income distribution, poverty line, and poverty.

to have an analytic, or "parametric," representation of the distribution. Moreover, we want a representation from which we can conveniently compute specific deciles or quintiles (thereby reconstructing the Lorenz curve) and also compute key poverty measures like the headcount.

The most widely used parametric representation is the lognormal density. A **density curve** captures the percentage of the population that earns or consumes a given amount (unlike a distribution that captures the cumulative percentage of the

● *The Lorenz curve and Gini usefully portray income distribution—the lognormal distribution is a bridge to forecasting poverty.* ●

If $f(x)$ denotes the distribution of income or consumption x, then the proportion of the population with income or consumption less than or equal to a given poverty line z, $H(z)$, is

$$H(z) = \int_0^z f(x)dx.$$

If the population is given by n, the headcount ratio can be converted into the poverty headcount using

$$h(z) = nH(z).$$

The distribution of income or consumption is often represented by parameters, in practice using the lognormal distribution, which is completely characterized by its mean, μ_x, and its standard

Source: Aitchinson and Brown (1963).

deviation, σ_x. Given the mean income or consumption μ, and the Gini coefficient, G, gathered from data, the parameters of this lognormal distribution follow

$$\mu_x = 1n(\mu) - \frac{1}{2}\sigma_x^2$$

$$\sigma_x = \sqrt{2}\Phi^{-1}\left(\frac{G+1}{2}\right),$$

where Φ is the standard normal distribution. If we denote the lognormal cumulative distribution by $\Lambda(\mu_x, \sigma_x)$, the headcount ratio for the poverty line z is given by

$$H(z) = \Lambda(z \mu_x, \sigma_x)$$

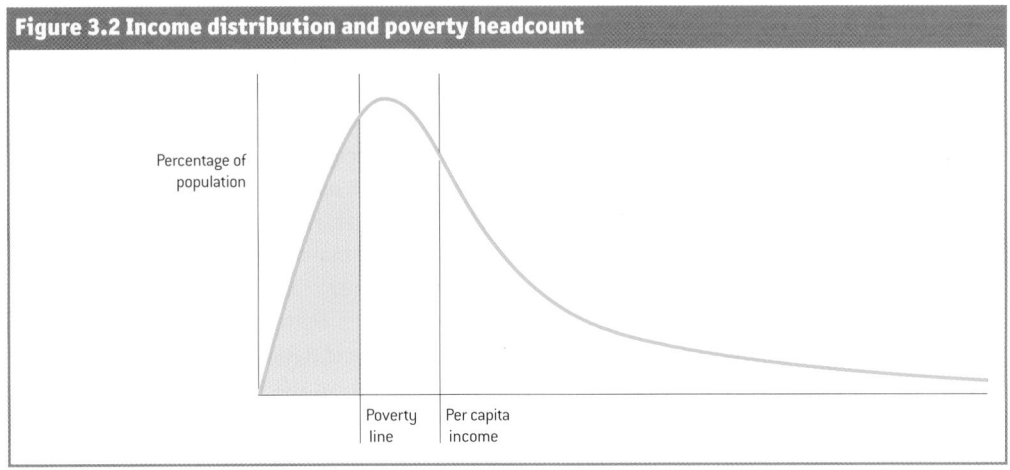

Figure 3.2 Income distribution and poverty headcount

Percentage of population

Poverty line

Per capita income

The income distribution and population also make possible calculation of the poverty gap and relative poverty. With respect to relative poverty, suppose the poverty line were set at one-third the average per capita income. The poverty line would then be drawn at this level instead of the fixed $1-per-day level. The area to the left of the poverty line would give the proportion of the population living in relative poverty and, when multiplied by the population, would provide the number of people living in relative poverty.

What is the role played by economic growth—the third vertex of the triangle discussed by Bourguignon (2003)—in calculating poverty? The discussion up to now has focused on calculating poverty at a particular point in time, when the distribution and population are known.

Economic growth is related to the evolution of poverty over time.

Although economic growth usually refers to an increase in per capita income (the average of the income distribution) over time, the process of growth should be more generally understood as affecting the entire income distribution. The incomes of different segments of the population will grow at potentially different rates. Figure 3.3 illustrates how the ensuing change in distribution will affect poverty.

In Figure 3.3, the second vertical line shows the distribution for a given point in time, say year 1. The dashed vertical line shows the distribution for a subsequent time, say year 2. The two vertical lines together show growth from year 1 to year 2 in per capita income, the average of the respective distributions. The area of hatched, dashed lines to the left of the

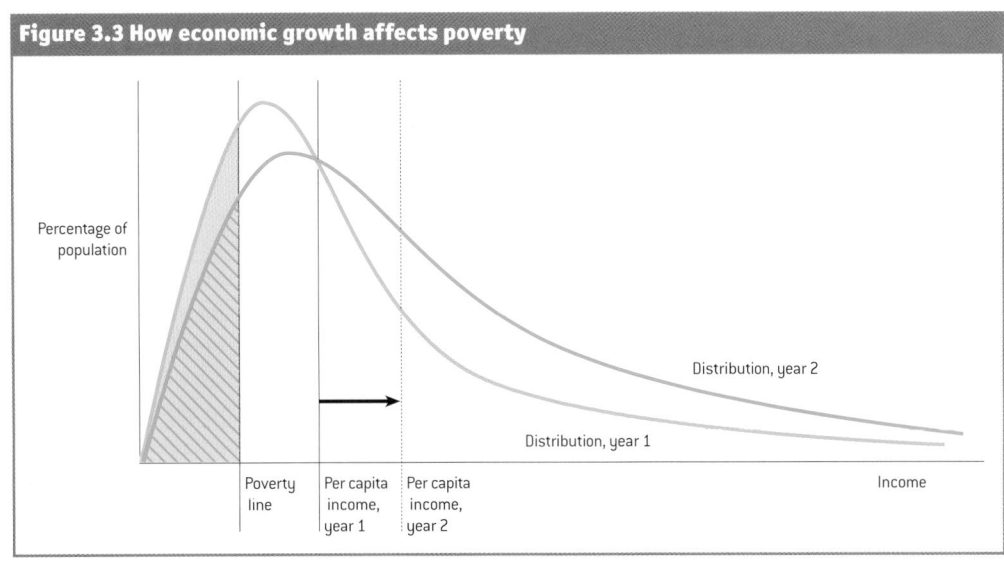

Figure 3.3 How economic growth affects poverty

Percentage of population

Distribution, year 2

Distribution, year 1

Poverty line

Per capita income, year 1

Per capita income, year 2

Income

poverty line in the new distribution shows the new poverty headcount ratio. This area is smaller than the area under the year 1 distribution, and the poverty headcount ratio has decreased. What happens to the poverty headcount number depends on the how the population has changed from the first year to the second. If the population increases significantly, the headcount number can increase even if the headcount ratio decreases.

In this illustration, economic growth gives rise to a decrease in the poverty rate, since the left-hand tail of the distribution becomes smaller. That need not always happen. In order to understand the effects of growth and distribution on the dynamics of poverty, we need next to decompose poverty changes into growth and distribution effects.

Decomposition of poverty changes into growth and distribution effects

The exact way in which the income or consumption distribution changes over time will clearly affect the poverty numbers. Economic growth increases the mean or per capita income by shifting parts or all of the distribution to the right. If the entire distribution shifts right without changing shape, or changes shape such that the left tail of the distribution becomes thinner, then growth will necessarily reduce poverty for a fixed poverty line. Otherwise, poverty could increase even if the per capita income grows.

Bourguignon (2003: 3) describes a decomposition of changes in poverty into growth and distributional changes as follows (see also Datt and Ravallion 1992):[1]

> A change in the distribution of income can be decomposed into two effects. First, there is a proportional change in all incomes that leaves the distribution of relative income unchanged, i.e., a *growth* effect. Second, there is the effect of a change in the distribution of relative incomes, which, by definition, is independent of the mean, i.e., a *distributional* effect.

What is the evidence on poverty changes arising from the interaction of growth and distributional effects? There is evidence that

growth tends to be "distribution neutral" on average; Martin Ravallion and Shaohua Chen (1997), Ravallion (2001), and Dollar and Kraay (2002a), find almost no correlation between changes in inequality and economic growth. Those findings are consistent with the evidence that the growth effect dominates and that growth tends to reduce absolute poverty (Fields 2001; Kraay 2004; Ravallion 1995; Ravallion and Chen 1997; and World Bank 1990). The World Bank (2001) and Ravallion (2004b) suggest that the "elasticity" of the $1-per-day poverty rate to growth is –2; an increase in the growth rate by 1 percent is associated with a decrease of 2 percent in the headcount index of poverty.

Although there is general consensus that growth is good for poverty alleviation, a few voices of caution can be heard. The actual reduction in poverty is arguably lower than might be expected, given recorded rates of economic growth. This has been termed "the paradox of persistent global poverty" (Cline 2004: 28). Poverty in the 1990s declined by less than would have been predicted with a poverty growth elasticity of around –2. Haider Khan and John Weiss (2006) warn that the elasticity of poverty to growth can vary widely—only –0.7 for the Philippines compared to –2.0 for Thailand—depending on the initial inequality and changes in inequality over time. Ravallion (2004) lists a few reasons to be cautious about the distribution neutrality of growth: measurement error in changes in inequality, possible churning under the surface with winners and losers at all income levels, and possible increases in absolute income disparities. Moreover, a few countries and regions could experience poverty increases from distributional changes, even if on average there is neutrality.[2]

In addition to uncertainties introduced by income inequality effects, the elasticity approach to anticipating poverty decline with income suffers from a problem that Chapter 2 discussed. A given rate of economic growth will have a bigger impact on poverty headcount when the poor are clustered closely around the poverty line than when their incomes fall markedly below the line. In some countries this phenomenon might explain the weaker-than-expected response of poverty levels to growth in the face of only modest changes in overall inequality.[3]

■ *Significant difficulties surround the use of income elasticities in understanding or forecasting poverty reduction.* ■

The lognormal approach for forecasting poverty in this volume eliminates the elasticity approach. In fact, lognormal specifications could be used to calculate variable poverty elasticities across countries and time.

Pro-poor growth

If growth in general reduces poverty, are certain types of growth patterns particularly helpful? The idea of **pro-poor growth** is at the heart of many a poverty reduction strategy. Ravallion (2004) uses the decomposition of poverty into growth and distribution components to formalize the notion of pro-poor growth. One usage defines growth as pro-poor only if poverty falls by more than it would have if growth were distribution-neutral (Baulch and McCulloch 1999; Kakwani and Pernia 2000). In other words, pro-poor means that the poor experience higher growth than the nonpoor. Policy prescriptions associated with pro-poor growth typically include rapid job creation for the relatively unskilled; public expenditure on infrastructure, health, and education disproportionately oriented toward the poor; and "narrowly targeting" measures to provide special support to the poor.

As an alternative, Ravallion and Chen (2003) define "distributional correction" as the ratio

of actual poverty over time to the poverty that would have resulted under distribution neutrality. If the distribution shifts in favor of the poor, it would be greater than one, and if it shifts in favor of the rich, it would be less than one. The formulation becomes:

Rate of pro-poor growth = Distributional correction x Ordinary growth rate.

Their definition is less restrictive in the sense that the rate of pro-poor growth can be high even if the distributional correction is less than one (distribution shifts in favor of the rich), provided the ordinary growth rate is high enough. They argue it is the right way to measure pro-poor growth when the objective is to assess poverty reduction caused by growth.

The Deep Drivers of Poverty

Given that growth, inequality, and population are the proximate determinants of poverty, what are the factors that in turn drive these determinants? Montek S. Ahluwalia, Nicholas Carter, and Hollis Chenery (1979) undertook an early effort in mapping both proximate and deep drivers, as well as some of the policy levers that might move the deep drivers. The bold lines in

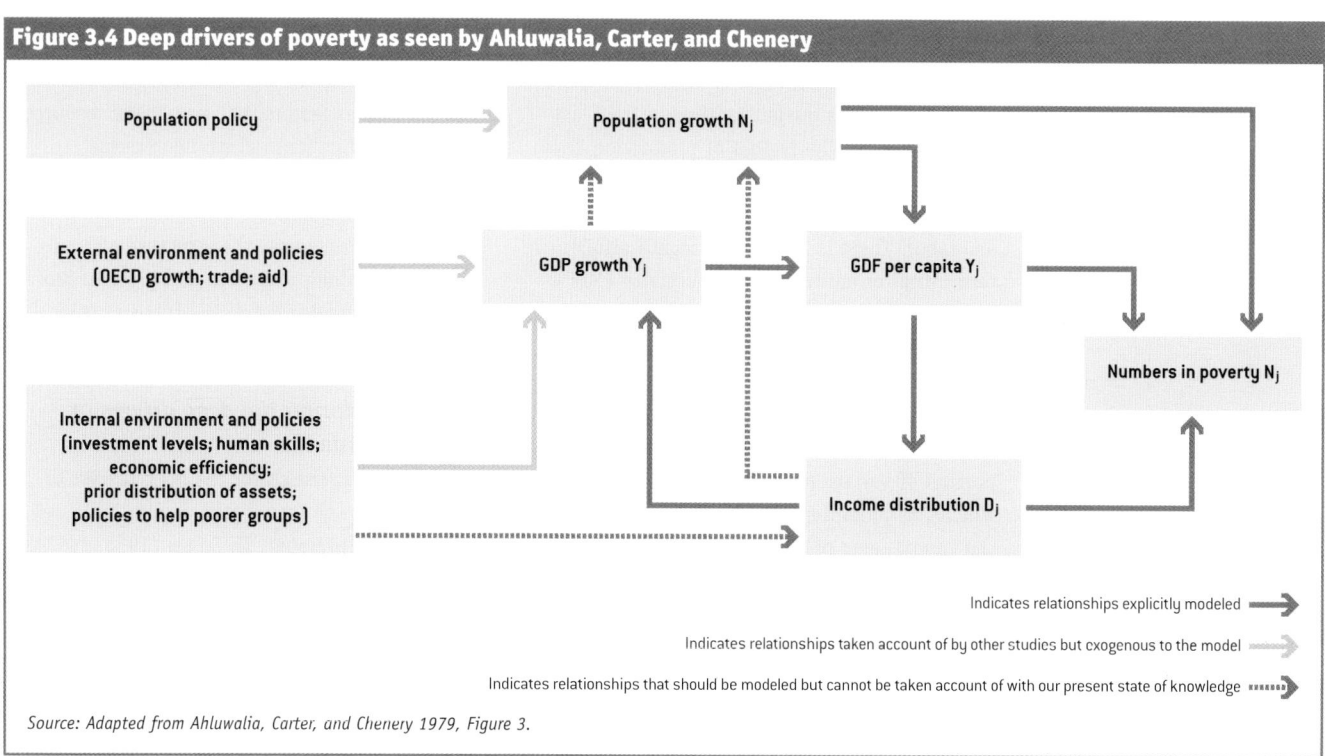

Figure 3.4 Deep drivers of poverty as seen by Ahluwalia, Carter, and Chenery

Indicates relationships explicitly modeled ⟶

Indicates relationships taken account of by other studies but exogenous to the model ⟶

Indicates relationships that should be modeled but cannot be taken account of with our present state of knowledge ┅⟶

Source: Adapted from Ahluwalia, Carter, and Chenery 1979, Figure 3.

Figure 3.5 The deep drivers of growth as seen by the Millennium Project

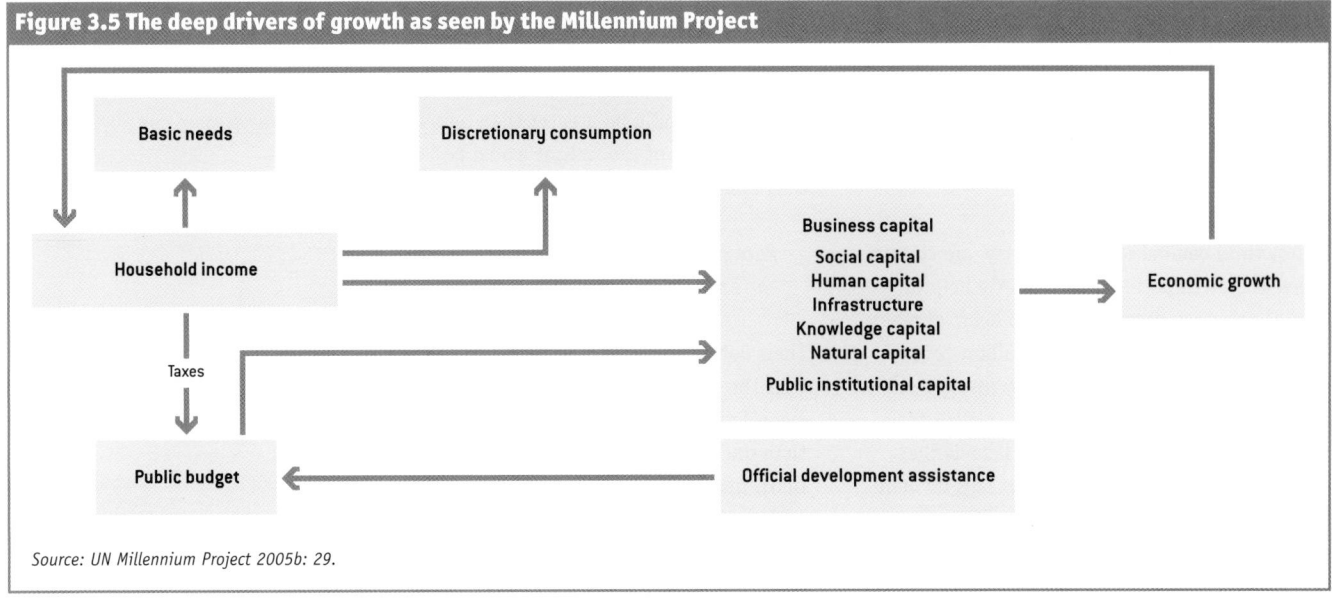

Source: UN Millennium Project 2005b: 29.

Figure 3.4 trace the connections between the proximate drivers and poverty. The figure also identifies deep drivers such as investment levels, human skills, and economic efficiency.

The UN Millennium Project (2005a) also identified deep drivers of economic growth (see Figure 3.5). In order to develop and present its "practical plan" for achieving the Millennium Development Goals (MDGs), the project elaborated a causal understanding of change in levels of poverty, hunger, education, and other variables related to the goals. The **production function** with which most growth economists model a country's output motivated their list of deep drivers. The factors of production that typically enter this function are business or physical capital (equipment and structures) and labor. There is also an aggregate efficiency term, total or multifactor productivity (MFP). In highly reduced form approaches, the MFP is a residual that captures everything that is not measurable physical and human input. However, quantitative studies show that these measurable inputs account for only a small portion of variations in growth and income, which has prompted calls to better understand the components of this residual (Klenow and Rodriguez-Clare 1997a; Prescott 1998). The inclusion of factors such as human capital, social capital, infrastructure, knowledge capital, and institutional capital in Figure 3.5 captures the attempts to get into the black box of productivity.

Listing deep drivers of economic growth

Figure 3.6 further elaborates on this theme. The figure shows that MFP, labor supply, and physical capital determine growth. In other words, the figure captures the production function. Although growth in all these inputs can cause economic growth in the short run, growth in MFP is primarily responsible for sustained long-run growth. MFP responds to changes in human capital, social capital and governance, infrastructure capital, natural capital, and knowledge. The schema is broad enough to allow for the contribution that infrastructure makes to MFP, as well as factors such as natural resources and the environment, which neoclassical economic analyses of growth do not typically include. The IFs model that we use to simulate poverty over time uses the structure of Figure 3.6 to determine production and growth. Box 3.2 describes in greater detail the types of capital depicted in Figure 3.6.

Further exploring the deep drivers of economic growth

The systematic search for the deep drivers of economic growth (see, again, Figure 3.5) goes back at least to Robert M. Solow (1956, 1957), who demonstrated that an economy cannot grow by accumulating capital alone. Diminishing returns on capital—the tenth machine in a factory with a constant labor force will produce proportionately less extra output than the first one—means that growth will eventually taper

Figure 3.6 Factors influencing economic growth

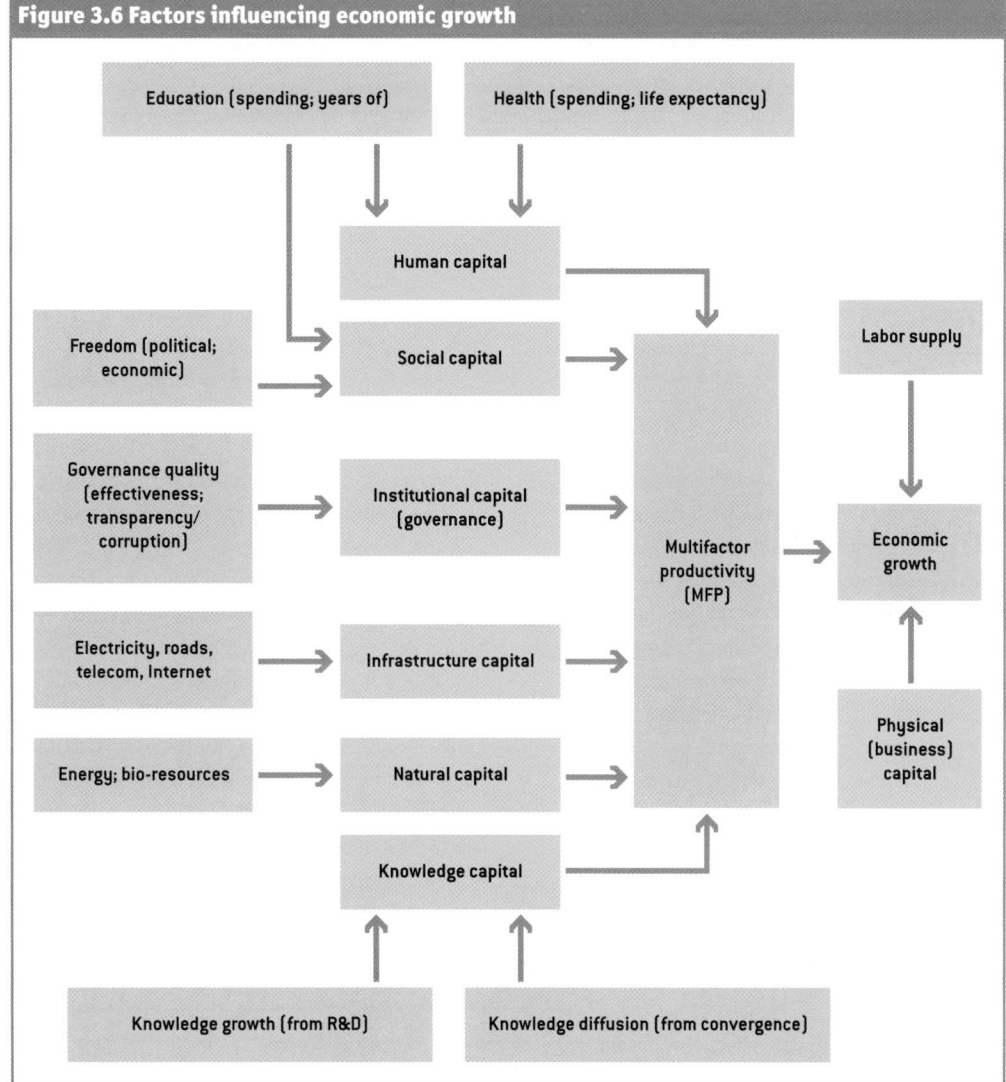

Box 3.2 The various types of capital

Physical Capital: Equipment and structures used in the production process. A broad conception of physical capital might include land as well as residential structures and commercial ones. Investment augments capital.

Human Capital: Broadly, the quality of labor used in the production process. Expenditures on child rearing, education and health, and time devoted to on-the-job training and learning by doing augment human capital.

Social Capital: The quality of *interactions* among individuals. This measure captures the benefits accruing to individuals through their membership in groups and social networks. Social capital has served as an umbrella term for a variety of concepts, such as transactional efficiency, trust, social networks, honesty, and civic engagement. Education, development of social norms and institutions, and culture are a few of the determinants of social capital.

Institutional Capital (Governance): The institutions and processes by which a social grouping manages itself, specifying power distributions and usage, including citizen participation. The quality of governance depends heavily upon the extent of social capital.

Infrastructure Capital: Roads, airports, and public transportation, and other public goods, where use by one party does not exclude its use by others. In most countries, the government is heavily involved in infrastructure investment and provision. Infrastructure also includes utilities such as electricity and water. Use of these utilities by one precludes use by others, and therefore the private sector can in principle provide these services. Given the scale of investment and operation involved, however, the government provides them in most developing countries.

Natural Capital: The physical and biological environment. Minerals, fossil fuels, and publicly held land, such as national parks and wildlife preserves, are types of natural capital. Although the amount of natural capital is fixed in a country, investments can be made in mineral exploration to discover new sources and in improvements of environmental quality.

Knowledge Capital: Knowledge not embodied in an individual or equipment. It is typically "nonrival"; use of, say, blueprints by one person does not preclude their use by another. R&D, expenditures in research institutions, and institutions of higher learning constitute investment in knowledge capital.

off. Only growth in MFP will sustain growth in the long run. Indeed, exercises in "growth accounting" reveal that there is a large portion of growth for which measurable inputs in capital and labor cannot account. Solow did not take a stance on how this productivity growth arose; it was exogenous to his framework, beyond the control of economic agents.

A series of papers in the 1980s by Paul M. Romer (1986, 1987) and Robert E. Lucas (1988) ushered in a new era in the research and understanding of economic growth. These "new growth theories" view growth as endogenous, arising from intentional actions of economic agents and governments. Romer posited that increasing returns, resulting from the use of specialized inputs in production or externalities in the use of capital, can overcome the stumbling block of diminishing returns and sustain long-term growth. Lucas posited that there are no diminishing returns on the accumulation of human capital used in production and that it can sustain growth in the long run.

The implications of endogenous growth are profound. Taking a stance on the reasons ("engines") for growth allows one to recommend policies to increase growth. For instance, if externalities associated with human capital result in underinvestment in education and other forms of human capital, subsidies for such investment can increase growth. Exploring endogenous growth also offers the possibility of getting into the black box of productivity and understanding its origins. Indeed, numerous factors have been suggested and studied as engines of growth since the 1980s. We offer a very brief and necessarily incomplete survey of these engines of growth, in order to provide an elaboration of the deep drivers in the previous two figures.

Forecasting many drivers of multifactor productivity helps endogenize economic growth.

Human capital

The origins of "human capital," the idea that investment in oneself is akin to investment in capital such as machines, can be traced back to Theodore W. Schultz (1963) and Gary S. Becker (1964). Lucas (1988) pioneered the notion of human capital as an engine of growth.[4] In his framework, externalities in production arising from human capital account for any residual in growth for which growth in measurable inputs cannot account.

Evidence on the causal connection between human capital and growth is mixed. N. Gregory Mankiw, David Romer, and David N. Weil (1992), Jess Benhabib and Mark M. Spiegel (1994), and Krishna B. Kumar (2003) found that educational measures (enrollment and attainment) cause growth. However, Peter J. Klenow and Andres Rodriguez-Clare (1997a), Edward C. Prescott (1998), and Mark Bils and Peter Klenow (2000) question the role of human capital in growth; they found that differences in human capital account for little of the cross-country variation in economic growth and income. William Easterly (2001) also provided a skeptical view of human capital. One problem with obtaining decisive evidence on the role of human capital in growth is the difficulty in measuring it. Even though educational variables are typically used as proxies, human capital encompasses more—improvements in labor productivity arising from repeated production ("learning by doing," as in Arrow 1962), on-the-job learning, and the knowledge of institutions (Kumar and Matsusaka 2006) to name just a few. As the following example from Lucas (2002: 13) shows, human capital is a very broad concept and therefore difficult to measure: "The idea that it will help business to smile at customers is not patentable or publishable, but whenever someone remembers and implements it, it shows up in profits and total factor productivity as well."

Knowledge base/technologies

Human capital, by definition, is embodied in individuals. Romer (1990) suggested that the growth in disembodied knowledge (technological blueprints) is an engine of economic growth. In his framework, intentional R&D by monopolistically competitive firms results in the discovery of new goods and specialized inputs. Human capital is viewed as an input into technology or knowledge production.[5]

Romer (1989) provided evidence for the R&D-based view of growth. Economic openness or an external orientation is an alternative to doing R&D to gain access to new technologies, and especially so for developing countries, which do not have the resources to engage in original R&D.[6]

Social capital and governance

Even though the concept of social capital appears to have originated in the early twentieth century (Hanifan 1916, 1920), it attracted the attention of economists and sociologists only recently. Joel Sobel (2002: 139) defined social capital succinctly as follows: "Social capital describes circumstances in which individuals can use membership in groups and networks to secure benefits."

Social capital has served as an umbrella term for a variety of concepts, such as trust, social networks, honesty, and civic engagement, to name a few (Coleman 1988; Fukuyama 1995, 1999; Putnam 1995). On the ability of social capital or social infrastructure to account for some of the unexplained variation in cross-country incomes, see La Porta et al. (1997), Knack and Keefer (1997), and Hall and Jones (1999).[7]

Despite ongoing debates about its measurability and ability to explain growth, social capital has been useful in conceptualizing the role of formal and informal institutions (and thus governance) in economic growth. It has also allowed researchers to think about human capital, the deep driver discussed above, in different ways. Education does more than increase the productivity of labor in goods production. For instance, Krishna B. Kumar and John G. Matsusaka (2006) viewed social capital as human capital, or the knowledge of how to use institutions. Education also politically empowers people and improves freedom, and therefore the "capability to function" in the sense used by Amartya Sen (1999).

Social capital, broadly construed, also deals with issues of governance and with institutions in general. Daron Acemoglu and Simon Johnson (2005) found, for instance, that institutions that define and enforce property rights have an important effect on economic growth. Edward L. Glaeser and his colleagues (2004) were skeptical of this view, and found that human capital, rather than institutions, is a more fundamental force for growth. Kumar and Matsusaka (2006) argued that the human capital versus institutions debate might be too narrowly framed, because human capital *about* the functioning of institutions is an important facet of economic development.

Infrastructure and natural resources
Infrastructure is a public good that improves the efficiency with which other productive, private inputs are combined with one another.

Therefore, infrastructure rightly deserves to be considered a crucial component of MFP. The World Bank (1994) studied the role of infrastructure in economic development. It surveyed the recent studies on the impact of infrastructure on economic growth and found very high rates of return on investment, sometimes up to 60 percent. It is possible that these returns could be overstated because of omitted factors and two-way causation between infrastructure and growth. However, based on studies of cost reduction resulting from infrastructure improvements, such as by David A. Aschauer (1993), the report concluded that the role of infrastructure in growth is "substantial, significant, and frequently greater than that of investment in other forms of capital."

Although theoretical treatments of natural resources, the environment, and growth are rare (see, for example, Stokey 1998 on the limits to growth), a few empirical studies have investigated the connection between natural resources and growth. Jeffrey Sachs (1995) and Sachs and Andrew M. Warner (1997) found a strong negative connection between use of natural resources and growth. An increase in the share of natural resource exports in GDP from 10 to 20 percent reduces the annual growth rate by 0.33 percentage points. They speculated that there might be greater incentives for rent-seeking in resource-rich economies, that natural resources might provide a false sense of security and postpone economic reforms conducive to growth, or that the economies could be suffering from a form of "Dutch disease" (the surge in raw material exports drives up the real exchange rate or real wages and hurts other exports). Thorvaldur Gylfason (2001) presented evidence to argue that natural capital slows economic development because resource-rich countries inadvertently or deliberately neglect expenditures on human capital.

The availability of natural resources can have a positive effect on growth. For instance, exhaustible resources such as oil are usually a bottleneck in production, and their extra availability will increase output. Likewise, the availability of water and fertile soil are crucial for agricultural production. But the above literature also alerts us that natural resources can be used as a tool of abuse.

Inequality

Inequality, a proximate driver of poverty, could itself affect growth, another proximate driver. Bourguignon (2003) surveyed theories as to how inequality could affect growth. Credit market imperfections (liquidity constraints, collateral requirements, enforcement difficulties) could cause investment to be undertaken only by those with enough initial wealth, whereas other, potentially more productive projects do not get initiated for lack of funding. In such cases, redistribution from the wealthy to the poor could enhance growth. Oded Galor and Joseph Zeira (1993), Abhijit V. Banerjee and Andrew F. Newman (1993), and Philippe Aghion and Patrick Bolton (1997) provided formalizations of this idea. Elizabeth M. Caucutt and Krishna B. Kumar (2006c) considered a similar situation but highlighted redistribution from low-ability to high-ability individuals in a stagnant economy where wealth-based redistribution is not possible. A second line of explanation argues that greater inequality would increase the political will for higher taxes and redistribution, taking resources away from growth-causing activities such as investment (Alesina and Rodrik 1992; Persson and Tabellini 1992). A third explanation is that high inequality can lead to political instability and therefore lower investment and growth (Alesina and Perotti 1996).

Aggregate cross-country evidence for the inequality-growth connection is also inconclusive (Forbes 2000). Bourguignon (2003) argued for tests of the micromechanisms suggested by the theoretical works.

Surveying deep drivers of population

The deep drivers of population growth, one of the proximate drivers of poverty, also influence the total production of a country via the amount of labor. Fertility rate and life expectancy, and to a lesser degree migration, affect population growth. Per capita income, the education level of women, and advances in medical technology influence in turn these drivers of population. In addition to population size, the cohort structure of population, retirement patterns, and female participation rates determine the labor supply. Figure 3.7 captures these interconnections.

The economic analysis of fertility can be traced back to Becker (1960), who introduced the quantity-quality trade-off inherent in fertility decisions. Given their income and time endowments, parents can either have many children but afford to impart to each child only small amounts of education or human capital, or have few children but provide each with large

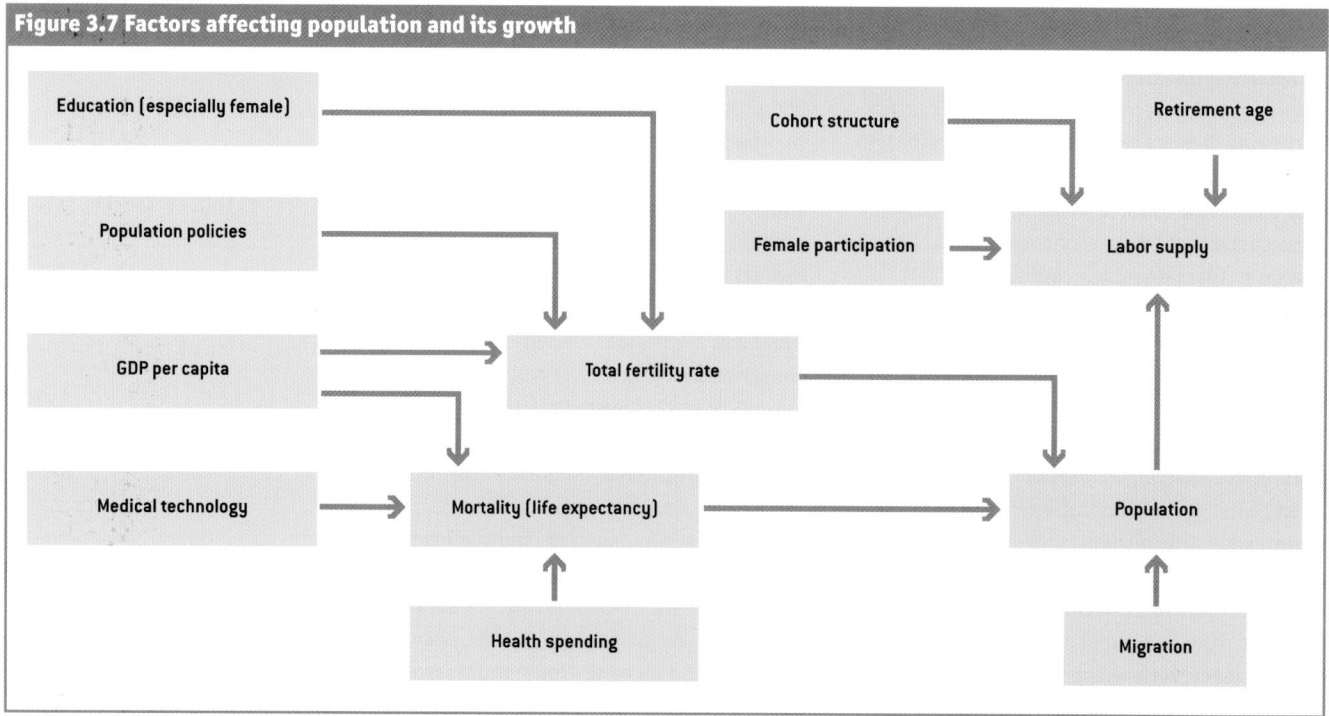

Figure 3.7 Factors affecting population and its growth

amounts of human capital. Robert J. Barro and Gary S. Becker (1989) analyzed fertility in the context of economic growth. Becker, Kevin M. Murphy, and Robert Tamura (1990) argued that, given the fixed costs inherent in childbearing and child rearing, an economy can either stagnate in a "Malthusian" state with high fertility and low human capital, or experience sustained growth with low fertility and high human capital. Oded Galor and David N. Weil (2000) provided a unified framework to analyze the transition from Malthusian stagnation to a situation with moderate growth and high fertility and eventually to high growth and low fertility.

The World Bank (1980) reported that socioeconomic factors, such as income, literacy, and life expectancy, account for a significant variation in fertility changes in developing countries. As opportunities for education and employment improve for women, the value of their time increases. They tend to marry later and prefer to have fewer children. When infant mortality is high, poor families tend to have many children as "insurance" against the expected loss of children.

In the same report, the World Bank listed the purchasing power of basic necessities, conditions of the environment (including sanitation), and an understanding of nutrition, health, and hygiene as the basic determinants of health. It also noted that a major problem with mortality of children in poor countries is the interaction of infectious diseases with malnutrition.

Surveying deep drivers of inequality

Individuals who differ in the amount of assets they possess earn different incomes. Access to markets and institutions that allow individuals to acquire these assets in the first place also varies widely across and within countries. The distribution of intrinsic ability would no doubt be responsible for some of the differences in outcomes. In this sense, some amount of inequality is inevitable. However, the inequality in ability could interact with, and sometimes be amplified by, constraints imposed by the environment. Since these constraints are most likely to apply to the poorest people, they induce a degree of persistence in poverty.

For instance, financial constraints—limits on borrowing, the need for collateral, and so on—can severely limit access to entrepreneurial

projects and other productive activities. Even if productive or educational ability is distributed independently from generation to generation, the presence of such constraints can cause persistence in inequality. Glenn C. Loury (1981) is an original influence in highlighting such persistence; see Elizabeth M. Caucutt and Krishna B. Kumar (2006a) for a more recent example. Richer and more educated parents can afford to educate their children more, even if the children are not intrinsically able. In contrast, even high-ability children of poor parents might not receive education because their parents, who find education unaffordable, cannot borrow to cover costs.

The existence of credit constraints implies that one's inheritance—the initial distribution of assets—matters for what activities one can undertake. Only the wealthy can engage in productive activities and can afford to make large enough bequests to their children. The poor will either subsist or work for low wages, and cannot make sizable bequests to their children. A persistence of inequality results.[8]

Even where the government steps in to address such constraints, say, through public expenditures, differences in access to publicly provided services can cause inequality to persist. A bias in expenditures toward urban schools, hospitals, financial institutions, and infrastructure can severely limit access to these public services for the rural poor. For instance, Kremer et al. (2005) found that lack of proper roads is one of the main reasons for the rampant teacher absenteeism in Indian public schools. Since the poor rely more heavily on public schools, they are more likely to be affected by this negligence. For that reason Khan and Weiss (2006) advocated public expenditure on infrastructure, health, and education disproportionately oriented toward the poor. Discrimination by gender, race, skin color, or caste can also limit access to publicly provided services.

A related cause for the persistence of or rise in inequality is poor governance. Misappropriation or misallocation of public funds can alter the distribution of factor endowments and skew access to public services. For instance, Sanjeev Gupta, Hamid Davoodi, and Rosa Alonso-Terme (2002) found in a cross-country sample that corruption increases

Figure 3.8 The deep drivers of inequality

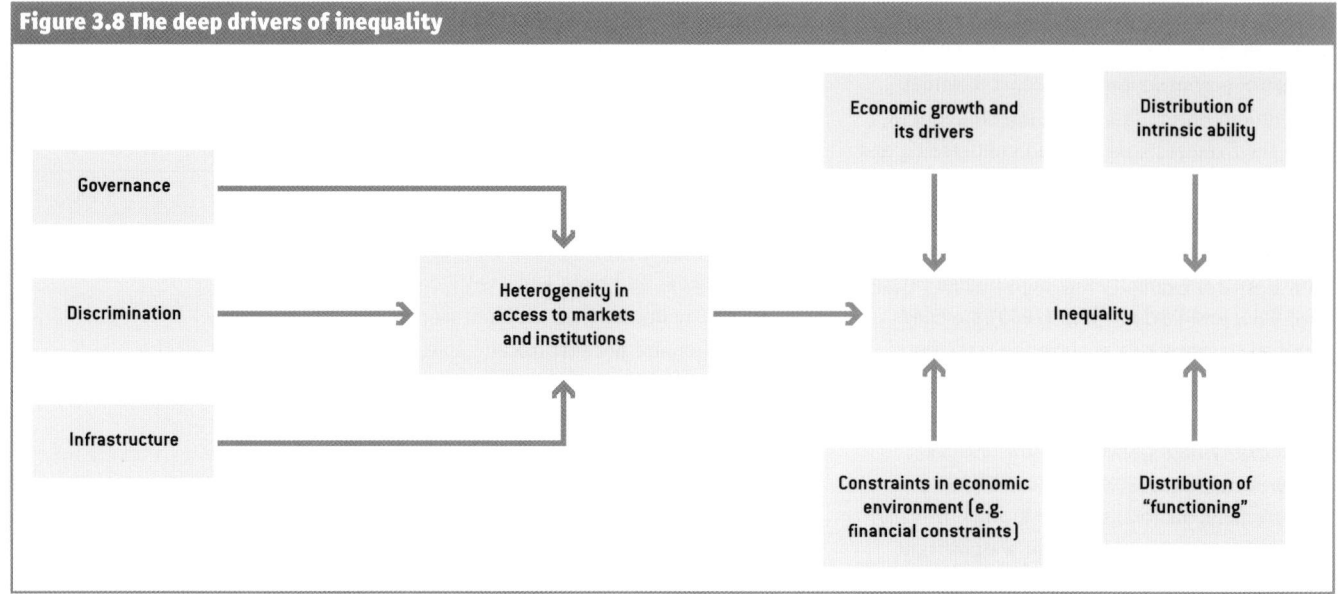

inequality in education and land distribution, decreases social spending, and decreases the progressiveness of taxes, thereby contributing to increased income inequality and poverty.

Poverty can be characterized as the deprivation of "capabilities"—freedom, social functioning, education, and health—that are intrinsically important, according to Sen (1984, 1999). In this view, income is only instrumental; how this income translates into capabilities varies by individuals or groups of individuals, and this variability captures a dimension of inequality not captured by inequality in income alone.[9] Figure 3.8 depicts the deep drivers of inequality discussed above.

In general, different policy levers that affect growth would therefore also have implications for inequality. For example, accumulation of human capital by the poor would increase their chances of upward mobility and decrease inequality. Likewise, investments in infrastructure or institutional improvements (social capital), if done in a way to benefit the poor, would also decrease inequality. We turn to surveying such policy levers next.

Policies to Reduce Poverty: A Selective Survey

A wide range of policy levers have the potential to reduce poverty. To identify those policies, we rely heavily on policy positions and documents from development institutions that are on the front lines of fighting poverty. As measured by

the headcount of people living on less than $1 per day, more than 85 percent of the world's poor live in China, South Asia, and sub-Saharan Africa. (The figure is a little over 80 percent if the $2-per-day measure is used.) Therefore, policies that have been suggested and used for these regions are of particular interest and importance.

Our aim is twofold. The first is collation: we list policy levers suggested by major sources. The second is extraction and synthesis: we identify strategic orientations, conceptualizations, and philosophies that various organizations follow in fighting poverty. Extracting these orientations allows us to consider packages of policies in the next section.

An early framework

As discussed earlier (see, again, Figure 3.4), Ahluwalia, Carter, and Chenery identified sets of policies to address poverty in 1979: population policy, policies relating to the external environment (poverty alleviation via international trade, increased high-income country growth, and foreign aid), and policies relating to the internal environment (investment, human capital, policies to directly help poorer groups, and policies that affect distribution of income).

We have learned much since that study, but the schema is a strong one overall. Specifically, the division of policies into internal versus external is a natural classification, one that

recurs in other prescriptions. One can see in these sets the possibility of an "inward," do-it-yourself orientation; an "outward," economically open orientation; and an orientation based on foreign assistance. Some of these policies are at the discretion of the developing country itself—for instance, whether to adopt an open stance or not. Some require coordination among developed countries—for example, the degree of free trade among countries and coordinated Organization for Economic Cooperation and Development (OECD) policies that increase world growth.

The World Bank's policies

The World Bank has been more extensively involved in global poverty alleviation than any other organization. From Robert McNamara's announcement in 1968 that the fundamental work of the Bank was to improve the lives of the poor to the adoption of "a dream of a world without poverty" as the Bank's motto by then-president James Wolfensohn, the intentions of the institution have been clear. However, the Bank's philosophy and approach to fighting poverty have evolved over time.

For over three decades the World Bank viewed development as an issue of economic growth (Birdsall and Londono 1997). In the 1960s, its lending focused on transportation and power, agriculture, industry. Poverty alleviation became a goal in itself in the 1970s, though lending continued to be aimed at filling infrastructure and external financial gaps to stimulate growth. In the 1980s, though distracted by adjustment demands caused by the debt crises, the Bank recommended reallocation of public spending to human capital, primary education, and health (World Bank 1980). The focus returned directly to poverty reduction in the 1990s, with strategies for pro-poor growth, social services targeted to the poor, and the creation of safety nets. Below we consider three landmark *World Development Reports* on poverty, released in 1980, 1990, and 2000–2001.

World Development Report, 1980

During the 1970s, as it became clear that economic growth alone would not reduce poverty at an acceptable speed, the World Bank and other organizations gave attention to four strategies: increasing employment, meeting basic needs, reducing inequality,

and raising the productivity of the poor. The 1980 report combined these approaches with a strong concern for growth, and it integrated them with human development, recognizing it as an end as well as a means for economic progress. As ways to raise incomes of the poor, it suggested land reform and tenure; public investment (such as irrigation projects) and private investment by nonpoor; improved education, health, and nutrition; a decrease in fertility; research into technology appropriate for poor countries (such as the introduction of high-yield seeds); migration by people to places where there are better opportunities; and transfers and subsidies.

The policies tend to be "progrowth," with improvements in education, health, nutrition, and fertility intended to increase growth. However, the report did pay attention to "human development" as an end in itself. Associating poverty with low levels of human development is substantively important. Ravi Kanbur and Lyn Squire (1999: 2) noted: "As more aspects of poverty are recognized, so more policies become relevant to fighting poverty—moving beyond income to health, for example, introduces a new set of policy instruments."

One can also see pro-poor policies in the attempts to increase the incomes of the poor. However, not until the 1990 World Development Report do we see a strong emphasis on growth in which the poor can participate.

World Development Report, 1990

The three pillars of poverty alleviation outlined in this report were encouraging patterns of growth that use labor more efficiently, targeting basic social services to the poor, and using transfers and social safety nets.

In order to encourage efficient use of labor, the report suggested avoiding excess taxation of agriculture, partly by avoiding overvalued exchange rates, providing strong support for rural infrastructure, making technical innovations accessible to small farmers, and fostering urban job creation by minimizing distortions in the product and factor markets and by providing suitable urban infrastructure.

The report also suggested that growth would be "poverty reducing" if the poor had access to land (improving property rights, tenancy), credit (microcredit and informal channels, rather

The World Bank has been at the forefront of efforts to reduce poverty, and its understanding has evolved over time.

than government-subsidized formal credit), and public infrastructure and services (adapting technologies to small farmers and improving rural infrastructure).

Under the umbrella of social sector policies ("investing in people"), the report included family planning to help reduce fertility, expanding the education system and improving the curriculum, and improving health.

Regarding transfers (for the poor who will need time to fully participate in the economy) and safety nets (for the poor who will be affected adversely by shocks), the report recommended attention to food pricing and distribution, public employment schemes, and social security. The report also highlighted the need for macroeconomic stability to encourage private investment and quick adjustments to shocks. On the external front, it pointed out the need for liberalization by industrialized countries. The developing countries need relatively undistorted sectoral terms of trade to avoid bias against agriculture. The aim is to promote labor-intensive growth through economic openness. It suggested that debt relief and foreign aid be tied to policy reforms.

One can see "poverty-reducing growth" emerge as a strategic priority in this report. That is, growth is still seen as important for poverty reduction, but this growth needs to allow the poor to participate, via increased employment and access. The goal of "human development" or "investing in people" was solidified, with education, health, and fertility reduction emerging as strong priorities. There was an emphasis on "openness." One also sees the emergence of an "efficiency first" call for a distortion-free environment—lower agricultural taxes and removal of distortions in sectoral terms of trade, industrial policy, exchange rates, and product and factor markets in general. Likewise, the issue of political feasibility arose in many a context—land reform, choice of macroeconomic policy, and so on. Even though "improved governance" was not a major theme, one can see hints of it throughout the report. Cooperation from the industrialized countries in the form of trade liberalization was mentioned, but calls for debt relief and aid from them were highly nuanced and tentative.

World Development Report, 2000–2001
This report reflected the movement to center stage in the 1990s of governance, institutions, and vulnerability of the poor. It proposed a three-pronged, complementary strategy for attacking poverty.

- Promoting opportunities by encouraging effective private investment, through macroeconomic stability, sound financial systems, and the rule of law; expanding into international markets; building the assets of the poor; addressing socially based asset inequalities; and getting infrastructure and knowledge to poor areas.
- Facilitating empowerment by providing a political and legal basis for inclusive development, enabling inclusive decentralization and community development, promoting gender equity, tackling social barriers, and supporting poor people's social capital.
- Enhancing security for the poor in the face of economy-wide and regionwide risks by formulating a modular approach to help poor people manage risk, providing national programs to prepare for and respond to macro shocks, designing social risk management programs that are also progrowth (such as unemployment insurance that does not compromise the incentive to work), addressing civil conflict, and tackling the HIV/AIDS epidemic.

The report noted the need for international action in these areas in addition to domestic implementation. Increased focus on debt relief and effective aid contingent on sound domestic policy are needed. Industrialized countries must open their markets to developing country imports in agriculture and in labor-intensive manufacturing and services. Poor countries need a greater voice in international forums, and international financial institutions should also strengthen the financial architecture to lessen economic volatility. Still further, international cooperation is needed in developing vaccines and technologies specific to the poor and in protecting the environment.

Growth was still the overarching poverty reduction tool in this report, but pro-poor growth was emphasized. "Improved governance"

took center stage as a poverty reduction strategy as well. Policies to promote "stability" at the individual level (insurance against risks) and at the macroeconomic level (sound economic architecture and policies to minimize shocks and deal with them when they happen) were given considerable importance. And instead of viewing domestic self-help and external assistance as alternate strategies, the report viewed "domestic self-help *plus* external assistance" (for example, opening of markets by industrialized countries) as a complementary strategy. "Environmental sustainability" also received attention.

Poverty Reduction Strategy Papers

The need for concerted action on the strategies outlined in these reports prompted the World Bank and the International Monetary Fund (IMF) to initiate the Poverty Reduction Strategy Papers (PRSP) in 1999 to facilitate a "comprehensive country-based strategy for poverty reduction." The IMF's website describes the papers as follows:

> Poverty Reduction Strategy Papers (PRSPs) are prepared by governments in low-income countries through a participatory process involving domestic stakeholders and external development partners, including the IMF and the World Bank. A PRSP describes the macroeconomic, structural and social policies and programs that a country will pursue over several years to promote broad-based growth and reduce poverty, as well as external financing needs and the associated sources of financing. ... PRSPs provide the operational basis for Fund and Bank concessional lending and for debt relief under the Heavily Indebted Poor Countries (HIPC) Initiative.[10]

The PRSP process thus emphasizes wide domestic ownership of a plan that combines growth and pro-poor orientations with identification of the external assistance needed.

Other World Bank documents

Guillermo E. Perry and his colleagues (2006) provided a detailed survey of the empirical literature on the effect of various polices on growth and inequality. Within that literature, policies to increase economic growth (and decrease inequality) divide into the categories of structural policies (and institutions) and stabilization policies. The structural policies involve improvement in education and governance; increases in financial development, infrastructure, and trade openness; and decreases in the size of government. Macroeconomic stabilization, a reduction in external imbalances, and minimization of financial turmoil are the suggested stabilization policies.

Despite occasional disagreements, there is a fair degree of empirical consensus that these policies increase growth. There is less consensus on whether three of the policies—financial development, openness, and government burden, or size—decrease inequality.

Financial development can ease credit access for the poor, who are often liquidity-constrained, and thereby decrease inequality. However, financial assets are mainly held by the rich and financial institutions concentrated in the high-income urban centers; thus some "improvements" in the financial arena can actually increase inequality. Alessandra Bonfiglioli (2005) presented evidence that inequality increases with financial development up to a certain level and declines after that.

Trade and openness are viewed as key elements of high growth, but if capital goods become cheaper to import and cause workers to lose jobs because capital is substituted for labor, inequality will increase. Capital-skill complementarity will further magnify this effect. Although some studies find that the positive effect outweighs or is at least as strong as the negative, Branko Milanovic (2005) found that openness reduces the income share of the bottom eight deciles and increases the share of the top two deciles. Only beyond a certain level of economic development do the poor and middle class benefit from trade.

Government spending via taxation can be distortional and inefficient, but if the spending is done on health care, primary education, and infrastructure, it can decrease inequality. Since *disposable incomes* matter more for poverty reduction than market income, Perry and colleagues (2006) surveyed the evidence on redistributive taxation and inequality. They found taxes and transfers have a greater impact

The Poverty Reduction Strategy Papers are comprehensive, country-owned strategies for reducing poverty.

on inequality in developed than in developing countries. However, they noted this important policy lesson: redistribution takes place largely through transfers rather than taxes (that is, tax progressivity). They suggested that attempts to address inequality and poverty should first address the composition and structure of existing transfer programs, and only then turn to obtaining more resources via taxes, minimizing distortions as much as possible.

These documents espoused the strategy of pro-poor growth, displaying strong concern for policies that increase growth *and* decrease inequality. These policies can also be viewed through the lens of "inward" versus "outward" strategies. A great deal of commonality exists between this set of policies and others mentioned previously, such as improved governance, increased education, increased openness, and macroeconomic stabilization. And yet again, there was a greater degree of consensus on policies that increase growth than on those identified as pro-poor.

The Asian Development Bank's policies

Given that over 65 percent of the $1-per-day poor live in Asia, strategies devised to address poverty in that region are of particular relevance. We therefore consider the policies that the Asian Development Bank (2000, 2004a, 2004b) has recommended. Three elements ("strategic pillars") guide its policies: pro-poor, sustainable economic growth; good governance; and social development.

Growth *can* reduce poverty, and labor-intensive growth can reduce it even faster. The policies that aid such growth include removal of market-distorting interventions (overvalued exchange rate, import and export restrictions, credit subsidies, and state ownership of enterprises), encouragement of microfinance, infrastructure development, sound macroeconomic management, encouragement of the private sector, and policies that enhance the health of the environment and the protection of natural resources.

Several actions support good governance: strengthened public expenditure management at the national level, policies to promote equity (progressive taxation and adequate allocation of expenditures for basic education, health, and public services), and delegation of responsibility for the provision of public services to the lowest appropriate level of government.

Addressing the needs of specific groups aids social development. The budget allocation has to provide for human capital development (access to basic education, primary health care, and other services), early childhood development, population policies (universal education for girls, accessible reproductive health services), social capital development, gender parity, and social protection (unemployment insurance, old age pension, safety nets).

The strategy of the Asian Development Bank relies heavily on microfinance as a way to increase incomes and access. John Weiss and Heather Montgomery (2004) reached a nuanced conclusion about the effectiveness of microfinance in reducing poverty. The evidence suggests that microfinance has positive impacts on poverty reduction, but it is unlikely to be a panacea, since those considered to be high risks for formal credit are also likely to be high risks for microfinance and might be denied access. The bank's view that the microfinance strategy can also aid in building participatory institutions is a more subtle argument, even if challenging to evaluate.

Given clearly articulated strategic pillars, the Asian Development Bank's policies naturally fall into those that increase growth (pro-poor growth), decrease inequality (human development), and address institutional changes that aid both goals (improved governance). The bank's strategy also suggests that its policies have been assigned to the following groups: (1) "population" (discussed under social development), (2) "outward" (labor-absorbing, trade-led growth, removing distortions such as overvalued exchange rate and import and export restrictions, sound macroeconomic management, and regional cooperation) and (3) "inward" (the remaining policies). We can also see that the policies reviewed thus far have similar views on the deep drivers of growth.

The United Nations and the Millennium Development Plan

The Millennium Project's understanding of growth drivers, presented in Figure 3.5, focuses on both the internal and external elements of policy. Taxes collected from the developing country's citizens are the internal source of funds for the public budget, and official development assistance (foreign

● *The Asian Development Bank fights extreme poverty in the region of its greatest incidence.* ●

aid) forms the external source of funds. The public budget is then used to fund accumulation of various forms of capital that constitute the deep drivers of growth, especially forms such as infrastructure, which are public goods.

The UN Millennium Project (2005a) listed more details of interventions that would allow the MDGs to be met. Some of these interventions, like the MDGs themselves, reach well beyond poverty reduction. However, many interventions, such as investments in rural development, urban development, and slum upgrading, the health system, education at all levels, gender equality, and environmental sustainability, are relevant to poverty reduction.

With its emphasis on health and education, the UN Millennium Project was clearly advocating a strategy of human development that is pro poor. Its distinction between rural and urban policies suggested strategies of rural development and urban development. The former might be particularly important, given that the vast majority of the poor live in rural areas. However, since the rise of megacities with a large population of slum dwellers, urban policies have also become specific targets for intervention. As with the Asian Development Bank, "environmental sustainability" is a major concern.

Policies: A summary table

We summarize the policies discussed in the earlier subsections in Table 3.1.

> ● *Then–UN Secretary-General Kofi Annan charged the UN Millennium Project with developing an integrated plan for the MDG-related assault on poverty.* ●

Table 3.1 A summary of policies to reduce poverty

Policy	Proximate driver(s) affected	Deep driver(s) affected	References	Comments and discussion
Increased access to reproductive health services (family planning)	Population	Fertility	ADB, WB	
Investments in rural development (water, sanitation, etc.)	Population, inequality	Mortality	ADB, Millennium Project, Oxfam	
Increased education expenditure for girls	Population, growth, inequality	Human capital, fertility	ADB, Millennium Project, Oxfam, WB	
Increased non-OECD R&D expenditures	Growth	Knowledge capital	Millennium Project	
Increased investment	Growth	Physical capital	Ahluwalia et al.	Is it directly needed, or will it happen via other channels? Can it be caused by an investment subsidy?
Privatization	Growth	Physical capital, human capital	ADB	Affects MFP if public and private enterprises have different efficiencies.
Export promotion	Growth	Knowledge capital, human capital	ADB, WB, Oxfam, Ahluwalia et al.	
Increased R&D in OECD countries on technologies relevant to non-OECD countries (including increased technology transfers)	Growth	Knowledge capital, human capital	Ahluwalia et al.	
Increased foreign direct investment (FDI), portfolio investment	Growth	Knowledge capital, human capital	ADB, WB, Oxfam	
Removal of other external distortions such as overvalued exchange rates	Growth	Knowledge capital, human capital	ADB, WB, Oxfam	
Decreased product market and factor market distortions	Growth	Physical capital, labor	WB	
Decreased agricultural taxes	Growth	Land, physical capital, labor	WB	
Increased investment in primary health care	Growth, Population	Mortality, human capital	ADB, Millennium Project, Oxfam, Khan and Weiss	
Increased education expenditure	Growth, inequality	Human capital, fertility, social capital	ADB, WB, Millennium Project, Oxfam, Ahluwalia et al, Khan and Weiss	Some argue supply-side push for education has not been effective (Easterly 2001).

Table 3.1 A summary of policies to reduce poverty *continued*

Policy	Proximate driver(s) affected	Deep driver(s) affected	References	Comments and discussion
Improved governance (economic freedom, governance effectiveness, decrease corruption)	Growth, inequality	Social capital	ADB, WB, Oxfam	Costs of effecting these changes are unclear.
Increased expenditure on infrastructure (roads, electricity, telecommunications, etc.)	Growth, inequality	Physical capital	ADB, WB, Millennium Project, Oxfam	
Enhanced quality of environment and protection of natural resources	Growth, inequality	Physical capital	ADB, Millennium Project, Oxfam	Unclear how this policy is put into operation. Via development of renewable energy?
More microfinance	Growth, inequality	Physical capital, social capital	ADB, WB	See Montgomery and Weiss (2004) for an assessment.
Financial development (private domestic credit)	Growth, inequality	Physical capital, human capital	ADB, WB	
Increased soundness of macroeconomic management (low inflation, minimal distortion to interest rates, decreased fiscal deficit)	Growth, inequality	Physical capital	ADB, WB	
Increased expenditure on early child development	Growth, inequality	Human capital	ADB	
Increased expenditure on urban development and slum upgrading	Growth, inequality	Human capital, social capital	Millennium Project	
Increased openness via decrease in import duties, tariffs, quotas	Growth (+), inequality (-)	Knowledge capital, human capital	ADB, WB, Oxfam, Ahluwalia et al	
Lowered corporate and marginal taxes	Growth (+), inequality (-)	Physical capital, human capital	WB	
Decentralization, community-based governance	Inequality	Social capital	ADB, Oxfam	Costs of effecting these changes are unclear.
Increased budget expenditures on services specifically for the poor (education, health care, public services, etc.)	Inequality	Human capital, social capital	ADB, WB, Millennium Project, Oxfam, Ahluwalia et al., Khan and Weiss	Assume the negative trade-off on growth, if it exists, is minimal (Khan and Weiss, 2006).
Increased transfers to poor households (such as food subsidies)	Inequality	Human capital	WB	
Increased expenditure on social safety nets	Inequality	Human capital	ADB, Oxfam	
Increased public employment	Inequality	Labor	WB	
Reduced social barriers	Inequality	Social capital	WB	
Greater poor people's social capital	Inequality	Social capital	WB	
Increased female participation in labor force	Inequality, growth	Labor	ADB & Millennium Project (under gender parity)	Costs of effecting these changes are unclear.
Progressive taxation	Inequality (+), growth (-)	Physical capital	ADB	
Increased immigration/labor mobility, leading to increased worker remittances	Inequality, growth	Human capital	WB	
Increased foreign aid	Inequality, growth	All types of capital	Millennium Project, Ahluwalia et al.	
Land reform	Inequality, growth	Land, physical capital	WB	
Social risk management	Inequality, growth	Social capital, human capital	WB	

Note: ADB refers to Asian Development Bank; MFP, multifactor productivity; OECD, the Organization for Economic Cooperation and Development; WB, the World Bank.

Poverty Reduction Strategies: Search for Silver Bullets?

The search for silver bullets in the fight on poverty, for those measures that can have the greatest impact, ideally with the lowest cost, is unending. Identification of prospective silver bullets changes over time and across philosophical viewpoints.

As a field, development has always been subject to arguments about the relative merits of various philosophical tendencies, and different strategic orientations have had prominence over time and retained considerable support. As mentioned earlier, analysts considered economic growth synonymous with economic development up to the 1970s. When it became clear that growth alone did not reduce poverty at an acceptable speed, attempts were made to target the poor directly. The approach changed from progrowth to pro-poor and human development. The elements of participatory growth by and for the poor were then integrated into the strategy of pro-poor growth. The success of the East Asian economies' export-led growth in reducing poverty gave rise to "outward" strategies based on openness. The East Asian crisis gave rise to calls for "stability." In recent years, in addition to the traditionally suggested strategies of trade and financial flow liberalization, other prominent strategies have surfaced. Stagnation and conflict in Africa, rampant corruption in Africa, and the role of weak institutions in the Asian crisis

Table 3.2 Strategic orientations and constituent policies

Strategic orientation	Source	Constituent policies
Major strategic orientations		
Inward, self-sufficient	ACC, ADB	All, except increased openness, export promotion, increased FDI, increased foreign aid
Outward, open	ACC, WB (WDR 1990), ADB	Increased openness, export promotion, increased FDI, increased immigration and remittances, removal of external distortions
Foreign assistance	ACC	Increased foreign aid, increased R&D in OECD countries on non-OECD technologies
Strategic components		
Inward + foreign assistance	WB (WDR 2000/2001)	All inward policies plus foreign assistance policies
Progrowth	WB (WDR 1980)	Increased expenditure on education, health care, infrastructure, R&D expenditures, investment; improve governance, privatization, financial development, sound macroeconomic management, increased openness, export promotion, increased FDI, removal of external distortions
Human development	WB (WDR 1980, 1990), ADB, MP	Increased expenditure on girls' education, increased access to reproductive health, investments in rural development, increased investment in primary health care, increased expenditure on early child development
Pro-poor	WB (WDR 1980), MP	Increased budget expenditures on services specifically for the poor, increased expenditure on social safety nets, transfers such as food subsidies, land reform
Pro-poor growth	WB (WDR 1990, 2000/2001), ADB	All progrowth policies plus encouragement of microfinance, increased education expenditure for girls, increased investment in primary health care, increased female participation in labor force
Efficiency first	WB (WDR 1990)	Increases soundness of macroeconomic management, removal of external distortions, decreased product and factor market distortions, lower corporate and marginal taxes
Improved governance	WB (WDR 1990, 2000/2001)	Improved governance, decentralization, support for poor people's social capital, corruption reduction
Stability	WB (WDR 2000/2001)	Increased soundness of macroeconomic management, increased expenditure on social safety nets, increased transfers such as food subsidies, microcredit
Environmental sustainability	WB (WDR 2000/2001)	Enhance quality of environment and protect natural resources
Population	MP	Increased education expenditure for girls, increased access to reproductive health services, increased female participation in the labor force
Rural and urban poor development	MP	Investments in rural development, increased expenditure on rural infrastructure, increased expenditure on urban development and slum upgrading

Note: ACC refers to Ahluwalia, Carter, and Chenery 1979; ADB, Asian Development Bank; FDI, foreign direct investment; MFP, multifactor productivity; MP, Millennium Project; OECD, the Organization for Economic Cooperation and Development; WB, the World Bank; WDR, World Development Report.

led to "improved governance" (a term typically connoting a combination of reduced corruption, increased protection of property rights, and liberalized markets) taking center stage. The drive toward debt forgiveness and increased but more effective foreign aid (especially for meeting the MDGs of the Millennium Project) by Jeffrey Sachs and others has brought to the fore the strategy of "external assistance."

These are all outlooks on or orientations toward poverty reduction. Policies are the flesh and body that give these skeletal conceptualizations shape and life. In Table 3.2, we list combinations of policies taken from Table 3.1 that capture the intent of these strategic orientations and can translate these ideas and philosophies into plans of action.

We divide these strategic packages into three major orientations—clusters of initiatives frequently recurring in policy prescriptions, which taken together encompass all the policies listed in Table 3.1—and into strategic components that countries might choose to implement in different combinations.

The inward, self-sufficient, or domestic self-help orientation heavily emphasizes improved governance, at least in its latest incarnation. The argument is that external resources and even internal expenditures are very often wasted if governance quality is inadequate. Corrupt regimes that divert resources to offshore bank accounts sap, if not fatally wound, development efforts. Likewise, well-defined property rights are essential to encourage entrepreneurial behavior. Earlier incarnations of this prescription more often focused on the development of human capital (as opposed to wasteful military expenditures) or basic infrastructure (in contrast with large-scale show projects or palaces for the privileged elite).

The outward, open, or external market orientation emphasizes the benefits of export promotion, increased trade as opposed to import substitution, and the encouragement of foreign direct investment. A contemporary variation of the general theme of external orientation concerns worker remittances and "brain circulation." In contrast to the fears of brain drain that characterized those tuned to domestic self-help, the arguments are that the remittances have often proven substantially larger than other international flows and that migrants frequently return with new skill sets and entrepreneurial behavior patterns.

The orientation of foreign assistance or international transfers is driven by the belief among many analysts that domestic self-help, and often even external market orientation, are difficult to pursue without some external resources to jump-start the process. The target of 0.7 percent foreign aid is one of the longest-standing specific prescriptions in development (UN Millennium Project 2005a: 252). The need to address high levels of indebtedness, especially for the poorest countries, also receives regular attention.

Table 3.2 associates the strategic orientations with the various sources reviewed here and also elaborates some of their strategic components. Chapter 7 returns to the orientations and explores their potential for poverty reduction.

---

1   Bourguignon (2004) developed graphics that explain these effects more extensively. Perry et al. (2006) and Foster, Greere, and Thorbecke (1984) provided mathematical decomposition.

2   Perry et al. (2006) pay particular attention to inequality in their examination of poverty in Latin America. They argue that the growth elasticity of poverty decreases (in absolute value) with inequality. Since poverty in richer, more unequal countries is more reactive to changes in inequality, while poverty in poorer, more equal countries is more reactive to changes in growth, different policies might be needed to address poverty in different countries. Also see Ravallion and Chen (1997), Ravallion (2001a), and Kraay (2004) in this regard.

3   Cline (2004) uses this explanation for his "cross section paradox" that poverty levels are higher than expected on the basis of a standard form of income distribution in some of the large, higher-income countries like China, India, and Mexico. Technically, it means that the share of inequality taken by those around the poverty line is greater than would be found in a lognormal form of income distribution.

4   Becker, Murphy, and Tamura (1990), Stokey (1991), and Tamura (2001) also developed frameworks in which human capital is an engine of growth. The introduction to Lucas (2002) is a highly readable summing up of the literature and an articulation of why human capital is important for growth.

5   Grossman and Helpman (1991a, 1991b), Aghion and Howitt (1992), Aghion et al. (1998), and Stokey (1995) also studied the role of R&D in economic growth.

6   Romer (1993), Lee (1993, 1995), Klenow and Rodriguez-Clare (1997b), Borensztein, De Gregorio, and Lee (1998), and Kumar (2003) provide evidence in support of openness-induced technological change and growth. However, for a skeptical view of this literature, see Rodríguez and Rodrik (2000).

7   For a survey of the social capital literature, see Durlauf and Fafchamps (2005). Sobel (2002) provided a critical survey.

8   This point is made in various forms in Galor and Zeira (1993), Banerjee and Newman (1993), and Aghion and Bolton (1997). Birdsall and Londono (1997) find evidence that initial inequality in land and human capital has a negative effect on the income growth of the poorest.

9   See the discussion of capabilities in Chapter 2 for more details.

10 See http://www.imf.org/external/np/exr/facts/prsp.htm.

Tools for Exploring the Future of Global Poverty

If poverty can be reliably defined and measured, and if the historical path of change in the incidence of global poverty can be reliably assessed, there is a basis for attempting to anticipate and then to influence poverty levels in the future. In spite of the debates over concepts, measurement, and analysis sketched in the preceding chapters, we understand the breadth and depth of global poverty and the dynamics of progress in its reduction better now than we did in past decades. Thus, even though a knowledge basis for exploring the future of poverty remains a bit shaky, it exists. In this chapter we review the tools developed for such exploration and the insights generated with them. We also sketch the tools that this volume brings to the effort.

Thinking about the future can and often does begin with a first step of simple **extrapolation**, helping us extend existing trajectories of change and anticipate where they might be taking us. Yet, if it is to be useful in the evaluation of

alternative intervention options, **forecasting** (see Box 4.1) must fairly quickly move beyond univariate extrapolation into causal analysis. Much analysis of poverty has taken this second step into causal analysis, the examination of the dynamics also of the proximate drivers identified in Chapter 3 (economic growth, income distribution, and population) so as to develop more sophisticated econometric forecasts. These forecasts often rely on multivariate equations linking the proximate drivers to the poverty level.

Such forecasts are helpful, but analysts and policy makers want to take still another step, into consideration of the deep drivers of these proximate drivers, so as to come closer to understanding poverty at the level of human agency and in order to examine potential levers for policy intervention. The deep drivers often interact with each other and the proximate drivers in a complex fashion, requiring considerably more elaborate causal modeling. This third step is at the frontier of

The concept of, measurement of, and analytical foundations for forecasting poverty have improved considerably.

●Ahluwalia, Carter, and Chenery helped lay a strong foundation for forecasting. ●

poverty forecasting and analysis and is the purpose for this book. To accomplish this goal, we use dynamic computer simulation modeling of poverty and poverty reduction. In this chapter we therefore consider the desirable characteristics of such simulation modeling and the tools available to us.

Foundational Forecasting

Just as Montek S. Ahluwalia, Nicholas Carter, and Hollis Chenery (1979) were leaders in establishing a measure of poverty linked to purchasing power parity (PPP) and therefore comparable across multiple societies (see Chapter 2), they were pathbreakers in the forecasting of poverty levels. Table 4.1 is from their work. The analysis suffered from the absence of information at that time from China but otherwise covered most of the world's population.

The authors computed that the portion of populations that they defined as poor in less developed countries other than China had fallen from 50.9 percent in 1960 to 38.0 percent in 1975. Relying only on extrapolation, they foresaw that the poor in their country set would fall to 20.2 percent of population in 2000. Using population forecasts from the UN 1975 population projections, basing future economic growth prospects on rates between 1960 and 1975, and forecasting income distribution in deciles (using the then-popular Kuznets curve to anticipate change in distribution), they expected that the number of poor would decline even more in their more dynamic base case, falling to 16.3 percent in 2000.

The forecasts of Ahluwalia, Carter, and Chenery (ACC) for the year 2000 were remarkably prescient, not only in direction of change but even in general order of magnitude. Clearly the poverty measure used by ACC was not identical to the contemporary extreme poverty measure; our analysis estimates their poverty line to have been about $.81 rather than $1.08.[1] Using IFs calculations (based on data from the World Bank) for those living on less than $.81 and looking at the set of countries they examined, the percentage of population at that level in 2000 was 16.5 percent. The forecasts for specific income groups did not prove quite as successful, but still proved remarkably good. Their biggest error was in the middle income category, into which they placed Nigeria. Because of its demographic size and abysmal performance in poverty reduction (Chapter 8 will explore that further), the ACC middle income group actually now has a slightly higher poverty rate than does their low income group.

The ACC study took one additional important analytic step by examining the likely impact on poverty levels of alternative assumptions about their three proximate drivers: population growth rate, mean income, and income distribution. Specifically, they looked at the possible impact of reduced population growth (the low UN estimate for their countries was 1.97 billion, versus 2.21 billion in the base case), of accelerated income growth (1 percent higher than in their base case), and improved income distribution (45 percent higher income for the bottom 60 percent, at a cost of 0.5 percent in overall economic

Table 4.1 Forecasts of poverty rates for 2000 produced in 1979

	ACC 1960 estimates	ACC 1975 estimates	ACC forecasts for 2000 Historical trend	ACC forecasts for 2000 Base case	IFs 2000 calculations
Low income	61.7	50.7	29.5	22.4	18.7
Middle income	49.2	31.0	11.4	14.2	20.4
High income	24.9	12.6	5.4	4.0	7.7
All LDCs	*50.9*	*38.0*	*20.2*	*16.3*	*16.5*

Note: ACC refers to Ahluwalia, Carter, and Chenery; IFs, International Futures; LDCs, less developed countries.

Sources: Ahluwalia, Carter, and Chenery 1979: Table 3; IFs Version 5.47.

growth). These changes in assumptions reduced their forecasts of poverty rates in 2000 for all less developed countries to 14.9 percent, 11.5 percent, and 10.5 percent, respectively. They calculated that were all three changes possible, poverty rates would fall to 8.1 percent.

Their alternative forecasts were clearly overly optimistic and contain a lesson for us today: it is not easy to change the underlying trajectory of growth and poverty reduction. Although their simulation methods did not allow ACC to pursue the more extensive, policy lever–based analysis they suggested, the ACC study also identified many of the key deep drivers that are of interest to the current study (see, again, Figure 3.4). Their foundational work was remarkably innovative.

Contemporary Forecasting and Simulation

Somewhat surprisingly, forecasting of poverty futures was mostly interrupted for two decades following the work of ACC. In the interim, analysts devoted attention to the refinement of poverty concepts and measures, as described in Chapter 2. Moreover, the UN and the World Bank have resumed forecasting.

The UN Development Programme (UNDP)

The declaration of the Millennium Development Goals (MDGs) pushed analysts into attempting to anticipate progress toward them. In one of the first recent steps, the UNDP's *Human Development Report 2003*, titled *Millennium Development Goals: A Compact Among Nations to End Poverty*, undertook simple extrapolation to compare extended trajectories of global regions with the path necessary to move toward accomplishing the goals by 2015.[2] Figure 4.1 shows the results with respect to the two most widely used indicators on the first MDG.

Although extrapolations tend to be a best first step in most forecasting, their limitations are obvious. For instance, in Figure 4.1, it is

---

Figure 4.1 Simple extrapolations of poverty trends relative to the first MDG

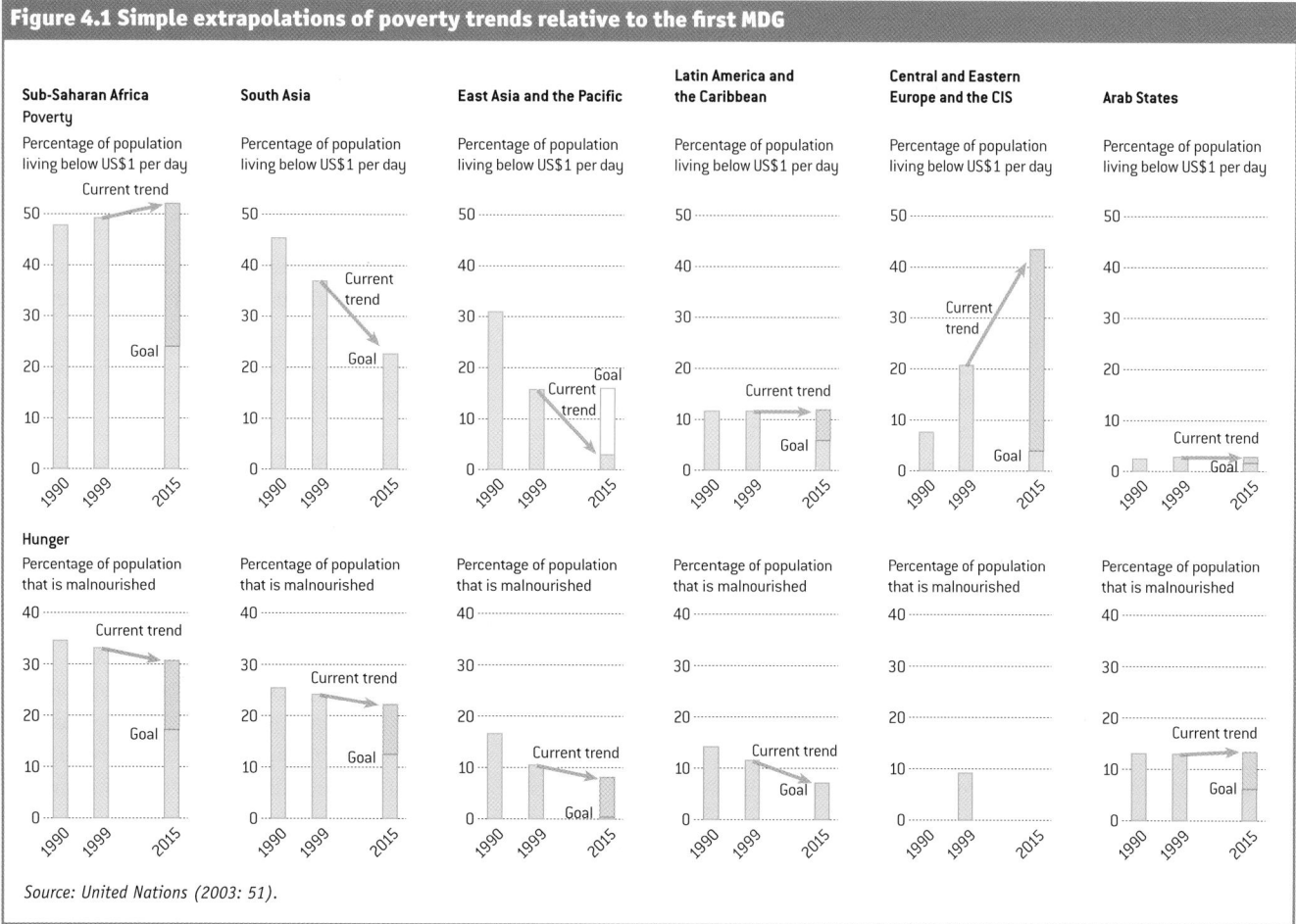

Source: United Nations (2003: 51).

Table 4.2 Forecasts of poverty head count in 2015 (millions)

	Dikhanov values and forecasts				World Bank
	1970	1990	2000	2015	2015
World	1,409	1,355	1,172	689	624
Latin America	43	43	43	37	34
East Asia	784	530	380	95	40
South Asia	427	494	325	92	217
Sub-Saharan Africa	145	267	288	430	290
Eastern and Central Europe	1	0	8	0	2

Note: Dikhanov used $700 per year in 1999 PPP terms, declaring it to be approximately $1 per day when adjusted from 1985 to 1999; thus the numbers were meant to be comparable.

Sources: Dikhanov 2005: 34; World Bank 2008: 46.

unbelievable that the reduction of poverty in East Asia and the Pacific will continue on a straight line to zero in 2015. Saturation effects will almost certainly preclude such an outcome. That is, assuming that poverty reduction continues, progress will become more difficult in pockets of chronic poverty within countries throughout the region. This point reinforces the facts that (1) representing the distributional characteristics of income, ideally within different population subgroups, is highly desirable in exploring the future of poverty; and (2) that forecasts should generally go beyond simple extrapolative techniques. Illustrating a different variation of the risks associated with simple extrapolation, given the increased economic growth of recent years, it is quite possible that the downward trajectory shown in Figure 4.1 for South Asia (primarily India) could accelerate. There have also been some signs in recent years of accelerated economic growth in sub-Saharan Africa, which could slow or reverse its upward trend in poverty rates.

In short, more sophisticated analysis must move at least to the key proximate drivers of poverty reduction. The Human Development Report Office has, in fact, done that. In support of the *Human Development Report 2005*, Yuri Dikhanov (2005) produced a study of change in global income distribution with forecasts to 2015. In addition, he began to manipulate the forecasting model, specifically by creating a pro-poor growth scenario.

Table 4.2 shows the Dikhanov report's 2015 forecast for regional and global poverty using UN population projections to 2015, economic growth rates mostly at the 1990–2002 rates, and unchanged national income distributions. The economic analysis assumed that growth in Eastern and Central Europe would increase, so as to compensate for the 1990–2002 declines (Dikhanov 2005: 6). Further, the study struggled with many of the issues raised in Chapter 2 about measuring historical poverty levels, and among other decisions, it reduced the economic growth rate of China from official data by nearly 3 percent, using numbers from Angus Maddison (2001).

Table 4.2 also includes forecast values from the World Bank's *Global Economic Prospects 2008*. The global numbers are comparable for 2015, but Dikhanov forecast a much lower headcount for poverty in South Asia and a considerably higher count for Africa.

Dikhanov's pro-poor growth scenario assumed that the incomes of the population below $700 at PPP would grow at twice the average rate of income growth. The assumption was a blunt manipulation of this proximate driver, clearly not tied to any particular intervention with respect to policy. The analysis calculated that it would take nine years to reduce global poverty to the MDG level in the pro-poor growth (PPG) scenario, compared to fifteen years in the distribution-neutral growth (DNG) scenario. The comparable numbers for Africa alone were twenty-two and more than thirty years. Thus the MDG for poverty would be met by 2015 in either case for the world as a whole, but in neither case for Africa.[3]

The World Bank

Because freeing the world from poverty is central to the World Bank's mission and the Bank collects the data that map progress toward that goal, it is hardly surprising that the Bank has produced most poverty forecasts, beginning with those by ACC. The number of the Bank's forecasts is not large, however, and they do not contain a great deal of geographic detail.

Among the Bank's analyses on poverty and poverty reduction are two World Development Reports titled *Poverty* (1990) and *Attacking Poverty* (2000–2001). Table 4.3 contains poverty forecasts and two social forecasts from the 1990 volume. In each case the table shows data for 1985 (as understood in 1990), a forecast to 2000, and data for 2000.

	Number of poor (millions)			Net primary school enrollment Percentage			Under 5 mortality (per thousand)		
	1985	2000	2000 data	1985	2000	2000 data	1985	2000	2000 data
Sub-Saharan Africa	180	265	291	56	86	59	185	136	170
East Asia	280	70	274	96	100	96	54	31	43
China	210	35	209	93	95	99	44	25	41
South Asia	525	365	484	74	88	85	150	98	97
India	420	255	359	81	96	89	148	94	94
Eastern Europe	5	5	21	90	92	88	25	16	32
Middle East, North Africa, Other Europe	60	60	13	75	94	88	119	71	55
Latin America and the Caribbean	75	60	52	92	100	89	75	52	34
Total	*1,125*	*825*	*1,104*	*84*	*91*	*87*	*102*	*67*	*73*

Source: World Bank 1990: 139; IFs Version 5.47 (for data).

The poverty forecast, rooted in a quantitatively informed but primarily qualitative analysis, anticipated that extreme poverty in the developing world would fall to 18 percent in 2000, leaving 825 million living on less than $1. Building on the most recent World Bank surveys, we calculate the actual rate for the set of countries that the Bank now defines as developing to have been 21.5 percent in 2000, for a total of 1,104 million. The bank's forecast set proved to be somewhat optimistic, suggesting a reason for conservatism with respect to poverty forecasts.

Chapter 2 emphasized, however, that poverty is much more than a matter of income and certainly cannot be captured only by a measure of those living on less than $1 or $2 per day. We should look also at capabilities and functioning, using forecasts of education, health, and measures of aggregate well-being such as the human development index to help broaden the perspective.

The World Bank analysis of 1990 also provided forecasts of net primary school enrollment and of under five mortality. The forecast of net primary enrollment also proved optimistic. According to data from the Bank's *World Development Indicators* (WDI), originally from the UN Educational, Scientific, and Cultural Organization (UNESCO), the population-weighted average of net primary enrollment for the same set of countries in 2000 proved to be 87 percent instead of the anticipated 91 percent. The

largest error was clearly for sub-Saharan Africa, where the value in 2000 was 59 percent instead of the forecast of 86 percent. The optimism, or inaccuracy, was partly a result of errors in the 1985 data. The IFs database, using more contemporary UNESCO-based numbers, suggests that the value for Africa in 1985 was actually 47 percent, not 56 percent.

Similarly, Table 4.3 suggests that forecasts for reduction of under five mortality rates were mostly too optimistic, although the error was less substantial than for the other two series. One interesting finding is that the Middle East and North Africa performed relatively well compared to expectations on all three variables, actually doing better than anticipated in two instances, as did Latin America. It clearly was Africa that primarily disappointed expectations.

The World Bank's 2000–2001 report, *Attacking Poverty,* did not forecast the number in poverty, presenting only a figure showing global progress from 1990 through 2000 toward the first seven MDGs in comparison with the paths needed to accomplish the goals. Forecasts are almost inevitably wrong, and the World Bank has understandably been cautious in making them.

Still, the need for forecasts is great. The Bank resumed making and publishing forecasts of global poverty in its annual series, *Global Economic Prospects*. Table 1.1 showed the full set of forecasts from its 2008 volume. Those forecasts suggest that the world as a whole will fairly easily meet the first MDG. The developing world beyond China may fail to meet the goal, however, because sub-Saharan Africa will be short of the target.

The *Global Economic Prospects* series is annual, making it possible to obtain some sense of the evolution of World Bank forecasting over time (see Table 4.4). The forecasts in the 2000 volume extended only to 2008, so that a comparable forecast series extending through 2015 begins only with the 2001 volume. The table suggests that the World Bank's forecasts have changed relatively little over that seven-year period.[4] The biggest absolute swings have been in the forecasts for sub-Saharan Africa, with higher values forecast in 2003–2004 but lower ones in recent years as economic growth in the region accelerated.

The methodology has evolved somewhat over time.[5] Typically, the LINKAGE model (van der Mensbrugghe 2005) provided gross domestic product (GDP) and consumption forecasts based on exogenous assumptions concerning demographics, savings, investment, and technological progress. The World Bank's poverty team combined the economic forecasts with their household surveys (represented by three-parameter Lorenz curves) to compute poverty headcounts for 2015. For the 2007 volume they assumed Gini coefficients to be constant over time, except for India and China; in the case of China they assumed both rural and urban Gini coefficients to

deteriorate 10 percent by 2015, accounting for the higher poverty forecast for China than in the 2006 volume of *Global Economic Prospects*. Forecasts in 2007 for 2030 did not use the same method, turning instead to forecasts of economic growth and income elasticities for poverty.[6]

The Bank's approach has sometimes used alternative scenarios related to specific deep drivers whose effect on the proximate drivers can be estimated. For instance, the theme of the 2006 volume was remittances and migration. Building on analysis of the effect of remittances on GDP, the formulation allowed an estimate of their impact on poverty headcount. The study calculated, for example, that for the countries with the highest remittances and highest poverty headcount, the impact of the remittances on the headcount rate could be as high as 20 percent.

Weaknesses in Our Tools for Thinking About the Future of Poverty

With the World Bank, in particular, leading the way, the ability to forecast poverty rates has improved considerably. Because the forecasting approaches described above generally rely only on the proximate drivers of poverty, however, they do not facilitate extended policy-oriented analysis of poverty reduction.

The World Bank is hardly alone in struggling with such limitations. Deeper analysis, such as that which motivated the

Table 4.4 Sequential World Bank forecasts of extreme poverty rates in 2015	2001	2002	2003	2004	2005	2006	2007	2008
East Asia and the Pacific	3.1	2.8	3.9	2.3	0.9	0.9	2.8	2.0
China			5.3	3.0	1.2	1.2	3.6	2.1
Rest of East Asia and Pacific	1.3	0.9	1.1	0.5	0.4	0.4	1.1	1.6
Europe and Central Asia	1.3	0.8	1.4	1.3	0.4	0.4	1.0	0.7
Latin America and the Caribbean	6.9	9.7	7.5	7.6	6.9	6.9	6.1	5.5
Middle East and North Africa	1.3	1.5	2.1	1.2	0.9	0.9	0.7	0.7
South Asia	17.7	16.7	15.7	16.4	12.8	12.8	16.2	15.1
Sub-Saharan Africa	39.5	39.3	46.0	42.3	38.4	38.4	37.4	31.4
Total	*12.6*	*12.3*	*13.3*	*12.5*	*10.2*	*10.2*	*11.8*	*10.2*
Excluding China	*15.0*	*14.8*	*15.7*	*15.4*	*12.9*	*14.2*	*14.2*	*12.6*

Source: World Bank, Global Economic Prospects *(2008: 46; 2007: 60; 2006a: 9; 2005a: 21; 2004: 46; 2002: 30; 2001: 42. The 2004 volume also included* Global Economic Prospects *forecasts for 2003*

authors of the UN Millennium Project (2005b), requires turning to deeper drivers. In order to develop and present *Investing in Development: A Practical Plan to Achieve the Millennium Development Goals,* the authors needed to elaborate the causal drivers of economic growth and to explore leverage with respect to them (see, again, Figure 3.5). They relied heavily on their causal understandings in extended analysis, and as experts with respect to development, their mental models were very rich. In the course of elaborating their plan, they implicitly made forecasts with respect to the magnitude of possible changes in human capital, social capital, governance, knowledge capital, and other productivity-enhancing factors and the collective impact of the changes on economic growth. They also thought deeply about the causal implications of official development assistance for public budgets and for investments in human capital and other drivers of growth.

What the authors of the Millennium Project (2005b) could not do was quantitatively tie analyses of the future of poverty to their understandings of the global development system. As rich as their mental models were, they were not sufficiently well elaborated and formalized to allow detailed analysis. When the authors turned in Part 4 of *Investing in Development* to a discussion of the costs and benefits of their proposals for achieving their goals, they were generally able to consider explicitly the costs of individual actions but not to match costs directly with benefits. They could not systematically investigate trade-offs, synergies, reinforcing, or perverse effects of their proposed interventions, nor could they explicitly address the many differences among the mental models of individual team members or the differences between the general approach of the team and other development experts.

In short, as much progress as the United Nations and the World Bank have made in understanding the foundations of poverty and thinking about alternative futures for it, there are substantial limitations in our forecasting capabilities. It would clearly be useful to have a more extensively elaborated model to serve as a thinking tool for such analysis. What might such a tool look like?

Desired Model Structure and Capabilities

A simulation tool or toolkit that could be useful in analysis of trends in and options for poverty reduction would allow user manipulation of the three proximate drivers of poverty: economic growth, economic distribution, and population growth. It would be highly desirable, however, if each proximate driver were, in turn, linked explicitly to a substantial number of deep drivers. In the case of economic growth, endogenous growth theory looks not just at labor and capital deepening but at the advance of human capital (such as education and health), the quality of social capital and governance (including such aspects as social trust levels, lack of corruption, the definition and protection of property rights, and the quality of day-to-day policies), the sustainable use of natural capital, and the development and acquisition of knowledge (see, again, Figure 3.6).

In the case of economic distribution, the model should explicitly represent the various social agents, including government, households, firms, and nongovernmental organizations (NGOs). Households vary greatly across dimensions such as rural/urban, levels of education, and employment categories. Households also vary in terms of their membership in various socially excluded groups, sometimes defined in terms of ethnicity and other times in other ways (such as the scheduled castes in India). With respect to population, the ideal tool's endogenization should represent not just the stocks of age- and sex-specific cohorts, but the manner in which fertility and mortality change, in significant part as a result of economic growth and distributional change.

The overall system would rely heavily on data and be deeply rooted in theory. With respect to the latter, the theoretically based economic model would most likely be some form of dynamic general equilibrium model in which interagent flows are represented by a social accounting system to capture many of the distributional elements. The demographic model would be a dynamic cohort-component system. The system would be geographically rich, with separate representation of at least the larger developing countries (and ideally with division of the largest developing countries into

Forecasting of poverty has overwhelmingly used proximate drivers and has seldom built on analysis of deep drivers.

subregions). The system and its data would be accessible to users, and its structures would be both transparent and open to change.

Even if such a tool did exist, analysts should be wary. There would be advantages: rich empirical models can facilitate explicit forecasts and can handle the calculations of secondary and tertiary effects that address trade-offs, synergies, and other effects; they can also allow investigation of possible futures with and without interventions, both selected individual ones and strategic packages.

Such models come, however, with great costs and disadvantages of their own. They suffer from shortages of and inadequacies in data and theoretical understanding. The richer and more complex they are, the more difficult it becomes to understand the precise paths by which interventions give rise to outcomes (one needs a model of the model) and the more subject they are to undiscovered errors in specification. In short, no one should ever take at face value the results of a formal, computerized simulation of development processes or the simulated results of human intervention—just as no one should ever take for granted the forecasts of those who base them on individualized and implicit mental models, whether simple or complex.

The motivating assumption behind this volume, however, is that explicit and formal computer models can contribute to thinking about strategies for poverty reduction, adding to and interacting with analyses based on more qualitative and expert judgment. Computer models are usually more explicit than mental models and more easily changed across runs or scenarios. Computer models often benefit from very extensive and up-to-date empirical information. They can enhance the ongoing dialogue about policy options, one in which refinements of mental models is also still an evolving process.

The next two sections will describe the computer simulation called International Futures (IFs), used for the analysis of poverty

> ● *Richly specified computer models, in spite of their limitations, can complement rich mental models in forecasting poverty.* ●

reduction in this study. Although a complete system like the ideal one sketched above does not exist, the IFs model has a substantial number of the desired characteristics. The first of the two sections provides general information about IFs, and the second focuses on the manner in which it provides alternative simulations of future poverty levels.

The International Futures Modeling System

International Futures is a large-scale integrated global modeling system representing 182 countries. Its broad purpose is to serve as a thinking tool for the analysis of near-term through long-term country-specific, regional, and global futures across multiple, interacting issue areas. IFs allows variable time horizons for exploring human leverage with respect to the pursuit of key goals in the face of great uncertainty.

Three sets of values and goals with which few would disagree increasingly frame global initiatives and the structure of IFs (see Table 4.5). First, humans as individuals should be able to develop their capabilities as fully as possible, attaining literacy, securing nutrition and health care that allow a reasonable life expectancy, and gaining access to a basic level of economic resources. The broader purposes of these capabilities are to allow individuals substantial freedom of choice in their pursuit of a fulfilling life (Sen 1999). Second, humans in their interactions with one another desire peace and security (Kant 1897) and also basic fairness and justice (Rawls 1971). Third, humans in their interactions with a broader biological and physical environment should be able to live in a sustainable manner so that lifestyles and choices do not jeopardize the life conditions of their own futures and those of subsequent generations (United Nations 1987). Collectively, these goals have increasingly come to be recognized as the pillars of sustainable human development, the overarching goal or metagoal of most who think about and act to enhance global futures.

The modules within IFs support thinking about and exploration of long-term change and human development with respect to these goals. Figure 4.2 shows the IFs modules and a small, selected set of connections among them.

Table 4.5 The value and conceptual foundations of IFs	
Humans as individuals	Personal development/Freedom
Humans with each other	Peace and security/Social fairness
Humans with the environment	Sustainable material well-being

Although the elements of particular utility to this study are those in the top half, including the population, economic, education, and sociopolitical modules, the full, integrated system will enhance the analysis.

In quick summary, the modules have the following basic structures:

The population module
- represents twenty-two age-sex cohorts to age 100+ in a standard cohort-component structure;
- calculates change in cohort-specific fertility of households in response to income, income distribution, education levels, and contraceptive use;
- calculates change in mortality rates in response to income, income distribution, and assumptions about technological change affecting mortality;
- separately represents the evolution of HIV infection rates and deaths from AIDS;
- computes average life expectancy at birth, literacy rate, and overall measures of human development (HDI); and
- represents migration, which ties to the flows of remittances.

The economic module
- represents the economy in six sectors: agriculture, materials, energy, industry, services, and information/communications technology or ICT. Other sectors could be configured because the system uses raw data from the Global Trade Analysis Project (GTAP) project with fifty-seven sectors in Release 6;
- computes and uses input-output matrixes that change dynamically with development level;
- is a general equilibrium-seeking model that does not assume exact equilibrium will exist in any given year; rather it uses inventories as buffer stocks and to provide price signals so that the model chases equilibrium over time;
- contains a Cobb-Douglas production function that (following the insights of Robert M. Solow and Paul M. Romer) endogenously represents contributions to growth in multifactor productivity from human capital (education and health), social capital and governance, physical and natural capital (infrastructure and energy

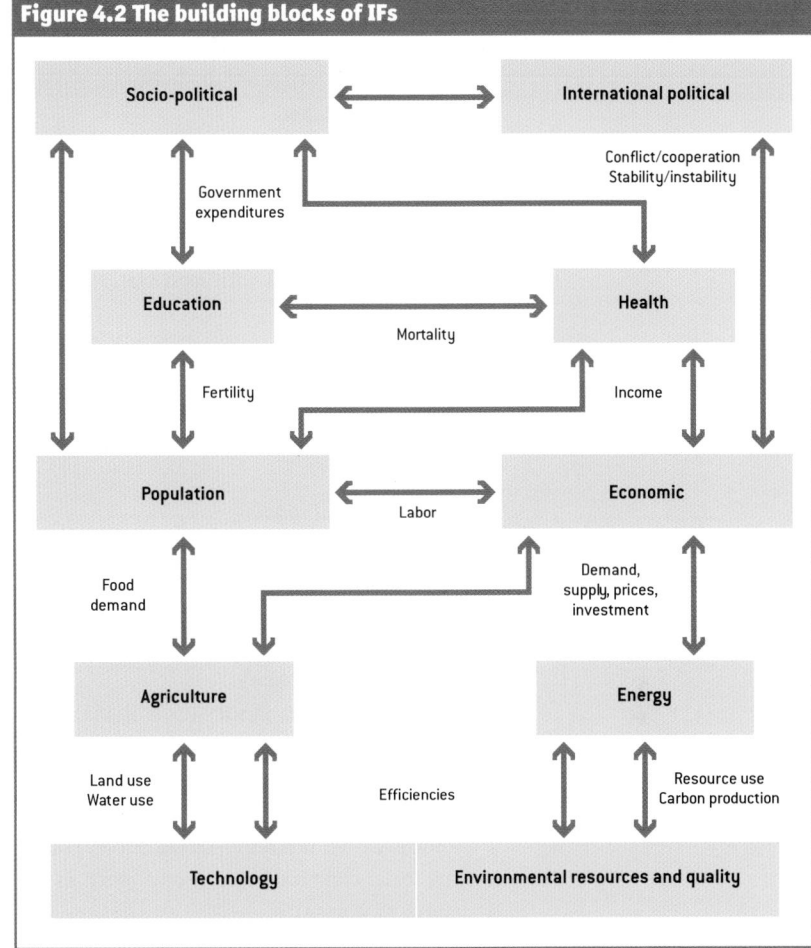

Figure 4.2 The building blocks of IFs

prices), and knowledge development and diffusion (R&D and economic integration with the outside world);
- uses a linear expenditure system to represent changing consumption patterns;
- utilizes a "pooled" rather than bilateral trade approach for international trade; and
- has been imbedded in a social accounting matrix (SAM) envelope that ties economic production and consumption to a very simple representation of intra-actor financial flows (it represents only the skilled and unskilled households of the GTAP project).

The education module
- represents formal education across primary, secondary (lower and upper separately), and tertiary levels;
- forecasts intake or transition from lower levels, rates of survival and/or completion, as well as net and/or gross enrollment;

- differentiates males and females;
- is fully linked to population; and
- computes education or human capital stocks by adult age cohort.

The health module (early in development)
- differentiates mortality causes by communicable disease, noncommunicable disease, and injuries with multiple subcategories; and
- uses World Health Organization Global Burden of Disease distal driver formulations and introduces assorted proximate drivers for policy intervention.

The sociopolitical module
- represents fiscal policy through taxing and spending decisions;
- shows six categories of government spending: military, health, education, R&D, foreign aid, and a residual category;
- represents changes in social conditions of individuals (like fertility rates, literacy levels, or poverty), attitudes of individuals (such as the level of materialism/postmaterialism of a society from the World Values Survey), and the social organization of people (such as the status of women);
- represents the evolution of democracy; and
- represents the prospects of state instability or failure.

The international political module
- traces changes in power balances across states and regions, and
- allows exploration of changes in the level of interstate threat.

The agriculture module
- represents production, consumption, and trade of crops and meat; it also carries ocean fish catch and aquaculture in less detail;
- maintains land use in crop, grazing, forest, urban, and "other" categories;
- represents demand for food, livestock feed, and industrial use of agricultural products;
- is a partial equilibrium model in which food stocks buffer imbalances between production and consumption and determine price changes; and
- overrides the agricultural sector in the economic module unless the user chooses otherwise.

The energy module
- portrays production of six energy types: oil, gas, coal, nuclear, hydroelectric, and other renewable energy forms;
- represents consumption and trade of energy in the aggregate;
- represents known reserves and ultimate resources of fossil fuels;
- portrays changing capital costs of each energy type with technological change as well as with drawdowns of resources;
- is a partial equilibrium model in which energy stocks buffer imbalances between production and consumption and determine price changes; and
- overrides the energy sector in the economic module unless the user chooses otherwise.

The environmental resources and quality module
- allows tracking of the remaining supplies of fossil fuels, of the amount of forested land, of water usage, and of atmospheric carbon dioxide emissions.

The technology module
- is distributed throughout the overall model;
- allows changes in assumptions about rates of technological advance in agriculture, energy, and the broader economy;
- explicitly represents the extent of electronic networking of individuals in societies;
- is tied to the governmental spending model with respect to R&D spending.

A menu-driven interface facilitates use of the model. Large numbers of intervention points allow access for the user to all parameters (for scenarios) across all the modules. An extensive database supports model development and use.

For detail on the International Futures system beyond this brief introduction, see the IFs website at www.ifs.du.edu. That site provides the web version of the full model, as well as a full downloadable version for use on Windows machines. The most important source of documentation for the model is its extensive help system, available with both web-based and downloadable versions. The help system provides assistance with the user interface and also includes flow charts, equations, and complete computer code for

The philosophical foundation of IFs is a broad conceptualization of sustainable human development.

all sections of the model. Barry B. Hughes and Evan E. Hillebrand (2006) provided a basic introduction to the model with a focus on facilitating its use. In addition, a substantial set of project reports and working papers are on the project website.

Where is the IFs system particularly weak with respect to the poverty analysis goals of this volume? IFs does not represent in any real detail the agents that determine poverty distribution within countries. There are no NGOs and there are only the two types of households (based on skilled and unskilled labor) for which the Global Trade Analysis Project provides data. Household distinctions by rural/urban residence and by work or profession do not exist in the model and would be very helpful for forecasting distributional change and analyzing chronic poverty. More generally, although the IFs model does contain a substantial number of important specifications that tie specific interventions or deep drivers to the proximate drivers and to the calculation of poverty, as with all models it is impossible to be fully confident about many of those. Models are always flawed representations of complex systems, which is why forecasts are inevitably useful only as one element in thinking about the future, not as substitute for such thought.

The Foundations in IFs for Poverty Analysis

This section prepares for the use of IFs in subsequent chapters for analyzing poverty by explaining the formulation(s) linking proximate drivers to poverty and by providing basic information about how the model specifies the linkage of deep drivers and action levers to the proximate drivers.

Initialization of poverty levels

The IFs model begins its calculations in 2000 and annually updates values for all driver variables and for poverty rates and levels, as well as for the poverty gap and human development index components. Initial poverty rates in the year 2000 and those computed thereafter are country-specific. The processes to set initial values used survey data from the World Bank, specifically from its *World Development Indicators* and the PovcalNet website (which, unlike the WDI, is constantly updated).[7] For

months and countries in which there were no surveys for 2000, linear interpolation across values before and after 2000 was used. When there were no values bracketing 2000 on which to anchor interpolations, extrapolations from values before or (ideally) after 2000 set the value in 2000.[8] For those countries having no surveys to draw upon, a cross-sectional relationship against GDP per capita (at PPP) provided estimates for 2000. Whenever this volume presents poverty rates for groupings of countries, the values are population-weighted averages from the country level.

Because the model calculates values in future years for all economic variables in 2000 dollars (both at market exchange rates and at PPP), it would have been ideal to convert the global poverty levels from 1993 dollars to 2000 dollars. Such conversion is, however, as discussed in Chapter 2, a nontrivial and potentially controversial process. Instead of attempting such a process in advance of the World Bank undertaking it again, IFs computes a country-specific scaling factor during the first model year to convert calculations driven by consumption in 2000 dollars to the values initialized as described above. That scaling factor ensures that data in the initial year override calculated values and also scales values calculated in future years.

Income poverty formulations

IFs uses two mechanisms to forecast rates of income poverty as a function of income and distribution, one tied to lognormal analysis and one based on cross-sectional analysis. Both formulations rely upon the broader model of IFs to generate driving forecasts of GDP per capita and the consumption share of GDP. They also rely on the IFs economic module or exogenous specification to generate forecasts of the Gini index as a measure of income distribution (with initial conditions for the Gini coefficient coming from the World Bank and therefore tied again to the survey data).

On the surface, it might seem that the clearly superior forecasting formulation would be based on the shifting of the lognormal distribution over time with change in average incomes and the Gini coefficient, as Chapter 3 described. The cross-sectional formulation serves two purposes, however. First, it helps estimate initial poverty

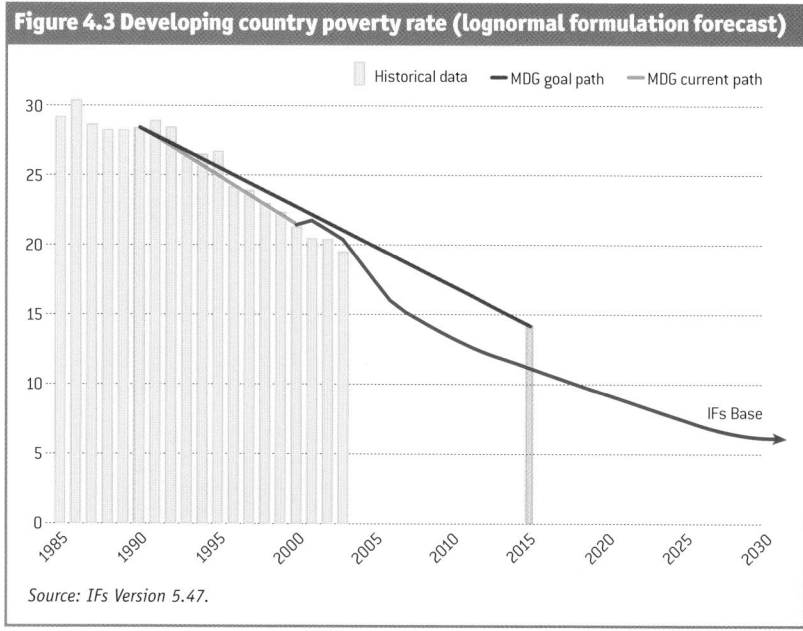

Figure 4.3 Developing country poverty rate (lognormal formulation forecast)

Source: IFs Version 5.47.

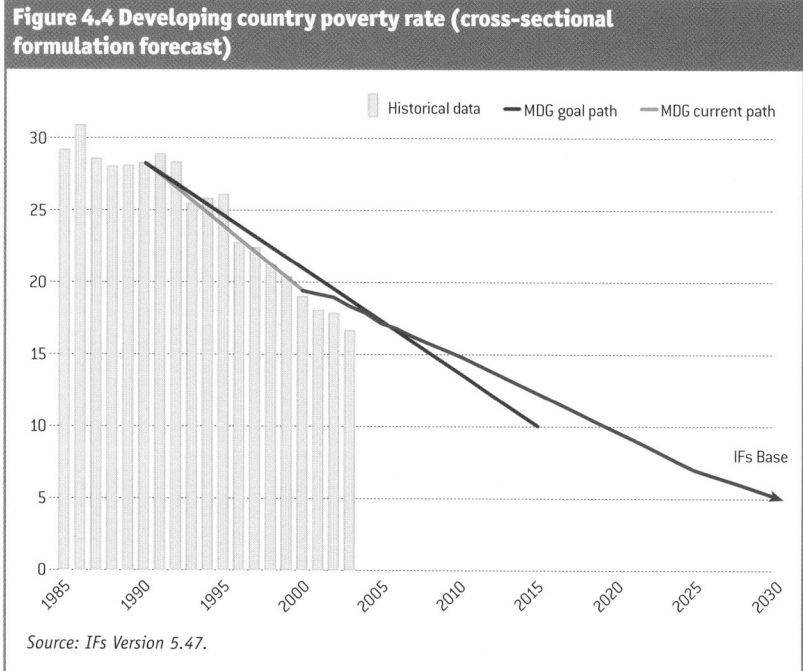

Figure 4.4 Developing country poverty rate (cross-sectional formulation forecast)

Source: IFs Version 5.47.

known phenomenon and often persist among disadvantaged subpopulations in spite of the economic advance of the average population. That is, there may be a tendency for the left-hand tail of the lognormal distribution to display some inertia with economic transformation, leaving some additional number of people at or below the poverty line. Even though the lognormal forecasting formulation may not pick up those pockets of chronic poverty, the cross-sectional formulation may be responsive to them.

In fact, the cross-sectional formulation could potentially be responsive to a number of factors not picked up in the theoretically elegant and simple lognormal approach. Figures 4.3 and 4.4 reinforce this point by showing base year forecasts of global poverty through 2030 with the two formulations. The two figures show, of course, the same historical profile of reduction in rates of global poverty. The bars are built from a combination of survey data and filling of the holes in those data with the cross-sectional formulation.[9] The solid lines represent the path from 1990 values to the MDG goal of reducing 1990 poverty rates by 50 percent by 2015. The marked pink lines are the base case forecasts in IFs.

The cross-sectional formulation shows slower rates of poverty reduction and a clear failure to meet the goal, while the lognormal formulation shows progress of poverty reduction below the goal path. The lognormal forecast is closer to the current conventional wisdom within the development community. In addition to the possible persistence of chronic pockets of poverty, is there any further basis for the more conservative path of the cross-sectional formulation? One basis is in the earlier finding that the 1990 forecasts of poverty for 2000 appear to have overestimated reduction rates.

The key point, however, is to stress the uncertainty with respect to any formulation, which reinforces the desirability of considering multiple ones. Appendix 1 of this volume provides more information on the two formulations. Appendix 3 explains the endogenization of economic growth and income distribution as a function of deep drivers in the model.

levels for countries for which there are no survey data. That set contains a small number of generally less populous countries, but in global analysis it is desirable to be as comprehensive as possible. Second, there is a logical basis on which to question the persistence of a pure form of the lognormal curve as average income improves (even when aggregate measures like the Gini coefficient change very little). For instance, pockets of chronic poverty are a well-

Conclusion

There is a triangle of activities involved in this volume's discussion of the assault on poverty. The first activity, discussed in Chapter 2, is assessment (conceptualization and measurement). Because of the great debates that the chapter sketched, we much better understand the breadth and depth of global poverty and the progress in its reduction than in past decades. The second activity, which Chapter 3 introduced, is framing possible action or intervention.

The third activity of the triangle is exploration of possible futures, with and without interventions. The purpose of this chapter was to describe the foundation for such exploration. Herein we reviewed forecasts of poverty reduction that have emerged to date and the methods behind them. We also sketched the tools that this study brings to the effort and how they will facilitate more extensive analysis. Chapter 5 will take us further down the road of that causal analysis.

● Alternative formulations for forecasting poverty can help map the range of uncertainty in our forecasts. ●

---

1 See Chapter 2 for more on the setting of the ACC poverty line based on that of India, further linked to food availability of about 2,250 calories per day. By one estimate, that corresponded to about $23.14 per month in 1985 relative to the $31 per month used subsequently by Ravallion as $1 per day (*Economist*, "Economic Focus: Another day, another $1.08," April 28, 2007: 90). The ratio of the two suggests that the ACC line was very roughly ($23.14/$31.00) * ($1.08/$1.00) or $.806.

2 A variety of other forecasts for specific regions and countries have similarly relied primarily on extrapolation. See UN ECLAC 2004 and 2005; UN ECAF 2005.

3 The UNDP study by Dikhanov produced other results of significance. For instance, it sketched the global distributions of income historically and in the base forecast to 2015. Interestingly, the strongly bimodal character of global income distribution in 1970 had already eroded considerably by 2000 and was forecast to erode further by 2015, beginning to approximate the lognormal form characteristic of most countries. Dikhanov anticipated generally lognormal distributions but used a polynomial estimation approach to fit distributional curves to data.

4 As discussed in Chapter 2, it bears repeating that forecasting depends heavily on the measurement

of initial conditions and the assessment of past patterns. For instance, Bhalla (2002: 170) forecast that in 2015 the portion of the developing world living on less than $2 per day would be 10.1 percent, about one-third of the percentage that the World Bank (see again Table 1.1) expects to be living at that level. His forecasting method was not dramatically different from that of the World Bank, using assumptions of per capita economic growth averaging 2.5 percent and constant income distribution as key drivers of the forecasts. How, then, could his forecast be so different? Although Bhalla used World Bank data from Deininger and Squire (1996), he imposed his own calculation of the poverty line on them, estimating that in 2000 only 23.3 percent of the developing world lived on less than $2 per day, rather than the approximately 50 percent value used by the Bank. In fact, Bhalla's estimate for poverty at $2 per day at the beginning of the century was very close to the Bank's estimate for poverty at $1 per day, making it no surprise that his forecast for levels at $2 per day in 2015 were actually quite close to the Bank's forecast at $1 per day.

5 The forecasts of the *Global Economic Prospects* 2006 used a cross-country poverty change model driven by GDP per capita and Gini coefficients (see World Bank 2006: 119 for the specification). For more detail on the technique the Bank used, as illustrated by its

analysis of poverty change in response to different assumptions about remittances, see Annex 5.1, pages 127–129.

6 Dominique van der Mensbrugghe, in an e-mail from January 2007, explained some of the details of the approach used in the analysis for 2007, supplementing the explanation of the volume (World Bank 2007: 63, footnotes 26 and 27). Chapter 3 of the 2007 volume also explained the processes used to build a global income distribution for 2030 and to explore the emergence of a global middle class. See also Bussolo et al. (2007).

7 For countries, such as China and India, and for years in which PovcalNet broke data on poverty rates into urban and rural subsets, national values are weighted sums of those two populations.

8 To illustrate, if the nearest survey-based estimate of the World Bank to 2000 was for 2003, that value helped estimate poverty headcount rate for initialization in 2000. A cross-sectional formulation provided the anticipated poverty decrease (or sometimes increase) as a result of difference in GDP per capita in 2000 and 2003, and that difference was used to adjust poverty headcount ratio from 2003 to 2000.

9 Surveys for 2004 were only partially available at the time of writing, so the graph omits that year.

The IFs Base Case: A Foundation for Analysis

The future is uncertain, and our tools for thinking about it are imperfect. These basic truths require us to avoid making predictions about what will happen and explore instead the range of what could happen. Moreover, human choices influence social futures, and our ultimate analytic purpose is to improve those choices in pursuit of human development goals. Thus, analysis of the future prospects for poverty reduction requires scenario analysis, the elaboration of alternative stories about the future. The assumptions that differentiate scenarios from each other should be made explicit, whether they concern uncertainties largely beyond human control, such as the fragility or robustness of natural systems in the face of human action, or whether they concern uncertainties largely under human control, such as the portion of children who attend elementary school.

⬛ *The assumptions that differentiate scenarios should be explicit, whether they concern uncertainties largely beyond human control or uncertainties largely under human control.* ⬛

When a large-scale computer simulation is used in forecasting, however, the assumptions that differentiate the scenarios elaborated in its use are typically a small fraction of the total assumptions made. The model structure and most of its parameters involve assumptions that may be common to the scenarios. Even when documented, complex models are difficult to understand, and examination of their behavior becomes an important part of such understanding. Most often that examination begins by looking at the behavior of a model in the absence of interventions and proceeds only thereafter into scenario analysis. The forecasts of a model without interventions are typically called the base case or reference run (see Box 5.1).

The purpose of this chapter is to explore the base case of the International Futures (IFs) with Pardee model. Our analysis will focus on the behavior of the proximate drivers of poverty (see Chapter 3) and on the unfolding of the base case forecast of poverty itself. We will compare the forecasts to others made of the proximate drivers and of poverty. Typically models are calibrated in their development to such alternative forecasts because doing so provides some evidence of their credibility.

There is an important point to make about the processes of (1) base case elaboration with (2) subsequent scenario elaboration, because to nonmodelers the steps may seem technical and perhaps even artificial. Specifically, we should develop forecasts based on mental models with the same exacting processes. Foundationally, we should subject the fundamental structure of the mental model to examination in some detail, and the assumptions and relationships of the model should be transparent. Further, we should review the base case forecast of a mental model and compare it to forecasts that others generate. Mental models should also then produce alternative scenarios about the future, as well specified and differentiated as possible. In short, these processes are part not just of thinking about the future with computer models, but much more generally part of thinking about the future.

Population Growth

The forecasts of the UN Population Division are the most widely used and cited of all population forecasts. Therefore, this section will primarily compare the base case forecasts from IFs with the UN's most recent forecasts, those from the 2006 revision.[1] Other institutions that provide population

forecasts with global coverage include the U.S. Census Bureau and the International Institute of Applied Systems Analysis (IIASA).[2] Another important information resource for understanding population data and forecasting is the Population Reference Bureau (e.g., O'Neill and Balk 2001).[3]

The IFs base case does not use the forecasts of any other source (except UN forecasts for migration) because the model uniquely generates its own. The most important difference between the forecasts from IFs and other sources is that the demographic module in IFs is integrated with the other modules of the system, including those for economics, education, and sociopolitical systems. That integration has allowed the development of formulations for fertility and mortality driven endogenously by variables such as gross domestic product (GDP) per capita (at purchasing power parity), years of education, and spending on health care. It is this characteristic that will make it possible in subsequent chapters to explore the impact on population, and therefore on numbers in poverty, of interventions such as changes in governance quality.

This "broad and deep endogeneity" of IFs also means that the forecasts of IFs, both the base case and the scenarios built around it, will never be identical to the forecasts of any other system. Nonetheless, IFs should generate values in its base case similar to those of experts on their respective issues.

The United Nations produces its well-known medium variant forecast, in combination with high and low variants. Even though global fertility rates are on a steep downward trend, the UN also always shows a constant fertility variant with especially high population growth rates. The IFs project does not normally compute high and low variants, which the UN creates by assuming fertility rates about one-half child above and below the medium variant. Instead, IFs generates scenarios by interventions in deeper drivers, such as those that affect economic growth rates and education levels. To allow some comparison with the alternative UN scenarios, however, Figure 5.1 shows the IFs base case and two scenarios prepared for the analysis of this volume. Chapter 6 will discuss these

We should subject forecasts from mental models to the same exacting analyses of specifications that we apply to thinking about the future with computer models.

Although the "broad and deep endogeneity" of IFs means that its forecasts will differ from others, values from the base case of IFs should be similar to those of experts.

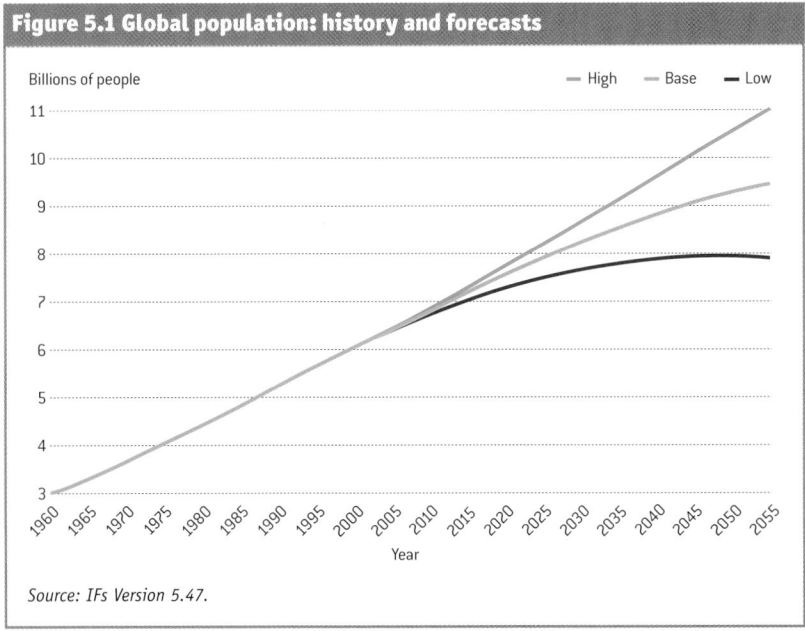

Figure 5.1 Global population: history and forecasts

Billions of people

— High — Base — Low

Year

Source: IFs Version 5.47.

Table 5.1 Comparison of United Nations median variant forecasts, 2006 revision, with IFs Base Case

	Population in 2050 (millions)	
	UN	**IFs**
More Developed (OECD)	1,245	1,262
Less Developed (non-OECD)	7,946	8,016
Oceania	49	45
World Total	*9,191*	*9,279*

Source: UN Population Division (2006), Table 1.1; and IFs Version 5.47.

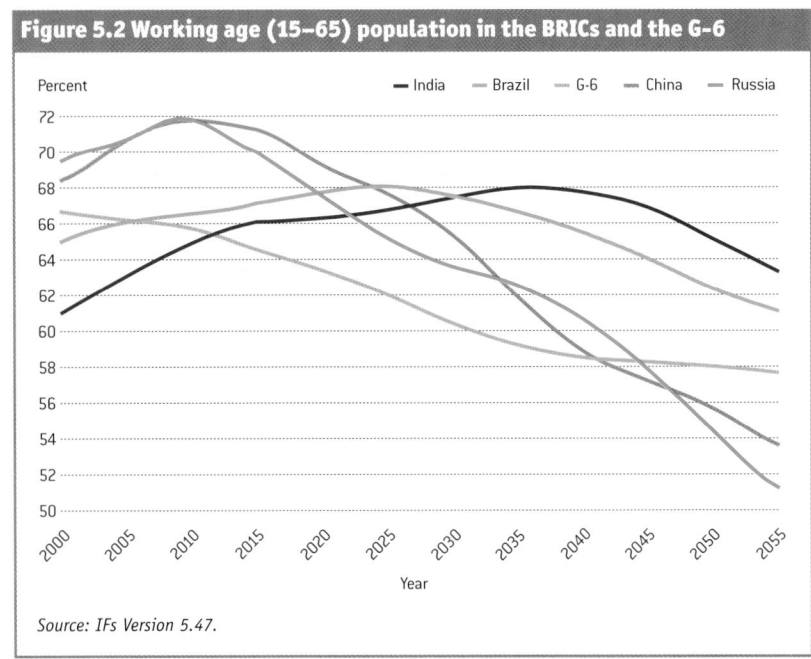

Figure 5.2 Working age (15–65) population in the BRICs and the G-6

Percent

— India — Brazil — G-6 — China — Russia

Year

Source: IFs Version 5.47.

IFs high and low population scenarios in more detail. The three scenarios generate populations in 2050 of 10.6, 9.3, and 8.0 million, respectively, compared to values from the UN's 2006 forecast revision of 10.8, 9.2, and 7.8 million in their high, median, and low variants.[4]

For more than a decade the forecasts of IFs (and IIASA) tended to be lower than those of the United Nations, and subsequent UN revisions brought down successive medium variants as it recognized the rapid pace of fertility decline, ultimately bringing its midcentury forecast below that of IFs. There is, however, now some reason to begin questioning whether fertility and growth rates will continue their sharp declines, especially in light of population growth rates that are moving fairly steadily to and below zero in many countries (see Figure 6.1 for the population growth rates corresponding to Figure 5.1). Moreover, AIDS mortality forecasts are declining. The UN median variant forecast for 2050 increased from 9.08 (2004 revision) to 9.19 billion (2006 revision).[5]

Turning to the population in regions of the world, Table 5.1 presents the breakdown by the United Nations of its median variant in comparison with the IFs base case. They are not completely comparable, because the more and less developed regions of the UN have been represented in IFs by members and nonmembers of the Organization for Economic Cooperation and Development (OECD). The regional breakdown, which is identical, shows that IFs forecasts marginally higher populations in Africa and Asia by 2050 than does the United Nations.

A full cohort-component population module, like that of IFs, provides a wide range of numbers that are important to the economic and other modules. Figure 5.2 from the IFs base case shows values for one such linkage, namely the size of the labor force relative to total population in Brazil, Russia, India, and China (the BRICs) and the Group of 6 (the G-7 without Canada). Growth in labor force share constitutes a "demographic dividend" that supports economic growth. The dividends being reaped by the BRICS are clearly evident (compare with the analysis of Goldman Sachs 2003: 8).

Economic Growth

Economic forecasts are more difficult to create than those for population. In the longer term, there can be substantial variation in savings rates, international investment flows, and technological change. Business cycles and financial panics are frequently apparent in short- and midrange economic data.

Because of the great importance of near-term economic forecasts for investors, companies, and governments, there are many forecasting services that create them in spite of the challenges. For instance, Oxford Economics provides forecasts for up to 175 countries, as well as models for use by its clients; the time horizon generally extends up to ten years. Similarly, Goldman Sachs provides forecasts as part of its research service. On occasion its forecasts have been more truly long term, as when they produced a report on the BRICs through 2050. The OECD mostly provides short-term forecasts, such as its semiannual series looking out two years, the *OECD Economic Outlook*.[6] The International Monetary Fund (IMF) also mostly provides short-term forecasts, extending about two years, as in its semiannual *World Economic Outlook*.

The interest of our analysis lies, however, in longer-term economic forecasting. Because of the challenges in creating them, no sets of regular long-term forecasts, like those of the UN and the U.S. Census Bureau for populations of countries, exist for economies.

IFs long-term forecasts

Figure 5.3 provides historical growth rates and IFs forecasts for GDP per capita growth at market exchange rates (MER) and purchasing power parity (PPP). Those figures place the IFs forecasts in the context of historical data, as a prelude to comparison with other forecasts. Because global population growth rates are trending downward and will likely be nearly 2 percent lower by 2050 than they were in 1970, the figure presents GDP per capita values.

It is useful to comment on several aspects of the forecasts of IFs and their relationship to past growth patterns:

- Forecasts are smoother than past patterns, because IFs is a long-term model that makes no attempt to anticipate short-term business cycles or other perturbations. Forecast rates are not completely flat or smooth, however, because many driving forces interact across all the submodels of IFs.

- World economy growth rates were quite a bit higher in the 1960s than in the 1970s and thereafter. Angus Maddison (1995) called the 1950s and 1960s the "Golden Age" of global growth. The per capita rates in IFs forecasts tend to fall somewhat between those of the Golden Age and those of later decades.

- The rise in global growth rates forecast in the early part of this century is in substantial part a result of the continued rapid growth of China and India, which, as their weight in the world economy rises, pushes global rates upward. Conversely, the increasing convergence toward midcentury of GDP per capita levels in middle-income countries with those in rich countries will slow global per capita growth rates, as may the passage of the world through the years of peak oil and gas production.

One aspect of Figure 5.3 merits special comment. The World Bank and Global Insights, whose forecasts the next section will review, anticipate that world GDP will grow faster at purchasing power parity than at market exchange rates. The reason for that expectation is that developing countries have higher GDPs at PPP than at MER; given their higher growth rates, composition

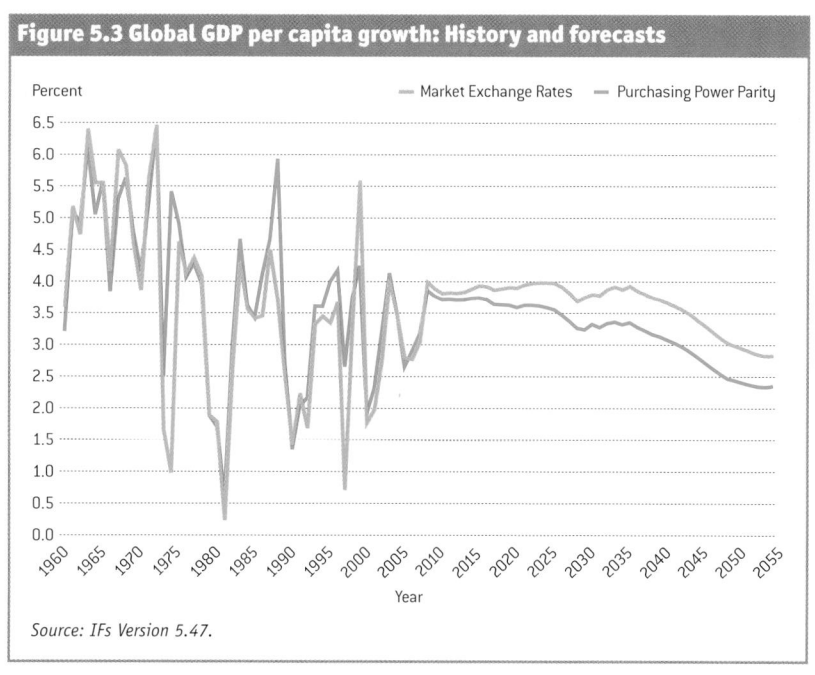

Figure 5.3 Global GDP per capita growth: History and forecasts

Source: IFs Version 5.47.

effects (the increasingly high weight assigned to developing countries in the global average) will, ceteris paribus, give rise to faster global PPP growth. In the World Bank analysis all else is, in fact, equal, because the ratio of GDP at PPP and MER does not change for any country or region; GDP in both cases is considered real GDP and subject to the same growth rate.

In IFs, that composition effect is also present. In addition, however, IFs posits that GDP at PPP and at MER will converge as countries become richer. For instance, the value of China's GDP at PPP is nearly 2.0 times that of its GDP at MER and India's GDP at PPP is 2.5 times its GDP at MER.[7] The values of GDP at PPP and MER for the richest countries of the system seldom differ by more than a factor of 1.5. As China continues to develop, further strengthen its economic ties with the world, and move toward a floating currency, the two measures of its GDP should also converge. That can only happen if GDP at MER grows faster than GDP at PPP. One might argue that forecasting such convergence violates the treatment of GDP at MER and PPP in real terms. We argue here that such convergence is a phenomenon of such importance that analysis should include it.[8] The result is a forecast for global growth at PPP that is slower than that at MER.[9]

Midrange forecasts for comparison

Three sets of forecasts provide the best comparative basis for the base case of IFs.

Compared to most organizations, the World Bank tends to take a longer view, and it frequently presents forecasts in its *Global Economic Prospects* series. The 2003–2006 volumes produced global and regional GDP forecasts through 2015 (as well as its forecasts for poverty reduction, reported in Chapter 4). The 2007 volume provided estimates of regional growth rates from 2008 to 2030 and of poverty rates through 2030 (the 2008 volume did not provide a table of long-term forecasts). The International Energy Agency (IEA) uses economic forecasts for its analysis of global energy, most recently through 2030. Global Insight supplies forecasts for the U.S. Department of Energy through 2030 for its annual International Energy Outlook series.[10]

Table 5.2 shows forecasts of the World Bank, the IEA, and Global Insight for growth rate in GDP through 2030, in comparison with those of the IFs base case. The World Bank revised its forecasts downward somewhat in recent volumes as the decade has progressed and the ravages of the financial market collapse and events such as 9/11 took their toll on actual growth. Nonetheless, the bank remains optimistic that growth rates in the developing world will exceed the growth rates of the 1990s. They argue that a variety of economic reforms have positioned many developing countries for acceleration. The forecasts of IFs not only echo that logic but add a bit more optimism for developing countries.

The forecasts of regional growth rates in IFs (at PPP) are very similar to those of the World

Table 5.2 Regional GDP growth rate forecasts from various sources

	GDP growth rate through 2030				
	World Bank	IEA	Global Insight/ Energy Information Agency	IFs Base (PPP)	IFs Base (MER)
High-income countries	2.4	2.2	2.6	2.3	2.6
Developing countries	4.0	5.1	5.3	4.6	6.3
East Asia and the Pacific	5.1	5.6	5.8	5.5	8.1
Europe and Central Asia	2.7	3.6	4.3	3.3	4.5
Latin America and the Caribbean	3.0	3.2	3.9	3.3	4.0
Middle East and North Africa	3.6	4.0	4.2	4.6	6.1
South Asia	4.7	5.6	5.8	4.8	6.4
Sub-Saharan Africa	3.3	3.9	4.9	4.0	5.0
World total	*2.9*	*3.6*	*4.1*	*3.4*	*3.6*

Notes: Starting years of forecasts vary somewhat; Global Insight and World Bank forecasts use PPP weights.

Sources: World Bank 2007: 3 (Table 1.1); International Energy Agency 2007: 62 (Table 62); DOE 2007: 10 (Table 2); IFs Version 5.47.

Bank[11] and Global Insights,[12] generally falling between them, with a few exceptions. First, IFs anticipates considerably higher economic growth in the Middle East and North Africa, largely due to the impetus of higher energy prices. The economic model of IFs is connected to an energy module, and 2030 is near the anticipated peak of global oil production, putting upward pressure on prices and import revenues. Second, except for the World Bank, IFs anticipates somewhat lower growth in both East and South Asia (again, in the important PPP terms; the IFs rates at MER are higher in each case). Interestingly, the World Bank (2008: 43–45) significantly revised upward growth expectations for developing countries in its 2008 analysis. Although it did not provide an updated table, the Bank increased expectations for per capita growth in Africa to 3.2–3.4 percent in coming decades; adding population growth averaging more than 2 percent would raise the bank's GDP forecasts from the lowest in Table 5.2 to the highest. Similarly, for developing countries as a whole, the bank's per capita expectations for the next two decades convert into GDP growth rates of nearly 4.5 percent.

Long-range forecasts for comparison

When one looks for economic forecasts beyond 2030, the universe shrinks. Shell International (2001: 60) built its energy scenarios through 2050 on assumptions of growth in global GDP at PPP of 3.2 percent from 2000–2025 and 2.4 percent from 2025–2050. These figures compare with 3.4 percent and 3.1 percent in the IFs base case. One of the key reasons for higher IFs forecasts in out-years is a composition effect—as developing countries become a larger share of global GDP, their higher growth rates raise the global average. IFs posits technological convergence of middle-income developing countries with rich countries, keeping the growth of that country set quite high.

Projects that analyze long-term energy demand/supply and environmental issues, especially greenhouse gas emissions, have created most sets of economic growth scenarios that extend to or beyond 2050.[13] The Special Report on Emissions Scenarios (SRES) of the third and fourth assessment rounds of the Intergovernmental Panel on Climate Change (IPCC) contain perhaps the best-known set of

scenarios.[14] Interestingly, three of those four scenarios show some acceleration of global growth in 2020–2050 compared to earlier years in part because, like IFs, they posit increasing North-South convergence.[15] The annual growth rates in the four IPCC scenarios range from 2.26 to 3.38 percent between 1990 and 2020 and from 2.34 to 4.04 percent from 2020 to 2050.

In general, the growth rate of the world economy has quite steadily accelerated since the beginning of the Industrial Revolution, significantly reflecting the cumulative impact of technological development and its diffusion. The great surge from 1950 to 1973 and the falloff thereafter, however, suggest the uncertainty of forecasting in the current century. The convergence of productivity in Europe to levels in the United States was a major driver of growth in the Golden Age, and a possible convergence of larger middle-income country growth rates with OECD rates could similarly now boost global growth through midcentury. On the downside, in addition to possible resource scarcities, it is important to remember that forecasts for the twenty-first century anticipate substantial declines in population growth rates.

It is, of course, ultimately important to consider the position of longer-term base case forecasts of IFs in the broader universe of such forecasts, not just for the world, but for major countries and regions. In this context, it is useful to turn to the numbers produced by Goldman Sachs, which tend to be more optimistic for the BRICs, in particular, than either IFs or the World Bank. In fact, Goldman Sachs concluded that "in less than 40 years, the BRICs economies together could be larger than the G6 in U.S. dollar terms."[16]

Strikingly, the compound growth rates over the first half of this century in the Goldman Sachs analysis are 7.7 percent for China, 8.5 percent for India, and 2.6 percent for the United States.[17] By 2050, China's GDP per capita reaches 90 percent of the level of the United States in 2000, and in that same year Russia's GDP per capita surpasses the value Goldman Sachs anticipates for the United States in 2020. Direct comparison with the IFs base case is possible. In the IFs base, the total GDP of the BRICs reaches about 85 percent of that of the G-6 by 2050, a remarkable increase in the ratio from 12 percent in 2000, but well short of the Goldman Sachs expectation of overtaking the G-6 by 2040.[18]

Overall, it bears repeating that there is nothing comparable in the economic arena to the near-consensus about population growth forecasts. Nonetheless, it is clear that IFs falls well within the range of forecasts presented by others.

Economic Distribution

Once upon a time, the Kuznets curve was the primary basis for making forecasts of change in national income distribution. That inverted U-shaped curve nicely portrayed a widely believed story line that countries typically move from heavily agricultural socioeconomic structures in which almost everyone is somewhat equally poor, to less egalitarian industrial structures in which a portion of the population controls most capital and its income, to service structures in which the spread of human capital and government intervention helps society move again toward more equal distribution. Cross-sectional evidence seemed to support the proposition.

Longitudinal data, however, as often contradicted as supported the Kuznets curve within countries over time. Moreover, the slowness of change in income distributions became even clearer than it had been. The most recent cross-sectional plots of the two variables (see Figure 5.4) show a global pattern more like either (1) a downward sloping line suggesting that largely agricultural societies are

not so egalitarian as in the story line or (2) two different patterns within groupings of countries separated by GDP per capita of roughly $10,000. It has become common to explain the apparent inverted U of the world in the 1960s in terms of the special position then of Latin American economies as middle-income and persistently inegalitarian (at least in part from the lingering effects of colonial land distribution).

Forecasting domestic inequality

In the face of disillusionment with the Kuznets' curve, there is unfortunately no consensus on any new, much less any simple story with respect to the likely change in income distribution over time. There are, therefore, practically no longer-term forecasts of income distribution within countries around the world. One exception is work reported by Maurizio Bussolo and Denis Medvedev using survey data and microsimulation. They forecast that "more than two-thirds of low- and middle-income countries" will experience a growth in inequality by 2030 (World Bank 2007: 83) and provide estimates by country.

Survey-based microsimulation approaches cannot easily be integrated with larger systems such as IFs. One promising alternative approach is the portrayal of socioeconomic systems in terms of multiple categories of households and other agents (especially firms and governments), each with its own pattern of human capital, accumulated wealth, and income, and all interacting via financial flows. Such social accounting matrixes (SAMs) can be a basis for computing measures of distribution such as the Lorenz curve and Gini coefficient, thereby assisting in their forecasting. As discussed in Chapter 4 (see also Appendix 3), the IFs project generalized a basic SAM structure to all its countries and developed a dynamic forecasting approach. The approach uses data from the Global Trade Analysis Project (GTAP), which unfortunately specify only skilled and unskilled labor categories and limit forecast credibility. The base case forecast produces an essentially flat population-weighted Gini coefficient of non-OECD countries through 2050, but with an increase in Africa of about 0.015 points. Interestingly, the World Bank forecast (2007: 84) similarly anticipates that a large number of African countries will experience increasingly

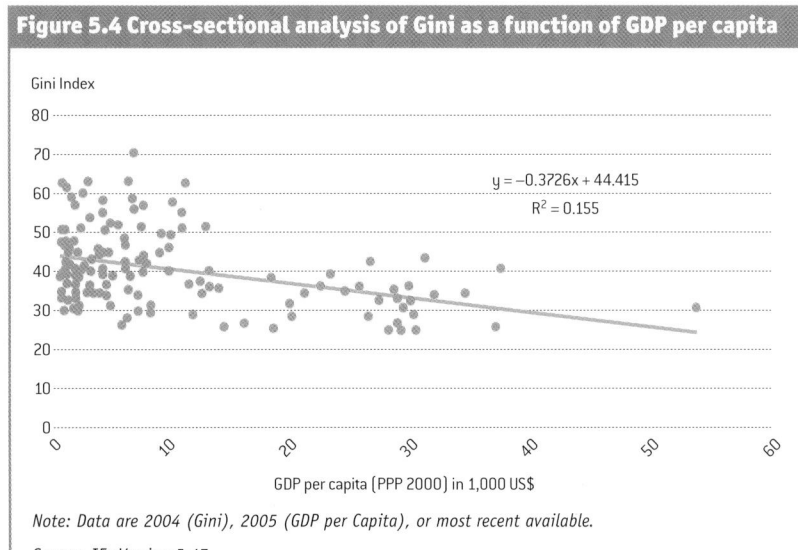

Figure 5.4 Cross-sectional analysis of Gini as a function of GDP per capita

Gini Index

$y = -0.3726x + 44.415$
$R^2 = 0.155$

GDP per capita (PPP 2000) in 1,000 US$

Note: Data are 2004 (Gini), 2005 (GDP per Capita), or most recent available.

Source: IFs Version 5.47

inequality and that none will experience decreases in inequality.

The important conclusion to draw from considering the future of domestic inequality is that there is very weak basis for forecasting. Future chapters rely heavily upon scenarios as a way of treating the variable.

Forecasting global inequality

Although it may seem a digression from the line of discussion in this chapter, the pattern of equality and inequality across the global population as a whole is a very important related topic—remember that Amartya Sen and others have identified inequality as at least a foundation for, if not a manifestation of poverty. The place to begin such a consideration is with a conceptual understanding of global inequality and associated approaches to building a global Lorenz curve and to calculating a global Gini coefficient. Branko Milanovic (2005) very usefully differentiated three concepts of global inequality. Although he regularly referred to them by concept numbers, it is useful to give them names.[19] In each case quantitative assessments normally use GDP per capita at PPP, although they could also build on income or consumption per capita.

Concept 1: Country-based global inequality
Using this approach, China and Barbados have the same weight, obviously a questionable approach to assessing levels of global distribution, but one sometimes used.

Concept 2: Country population–based global inequality
Using this approach, each individual within China is given as much weight as each within Barbados, but the average GDPs per capita or incomes of their countries represent all citizens of each. This approach is frequently used as a basis for measurement of global distribution.

Concept 3: Individual-based global inequality
Now that survey-based data on income or consumption distribution are available for most countries, it is possible to compute a global distribution that effectively captures the human income distribution globally, independent of countries. Milanovic (2002, 2005), Xavier Sala-i-Martin (2002a, 2002b), and others have used this approach.

Milanovic (2005) carefully examined the evolution since 1820 of global distribution with reference to each concept. He found that country-based global inequality rose significantly during the first globalization century, from a Gini of 0.20 in 1820 to 0.37 in 1913. It then fell slightly through the interwar period, rising sharply to the mid-0.40s with the outcomes of World War II, and growing especially in the 1980s and 1990s, ending at 0.54 in 2000.

The pattern for country population–based global inequality was quite different. Although the historical pattern was similar to that for country-based inequality until World War I, with Gini rising from 0.12 in 1820 to 0.37 in 1913, country population–based Gini continued upward to 0.40 in 1938 and then shot up to 0.57 in 1952. The reasons for the dramatic shift have much to do with the economic decline of populous, poor countries like China before and especially during World War II and with the rise of an also populous United States during and after the war. Since 1950, the country population–based Gini has generally trended downward, falling to 0.50 in 2000. The fall has much to do with the economic renaissance of China and would have been greater except for the economic strength of the United States.

Historical computations for individual-based global inequality are much more difficult and uncertain. The key finding is that at the individual level, global inequality was already very high in 1820, with a Gini of 0.50, attributable to great intracountry inequality at that time, even though intercountry inequality was much less than in later years. The Gini calculated at the individual level continued to rise, to 0.61 in 1913 and 0.64 in 1952. Since then it has been relatively stable.

Milanovic concluded that there was a sweeping historical transition between 1820 and 1950 characterized by three elements: "First, rising differences among countries' mean incomes; second, relative decline of poor and populous countries; and third, diminishing within-country inequalities" (2005: 144). The first two of these forces interacted to give rise to increasing individual-level inequality. Since 1950 the divergence among countries has been less rapid overall, while populous and poor countries (India and especially China) have begun to close the economic gap. Any growth of inequality

Individual-based global inequality was already high in 1820 with a Gini of 0.50, but rose to 0.61 in 1913 and 0.64 in 1952; since then it has been relatively stable.

within countries has been offset by such rise of the populous poor countries, so as to keep global individual-level inequality quite stable.

What might be the future of global inequality? On the one hand Milanovic (2005: 148) inveighs against projections because he feels them to be too uncertain, but on the other hand (2005: 162) he concludes that movements toward global community and democracy will lead humanity to reduce economic disparities. Others have been less ambivalent about forecasting. For example,

Glenn Firebaugh (2003) argued that the decline in inequality across countries is more than offsetting greater inequality within them, and the trend of reduced individual-based inequality is the "new geography." Sala-i-Martin (2002a) argued that the future of global distribution at the individual human level depends heavily on sub-Saharan Africa. Assuming that the incomes of Africans stagnate, "The main lesson is that world income inequality is expected to fall for a few more years and then, when the Chinese (and Indian) convergence-to-the-rich effect is over, inequality is expected to rise again as the divergence-from-the-poor effects begins [sic] to dominate" (2002a: 37).

Figure 5.5 shows the calculation by IFs of individual-based global inequality (Milanovic's Concept 3). Because that forecast requires forecasts of GDP growth and of domestic Gini coefficients, as well as the assumption that income distribution is lognormal, it should be considered cautiously. The pattern does, however, generally support the expectations of Sala-i-Martin, tracing a slow and not very substantial erosion in global inequality over most of the first half of the twenty-first century, followed by a flattening as the convergence effects of China and India play out.

An emerging global middle class

Figure 5.6 shows a representation from IFs of the global Lorenz curve for GDP at PPP in 2000. The Lorenz curve is of country population–based global inequality (Milanovic's Concept 2), not of individual-level inequality. The figure also forecasts the Lorenz curve in 2025 and 2050, using base case forecasts of population and economic growth. It is easy to see the implications of continued rapid economic growth in China, India, and the transition economies in the upper-middle range of the population distribution. That forecast of middle-income growth brings Gini down from 0.549 to 0.515 by 2025. A global middle class is growing, and the number of people globally who have incomes between the average incomes of Brazil and Italy in 2000 ($3,914 and $16,746 at PPP) may grow from 440 million to 1.2 billion by 2025 (Bussolo et al. 2007: 26). It is also possible to see the implications of Sala-i-Martin's analysis in the slowing of change in the distribution and the Gini after 2025, even though the IFs base case

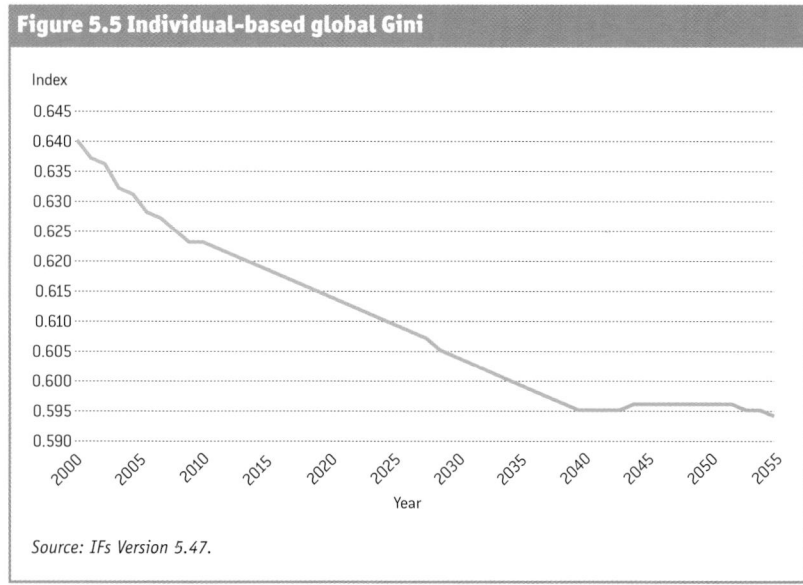

Figure 5.5 Individual-based global Gini

Index

Source: IFs Version 5.47.

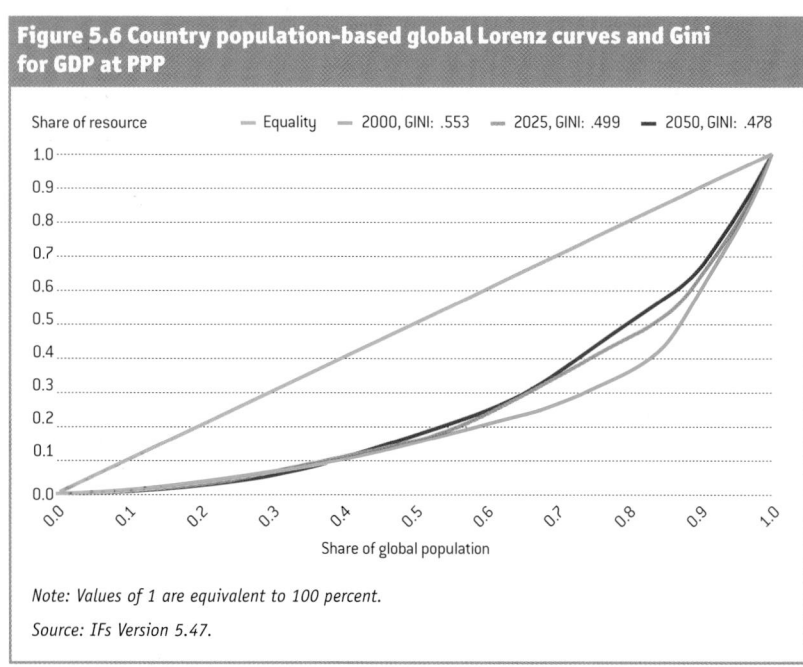

Figure 5.6 Country population-based global Lorenz curves and Gini for GDP at PPP

Note: Values of 1 are equivalent to 100 percent.

Source: IFs Version 5.47.

does not assume stagnation in African GDP per capita through 2050.

Overall, forecasts of changes in income distributions, both within and across countries, are rare for good reasons: the uncertainty about changes in those distributions is very great. In subsequent chapters of this book, we are attentive to the implications of change in distribution for their impact on poverty, but we also often treat those changes via scenario-based assumptions.

Poverty Levels

Chapter 4 reviewed the approaches and tools that have been used by others (including Dikhanov 2005) to forecast poverty and presented the forecasts that have been made with them. Table 5.3 reproduces the poverty rate forecasts of the World Bank's *Global Economic Prospects 2007*, which are the best-known and

most authoritative (see Table 1.1).[20] The table also shows the numbers from IFs with Pardee for the same regional groupings, allowing a direct comparison of base case results from IFs with the forecasts of the World Bank in 2015 and 2030 (and their downward revisions in 2008 of forecasts for 2015).

Most of the numbers for 2015 in the World Bank and IFs lognormal forecasts are quite close, including those for the total developing world at both $1 and $2 per day. There are, however, some important differences between the World Bank and IFs lognormal forecasts, especially for extreme poverty in sub-Saharan Africa. The three variations that might account for such differences occur in drivers, formulations, and initial conditions.

With respect to drivers, we saw earlier that in 2008 the World Bank revised its anticipated economic growth for sub-Saharan Africa

Table 5.3 World Bank and IFs forecasts of poverty rates

| | Percentage of population living on less than $1 a day | | | | | | |
| | 2015 | | | | 2030 | | |
	WB-07	WB-08	IFs-LN	IFs-CS	WB-07	IFs-LN	IFs-CS
East Asia and the Pacific	2.8	2.0	3.8	7.4	0.8	1.4	1.9
China	3.6	2.1	2.7	6.6	1.1	0.3	0.0
Europe and Central Asia	1.0	0.3	0.6	1.8	0.6	0.3	0.8
Latin America and the Caribbean	6.1	5.5	7.1	8.1	4.1	4.6	5.4
Middle East and North Africa	0.7	0.7	1.3	4.0	0.2	1.5	2.3
South Asia	16.2	15.1	13.7	20.2	8.1	4.5	10.2
India		17.6	16.0	24.0		3.1	9.5
Sub-Saharan Africa	37.4	31.4	29.4	39.4	29.9	20.5	33.3
Total Developing Countries	*11.8*	*10.2*	*11.1*	*16.1*	*7.8*	*6.1*	*10.6*
	Percentage of population living on less than $2 a day						
	2015				2030		
	WB-07	WB-08	IFs-LN	IFs-CS	WB-07	IFs-LN	IFs-CS
East Asia and the Pacific	15.5	14.5	16.3	29.4	6.7	7.7	10.2
China	16.5	13.4	10.7	25.2	7.3	2.2	2.5
Europe and Central Asia	8.4	3.4	7.4	11.9	5.5	4.1	5.6
Latin America and the Caribbean	18.8	16.3	19.1	20.7	14.2	14.1	14.2
Middle East and North Africa	12.3	10.3	10.4	21.7	6.5	9.2	14.5
South Asia	60.2	59.0	60.3	54.1	46.0	30.7	35.8
India		62.7	56.4	59.5		23.5	34.7
Sub-Saharan Africa	66.5	61.5	66.6	69.2	58.0	56.0	60.2
Total Developing Countries	*35.1*	*32.9*	*35.0*	*41.1*	*26.7*	*23.0*	*27.8*

Note: LN refers to lognormal formulation; CS, to cross-sectional.

Source: World Bank 2007: 60 (Table 2.3); World Bank 2008: 46 (Table 1.5); IFs Version 5.47.

significantly upward. Prior to that revision, the IFs forecast of extreme poverty for the continent in 2015 was substantially lower than those of the Bank. Now they are quite comparable, although that from IFs for those living on less than $2 per day is now higher than that of the Bank.

IFs also anticipated lower poverty in China than did the Bank, especially at $2 per day. It is likely that the IFs forecast for economic growth in China was higher than that of the World Bank, especially through 2030. The differences with the Bank's values in 2008 are much less. Expected income distribution definitely makes a difference in drivers. IFs endogenously forecasts change in the domestic Gini coefficient. The Gini for China rises in the base case from 0.469 in 2000 to 0.474 in 2015, considerably less than the 10 percent deterioration posited by the Bank.

With respect to formulation, the differences through 2015 between the Bank's approach and the lognormal formulation of IFs are not great; although the Bank uses a three-parameter representation of the Lorenz curve instead of the lognormal representation, the two approaches are analytically very similar. The World Bank and IFs lognormal formulations vary somewhat more in the longer run. The World Bank numbers after 2015 are largely extrapolative, using poverty elasticities with income growth, whereas the IFs numbers reflect the functioning of the full, integrated modeling system. Although the two forecast sets remain quite similar, it is not surprising that they differ more for 2030 than for 2015. Differences in both drivers and formulations explain the increasing divergence.

The IFs cross-sectional forecasts are generally higher than the other two sets, something that Chapter 4 explained in terms of the formulation's potential responsiveness to chronic poverty in disadvantaged groupings. Because neither the Bank's approach nor that of IFs explicitly builds upon the heterogeneity of populations, this characteristic could be useful.

How much difference does the cross-sectional formulation make in baseline forecasts of poverty? Table 5.3 indicates that the magnitude is very substantial. In fact, the cross-sectional formulation suggests that the global goal for extreme poverty reduction will not be met in 2015. Rather, 16 percent of the population of developing countries would still be living on less than $1, in contrast to the 10 percent and 11 percent forecast by the Bank and IFs, respectively, using more traditional approaches.

With respect to initial conditions, the values used by the World Bank will inevitably differ somewhat from those used by IFs, partly because of different procedures for filling the large number of data holes. Only a few countries actually have surveys in any specific year (large countries mount surveys about every third year), so both the World Bank and the IFs project had to use assorted mechanisms, such as interpolation, for filling holes and providing global pictures for any given year. Because there are so many countries in sub-Saharan Africa and a relatively small number of surveys in any given year, it is likely that the largest differences in initial values for the World Bank and IFs would be for that continent, and they are. The World Bank (2007: 60) calculated the extreme poverty level of sub-Saharan Africa in 1990 at 44.6 percent, whereas IFs uses 43.7 percent. This discrepancy is obviously too small to account for the forecast differences but contributes to them.

Overall, the forecasts of poverty from the base case of IFs are not greatly different from those of the World Bank. Moreover, the differences are understandable in terms of variations in driver specification, formulation, and, to a much lesser extent, initial conditions. The basis for further analysis appears solid.

Before moving on to a more extended discussion of poverty, it is important to consider the information presented in Figure 5.7. Using the

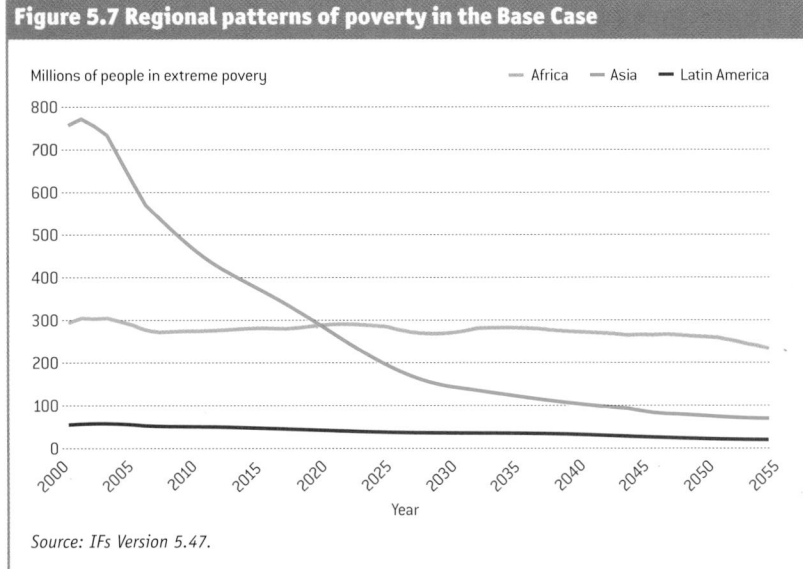

Figure 5.7 Regional patterns of poverty in the Base Case

Millions of people in extreme poverty

— Africa — Asia — Latin America

Year

Source: IFs Version 5.47.

lognormal formulation, the IFs base case suggests that by about 2020, the ongoing processes of rapid reduction in poverty throughout much of Asia and considerably less progress in Africa will lead to the latter continent having the greatest number in poverty and by far the highest rates (not shown). The results for the cross-sectional formulation delay the crossover point for Africa and Asia to about 2040, but the implication is the same. As the attention of this book shifts to human intervention, it will need to focus more and more on Africa.

Moving beyond $1 and $2 per day

The world will soon begin to look beyond 2015 and, before many years, also beyond $1 and $2 per day as critical poverty lines. What might poverty rates be through midcentury? And might analysts want to begin focusing more attention on the number of people who live on less than $5, $10, or perhaps even $25 per day (corresponding to roughly $2,000, $4,000, and $9,000 per year)? In an early study of economic and social structure change, Hollis B. Chenery and Moises Syrquin (1975: 19) concluded that "75 to 80 percent of the total structural change takes place within" a range topped by about $1,000 in 1964 dollars at MER, about $7,000–8,000 per year at PPP in 2000 dollars. For instance, when countries reach such levels of average income, the agricultural share of GDP tends to fall below 10 percent, fertility generally drops to replacement levels, life expectancy typically reaches seventy or above, primary education completion normally exceeds 90 percent, access to safe water and improved sanitation nears 100 percent, and much more (Hughes 2001).

Countries actually accomplish a very large portion of that transformation below a lower level of about $10 per day, roughly the level at which people demonstrate the satisfaction of more basic needs by looking seriously at the purchase of an auto. The definition of entry into the global middle class is marked by reaching an income of about $4,000, or about $11 per day (World Bank 2007: 73). Thus, barring global catastrophes that set back long-term global growth patterns, our desire that humans attain basic capabilities to escape poverty will ultimately require attention to such levels, well above $1 or $2 per day.

Figure 5.8 provides forecasts through midcentury of the number of humans who will be living in poverty defined by five different poverty lines.[21] Hopefully, the world will not increasingly ignore the 350–500 million people who may remain rather persistently in extreme poverty between 2025 and 2055. And it certainly will not be able to turn its eyes from the more than 1 billion people likely to be living on $2 per day or less by midcentury. In fact, it is likely that $2 per day will replace $1 per day as the primary focus of attention. If another line becomes important in discussion of global poverty, it may well be $5 per day. Even by 2055, nearly one-third of humanity is likely to live on less than that amount.

Table 5.4 takes a first cut at exploring in regional detail how the world now looks and how it might appear from the perspective of a poverty line of $5 per day. It suggests that about 70 percent of the global population lived below that level at the beginning of this century and more than 90 percent in both sub-Saharan Africa and South Asia. Given the growth patterns of the base case, those rates could be dramatically lower almost everywhere by midcentury, although the rate in sub-Saharan Africa may still be about 70 percent.

▬ Attention to the emergence of a global middle class requires looking at incomes above $10 per day. ▬

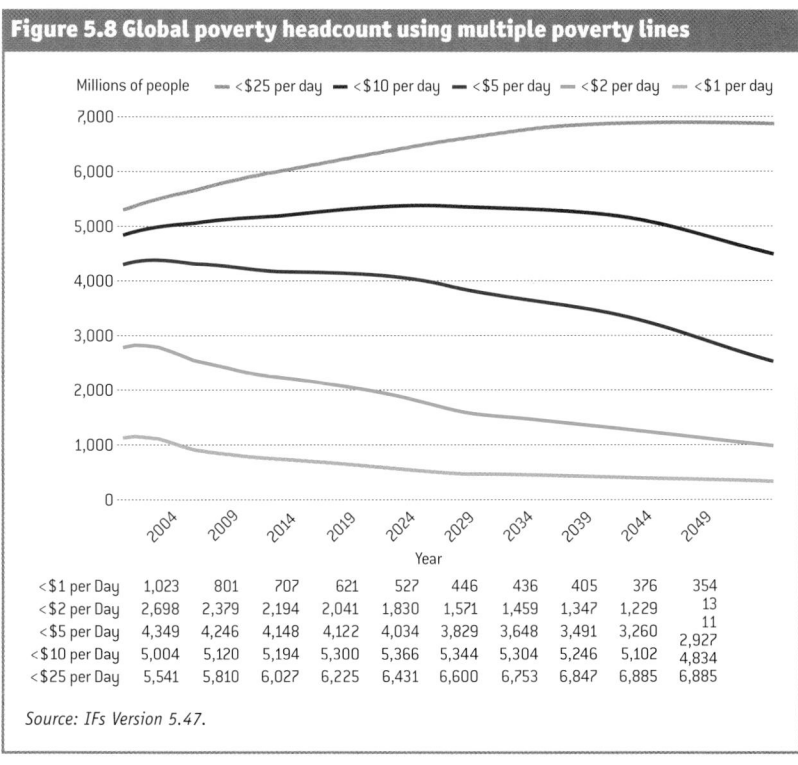

Figure 5.8 Global poverty headcount using multiple poverty lines

Millions of people — <$25 per day — <$10 per day — <$5 per day — <$2 per day — <$1 per day

	2004	2009	2014	2019	2024	2029	2034	2039	2044	2049
<$1 per Day	1,023	801	707	621	527	446	436	405	376	354
<$2 per Day	2,698	2,379	2,194	2,041	1,830	1,571	1,459	1,347	1,229	1,131
<$5 per Day	4,349	4,246	4,148	4,122	4,034	3,829	3,648	3,491	3,260	2,927
<$10 per Day	5,004	5,120	5,194	5,300	5,366	5,344	5,304	5,246	5,102	4,834
<$25 per Day	5,541	5,810	6,027	6,225	6,431	6,600	6,753	6,847	6,885	6,885

Year

Source: IFs Version 5.47.

Table 5.4 Forecasts of poverty rates at $5 per day (lognormal formulation)

	Poverty rates at $5 per day		
	2000	2030	2055
World	70.7	46.0	26.6
High-income countries	1.7	0.6	0.1
Developing countries	83.3	52.4	29.8
East Asia and the Pacific	85.6	32.9	12.1
China	84.5	23.3	7.1
Europe and Central Asia	62.2	14.5	6.2
Latin American and the Caribbean	57.4	37.0	19.5
Middle East and North Africa	66.3	31.0	10.3
South Asia	93.7	67.4	29.7
India	98.6	71.0	19.5
Sub-Saharan Africa	94.2	82.0	62.5

Source: IFs Version 5.37.

Moving up one step further in income, on a global basis, IFs calculates that nearly 5.1 billion were living on less than $10 per day in 2000. How might global poverty at that level, roughly the bottom of middle-class status, unfold across the next fifty years? Figure 5.9 shows the IFs base case forecast. Economic and population growth clearly interact in producing that forecast. Because of strong economic and low population growth forecasts, the number in East Asia and the Pacific living on $10 per day or less may decline

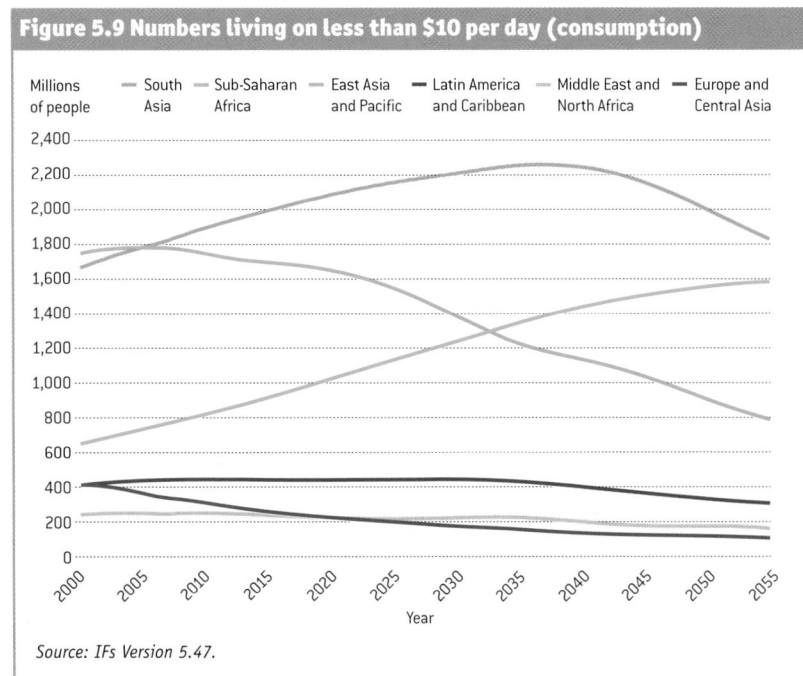

Figure 5.9 Numbers living on less than $10 per day (consumption)

Source: IFs Version 5.47.

quite substantially. In contrast, the number below $10 in South Asia will probably continue to grow until about 2035. As the number in South Asia ultimately begins to decline, the number living below $10 per day in Africa may overtake the region. Interestingly, in 2055 the IFs forecast is that about 5.1 billion people globally will still live at or below $10 per day, even though the percentage may decline from 79 percent of global population to 54 percent.

This discussion has begun to move from consideration of poverty in absolute terms to exploration of it in relative terms. Figure 5.10 takes another step in doing so. Looking inside each of the world's developing regions, it portrays the number of dollars per day available to the bottom 20 percent, as opposed to the dollars available to those who control more buying power. By midcentury, that line may approach $7 per day in East Asia and in the Middle East and North Africa. Yet in Africa it may still hover around $1 per day, which means that the $1-per-day measure may continue to be very relevant for that region even then.

In the richest countries of the world, such as the original members of the European Union and the United States (not shown in Figure 5.10), the dividing line between the poorest 20 percent of the population and those with higher daily consumption levels is already about $20 per day (2000 dollars at PPP).[22] In relative terms, those societies would consider many or most in that bottom 20 percent to be living in poverty.

Moving beyond income poverty

Chapter 2 emphasized that poverty is a much more complex phenomenon than simple income measures can capture. Thus it is important in this volume that we use a variety of measures, supplementing income ratio and headcount with measures such as the poverty gap, but also looking much more broadly to capabilities-based measures like the noneconomic contributions to the human development index (HDI), as well as the HDI itself.

Figure 5.11 shows the average years of education of people twenty-five years of age or older in non-OECD and OECD country groupings (those who wish to see regional and country detail can check the appendixes to this volume). The Robert J. Barro and John Wha Lee (2000) dataset provided the historical data. The forecasts are from the IFs cohort-based model of formal education at primary, secondary, and tertiary levels, developed by Mohammod Irfan. As Sen (1999) has stressed, an increase in educational levels plays a critical part in developing human capabilities that provide the foundation for true freedom. Thus the second volume in this series will focus directly on enhancing educational attainment.

Interestingly, Figure 5.11 could support the same kind of alternative interpretations of global inequality that global GDP per capita often does. Those who see the glass as half empty will likely point to the fact that no significant closure of the nearly four-year gap in educational levels of 1960 between OECD and non-OECD countries has occurred or is anticipated in the base case. At the same time, those who see it as half full will note that the ratio of years of education in the OECD to years of education in non-OECD countries, which has been steady at about 1.9, is forecast to decline below 1.5 by midcentury. Moreover, the average years in school of populations in non-OECD countries will likely reach nine years.

Table 5.5 shows the rise in the human development index for developing regions in the base case forecast of IFs through midcentury. The impact of HIV/AIDS on life expectancy in sub-Saharan Africa, and therefore on HDI, has been substantial. Extending African performance in the 1980s and early 1990s that was already anemic, AIDS has helped cut growth in the HDI for the continent to nearly nothing in the last decade and will help keep it fairly low even through 2030. It appears likely that East Asia and the Pacific will overtake Latin America and the Caribbean within the next two decades, very likely advancing toward the top of the (currently configured) HDI scale by midcentury.

Moving beyond income even in relative terms, Table 5.5 shows two key measures more closely linked to capabilities and functioning. The HDI is fairly well-known: it averages measures of a long and healthy life, knowledge (literacy and educational enrollment) and a decent standard of income. By midcentury the developing world may largely catch up with the current level of countries in the Organization for Economic Cooperation and Development. Some developing regions will be near the top of that index's current range.

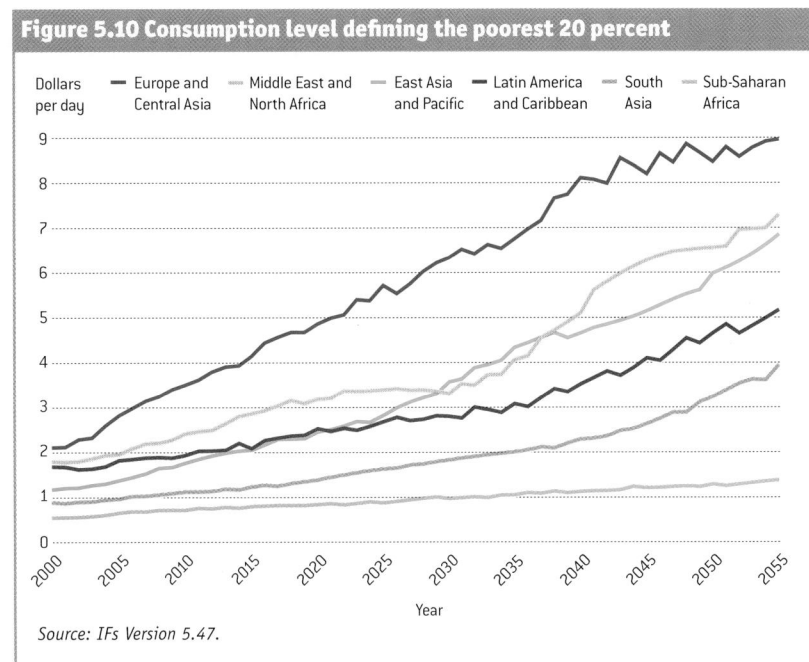

Figure 5.10 Consumption level defining the poorest 20 percent

Source: IFs Version 5.47.

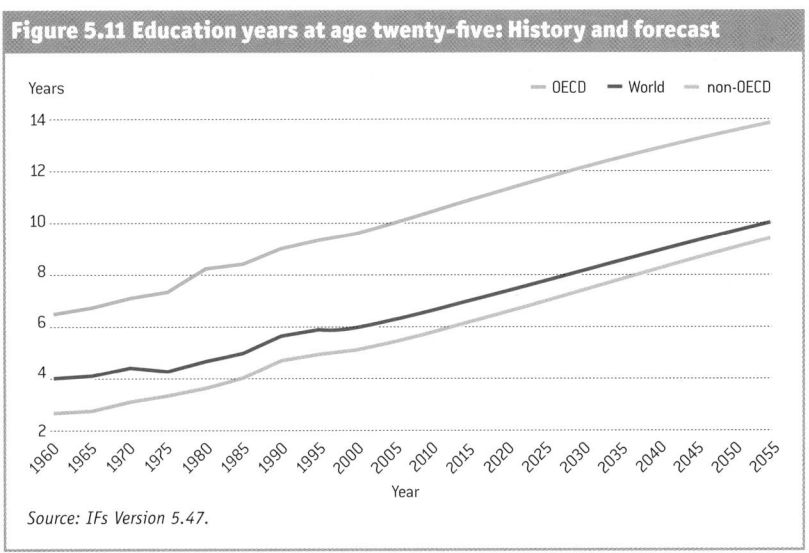

Figure 5.11 Education years at age twenty-five: History and forecast

Source: IFs Version 5.47.

Although the HDI tells us much about average capabilities and human development, the first version of the human poverty index (HPI-1) better links functioning and poverty by its attention to deprivation. It focuses on the percentage of a population that fails to attain capabilities and functioning. Specifically, it averages (1) the portion of a population not reaching age forty, (2) the adult illiteracy rate, and (3) a subindex averaging of the portions of population not having sustained access to improved water and the number of underweight children. The HPI-1 paints quite a different picture from the HDI. For

Table 5.5 Human development index (HDI) and human poverty index (HPI)

| | Poverty measures related to capabilities and functioning | | | | | |
| | HDI (scale is 0–1) | | | HPI-1 (scale is 0–100%) | | |
Developing Regions	2000	2030	2055	2000	2030	2055
East Asia and Pacific	0.74	0.83	0.97	15.0	8.2	2.5
China	0.76	0.86	1.00	13.1	6.3	1.7
Europe and Central Asia	0.79	0.85	0.97	7.4	5.2	2.2
Latin America and the Caribbean	0.78	0.83	0.95	11.5	8.0	2.9
Middle East and North Africa	0.67	0.74	0.91	22.8	16.1	7.1
South Asia	0.58	0.64	0.84	33.1	27.8	17.1
India	0.58	0.64	0.88	34.2	28.6	17.7
Sub-Saharan Africa	0.45	0.52	0.72	41.3	37.5	232.3
Developing world total	*0.66*	*0.72*	*0.89*	*23.2*	*19.0*	*12.3*
Developed world (OECD)	*0.92*	*0.95*	*1.00*	*3.6*	*2.5*	*1.1*

Note: HPI refers to Human Poverty Index.

Source: IFs Version 5.47.

● *Although poverty measures are correlated, they tap very different aspects of the phenomenon.* ●

instance, in 2055 the developing world as a whole may still lag considerably behind the developed world's current values.

Remarkably, the scaling of the HPI-1 is such that it corresponds in this decade very closely to $1 per day. In the developing world as a whole in 2000, the IFs calculation of the income level that separates the lowest 23.2 percent (the HPI value in that year) from the rest of society is about $1.04, very nearly the official $1.08. Similarly, the value that separates the lowest 41 percent in sub-Saharan Africa from others is about $1.10, as is the value that separates the lowest 33 percent of South Asians from others. In spite of these similarities in the aggregate, the people who live below $1 would not always be the same as those designated as deprived by the HPI-1.

The HDI, HPI-1, and income measures demonstrate, however, quite different patterns when one looks forward—although correlated, they tap very different aspects of poverty and human development. For instance, IFs calculates that the line separating the bottom 12.3 percent of the developing world (the HPI-1 forecast for 2055) from the more well-to-do population will be about $2 per day, not $1.1. That is, deprivation will not decline as quickly as incomes will rise, a phenomenon consistent with the continued persistence of a chronic core of poverty. The stories of poverty now and in the future are very much multifaceted. Forecasts with alternative measures in this volume break

new ground (see, especially, the forecast tables at the end of this volume). The development and use of a wide range of measures must continue.

Conclusion

The base case forecasts of IFs with Pardee are generally and purposefully not very different from those of other long-term forecasting models. Those of IFs have the added advantage of representing an integrated system across demographic, economic, sociopolitical and other modules. They also reach beyond the two basic measures of global income poverty. Thus the base case forecasts provide a useful foundation for subsequent chapters, which explore interventions relative to the base.

It is not too strong a statement to say that forecasts of complex human systems are nearly always wrong, whether in the short or long run. Why, then, build anything further on the base case of IFs in subsequent chapters? As we argued in Chapter 1, for those interested in the possibility of actions that might enhance the global human condition, there is no alternative to forecasting. It is necessary to make one's best estimates about that condition, with and without various interventions. In fact, the real value added of forecasting is precisely around such interventions. So, caveats in place, it is time to move forward.

1 Population Division of the UN Department for Economic and Social Affairs. The UN releases revisions of its forecasts biannually under the title *World Population Prospects* (see UN Population Division 2006 concerning the 2004 revision) and http://www.un.org/esa/population/publications/ wpp2006/wpp2006.htm for the 2006 revision. The coverage is global, built up from countries. The forecast horizon is normally through 2050, but in late 2003 the UN released forecasts through 2300, under the title World Population in 2300. In addition, the UN has also prepared a database on migration with forecasts through 2050.

2 The U.S. Census Bureau began publishing global forecasts with a 2050 horizon by country in 1985 and does so periodically in its *Global Population Profile* (for the 2002 report, see U.S. Census Bureau 2004). The coverage of IIASA's population forecasting is global, although often with a focus on thirteen global regions and variously through 2050 or 2100 (Lutz, Sanderson, and Scherbov 2004).

3 Although its does not provide global forecasts, the Population Matters program of RAND produces targeted demographic forecasts of importance. See, for instance, Bloom, Canning, and Sevilla, *The Demographic Dividend* (2003) and Cook, Demographic Trends Alter the National Security Scene (2000).

4 For further reference, the Millennium Ecosystem Assessment (MA) (2005: 306) scenarios generate global populations in 2050 that range from a high of 9.6 billion for Order from Strength to a low of 8.1 billion in Global Orchestration. There is no base case in the MA. The MA scenarios were generated by the IIASA population model.

5 The median forecast for 2050 in 1994 was 9.8 billion, in 1996 it was 9.4 billion, in 2000 it was 9.3 billion, and in 2002 it was 8.9 billion. But in 2004 it increased to 9.1 billion. The 2002 revision brought the UN forecasts more in line with those of IIASA in 2001 (as reported in *Nature,* January 9, 2005), namely peaking by 2070 at about 9 billion and declining to 8.4 billion in 2100.

6 The OECD also periodically provides forecasts with a longer range. In 1979 it released *Interfutures: Facing the Future*. In 1991 it published a collection of articles in Long-Term Prospects for the World Economy with some horizons through 2010 and 2015. Sadly, but with importance as a warning to contemporary forecasters, the seeming inability of the United States to shake off low productivity and the great success of Japan in racing ahead appeared for authors at that time to be patterns unlikely to change. By the late 1990s, the OECD (1999) had turned some attention to analyzing the "Long Boom" in a collection of articles looking to 2025 and other horizons, and in 2006–2007 the OECD (2006) undertook a large-scale integrated environmental outlook to 2030 and prepared global economic forecasts in the process.

7 In 2008 the International Comparison Project revised its estimates of GDP at PPP based on new surveys in China and India, greatly narrowing earlier estimates of the gaps between values at PPP and MER; the IFs formulations expect narrowing to continue.

8 Without the representation of convergence, the Chinese growth rates at MER would be unrealistically passed through to PPP and result in many perverse effects, including overly rapid reduction in poverty and unreasonable growth in energy demand. The need to recognize more modest rates of increase in GDP at PPP is one reason some analysts arbitrarily adjust downward Chinese growth at MER.

9 The relationship between MER and PPP accounts is both complicated and controversial (see Castles and Henderson 2003 for some of the controversy). Nordhaus (2005) sorts the relationship out particularly well. Nuxoll (1994) found, similarly to the IFs forecasts, that developing country growth rates at PPP tend to be lower than at MER.

10 In 2011 Data Resources Inc. (DRI) and Wharton Econometric Forecasting Associates (WEFA) merged to become Global Insight.

11 Given the much greater economic weight of other developing regions, the anticipated growth of developing countries as a whole is nonetheless quite similar in the World Bank and IFs forecasts. One surprising element is the considerable difference in world rates. Because the developing countries have a slightly greater GDP throughout most of the forecast horizon, one would expected the weighted average to be somewhat closer to the value of the developing countries, which is not true for the value provided by the World Bank. One possible explanation is that the World Bank may have weighted the global calculation with GDPs only early in the forecast horizon, not with GDPs throughout it.

12 One noteworthy feature of the forecasts of GDP per capita from Global Insights is that the rates for 2015–2030 are consistently lower than those for 2000–2015, in contrast to the forecasts of IFs (see Figure 5.4). Limited explanation of the forecasts is available in the *International Energy Outlook 2006* except for (1) a footnote indicating an analyst-based downward adjustment of rates in India and China and (2) an argument (DOE 2006: 13) that labor force growth rates are anticipated to decline in other non-OECD Asia. In fact, although labor force growth rates are likely to decline in most developing countries, labor force as a share of the total population, normally growth enhancing, is likely to continue rising for many, especially in Africa. Global Insights has also created high and low economic forecasts for the period through 2030. The high-growth scenario assumes OECD and non-OECD growth rates 0.5 and 1.0 percent higher, respectively, with a raise by 1.5 percent in Russia. The low-growth scenario assumes reductions of the same magnitude.

13 Those interested in energy tend to adopt forecast horizons between 2015 and 2050 (e.g., U.S. Department of Energy 2006 and Shell 2001), whereas those interested in climate change have horizons that reach to 2100. With respect to climate change, in 1998 the International Institute for Applied Systems Analysis produced global economic forecasts through 2100 in cooperation with the World Energy Council (WEC) titled *Global Energy Perspectives* (Naki enovi , Grübler, and McDonald 1998). Building in part on IIASA and WEC foundations, the IPCC has needed economic growth forecasts through 2100 as a foundation for its energy and environmental analyses. These are available in the IPCC Third Report Emissions Scenarios (2001). The Millennium Ecosystem Assessment (MEA) in 2005 forecast to 2100, and the UN Environment Programme's Global Environmental Outlook 4 will look out to 2050 (using IFs with Pardee for the economic forecasts).

14 Van Vuuren and O'Neil (2006) have analyzed these numbers and compared them with other economic forecasts, including those of Richels, Manne, and Wigley (2004) who, in working with the Stanford-based Energy Modeling Forum, forecast growth for the twenty-first century between 1.7 and 2.8 percent, with 2.4 percent as the medium case.

15 Another primary source of long economic forecasts is the Millennium Ecosystem Assessment (2005; see Chapter 9, page 309 for tables of forecasts). Its four scenarios come in substantial part from the IMAGE Team (2001) with help in regional disaggregation from procedures developed by Bollen (2004) and the World Scan model. All of the MEA scenarios anticipate higher per capita global economic growth in the 2020–2050 period than in the preceding 25 years, with rates from 1.0–3.0 percent (the IFs base case is at the high end of this range).

16 Goldman Sachs 2003: cover page; for detailed forecasts, see page 9.

17 Methodologically, the Goldman Sachs model is driven substantially by an assumption of 1.5 percent annual convergence of total factor productivity in the BRICs with the United States (Goldman Sachs 2003: 18).

18 The Goldman Sachs analysis attributed about one-third of the gap closure to appreciating currency values of the BRICs. This reflects their recognition that BRICs have relatively higher GDP at PPP than at MER. Our own analysis concurs with their expectation that GDPs at PPP will likely converge with those of the G-6 by midcentury and that, with likely currency appreciation added, GDPs at MER may also do so.

19 The World Bank calls them intercountry, international, and global inequality, respectively.

20 Chapter 4 pointed out that, although initial conditions for Bhalla's forecasts (2002: 170) differ from those of the Bank as a result of different measurement approaches for 2000, the trajectories of his forecasts are very similar to those of the Bank.

21 The lognormal formulation currently allows at least crude estimates of poverty at any specified poverty line. A specialized display form within IFs allows exploration of poverty at different daily consumption levels and consideration the thresholds that divide different percentiles of population from each other.

22 Estimates within IFs of poverty numbers in percentiles of societal distributions and of numbers falling below poverty lines other than $1 and $2 do not tie directly to survey data as do initial conditions for poverty at those two standard analysis levels. Instead, they draw upon the lognormal formulation, anchored by average societal consumption levels and the income distribution of Gini coefficients. For consistency, we adjusted the lognormal formulation to $2-per-day poverty rates from available surveys before calculating higher poverty levels.

6

The Future of Poverty: Framing Uncertainty

Exploring reasonable ranges for proximate drivers will frame the uncertainty of poverty forecasts and the likely outer range of human leverage.

How much leverage is available in reducing poverty globally and in specific regions and countries of the world? Another way of asking the same question is, how rapidly and substantially can we shift patterns of base case forecasts of poverty like those in Chapter 5? The proximate drivers (economic growth, population growth, and income distribution) can help frame an answer to the question. We have some understanding of the general range of uncertainty for each of those drivers. Varying them accordingly, one at a time and collectively, will frame the range of uncertainty about the future of poverty. That is the purpose of this chapter.

This volume has emphasized, however, that the search for levers and strategies of actions must focus on the deeper forces that drive economic and population growth and of income distribution. Human action, such as passing laws or changing government spending patterns, does not directly increase income or make income distributions more equitable. Such action can,

however, lead to improved governance, more investment in education or R&D, or increased transfer of tax receipts from rich to poor, all of which in turn can indirectly change income and its distribution. The next two chapters will therefore explore the relationship between strategies of intervention, as individual actions or in poverty reduction packages (see, again, their discussion in Chapter 3), and the proximate drivers. Chapter 7 will do so at a high level of geographic differentiation and Chapter 8 at the level of country groupings, countries, and even regions within countries.

Framing Uncertainty with Proximate Drivers

Average income and income distribution are proximate drivers of poverty. That is, of course, true with respect to the poverty *rates* within a population, but not true with respect to the *absolute number* of people living in poverty. To incorporate into the analysis the number of people living in poverty requires the addition of population size to the proximate driver list. That addition is also important because of the many interactions between demographic and economic growth.

Population

Chapter 5 compared the base case of International Futures (IFs) with Pardee with the population forecasts of the United Nations and others. Two additional forecasts built around the base case can provide reasonable higher and lower estimates for global and regional populations between now and midcentury and identify the impact that such framing scenarios might have on poverty. Figure 6.1 shows the global growth rates of population historically and in the frame-building forecasts. The interventions to create the high and low population forecasts were variations on the endogenous fertility rate forecasts of the base case, scaled so as to create something close to the well-known UN high and low population forecasts.[1] Interventions to the model for these and all other framing scenarios began in 2000, so as to represent the maximum variation that was possible beginning in the year during which the global community set the Millennium Development Goals (MGDs).

The UN high variant scenario appears very improbable, because it would require a bit more than 1.1 percent global annual population growth through 2050. The global rate in 2005 was 1.2 percent, and that rate has been falling quite sharply. That is, the UN high forecast would require something very close to today's global population growth over the first half of this century, following forty years during which the global rate dropped by nearly half and momentum for further decline has built.

Figure 6.2 shows the implications that alternative population forecasts have on the total number of people living on less than $1 per day, using the lognormal formulation. The difference is relatively modest by 2015, but very substantial by 2050.

Population growth rates affect not just the number of people living on less than $1 per day. They affect also the percentage of people in poverty, which is lower in the low population scenarios. Although higher population contributes to somewhat higher total economic growth, it also places many burdens on developing societies that can slow

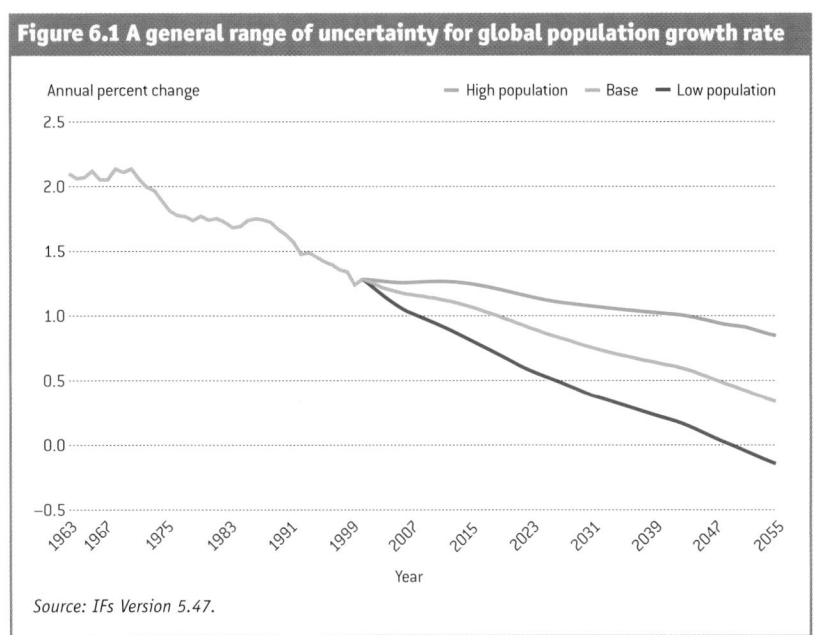

Figure 6.1 A general range of uncertainty for global population growth rate

Annual percent change — High population — Base — Low population

Year

Source: IFs Version 5.47.

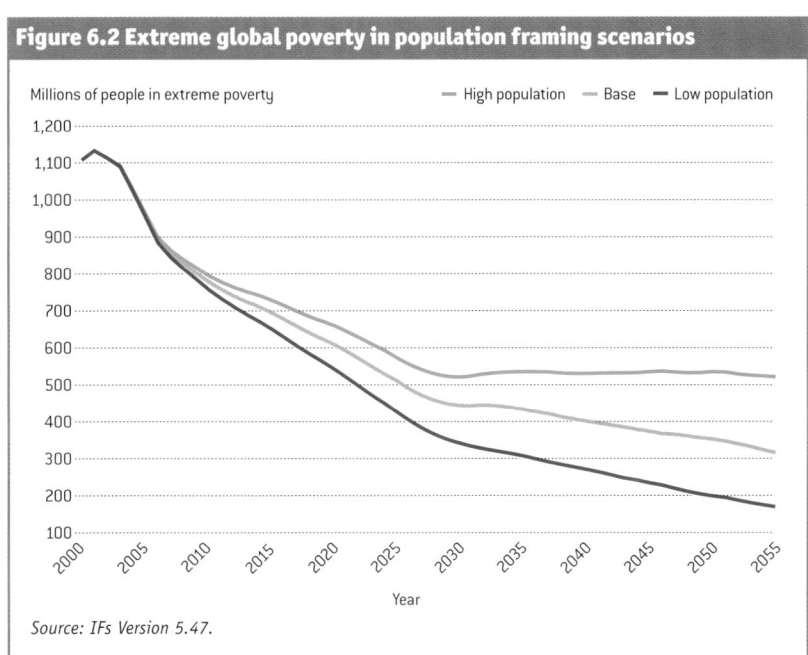

Figure 6.2 Extreme global poverty in population framing scenarios

Millions of people in extreme poverty — High population — Base — Low population

Year

Source: IFs Version 5.47.

per capita growth. For instance, it requires higher educational expenditures and places more demand on agricultural land. In contrast, slower demographic growth can make such expenditures and resources available at higher levels per capita and can also increase the portion of the population in their working years (a demographic dividend) across many years of the forecast horizon. Not surprisingly, the variation in the rate of poverty is not as great across demographic scenarios as the variation in the headcount. Yet it is significant, reaching more than 3 percent by 2050, reinforcing the importance of looking at population not just as a driver of numbers living in extreme poverty but as a driver of poverty rates.

Economic growth

The interventions made to create the high and low economic forecasts were variations on the multifactor productivity forecasts of the base case, scaled globally so as to create something close to rates of gross domestic product (GDP) growth 1 percent faster or slower than those in the base case (refer to Figure 5.3 for rates in the base case). Because of greater uncertainty, we increased or decreased the rates of growth in sub-Saharan Africa, South Asia, and Latin America by about 1.5 percent. Because the historical pattern of economic growth, to which the base case is tied, has been so high for China, we increased its high case by only 0.5 percent and decreased its low case by 2.0 percent.

The framing cases represent annual global growth rates that range from 2.1 to 4.2 percent. Angus Maddison (2001: 126; see also Maddison 1995) estimated that the world economy grew at a rate of 1.6 percent from 1820 to 1950, at 3 percent between 1973 and 1998, and at 4.9 percent during the Golden Age from 1950 to 1973. It is important to reiterate that the forecasts in this book for the first half of the

twenty-first century are scenarios for a period in which population growth rates are expected to continue a fairly substantial decline, in contrast to the history of most of the twentieth century, which included a rapid rise, peaking, and then some important initial decline in population growth rates. The three frame-building forecasts appear to capture the broad range of historical patterns fairly well.[2]

Figure 6.3 shows the possible implications of the three different GDP forecasts on poverty rates, using the lognormal formulation. Clearly, the headcount differences across GDP forecasts are substantial.

Not surprisingly, the alternative economic forecasts have a greater impact on poverty reduction than do the different population forecasts. For example, the variation in the percentage of people living in poverty in 2050 reaches 8–9 percent (within a given formulation), more than twice the variation seen across the population forecasts. Still, the variation in rates by 2015 within formulations is only about 2–4 percent, raising some serious questions about the extent of human leverage in poverty reduction over such a horizon, a theme to which we will return.

Distribution

Although global distributions of income across countries and among individuals regardless of their geographic location are very much of interest (we discussed them in Chapter 5 and will return to them in Chapter 7), the society is the basic level for calculation of poverty and therefore the appropriate level of analysis for framing scenarios around the implications of distribution.

The endogenous forecasts of income distribution within IFs are not strong enough to carry much weight in the analysis of future poverty levels. That is not a criticism of IFs relative to other forecasting efforts, but rather an absolute statement—authoritative long-term forecasts of domestic income distributions simply do not exist. Montek S. Ahluwalia, Nicholas Carter, and Hollis Chenery (1979) attempted to create distributional forecasts by relying upon the inverted U of the Kuznets curve, found in early cross-sectional analysis, but longitudinal analysis and even recent cross-sectional work has largely discredited that pattern.

Figure 6.3 Extreme global poverty in economic framing scenarios

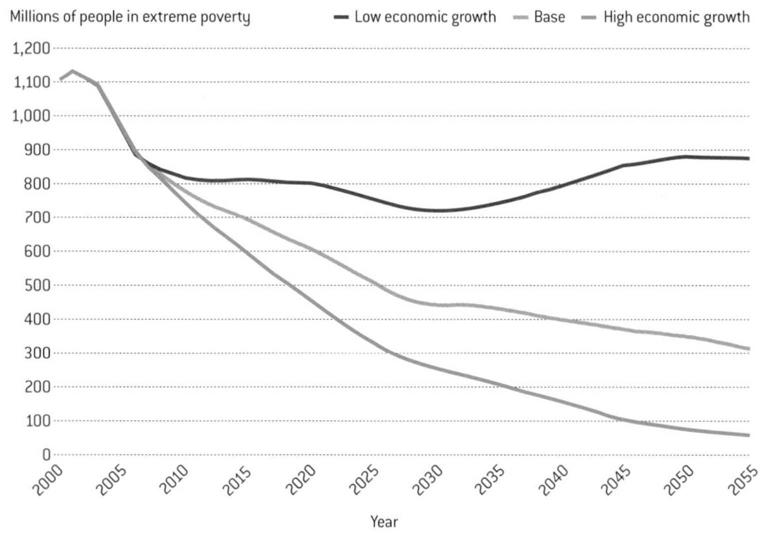

Millions of people in extreme poverty — Low economic growth — Base — High economic growth

Source: IFs Version 5.47.

Given both the weak basis for forecasting and slow change historically in domestic distributions, a fundamentally flat forecast is a reasonable pattern for the base case. As with population and economic growth, framing cases were created that attempt to provide general outer boundaries for change in average Gini coefficients in the first half of the century. In both framing cases, exogenous changes in domestic distributions enter gradually over the entire fifty-year period, cumulatively shifting initial Gini coefficients upward or downward by about 0.06 points, or 15 percent, relative to the base case.[3]

Figure 6.4 begins the analysis of the impact that different forecasts of distribution can have on forecasts of poverty levels, looking once again at the number of those living in extreme poverty as calculated by the lognormal formulation. One of the most interesting aspects of it (and the patterns with the cross-sectional formulation also) is the asymmetry between the impact of greater inequality and greater equality relative to the base case. In the early years, the asymmetry is largely a function of the turn of the base case toward somewhat greater inequality. That is partially a composition issue, because the global computation is weighted by population, which is growing more rapidly in developing countries where inequality tends to be higher. In the longer run, however, the global average of domestic Gini coefficients in the base case returns to a value close to initial conditions, which suggests that there must be a deeper basis for the asymmetry.

The core of the explanation involves Africa. An increasingly large share of the global poor over time are in sub-Saharan Africa. In the IFs base case forecast, African income distributions become somewhat worse, while those in other parts of the world improve. It is important to inveigh again against attributing too much credibility to such a forecast, but accelerated economic development often does increase inequality. If it were to happen in Africa, the difference in poverty level forecasts between the base case and the high inequality case would be relatively small.

Comparing only the high and low inequality forecasts (so as to avoid the complications of the pattern of inequality in the base case), the differences in poverty rates for the lognormal formulation in 2015 are 3.2 percent. That is

quite comparable to the differences by 2015 across the economic growth scenarios. In contrast, the differences by 2050 are less great across forecasts based on differing income distribution than they are across different growth forecasts. This result has implications for the next chapter, in which different types of interventions are considered. Specifically, distribution changes can be as important as growth in the short run in lowering poverty rates, but growth will prove more important than distributional changes in the longer run.

Proximate drivers in combination

Attention to the combined impact of the proximate drivers completes the framing of futures for poverty reduction. Although it is, of course, extremely unlikely that the world would experience, for instance, a combination of high population growth, low economic growth, and worsening inequality, such a forecast helps us understand the likely upper limits for poverty through the first half of the century—the "worst case." Similarly, a combination of low population growth, high economic growth, and decreasing inequality lets us examine the likely lower limits for poverty—the "best case."

The worst case and the best case are the worst and best only in the limited terms of the sets of individual drivers that have been examined in this chapter. One can, of course,

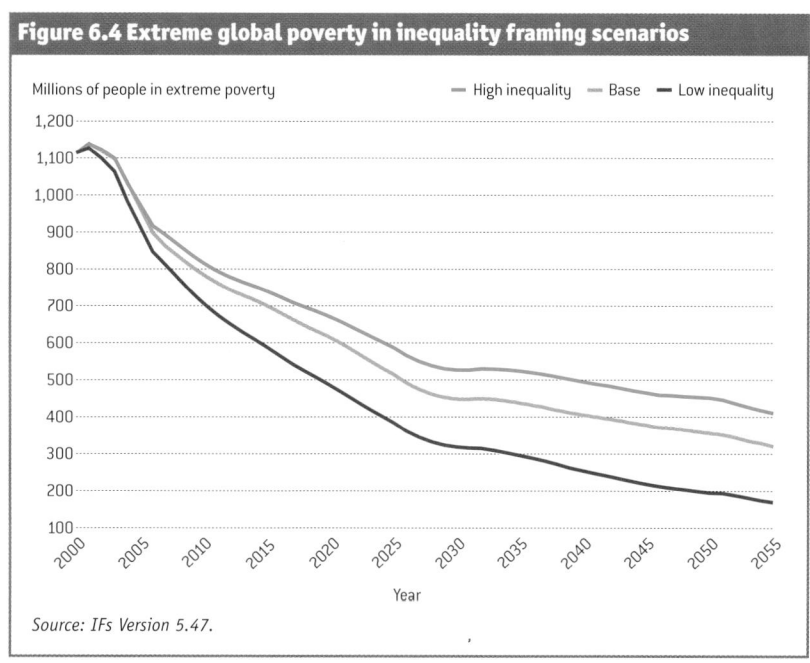

Figure 6.4 Extreme global poverty in inequality framing scenarios

Millions of people in extreme poverty

— High inequality — Base — Low inequality

Source: IFs Version 5.47.

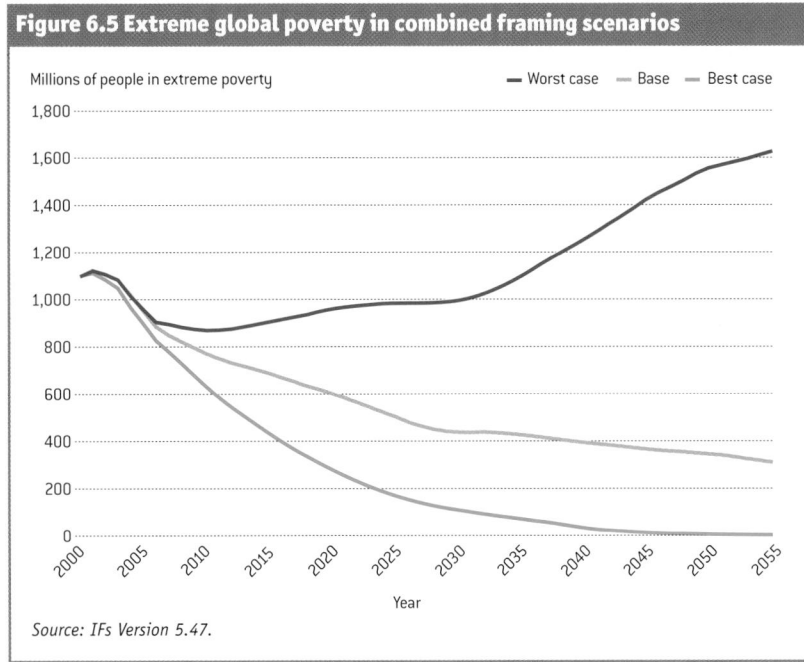

Figure 6.5 Extreme global poverty in combined framing scenarios

Millions of people in extreme poverty

— Worst case — Base — Best case

Source: IFs Version 5.47.

the three scenarios for global headcount of those living on less than $1 per day. Table 6.1 summarizes the numerical forecasts of global poverty, across formulations as well as across time and by headcount and rate. In the best case scenario, both lognormal and cross-sectional formulations suggest that extreme poverty could be nearly eliminated by midcentury. Remember that extreme poverty kills through malnutrition and bad health, so that is a marvelous prospect—a slaying of one Horseman of the Apocalypse that all cultures recognize as fundamentally threatening. At the same time, remember also that crawling out of that condition requires only an income of $1 per day, hardly suggesting that the world's poor would be doing very well in absolute terms. The last section of this chapter returns to the richer portrait of what the different scenarios mean with respect to poverty defined more broadly.

Even in the worst case, it appears very probable that the numbers and percentage of those living in the worst poverty will decline for the next ten to fifteen years. That has a great deal to do with the momentum of economic growth in China and India; growth rates a percent or two below recent levels would not fully stop their forward movement. In contrast, however, the longer-term future of poverty reduction has much to do with sub-Saharan Africa, where what seem reasonable swings in economic growth could make a substantial difference. In the worst case, numbers in poverty could actually rise again, and the percent living in poverty could flatten out.

One of the remarkable aspects of Table 6.1 is that, even in the worst case scenario, the lognormal formulation suggests that humanity

imagine a future in which economic growth of most of the developing world collapses, even reversing the gains of China and India, perhaps as a result of a massive global wave of avian flu or great political unrest. Similarly, the worst and best cases obviously diverge substantially on either side of the base case, psychologically conferring more credibility to it. Presumably, the unfolding reality of the next fifty years is more likely to be close to the base case than to the extreme cases, but the base case also remains a very low probability forecast. The analyses in this study should help us think about possible futures, not lead us to believe that we can predict them.

Figure 6.5, using the lognormal formulation, shows the wide range of possible futures in

Table 6.1 Extreme poverty in combined framing scenarios

	Combined proximate driver framing scenarios					
	Worst case		Base case		Best case	
Poverty numbers (millions)	2015	2050	2015	2050	2015	2050
Lognormal	913	1,561	692	350	437	10
Cross-sectional	1,151	1,654	998	569	799	112
Poverty rates (percent)						
Lognormal	14.5	16.1	11.2	3.7	7.2	0.1
Cross-sectional	18.3	17.0	16.1	6.9	13.2	1.6

Source: IFs Version 5.47.

will come very close to accomplishing the first Millennium Development Goal of bringing the poverty rate down by half by 2015. (As we proceed through the discussion of this chapter, it will be useful for the reader to keep in mind the MDG target for extreme poverty; given the World Bank (2008: 46) estimate of 28.7 percent in 1990 for developing countries, that target is 14.3 percent in 2015.) Goals set by the global community have historically been almost always missed. But this global goal is very likely to be achieved, thanks substantially to the progress in China. Regional attention to South Asia in the shorter run and sub-Saharan African throughout the forecast horizon is, of course, needed, and later sections and chapters will provide it.

Insights from the analysis of framing scenarios with proximate drivers

The analysis of frame-building forecasts provides overall insights about the combined impact of the proximate drivers of poverty:

- There is great uncertainty with respect to the course of human poverty, but there appears to be a considerably higher probability that both numbers in poverty and rates of poverty will fall than that they will rise (sub-Saharan Africa excepted, and subject to further analysis).
- Uncertainties related to forecasting formulations are considerable, even in the relatively near-term horizon of 2015.[4] The lognormal and cross-sectional formulations vary by 5–7 percent in their anticipated reduction of global poverty rates by 2015. Somewhat surprisingly, they exhibit less variation by midcentury, in part because of the boundary effects of approaching zero extreme poverty.
- Uncertainties related to drivers are also very considerable and give rise to estimates of poverty that vary as much as 5–7 percent by 2015 and 16 percent by 2050.
- To put in contexts such ranges of uncertainty surrounding formulations and drivers, the ones through 2015 are, although important, less than about half of the absolute reductions anticipated in the base case between 2002 and 2015 by either the World Bank or IFs.

- Given that each of the proximate drivers is subject to very considerable human influence via collective and conscious action, humanity appears to have had (from the perspective of 2000) considerable influence with respect to poverty levels and rates, most likely within the same general range of 5–7 percent before 2015 and 16 percent by 2050.
- The variation in poverty rates of 5–7 percent by 2015 is, however, the result of contrasting extreme assumptions about all proximate drivers. Because conscious human action is unlikely to cause swings in the proximate drivers nearly as large as the ranges selected for this frame-building analysis of the drivers, it is likely that potential human influence on poverty rates is considerably less than those outer-range values. In fact, it might be reasonable to guess that incremental human action is unlikely to result in swings of much more than half those magnitudes, perhaps 3 percent by 2015 and 8 percent by 2050. This is important context for the analysis in Chapter 7 of the power of deep levers.

Framing Uncertainty with Integrated Scenarios

The purpose of this chapter is to frame the potential scope of human leverage with respect to poverty reduction. The method used in the last section, namely varying each proximate driver toward the outer limits of what seems likely, is very helpful. It is also, however, somewhat crude. The best and worst case scenarios, a simple summing across the three drivers, are extreme. Moreover, they are not tied to any fundamental assumptions about human decisions or constraints imposed by technology or the environment.

Another approach to framing the future of poverty is the use of coherent, integrated scenarios. Forecasters have developed many different scenario sets for global futures.[5] Those sets are of interest for several reasons. First, they normally try to map a broad range of likely human futures. Second, those alternative futures often reflect implicit or explicit assumptions about different patterns of human development, including alternative beliefs concerning the extent to which humans can steer their own systems.

Even in the worst case scenario, the world will probably reach the Millennium Development Goal for poverty in 2015.

We may have the ability to reduce global extreme poverty by about 8 percent by 2050 relative to an already strong downward trend.

Third, however, those scenarios also remind us that the future is not simply a matter of different human action patterns. Within good scenarios of the long-term future, some broad aspects of uncertainty are not particularly susceptible to human action and have the character of physical unknowns. For instance, the fragility of the global biological and physical environment, so that human actions might disturb equilibria and tip systems, is to a considerable degree unknown. So are ultimately recoverable fossil fuel resources and rates of advance in technology.

In 1995 the Stockholm Environmental Institute convened one of the most influential efforts to think deeply about long-term futures, the Global Scenario Group (GSG), "as an independent, international and interdisciplinary body to engage in a process of scenario development." [6] The GSG process gave rise to three scenario classes, or families, widely used in longer-term global analysis. Its Conventional Worlds scenarios (Market Forces and Policy Reforms) serve as something close to base case portrayals of global futures. Its Barbarization scenarios (Breakdown and Fortress World) provide detail on how things could go badly wrong. And its Great Transitions scenarios (Eco-Communalism and New Sustainability Paradigm) convey visions for long-term futures that give priority to human development, social stability, and environmental quality as pillars of sustainable development.

Building on the global scenario group: The Global Environment Outlook

The GSG scenarios were one of the key sources of inspiration for a set of four related scenarios elaborated in the UN Environment Programme's (UNEP's) *Global Environment Outlook 3* and again used in the *Global Environment Outlook 4*. Box 6.1 describes the variations developed by the UN Environment Programme (2002).

Although environmental issues obviously have a prominent place in the analysis done for GEO scenarios, their framing of uncertainty extends widely to key issues such as demographic and economic growth and technology and globalization processes. As true scenarios, rather than simpler alternative forecasts, each represents a quite different but potentially coherent pattern of global evolution with associated human interventions: (1) focusing on free markets and globalization processes, (2) intervening with policies directed toward human capital and environmental quality, (3) changing cultural and behavioral patterns toward sustainability, and (4) separating into competing groups within and across countries.

Box 6.1 Global Environment Outlook scenarios

Markets First. "The private sector, with active government support, pursues maximum economic growth as the best path to improve the environment and human well-being. Lip service is paid to the ideals of the Brundtland Commission, Agenda 21, and other major policy decisions on sustainable development. There is a narrow focus on the sustainability of markets rather than on the broader human environmental system. Technological fixes to environmental challenges are emphasized at the expense of other policy interventions and some tried-and-true solutions." (UNEP 2007: 400)

Policy First. "Government, with active private and civil sector support, initiates and implements strong policies to improve the environment and human well-being, while still emphasizing economic development. *Policy First* introduces some measures aimed at promoting sustainable development, but the tensions between environment and economic policies are biased towards social and economic considerations. ... The emphasis is on more top-down approaches, due in part to desires to make rapid progress on key targets." (UNEP 2007: 400–401)

Security First. "Government and the private sector complete for control in efforts to improve, or at least maintain, human well-being for mainly the rich and powerful in society. *Security First*, which could also be described as *Me First*, has as its focus a minority: rich, national, and regional. It emphasizes sustainable development only in the context of maximizing access to and use of the environment by the powerful." (UNEP 2007: 401)

Sustainability First. "Government, civil society and the private sector work collaboratively to improve the environment and human well-being, with a strong emphasis on equity. Equal weight is given to environmental and socioeconomic policies, and accountability, transparency and legitimacy are stressed across all actors.{AU: Sectors? ED} As in Policy First, it brings the idealism of the Brundtland Commission to overhauling the environmental policy processes at different levels"[1] (UNEP 2007: 401).

1 Compare this also with the sustainability scenario developed in European Commission–sponsored TERRA project (Hughes and Johnston 2005).

Many experts helped create the GSG scenarios, develop the GEO versions of them, and examine the specific implementations of those scenarios within IFs. For instance, the GEO-4 process relied on regional teams to consider the forecasts produced within each scenario, as well as the specific assumptions that generated model results, and to provide feedback for improvement of the story lines. GEO-4 used IFs to map demographic and economic drivers and to add richness to the stories of alternative technological and social futures.

Comparison of the UNEP GEO scenarios with best and worst case forecasts

Are these integrated scenarios associated with significantly different forecasts of poverty? If so, what is the character of that association? How does the range of poverty vary across the integrated scenarios relative to the broad framing scenarios?

Table 6.2 helps address those questions. It provides poverty forecasts (using the lognormal formulation) from the UNEP GEO scenarios in comparison with the best and worst case forecasts.[7] The first two columns look at the World Bank's set of developing countries as a whole. The UNEP GEO scenarios capture much of the same variation in the GDP and population drivers as the best and worst cases, although that variation tends to be narrower.

None of the GEO scenarios produce GDPs in 2050 as high as the best case scenario, and none produce population in 2050 as high as the worst case scenario. Because the driver range is narrower in the UNEP forecasts, and because the

UNEP forecasts exhibit very little variation on income distribution, it should not be a surprise that the variation in their poverty forecasts is more limited than that of the best and worst case forecasts. Already by 2015, that variation is reduced in developing countries as a group from about 7 percent between best and worst cases to only 3 percent. And by 2050 the range is narrowed from nearly 16 percent to just over 7 percent. Because the four GEO scenarios purposefully span a wide range of possible futures, this result reinforces the earlier conclusion that the impact of incremental human leverage (remember that the base case already represents much applied leverage) might be less significant than often argued, especially by 2015. And it reinforces the expectation that packages of interventions might only swing poverty rates about half as much as the total difference between worst and best cases. Yet not surprisingly, all four of the GEO scenarios suggest levels of extreme poverty in the developing world as a whole that fall below the MDG target of 14.3 percent by 2015.

Turning to sub-Saharan Africa, Table 6.2 suggests much the same set of conclusions. The two proximate drivers that vary across the four UNEP GEO scenarios, GDP and population, lead to poverty reduction that is within the general range of the best and worst cases, but the variation is very considerably less. The World Bank's (2008: 46) estimate of poverty rates for sub-Saharan Africa in 1990 was 44.6 percent, setting up an MDG of 22.3 percent. None of the GEO scenarios achieve that by 2015, although "policy first" and "sustainability first" do bring the rates to about 25 percent.

The variation in UNEP GEO scenarios is similar to, but somewhat less than, that of the worst and best case scenarios.

Table 6.2 Extreme poverty (percent) in the GEO and IFs framing scenarios						
	Developing countries		Sub-saharan Africa		South Asia	
GEO Scenarios	**2015**	**2050**	**2015**	**2050**	**2015**	**2050**
Markets first	11.1	3.7	29.8	12.8	13.6	1.9
Policy first	10	1.8	25.3	8.5	12.7	0.9
Security first	12.5	8.6	30.1	28.2	16.1	5.4
Sustainability first	9.8	1.5	24.5	7.8	12.5	0.7
Framing Scenarios						
Best case	7.2	0.1	21.7	0.6	7.8	0.5
Base case	11.2	4.2	29.4	14.2	13.7	2.2
Worst case	14.5	16.1	33.8	40.5	18.1	11.5

Source: IFs Version 5.47.

Looking at South Asia, all the above conclusions remain valid. The World Bank's (2008: 46) estimate for poverty in the region in 1990 was 41.3 percent. All four GEO scenarios cut that by more than half in 2015. Although the GEO scenarios by 2015 tend to be closer to the IFs base case or the worst case framing scenario than to the best case, by 2050 all four scenarios show near elimination of extreme poverty.

These scenarios and their implementation in the IFs system all have weaknesses, of course. Consider one significant example for South Asia. Global oil prices rose rapidly after 2000 and in 2007–2008 reached more than $130 per barrel, about five times the price of 2000 in real terms. There is much uncertainty about how prices will change through 2015, much less 2050. The U.S. Department of Energy's Energy Information Agency publishes *International Energy Outlook* annually, and the 2007 volume presented three pricing scenarios through 2030, with prices in that year of $36, $59, and $100 per barrel in 2005 dollars (U.S. Department of Energy 2007: 12–13).

The base case of IFs builds in very little economic impact from higher oil prices. If the price spike of 2007–2008 were to persist for several years, however, even eroding over time to as low a value as $36, it could have substantial impact on developing countries, especially regions as dependent on imported oil as South Asia. In 2015 the region's poverty rates could be 18.5 percent instead of the 13.7 percent of the base case. Interestingly, such a rate would actually be higher than the worst case scenario of Table 6.2, already said to be worst only in the context of the assumption set explored earlier.

Table 6.2 merits a final comment. Since each of the GEO scenarios that reduce poverty relative to the base case have different orientations, one might conclude that the potential exists for combinatorial intervention packages that are more positive than any one of them alone. We should recognize, however, that some aspects of the integrated GEO-4 scenarios may be incompatible, at least philosophically, if not in terms of directly conflicting actions. The fact that each constitutes a plausible world is one of their greatest strengths in helping frame the study of the future of poverty. The GEO scenarios thus suggest that we should temper expectations for very large impacts from incremental interventions beyond the processes already set in motion in the base case. Let us keep this recognition in mind as we explore specific interventions and packages of them in Chapter 7.

Framing the Future of Poverty More Fully

Until this point in this chapter, our focus has been on developing countries as a whole, and we need to begin the geographic disaggregation that the next two chapters will continue. In addition, although the $1 per day measure of income poverty is very useful and the first Millennium Development Goal greatly popularized it, poverty is a much more complex phenomenon than rates of extreme poverty alone can assess. Consideration of additional poverty measures can more fully frame our understanding of the range of possible poverty futures and the leverage available to shape them.

A more extensive look at income poverty

Table 6.3 moves beyond extreme poverty by looking at two other income poverty measures, the percent of those living on less than $2 per day and the poverty gap. It provides 2000 data, along with framing forecasts for 2030 and 2055 across the set of developing-country regions normally used by the World Bank in its analysis, breaking out the Chinese and Indian giants. The insights from that table concerning extreme poverty include the following:

- Absolute poverty rates in 2000 were not greatly different in India and sub-Saharan Africa, but the future of those rates is very different in scenarios from the worst case to the best case. The reason lies largely in the higher economic growth rates of India, but India's lower population growth rates also make a positive contribution to poverty reduction.
- Even in the worst case, India will almost certainly greatly reduce extreme poverty by 2030 and be well on the road to eliminating it by 2055.
- In addition to sub-Saharan Africa, the region most in danger of stagnation with respect to poverty reduction may be Latin America and the Caribbean. The reason lies again in relatively low per capita economic growth.

- The developing countries of Europe and Central Asia, as well as those of the Middle East and North Africa, suffer quite low rates of extreme poverty and are making considerable progress in reducing even those.

Life on less than $1 per day is called absolute or extreme poverty because such income is considered the borderline for survival. It is no coincidence that about 1 billion people live at that level and that about 800 million global citizens, roughly the same number, are considered

Table 6.3 Income poverty in combined framing scenarios

| | Percent of people living on less than $1 per day | | | | |
| | | Worst case | | Best case | |
	2000	2030	2055	2030	2055
East Asia and the Pacific	15.2	4.4	3.3	0.4	0
China	16.5	2.9	2.2	0.1	0
Europe and Central Asia	4.5	0.8	0.9	0.1	0
Latin America and the Caribbean	10.2	11.2	8.7	1.4	0.2
Middle East and North Africa	4.8	3.2	1.9	0.1	0
South Asia	28.5	12.3	10.5	1.1	0
India	35.4	10.7	3.2	0.2	0
Sub-Saharan Africa	43.9	33.4	39.2	6.4	0.4
Total developing countries	*21.5*	*13.1*	*15.9*	*1.7*	*0.1*
	Percent of people living on less than $2 per day				
		Worst case		Best case	
	2000	2030	2055	2030	2055
East Asia and the Pacific	49.7	19.1	13.7	3.0	0.1
China	49.2	15.1	11.4	1.4	0.0
Europe and Central Asia	19.5	5.2	5.9	0.5	0.0
Latin America and the Caribbean	25.7	25.6	19.6	5.4	0.8
Middle East and North Africa	26.2	17.0	8.4	1.6	0.0
South Asia	70.0	44.5	33.4	8.2	0.6
India	79.9	44.6	20.9	6.1	0.0
Sub-Saharan Africa	76.2	65.7	65.1	25.6	7.0
Total developing countries	*53.9*	*36.6*	*34.6*	*8.6*	*1.6*
	Poverty gap relative to the $1 per day poverty line				
		Worst case		Best case	
	2000	2030	2055	2030	2055
East Asia and the Pacific	5	1.4	1.9	0.1	0
China	5.5	0.8	0.6	0	0
Europe and Central Asia	1.1	0.2	0.2	0	0
Latin America and the Caribbean	3.7	4.5	3.6	0.5	0
Middle East and North Africa	1.4	1	0.6	0	0
South Asia	9.2	3.7	3.6	0.3	0
India	11.6	2.9	0.8	0	0
Sub-Saharan Africa	19.6	14.7	18.9	2	0.1

Source: IFs Version 5.47.

malnourished. Obviously, however, even doubling that income threshold to $2 per day leaves those who live below it at very considerable risk. Approximately 2.5 billion people, nearly 40 percent of humanity, live below that level, sometimes referred to as moderate poverty. Approximately half of those in the developing world live below $2 per day. Again, the forecasts suggest a number of insights:

■ Not surprisingly, poverty at $2 per day will be more persistent than poverty at $1 per day. Reductions by 2030 are proportionately smaller, and it persists in sub-Saharan Africa through 2055 even in the best case.
■ More surprisingly, poverty at this level should be reduced by 2055 to one-third or less of populations in regions other than sub-Saharan Africa, even in the worst case.
■ Even though the Middle East and North Africa, including many very oil-rich countries, do not have a very large percentage of people living on less than $1 per day, they have a great many living below $2.
■ In scenarios involving significantly slower economic growth, like those around the worst case framing scenario, the developing world could still be burdened with more than one-third of its population in moderate poverty by 2055. Even China could have quite high levels by then.

One of the key difficulties with headcount measures of poverty is that they give no idea of how far below the identified poverty line individuals might be. In contrast, the poverty gap measure assesses the mean shortfall from the poverty line, treating those above the poverty line as having zero shortfall. The measure expresses the shortfall as a percentage of the poverty line. Thus in Table 6.3, the mean shortfall in sub-Saharan Africa in 2000 is nearly 20 percent, almost twice that of India. In contrast, the extreme poverty headcount percentage for sub-Saharan Africa in 2000 was 43.9 percent, not that much more than the 35.4 percent for India. Thus the poverty gap measure indicates that the depth of poverty in Africa is considerably greater than in India. In addition to higher forecasts of economic growth in India, that

recognition helps us understand why Africa, unlike South Asia, is unlikely to meet the MDG goal for poverty headcount rate by 2015 even in the best case scenario and why, in the worst case scenario, extreme African poverty stays very high.

Turning to capabilities

Chapter 2 emphasized that poverty, in the widely accepted conceptualization of Amartya Sen, is ultimately rooted in human capabilities and that it is important, therefore, to look at a broad set of such capabilities when assessing the extent and depth of poverty. The most recognized set of capabilities is that tapped by the UNDP's human development index (HDI).[8] Specifically, the HDI aggregates capabilities on three subdimensions: a decent standard of living, a long and healthy life, and knowledge. Indicators used by the UNDP for those three dimensions include, respectively, GDP per capita at purchasing power parity (logged); adult literacy and gross aggregate enrollment rates at the primary, secondary, and tertiary levels; and life expectancy. Table 6.4 reports conditions in 2000, as well as framing forecasts for the same three dimensions and approximately the same indicators.

Not surprisingly, given the breadth of poverty indicated by headcount percentage and the depth as indicated by the poverty gap (see, again, Table 6.3), the GDP per capita of sub-Saharan Africa in 2000 fell below that of other regional groupings. The low GDP per capita in sub-Saharan Africa relative to that of India helps explains the greater relative severity of poverty in Africa. At the other end of the spectrum, both developing Europe and Central Asia, and Latin America and the Caribbean, had GDPs per capita in 2000 at or above $6,500 at purchasing power parity. Those levels are totally consistent with the low rates of extreme poverty and the relatively small size of the poverty gap within the developing countries of Europe and Central Asia. In the case of Latin America, however, the rates of extreme poverty are more than double those of developing Europe and Central Asia, in spite of a slightly higher per capita GDP. Great intercountry variation within Latin America explains part of the combination of relatively high income and high poverty, but not all of it. Very substantial domestic inequality also explains much of the phenomenon. Brazil is an obvious example. In 2000 it had a GDP per capita of over $7,300, but still had an extreme poverty rate of about 8 percent and a poverty gap of nearly 3 percent. Even Argentina, with a GDP per capita in 2000 of $12,000, had a poverty rate of nearly 5 percent.

The Middle East and North Africa demonstrates a pattern with a different combination of income and poverty. Although the GDP per capita in 2000 was only $4,200,

Table 6.4 HDI components in combined framing scenarios

GDP per capita at purchasing power parity (in 1,000s of dollars)

		Worst case		Best case	
	2000	2030	2055	2030	2055
East Asia and the Pacific	3.8	9.8	12.8	17.6	40.5
China	3.9	11.5	15.2	21.2	48.7
Europe and Central Asia	6.3	13.6	18.5	19.9	48.3
Latin America and the Caribbean	7.1	9.2	12.0	18.5	50.7
Middle East and North Africa	4.2	7.5	10.2	13.0	38.7
South Asia	2.6	4.9	7.3	9.9	35.0
India	2.4	5.1	9.1	10.7	42.3
Sub-Saharan Africa	1.6	1.8	2.3	3.9	13.7
Total developing countries	*3.8*	*6.9*	*8.5*	*13.3*	*35.9*

Life expectancy (years at birth)

		Worst case		Best case	
	2000	2030	2055	2030	2055
East Asia and the Pacific	67	76	80	81	87
China	69	79	83	85	89
Europe and Central Asia	64	73	79	77	83
Latin America and the Caribbean	68	72	76	78	85
Middle East and North Africa	66	72	76	77	87
South Asia	62	68	73	75	86
India	62	70	77	76	89
Sub-Saharan Africa	45	56	58	62	73
Total developing countries	*63*	*69*	*71*	*75*	*84*

Primary education completion rates (percent)

		Worst case		Best case	
	2000	2030	2055	2030	2055
East Asia and the Pacific	107	100	98	102	100
China	112	102	100	102	100
Europe and Central Asia	96	100	99	101	100
Latin America and the Caribbean	103	98	97	101	100
Middle East and North Africa	93	101	99	103	100
South Asia	68	98	98	105	104
India	63	105	102	107	106
Sub-Saharan Africa	61	78	90	91	98
Total developing countries	*87*	*95*	*96*	*101*	*101*

Source: IFs Version 5.47.

the poverty rate was a relatively modest 5 percent, half that of Latin America and even below that of Europe and Central Asia, two regions with considerably higher average incomes.

Different contemporary patterns help shape the forecasts. The broad and deep poverty of Africa makes it likely to be persistent. The broad but somewhat less deep poverty of South Asia and India's high economic growth make the region the likely location for the greatest poverty reduction in the coming decade or two. Just as most analysts today are saying something along the lines of "global poverty reduction is very impressive, but attributable primarily to China—look at the problems of sub-Saharan Africa," in 2030 analysts may well be declaring how impressive global reduction is, attributing it primarily to South Asia, and saying "look at the problems of sub-Saharan Africa."

The second dimension of the human development index is a long and healthy life. In 2000 the values for all regions except South Asia and, especially, sub-Saharan Africa, were at or above global averages. The African values once again reinforce the breadth and depth of the continent's poverty. Moreover, in part because of HIV/AIDS, even the best case forecast does not exhibit much progress by 2015.

The third dimension of the HDI is knowledge. The UNDP puts two-thirds weight on the literacy indicator of knowledge and only one-third on the combined enrollment ratio across primary, secondary, and tertiary education levels. Literacy is difficult to measure consistently, however, and many analysts look to completion of primary education as a proxy measure of it. It is also one of the targets of the second MDG.

Table 6.4 shows the completion rates for primary education (those rates can exceed 100 percent when overage students return to complete primary school). On this measure, sub-Saharan Africa in 2000 actually was not far below South Asia. Both best and worst framing cases, however, suggest slippage by Africa by 2030. In fact, Africa appears highly unlikely fully to meet the MDG of universal primary education completion by 2030, much less 2015.

Having looked at all three dimensions of capabilities in the HDI, the reader may wish to glance back at the base case forecast of the measure in Table 5.5. Obviously, as an equally weighted index based on the three dimensions reviewed, its characteristics are an average of those seen on the individual dimensions and their indicators. In aggregate, the extent of poverty in sub-Saharan Africa is as clear from the HDI as from measures of individual capabilities, with South Asia in a better current position, but in turn quite far behind middle-income regions. Forecasts for Africa suggest a gap with all other regions that fails to narrow by midcentury, in spite of very considerable progress.

One size does not fit all. This cliché of development policy analysis deserves the regular repetition it receives. The starting points of different regions, and obviously of the countries within them, are very different. They differ not just on the level of poverty but on its character, as illustrated by different patterns across the various dimensions of poverty. Moreover, their current trajectories, and their possible or even likely patterns of development in coming decades, are quite different. The next chapters will need to be sensitive to that in looking at strategies for intervention.

Conclusion

Previous chapters demonstrated the importance of measurement and formulation when assessing historical data on poverty and when attempting to forecast future levels and rates of it. This chapter took the additional step of investigating the impact of very different economic and demographic growth patterns for the proximate drivers of poverty. It mapped the likely range of poverty by creating two framing forecasts, titled worst and best cases, but explained to be in reality better and less good (relative to the base case), since the future could potentially slip in either direction outside the boundaries set by them. It further explored the importance of deep drivers by looking at the possible influence on poverty of four integrated framing scenarios. Finally, it sketched some of the very large differences in poverty across regions and dimensions of poverty.

The findings should help shape our expectations for the more detailed and focused exploration of human leverage in the next chapter. We list the most important findings below:

- Because conscious human action is unlikely to cause swings in the proximate drivers as large as the ranges selected for them in the first section of this chapter, it is likely that human influence on extreme poverty rates for the developing world will be less than 5 percent. In fact, the integrated framing scenarios suggest that leverage is unlikely to result in swings of more than half those magnitudes, perhaps in the neighborhood of 2–3 percent relative to the base case. (Within sub-Saharan Africa, with its high poverty rates, however, the leverage appears considerably greater.)

- Incremental human leverage, on top of already substantial and critical efforts to reduce poverty, should not be downplayed or ignored simply because the likely swings in poverty rate as a result of applying it may not always appear huge. Reductions of 2–3 percent in the poverty rate of developing countries would mean the lifting of 150–250 million more people out of extreme poverty, the poverty that kills.

Human choices have the potential by 2050 to reduce the headcount of extreme poverty, the poverty that kills, by 150–200 million.

1   Specifically, the high population scenario increases fertility relative to the base case gradually over time, bringing it to values 50 percent higher than the base case in 2050. The low population scenario reduces fertility slowly relative to the base case for non-OECD countries only, bringing it down by 40 percent relative to the base case in 2050, while allowing OECD countries to stabilize long-term fertility rates at as low as 1.6, rather than at 1.8 in the base case.

2   The International Institute of Applied Systems Analysis (IIASA) and the World Energy Council (WEC) produced long-term scenarios of gross world product (Naki enovi , Grübler, and McDonald 1998: 6) with implicit annual growth rates between 2.2 percent and 2.7 percent. The Intergovernmental Panel on Climate Change (IPCC) scenarios from the third assessment report had annualized growth rates between 2.4 percent and 3.8 percent. Again, the framing forecasts above appear sufficiently broad so as to capture the range of futures that most analysts believe reasonable.

3   Using the Gini coefficient, income distribution in China worsened after 1980 by 0.15 or more. The distribution in India has remained much more stable.

4   Interventions to the model for these and all other framing scenarios began in 2000.

5   Hughes (2004b) mapped many of the scenario sets used in longer-term forecasting projects across different dimensions of uncertainty.

6   See http://www.gsg.org/gsgintro.html. Full documentation is in *Bending the Curve: Toward Global Sustainability* by Raskin et al. (1998) and *Great Transition: The Promise and Lure of the Times Ahead* by Raskin et al. (2002). See also *Which World? Scenarios for the Twenty-First Century* by Hammond (1998).

7   Dale Rothman of the International Institute for Sustainable Development (IISD) built upon the basic implementation of the GEO scenarios by the IFs team and refined and extended it with input from several of the modeling and regional teams that contributed to the GEO-4 process.

8   Although Sen was an adviser in the development of the HDI, he has often commented on its inadequacies as a measure. It is given prominence here for lack of an obviously better alternative.

7

Changing the Future of Poverty: Human Leverage

▰ Within the
total range of
possible human
leverage, how
powerful are
specific choices? ▰

Human leverage has great potential to reduce global poverty. Much action is already underway to apply leverage, and the base case forecast presumes that such action will continue. Chapter 6 framed the general magnitude of possible incremental leverage by examining a reasonable range of variation in the proximate drivers of poverty. The purpose of this chapter is to explore the choices that might most effectively exercise that discretionary leverage—to drill down toward policy one more level from the framing discussion. The first several sections seek to identify the points of leverage, those actions that can further influence the proximate drivers of poverty, and to map reasonable magnitudes for intervention.[1] Then we explore whether there are any silver bullets available, any actions that hold disproportionate potential for accomplishing incremental poverty reduction.[2] The final subsection turns to packaging of multiple actions and to looking at synergies and trade-offs among them.

Operationalizing the Levers

The International Futures (IFs) with Pardee model explicitly represents by no means all the structures and drivers desirable for a full analysis of human leverage with respect to economic and population growth and distribution (see Table 3.1 for an extensive listing), but it does contain substantial numbers of them. In reality, many of the identified "levers" of this discussion will remain rather aggregated, more "subdrivers" than true policy levers.

Levers below the proximate drivers often affect more than one driver. For instance, investments in human capital affect population, economic growth, and distribution. Increased international trade can affect both economic growth and distribution. It therefore makes little sense to proceed by discussing levers as if they were related to single proximate drivers. Instead, as discussed also in Chapter 3, although the distinctions are also not always clear between largely domestic and largely international actions, that division is generally apparent and organizes our discussion. The same reality lies behind the ordering of the Millennium Development Goals (MDGs), the first seven of which focus on primarily domestic measures and the last of which, the global compact, turns to largely international leverage.

Tailoring the interventions: Geographic focus

"One size does not fit all" is one of the many clichés of the development world. Clearly, appropriate intervention packages for development generally and for poverty reduction specifically vary by region of the world, by country, and even by subregions within countries. Because of the global and long-term focus of this volume and the IFs simulation on which it builds, this chapter will not take analysis down to the country level. Instead it will stay at the regional (subcontinental) level, and Chapter 8 will consider selected countries.

What regional breakdown of the globe can be helpful in our analysis? Chapters 5 and 6 used the World Bank regions to provide some continental level information on poverty and to make comparison with World Bank results possible, but those units are too highly aggregated for policy analysis. Similarly, the six basic groupings of the UN are continental: Africa, Asia, Europe, Latin America (including the Caribbean), North America, and Oceania. The United Nations' regions and subregions for statistical reporting are, however, much closer to what is needed (see Appendix 4 to this volume).[3] For instance, that set divides Africa into Eastern, Middle, Northern, Southern, and Western. It divides Asia into Eastern, South-Central, South-Eastern, and Western (covering the Middle East up through the Caucasus).

No geographic representation is perfect for every purpose, and the divisions of the UN have obvious limitations in analyzing poverty or other Millennium Development Goals. For instance, the UN region of Eastern Asia puts Japan together with China. For the purposes of this analysis, we have put Japan, along with Hong Kong, the Republic of Korea, and Taiwan (not a member of the United Nations and its regionalization but represented in IFs) into an Eastern Asia Rich region and left China together with North Korea and Mongolia in Eastern Asia Poor. That serves us better because

it separates countries essentially without extreme poverty from those with significant rates of it. Similarly, we have put Australia and New Zealand into a new Oceania Rich, leaving the mostly Micronesian countries in Oceania Poor. We placed Mexico with the United States and Canada in North America, partly to prevent it from dominating Central America in statistical analysis. Weaknesses remain, such as the inclusion of Israel with considerably poorer countries of the Middle East. Ultimately, country-level analysis, such as in the appendixes to this volume, is necessary. Yet the rest of this chapter will show that regional analysis can generate many insights.

Tailoring the interventions: Magnitude

The exploration for reasonable magnitudes of policy intervention will draw on cross-sectional analyses like that of Figure 7.1, showing contemporary conditions in regions as a function of gross domestic product (GDP) per capita. Specifically, we will look for typical structural patterns and how regions perform with respect to them. Such analysis follows a tradition going back at least to Hollis Chenery and Moises Syrquin (1975) and picked up again by Jeffrey Sachs (2005: 74–89) in his recommendations for clinical analysis of development patterns. Sachs emphasized that it is unreasonable to

Leverage needs to be tailored to the specifics of regions and situations.

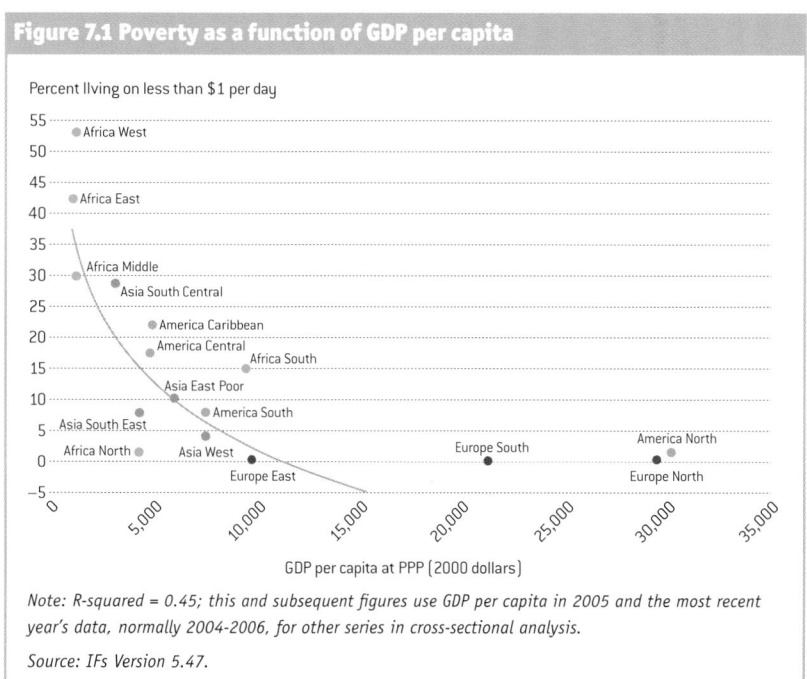

Figure 7.1 Poverty as a function of GDP per capita

Percent living on less than $1 per day

Note: R-squared = 0.45; this and subsequent figures use GDP per capita in 2005 and the most recent year's data, normally 2004-2006, for other series in cross-sectional analysis.

Source: IFs Version 5.47.

assume that the poorest countries can attain the same levels of performance on many key lever variables, such as governance quality, as can rich countries. Economic development level often poses significant resource and capability constraints on what is likely or probable—even on what is possible.

For instance, in Figure 7.1 a steeply downward sloping relationship relates GDP per capita and poverty rates, with extreme poverty largely disappearing by $10,000 per capita. The composition of countries within regions confuses this somewhat because the Baltic republics introduce some poverty into northern Europe, as Mexico does with North America; our statistical analysis, in contrast to our displays, is always at the country level. Yet it is striking that Southern Africa has a considerably higher poverty rate than Northern Africa, even at a higher level of GDP per capita. That suggests a structural problem, namely distribution.

The unfolding analysis in this chapter will, of course, focus on structural patterns of variables offering potential policy leverage. When regions (and later countries) appear to underperform relative to their peers at comparable economic levels, for instance with respect to educational spending or economic freedom, that will suggest at least the possibility that interventions on that dimension may be possible and productive. The extent of deviation from typical patterns will suggest also the rough magnitude of feasible change.

Primarily Domestic Drivers and Levers

Most domestic leverage potentially enhances economic growth, which in the long run has the greatest impact on poverty. This section will, however, look first at leverage with respect to population size. It then turns to economic growth, initially focusing on the traditional drivers of labor force and capital stock and then shifting attention to the critical drivers of productivity growth. Attention directly to distribution will close the domestic analysis.

Fertility

With respect to population size, the key drivers are fertility rate and life expectancy, and to a lesser degree migration. Most leverage with respect to fertility operates through improvements in human capital, and the discussion of economic growth will return to that. Here the primary focus is on fertility rate.

Figure 7.2 shows the contemporary relationship between GDP per capita and fertility across world regions. Although many country-level exceptions persist, note that all but four regions have already reduced total fertility rates (TFR) to 3.5 or below. The exceptions are Middle (or Central) Africa, Western Africa, Eastern Africa, and the poorer countries of Oceania. The base case of IFs forecasts that fertility rates above replacement levels may still characterize these regions by midcentury, respectively about 3.6, 3.2, 2.8, and 2.2. In contrast, all other developing regions reach replacement fertility by 2050.

It is, of course, no accident that the three regions with the highest fertility also have the lowest GDP per capita. Yet in the IFs base case, the three African regions reach GDP per capita levels between $2,300 and $5,000 by 2050, putting them at the approximate level of Southeast Asia today, a region that has already approached replacement fertility. Achievement of fertility rates near replacement thus appears a realistic goal for these African regions. The intervention structured for IFs posits the reduction of TFR in Eastern Africa, Western Africa, and poorer Oceania by 33 percent relative to the base case, phased in over thirty years,

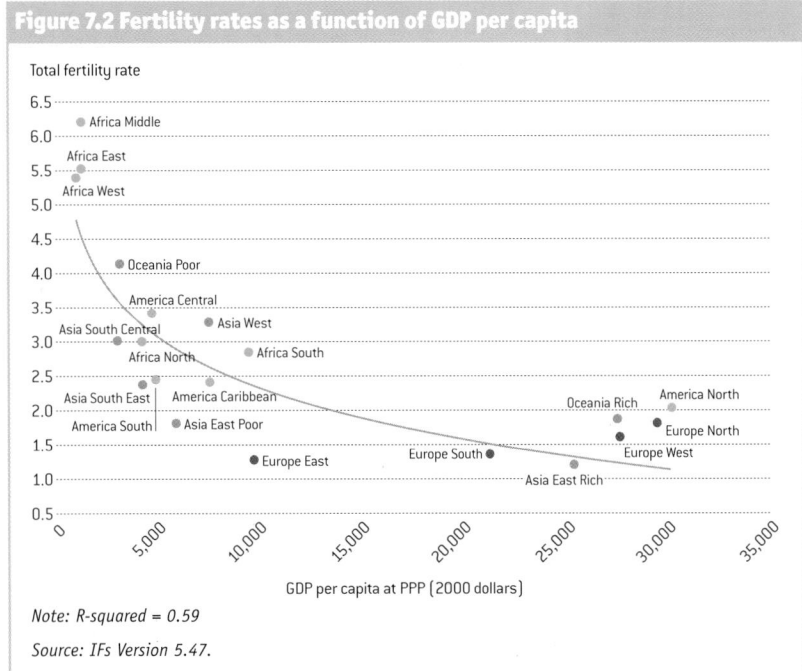

Figure 7.2 Fertility rates as a function of GDP per capita

Total fertility rate

Note: R-squared = 0.59

Source: IFs Version 5.47.

and a reduction in Middle Africa by 45 percent, phased in over forty-five years. Thus fertility for each of those regions is brought to replacement levels by 2050.[4] It would be possible to posit accelerated TFR reduction in a number of other regions shown in Figure 7.2, but because their rates are already fairly low and dropping, the impact on population growth relative to patterns of the base case would not be terribly great.

Does the leverage exist to make such a demographic intervention realistic? Past experience has definitely shown that active family planning programs or population policies, especially in association with activities to support maternal and child health and women's status more generally, can influence fertility independently of GDP per capita and historical cultural patterns, the two variables sometimes argued to determine fertility. Figure 7.3 indicates how strong such effects can be. It shows cross-sectional relationships between GDP per capita at PPP and total fertility rates in 1960, 1980, and 2005. There has been a sharp downward shift in those functions, especially after 1980. At all levels of GDP per capita, women in countries around the world are, on average, having about two fewer children across their lifetimes than they did in 1960. That is, not only income changes fertility—many other policies and practices offer leverage.

Labor and capital

With regard to economic growth, almost all contemporary models of it (IFs included) build on three immediate drivers: supplies of labor, levels of production capital, and multifactor productivity. The next subsection will return to the multiple factors that drive productivity.

Looking first at the labor force, there are multiple paths to increasing its size within the population. A number of the paths involve putting the unemployed and underemployed to work. Such efforts are essential for poverty reduction. In the long run, however, the size of the economically active population determines labor force size. In more developed countries, increasing retirement age has become or is becoming an important issue, but that is not such a significant issue in developing countries, where the greater issue is often female participation.

Female participation rates present a point of potentially substantial leverage for

many countries and regions (see Figure 7.4 for subregional detail). In Organization for Economic Cooperation and Development (OECD) countries, the female share of the official labor force (not counting unpaid domestic or farm labor) is nearly 43 percent. Surprisingly, for developing countries as a whole it is nearly 40 percent, and in China it is 45 percent.

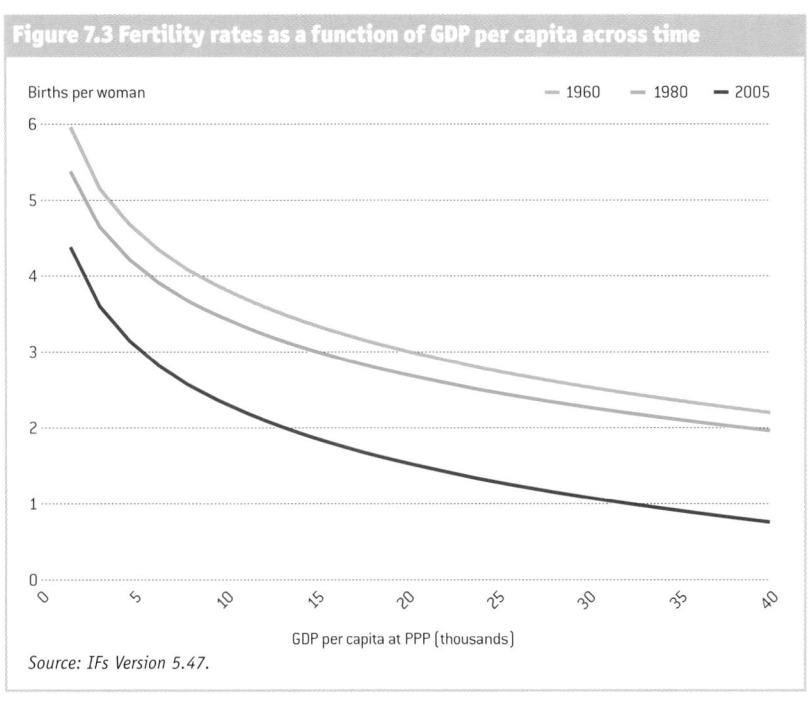

Figure 7.3 Fertility rates as a function of GDP per capita across time

Births per woman

— 1960 — 1980 — 2005

Source: IFs Version 5.47.

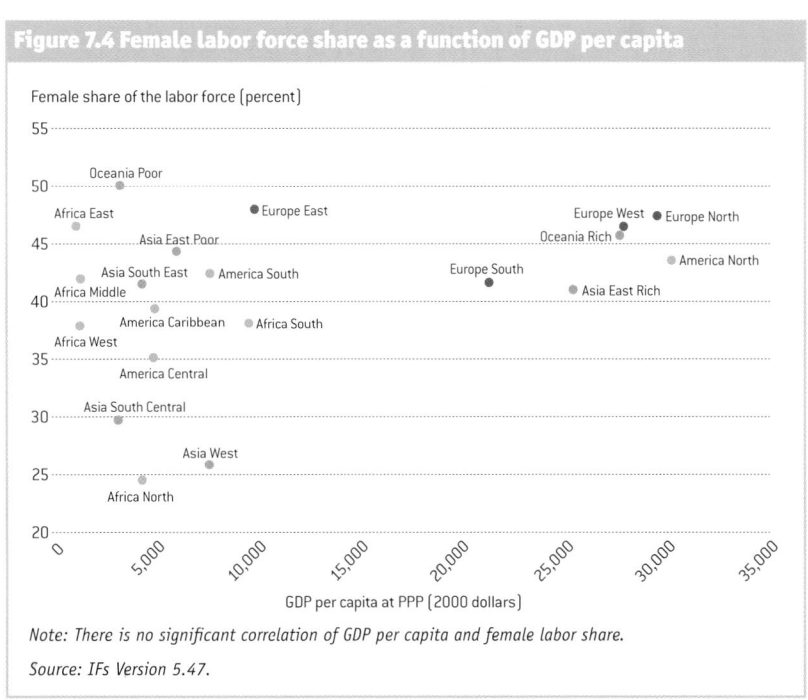

Figure 7.4 Female labor force share as a function of GDP per capita

Female share of the labor force (percent)

Note: There is no significant correlation of GDP per capita and female labor share.

Source: IFs Version 5.47.

But for India and the rest of South Asia, the female share of the labor force is only 33–34 percent, for Latin America and the Caribbean it is 36 percent, and for the Middle East and North Africa, it is very near 30 percent. Although statistics show it at 42 percent for sub-Saharan Africa as a whole (a total labor female share nearly as high as that for OECD countries), there appears to be considerable headroom for increase in female participation in official labor across much of the developing world.

From Figure 7.4, it is clear that the regions where increased female participation might be particularly significant are Northern Africa, Western Asia (the Middle East), South-Central Asia, and Central America, with less leverage in Western Africa, Southern Africa, and the Caribbean countries. In some of those regions the female labor shares have been rising. For instance, in Central America they have risen from about 19 percent in the early 1960s to over 35 percent.

The base case of IFs already builds in such increases, even in Northern Africa and Western Asia, where historical patterns have been quite flat and where the *Arab Human Development Report 2002* called for drawing on the half of populations now substantially excluded from the economy and many aspects of broader society. Thus the intervention structured for analysis on this lever is very modest, increasing female participation in the formal labor force by only an additional 2–5 percent over fifty years, relative to the ongoing increases in the base case for the four lagging regions.

A central emphasis of development analysts over many, many years has been on increasing savings and investment rates. The reality now, however, is that the non-OECD countries invest a higher percentage of their GDPs than do OECD countries. China's exceptionally high rates stand out (see Asia–East Poor in Figure 7.5). Even India and South-Central Asia more generally, however, have investment rates that match or exceed those of most developed countries.

Nonetheless, investment rates in sub-Saharan Africa lag in absolute terms, and those in South Asia could almost certainly rise somewhat above current rates, which are very modest by standards of the Asian tigers and China.[5] The intervention lever doubled savings and investment rates in Eastern Africa, Oceania Poor, and Central America over twenty-five years relative to the base case. The reason for the slow phase-in of the intervention, in addition to the fact that such changes are generally very slow in coming about, is that rapidly increasing rates of savings in poor countries will, of course, reduce consumption, at least in the interim, and therefore actually increase rather than decrease consumption-based poverty rates. The intervention increased savings/investment rates for Southern Africa and for the Caribbean by 50 percent over twenty-five years (raising, for example, a rate of 18 percent to 27 percent). It increased rates for South Central Asia, South America, Western Asia, Eastern Europe, Northern Africa, Middle Africa, and Western Africa by 30 percent.

One significant problem with any direct intervention on behalf of higher savings and investment rates is that the actual policy levers are not at all clear. Raising savings and investment is not like increasing educational spending. In fact, doing so may require improved governance, enhanced human capital, and much else.

Driving productivity: Human capital

Figure 3.6 elaborated the key multifactor productivity term, initially by dividing its drivers into six types of capital: human capital, social capita, institutional capital (governance),

Figure 7.5 Savings as portion of GDP as a function of GDP per capita

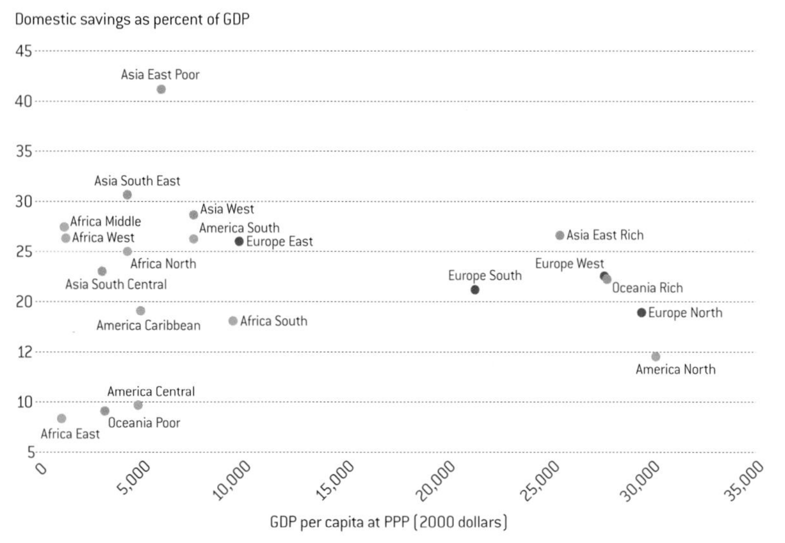

Domestic savings as percent of GDP

Note: R-squared (country-based, unweighted) = 0.23

Source: IFs Version 5.47.

infrastructure capital, natural capital, and what might be called the stock of knowledge, or knowledge capital. They, in turn, have drivers and levers that influence them. To explore the details of potential leverage, we start with human capital, specifically education and health, and move progressively through other forces that drive multifactor productivity.

The lever manipulated in IFs with respect to education is government spending on education and health (see Appendix 5 to this volume for more information on all the levers explored herein). Figures 7.6 and 7.7 show the rates of public spending on education and health as portions of GDP by global region. Like most figures in this analysis, they draw upon data from the World Bank's World Development Indicators.

Weighted by economic size, the governments of the world spend about 4.3 percent of economic product on education, a rate that has been fairly stable since the mid-1990s and was higher in earlier years. In comparison, they spend about 6 percent of economic product on health, up from about 5 percent in the early 1990s. (Both can be compared with about 2.4 percent on military spending, down very considerably since the end of the Cold War.) The developing regions of the world that fall considerably below average educational spending rates are Western Africa, Middle Africa, and the poorer countries of East Asia.[6] Because of the dominance of China in the latter grouping and the common perception that Chinese investment in human capital is high, that may be surprising. But, in fact, China has set a relatively near-term goal of spending 4 percent of GDP on education, up from only about 2 percent for most of the 1990s and through 2004.[7]

For the intervention, a multiplier ramped up spending increases on education to bring those regions below 4 percent of GDP up to about that level. Specifically, for Western Africa, Middle Africa, and Asia–East Poor, the increases were 80 percent of their base, phased in over fifteen years. The reasoning behind the phase-in of the intervention is that it is difficult or impossible, both in terms of the supply of funds and in terms of plans for school expansion or improvement, to introduce major increases immediately. For Southeast Asia and Central America, the increase was 35 percent over fifteen years. For the regions of South-Central Asia, Eastern Africa, Northern Africa, Eastern Europe, and South America,

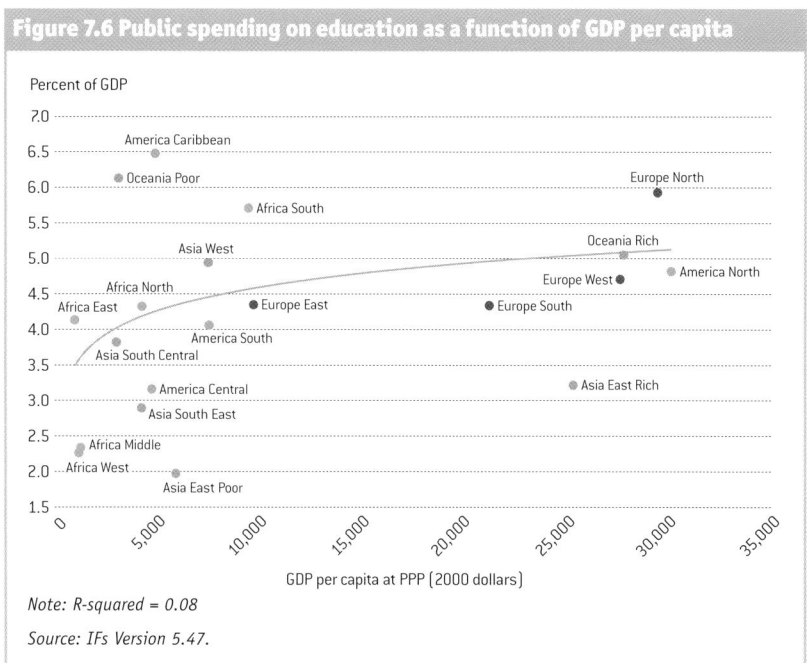

Figure 7.6 Public spending on education as a function of GDP per capita

Percent of GDP

Note: R-squared = 0.08

Source: IFs Version 5.47.

increases of 20 percent were phased in over ten years. The logic behind intervening also in this second set of countries is that, even though they are close to the global average, additional spending may be beneficial.

Higher levels of education are often goals in and of themselves, as in the MDGs. And education has a wide range of potential benefits beyond enhancing economic productivity, including impacts on fertility and socialization. Yet major debates rage in the development literature around the degree to which higher education spending can achieve development goals such as increased economic productivity and poverty reduction. Among others, William Easterly (2001) concluded that the supply-side push for education has not been effective, at least in the absence of other types of developmental activities focused heavily on encouraging and supporting entrepreneurial activities that put education to work. Another supply-versus-demand debate focuses within education itself over whether providing educational opportunity really works in comparison to demand-side emphases such as providing assistance to families who send their children to school. This study cannot fully address the debates that surround all the interventions explored here.[8] In brief, the IFs model does include a positive relationship between the educational level of the working-age population and economic growth (via productivity; see Hughes 2005a), based on empirical studies such as Robert J. Barro (1999b), Barro and Xavier Sala-i-Martin (1999), Barry Bosworth and Susan M. Collins (2003), Emanuele Baldacci et al. (2004), and Derek Chen and Carl Dahlman (2004).

The implementation of higher spending on education within IFs has trade-offs, because spending on education competes with spending for other purposes such as health and the military. In addition, because of the cohort structure of those being educated and the population more generally, the payoff of education, in terms of larger portions of the population with more years of education, requires considerable time to manifest itself (spending is a flow, but human capital is a slowly accumulating stock).

Figure 7.7 portrays a relationship between the rates of spending on health and GDP per capita that is quite different from the one underlying spending on education. Specifically, there is a clear upward-sloping relationship between economic development level and health spending around which the regions of this analysis cluster relatively closely. South-Central Asia and Southeast Asia are below the line of that relationship, as are Western and Middle Africa, while Central America, the Caribbean, and Eastern Europe are above it. On the basis

of the clear upward slope of the relationship, it is reasonable to argue that health is so fundamentally important that countries simply spend what they can, consistent with overall philosophies of the roles that government should have in social spending (the Asian societies actually spend proportionately less than the African ones). Spending levels do not appear to reflect differential burdens of disease faced by the societies (e.g., the tropical disease burden of African countries).

Whatever the explanation for positioning of regions on Figure 7.7, the basis for differentiating interventions by region is not as obvious as for education. Instead of targeting specific values by region, the intervention ramped up a 20 percent increase in health spending relative to the base case for all developing countries over a ten-year period. With respect to the magnitude of the intervention, non-OECD countries spend about 3 percent of their GDP on health. On top of natural increases tied to higher GDP per capita, the intervention raises that portion to more than 4 percent by midcentury, still quite a bit below that of OECD countries. The implementation within IFs again sets up trade-offs and some time lags (for instance, in affecting life expectancy levels). Not surprisingly, significant debates characterize the development literature around the developmental benefits of health spending, just as they surround investment in education.

Driving productivity: Social capital and governance

Moving from human capital to social capital and governance, there are multiple elements of the way in which societies are organized and governments function that fall generally under those rubrics. Deep cultural patterns, such as levels of social trust, define social capital. The focus here, however, is heavily on (1) governance, both the quality of it (effectiveness and level of corruption) and (2) freedom or openness, political and economic.

The World Bank's project on governance has usefully distinguished among three aspects: (1) the process by which governments are selected, monitored, and replaced; (2) the capacity of the government to effectively formulate and implement sound policies; and (3) the respect of citizens and the state for the institutions that govern economic and social

Figure 7.7 Public health spending as a function of GDP per capita

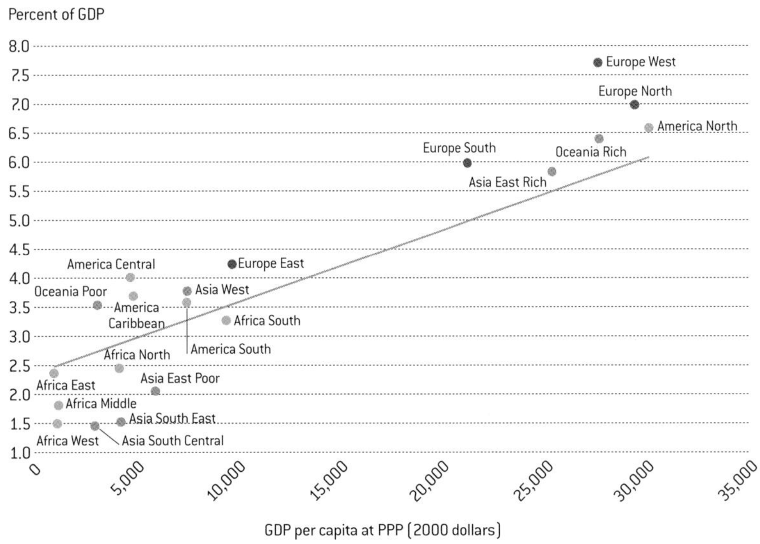

Percent of GDP

Note: R-squared = 0.41

Source: IFs Version 5.47.

interactions among them (Kaufmann, Kraay, and Mastruzzi 2003: 2; see also Kaufmann, Kraay, and Zoido-Lobatón 1999).

Interestingly, and rather disappointingly for most democrats, the empirical literature has found that it is only the second and third of these three dimensions that appear to have a significant impact on productivity, not the first (Hughes 2005a).

This analysis explores three elements related to governance. First, and directly related to the second dimension of the Bank's categorization, is governance effectiveness. On the World Bank's five-point scale, OECD countries are about 1.2, and non-OECD countries are about –0.3 (see Figure 7.8). A 20 percent, or about 0.5-point shift, was introduced for developing countries (as defined by the World Bank).[9]

Second, and related to the "sound policies" of the Bank's second dimension, analysts widely believe economic freedom (Gwartney, Lawson, and Holcombe 1999; Gwartney et al. 2007) affects economic performance. On a ten-point scale, OECD countries now average about 7.6, and non-OECD countries average about 6.3. Both sets have been quite stable since 2000 but over a longer period have moved toward greater economic freedom (see Figure 7.9). The intervention accelerates the upward shift in the non-OECD world by 20 percent (about 1.2 points) over ten years.

Third, and directly relevant to the World Bank's third dimension of governance, studies have found government corruption to be significantly related to economic performance. Both the World Bank's scale and Transparency International's (TI's) corruption perception index measure its level.[10] On the TI measure, the OECD countries average about 6.6 (higher values indicate better transparency), and the non-OECD countries average about 3.0. There thus appears to be even more "headroom" on reducing corruption than on other governance measures. The intervention introduced is a 30 percent improvement on base case values, but over twenty years instead of ten.

Figure 7.10 focuses on corruption only for the developing regions. It is obvious that Middle Africa and Eastern Europe are the farthest below the upward-sloping pattern created by the regions shown. The intervention for the former was an improvement of 40 percent; for the latter it was 60 percent.

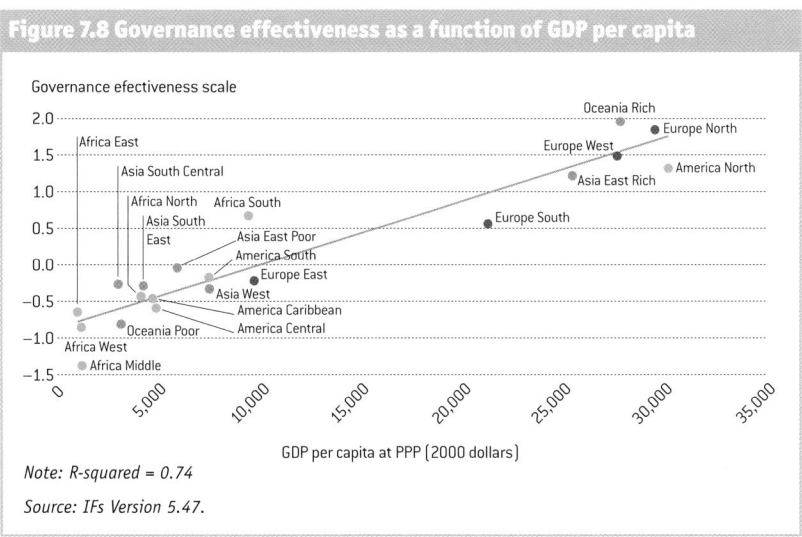

Figure 7.8 Governance effectiveness as a function of GDP per capita

Note: R-squared = 0.74

Source: IFs Version 5.47.

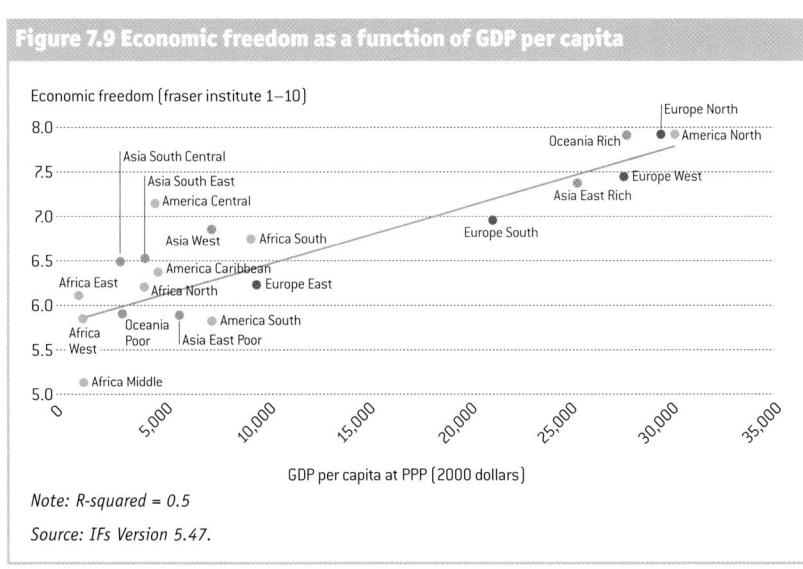

Figure 7.9 Economic freedom as a function of GDP per capita

Note: R-squared = 0.5

Source: IFs Version 5.47.

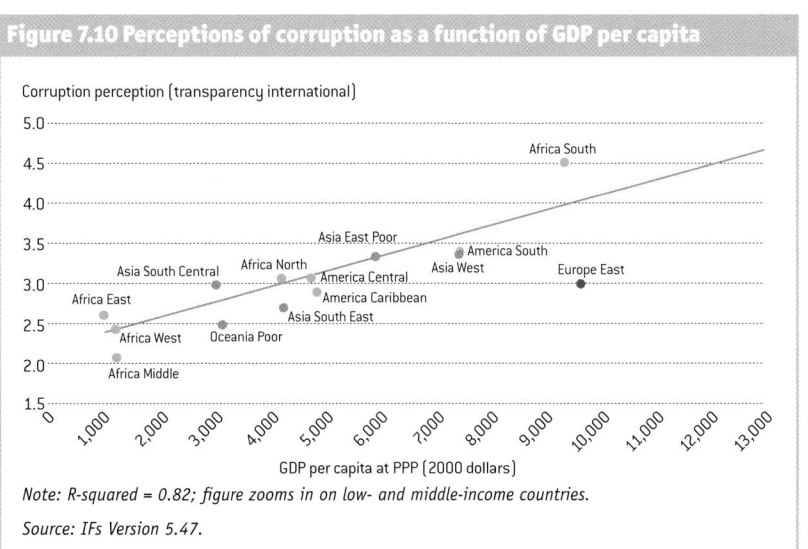

Figure 7.10 Perceptions of corruption as a function of GDP per capita

Note: R-squared = 0.82; figure zooms in on low- and middle-income countries.

Source: IFs Version 5.47.

The analysis could have tapped many other measures of governance and the broader concept of social capital. For instance, Hernando de Soto (2000) and others have pointed to the definition and protection of property rights as especially important. And we must raise one important caveat with respect to the interventions around governance as now implemented in International Futures—there is no cost associated with them. That may not be dramatically unrealistic, because many of the interventions "simply" require turnover in government and perhaps some domestic and outside pressure. But the path to achieving improved governance and the costs of following that path are unclear. Unfortunately, the extensive calls in academic and policy literature for improvement of governance inadequately identify the still deeper levers that will accomplish it.[11]

Driving productivity: Infrastructure capital
Developing countries often have substantially underdeveloped infrastructures of many kinds, a weakness especially associated with poverty in rural areas and remote regions. IFs includes representations of infrastructure for roads (not for other transportation infrastructure, so roads must be a proxy), electricity, telecommunications, and modern computing (including networking).

The level of infrastructure development in OECD countries is generally vastly superior to that in non-OECD countries. Because infrastructure consists of so many different elements, however, it is not easy to assess the differences. The World Economic Forum (WEF) used surveys to build a seven-point scale of perceived infrastructure quality (Figure 7.11). As with so many other measures of development, there is a close relationship between it and GDP per capita, upward-sloping and generally linear.[12] The regions at the bottom of the tail (Eastern, Western, and especially Middle Africa) have the most obvious infrastructure deficiencies. So, too, does Southern Europe, although given that survey respondents ranked its infrastructure well below that of Southern Africa, they may have applied somewhat different expectations, a danger of perception-based measures.

The intervention involved improving the infrastructure of non-OECD countries generally by a factor of 1.2 (20 percent), with that in Middle Africa targeted for an 80 percent improvement. Developing infrastructure takes time, so the increase relative to the base would be phased in over thirty years. One significant analysis risk of this particular intervention is that, as with governance, the model does not yet represent any cost of the improved infrastructure; there will eventually be a flow of government and/or private funding that, like expenditures on health and education, will restrict spending elsewhere. Thus the net benefits are almost certainly exaggerated in this analysis, unless substantial outside resources are available.

Driving productivity: Natural capital
It is possible to define a natural capital category in addition to human and social capital. That category can include the stock of biological and physical resources available to the society, such as forests, fossil water (from slowly or nonrecharging aquifers), and fossil fuels. Many analysts frame any discussion of natural capital in terms of the economy's draw upon environmental services (Banzhaf and Smith 2002; Millennium Ecosystem Assessment 2005). Others have sought to define a "real" or "green" GDP that excludes the drawing down of stocks of natural capital such as that implicit in deforestation's contribution to GDP.

The IFs model does not represent environmental services or green GDP. Nonetheless, one of the

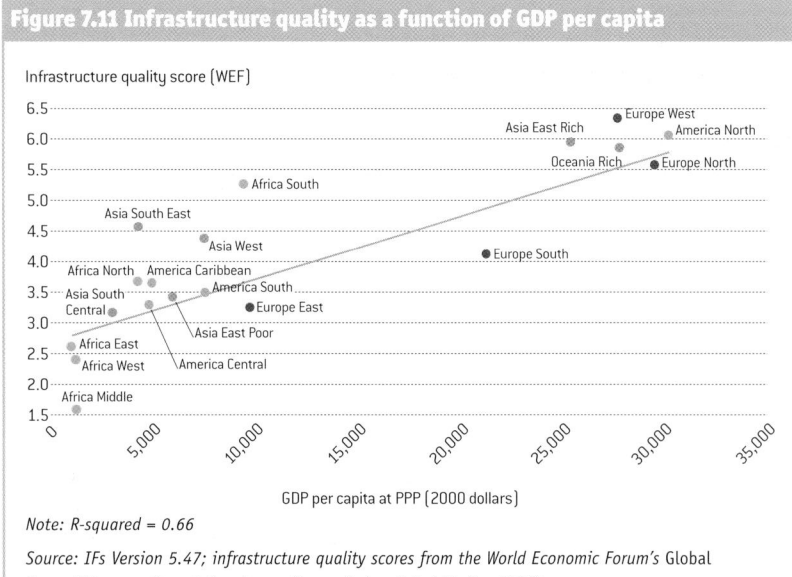

Figure 7.11 Infrastructure quality as a function of GDP per capita

Infrastructure quality score (WEF)

GDP per capita at PPP (2000 dollars)

Note: R-squared = 0.66

Source: IFs Version 5.47; infrastructure quality scores from the World Economic Forum's Global Competitiveness Report (see Lopez-Claros, Porter, Sala-i-Martin, 2006).

most significant inputs to the economy from natural capital is energy. And when supplies are restricted and prices rise, as in the 1970s and in 2006–2008, the economy can suffer considerably. In part, higher energy prices make inefficient a portion of the productive capital of the economy and can lead to its removal from production. IFs includes a rough calculation of such an effect so that an intervention affecting energy price does affect productivity. In addition, of course, higher prices set in motion financial transfers domestically and internationally.

To explore the relationship between energy and poverty, this study considered the implications should non-OECD countries substantially accelerate the pace of development of renewable energy. Since the contribution of renewables is so low in the base case, the intervention steadily increased the production of them relative to the base case, rising to a 50 percent increase in 2050. The intervention helps protect non-OECD countries from the energy price increases of the base case as global fossil fuel supplies are run down (global peak oil is reached and passed by midcentury); it has the additional benefit of improving trade and current account balances.

Driving productivity: Knowledge

Moving from natural capital to knowledge stock, expenditures on R&D by non-OECD countries are important to both knowledge creation and acceleration of its diffusion from high-income countries. Whereas R&D spending as a portion of GDP is in the 2.5 percent range for OECD countries, it is closer to 1.0 percent for non-OECD countries (see Figure 7.12). The intervention assumed a 20 percent increase on that base for non-OECD countries, phased in over twenty years. Educating the skilled personnel and creating the facilities needed are slow processes.[13]

Openness to trade (and financial flows) is another important mechanism for knowledge diffusion. Protectionist measures can harm developing countries by slowing the flow of new technology. The next subsection will explore global cooperation on opening markets, including actions by developed countries, but unilateral trade openness (thus making it primarily a domestic action) can reduce the costs of imports and the technology that selected imports carry.

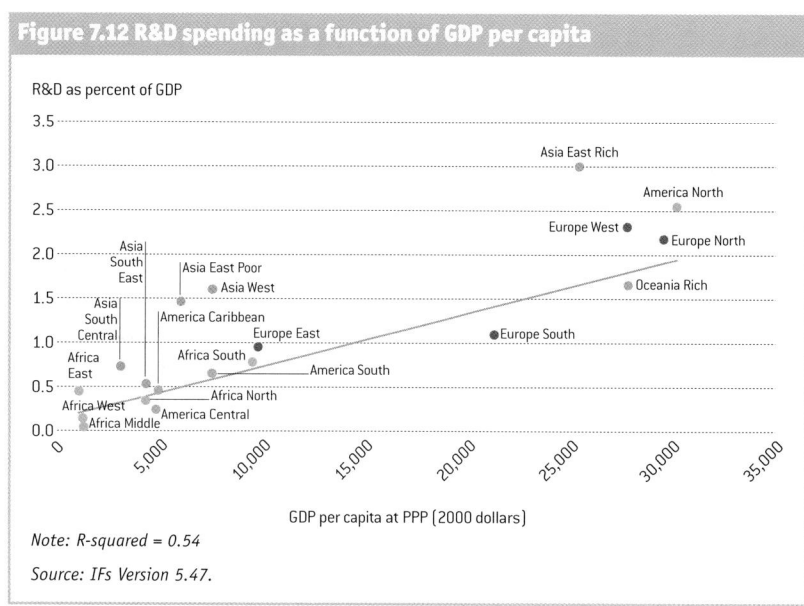

Figure 7.12 R&D spending as a function of GDP per capita

Note: R-squared = 0.54

Source: IFs Version 5.47.

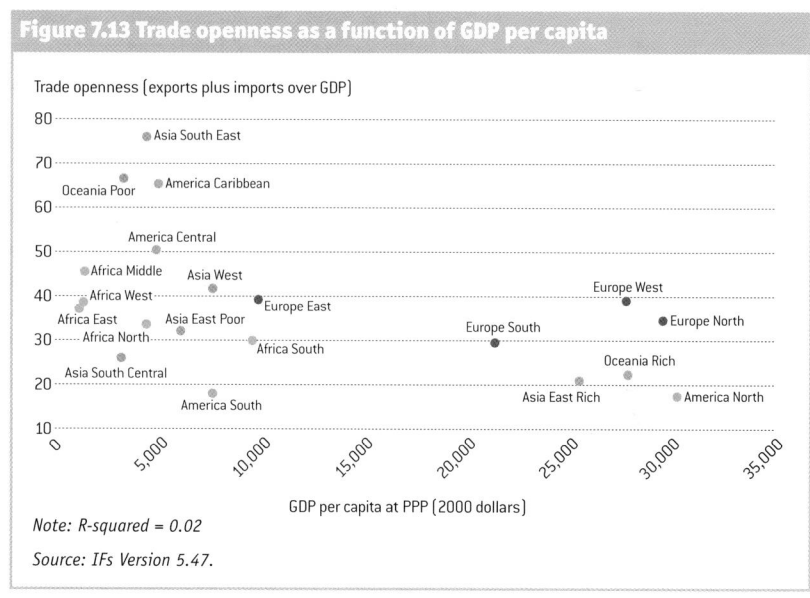

Figure 7.13 Trade openness as a function of GDP per capita

Note: R-squared = 0.02

Source: IFs Version 5.47.

Figure 7.13 shows a standard measure of trade openness: exports plus imports as a share of GDP. By that measure, low- and middle-income regions are, on average, as open as high-income countries.[14] Many are, of course, relatively small countries that depend on the outside world for a wide range of goods as well as for markets. A better but not easily available measure would be the extent of market protection. South-Central Asia, and especially South America, are not only relatively less open than other developing countries but, on the whole, relatively more protectionist. The intervention with respect to trade openness thus focused on those two regions and reduced the effective price of external goods and services in their markets by 20 percent over twenty years.

Domestic transfers

Domestic interventions discussed to this point have focused on increasing growth, implicitly assuming that income distribution, if not fundamentally unaffected, would at least not deteriorate enough to associate growth in the economy with an increase in poverty. Figure 7.14 shows, however, how dramatically income distributions vary across the developing regions; it is important to consider the prospects for improvements that would reduce poverty levels.

There are options for directly supporting the incomes of the poor. A very considerable literature discusses enhancing social protection and the social safety net for those who need it most in poor countries.[16] The consensus is that it is strongly desirable to adopt mechanisms that reinforce participation in the workforce (such as payment for labor on infrastructure development projects) or that directly target the health, education, and nutrition of the poor (such as food payments for the families of children attending school). Targeted conditional transfer (TCT) programs such as Progressa in Mexico, Bolsa Escola in urban Brazil, and PETI in rural Brazil have generally been quite effective (Sedlacek, Ilahi, and Gustafsson-Wright 2000).

The model distinguishes skilled and unskilled households, and the latter generally have lower incomes.[16] Thus transfers across those groups bring the Gini coefficient down. Because of the social accounting matrix (SAM) in IFs, the increase in transfers to the unskilled affects not just household accounts but also government accounts. For instance, the secondary impacts include reduced transfers to skilled households; decreased spending on items such as pensions, education, health care, or the military; and increased government spending overall with related higher taxes and impacts in other ways on firms and households. In short, the transfers are far from a free lunch, and growth-reducing effects via other paths in the model could partially or totally offset the direct benefits of them.

The intervention assumes away all the complications of actually setting up such transfers and simply increases the domestic transfers to unskilled households relative to the base case over twenty years. It doubles domestic transfers for seven clusters of countries where substantial improvements in distribution appear possible in Figure 7.14: Southern Africa, South America, Central America, the Caribbean, Middle Africa, Oceania Poor, and Asia–East Poor. For Western Africa, Eastern Africa, and Western Asia, it increases transfers by 50 percent.

Primarily International Drivers and Levers

Turning to primarily international deep drivers, most involve transfers across sets of agents. As Chapter 4 discussed, IFs with Pardee represents such transfers, domestic and international, in a social accounting matrix structure that links governments, households, and firms in a variety of financial interactions.

A survey

Figure 7.15 sketches many potential monetary flows between and within external and domestic environments. It is important to note that the flows are not just economy-to-economy linkages in the aggregate, or even government-to-government, but rather involve a broader range of agent classes of the kind that SAMs represent. For instance, the flows include the increasingly important remittances by workers to families and friends who most often reside in poorer countries and also the very important

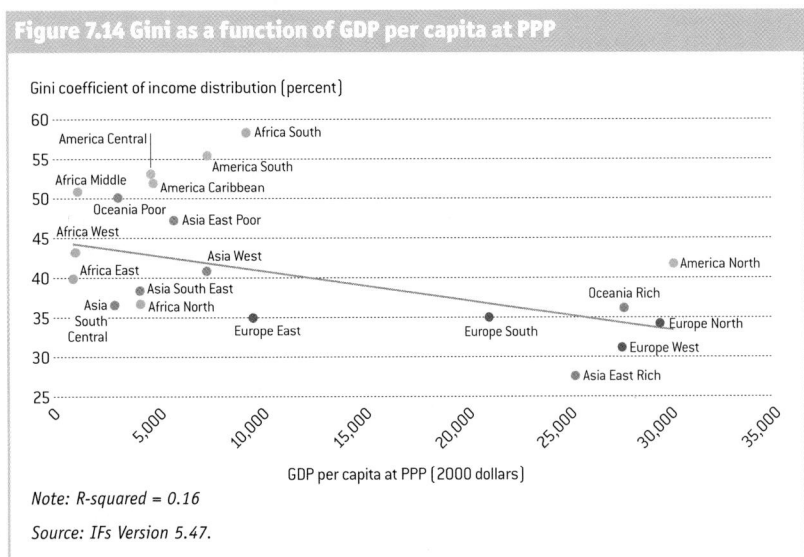

Figure 7.14 Gini as a function of GDP per capita at PPP

Gini coefficient of income distribution (percent)

Note: R-squared = 0.16

Source: IFs Version 5.47.

Figure 7.15 A schematic of key international transfers

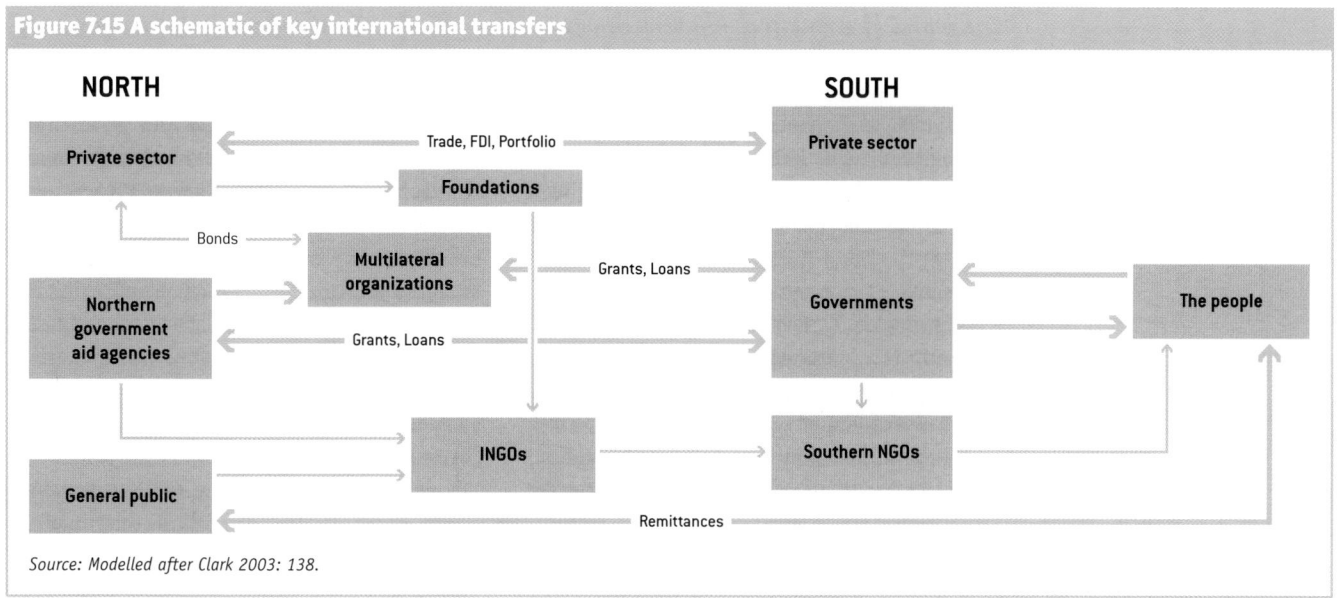

Source: Modelled after Clark 2003: 138.

foreign direct investment (FDI) and portfolio flows that occur among firms and households in more and less developed countries. Some international flows are overwhelmingly in one direction, but a large number of flows, such as bond purchases and FDI, accumulate over time and set up two-way flows or reversals of patterns over time. IFs represents and allows analysis of most of the larger flows in the diagram, those represented by bold lines.

Table 7.1 provides an approximate idea of the annual magnitude of some of the international flows during the early years of the twenty-first century. It identifies trade, foreign direct investment, worker remittances, portfolio investment, and foreign aid as giving rise to the greatest financial flows, roughly in that order, and therefore being especially important levers to explore.

Table 7.1 Rough magnitude of annual international transfers

Source/type	To all World Bank developing countries	Of which to sub-Saharan Africa	Nonfinancial issues/impact
Export receipts, total	$3,400 billion	$190 billion	Facilitates imports
Export receipts, agricultural	$180 billion	$8 billion	Poorest often earn
Net foreign direct investment	$200 billion ($285 billion in and $85 billion out; highly variable)	$8 billion ($10 billion in and $2 billion out; highly variable)	Carries technology
Worker remittances	$190 billion	$7 billion	Often to the poorest, but perhaps not in Africa
Net portfolio investment	$65 billion (highly variable)	$7 billion (highly variable)	Hot money; market and financial discipline, but also disruption
Bilateral aid	$57 billion (of which 55% is grants)	$20 billion (of which 80% is grants)	Often targeted, conditional
World Bank (IBRD and IDA)	Near balance in and out	Near balance in and out	Development consulting and direction
IMF	Near balance in and out	Near balance in and out	Technical assistance, conditionality
Context			
GDP	$8,200 billion	$420 billion	
Foreign debt	$2,700 billion	$215 billion	
Government spending	$1,700 billion	$120 billion	
Population	5,400 million	740 million	

Source: IFs Version 5.47 Database.

Trade and foreign direct investment

Trade interventions on behalf of poverty reduction can take two quite different forms. The first involves a multilateral movement toward trade openness (see again Figure 7.13) of the kind associated with past rounds of global trade negotiations and the proposals of the Doha round of the World Trade Organization.[17] In IFs freer trade is simulated across all sectors of the economy, reducing the effective prices of goods and services in trade without differentiating between the overt protectionism of duties and the more complicated manifestations of subsides and nontariff barriers to trade (Ferrantino 2006). For the purposes of this analysis, the effective prices were reduced by 20 percent over twenty years. The direct impact of that intervention on trade levels is substantial—by midcentury, global trade as a portion of GDP rises about 7 percent relative to the base case. The forward linkage of that higher trade to economic performance is largely via its impact on productivity.

The second type of trade intervention is export promotion, a pattern that has been very effective in a number of the rapidly growing Asian economies. Because export promotion has already been significant in much of East Asia, the intervention explored here focused on sub-Saharan Africa and South-Central Asia (including India). By midcentury, exports of the two regions rose by 25–30 percent relative to the base case.[18]

Foreign direct investment has fundamentally different characteristics than trade. A key difference is that it creates stocks that set up reverse flows of profits. Figure 7.16 shows those stocks as a portion of GDP. Some of the poorest regions of the world, including Middle Africa, have been substantial net recipients of such investment and therefore have large stocks, primarily in industries focused on extraction of raw materials. The fact that FDI comes in many different flavors with very different patterns of spillover to other economic sectors makes it difficult to evaluate the potential costs and benefits of increased flows. Moreover, FDI has a complicated relationship with local investment, sometimes supplementing it and sometimes replacing it (Moran, Graham, and Blomström 2005), as well as with the quality and transparency of local governance.

The intervention explored in this analysis is a doubling of FDI inflows to all non-OECD countries except China, to which base flows are already extremely high, and Middle Africa, for which base stock levels in extractive industries are already very high. The doubling is relative to the base case and is phased in over thirty years. The growth rate of total global FDI was increased over thirty years by 30 percent so as to prevent the intervention from simply diverting investment flows from among developed countries, where most global flows occur.

Although currently quite a bit smaller overall than FDI, portfolio investment to the emerging equity markets of developing countries has grown quickly in the last two decades. This path provides considerably "hotter" money, and the ease of reverse flows contributes to financial crises (Bouchet, Clark, and Groslambert 2003). Nonetheless, the prospects for further increases with development are strong, and the base case builds on them. The intervention doubles the net inflows relative to the base case for all non-OECD countries and increases the total volume of global flows by 30 percent so as to limit diversion effects. The real impact of portfolio investment will, however, be different from that of FDI and probably less beneficial. It tends not to carry as much incremental investment with it and also does not carry technology. In IFs it affects only current and capital accounts.

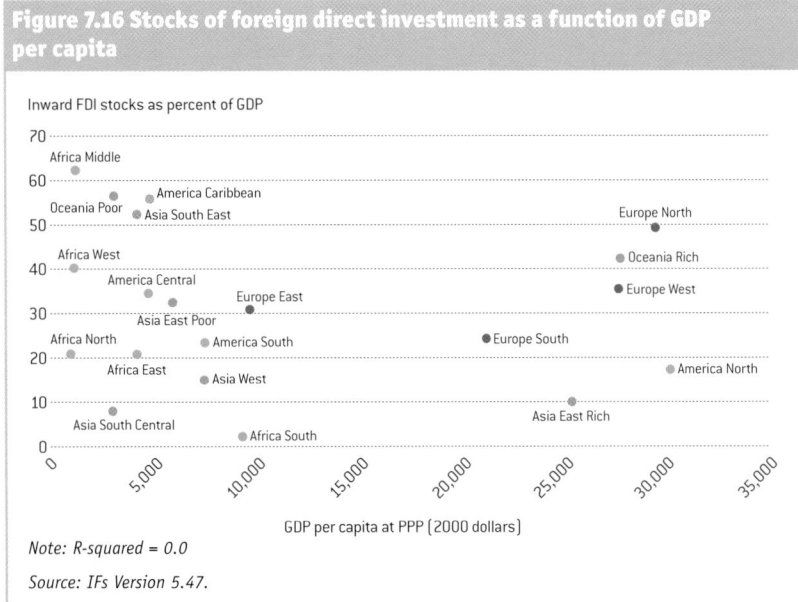

Figure 7.16 Stocks of foreign direct investment as a function of GDP per capita

Inward FDI stocks as percent of GDP

Note: R-squared = 0.0

Source: IFs Version 5.47.

Patterns of Potential Human Progress Volume 1: **Reducing Global Poverty**

Worker remittances

Worker remittances have increased dramatically in recent years and now rival FDI as a source of annual inflows.[19] They have come to be an especially importance source of development funds for several reasons. First, many remittances flow directly to the poorest families in recipient countries (although in some of the world's poorest countries, like those in Africa, it is the somewhat more well-to-do who emigrate and send back funds). Second, unlike the loan portion of foreign aid and unlike FDI, there are no future reverse flows tied to the remittances. Figure 7.17 shows the level of net worker remittance receipts as a portion of GDP. The Caribbean countries and Central America now obtain the most benefit, with Northern Africa in a fairly distant third place.

Remittances are tied heavily to levels and patterns of immigration. The intervention in this analysis increases global immigration by 50 percent over twenty years relative to the base case, which automatically increases remittances by similar proportions. Given the high number of immigrants already in many countries and some backlash against them, the increase might be unreasonably great. At the same time, however, aging populations in developing countries and fertility rates below replacement levels are creating offsetting pressures for such increases.

Foreign aid

Over most of the postcolonial period, a great hope of many proponents for accelerating development and poverty reduction has been foreign aid. At one point advocates called for rich countries to raise their aid as a portion of GDP to 1 percent. In recent decades the target of 0.7 percent has been repeatedly urged, and the inclusion of a Global Compact as part of the MDGs revitalized that call—see Figure 7.18 for the actual rate of donation as a portion of gross national income (GNI), by donor country. Because, however, of the very low rates of giving by the two largest global donor economies, United States and Japan, and because many other large developed countries like Germany are also significantly below that target, the OECD countries as a whole give something closer to 0.25 percent of GDP as aid.

The intervention investigated in this study is a more modest but still challenging rise

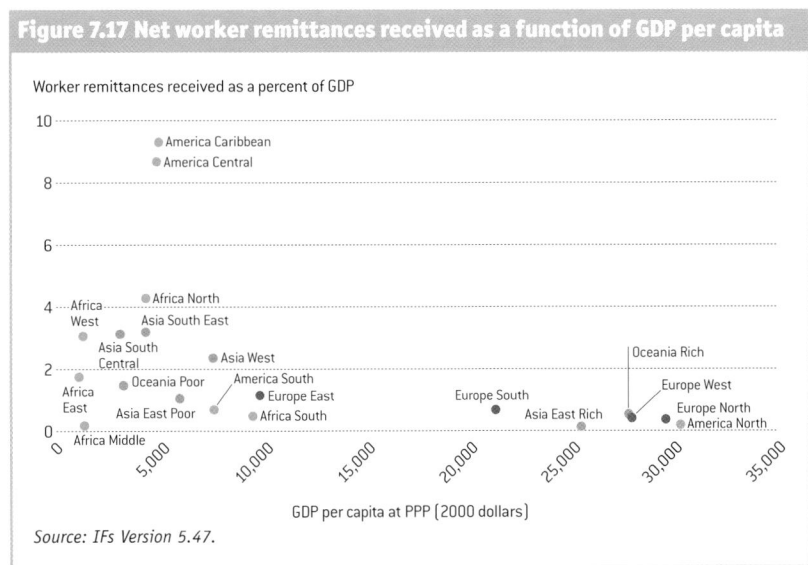

Figure 7.17 Net worker remittances received as a function of GDP per capita

Worker remittances received as a percent of GDP

Source: IFs Version 5.47.

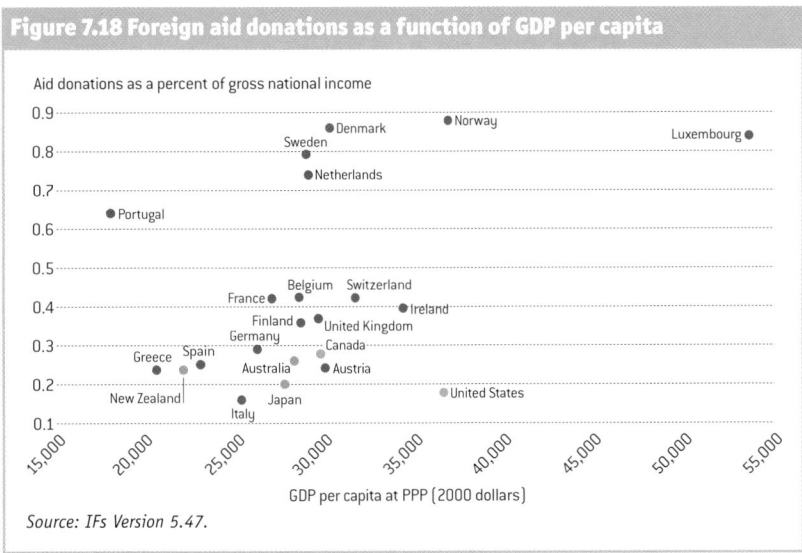

Figure 7.18 Foreign aid donations as a function of GDP per capita

Aid donations as a percent of gross national income

Source: IFs Version 5.47.

over fifteen years to 0.5 percent of GDP for all countries in Figure 7.18 who have historically been below that level. That intervention increases the annual flow of donations in 2010 by $50 billion relative to the base case and in 2020 by $100 billion (compare that with the Millennium Project's recommendation for a global partnership goal of an increase in the range of $40–60 billion).

To whom should the additional foreign aid funds flow? That is, of course, a recurrent and highly contested question of the policy world. Figure 7.19 shows the pattern of aid receipts as a portion of GDP in the early twenty-first century (2005). Only three African regions and the poorer countries of Oceania receive

Figure 7.19 Foreign aid receipts as a function of GDP per capita

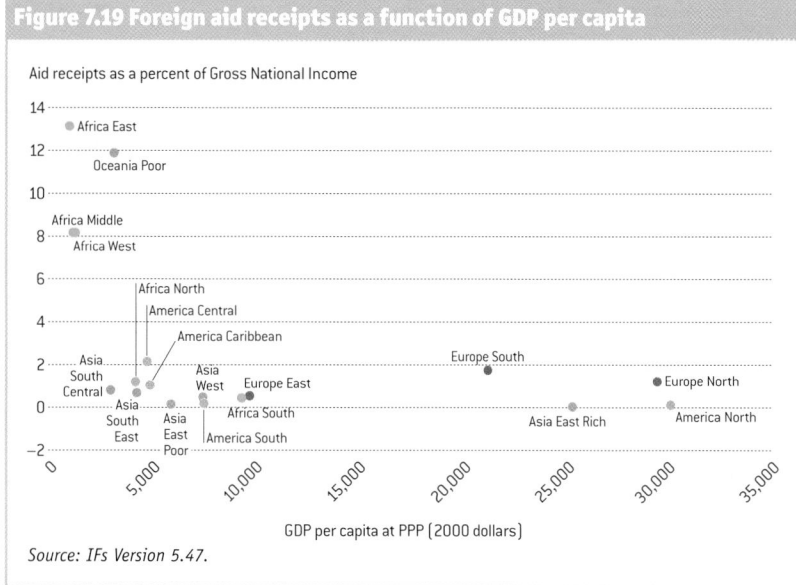

Aid receipts as a percent of Gross National Income

Source: IFs Version 5.47.

Beyond the magnitude of aid flows, increasing attention has been given to the effectiveness of them, partly due to recognition of distorting effects beyond those mentioned above.[20] For instance, a large portion of aid is tied to expenditures in the donor country, reducing its effective value. Another significant portion of "aid" takes the form of loans and therefore requires repayment. The intervention here does not assume changed quality of aid.[21]

In addition to the direct bilateral flows of aid from donor countries (and from individuals via nongovernmental organizations, a flow not captured by IFs), there are flows via multilateral international financial institutions (IFIs), such as the International Monetary Fund (IMF), World Bank, and Asian Development Bank. As indicated in Table 7.1, the actual dollar value of financial flows from these institutions to developing countries is very small compared to the other flows discussed up to this point. Moreover, large portions take the form of loans, so net flows can often actually be from developing countries to the IFIs. The reality is that the primary contributions of the IFIs to development lie in the quality of the advice that they provide to client countries (which some critics also question) and in the fiscal stamp of approval that their review and lending provides to other lenders and investors who control considerably greater financial flows. The intervention doubles flows over ten years, and the model represents only the financial impacts, not ancillary benefits.

Technology transfers

Until this point, all the internationally oriented interventions have focused on financial flows. Other kinds of international interventions are possible. For instance, flows of technology are partly related to trade and investment but also are based on the willingness of rich countries to allow access to intellectual property. Technology also often flows as a result of the rich and poor engaging in explicit activities that develop and transfer technology, such as the Consultative Group on International Agricultural Research (CGIAR). Nongovernmental organizations, such as those that focus on medical technologies, facilitate other flows of special interest to developing countries. It is very difficult both to quantify such flows and to say what kind

substantial portions of their GDP as aid. The argument over appropriate recipients of foreign aid is so intense in large part because these countries are (1) the poorest and thus prima facie the neediest and, (2) as shown in Figures 7.8–7.10, often the least well-governed. The intervention framed for this analysis simply left the pattern of recipients unchanged; variations in the pattern would be fairly easy to undertake with the IFs software for those who are interested.

There are, of course, many development experts such as Easterly (2001) who are very skeptical about foreign aid. Among the concerns raised is that it has several distorting effects upon recipients. One distortion is the so-called Dutch disease, normally associated with foreign exchange earnings from raw materials but also relevant to foreign aid. That is, aid receipts boost current accounts and put upward pressure upon exchange rates, undercutting the attractiveness of exports and thereby undermining the broad development of economic strength. IFs represents the working of these economic forces. Another distorting effect from aid is that of welfare dependency. Unearned income shapes incentive structures not just for individuals, but for societies. A particularly perverse variation of this can be the honeypot effect, whereby the access to flows by country leaderships leads to siphoning of the flows and more general corruption. IFs does not represent these sociopolitical forces.

of overall impact on growth they have. The earlier intervention built around FDI did not explicitly enhance the technological capabilities of recipients (only the financial effects are modeled), so the results of that intervention may underestimate the impact. It is not unreasonable to hypothesize that FDI increases, in combination with other measures to enhance technology flows, could add 0.2 percent to growth of multifactor productivity in developing countries. The intervention on technology studied here phased in that arbitrary impact over fifteen years.

Summarizing Drivers and Levers in IFs

Table 7.2 summarizes the levers identified in the above discussion for use primarily within countries (although many of them clearly have international ramifications) and those for use primarily across countries (although they all have domestic ramifications for developing countries). The appendix to this chapter, Summary of Interventions by Region, further elaborates the levers identified in this chapter and their specifications for implementation in the analysis to follow. Compare it with Table 3.1, which extracted a more complete list from the development literature. As that comparison will quickly illustrate, the levers available within IFs by no means exhaust the possible points of intervention in order to accelerate reductions in poverty rates. They do, however, touch on many interventions that development experts have identified.

As Archimedes pointed out long ago, not all levers have the same length and the same potential to move the world. The next section looks for those that offer the greatest leverage.

Silver Bullets?

Our uncertainty about the future is great. Our analysis of the weaknesses in our ability to measure poverty and to formulate relationships that accurately forecast it produced a wide range of possible futures for poverty in the framing exploration of Chapter 6. As we move from framing the ranges of poverty futures by continent using the proximate drivers, to exploring the sensitivity of poverty in subregions, to developing more policy-rooted levers for human action, the analysis may appear more precise, but great uncertainty remains. The ground shifts

from uncertainty about the assumptions that framed possible futures for demographic and economic growth and distribution to uncertainty about the relationships between deep drivers and such growth and distribution. The structures and parameters of the model are meant to represent much of what we know about such relationships theoretically and empirically, but they will inevitably be flawed.

As Chapter 1 emphasized, however, all action requires forecasting, even when the basis for it is less strong than we would like. Advocates of various policy positions sometimes provide estimates of the benefits from them (and should presumably always do so). For instance, in the early discussion of the potential benefits of the proposals in the Doha round of global trade negotiations, one World Bank estimate of their impact on poverty was that implementation could reduce the numbers in extreme poverty by 100 million. More recent analysis has considerably scaled back such estimates.[22] Given the discussion in Chapter 6, concluding

Table 7.2 Internal and external levers for poverty reduction	
Primarily Domestic Levers	**Primarily International Levers**
Factors of Production	Trade
Fertility reduction	High trade
High female labor	Export promotion
High investment	Foreign investment
Human capital	High FDI
High education spending	High portfolio flows
High health spending	Household transfers
Social capital/governance	High remittances
High government effectiveness	Government transfers
Low corruption	High foreign aid
High economic freedom	High IFI flows
Infrastructure capital	Technology
Extensive infrastructure	High technology
Natural capital	
High renewable energy	
Knowledge capital	
High R&D	
Low protection	
Domestic transfers	
High transfers	

that incremental human leverage might be able to move a maximum of 150–250 million from poverty, the original estimate assigned to trade alone appears improbably high.

The search for silver bullets in the fight on poverty, for those measures that can have the greatest impact, ideally with the lowest relative cost, is unending. Identification of prospective silver bullets changes over time and across philosophical viewpoints. In recent years the two most prominent candidates, in addition to the classics of trade and financial flow liberalization, tend to be (1) improved governance (by which is generally meant some combination of reduction of corruption, protection of property rights, and liberalization of markets) and (2) increased and more effective foreign aid (given considerable attention in the Millennium Project's recommendations for meeting the MDGs). In this section we want to give special attention to such potentially important levers but also explore more generally how a wide range of individual levers might contribute to the reduction of poverty.

In reading about the impact of various interventions in the sections to follow, it may be useful to review Table 1.1, which showed poverty headcounts and ratios in 1990, the base year for the Millennium Development Goals. In summary, in 1990 approximately 28.7 percent of the developing world's population lived on less than $1 per day; the percentages for the two regions of greatest concern, sub-Saharan Africa and South Asia, were 46.7 percent and 43 percent, respectively. The target values for 2015 are, of course, half those percentage levels. Given the populations of the IFs base case, roughly also the UN median variant, our calculations of target numbers in 2015 for total developing world and the two regions are 890, 223, and 459 million, respectively. Are there silver bullets that might get us close to those numbers or below?

Internal leverage

Table 7.3 shows the individual impact of each of the domestic leverage points identified earlier, as forecast by IFs. The lognormal formulation (see Chapters 3 and 4) was used for the table, and it provides the base case for comparison. The results of the cross-sectional formulation are not shown, but Chapter 6 documented that it would provide higher forecasts.

In interpreting tables on domestic interventions and all other forecast results in this volume, it is essential to remember once again the first rule of forecasting: always distrust the results. Models (mental or computer-based) are oversimplifications of reality, sometimes brutally so. They are always prone to various errors of construction and use. International Futures is intended to collect and synthesize, as much as possible within the limits of these realities, the collective knowledge of a wide range of experts and to tie that knowledge to data and theory. We should still view results as further input into a thinking process, not as a substitute for it. Within these limits, the analysis of individual and combined domestic interventions supports several conclusions.

First, the results strongly support the conclusion from Chapter 6 that the incremental leverage available for poverty reduction by 2015 (relative to the base case, which builds in much action already underway) was very limited for policies beginning to take effect in 2007, when this analysis was undertaken. There is, at least in the combination of interventions, however, some quite significant leverage for policies by 2050. On a global basis, perhaps nearly 250 million fewer people would live in extreme poverty at midcentury with a combined package of incremental domestic interventions beginning in 2007 than without such interventions. What this pattern suggests, however, is that as important as the focus of the MDGs on 2015 is, policy analysis must take a longer time horizon, at least to 2030 (results not shown) and probably, even though results become more uncertain, as far into the future as midcentury.

Second, there appears no silver bullet to reduce poverty among the set of interventions examined. Almost all the interventions make some contributions to that goal, but the reductions associated with each of them individually are fairly modest.

Third, direct transfers to the poor are among the most effective single measures, and perhaps the only one that makes a significant contribution by 2015. Interestingly, however, by 2050 other interventions are as important or more so, especially fertility reduction. This pattern suggests the necessity of exploring further the time paths of the effects of interventions. For instance, higher savings and investment actually have a detrimental impact in the near term, but that negative impact turns significantly positive over time. Because the intervention mentioned in Table 7.3 continues to ramp up investment over a long period, however, that pattern does not emerge clearly.

These time-dependent patterns reinforce one strategic argument about poverty and hunger reduction, namely the argument for a twin-track approach to pursuit of the MDG targets, as proposed by the UN Food and Agriculture Organization (UN FAO) and the World Food Program at the 2002 Monterrey conference on development financing (UN FAO 2005: 28).

Table 7.3 Internal levers explored (lognormal formulation)

| | Extreme poverty (millions) | | | | | |
| | Developing world | Sub-Saharan Africa | South Asia | Developing world | Sub-Saharan Africa | South Asia |
Scenarios	2015	2015	2015	2050	2050	2050
Base case	692	280	294	350	260	65
Fertility reduction	685	273	293	260	170	64
High female labor	691	280	293	347	258	64
High investment	724	293	311	324	241	58
High education expenditure	699	279	292	317	232	61
Effective govt.	686	278	290	311	232	58
Free markets	690	279	292	327	243	61
High infrastructure	691	279	293	327	244	61
High renewable	692	280	293	342	254	63
High R&D	691	279	293	343	256	63
Low protection	688	280	289	353	264	64
High transfers	673	265	293	275	180	64
All domestic combined	*680*	*270*	*296*	*106*	*57*	*37*

| | Extreme poverty (percent) | | | | | |
| | Developing world | Sub-Saharan Africa | South Asia | Developing world | Sub-Saharan Africa | South Asia |
Scenarios	2015	2015	2015	2050	2050	2050
Base case	11.2	29.4	13.7	4.2	14.2	2.2
Fertility reduction	11,1	29.0	13.7	3.3	11.6	2.2
High female labor	11.2	29.4	13.7	4.2	14.1	2.2
High investment	11.7	30.7	14.5	3.9	13.4	2.0
High education expenditure	11.1	29.3	13.7	3.8	12.8	2.1
Effective govt.	11.1	29.2	13.6	3.7	12.7	2.0
Low corruption	11.1	29.3	13.7	3.9	13.0	2.0
Free markets	11.1	29.3	13.7	4.0	13.3	2.1
High infrastructure	11.1	29.3	13.7	3.9	13.4	2.1
High renewable	11.2	29.3	13.7	4.1	13.9	2.1
High R&D	11.1	29.3	13.7	4.1	14.0	2.2
Low protection	11.1	29.4	13.5	4.3	14.4	2.2
High transfers	10.9	27.8	13.7	3.3	10.4	2.2
All domestic combined	*11.0*	*28.8*	*13.9*	*1.3*	*3.9*	*1.2*

Source: IFs Version 5.47.

The first track focuses on growth in the productivity and longer-term income of the poor; the second track creates social safety nets and provides direct food and other basic assistance to the poor. Another common strategic argument is that some external assistance might be useful or necessary in the interim, in order to help pay some of the costs of long-term investments of various kinds. The next subsection will begin exploring that possibility.

Fourth, in spite of limited geographic differentiation in Table 7.3, there is some evidence of differential contributions of interventions to different regions. In particular, fertility reduction is much more important in Africa through midcentury than in South Asia.

Once again, one size does not fit all with respect to development policies.

External leverage

As with the domestically focused interventions, the internationally oriented ones may have important synergies and trade-offs. For instance, there is a logic to the globalization process that says that many interventions are likely to cluster together (an issue to which the next section will return). Table 7.4 presents the forecasts for each individual international intervention and their combination, using the lognormal formulation.

Subject to the same caveats with respect to the inherent inaccuracy of forecasting that were

Table 7.4. External levers explored (lognormal formulation)

	Extreme poverty (millions)					
	Developing world	Sub-Saharan Africa	South Asia	Developing world	Sub-Saharan Africa	South Asia
Scenario	2015	2015	2015	2050	2050	2050
Base case	692	280	294	380	260	65
High trade	694	284	293	329	244	62
Export promotion	700	284	298	345	257	63
High FDI	697	282	295	333	245	64
High portfolio	691	280	293	348	258	65
High remittances	689	279	292	336	250	63
High foreign aid	684	273	295	278	202	52
High IFI flows	692	279	294	337	247	64
High technology transfer	684	278	289	303	222	59
Combined international	*686*	*278*	*293*	*194*	*145*	*32*
	Extreme poverty (percent)					
	Developing world	Sub-Saharan Africa	South Asia	Developing world	Sub-Saharan Africa	South Asia
Scenario	2015	2015	2015	2050	2050	2050
Base case	11.2	29.4	13.7	4.2	14.2	2.2
High trade	11.2	29.8	13.7	4.0	13.4	2.1
Export promotion	11.3	29.8	13.9	4.2	14.1	2.1
High FDI	11.2	29.6	13.8	4.0	13.4	2.2
High portfolio	11.1	29.3	13.7	4.2	14.0	2.2
High remittances	11.1	29.3	13.7	4.1	13.7	2.2
High foreign aid	11.0	28.6	13.8	3.4	11.1	1.8
High IFI flows	11.2	29.3	13.7	4.1	13.5	2.2
High technology transfer	11.0	29.2	13.6	3.7	12.2	2.0
Combined international	*11.1*	*29.1*	*13.7*	*2.4*	*8.1*	*1.1*

Source: IFs Version 5.47.

provided earlier, we can draw general conclusions from Table 7.4. The conclusions reinforce those drawn from analysis of domestic interventions.

First, the leverage available for poverty reduction by 2015 (with interventions beginning in 2007) is very limited. With the partial exception of higher foreign aid, which potentially provides immediate resources for recipient societies, none of the interventions significantly reduce poverty by 2015. The model may exaggerate the impact of foreign aid, however, by adding aid to government revenues and via transfers to household income, thereby raising average income and reducing poverty. That pass-through to poor as well as rich is by no means certain in the real world. For instance, Santosh Mehrotra and Enrique Delamonica (2007: 326) calculate that less than 10 percent of aid flows to basic social services.

Second, there is again quite significant leverage for policies by 2050. The combined impact could be a reduction in global poverty of more than 150 million people.

Third, there still appear to be no silver bullets. There is one clear leader in overall magnitude of impact both by 2015 and in 2050. That is significantly increased foreign aid (subject to the uncertain assumption of effective use). And there is a second intervention with very substantial impact

by 2050, namely the greater availability of technology. In reality, both fail to be fully convincing silver bullets—foreign aid because the model does not represent well some of the negative or distorting sociopolitical impacts of aid (although the model does capture Dutch disease implications); technology because the model does not parcel out its presumed greater availability to the true deeper drivers, such as greater FDI inflows and even the skills that might return with the same temporary emigrants who send home remittances.

Intervention Packages

With a rough map of the impact of individual interventions and of domestic and international packages of them, the next obvious step is to search for strategic packages that maximize the potential for reducing poverty.

Simple additive combination

The easiest first step is simply to combine the domestic and international interventions explored in the last section. Table 7.5 does that. One quite remarkable thing about combining the interventions is that there appear to be as many or more synergies as trade-offs, particularly in the impact on poverty forecasts for 2015. That is, the reduction in the number of the poor brought about by the simultaneous introduction of all

Table 7.5 Combined levers explored (lognormal formulation)						
	Extreme poverty (millions) using log-normal formulation					
	Developing world	Sub-Saharan Africa	South Asia	Developing world	Sub-Saharan Africa	South Asia
Scenario	2015	2015	2015	2050	2050	2050
Base case	692	280	294	250	260	65
All domestic	680	270	296	106	57	37
All international	686	278	293	194	145	32
Domestic and international	670	264	296	48	30	10
	Extreme poverty (percent) using log-normal formulation					
	Developing world	Sub-Saharan Africa	South Asia	Developing world	Sub-Saharan Africa	South Asia
Scenario	2015	2015	2015	2050	2050	2050
Base case	11.2	29.4	13.7	4.2	14.2	2.2
All domestic	11.0	28.8	13.9	1.3	3.9	1.2
All international	11.1	29.1	13.7	2.4	8.1	1.1
Domestic and international	10.8	28.0	13.9	0.6	2.1	0.3

Source: IFs Version 5.47.

interventions into the simulation is closer to the sum of the reductions from individual packages than to the larger reductions of the individual packages (which would imply overlapping effects or trade-offs across interventions).

This finding provides some independent support for the approach advocated by the Millennium Project under the leadership of Jeffrey Sachs. The plan proposed by that large team was not labeled "big push" by the writers of the report, but is in fact an exemplar of that development strategy and is an aggregation similar in many ways to the IFs combined scenario. Paul Collier (2006b: 121; 2007), while disagreeing with the emphasis Sachs puts on aid, also suggests the need for a big push "country by country."

Why would there be such synergies, and what are they? The most obvious and important one is that many of the interventions support economic growth. When one intervention increases economic growth relative to the base case, almost all other interventions take place on a higher base. For instance, educational and health expenditures rise with GDP, so an incremental percentage increase in a society already growing faster as a result of FDI or foreign aid will work from a higher base and have an even greater effect. There are also interacting positive feedback loops via broader human development variables, such as the impact of education on fertility.[23]

Table 7.5 also reinforces the earlier conclusion that interventions vary in their

effectiveness across regions of the world. Through midcentury, the domestically oriented interventions as a package have more impact on poverty reduction in sub-Saharan Africa than do the internationally oriented interventions. For South Asia, the two sets of interventions have a basically comparable impact.

How well does the combined scenario do in reducing poverty? Figure 7.20 helps address that question. Chapter 6 framed this analysis of poverty by exploring what appear to be the outer limits of human potential to accelerate poverty reduction. It did so by creating a "best case" scenario (as well as a "worst case") by direct manipulation of the proximate drivers of poverty, namely economic and population growth and distribution. Figure 7.20 shows the total number living in extreme income poverty in the base case, the best case, and the combined scenario.

The combined scenario reduces poverty considerably relative to the base case, pulling 285 million additional people out of extreme poverty by 2040 (270 million by 2055 as the numbers in the base case continue to decline). Not surprisingly, the combined scenario does not do as well as the best case, which was framed using costless assumptions about changed economic and population growth and redistributed economic well-being. In contrast, the combined scenario was built upward from large numbers of individual interventions, many of which do have real costs. As we have seen, for example, increases in savings and investment can actually reduce consumption and increase poverty in the short run. Thus it is quite impressive how well the combined scenario does over the longer term. The intelligent packaging of interventions does offer the opportunity to tackle poverty forcefully enough to push results toward the outer boundaries of reasonable expectations.

Strategic orientations

A future like that of the combined scenario is unlikely, however, for two related reasons. First, the full set of interventions would be very expensive. Although the costs to achieve the scenario would almost certainly be less expensive than the costs of continued poverty and lives lost, costs and benefits related to any policy intervention are seldom distributed

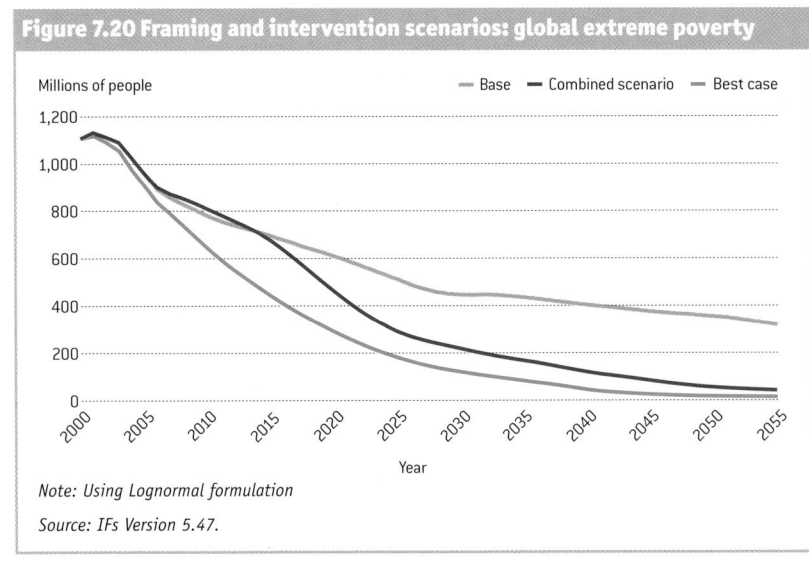

Figure 7.20 Framing and intervention scenarios: global extreme poverty

Millions of people

— Base — Combined scenario — Best case

Year

Note: Using Lognormal formulation

Source: IFs Version 5.47.

similarly across a population. Economists may talk about Pareto-superiority after compensatory transfers, but those asked to pay on the front end for benefits that quite obviously accrue to others will reasonably harbor doubts about ever receiving such compensation. Second, various philosophical tendencies divide development as a field, and practitioners support different strategic orientations. There are at least three easily identified clusters of initiatives that reappear in policy prescription. Chapter 3 (see especially Table 3.2) reviewed the components and some of the background of these strategies:

Domestic self-help

The most recent incarnation of this prescriptive orientation heavily emphasizes improved governance. The argument is that external resources and even internal expenditures are very often wasted if governance quality is inadequate. Clearly, corruption levels that divert resources to offshore bank accounts sap, if not fatally wound development efforts. Clearly, also, well-defined property rights encourage entrepreneurial behavior. Earlier incarnations of this prescription more often emphasized the development of human capital (as opposed, for instance, to military expenditures) or of basic infrastructure (in contrast for example, with large-scale show projects or, once again linking to governance, palaces for the privileged elite).

Outward, open orientation

The success of the Asian tigers drew everyone's attention to the possible benefits of export promotion, increasing trade (in contrast with import substitution), and the encouragement of large inflows of foreign direct investment. Advocates of globalization and liberalization have often pointed to this strategic orientation approvingly, although in reality many countries practicing export promotion have been ambivalent at best about the opening of domestic markets to trade or shorter-term financial flows. A contemporary variation on the general theme of external orientation concerns worker remittances and "brain circulation." In contrast to the fears of brain drain that characterized those tuned to domestic self-help, the arguments are that the remittances have often proven substantially larger than other international flows and the

migrants frequently return with new skill sets and entrepreneurial patterns.

Foreign assistance

Those who are exceptionally poor have limited choices. Their freedom of action is restricted. For that reason, there has been a strong belief among many analysts that domestic self-help, and even sometimes external market orientation, are difficult to pursue without some external resources to jump-start the process. The target of foreign aid reaching 0.7 percent of GDP is one of the longest-standing specific prescriptions in development. The need to address high levels of indebtedness, especially for the poorest countries, also receives regular attention.

Exploring these three strategic orientations is subject to considerable risk of both misinterpretation and criticism from those who adhere strongly to one perspective or another. The representations of important linkages within models, including IFs, are not sufficiently strong to settle the debates. Even the details of how intervention specifications should be associated with the perspectives are uncertain. In spite of the risks, there is value in tentatively exploring the three perspectives. The arguments within and across them are too important to ignore. Figure 7.21 shows forecasts for global income poverty reduction, using the $2 per day figure, for packages of the interventions clustered into the three strategic orientations and with the base case for reference.

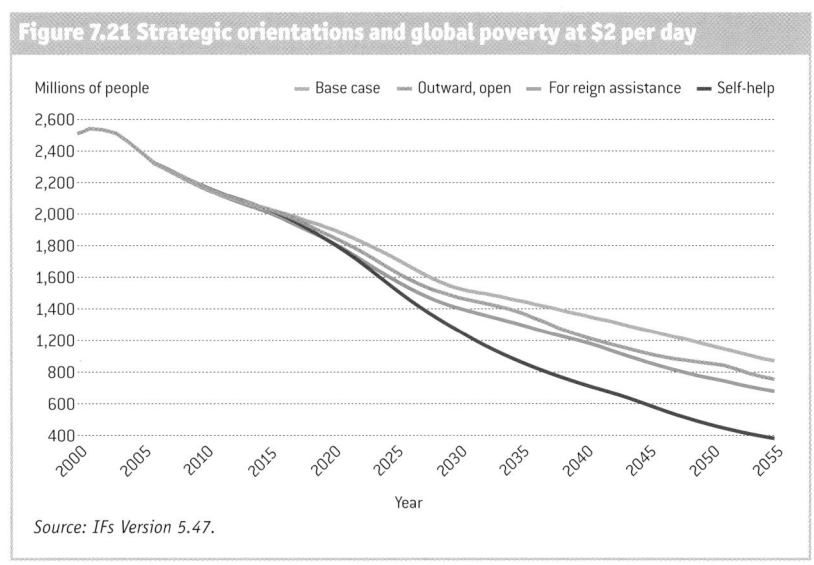

Figure 7.21 Strategic orientations and global poverty at $2 per day

Millions of people — Base case — Outward, open — Foreign assistance — Self-help

Source: IFs Version 5.47.

Most important, each package reduces global poverty relative to the base case. The outward, open orientation, at least as configured in this analysis and as represented in the IFs model, delivers the least improvement. Interestingly, it contributes more to middle-income countries than to those with the lowest incomes (such as countries in sub-Saharan Africa) and to the population living on less than $2 per day than to the population living on less than $1.

The foreign assistance package scenario delivers somewhat more reduction in poverty worldwide, primarily because of its positive impact on sub-Saharan Africa. In South Asia it makes a contribution similar to that of the outward, open orientation.

The self-help strategy provides the greatest benefits quite consistently across all developing regions. It is important to stress, however, two aspects of that finding. First, the combined scenario (not shown in Figure 7.21) would further reduce those living on less than $2 per day by more than 200 million by midcentury. Second, self-help is often actually attributable to the action of others. For instance, improved governance, reduced corruption, or more effective educational and health spending often benefit greatly from external examples, outside expertise, and even pressure brought to bear by the glare of a spotlight shone on self-serving or incompetent leadership and policies.

In short, each of the strategic orientations, although partisans frequently single them out as "the path" to reduced poverty and broader development, can make very important contributions. And the connections across them are sufficiently strong and mutually reinforcing that is it better to think of them as legs on a stool rather than as competitive perspectives. Human efforts to reduce poverty will benefit from resting on a stool with the stability provided by all three legs.

Conclusion
Substantively, there are significant interventions that can make great contributions to reducing global poverty. They require time to produce results, and because there are no true silver bullets, they achieve much more significant results in combination than individually. Are there packages of development proposals that, perhaps with

different combinations and better specification of possible interventions and strategic orientations, could better reduce poverty than any of those orientations individually and challenge the potential of the simple combined intervention scenario?[24] Almost certainly. For example, the UN Millennium Project (2005) developed *A Practical Plan to Achieve the Millennium Development Goals*, identifying many of the same interventions that this chapter has explored over a longer time horizon and elaborating them in considerable detail.[25]

Methodologically, there are inherent differences between the structures of such plans and the structure of the analysis undertaken here. Many such plans are not fully concrete with respect to the magnitude and timing of interventions proposed. Plan developers also seldom have the capacity to look very systematically and globally at proposals as integrated packages. That has been the added value of the analysis here. At the same time, however, a model like IFs necessarily functions at a more highly macro level than proposals that typically come out of extended development analysis. These differences make the two approaches complementary rather than strictly comparable.

Appendix: Summary of Interventions by Region
The world as a whole
Global increase in FDI by 30 percent over twenty years; global increase in portfolio investment flows over twenty years; R&D expenditures increased by 20 percent over twenty years; global increase in migration by 50 percent over twenty years.

Developed countries
Foreign aid donations of at least 0.5 percent of GDP within ten years.

International financial institutions
Doubling of lending over ten years.

World Bank developing countries as a whole
Health spending increased 20 percent over ten years; governance effectiveness improved by about 20 percent on World Bank scale over ten years; economic freedom increased by about 20 percent on Fraser Institute scale over ten years; corruption decreased by about 30 percent

on the Transparency International scale over twenty years; infrastructure improved by about 20 percent over thirty years; renewable energy production increased, reaching 50 percent above the base case in 2050; an increase of technologically based productivity growth by 0.2 percent over ten years.

Africa
Eastern
Education spending increased 20 percent over ten years; savings and investment rates doubled over twenty-five years; transfers to unskilled households increased by 50 percent over twenty years; export promotion push leading to export growth of 25–30 percent relative to the base case by 2050.

Middle
Movement to replacement fertility over forty-five years (45 percent change relative to the base case); increased savings and investment by 30 percent over twenty-five years (e.g., 18 percent to 24 percent); education spending increased 80 percent over ten years; corruption decreased by about 40 percent on the Transparency International scale over twenty years; infrastructure improved by about 80 percent over thirty years; doubled transfers to unskilled households over twenty years; export promotion push leading to export growth of 25–30 percent relative to the base case by 2050.

Western
Movement to replacement fertility over thirty years (33 percent change relative to the base case); increased savings/investment by 30 percent over twenty-five years (e.g., 18 percent to 27 percent); education spending increased 80 percent over ten years; transfers to unskilled households doubled over twenty years; transfers to unskilled households increased by 50 percent over twenty years; export promotion push of leading to export growth of 25–30 percent relative to the base case by 2050.

Southern
Movement to replacement fertility over thirty years (33 percent change relative to the base case); increased savings/investment by 50 percent over twenty-five years (e.g., 18 percent to 27 percent); doubled transfers

to unskilled households over twenty years; export promotion push leading to export growth of 25–30 percent relative to the base case by 2050.

Northern
Movement to equal female labor force participation over forty-five years; education spending increased 20 percent over ten years.

Asia
South Central
Movement to equal female labor force participation over forty-five years; education spending increased 20 percent over ten years; increased savings and investment by 30 percent over twenty-five years; reduced protectionism lowered the cost of imports by 20 percent over twenty years; export promotion push leading to export growth of 25–30 percent relative to the base case by 2050.

Southeast
Education spending increased 35 percent over ten years.

East Poor
Education spending increased 80 percent over ten years; doubled transfers to unskilled households over twenty years.

West (Middle East)
Movement to equal female labor force participation over forty-five years; increased savings and investment by 30 percent over twenty-five years (e.g., 18 percent to 24 percent); transfers to unskilled households increased by 50 percent over twenty years.

Oceania Poor
Movement to replacement fertility over thirty years (33 percent change relative to the base case); savings and investment rates doubled over twenty-five years; transfers to unskilled households were doubled over twenty years.

The Americas
Caribbean
Increased savings and investment by 50 percent over twenty-five years (e.g., 18 percent to 27 percent); doubled transfers to unskilled households over twenty years.

Central

Movement to equal female labor force participation over forty-five years; doubled savings and investment over twenty-five years (e.g., 12 percent to 24 percent); education spending increased 35 percent over ten years; transfers to unskilled households doubled over twenty years.

South

Movement to equal female labor force participation; education spending increased 20 percent over ten years; reduced protectionism

lowered the cost of imports by 20 percent over twenty years; transfers to unskilled households doubled over twenty years.

Europe

Eastern

Savings and investment doubled over twenty-five years (e.g., 15 percent to 30 percent); education spending increased 30 percent over ten years; corruption decreased by about 60 percent on the Transparency International scale over twenty years.

1   Disagreements about possible levels of action are inevitable. The IFs model and the library of interventions for this analysis are available for any who wish to explore variations.

2   The Poverty Action Lab at MIT and much research does this at a micro level, complementing the macro analysis of this chapter.

3   See http://www.un.org/depts/dhl/maplib/worldregions.htm#CAR for a full membership list. This is also the regional set used by the Population Reference Bureau. The UN's regional commissions are organized on a different basis, with Western Asia (the Middle East, including Egypt) broken out of Asia and Oceania added to Asia and the Pacific.

4   Rwanda has targeted a maximum of three children much sooner using positive incentives.

5   Goldman Sachs (Poddar and Yi 2007: 12–13) pointed out that World Bank data show the savings rate in India rising from 12 percent in 1961 to nearly 30 percent in 2003 and calculated that the savings rate has increased by about 0.8 percent for every 1 percent decline in the demographic dependency ratio (young and old dependent population as a percentage of total population). They therefore posit a continuing rise in the savings rate that is not in the IFs base case.

6   Countries within regions vary substantially, however, and the analysis should ideally be at the country level (to which we turn in Chapter 8). Among the most egregious examples is the Caribbean region of the Americas, where Haiti spent about 1.5 percent of GDP for education and Cuba spent over 8.0 percent.

7   China Daily story at http://www.chinadaily.com.cn/english/doc/2006-03/06/content_527242.htm.

8   Still other important issues surround (1) the balance of social spending between basic social services such as primary education and broader spending; (2) the equity of social spending across income categories; and (3) the efficiency of social spending (see Mehrotra and Delamonica 2007).

9   For use in IFs, this index has been rescaled from 0 to 5; non-OECD countries average about 2.3. A 20 percent change on that base is about 0.5 points.

10   The IFs project generally uses the TI measure because it provides a considerably longer historical series.

11   A variety of initiatives for transparency in government finance, such as Publish What You Pay, clearly tackle the issue.

12   Because many index-based and more physically based measures (like life expectancy) saturate, and GDP appears not yet to do so, logarithmic-shaped functions are common in looking at relationships between such measures and GDP per capita. Hughes (2001) explored such relationships.

13   In 2006 China developed a plan to move R&D from 1.23 percent of GDP to 2.5 percent by 2020, a much more aggressive intervention. Analysis by the *Economist* (August 5, 2006: 39) identified the same constraints indicated here.

14   A relationship drawn to fit the regions would actually be downward sloping, but a relationship fit to the underlying countries would be nearly flat.

15   The World Bank Social Protection Discussion Papers are a good entry point into the literature.

16   It would be desirable to have many more categories of households, but data at a more disaggregated level are not extensively available across countries. The Global Trade Analysis Project (GTAP) provides it for these two categories.

17   The treatment of trade within IFs uses a pooled rather than bilateral trade representation, and there are other tools available for more detailed, bilateral exploration of the impact of trade initiatives, including the models of the Global Trade Analysis Project.

18   Specifically, the intervention pushed export growth upward by about 4 percent per year beyond the base case. The cumulative increase over the half century is quite a bit less than the integral of that annual 4 percent, however, because as with many other interventions, equilibration mechanisms (such as the competition for markets inherent in global trade) resist such an ongoing intervention.

19   Adams (2007) identified some of the problems with data on remittances, including (1) the exclusion of remittances that do not flow through official

channels and (2) the classification by some central banks of remittances as other flows. Data may therefore underreport true flows. The study also importantly explores the use of remittances and concludes that they tend to support investment and entrepreneurial activity.

20   The OECD countries have set up a Network on Poverty Reduction (POVNET) to support implementation of the Paris Declaration on Aid Effectiveness.

21   The IFs model has a parameter to change the portion of aid that comes as loans, making such analysis possible.

22   *Economist,* December 10, 2005: 82. Another estimate was that implementation of Doha could reduce those living in poverty (using the $2 per day definition) by 150 million (reported in "Europe's Farms vs. Free Trade," Christian Science Monitor, December 15, 2005: 1). The second estimate suggested the reduction in those living in extreme poverty (below $1 per day) could be about 75 million.

23   Mehrotra and Delamonica (2007: 5) argue that such positive feedback loops across multiple dimensions of social and economic development operate at both micro and macro levels.

24   Experiments have been undertaken to link the Computer Assisted Reasoning System (CARS) of RAND and Evolving Logic (Lempert, Popper, and Bankes 2003) with IFs and to explore the space of interventions more deeply and systematically.

25   There is at least one key intervention that the Millennium Project did not highlight but that proved important here, especially for absolute numbers of the poor. Chapters 6 and 7 have shown how important family planning and associated population growth reduction could be in reducing poverty levels in sub-Saharan Africa by 2050. *The Practical Plan* did heavily emphasize rebuilding and strengthening networks of public health clinics, in part for the maternal care that does tend to reduce fertility rates. Yet the plan never really emphasized family planning's importance in its own right, and many political environments have been somewhat unfriendly to it in recent years.

8

The Multiple Faces of Poverty and Its Future

Poverty has many similarities wherever it is found, not least the degradation and limiting of options that it brings. Yet character and patterns of poverty differ widely across space and time. Past chapters have explored poverty at the global and continental region levels, with attention also to interventions for continental subregions. This chapter drills down to the country level, albeit focusing on selected larger countries, providing a transition to and foundation for the 182-country forecasts in the tables accompanying this volume. Given the complications of making generalizations about the more than 1 billion people each in India and China, however, the chapter also explores variation within the two demographic giants.

Ideally, poverty analysis and forecasting should range from aggregate and macro analysis to the microlevel characteristics of individuals. In doing so it should give attention to subpopulations determined by age, sex, urban or rural residence, ethnicity and religion, and much

more. The distinction in Chapter 2 between chronic and transient poverty, for instance, depends on such disaggregation. In reality, the gap between micro analysis, mostly undertaken with surveys and case studies, and aggregate analysis, done primarily with models, remains wide. Macro studies of global poverty have generally been undertaken at the aggregate regional or continental level, with some attention also to the Indian and Chinese giants.

Moving to the country level creates both challenges and opportunities. A key challenge is representation of the many features of individual countries that shape their variable prospects for addressing poverty. Potentially important country-specific features include demographic and economic structures, governance characteristics and quality, financial strength, whether a country is landlocked, natural resource levels (for better or for "resource curse" worse), and stocks of human capital. Yet scarcity and quality of data, especially for the poorest and smallest countries, plague analysis at the country level. So, too, does the possibility of tipping points, at which countries may actually move between progress and deterioration based on idiosyncratic elements such as the personality of specific leaders. Analysis at the continental level allows the sweeping of many such issues into the aggregations.

With respect to opportunities, differentiating countries by such features allows more subtle, path-dependent investigation of historically important driving forces. On balance, although the challenges of moving to subcontinental and country-specific analysis are great and those of moving inside countries to provinces or states are even greater, the potential payoffs are substantial.

Scanning Poverty Across Countries

Tables 8.1 and 8.2 provide an initial scan of country-specific patterns of income poverty.[1] Table 8.1 shows the eight countries of the world that have or may before 2055 come to have 25 million or more citizens living below $1 per day. Clearly, Afghanistan, Bangladesh, China, the Democratic Republic of the Congo, Ethiopia, India, Nigeria, and Uganda require special attention. If the threshold were dropped to 10 million people or more, the number would rise to twenty-three countries, and the list would include Brazil, Ghana, Indonesia, Kenya, Madagascar, Myanmar, Nepal,

Niger, Pakistan, the Philippines, Somalia, Sudan, Tanzania, and Zimbabwe.

The forecasts demonstrate multiple different patterns. Bangladesh, China, and India show declining numbers of the extremely poor over time, largely eliminating such poverty in each case over the next fifty years. In a mirror image, Afghanistan shows increasing numbers through midcentury. In contrast, the base case forecast for the Democratic Republic of the Congo, Ethiopia, and Uganda shows increasing numbers of the poor for some or many years and then decreases in their numbers. And in still a fourth pattern, numbers initially decrease in Nigeria, as a result of a forecast for higher oil revenues and positive use thereof that historical experience may well contradict, but then reverse and climb as the peak of production and export earnings is passed.

Table 8.2 shows six countries in which more than 65 percent of the population may live at some time in the first half of the century on less than $1 per day: Cambodia, Central African Republic, Eritrea, Nigeria, Uganda, and Zambia. If the threshold for inclusion were lowered to just 50 percent, the number of countries would rise to twenty-two, adding Afghanistan, Burundi, Ghana, Guinea-Bissau, Haiti, Liberia, Madagascar, Nicaragua, Niger, Rwanda, São Tomé and Principe, Sierra Leone, Somalia, Tanzania, Togo, and Zimbabwe. Again, different patterns are evident, with increasing frequency of poverty

Table 8.1 Countries with 25 million people living on less than $1 per day

	Millions living on less than $1 per day							
Year	Afghanistan	Bangladesh	China	DR Congo	Ethiopia	India	Nigeria	Uganda
2000	9.416	**53.24**	**208.7**	23.83	13.89	**359.1**	**87.26**	20.43
2005	11.05	**48.65**	**147.2**	**25.18**	12.84	**307.2**	**82.51**	23.36
2010	13.26	**42.35**	**71.83**	24.52	16.39	**244.9**	**60.57**	**25.89**
2015	15.28	**36.53**	**38.18**	**28.54**	23.64	**197.5**	**36.12**	29
2020	17.38	**29.76**	23.19	**31.33**	**26.73**	**137.5**	22.91	**32.73**
2025	19.99	22.98	11.36	**32.5**	**25.12**	**77.97**	17.42	**35.44**
2030	23.04	17.66	4.875	**35.65**	10.83	**43.34**	13.55	**35.81**
2035	**26.53**	13.52	2.692	**41.07**	12.88	**28.22**	13.85	**30.02**
2040	**30.74**	9.378	1.795	**44.11**	7.339	16.56	20.27	20.82
2045	**35.92**	5.894	1.09	**53.05**	3.686	7.094	**34.52**	14.66
2050	**40.44**	3.646	0.668	**49.56**	1.157	2.189	**56.17**	10.72
2055	**43.08**	2.294	0.467	**34.5**	0.099	0.712	**62.19**	7.711

Note: The table shows 25 million or more in bold.

Source: Base case forecast of IFs Version 5.47.

in the Central African Republic and Eritrea, but generally decreasing rates in all other countries. The contrast in patterns for Nigeria between increasing numbers of poor toward midcentury (see, again, Table 8.1) and a significant decrease in the rate of incidence over most of the period reinforces again the important impact on poverty of absolute population size and its growth.

Two important qualifications apply to Tables 8.1 and 8.2, with implications for all the forecasts. First, the initial rates and numbers of the poor are not actually known for some of the countries shown or named. The World Bank's database of countries in which surveys have been done since 2000 does not include Afghanistan, the Central African Republic, the Democratic Republic of the Congo, Djibouti, Eritrea, Guinea-Bissau, Myanmar, São Tomé and Principe, Sierra Leone, and Somalia. The very fact that estimation and forecasting places so many of these data-poor countries into the highest categories, however, suggests the importance of not only including them in this analysis but giving them some prominence. Chapter 4 discussed the process for the IFs model that uses the results of a cross-sectionally estimated function with income levels and income distribution to estimate initial values for such countries.[2] Second, the forecasts are, as always, subject to a high level of uncertainty.

Income poverty at these extreme levels has a broad range of consequences and correlations, something to which Chapter 9 will return. For instance, it is of interest to note the relationship between the countries with the highest numbers and, especially, rates of poverty and the incidence of what is sometimes called state failure, a complex syndrome of attributes. The Fund for Peace defines the characteristics to include "loss of physical control of its territory or of a monopoly on the legitimate use of force."[3] Indicators of it include high levels of corruption and criminal behavior, economic decline, demographic pressures, and frequent violence. In its 2007 study in association with *Foreign Policy* magazine, the list of thirty-two countries considered to be in critical condition by the Fund for Peace included many of those named above, specifically (from worst to less bad) Somalia, Zimbabwe, Democratic Republic of the Congo, Afghanistan, Central African Republic, Haiti, Pakistan, Myanmar, Bangladesh, Ethiopia, Burundi, Sierra Leone, Liberia, and Niger.

What, then, are the different faces of poverty in countries around the world and of prospects for its reduction? The remaining sections of this chapter explore that question by continent and regions within them. We begin with Africa, the continent facing the greatest rates of income poverty and by far

High poverty and state failure often coincide.

Table 8.2 Countries with 65 percent living on less than $1 per day						
	Percent living on less than $1 per day					
Year	Cambodia	Central African Republic	Eritrea	Nigeria	Uganda	Zambia
2000	**72.42**	63.46	38.79	**74.19**	84.04	71.04
2005	62.65	64.27	42.92	61.77	80.88	66.04
2010	48.67	64.5	56.88	40.23	75.73	62.17
2015	44.47	65.99	61.85	21.42	72.1	61.98
2020	39.35	68.28	60.53	12.2	69.8	61.96
2025	27.46	68.47	62.39	8.371	65.52	58.99
2030	18.57	69.34	67.14	5.905	58.13	55.7
2035	13.39	74.83	63.79	5.508	43.41	44.76
2040	8.57	75.68	64.02	7.405	27.26	32.37
2045	5.468	63.22	66.91	11.68	17.69	24.13
2050	3.785	52.28	64.56	17.74	12.12	18.31
2055	2.858	58.07	60.89	18.5	8.295	15.1

Note: The table shows poverty rates above 65 percent in bold.

Source: Base case forecast of IFs Version 5.47.

the greatest number of countries in extreme poverty. By the mid-1990s, gross domestic product (GDP) per capita in sub-Saharan Africa as a whole had fallen back to 1960s levels. Growth has only begun to return to the region, and because it is so dependent on raw materials, uncertainty about prospects remains very high.

Africa
Scanning the continent

There are fifty-one countries in the United Nation's definition of Africa. Analysts traditionally group them into regional clusters that carry some basic information about geography and thereby, perhaps, also some very broad similarity with respect to topology and climate. Because it is so widely adopted, this chapter uses the UN regionalization, despite its many limitations (see Map 8.1).[4] Table 8.3 shows poverty in those regions. The descending order for contemporary poverty rates across them is Western,[5] Eastern, Middle, Southern, and Northern Africa. Nigeria, Ethiopia, and the Democratic Republic of the Congo demographically dominate the first three of those regions, respectively, and those three high-poverty countries require much of our attention here. South Africa similarly dominates its region demographically, and although it is not as large or poor, also merits special attention.

Other regional groupings are possible and potentially useful. Julius Gatune has divided the continent into eight cultural regions, which overlap with the five standard geographic ones but helpfully further extract the clusters of states in the Horn of Africa, African Oceania, and the Sahel.[6] Removing the Horn from East Africa makes sense culturally and in terms of leaving the rest of the region roughly comparable in membership to the proposed East African Federation; again, however, we will stay with the UN regionalization.

Perhaps the best-known alternative disaggregation is that of Paul Collier and his colleagues. It builds on two dimensions related to countries' distinctive positions in the global system, namely whether they are landlocked and whether they are resource rich or poor. Collier has argued (2006a; 2007) that it is resource poor, landlocked states that suffer the greatest disadvantages.[7]

Clearly, having either a coastline or extensive natural resources positions a country to participate in global trade. Yet the two characteristics can proffer quite different advantages and, in the case of natural resources, some potential disadvantages. Although resource wealth offers at least the possibility of escape from poverty (as Botswana's good management of diamonds has shown), many analysts have stressed the syndrome of problems known as the **resource curse**, including the propensity

Table 8.3 Extreme poverty rates in African regions

	Percent living on less than $1 per day				
Year	Eastern	Middle	Northern	Southern	Western
2000	42.8	40.89	7.333	14.77	54.13
2005	38.25	32.09	6.13	11.75	47.06
2010	36.6	25.09	4.192	9.428	36.39
2015	37.61	24.68	2.674	8.704	28.3
2020	35.86	24.19	2.026	8.761	23.71
2025	31.17	22.68	1.721	8.791	20.71
2030	24.61	22.68	1.503	6.701	18.64
2035	21.72	24.34	1.279	4.446	18.26
2040	16.45	23.29	1.084	2.923	18.3
2045	12.51	22.78	0.99	2.213	17.98
2050	10.02	18.39	0.898	1.895	18.97
2055	8.371	12.34	0.533	1.651	17.42

Source: Base case forecast of IFs Version 5.47.

of plentiful resources to support corruption within elites and to support exchange rates high enough to choke off the development of more diversified export capabilities. Price fluctuations of materials on world markets also cause macroeconomic volatility that weakens growth potential (Addison and Wodon 2007).

Focusing on the impact of being landlocked, Figure 8.1 shows extreme (less than $1) poverty rates in the coastal and landlocked states of sub-Saharan Africa as defined by Paul Collier and Stephen A. O'Connell (2007: 46).[8] The landlocked countries have a poverty rate nearly 10 percent higher than that of the coastal countries. The much more well-to-do coastal countries bordering the Mediterranean have an extreme poverty rate of only about 7 percent, reinforcing the advantage that coastal states, especially resource-rich ones, typically have. The very large, oil-rich coastal population of Nigeria, with a poverty rate of 74 percent in 2000, constitutes an important exception to that pattern. Its inclusion in coastal

Map 8.1 African regions

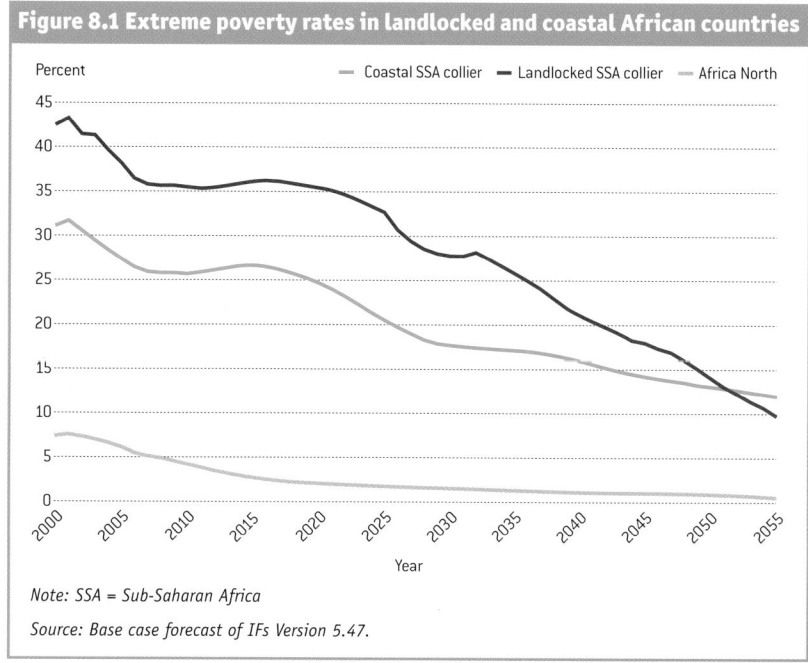

Figure 8.1 Extreme poverty rates in landlocked and coastal African countries

Note: SSA = Sub-Saharan Africa

Source: Base case forecast of IFs Version 5.47.

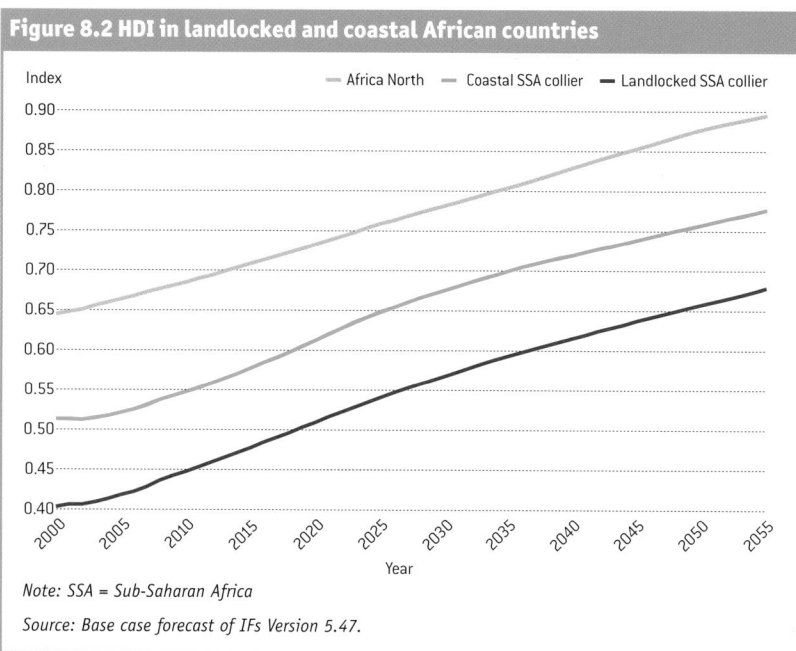

Figure 8.2 HDI in landlocked and coastal African countries

Note: SSA = Sub-Saharan Africa

Source: Base case forecast of IFs Version 5.47.

sub-Saharan Africa not only raises initial rates but also raises them midcentury because IFs forecasts some difficulties for the country as oil resources play out.

The values of the human development index (HDI) in the landlocked states even more definitively trail those of coastal states (see Figure 8.2). Life expectancy is somewhat lower in the landlocked states, and literacy is considerably lower. The low level of human

development in Ethiopia, even below that of the Democratic Republic of the Congo, tends to bring down that of the landlocked countries, just as Nigeria brings down that of the countries with ocean access. The fact that it is Ethiopia that particularly lowers the average of the human development index for the landlocked countries, however, somewhat undercuts the argument that being landlocked is a key determinant of a troubled economic situation—Ethiopia has been relatively poor for much longer than it has been landlocked (Eritrea won its long war for independence in 1991 and took away the Ethiopian coastline).

In general, a look at regions in Africa suggests that geographically differentiated analysis is important but that it must reach down to the country level, especially into the high population countries, for real insight. With 127 million people, Nigeria is the giant of both Western Africa and coastal sub-Saharan Africa. The 74 million people of Ethiopia dominate East Africa (especially its horn) and the landlocked category, as the 58 million of the Democratic Republic of Congo dominate Middle Africa and add to landlocked populations. South Africa, with 45 million people, similarly dominates southernmost Africa. Therefore looking at these four countries is particularly useful. Obviously, even though attention here is on the demographically largest states, all people of Africa are equally important in analysis of poverty reduction. This discussion will say very little about smaller countries like Botswana or Rwanda (with populations of about 2 and 9 million, respectively), but we hope that the discussion of the large-population countries can identify archetypal patterns for the entire continent. For other countries readers may turn to the forecast tables that conclude this volume.

Understanding the patterns of large countries

Figure 8.3 shows historical and forecast rates of extreme poverty in the biggest regional populations: Nigeria, Ethiopia, the Democratic Republic of Congo, and South Africa. In spite of the Congo's small outlet to the ocean, Collier characterized it as landlocked. All but Ethiopia have developed extensive natural resources, and

Ethiopia has identified very large natural gas resources in the Ogaden subregion. What might be their various prospects for poverty reduction?

Nigeria

Many factors will shape the prospects for Nigeria, including its ethnic and religious divisions and disease burden on the negative side, and relatively strong educational system on the positive side. The emergence of a very strong film industry, increasingly known as Nollywood, also testifies to a strong entrepreneurial culture and capability. Two factors, however, generally and appropriately receive special attention. The first is the availability of oil revenues. The second is the quality of governance, including the country's ability to use those revenues well.

Although OPEC member Nigeria is not an energy giant in the category of Saudi Arabia, Iraq, Iran, or Kuwait, its oil and natural gas reserves are both substantial, in the range of 25–30 billion barrels of oil equivalent, or approximately 3 percent of global totals. Its oil production, climbing up toward 1 billion barrels per year, provides a very substantial portion of its government budget and GDP. With the sharp rise in energy prices since 2004, that financial foundation has grown especially fast.

With the increases in oil production and prices, Nigeria has a window of opportunity for the effective use of revenues to tackle poverty and many other problems. Although ultimately, depletion of energy resources will close that window, troubles with rebels in the delta subregion could significantly interrupt production even earlier. In the base case of IFs, peak oil and gas production occurs in the period between 2025 and 2040, and Nigeria ceases being a net energy exporter before 2050. Future global energy prices probably will remain quite high through the period of global energy transitions associated with peaking oil and gas production around the world. Both the International Energy Agency (IEA) and the Energy Information Administration (EIA) of the U.S. Department of Energy make annual forecasts of longer-term energy prices, and in 2007 looked through 2030. Even in their low price scenarios, both organizations foresee prices through 2030 that are well above those of the 1990s (International Energy Agency 2007; U.S. Department of Energy 2007).

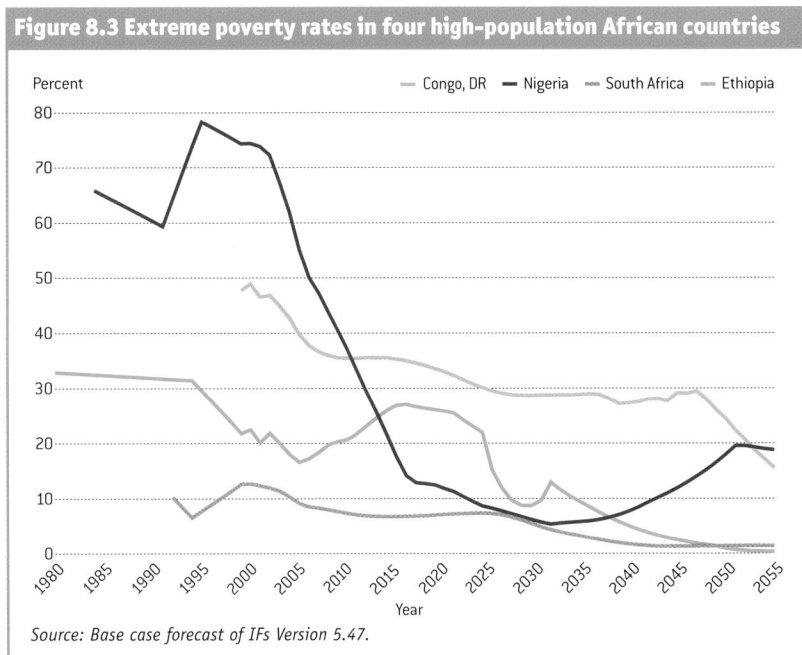

Figure 8.3 Extreme poverty rates in four high-population African countries

Source: Base case forecast of IFs Version 5.47.

How substantially might this windfall help Nigeria? Figure 8.4 indicates a base case forecast of very substantial net export revenues as a portion of GDP. Nigeria used the windfall in 2006 to settle its remaining Paris Club debt of about $4.6 billion (debt relief of $18 billion had been provided) and quite quickly to pay back most of its London Club debt of $2.4 billion in 2006 and early 2007. In 2006 Nigeria was able to obtain ratings from Standard & Poor's and Fitch.

As important as the debt settlements, in 2003 Nigeria put in place a substantial anticorruption effort in the form of its Economic and Financial Crimes Commission (EFCC), which after decades of general mismanagement and theft of oil revenues began to prosecute and convict even high officials, including state governors and the vice president.[9] Nigeria also managed in 2007 to hold a third civilian election for the presidency, in spite of very great irregularities in the process. Unfortunately the reassignment at the end of 2007 of the EFCC's crusading head, Malam Nuhu Ribadu, threw a heavy cloud over anticorruption efforts. Nigeria, long one of the most corrupt countries of the world, thus faces great political and financial uncertainty. The sharp and substantial reduction in extreme poverty forecast in Figure 8.3 depends on success in changing such patterns. And even with reasonable growth, it is likely to take Nigeria until about 2015 simply to recover its

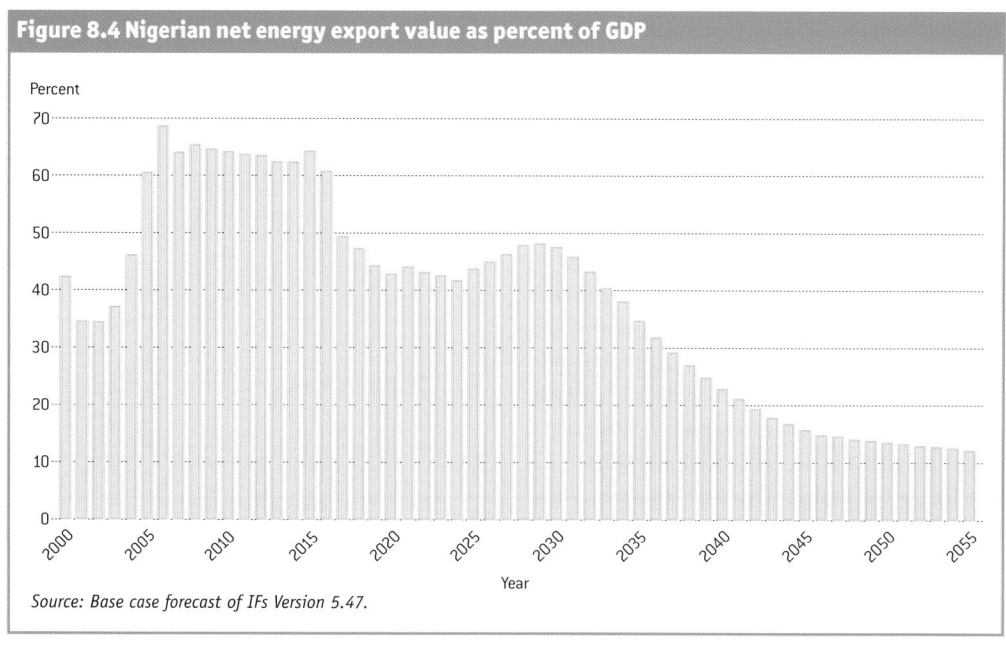

Figure 8.4 Nigerian net energy export value as percent of GDP

Percent

Year

Source: Base case forecast of IFs Version 5.47.

per capita GDP levels (at purchasing power parity, or PPP) of the late 1970s.

In the longer run, many other challenges face Nigeria. For instance, like the continent as a whole, total fertility rates (TFR) in Nigeria have dropped from around 7.0 in 1960 to near or below 5.5, and the trend is clearly downward. Yet even if the pattern follows the base case forecast in Figure 8.5 and reaches a TFR of near 3.0, the population of Nigeria will nearly triple between 2000 and 2050 to a total of about 320 million

people; the population of the continent might exceed 1.7 billion. Compared especially to Asia, most of Africa has been very slow to aggressively promote lower birth rates. There are indications of change. After the loss of 800,000 people in the genocide of 1994, Rwanda's population growth accelerated sharply, a common pattern after war or other disruption. In 2007 it began to explore mechanisms to reduce the fertility rate quickly from 6.1 to 3.0. Barring such substantial changes, however, the transition to such rates might well stretch to midcentury.[10]

Nigeria also must cope with high income inequality. A rebound like that in Figure 8.3 in the percentage of Nigerians living in extreme poverty could occur after 2030 as a result of either deterioration in income per capita or in income distribution.

South Africa

South Africa has the longest colonial history and most European institutions of all African countries. It is rich in resources and further substantially blessed by geography. In spite of the history of apartheid, South Africa has a much lower rate of extreme poverty than Nigeria and most of the rest of Africa (see, again, Figure 8.3). Yet around 30 percent of its population still lives on less than $2 per day. The key determinants of economic growth and poverty reduction may well, as with Nigeria, depend heavily on two factors. The first of

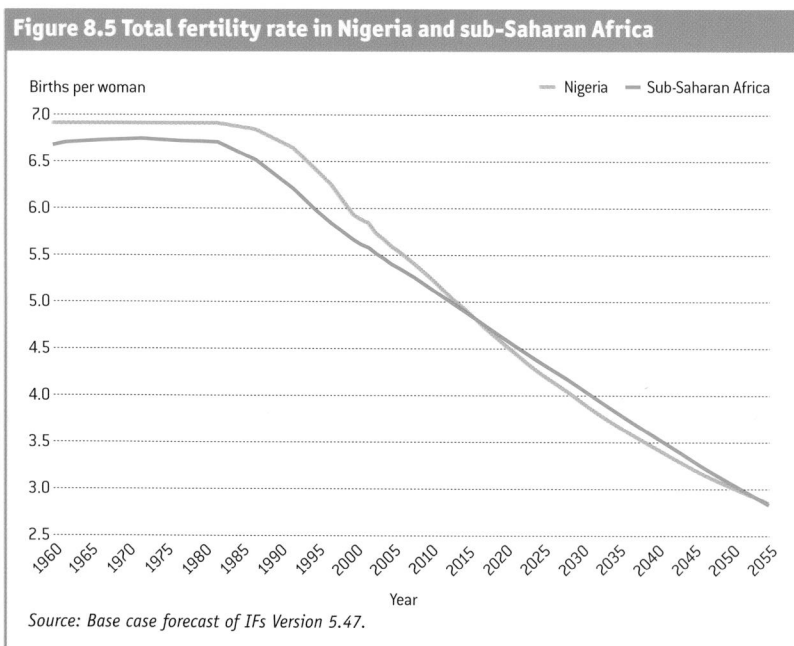

Figure 8.5 Total fertility rate in Nigeria and sub-Saharan Africa

Births per woman

—— Nigeria —— Sub-Saharan Africa

Year

Source: Base case forecast of IFs Version 5.47.

those, the challenge of HIV and AIDS, presents a window of threat rather than opportunity. The second is again governance, including the continued ability of the still-new postapartheid government to manage both the social and economic foundations of growth.

As in much of the southern region of Africa, the plague of HIV and the growing rate of AIDS-related deaths have very considerably reduced life expectancy. Figure 8.6 shows the historical pattern in South Africa and a forecast of recovery from the catastrophe in the IFs base case (tied to UNAIDS estimates).[11] It appears that a number of African countries have reached or nearly reached the peak year of HIV infection rates and have begun to reduce those rates. Uganda is often cited as such a success story, having reduced rates from perhaps 15 percent in the early 1990s to a UNAIDS estimate (2007: 17) of 7.5 percent among women and 5 percent among men in 2004–2005.

There remains very great uncertainty about the impact of HIV/AIDS on economies and broader societies. The costs of the epidemic include direct ones, such as prevention and treatment programs, and indirect ones, such as reduced labor force size and productivity and broader disruption to the social fabric. The United Nations Department of Economic and Social Affairs reviewed a substantial number of studies of the aggregate economic impact and found a wide range of calculations even for the same country, ranging "from 'small' to annual GDP growth rates of 2–4 percentage points lower than in the absence of AIDS" (UN ESA 2004: 89); on a per capita basis some studies have actually suggested accelerated growth.

Specifically for South Africa, the estimates of impact by two different studies ranged from a loss of less than 0.5 percent of annual GDP growth to a loss of 2.5 percent or more, as the country moves through the probable peak years of AIDS deaths (UN ESA 2004: 85). Although AIDS is almost certainly hurting South African growth, many other factors influence the probable future growth of the economy, including the price of various commodities, infrastructure adequacy, the impact of investments in human capital, the relationship among its various subpopulations, and, again, the quality of its governance. The IFs base case forecast is slightly higher than the historical pattern.

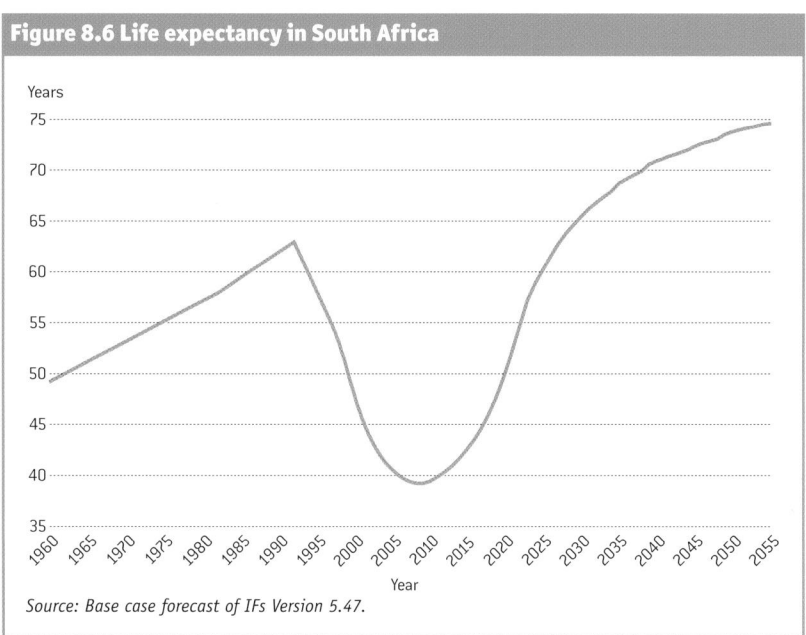

Figure 8.6 Life expectancy in South Africa

Source: Base case forecast of IFs Version 5.47.

Ethiopia

Ethiopia was the only country in Africa not colonized; in fact, it conquered other peoples.[12] It has a long and proud cultural history. It is also now landlocked and resource-poor, exemplifying the challenges of growth that Collier and others have associated with such characteristics. It entered the modern period with a divine monarch and feudal system, not particularly amenable to processes of modernization. A socialist system replaced that after 1974, and government land ownership remains a debilitating issue. It now faces a number of internal and external armed conflicts in the north, east, and south. In spite of its potential agricultural strength, drought has ravished it often. It may therefore not be surprising that its GDP per capita (PPP) is less than one-half that of sub-Saharan Africa as a whole.

The bases upon which economic growth might build are not obvious. Although the country is nearly twice the size of Texas, its population is nearly four times as large and overwhelmingly agricultural. The success of the struggle for independence by Eritrean rebels in 1991 not only eliminated the Ethiopian coastline, it set the stage for a long-term border dispute with its new neighbor, one that was especially bloody in 1998–2000.

Figure 8.7 shows that, despite all its problems, Ethiopia has posted slow economic growth since 1960 and some progress on the

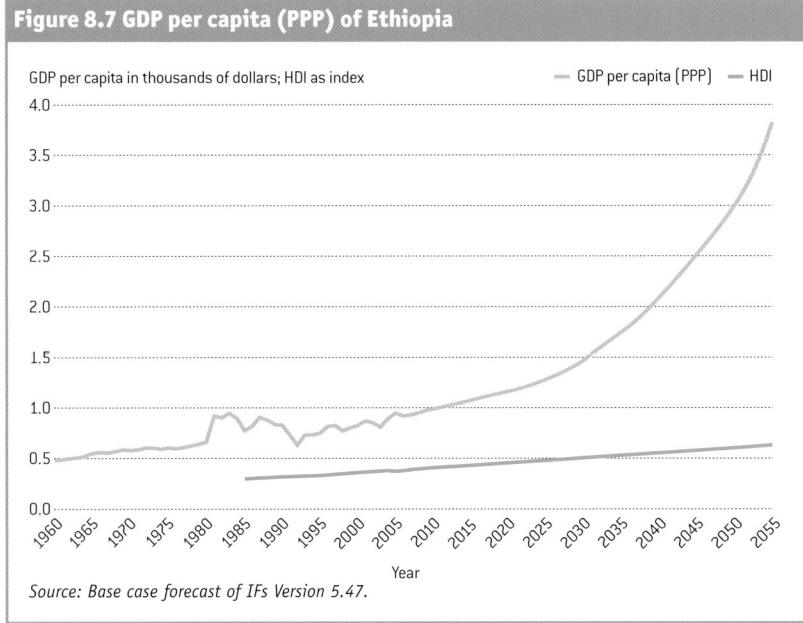

Figure 8.7 GDP per capita (PPP) of Ethiopia

GDP per capita in thousands of dollars; HDI as index

— GDP per capita (PPP) — HDI

Source: Base case forecast of IFs Version 5.47.

human development index. The base case of IFs continues that pattern. Moreover, the forecast suggests a gradual emergence of an industrial economy in the coming decades, facilitating a possible acceleration of economic growth through midcentury.

Democratic Republic of the Congo

In contrast to Ethiopia, the Democratic Republic of the Congo (DRC) had a colonial history among the most brutal and disruptive of the continent. When it gained independence from Belgium in 1960, it had a miserable legacy on which to build, and unfortunately Colonel Joseph Mobutu

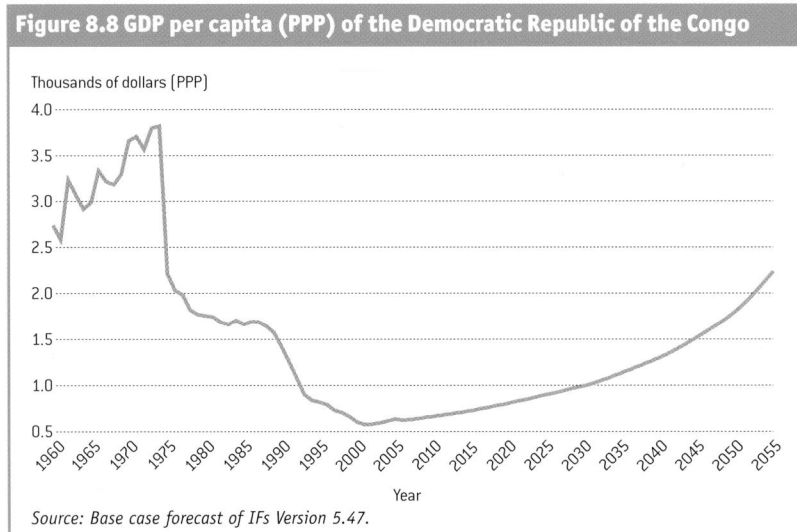

Figure 8.8 GDP per capita (PPP) of the Democratic Republic of the Congo

Thousands of dollars (PPP)

Source: Base case forecast of IFs Version 5.47.

raped rather than built. His overthrow in 1997 overlapped with a period of civil war, ultimately involving interventions by most of the country's neighbors. It is not surprising that the DRC has qualified for various lists of failed states in recent decades. The two top determinants with respect to its future progress might well be governance and conflict resolution, both of which interact closely with the high-priority issue of security sector reform.

After the election of 2006, violence died down enough to inspire hope, although it is far too early to judge whether that can truly be justified. Although UN forces entered in 1999, in 2007 some fighting continued, and there were still an estimated 1.1 million internally displaced persons. The vast geographic scope of the country, especially in the face of poor infrastructure, combined with both a wide range of ethnic groups and richness of natural resources, easily supports local conflict entrepreneurs (as among the Luba in Katanga) who can benefit from carving out their own strongholds. Figure 8.8 shows the historical collapse of GDP per capita (PPP), along with a base case scenario that only manages to regain the levels of the mid-1970s by 2055.

The experience of all four of these countries illustrates the great range of possible futures that Africa faces. Levels of GDP per capita have fluctuated sharply over the fifty years since the first of Africa's colonized regions gained independence. Promise appears substantial for some countries in the next fifty years, especially in the southern triangle of the continent. Risks appear huge for others, especially in the Horn of Africa. Look for more detailed forecasts on these and other countries in the volume appendixes.

Improvement in governance, an end to military conflicts, control of disease, and improvements in human capital and infrastructure look to be essential foundations for progress. The role of outside actors in making some of those possible or difficult may well also be substantial. For instance, China's push for secure access to raw materials has helped raise prices and economic growth rates, but created real anxiety around its impact on governance and other domestic foundations of long-term growth.

Extending the analysis

Returning to more integrated analysis of the continent, the United Nations Economic Commission for Africa (UN ECAF 2005) reviewed Africa's overall progress toward the Millennium Development Goals (MDGs). With respect to poverty, it calculated that the percentage of those in sub-Saharan Africa living in extreme poverty rose from 45 percent to 46 percent between 1990 and 2000, with absolute numbers climbing from 217 million to 290 million (UN ECAF 2005: 1). It also calculated that the completion rate for primary education fell from 57 to 55 percent between 1990 and 2000 (although attendance rose from 50 percent to 61.2 percent), and life expectancy declined from fifty to forty-six years. Although progress toward some of the MDGs did occur, including an increase in gender equity in education, a fall in infant mortality, and an increase in access to clean water, the overall prospects for meeting most MDGs in most African countries remain bleak. The UN ECAF did suggest (using primarily extrapolative methods) that Algeria, Botswana, Burkina Faso, Cameroon, Egypt, Ghana, Lesotho, Libya, Mauritius, Morocco, South Africa, Tunisia, and Uganda are likely to meet the first goal of halving the number in extreme poverty. The countries of Northern and Southern Africa obviously dominate that group.

What do the IFs scenarios suggest with respect, not just to 2015, but midcentury? Global progress toward the poverty target of the first MDG has been dominated by the great reduction in poverty within China. In somewhat analogous fashion, the discussion above has emphasized that what happens in Nigeria, Ethiopia, and the Democratic Republic of the Congo will heavily influence the extent of progress toward cutting the rate of extreme poverty by half within Africa.

There may be particular hope for two of the large-population countries and the regions they dominate. The earlier discussion indicated both the extreme level of poverty in Nigeria and the potential, which may not be fulfilled, for a substantial assault on it by 2030 with energy revenues. Gross governance failures and emergence of conflicts have created base case conditions so abysmal in the DRC that it is easy to imagine considerable bounceback in coming years. Table 8.4 shows how progress

in the broader regions of these two countries could reverse the continent's slight increase in extreme poverty during the 1990s. In fact, the commodity boom of the early twenty-first century has begun to do that for many countries. If such progress is maintained and spreads, the base case of IFs actually foresees the possibility that extreme poverty in sub-Saharan Africa could drop to 30 percent by 2015, well short of the reduction called for in the first MDG but still very meaningful. The 2015 goal for extreme income poverty might be met by 2025.

The per capita growth rates (PPP) underlying such a base case are hardly astonishing. In fact, after the losses in the 1990s, they involve very slow increases to about 2 percent annually in the late 2020s (with a continuing increase in the base case to about 3 percent by midcentury). Should such early growth be accomplished, the poverty gap would decline even more rapidly than would the percentage rate of extreme poverty, cutting the gap for sub-Saharan Africa as a whole from nearly 20 percent in 2000 to less than half that before 2025. Given the experience of the continent since independence and the failed hope of the commodity boom in the 1970s, caution is warranted in putting forward the possibility that this time might be different and that significant progress might be made against extreme poverty.

It seems quite likely that the setting of poverty goals globally beyond 2015 will begin shifting attention from $1 to $2 per day. Slightly more than three-quarters of the population of sub-Saharan Africa now lives below $2, and that percentage is unlikely to drop below 65 percent by 2015. Over 600 million people may still live on less than $2 per day, and the number will likely be rising. Table 8.4 suggests how slowly that higher level of poverty may decline. And when the spotlight does shift to $2, Egypt will fall within the beam. Although only about 2 percent of its population live on less than $1 per day, more than 40 percent live on less than $2, and the IFs base case places that number at 22 percent even in 2015.

Conceptualizations of poverty repeatedly emphasize that much more than income is involved. In particular, Sen has emphasized human capabilities. The second MDG calls for universal primary education completion, redundantly but usefully emphasizing that the

Table 8.4 Poverty and development indicators in African regions

Extreme Poverty Rate	Eastern	Middle	Northern	Southern	Western	SSA
2000	42.8	40.9	7.3	14.8	54.1	44.5
2015	37.6	24.7	2.7	8.7	28.3	30.2
2050	10.2	18.4	0.9	1.9	19.0	14.6
Moderate Poverty						
2000	77.8	77.9	34.5	35.3	84.1	76.8
2015	72.1	57.2	17.7	24.2	70.8	66.1
2050	23.0	54.3	4.4	6.8	54.9	40.1
Poverty Gap						
2000	18.8	16.7	2.3	5.9	25.9	20.1
2015	15.8	9.8	0.7	3.2	10.4	12.0
2050	4.1	6.5	0.2	0.6	6.9	5.4
GDP per Capita (PPP)						
2000	950	1,076	3,718	8,326	1,089	1,611
2015	1,258	1,339	5,072	9,856	1,899	1,458
2050	5,065	2,352	14,360	24,110	3,026	4,525
Net Primary Enrollment						
2000	54.8	51.2	80.7	88.2	56.8	54.4
2015	66.4	60.9	90.7	97.1	68.1	68.1
2050	88.5	83.1	98.3	99.7	89.4	88.2
Life Expectancy						
2000	44.8	43.5	66.9	47.5	46.9	45.6
2015	51.6	44.6	68.9	42.3	47.9	48.5
2050	67.6	60.3	80.4	73.8	63.8	65.0
HDI						
2000	0.44	0.45	0.65	0.65	0.43	0.45
2015	0.53	0.48	0.71	0.66	0.48	0.51
2050	0.73	0.64	0.88	0.91	0.66	0.70
HPI-1						
2000	42.8	41.0	26.3	27.5	43.5	41.6
2015	37.1	39.5	19.5	30.4	39.6	38.0
2050	22.7	26.3	10.1	14.9	27.6	24.9

Note: SSA = sub-Saharan Africa; HPI = human poverty index.

Source: Base case forecast of IFs Version 5.47.

goal applies to boys and girls alike. The UN ECAF (2005: 13) suggested that Algeria, Botswana, Cape Verde, Egypt, Gabon, Mauritius, Namibia, Rwanda, São Tomé and Principe, Seychelles, South Africa, Togo, Tunisia, and Zimbabwe are likely to meet the goal. Gross enrollment rates for that set of countries, including older than appropriated age students in primary school, are already at or above 100 percent, theoretically making it "only" necessary for them to bring net, of-age enrollments to 100 percent to accomplish the goal.

That list, however, excludes three of the four large countries in Africa that this chapter has explored in most depth. Thus it is not surprising that, as is now widely understood, the universal goal never was reasonable for Africa by 2015. In fact, Table 8.4 makes clear that it will be a real challenge for several regions of the continent even by 2050. Michael A. Clemens (2004) has pointed out that developing countries today are, in fact, making considerably more rapid progress toward 90 percent completion of primary education than did the currently developed countries a century earlier—and the last 10 percent is particularly difficult.

Life expectancy captures many capabilities and aspects of well-being fundamental to poverty. Beneath the numbers in Table 8.4 are three very different historical trajectories in African regions in the coming years. First, Northern Africa has been essentially unscathed by the AIDS epidemic and is on track to see life expectancies essentially converge with those of the world's richest countries. Second, Southern Africa, with a life expectancy above sixty in the early 1990s (roughly comparable to Northern Africa), has fallen back dramatically. The South may have difficulties reclosing the gap even if the epidemic wanes as anticipated in the IFs base case, but should regain considerable momentum. Third, life expectancy in most of the rest of Africa, although less devastated by HIV/AIDS, has never reached very high levels.

The human development index summarizes the state of human capabilities across health, knowledge, and income dimensions. The human poverty index (HPI-1) focuses on the portion of the population especially disadvantaged in terms of measures such as illiteracy and lack of access to clean water. In spite of the devastation of AIDS, the gap in Africa on these two broader measures of capabilities definitively separates the North and South from the rest of sub-Saharan Africa. The high income and life expectancy advantages of the North are offset by its significant disadvantage in literacy rates, which are quite comparable to those of Eastern, Western, and Middle Africa. As emphasized repeatedly, poverty is a many-faceted phenomenon.

Scenario analysis and African poverty

Chapter 7 explored a substantial series of interventions, domestic and international, that might have potential for reducing poverty, and it created a combined intervention scenario. The scenario included a large range of interventions involving both domestic and international action. In short, the scenario explored a "big push" with respect to global poverty reduction, but with interventions at regional levels that

were generally tailored to shortfalls relative to the benchmark levels of specific interventions based on GDP per capita.

The scenario demonstrated potentially significant power to reduce extreme global poverty faster than the current, already substantial course of reduction. Figure 8.9 shows the implications for Africa specifically. Through the horizon of the Millennium Development Goals, the scenario does not materially reduce poverty, for three primary reasons. First, the scenario introduced interventions relative to the base case only in 2007—the MDG horizons, as this volume has repeated stressed, are nearly upon us. Second, the scenario phased in interventions because it takes time to introduce policies and structures that are substantial changes from past patterns. Finally, change is disruptive and sometimes even costly; most notably, increasing investment rates in the scenario came with some midterm cost with respect to consumption levels, a key driver of poverty.

In the longer term, however, the scenario greatly reduces the forecast of extreme poverty in Africa below the relatively stable numbers of the base case. By midcentury, more than 200 million fewer people live in poverty.

There are, of course, an infinite number of possible future scenarios for Africa (Sall 2003 developed four important ones). Some might

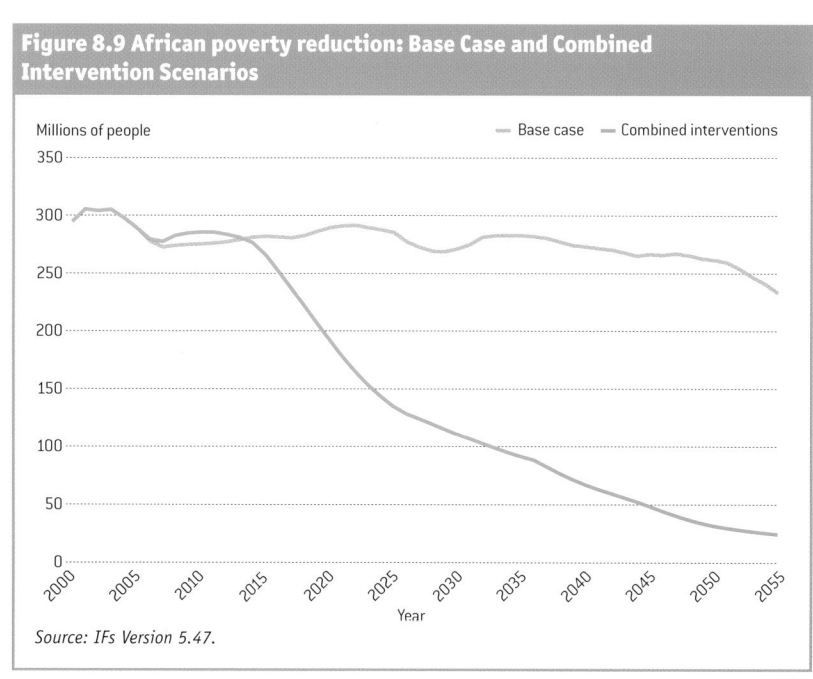

Figure 8.9 African poverty reduction: Base Case and Combined Intervention Scenarios

Millions of people

Base case — Combined interventions

Year

Source: IFs Version 5.47.

help accelerate poverty reduction even relative to the combined intervention scenario. For instance, should the planned movement toward an East African Federation in 2013 (to include Kenya, Uganda, and Tanzania and possibly of Rwanda and Burundi) succeed on the foundation of the East African Community Customs Union and a Common Market planned for 2010, advocates believe that the region would experience accelerated growth. Other regional integrative efforts are in various stages of planning and implementation, including the Southern African Development Community to which Tanzania also belongs. Historical experience with regional integration schemes among developing countries has, however, often found that economic spillback effects (concentration of benefits in already richer countries) compete with positive spillover effects, making it difficult to know whether such efforts can persist politically and succeed economically.

The acceleration of economic growth in Africa in the second half of the 1990s has raised hope that more positive scenarios for Africa, like the combined intervention scenario, could come to pass. Jean-Claude Berthélemy and Ludvig Soederling (2001) explored the possibility that six countries (Burkina Faso, Côte d'Ivoire, Ghana, Mali, Tanzania, and Uganda) might become African versions of emerging countries, adding 2–3 percent to their growth rates in coming years. Unfortunately, internal developments in some have already put such possibilities at risk.

We should also remember that some wild card scenarios could actually make poverty worse than in the base case. The IFs project has explored the possible implications for numbers living in poverty in South Africa in the base case and in a scenario positing a major failure to control HIV and AIDS, possibly as a result of adverse mutations in the virus. The specific assumptions in the scenario pushed the peak of the global epidemic from 2015 to 2035 and doubled the growth rate in infections in Africa. Instead of the numbers living in extreme poverty falling from 300 million at the start of the century as in the combined intervention scenario, they rise very substantially.

It might be reasonable to argue, nonetheless, that the African base case explored in this section is more likely to have erred on the side

> ● Current expectations make pleasant surprises in Africa and unpleasant ones in Asia more likely than the reverse. ●

of pessimism than of optimism. Simon Johnson, Jonathan D. Ostry, and Arvind Subramarian (2007) explored the possibility that a number of African countries have in place the fundamentals, including improvements in governance, to support takeoffs to sustained growth. The initial conditions and parameters of all models come from historical patterns, which have not been good for Africa in recent decades. As the next section will discuss with respect to Asia, the reverse might be the case there—rapid economic growth, especially in China and more recently in India, has led to very optimistic expectations for future poverty reduction, giving rise perhaps to more downside risk than upside potential relative to many contemporary forecasts.

Asia
Scanning the continent

There are fifty countries or political units in the UN's Asia region and forty-six in the IFs representation of Asia and the Pacific. Some in IFs, notably Hong Kong, Taiwan, and Palestine, have complicated political statuses and are not traditionally defined nation-states with sovereignty that the entire global community recognizes. Partly for this reason, our analysis uses the word "country" rather than "nation-state." These less well-defined entities, whatever their label, contain significant populations that merit our attention.

Together the countries of Asia and the Pacific contain nearly 4 billion of the world's people. They are also home to approximately two-thirds of those living in extreme poverty. In addition, nearly three-fourths of those who live on less than $2 per day are in Asia. Although poverty may be declining considerably more rapidly in Asia than in Africa, global poverty remains a heavily Asian phenomenon in terms of numbers.

The regions of Asia are, like those of Africa, not a fully fixed and universally recognized set. Four regions are nearly standard. See Map 8.2 for three of them: South-Central Asia, Southeast Asia, and East Asia. South-Central Asia includes not only the countries of the Indian peninsula but those that emerged from the Turkic republics of the former Soviet Union. The latter make up Central Asia. In terms of extreme poverty, the Indian Peninsula of South-Central Asia contains the greatest concentration of all

Map 8.2 Asian regions

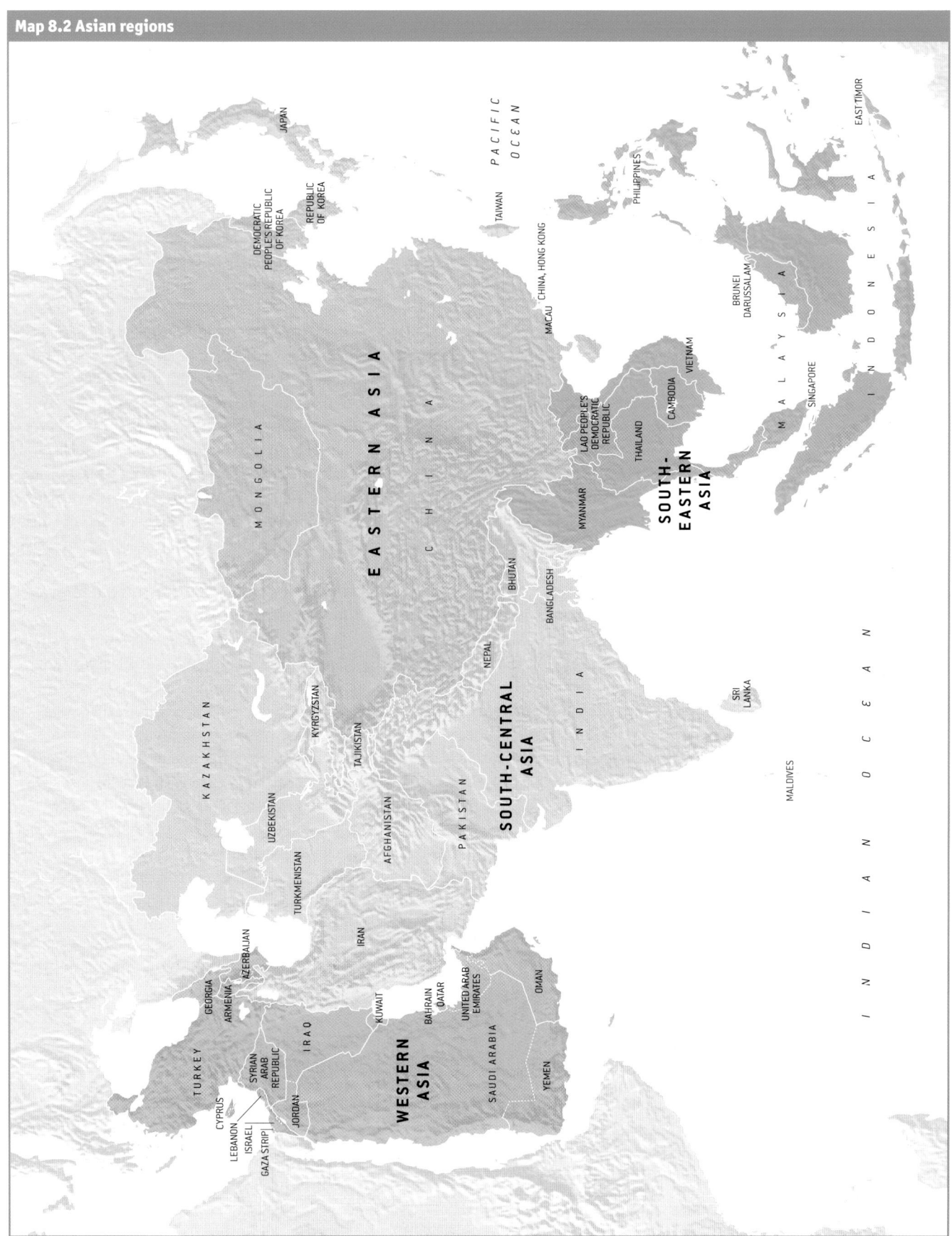

global regions, with especially large numbers in India, Bangladesh, and Pakistan. Indonesia is the demographically largest country in Southeast Asia. Although considerably smaller in population, Burma/Myanmar has a roughly comparable number of people living in extreme poverty. China dominates East Asia in population.

Western Asia, the least poor portion of Asia, contains the countries of the Middle East and the Caucasus.[13] Demographically, it is the smallest of the Asian regions, and Turkey is the largest of its countries. Asia and the Pacific (as opposed to Asia itself) contains another potential region of importance, namely Oceania, with Australia, New Zealand, and the small Pacific states. Populations and poverty numbers in that region are so much smaller than the rest of Asia that it will not be considered separately here.

Are there other important categorizations of countries in Asia like those that Collier and his colleagues defined for Africa? Only about 120 million of the nearly 4 billion people in the region live in landlocked countries, and some of those, in Central Asia, possess substantial oil and natural gas resources. The set of landlocked, resource-poor countries is small: Afghanistan, Armenia, Kyrgyzstan, Laos, Mongolia, Nepal, and Tajikistan. A number of them, especially Afghanistan, illustrate the development perils of that status. In contrast, however, Mongolia, although poor, demonstrates that geography has a complicated relationship with destiny.

Countries that have been racked by conflict, including Afghanistan, Cambodia, Indonesia, Palestine, and Sri Lanka, also could perhaps more productively be separated from the larger set for some special attention, but this analysis has not done so.

Thus Table 8.5 shows the percentage living in extreme poverty for the standard four Asian regions. The percentage within South-Central Asia is about twice that of East Asia, and the base case forecast is for it to decrease more slowly. Because the population of both those regions is near 1.5 billion, the number in extreme poverty in South-Central Asia was also nearly twice as high as that in East Asia early in this century, and, over time, that ratio is likely to increase considerably. The poverty percentages in the other two regions are lower, and the populations are much lower. Table 8.5 thus makes even clearer what we already knew: the study of poverty in Asia especially requires that we drill down into South-Central Asia and East Asia, looking especially at India and China.

Understanding the historical patterns of large Asian countries

Although China and India dominate the extreme poverty headcount in Asia, Bangladesh takes a clear third place. In terms of the numbers of poor, all three stand in a class by themselves in spite of great differences across them. At the beginning of the twenty-first century, IFs estimates the number in extreme income poverty in Bangladesh to have been nearly 50 million, that in China to have been over 200 million, and that in India to have been over 350 million. Other countries in Asia with more than 10 million people living in extreme poverty are Myanmar, Indonesia, Pakistan, and the Philippines. Except for Pakistan with 20 million, the others all have 15 million or fewer in that condition. Thus, in spite of the importance of poverty everywhere, this discussion will focus heavily on the big three.

China has the highly enviable status of being the country with the most rapid reduction of poverty in the world since the 1980s, bringing those in extreme poverty down from 33 percent of the population in 1990 to 10 percent in 2004 (World Bank 2008: 46), thereby already having greatly exceeded the first Millennium Development Goal. Although income distribution

Table 8.5 Extreme poverty rates in Asian regions

| Year | Asian regions | | | |
	Eastern	South-Central	Southeast	Western
2000	14.6	31.2	10.6	6.5
2005	10.0	25.3	8.5	4.1
2010	4.8	19.4	6.3	2.3
2015	2.7	15.5	5.4	1.7
2020	1.7	11.1	4.2	1.6
2025	1.0	6.9	3.4	1.7
2030	0.5	4.8	2.9	1.9
2035	0.4	4.0	2.4	1.3
2040	0.3	3.3	1.8	0.7
2045	0.2	2.7	1.4	0.4
2050	0.1	2.4	1.1	0.4
2055	0.0	2.2	0.8	0.4

Source: Base case forecast of IFs Version 5.47.

has deteriorated, the growth of GDP has been so rapid that the rate of poverty has plummeted. Thus before turning to the future of poverty in China and elsewhere in Asia, it bears asking how China has accomplished this remarkable feat.

One standard explanation for the success of China is the quality of its governance. A second and related one is the specific nature of the policies its government has adopted, including (1) the development of human capital and (2) China's economic openness to the outside world. Table 8.6 helps historically compare China to India and Bangladesh on these dimensions.

With respect to governance, the World Bank's project on Governance Matters has compiled six measures of governance for 213 countries from 1996 through 2006. The project facilitates comparison with other countries globally and in the same income category, which for China is lower-middle. China's percentile calculation on those measures varies from a low of 6.3 percent on voice and accountability (compare with an average of 40 percent for its income group) through 30.5 percent on control of corruption (compare with 39.1 percent) and 40.6 percent on the rule of law (compare with 38.6 percent) to a high of 52.2 percent on government effectiveness (compare with 39.9 percent).[14] In addition to the democratic deficit indicated by China's score on voice and accountability, it is this last measure, government effectiveness, on which China stands out from countries at comparable levels of income.

The definition of governance effectiveness includes such seemingly important attributes such as "the quality of public services, the quality of the civil service … [and] the quality of policy formulation and implementation."[15] Table 8.6 shows that China does, in fact, exceed the performance of its large and poor Asian neighbors on this measure. Yet the relative performance shortfall of India has narrowed substantially since the 1990s, perhaps one of the reasons for India's more recent acceleration of economic growth (and China's high score in 1996 should be considered in the context of a score of 48.3 in 1998).

The measure of governance that normally receives the greatest analytical and policy attention is corruption, the misuse of public office for personal gain. Corruption is not easily measured, but perceptions of it can be obtained from those who interact with a government. The most widely known measure of corruption perceptions is that of Transparency International (TI), which correlates very highly with that of the World Bank but offers a longer time series. Table 8.6 therefore uses the TI measure to show corruption perceptions (higher numbers are less corrupt) for the three high-poverty Asian countries. Note that China scores at very much the same level as India, both of which are well above Bangladesh. The World Bank also shows a substantial deterioration for China on this measure, with a fall from 52.5 percent in 1998 to 44.2 percent in 2000 and scores below 40 percent thereafter.

Table 8.6 Development drivers in Asian regions			
Effectiveness of governance	China	India	Bangladesh
1996	66.80	50.70	27.00
2000	55.50	52.60	38.40
2006	55.50	54.00	23.70
Corruption perception			
1983	5.1	3.7	0.8
1996	2.4	2.6	2.3
2006	3.3	3.3	2.0
Life expectancy			
1962	54	46	41
1982	69	61	58
2005	72	64	64
Adult literacy			
1970	53	33	25
1990	78	49	34
2006	91	61	43
Economic freedom			
1980	3.8	4.9	3.1
1990	4.2	4.8	4.2
2007	5.9	6.7	5.8
Trade openness			
1970	3.7	8.1	20.8
1990	31.9	15.7	19.7
2005	69.3	44.7	39.6
FDI inflows as % of GDP			
1980	0.03	0.04	0.05
1990	0.98	0.08	0.01
2003	3.78	0.71	0.20

Source: Base case forecast of IFs Version 5.47.

Thus overall, China's advantage in governance quality is not strikingly obvious, especially relative to India, unless that advantage is, in fact, authoritarian leadership by very progrowth elites (as in Singapore and Malaysia). A more obvious and less controversial advantage may be seen in some of China's policies. Table 8.6 shows the results of very strong emphasis in China after the communist revolution on the development of human capital. Life expectancy surged in China during the 1960s and 1970s, and literacy rates were already high and climbing in the 1970s, when economic growth accelerated sharply.

In addition to the investments that China made in human capital as a foundation for its recent economic success, it has become perhaps even more common to point to the transition that China made, especially since 1978, in its economic policies. Deng Xiaoping and other pragmatists began at about that time to structure "socialism with Chinese characteristics." Economic liberalization involved many elements of reducing the state role in the economy, such as allowing farmers to market surplus crops and opening China to the outside world. Table 8.6 shows the progression of all three of the highest-poverty Asian states toward economic freedom, defined by the Fraser Institute to emphasize the ability to acquire, use, and exchange property.

Interestingly, the shift toward economic freedom in China, as measured by the Fraser Institute and reinforced by the Heritage Foundation's measure of economic freedom, does not appear any more pronounced than that of India.[16] What is more clear-cut with respect to China is trade openness. The table therefore shows a standard measure of economic openness to the world, namely exports plus imports as a percentage of GDP. On that measure, China's transition from the most closed of the three countries to the most open is dramatic in magnitude and speed. It is also interesting that the levels that Bangladesh and India reached by 2005 were reached by China only in 1999 and 2000, respectively. That is, India and Bangladesh appear on a similar track, less than a decade behind.

If China's relative advantage in trade is striking, it is dramatic with respect to foreign direct investment. The Chinese began to distinguish themselves from India and Bangladesh in the early 1980s, very quickly after the initiation of economic reform, and thereafter greatly widened their lead. Taxes on foreign direct investment (FDI) that give it preferential treatment relative to domestic firms certainly has explained part of the attractiveness of China to external funds (and also has somewhat distorted the accounting by encouraging round-tripping of funds from China through Hong Kong and back to China). On this measure, Bangladesh and India lag behind China by twenty years.

In summary, the answer to the question of how China managed to greatly accelerate its economic growth and reduce poverty since 1980 is almost certainly more complex than sometimes suggested. Clearly, general economic reforms and governance quality have played roles. So, too, however, did attention to human capital development and some very specific policy initiatives.

Exploring Future Asian Poverty: The Case of India

What about the future of poverty in China, India, Bangladesh, and other Asian countries? Figure 8.10 continues the focus on the three Asian countries with the highest numbers of those living in extreme poverty and shows three quite different patterns in base case forecasts. In the case of China, the very rapid reduction of recent decades is likely to continue, driven by high economic growth rates. In the case of Bangladesh, the numbers living in poverty also may drop, but at a considerably slower rate. Still, even in Bangladesh, the goal of cutting the rate of income poverty in half before 2015 appears quite feasible.

In many respects, the most important and complicated case is India. It is fundamentally important because close to half of those living in extreme poverty in Asia and the Pacific are in India and because its poverty rate at the turn of the century was among the very highest in the region. It is complicated because (1) economic growth has accelerated considerably in recent years, but it has not yet established a pattern of longer-term high growth that provides high confidence in its continuation; and (2) India is, in essence, a continent of its own, with a population that will likely pass China to become the largest in the world by about 2050. India also is highly heterogeneous on many dimensions, so that it is especially difficult to explore poverty futures for the country as a whole.

India thus merits special attention as a case study on the future of poverty. Map 8.3 shows its states and union territories. One common aggregation of those (used, for instance, in the *Human Development Reports* for India) is into Middle India, North-Central India, Northeast India, Southern India, West Bengal, and West India. Middle India is of special interest to us. It contains the states of Bihar, Chhattisgarh, Jharkhand, Madhya Pradesh, Orissa, and Uttar Pradesh.[17]

The largest of the subregions, Middle India contains more than 400 million of India's more than 1.1 billion people. It contains about 190 million (more than half) of India's citizens living in extreme poverty, thereby accounting for more than one-fourth of the extreme poverty in Asia and the Pacific and about one-sixth of that globally.[18] Moreover, it has been growing less rapidly economically and more rapidly demographically than the rest of India.

The IFs base case forecasts for poverty across all subregions (see Table 8.7) shows that these various characteristics of Middle India also make it likely that, in contrast to all other subregions of the country, poverty numbers may be relatively unchanged through the MDG target year of 2015. In fact, by 2015 the subregion could account for about 45 percent of all extreme poverty in Asia and the Pacific, and by 2030 it could account for 50 percent.

There are a variety of reasons for the difficult situation of Middle India. The area is more agricultural than the rest of India but has a very high population density (more than 11 people per hectare of cropland, about twice that of India as a whole and seven times that of the United States). Its urban population is less than 20 percent of the total, compared to 30 percent nationally. The literacy rate of Middle India is about 50 percent, compared to over 60 percent for the country as a whole. Life expectancy is about three years less than India as a whole. Both the gender empowerment measure and the human development index are about 0.5 in Middle India, compared to 0.6 for all of India. Access to safe water is available to under 60 percent of region, more than in the Northeast or the North Mountainous areas, but about 6 percent below the national average.

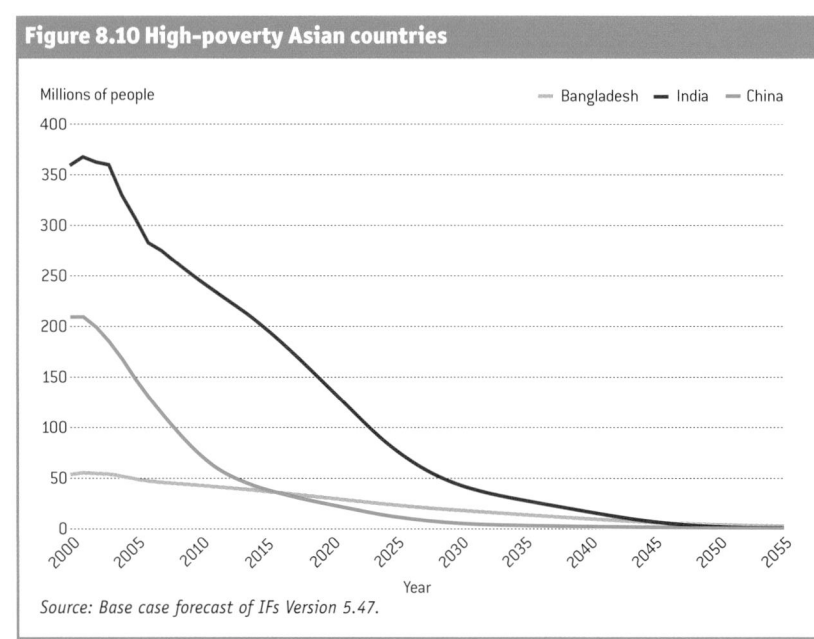

Figure 8.10 High-poverty Asian countries

Source: Base case forecast of IFs Version 5.47.

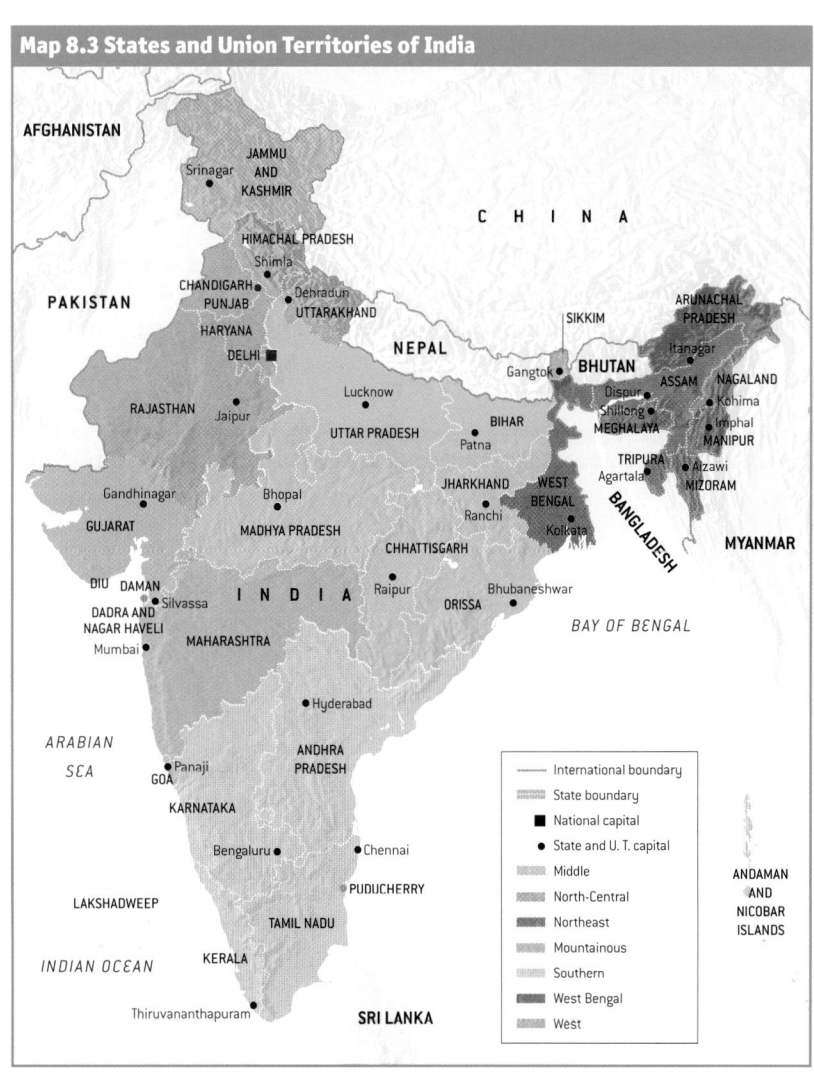

Map 8.3 States and Union Territories of India

Table 8.7 Poverty numbers in subregions of India

| Year | Millions of people living on less than $1 per day | | | | | | |
	Middle	North-Central	Northeast	Mountainous	Southern	West Bengal	West
2000	192.9	22.0	17.8	0.7	53.3	28.8	36.6
2005	186.7	17.6	14.9	0.6	43.3	23.3	23.7
2010	176.6	12.2	10.5	0.3	29.8	16.0	14.4
2015	174.6	8.3	7.1	0.2	19.8	10.5	8.8
2020	164.7	4.8	4.0	0.1	11.8	6.0	4.5
2025	134.3	2.1	1.8	0.0	5.9	2.8	1.6
2030	98.5	0.8	0.7	0.0	2.8	1.2	0.6
2035	73.0	0.3	0.3	0.0	1.2	0.5	0.2
2040	57.6	0.1	0.1	0.0	0.5	0.3	0.1
2045	43.2	0.0	0.0	0.0	0.2	0.1	0.1
2050	20.1	0.0	0.0	0.0	0.0	0.0	0.0
2055	6.3	0.0	0.0	0.0	0.0	0.0	0.0

Source: Base case forecast of IFs Version 5.47 (Special India Release).

Although the analogy should be treated very cautiously, there are some similarities between the states of Middle India and the landlocked countries of sub-Saharan Africa. Like those countries in Africa, the Indian states are sometimes resource-rich but generally suffer relative to coastal areas from access to global markets. Moreover, transportation infrastructure weaknesses and even interstate border controls disrupt the free flow of goods to the rest of India.

● *Middle India is the hard core of Indian poverty.* ●

Asian poverty: Now you don't see it, now you do

Even Middle India appears likely to experience diminishing extreme poverty after about 2015–2020. Relative to Africa, the fight against poverty in Asia has been and appears likely to continue to be a success story. The base case forecast of IFs shows extreme poverty numbers in Asia and the Pacific dropping below those of Africa before 2020. Many therefore consider the discussion about the future of poverty to be a discussion primarily of Africa.

Yet even if the superior economic performance of Asia relative to Africa prevails through midcentury, the populations in Asia are so large that the center of gravity with respect to global poverty may well remain there. Over time it is very probable that the focus on poverty among the poorest will shift from $1 and $2 per day to $2 and $5 or even $5 and $10 per day. Figure 8.11 forecasts the count of those living on less than $5 per day in Asia, Africa, and Latin America. Asia is likely to have the largest number of those living on less than $5 until midcentury. Even the crossover point for those living on less than $2 per day is unlikely before 2035.

Moreover, even the battle against extreme poverty will likely rage through midcentury in some parts of Asia. For example, Afghanistan and Pakistan are two of the most challenging countries in the continent. They have some of the most rapidly growing populations in the

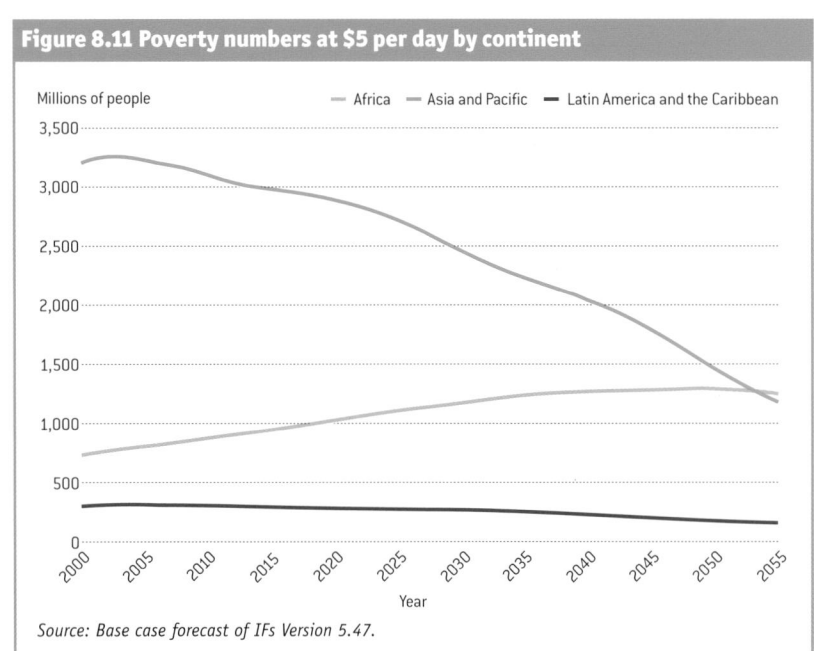

Figure 8.11 Poverty numbers at $5 per day by continent

Millions of people

— Africa — Asia and Pacific — Latin America and the Caribbean

Source: Base case forecast of IFs Version 5.47.

world. In the case of Afghanistan, the return of refugees has added to the weight of population, but both countries have total fertility rates near 5.0. In addition, both countries have youth bulges (the portion of population between fifteen and twenty-nine years of age) that exceed 45 percent. Both have suffered substantial internal conflict and governance problems that have often disrupted economic growth and have led them to be labeled either failed states or in danger of being such. The base case posits gradually accelerating growth in GDP per capita, assumptions that many observers might argue are overly optimistic. Nonetheless, the numbers in extreme poverty in Afghanistan climb steadily until 2030 and then stabilize, and those in Pakistan begin to fall only after 2020. The reader will find more details on these and other countries in the forecast tables that conclude this volume.

Scenario analysis and Asian poverty

The earlier discussion of Africa turned our attention back to the combined intervention scenario of Chapter 7, comparing its forecast for continental reduction in extreme poverty with that of the base case (see Figure 8.9). The combined intervention scenario has relatively little impact on the long-term profile of those living in extreme poverty in Asia because the numbers by midcentury are fewer than 100 million in either case. The combined intervention scenario does substantially reduce so-called moderate poverty in Asia relative to the base case, leaving nearly 250 million fewer people at $2 or below by midcentury.

Yet overall, the combined intervention scenario clearly has much less relative impact on Asia than it does on Africa, for straightforward reasons. The scenario interventions in Chapter 7 were built so as to bring performance of regions on a wide range of policy levers up to reasonable "good practice" values, given the levels of GDP per capita of the regions. In the case of much of Asia, performing at fairly high levels already, that meant considerably less aggressive assumptions for potential change than in Africa.

For the same reasons, the risk of error in the base case forecasts for Asia is to a greater degree being overly optimistic than it is for Africa, where it was argued that the base case might be overly pessimistic given the poor performance

of the continent in recent decades and therefore the substantial headroom for improvement.

How badly might the base case scenario itself overestimate the eventual course of poverty reduction for Asia? That is impossible to know, of course, but GDP per capita seldom grows for countries at more than about 2.5 percent per year for very long. China has been turning in rates closer to 7–9 percent for many years. The base case brings those rates down gradually to about 3 percent by midcentury. What if they were to drop much more precipitously, say to 2.5 percent by 2025? Similarly, India has moved its per capita growth rates (at market exchange rates, or MER) up toward 6 percent, and the base case allows those to stay near or above 6 percent until midcentury (per capita growth rates at PPP in the IFs base case are closer to 4 percent). What if, again, they were to decline to 2.5 percent by about 2025? A variety of forces that have operated historically, including domestic instability, international conflict, environmental problems, energy constraints, and plagues could function not only to bring rates down in such a fashion but even to push them down substantially faster or lower.

Figure 8.12 shows the quite dramatic implications of such assumption differences, especially for India. It looks at numbers living on less than $2 per day in the base case and what would happen if per capita growth in

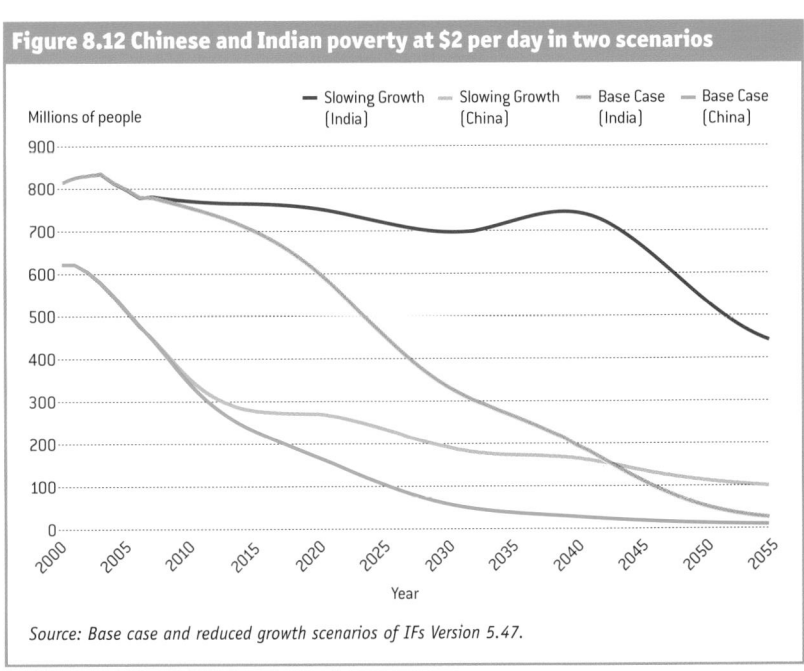

Figure 8.12 Chinese and Indian poverty at $2 per day in two scenarios

Source: Base case and reduced growth scenarios of IFs Version 5.47.

both countries were to slow to 2.5 percent by 2025. China's growth momentum and lower initial poverty gap (not shown) would allow poverty reduction to continue, albeit at a somewhat slower rate. In the case of India, however, numbers in poverty might essentially not change. Thus it bears repeating that if the IFs base case proves incorrect (which forecasts almost always are), the reality may prove to be more like the slow growth case than the combined intervention scenario.

The Americas
Scanning the continent

The geography of the Americas makes division of the continent into regions somewhat easier than is the case for Africa or Asia. An obvious and very common division is into North America, Central America, South America, and the Caribbean. For example, the United Nations divides the forty-one countries of the Americas into these groups.[19] For the purposes of analysis, one undesirable consequence of such partition is the common placement of Mexico with Central America, thereby overwhelming the demographically smaller members of the isthmus (Mexico's population is 2.5 times that of the other countries combined). For that reason, and because of the increasing integration of Mexico with the United States and Canada via the North American Free Trade Agreement (NAFTA), the analysis here uses the same basic four-part division but combines Mexico with North America (see Map 8.4).

Development-oriented international organizations like the United Nations and World Bank focus on Latin America and the Caribbean and generally exclude the United States and Canada from their analysis completely. That is the approach of the UN Economic Commission for Latin America and the Caribbean (ECLAC), whose analysis distinguishes the Caribbean countries from the rest of Latin America, treated often as a single region.

Are other potential divisions of the Americas of use in analysis of poverty? A focus on landlocked countries versus those with ocean access makes little sense, because only Bolivia and Paraguay lack direct access. There might be some basis for pulling out Bolivia, Ecuador, and Peru as poorer Andean countries, but Chile is both Andean and

relatively rich. There are, however, two divisions that observers inside and outside the region often see as important, especially when considering the future of poverty: (1) the size of indigenous populations, which tend to be most deeply mired in that poverty, and (2) the extent of foreign debt.

Indigenous populations make up about 10 percent of the total population of Latin America and the Caribbean, and poverty rates are considerably higher in the indigenous subpopulations of the region than in the larger population. For example, in Mexico predominantly indigenous municipalities were found to have a poverty incidence 4.5 times that of largely nonindigenous municipalities (Hall and Patrinos 2006). At the country level, ECLAC has estimated that the rate of poverty among indigenous peoples and Afro-descendents in Paraguay is 7.9 times that of the rest of the population (UN ECLAC 2005: 49). The multiples are 5.9 in Panama, 3.3 in Mexico, and 2.8 in both Guatemala and Chile. Across fourteen countries reviewed, only Costa Rica and Haiti have multiples at or near 1.0.

Although statistics on the size of indigenous populations are not very reliable, the rates are highest in Bolivia, Ecuador, Guatemala, Mexico, and Peru, each of which has more than 30 percent indigenous peoples, and all of which, except Mexico, are 44 percent or more indigenous. That set of countries does merit special attention. At the same time, however, many other countries in Latin America, including Chile, Colombia, the Dominican Republic, El Salvador, Nicaragua, Panama, Paraguay, and Venezuela, have high percentages of partly indigenous populations.

The second grouping of countries that may require special attention is that of heavily indebted poor countries (HIPC). Bolivia, Honduras, and Nicaragua have reached the completion points of the HIPC process, established to relieve some of that burden, and are therefore eligible for the full debt-relief available through it and also for further consideration under the newer Multilateral Debt Relief Initiative (MDRI). Haiti has reached the decision point in the HIPC process and is eligible for interim relief.

Scanning the poverty levels of the continent, regardless of how divisions of it are

Map 8.4 American regions

GREENLAND

C A N A D A

NORTH AMERICA

UNITED STATES OF AMERICA

BERMUDA (UK)

ATLANTIC OCEAN

MEXICO

CENTRAL AMERICA

CARIBBEAN

BELIZE
GUATEMALA   HONDURAS
EL SALVADOR   NICARAGUA
COSTA RICA

PACIFIC

OCEAN

PANAMA

VENEZUELA   SURINAM
GUYANA   FRENCH GUIANA

COLOMBIA

ECUADOR

SOUTH AMERICA

PERU   B R A Z I L

BOLIVIA

CHILE   PARAGUAY

URUGUAY

ARGENTINA

FALKLAND ISLANDS
(MALVINAS) (UK)

C A R I B B E A N

BAHAMAS

TURKS & CAICOS
ISLANDS (UK)

ANGUILA (UK)
BARBUDA
BRITISH   ANTIGUA
VIRGIN IS.
US (UK)   MONTSERRAT
VIRGIN IS.   (UK)
(US)
GUADELOUPE (F)

PUERTO
RICO (US)

CUBA   DOMINICAN
REPUBLIC

HAITI   DOMÍNICA
MARTINIQUE (F)
ST. KITTS & NEVIS   ST. LUCIA
BARBADOS
ST. VINCENT &
THE GRENADINES

CAYMAN
ISLANDS (UK)   JAMAICA

GRENADA
TOBAGO
TRINIDAD

CARIBBEAN SEA   ARUBA (NE)

NETHERLANDS
ANTILLES (NE)

made, requires that attention extend beyond the extreme level of $1 per day. Although 35 percent of Africans live on less than $1 per day, and 20 percent of Asians do so, only 6 percent in the Americas are at that level (10 percent when the United States and Canada are excluded). In its analysis of the region, the UN's ECLAC has chosen to use two alternative thresholds that it characterizes as indigence and poverty (see Table 8.8). The indigence line is defined in terms of the cost of a basic food basket. The poverty line has been defined as that income plus other resources for basic non-nutritional needs of households, estimated at 2 times the indigence line for urban areas and 1.75 times that line in rural areas (UN ECLAC

Table 8.8 UN ECLAC analysis of poverty

Percentages of poor and indigent population, measured by the International Line and National Lines (ECLAC), around 2000[a]

Countries	Populations living on less than US$ 1 per day		Indigent population		Population living on less than US$ 2 per day		Poor population	
Latin America	*9.5*	*2001*	*18.5*	*2001*	*24.5*	*2001*	*43.2*	*2001*
Argentina	3.3	2001	10.9	2001	14.3	2001	30.1	2001
Bolivia	14.4	1999	36.5	1999	34.3	1999	60.6	1999
Brazil	8.2	2001	13.2	2001	22.4	2001	37.5	2001
Chile	<2	2000	5,7	2000	9.6	2000	20.6	2000
Colombia	8.2	1999	26.8	1999	22.6	1999	54.9	1999
Costa Rica	2.0	2000	7.8	1999	9.5	2000	20.3	1999
Ecuador	17.7	1998	31.3	1999	40.8	1998	63.5	1999
El Salvador	31.1	2000	22.1	2001	40.8	2000	48.9	2001
Guatemala	16.0	2000	30.3	2002	37.4	2000	60.2	2002
Honduras	20.7	1999	56.8	1999	44.0	1999	79.7	1999
Mexico	9.9	2000	15.2	2000	26.3	2000	41.1	2000
Nicaragua	50.5	2001	42.3	2001	79.9	2001	69.4	2001
Panama	7.2	2000	10.7	1999	17.6	2000	30.2	1999
Paraguay	14.9	1999	33.9	1999	30.3	1999	60.6	1999
Peru	18.1	2000	22.4	1999	37.7	2000	48.6	1999
Dominican Republic	<2	1998	24.8	2000	<2	1998	46.9	2000
Uruguay	<2	2000	1.8	1999	3.9	2000	9.4	1999
Venezuela (Bolivarian Republic of)	15.0	1998	21.7	1999	32.0	1998	49.4	1999
Caribbean								
Grenada	4.7	1999						
Guyana	3.0	1998			11.2	1998		
Haiti	55.0	2001			76.0	2001		
Jamaica	<2	2000			13.3	2000		
Saint Lucia	25.4	1995			59,8	1995		
Saint Vincent and the Grenadines	5.6	1996						
Trinidad and Tobago	4.0	1992			20.0	1992		

Notes:

[a] The sources for the poverty estimates calculated using national and international lines are ECLAC and the World Bank, respectively (with the exception of the figures for some Caribbean countries.

Source: UN ECLAC, 2005, 27.

2004: 51). The numbers listed as indigent in Table 8.8 make clear that the indigence line is higher than the extreme poverty value of $1 per day. IFs calculates that a consumption level of about $1.55 per day produces the regionwide percentage of indigence reported by ECLAC and that $3.50 produces ECLAC's percentage that lives in poverty in 2000.

UN ECLAC is monitoring the progress of the region and its individual countries toward the MDGs, including that of reducing poverty rates as it defines them by one-half relative to 1990. As of 2004, fifteen of seventeen countries had made progress, the exceptions being Argentina and Venezuela. Unfortunately, UN ECLAC estimated the region as a whole to have progressed only 34 percent of the distance to the goal for 2015 while using 56 percent of the time period. The countries on target to reach the goal were Brazil, Chile (already having attained it), Ecuador, Mexico, Panama, and Uruguay. Countries lagging far behind the needed progress rate include Bolivia, Colombia, Honduras, Paraguay, and Peru (UN ECLAC 2005: 36). World Bank data, used in analysis with its PovcalNet tool, yield very similar results for the more common measure of extreme poverty. Given the nearness of 2015, this overall pattern is unlikely to change dramatically.

What about the longer-term future? Figure 8.13 shows the IFs base case forecasts through 2055 for the percentage living in poverty in Latin America and the Caribbean at $1, $2, $3.50, and $5 per day. All exhibit generally the same pattern of reduction. By midcentury the percentage living below $5 per day could well be reduced to about the level of those living at or below $2 in 2000.

Are the forecasts reasonable? In 2015 the base case of IFs anticipates that about 7 percent of the region will still be living in extreme income poverty compared to 10 percent in 1990 (World Bank 2008: 46). That is, the forecast is that the first MDG will not be met for the continents as a whole. Instead, about three-quarters of the distance toward cutting rates in half will have been traversed. That is generally comparable with the estimates above made by the UN ECLAC for progress through 2004, showing that progress through that year was about 61 percent of that needed to be on track to the goal. The IFs base

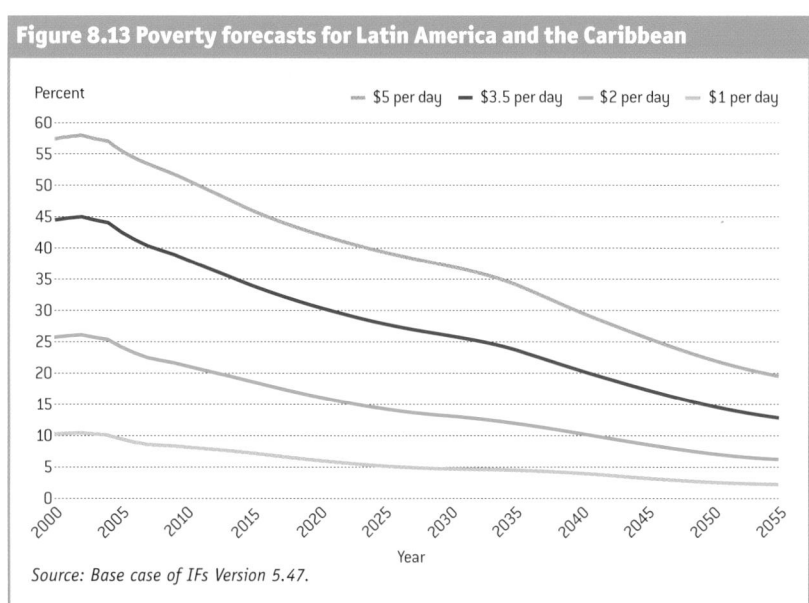

Figure 8.13 Poverty forecasts for Latin America and the Caribbean

Legend: $5 per day, $3.5 per day, $2 per day, $1 per day

Source: Base case of IFs Version 5.47.

case is therefore anticipating an acceleration of progress relative to the 1990–2004 period. Given the economic disruptions of those years, such a forecast may be optimistic but certainly not unreasonably so.

Table 8.9 disaggregates the continents, and the results are striking. Progress in South America is anticipated to be very substantial. In North America the $1 income poverty level only really picks up Mexico, but progress there, too, will likely be significant.[20] In sharp contrast, the forecasts for Central America and the Caribbean are for little change in poverty

Table 8.9 Forecasts of poverty by region of the Americas

| Year | Percent living in extreme income poverty | | | |
	Caribbean	Central	North	South
2000	21.0	17.3	1.4	9.4
2005	20.7	18.1	1.4	8.2
2010	22.9	19.6	1.1	6.3
2015	22.3	20.3	0.9	5.0
2020	17.1	17.9	0.7	4.2
2025	15.4	15.0	0.6	3.5
2030	15.0	14.9	0.5	3.0
2035	15.2	15.8	0.3	2.7
2040	15.8	14.1	0.3	2.1
2045	15.0	10.8	0.2	1.5
2050	12.6	9.2	0.2	1.0
2055	11.5	8.7	0.1	0.7

Source: Base case forecast of IFs Version 5.47.

rates through 2015. These forecasts contrast distinctly with the situation in the 1990s. During that decade, the percentage of those living in poverty in Central America dropped considerably, while the percentage in South America was relatively stable overall, actually climbing somewhat near the end of the decade, in part because of the loss of ground in Argentina and Venezuela.

Central America and the Caribbean contain a substantial number of the countries in the Americas with high levels of indigenous population and with high historical indebtedness. Earlier discussion noted the relatively high poverty rates in indigenous populations. It did not emphasize, however, that those poverty rates also appear especially resistant to change with GDP levels, whether GDP increases or decreases. World Bank analysis found that between 1994 and 2004, ironically identified as the Indigenous Peoples' Decade, "virtually no reduction occurred in the share of indigenous people in poverty" in four of five countries studied (World Bank 2006a: 4).

In addition, of course, high levels of indebtedness tend to lessen growth prospects and also mean that countries will endure structural reforms that often weaken household incomes relative to the overall size of the economy. For these reasons, the analysis here will focus especially on these two regions of the Americas.

The future of poverty in Central America and the Caribbean

Based on head counts and annual rates of income poverty for Central America and the Caribbean, the countries that require special attention when thinking about the future of poverty are Nicaragua, El Salvador, Guatemala, Honduras, and Haiti, especially the first and the last. Table 8.10 shows the IFs base case forecast for the number in extreme poverty in those five countries. Although the percentages living in poverty are likely to decrease significantly for all five before 2055, the absolute numbers living in poverty could well increase in all countries in coming years and, except for El Salvador, be worse or little improved by midcentury.

There are several reasons that these countries may fail to make greater strides against poverty. One is that population growth rates remain quite high. Although the rates are now coming down fairly rapidly, Central America is growing at just over 2 percent each year, and Nicaragua's rate is near 2.4 percent. In the Caribbean as a whole, the rate is closer to 1 percent, but Haiti is growing at about 2 percent. Per capita GDP growth in the last two decades of the twentieth century was quite weak.

The forecasts of IFs are, however, for generally stronger per capita growth in the first two decades of the twenty-first century. Among the sources of relative optimism for the region is the debt relief that has been put into place in recent years. At the turn of the century, the external debt burden of Honduras was near 100 percent of GDP and that of Nicaragua was an astounding 175 percent of GDP (by 2006 these numbers had fallen to 66 and 70 percent, respectively).[21] Haiti's debt burden is significant but not so large (22 percent in 2006), but that is because, as the poorest country in the Western Hemisphere and one that often is placed on lists of failed states, lending to it has been more limited.

Optimism with respect to the positive implications of debt relief might be somewhat misplaced, however, because such relief by itself will not significantly address the root problems of the two regions. Although calls for structural adjustment by the International Monetary Fund (IMF) and others may not be popular with the opponents of what they often term neoliberalism, there are some structural issues of

Table 8.10 Poverty in selected Central American and Caribbean countries

| Year | Number in extreme income poverty (millions) | | | | |
	El Salvador	Guatemala	Haiti	Honduras	Nicaragua
2000	1.2	1.2	4.2	1.2	2.3
2005	1.3	1.5	4.7	1.5	2.7
2010	1.5	1.8	5.3	1.8	3.4
2015	1.5	2.1	6.0	2.1	4.2
2020	1.3	2.0	6.4	2.0	4.2
2025	1.2	1.8	6.4	1.9	3.8
2030	1.2	1.8	6.3	2.2	4.2
2035	1.1	1.9	6.8	2.4	5.2
2040	0.9	1.7	7.5	2.0	5.3
2045	0.8	1.4	7.3	1.7	4.2
2050	0.7	1.1	6.2	1.6	3.8
2055	0.6	1.0	5.8	1.3	4.1

Source: Base case forecast of IFs Version 5.47.

significance for the region, in addition to rapid demographic growth, that require attention.

Among those structural problems are imbalances in trade and government accounts. Trade deficits are significant for many countries, with the resulting holes in external accounts traditionally filled by foreign aid, worker remittances, and borrowing. At the beginning of the twenty-first century, trade balances for the five countries of focus here ranged from a deficit of 11 percent in Guatemala to a deficit of 28 percent in Nicaragua. Similarly, in 2000 government revenue, excluding aid receipts, was in surplus relative to expenditures only in El Salvador and otherwise ranged from a deficit of 1.1 percent in Haiti to a deficit of 10.7 percent in Nicaragua. With aid receipts, most government balances were in surplus, but much of that aid was helping to cover payments on external debt, and provision of it may well be less generous in a future after debt relief. Household consumption ranged from 73 percent of GDP in Honduras to 87 percent in El Salvador, averaging 78 percent for the Caribbean and 76 percent for Central America, whereas South American countries as a whole averaged 63 percent. Such high household expenditure rates leave relatively little room for government spending and investment.

When structural imbalances such as those begin to correct, as they must either in agreements structured around debt relief or as foreign aid flows decline, all expenditure components can be squeezed and households almost invariably lose consumption power. Because the calculation of poverty in Table 8.10 is tied to consumption expenditures (as it is more generally in the analysis of this volume), the adjustment processes that are now or will soon be underway can give rise to lower consumption and greater poverty, even as GDP continues to grow. That is exactly the situation in the midrange forecasts presented here for much of Central America and the Caribbean. In the base case, the number of Central Americans living in extreme income poverty actually grows through 2015.

Yet, not all is bleak for the region. In contrast to the numbers living in extreme income poverty, the trajectory of the human poverty index (HPI-1) is steadily downward. Even in the base case, the forecast is for considerable improvement as the rate of death under forty declines, illiteracy falls, and access to safe water increases.

One substantial uncertainty with respect to the future of economic growth and poverty reduction in the region is the impact of the Dominican Republic-Central America Free Trade Agreement (DR-CAFTA), committing Costa Rica, the Dominican Republic, El Salvador, Guatemala, Honduras, and the United States to free trade. An analysis by the World Bank's Central America Department and Office of the Chief Economist for the Latin America and the Caribbean Region (undated) concludes that it will enhance growth and reduce poverty in the region, even in the near term. The analysis recognizes, however, a variety of structural adjustments that will inevitably occur and acknowledges the complications of understanding the dynamics of their unfolding, especially in interaction with substantial government budget constraints and therefore uncertain policy responses. The analysis here places more weight on the cost of the structural adjustments but also sees them as inevitable, with or without DR-CAFTA.[22]

Other stratifications that affect poverty in the Americas

Prominent among other important stratifications is the urban-rural division. Many who travel from richer to poorer countries and see the massive slum areas that often grow up around cities in developing countries conclude that poverty is primarily an urban phenomenon and that the urban poor would certainly live better in rural areas, with land to grow food and to support themselves. The reality is different. Very often urban slum dwellers have escaped from even greater rural poverty, where they had no land of their own or labored to eke out a living from small, poor-quality plots, to an environment in which they frequently have greater opportunity. Statistics bear out the urban-rural contrast. UN ECLAC (2005: 42) calculated the ratio of rates of indigence in rural to urban areas in thirteen Latin American countries and found them to range from 1.4 in Chile to 5.2 in Peru, with an unweighted average of 2.6. Clearly, this dimension of stratification interacts with the reality that the indigenous population tends more frequently to be rural.

Structural imbalances and the status of indigenous peoples pose a continuing threat to poverty reduction in Central America.

Another social stratification of great importance is sex. UN ECLAC (2005: 44–45) reports that, in rural areas of Latin America, 37 percent of women have no independent source of income, compared to 20 percent of men. In urban areas the percentages are 21 and 22, respectively, but other data show that women suffer greater poverty in urban areas as well, presumably as a result of lower incomes. A substantial climb in the workforce participation rate of women in the 1990s did occur, and further climbs could ameliorate income differentials.

Still another stratification of relevance to poverty is age. Poverty rates for children, for young adults between fifteen and twenty-four years of age, and for the elderly are substantially higher than for adults at the peak of their working years (UN ECLAC 2005: 45–48). Poverty among children often sets up a vicious cycle, as they move prematurely out of education and into efforts to earn a living, thereby impairing future prospects for themselves and their own children.

More generally, social stratifications, particularly those that are inherently persistent, like the distinction between indigenous and other populations, give rise to the chronic forms of poverty that Chapter 2 juxtaposed with more transient poverty. The importance of such stratification in Latin America might mean that forecasts of poverty reduction made using formulations that do not explicitly differentiate population subgroups (like those in Figure 8.13 and Table 8.9) are overly optimistic.

Foundations for future poverty reduction and the potential for acceleration

Although there are many factors, especially in Central America and the Caribbean, that may work to slow down the process of poverty reduction, there are also many factors at work that will facilitate it. For instance, a heavy emphasis on education throughout the Americas is building a base for higher productivity. In South America, the average years of education of those twenty-five years of age and older is likely to climb from about 5.6 years in 2000 to 7.1 in 2015 and 8.7 in 2030, a rapid rate of increase. Gains in Central America and the Caribbean will be somewhat slower, still adding about 1.1 years of education to the average by 2015. Health conditions have improved fairly steadily in the Americas, with life expectancy, a good summary indicator, having reached at least sixty-eight years in all regions. The human development index has been climbing across the regions of the Americas.

Overall, the HPI-1 is declining (see Figure 8.14 for values and the annual *Human Development Reports* for details of index construction). The combined intervention scenario could bring it down even more rapidly. The combined interventions could also considerably accelerate reduction in extreme poverty relative to the base case, cutting it about two-thirds by 2040 and removing an additional 20 million people from that condition. It could similarly reduce the percentage of those living on less than $2 daily and lift 40 million above that threshold.

Europe
Scanning the continent

As for other continents, the basic regionalization of Europe adopted here is that of the United Nations, which allocates forty-seven political entities into Eastern, Northern, Southern, and Western Europe (see Map 8.5). Eastern Europe consists entirely of formerly communist countries and former republics of the Soviet Union; Russia accounts for nearly one-half its people. Northern Europe includes the Baltic republics and Scandinavia, but the United Kingdom accounts for more than 60 percent of its population. Italy and Spain have two-thirds of the population in Southern Europe. Germany and France make up three-fourths of the Western European population.

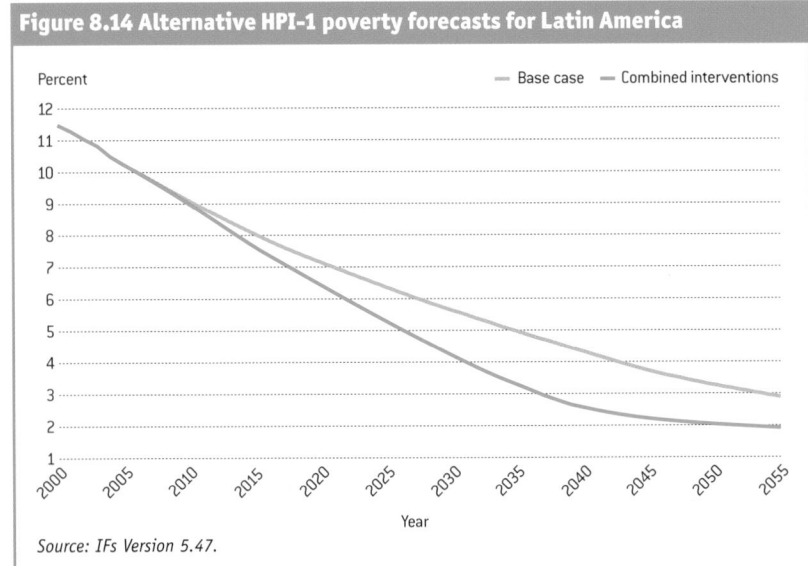

Figure 8.14 Alternative HPI-1 poverty forecasts for Latin America

Source: IFs Version 5.47.

Map 8.5 European regions

ARCTIC OCEAN

ICELAND

FAEROE ISLANDS

ATLANTIC OCEAN

SWEDEN

FINLAND

NORWAY

NORTHERN EUROPE

NORTH
SEA

ESTONIA

LATVIA

RUSSIAN
FEDERATION

DENMARK

LITHUANIA

RUSSIAN FED.

IRELAND

ISLE OF
MAN (UK)

UNITED
KINGDOM

BELARUS

NETHERLANDS

CHANNEL ISLANDS

BELGIUM

LUXEMBOURG

GERMANY

POLAND

EASTERN EUROPE

UKRAINE

CZECH REP.

SLOVAKIA

WESTERN EUROPE

LIECHTENSTEIN

SWITZERLAND

AUSTRIA

HUNGARY

REPUBLIC OF
MOLDOVA

FRANCE

SLOVENIA

ITALY

CROATIA

ROMANIA

MONACO

SAN MARINO

BOSNIA AND
HERZEGOVINA

PORTUGAL

ANDORRA

SERBIA

BULGARIA

MONTENEGRO

SPAIN

HOLY
SEE

MACEDONIA

SOUTHERN EUROPE

ALBANIA

GIBRALTAR (UK)

GREECE

MEDITERRANEAN SEA

MALTA

Table 8.11 Poverty in European regions

	Europeans living on less than $5 per day (millions)			
Year	Eastern	Northern	Southern	Western
2000	168.0	4.8	16.8	0.1
2005	105.8	3.9	16.3	0.1
2010	66.5	3.2	16.2	0.1
2015	47.6	2.6	15.3	0.0
2020	36.0	1.6	13.4	0.0
2025	26.8	1.1	12.3	0.0
2030	19.8	0.8	11.3	0.0
2035	16.2	0.5	8.0	0.0
2040	11.7	0.3	5.6	0.0
2045	9.7	0.2	5.3	0.0
2050	8.6	0.1	4.2	0.0
2055	7.6	0.0	3.0	0.0

Source: Base case forecast of IFs Version 5.47.

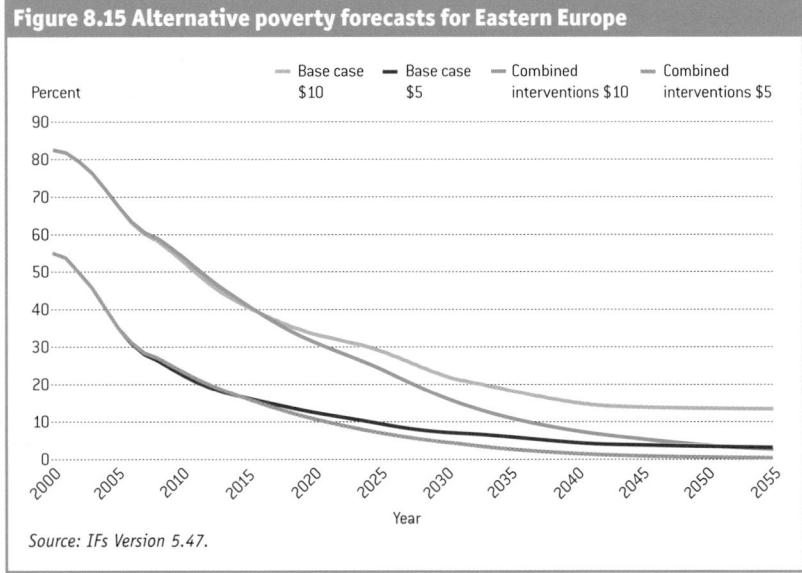

Figure 8.15 Alternative poverty forecasts for Eastern Europe

Source: IFs Version 5.47.

Relatively few Europeans survive on less than even $2 per day, much less $1 per day. World Bank surveys therefore do not even cover most of the European countries, primarily providing information on Eastern Europe and the formerly communist countries of Southern Europe. So for most of the European countries, we rely on estimates of IFs based on data for GDP per capita and income distribution, along with the presumption that income is distributed lognormally.[23]

With the exception of Albania, Bosnia, and Serbia in Southern Europe, almost all Europeans who live on less than $2 are in Eastern Europe. Russia has dominated the total European headcount of those below $2 per day, with 23 of 50 million in 2000.

The big story with respect to income poverty in Europe, however, is the rapidity with which it has declined in recent years as the transition economies of Eastern Europe have bounced back from the economic shocks that accompanied the end of communism. Table 8.11 shows that decline as calculated in IFs. There are, however, many elements of rebound that are far from complete. Russian life expectancy, which had reached sixty-five years in 1987, fell to under sixty years by 2000. Although it may have reached sixty-six in 2005 (UN Population Reference Bureau), it remains far below that of most other European countries.

Scenario analysis and Eastern European poverty

The rapid reduction anticipated in poverty in Eastern Europe at $5 per day is echoed by the likely reduction in poverty at $10 per day. Most of the region's countries have now joined the European Union and have already begun to enjoy the economic benefits of doing so. Russia has extraordinary energy wealth and most likely also has the governance capacity to manage many of the problems that such wealth has brought to the weaker states of Africa. Figure 8.15 shows the possible path of poverty reduction in both the base case and the combined intervention scenario. The latter could somewhat further accelerate poverty reduction, but the incremental leverage it offers is not nearly that seen earlier for countries in Africa, Asia, or Latin America.

The formerly communist countries of the Balkans may have somewhat more difficulty and are the countries that require attention. While Croatia is negotiating its entry and Macedonia is a candidate member, Albania, Bosnia and Herzegovina, Montenegro, and Serbia are only potential candidates for the European Union. Very great steps have been taken in the Balkans toward resolution of the conflicts that followed the breakdown of the former Yugoslavia, but ethnic relations throughout the region are not yet stable. The region has long been said to have had more history than it could absorb on its own, and its affairs still spill over widely throughout Europe.

Yet the per capita economic growth rates anticipated within the base case for the Balkan region are higher than those for Southern Europe as a whole, even if they are lower than those expected for Eastern Europe. Thus income poverty reduction is likely to continue relatively steadily across Europe.

Conclusion

Each of the regions reviewed in this chapter faces rather different poverty reduction challenges. The forecast tables at the end of this volume help elaborate not only regional, but country-specific aspects of development patterns.

In Africa, issues of governance belong high on the list of those that need to be addressed, as the New Partnership for Africa's Development (NEPAD) initiative acknowledges the region itself to understand. A special instance of governance challenge faces many African countries in the form of the need to develop capabilities for handling the concentrated, high rents associated with natural resources, especially energy. Corruption and poor governance have plagued the region. The region also faces major challenges with respect to the development of human capital, including broad health issues well beyond HIV/AIDS and very low levels of education. Population growth rates remain unfortunately high across much of the continent. Infrastructure and technological capabilities are also substantially underdeveloped. Conflict in many areas continues to simmer or boil. As if this list were not long enough, Africa further faces challenges of strengthening its relationship with the global economy, but doing so on terms that allow it to progress with respect to all the other issues. It is not surprising that forecasts anticipate that Africa as a whole will fail to meet most of the MDGs by 2015. In fact, the first half of the century will likely be needed for truly significant progress on many of the underlying measures.

Asian countries mostly find themselves in substantially better positions as they move into the final few years of the MDG target period and position themselves for continued progress on broad fronts. The general quality of government policy in China, including its support for human capital development, infrastructure development, and active engagement with the global economy, has served it very well.

India, Vietnam, and several other countries are largely following similar paths. Within some of these very large countries and economies, intracountry differences in well-being and rates of poverty reduction offer some of the most significant challenges, as the analysis of Middle India made clear. Nonetheless, the trajectory of much of developing Asia is such that attention is increasingly likely to turn from the reduction of extreme poverty to the amelioration of it at higher development levels. Goals for the reduction of those who live on less than $2 and $5 per day will almost certainly follow rapid progress on the current ones. Nonetheless, all is hardly rosy for the region. Selected countries, such as Afghanistan and Pakistan, either fall into the category of failed states or easily could. And given the success of the region in recent years, surprises with respect to the pace of poverty reduction may be more likely on the negative than on the positive side.

The Americas, notably the countries of Latin America, present still a different pattern. Like Africa, it is unlikely that the region as a whole will meet the MDG for poverty reduction. Issues of governance, human capital development, and infrastructure also face countries throughout the region. But to a greater degree than either Africa or Asia, Latin America has also struggled with its role in the larger global economy and has often understood its economic interactions as harmful rather than helpful. This ambivalence, with roots in an exploitative colonial heritage, has been strongly reinforced in recent years by a complex interacting pattern of high levels of domestic inequality, high levels of international debt, and substantial external pressure for changes in domestic policies. The existence of fairly deep and not always fully acknowledged social stratifications, including those emanating from the existence of especially poor indigenous populations, interacts with these entwined issues. The emergence in much of the region of strengthened movements on behalf of those peoples and ongoing accommodations with the global political economy may be bringing some of these elements to a head. Although there is much basis on which to forecast continuing and substantial poverty reduction, economic and sociopolitical setbacks have characterized the region too often to allow complaisance.

All global regions and countries within them face unique changes in poverty reduction.

Poverty in Europe has still another face. Very little of it is so deep as to be labeled extreme poverty, that which limits the ability of people to meet nutritional needs and is life-threatening. Most poverty at more moderate levels has been concentrated in the formerly communist countries of Eastern and Southern Europe, and the rebounds in GDP and income since the immediate aftermath of the transition from communism have been substantial. Yet the countries remain transition economies and societies. Many probably yet face a long road to achieving the status of what their peoples have often referred to as being a "normal country."

Regardless of the location of poverty around the world, the intervention set that Chapter 7 developed and labeled the combined intervention scenario has potential power to reduce rates and levels below those of the base case. The costs of poverty to individuals and their families are simply too great not to make such reduction one of humanity's very highest goals.

1   The World Bank's data and country-specific assessments are the foundation of almost all country-specific work on poverty, including that done here. See its PovcalNet web site. The large number of country-based studies are an incredible resource.

2   For many other countries, interpolation or extrapolation was necessary to determine values for the common base year of 2000.

3   See the Fund for Peace website at http://www. fundforpeace.org/programs/fsi/fsifaq.php#q5 and the May–June 2006 issue of *Foreign Policy*.

4   See http://www.un.org/depts/dhl/maplib/ worldregions.htm. The UN Economic Commission for Africa is organized also into five regions, but it uses Central rather than Middle Africa and puts the Democratic Republic of the Congo into East Africa. Except for the exclusion of Mauritania, the Economic Community of West African States (ECOWAS) has membership identical to the UN's West Africa.

5   Wodon (2007) studied the history of poverty reduction in six countries of West Africa.

6   Gatune's eight regions are available for analysis in IFs as African cultural groupings.

7   Collier and others have also drawn attention to the often overlapping distinction between countries with substantial histories of internal conflict (such as the Democratic Republic of the Congo and Angola) and those without that burden; still another typology for thinking about African states might divide those with high rates of HIV infection and those without. Still another would be between those countries with the highest continuing dependence on agriculture (Sierra Leone, Tanzania, and the Democratic Republic of the Congo rank among the highest, with Uganda, and Eritrea, Guinea Bissau, Somalia, and Uganda not far behind) and those with more diversified economies.

8   The figure uses Collier and O'Connell's (undated) definition of landlocked, which includes the Democratic Republic of the Congo in spite of its very limited access to the ocean; includes the Sudan, which has access to the Red Sea and a rail line from Port Sudan to the Nile; but excludes Swaziland. The IFs system allows comparison,

however, of their country grouping with a more strictly defined landlocked one and finds the extreme poverty rates nearly identical. IFs data analysis does not, however, support their conclusion that being coastal augments growth by 1.5 percent (Collier and O'Connell 2007: 5). Looking at sub-Saharan Africa only (because the oil and gas of the Mediterranean states put them in a special category), between 1960 and 2005 the GDP per capita at purchasing power parity of landlocked countries, using the Collier and O'Connell definition, grew just 0.3 percent slower than the coastal set. Overall, the traps of being landlocked and either resource-poor or resource-rich may not be as pronounced as sometimes argued. Africa as a whole has simply not done well.

9   Although generally seen as targeting actual corruption, the prosecutions have also been recognized as targeting political opposition.

10 Patterns vary substantially across Africa. Countries like Botswana, Ghana, Kenya, Namibia, and Zimbabwe have already reduced fertility rates to near 4.0 as a group. Except for Zimbabwe, they also tended to experience faster economic growth in the 1990s (UN ECAF 2005: 131–132).

11 In late 2007 UNAIDS (2007) revised its infection and death numbers downward, meaning that the turnaround for life expectancy in South Africa may happen at a somewhat higher level and faster rate.

12 Liberia gained its independence in the mid-1800s. Semantically the returning American blacks may not have been colonizers, but they were in practice.

13 Because extreme income poverty in the Middle East is relatively low and because fortunes in coming years depend so much on both uncertain energy revenues and governance (Noland and Pack 2007), this discussion of Asia gives the region less attention than it deserves.

14 An interactive display of performance is available at http://info.worldbank.org/governance.

15 http://info.worldbank.org/governance/kkz2005/ pdf/ge.pdf.

16 The Heritage Foundation series began only in 1995. In 2006 it ranked China, India, and Bangladesh

at positions 111, 121, and 141, respectively, with especially little distance in underlying scores between the first two.

17 Aromar Revi has created a nine-region representation of India that better divides the country by economic, cultural, and geophysical characteristics; it is also available in IFs.

18 State-specific poverty values were taken from India's *National Human Development Report 2001* and normalized to World Bank values for India as a whole.

19 IFs represents only thirty-three of these countries; those missing are almost entirely the smaller countries of the Caribbean, such as Anguilla, Antigua and Barbuda, and Aruba.

20 In 2007 the official poverty line for a single person in the United States was about $27 per day, and that for members of a family of four was just under $14 per day per person.

21 Numbers for 2006 are estimates from the CIA's online *Factbook*.

22 The Office of the U.S. Trade Representative, while obviously writing to convince a domestic audience of the benefits of the agreement, emphasizes that U.S. markets are largely already open to Central America and that the agreement will primarily open Central American markets to the United States, presumably reinforcing the analysis that both the interim costs of adjustments and the longer-term potential benefits might fall heavily on the smaller partners. See http://www.ustr.gov/Trade_ Agreements/Bilateral/CAFTA/Section_Index.html.

23 The Bank has undertaken extensive individual country analyses on at least thirteen countries in Eastern and Southern Europe. See http://web. worldbank.org/WBSITE/EXTERNAL/TOPICS/ EXTPOVERTY/EXTP/ 0,,contentMDK:20204084~men uPK:443282~pagePK:148956~piPK:216618~theSit ePK:430367,00.html. Some of the Bank's surveys, like that for Bosnia-Herzegovina, have relied on measures that vary somewhat from the $1 and $2 per day categories and provide numbers that may differ from those estimated by IFs.

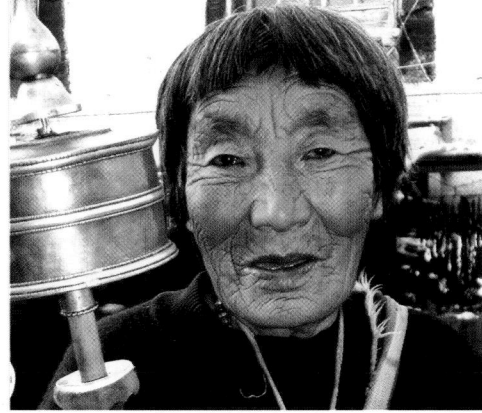

9

Poverty in a Broader Context

In this penultimate chapter, we come full circle to the broad-based discussion of poverty in our initial chapters. Although the model-based findings and analysis from the intervening chapters inform our discussion, they do not confine us. This allows us to take stock of what we have been able to accomplish, as well as to lay out issues that await research and analysis in the future.

In this spirit, we focus on a few substantive elaborations of the analysis in previous chapters. We expand the discussion by including attention to aspects of proximate and deep drivers that currently challenge or even defy quantitative measurement and analysis and by broadening the focus from drivers of poverty to impacts of poverty. Among the topics that deserve greater attention than past chapters afforded them are the implications of natural resources and the environment for poverty reduction, as well as the consequences of poverty levels for the environment. Similarly, conflict/stability and governance/sociopolitical institutions

have consequences for poverty and, in turn, are influenced by poverty. An ancillary topic for discussion is the external involvement of governments, intergovernmental organizations, and other actors in poverty reduction efforts; such involvement has a wide range of consequences and trade-offs.

Natural Resources, the Environment, and Poverty

We recognize that poverty, environmental degradation, and population growth are inextricably related and that none of these fundamental problems can be successfully addressed in isolation. We will succeed or fail together. (World Commission on Environment and Development 1987: 45)

Investment in environmental assets is essential for poverty reduction. (Poverty-Environment Partnership 2005c)[1]

> *Many phenomena that we cannot model affect and are, in turn, influenced by poverty.*

Eliminating poverty and hunger and protecting the environment are inseparable. (Kermal Davis, UNDP administrator, at the launch of the joint UNEP and UNDP Poverty and Environment Facility, 2007)[2]

In this section we turn to the linkages between poverty and natural resources and the environment. What are they, and what might be their implications for the earlier analysis in this volume?

We best know the World Commission on Environment and Development (WCED) for popularizing the term **sustainable development**, defined as development that "meets the needs of the present without compromising the ability of future generations to meet their own needs." At the same time, the quotation from the WCED indicates that the commission clearly understood the fundamental relationship between poverty and the environment in the present as well as the future.

Many other bodies have recognized these connections, including the 1992 United Nations Conference on Environment and Development, the 2000 Global Ministerial Forum, the 2000 Millennium Summit, the 2002 World Summit on Sustainable Development, and the 2005 World Summit. This recognition, along with the establishment of Millennium Development Goals (MDGs) and assorted formal resolutions, has led to the establishment of institutions and networks to consider the relationships between poverty and the environment.[3] A key example is the Poverty and Environment Initiative (PEI) of the UN Development Programme (UNDP) and the UN Environment Programme (UNEP).[4] This partnership, established in 2005 to scale up investment and capacity development support for mainstreaming the environment in country-led MDG processes, has garnered further support, in part through the setting up of the joint UNEP and UNDP Poverty and Environment Facility in Nairobi. Less formal, but working closely with the PEI, is the Poverty-Environment Partnership (PEP), a network of development agencies established in 2001.[5]

The role of the environment in poverty reduction has also received attention in the World Bank's guidance documents on poverty reduction strategies (Bojö et al. 2002), the work of the UN Millennium Project (UN Millennium Project 2005), the establishment of

the Poverty and Environment Program of the Asian Development Bank, and country-specific analyses of the relationships between poverty reduction and environmental priorities (see, for example, Sánchez-Triana, Ahmed, and Awe 2007). The Millennium Development Goals formally recognize the poverty-environment connection, most directly in the goal of ensuring environmental sustainability, but the quality of the natural environment also strongly influences many of the other goals. The survey of policies to reduce poverty in Chapter 3 of this report, as summarized in Table 3.1, also includes, inter alia, policies to enhance the quality of the environment and protect natural resources.

The next subsection conceptualizes the relationship between poverty and the environment, paying careful attention to the role of the natural environment as a source of assets, in the form of goods and services, for individuals and society. That beginning leads to an exploration of the links between this general understanding and the deep and proximate drivers of poverty. We then consider how more careful attention to the natural environment would enhance our understanding of these drivers and the subsequent analysis of plausible futures for their evolution and therefore the evolution of poverty itself.

Conceptualizing the links between poverty and the environment

Underpinning the more directly policy-related efforts noted above has been (1) the development of frameworks to help conceptualize the connections between poverty and the environment and (2) empirical analyses aimed at better understanding how they are manifested in the real world.[6] The frameworks see the relationship between poverty and the environment as being inherently bidirectional. On one side, a healthy, functioning environment is a prerequisite for poverty reduction; on the other, poverty can force people to behave in such a way as to degrade the environment upon which they depend. The potential for poverty and environmental degradation to feed upon each other in a negative fashion has been referred to as a "poverty trap" (Carter et al. 2007; Prakash 1997), "downward spiral" (Durning 1989; Scherr 2000), and perhaps most ominously, an "optimal path to extinction" (Perrings 1989).

An increasing range of institutions address the poverty-environment nexus.

The story is, however, not so simple. We cannot ignore social, political, and cultural factors in explaining the complex web of relationships between people and their environment.[7] Figure 9.1 illustrates the possible relationships in what is increasingly referred to as the poverty-environment nexus.[8]

In this particular conceptualization, the feedback loop shown by R1FB and R4 reflects the orthodox view of poverty leading to environmental degradation and vice versa. Relationships R2, R3A and R3B highlight the fact that environmental degradation can have many other root causes: power, wealth, and greed; institutional failures; and market failures. Furthermore, via R4, those causes can further affect poverty.[9]

The adoption of a more complex perspective on the poverty-environment nexus also belies the common assumption of an inherent trade-off between poverty alleviation and environmental protection.[10] At the heart of this perspective is the recognition that, through its interactions with individuals and society, the natural environment provides assets that are fundamental to all social and economic development but are of particular importance to the poorest persons in society.[11]

Beginning with Rudolf S. de Groot (1992) and Gretchen C. Daily (1997), a number of efforts have been made to define and spell out the goods and services that the natural environment provides (see Boyd and Banzhaf 2006 for a recent review). Perhaps the most influential is the approach that the Millennium Ecosystem Assessment (MA) spelled out, using the term "ecosystem services." The MA defines them as "the benefits people obtain from ecosystems" (Millennium Ecosystem Assessment 2003: 211). It distinguishes four categories of services—provisioning, regulating, cultural, and supporting—as shown in Table 9.1.

Some of the goods and services provided by the natural environment contribute directly to people. Others contribute indirectly by allowing for the continued provision of other goods and services. The direct contributions can involve either transformative or nontransformative uses of the environment. In the case of the former (provisioning services), such as the provision of firewood for cooking or providing warmth, there is a physical change in the environment; with the latter (cultural services), such as a birdsong that brings joy to those who hear it, there is not. The indirect contributions derive from services that allow for the continued provision

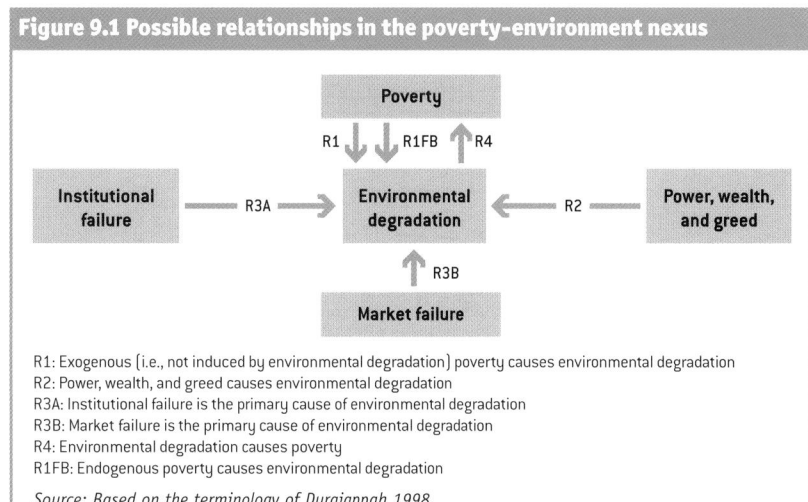

Figure 9.1 Possible relationships in the poverty-environment nexus

R1: Exogenous (i.e., not induced by environmental degradation) poverty causes environmental degradation
R2: Power, wealth, and greed causes environmental degradation
R3A: Institutional failure is the primary cause of environmental degradation
R3B: Market failure is the primary cause of environmental degradation
R4: Environmental degradation causes poverty
R1FB: Endogenous poverty causes environmental degradation

Source: Based on the terminology of Duraiappah 1998.

> ■ The poverty-environment nexus involves many other forces, including governance, markets, and social relationships. ■

Table 9.1 Ecosystem services as defined in the Millennium Ecosystem Assessment

Ecosystem Services		
Provisioning Services *Products obtained from ecosystems* • Food • Freshwater • Fuelwood • Fiber • Biochemicals • Genetic resources	**Regulating Services** *Benefits obtained from regulation of ecosystem processes* • Climate regulation • Disease regulation • Water regulation • Water purification	**Cultural Services** *Nonmaterial benefits obtained from ecosystems* • Spiritual and religious • Recreation and ecotourism • Aesthetic • Inspirational • Educational • Sense of place • Cultural heritage
Supporting Services *Services necessary for the production of all other ecosystem services* • Soil formation • Nutrient cycling • Primary production		

Source: Millennium Ecosystem Assessment 2003: 57.

of other services. These other services may themselves contribute either directly (regulating services) or indirectly (supporting services) to human well-being. For example, consider the purification of water: the purified water may be directly consumed, but it may also support a fish population that is a source of protein. Finally, please note that the contributions from the environment need not always be beneficial to human well-being. Dirty air and water, not to mention events such as hurricanes or a snake bite, can negatively affect human well-being.

The approach used in the MA explicitly focuses on biological resources that are renewable over relatively short time scales. Note the careful use of the term "fuelwood" rather than "fuel" in Table 9.1. Similarly, the concept of ecosystem services does not include minerals and metals. Thus it does not include key aspects of natural capital as defined in Chapter 3 of this report. (Although that chapter defined natural capital broadly, the forecasts of poverty in this report by no means fully reflect the elements in that definition.) For this reason we use the term "environmental goods and services," rather than either "ecosystem services" or "natural capital," to represent the full range of contributions from the natural environment.

Connecting the environment to the drivers of poverty

Chapter 3 of this report explored the deep and proximate drivers of poverty. It specified the latter as levels of economic activity, population, and inequality, with changes in them driving changes in poverty. In turn, it examined the deep drivers of each of the proximate drivers, which later chapters then used as the basis for exploring plausible futures of poverty. A number of the deep drivers of poverty depend strongly upon environmental goods and services. In turn, poverty itself, and efforts to eradicate it, positively or negatively affect a number of environmental goods and services.

This subsection will focus on various ways in which increased attention to the role of the environment could enhance the projections of plausible futures of poverty, specifically (1) environmental goods and services as determinants of health, including fertility and mortality; (2) environmental goods and services as actual products or components of products;

and (3) environmental goods and services as general factors of production. Finally, it will separately address the particular relationship of the environment and inequality.

Health, including fertility and mortality

Through its program on quantifying environmental health impacts, the World Health Organization (WHO) has been producing a series of publications on the environmental burden of disease, including country profiles.[12] Since the World Summit on Sustainable Development in 2002, WHO has also partnered with UNEP in carrying out the Health and Environment Linkages Initiative (HELI), a global effort "to support action by developing country policymakers on environmental threats to health").[13]

Annette Prüss-Üstün and Carlos Corvalán (2006) estimate that globally 24 percent of the disease burden (healthy life years lost) and 23 percent of all deaths (premature mortality) are attributable to environmental factors; among children up to age fourteen, the figure for deaths is as high as 36 percent. The diseases with the largest absolute burden attributable to modifiable environmental factors are diarrhea, lower respiratory infections, "other" unintentional injuries (workplace hazards, radiation, and industrial accidents), and malaria. Related to this, HELI identified the priority environment and health risks as vector-borne diseases, urban air pollution, indoor air pollution, unsafe water and sanitation, climate change, and toxic substances. It is not surprising that many of these same concerns appear in the Millennium Development Goals. Various studies, such as John Luke Gallup and Jeffrey Sachs (2001), Sachs and Pia Malaney (2002) and Yohe et al. (2007), have attempted to estimate the economic and social costs of a number of these environmentally related health risks.

Turning to the conceptual framework used to project future economic activity and poverty in this report, Figure 3.6 showed health as an input into human capital, which in turn influences multifactor productivity and economic growth. (The figure leaves implicit the importance of the size of the population, as well as its general health, for the labor supply.) Figure 3.7 highlighted the roles of fertility and mortality in determining population, but, somewhat surprisingly, it shows health explicitly only in terms of the impact of health spending on mortality. Significantly, neither of these figures draws attention to the role of the environment. Furthermore, although increased mortality can reduce the labor supply and life expectancy influences human capital, the potential impact of morbidity on economic activity, and therefore poverty, is missing.

In its current form, IFs captures limited impacts of environmental change on health. It represents a linkage from food availability to malnutrition levels, which in turn affects the human poverty index, but does not consider other impacts.

Environmental goods and services as actual products or components of products

In the form of provisioning and cultural services (food, timber, fossil fuels, and recreational opportunities), environmental goods and services have traditionally provided economic commodities, thereby making a direct contribution to economic activity and economic growth. Environmental goods and services are also the basic building blocks of many other products (clothing, furniture, and pharmaceuticals). With the advent of more recent institutions, such as markets for greenhouse gas credits, even some regulating and supporting services are beginning to enter economic markets directly.

IFs makes some attempt to incorporate the role of environmental goods and services as economic commodities or components of economic commodities. Three of its six economic sectors are agriculture, primary energy, and raw materials, which directly embed environmental goods and services into their products. An input-output structure connects these sectors to each other and to the three other sectors of the model. Theoretically, restrictions on environmental goods and services could therefore affect the ability to constitute other goods and services. With one exception, however, the model does not attempt to represent such constraints, partly because of the highly aggregate nature of these sectors. The single exception is that, if energy supplies are abruptly reduced (as by the shocks of the 1970s), the ability to constitute other goods drops proportionately. More generally, however, the model looks to the availability of environmental goods and services, especially energy, as a factor

of production that may influence economic activity and, in turn, poverty.

Environmental goods and services as general factors of production

Even when they do not appear as products or components of products, environmental goods and services play a key role as general factors of production. Energy may be the most obvious example, but those aspects of a quality environment hinted at by the supporting and regulating services (healthy air, water, and soil and a relatively stable and predictable climate) are also significant factors of production for many economy sectors.

Figure 3.6 identified six forms of capital as being fundamental to economic activity and growth.[14] Of these, only natural capital is, on the surface, directly related to the natural environment. One other— infrastructure capital—clearly traces its roots back to the natural environment, however, because its physical form consists of transformed parts of the natural environment. Finally, human, social, institutional, and knowledge capital, as well as labor, are embedded in single individuals or groups of individuals, who also ultimately depend on the natural environment for their continued existence. Thus environmental goods and services theoretically support all factors of production.

Within IFs, separate agriculture and energy modules represent physical production based on physical factor inputs. For instance, land withdrawn for urban use is unavailable for agricultural production, and depletion of nonrenewable energy resources ultimately constrains production of them. Thus environmental goods and services directly shape production of those sectors.[15] In addition, the price of energy directly enters into the calculation of broader productivity for all sectors, representing the rendering of some capital obsolescent when energy prices rise. In addition, climate, via changes in the levels of atmospheric carbon dioxide, has the potential to influence crop yields, but only via scenarios introduced by users willing to specify the parameters for the linkage.

Thus the representations of IFs omit much in the potential representation of environmental goods and services in economic production. For example, the model ignores the potential

Environmental goods and services contribute much to economic growth.

impacts from changing temperature and precipitation patterns. Similarly, it does not consider explicitly the role of other key environmental factors (water availability, water quality, land quality, and air quality). To the extent that these influence economic activity, and therefore poverty, the results presented in this report may be misleading.

Inequality

Thus far, we have dealt with the role of the environment at a fairly macro level, emphasizing in particular its potential impact on overall economic activity and, to a lesser extent, population. Perhaps even more significant, though, is the role the environment can play with respect to inequality, the third proximate driver of poverty.

Poorer people, particularly in rural areas of developing countries, heavily depend upon environmental goods and services for their livelihoods (e.g., Cavendish 1999b, 2000; Narain, Gupta, and van 't Veld 2005; Nunan et al. 2002; Poverty-Environment Partnership 2005a, 2005b, 2005c; World Resources Institute 2005). In addition, the poor often suffer from unequal rights and insecure access to these resources (Poverty-Environment Partnership 2005a, 2005b, 2005c). Related to that is the importance for the poor of resources they hold in common. Further, the poor tend to live in more ecologically fragile areas (Narain, Gupta, and van 't Veld 2005; World Resources Institute 2005), making them the most vulnerable to human-made and natural disasters (Department for International Development 2002; Scott 2006).

Finally, even among the poor, the links between poverty and the environment varies across different groups. Bina Agarwal (1997) and the Organization for Economic Cooperation and Development (OECD 2001) have explored the links among gender, poverty, and the environment. Some mechanisms by which their relationship to the environment may more substantially affect women and children than men are fairly straightforward, such as less access to private resources and greater exposure to indoor air pollution. Others are subtler, such as the fact that environmental degradation increases burden on women and children, especially girls, to collect water and fuel wood, reducing time for education and income-generating activities.

Taken together, all these factors suggest that environmental changes may result in changes in the distribution of income within a country and not just average levels of income. This potential for environmental change to influence the distribution of income adds to the vulnerability of the poorest segments of society. The discussion in Chapter 3 on the deep drivers of inequality does not really address that potential. And Chapter 5 noted the difficulties in general and for IFs specifically in forecasting changes in inequality. Thus, it is not surprising that IFs does not capture the potential effect of environmental change on the distribution of income. Because of the knife-edge property of the most common measure of poverty, $1 per day, however, even small shifts in the distribution of income at the lower end could have a large influence on the total number of the poor.

Implications

We should not underestimate the challenge of delving into the potential implications of incorporating the environment more explicitly into analysis of future poverty levels. Michael Toman (2003: 15) notes that although a fair amount of empirical work has been done on the effects of human and economic activity on the environment, "less is known empirically about the effects of environmental quality on economic growth." Anthony J. McMichael and Rosalie E. Woodruff (2005) and Colin Butler (2005), respectively, chose the somewhat provocative titles "Detecting the Health Effects of Environmental Change: Scientific and Political Challenge" and "Peering into the Fog: Ecological Change, Human Affairs, and the Future" for contributions to the journal EcoHealth. Hence it is not a surprise that the design of integrated models such as IFs does not address issues of poverty and the environment at the level of detail, in terms of their representations of both the environment and society, required to capture the key relationships that make up the poverty-environment nexus.

Even still, it is possible to indicate the effect of taking more account of the environment in our projections. Most of the evidence points to the importance of addressing environmental issues as part of efforts to alleviate poverty. Environmental improvements, if shared equitably, will enhance the earning potential of the poor. Alternatively, the poor are the most likely to suffer from environmental degradation. As such, efforts to increase economic development without proper consideration of the environment may lead to increased levels of poverty, even as average incomes rise.

As discussed throughout this section, IFs does not contain a particularly strong representation of the environment. Moreover, the environmental module is almost entirely a satellite of other modules, affected by them but not providing many inputs to them. The only indicators that may look explicitly at the state of the environment are the atmospheric concentrations of carbon dioxide (CO_2), land use (especially forest area), and remaining fossil fuel resources.[16] Other indicators (mostly flows rather than stocks) do provide, however, some indication of pressures placed on the environment. These include energy demand, carbon emissions from energy use, water use, and livestock herds.

Table 9.2 looks at a few of these indicators in the IFs base case and the combined intervention scenario, which contains all domestic and international interventions to reduce poverty. As a primary means of reducing poverty, the combined intervention scenario involves considerably stronger economic growth in developing regions of the world than does the base case. It also involves, however, considerable technological advance in systems with the greatest effect on the environment (both in IFs and the real world), including agriculture and energy.

The relative impact that we should anticipate of the poverty-reducing scenario on the environment is therefore not immediately obvious. Table 9.2 shows it to be mixed. It increases energy demand considerably relative to the base case, especially in the developing world, so that relative oil and gas reserves are lower, while carbon emissions and atmospheric buildup of carbon are higher. But the scenario also relatively increases the use of renewables (not shown, but built into the scenario), so that the difference in environmental impact is not dramatic. Similarly, livestock herds increase substantially more in the developing world in the combined intervention scenario. Yet water use is not greatly different between the scenarios, and forest area is actually

somewhat larger in the combined intervention scenario. These results depend on a forecast of considerable improvement in agricultural productivity. In short, the combined intervention scenario is not significantly more environmentally friendly or damaging than the base case, giving us reason to believe that the failure of the model to include forward linkages from the environment affects both scenarios in much the same manner.

Overall, the significantly larger increases in energy demand and livestock herds in the combined intervention scenario also point to the potential for pro-poor policies to (inadvertently) increase pressures on the environment. Yet Table 3.1 includes a number of possible policy interventions that represent environmental sustainability as one strategic thrust in poverty reduction. The analysis in Chapter 7 was only able to incorporate greater attention to renewable energy. Other policies that IFs cannot explicitly represent, such as land reform, microfinance, and support for poor people's human capital, do address many of the social, political, and cultural factors at the center of the poverty-environment nexus. In this way, they can have impacts that go beyond simply raising average incomes. Thus Chapter 7 and the combined intervention scenario may well underestimate the positive effects of poverty reduction efforts on the environment.

Moving away from comparison, it is important to emphasize that, as currently configured,

● *Both base case and combined intervention scenarios would have great impacts on the environment, some negative and, via poverty reduction, some positive.* ●

Table 9.2 Selected environmental forecasts from IFs					
	2000	2030		2055	
Indicator		Base case	Combined intervention	Base case	Combined intervention
World					
Atmospheric CO_2 (ppm)	372.0	459.6	463.5	547.9	554.0
Carbon emissions from fossil fuels (billion tons)	6.88	12.05	12.50	9.15	8.50
Oil and gas reserves (billion barrels of oil equivalent, or BOE)	2,230	1,999	1,951	819	785
World Bank—Developing Economies					
Energy demand (billion BOE)	29.3	80.2	97.6	118.2	191.8
Water use (cubic kilometers)	2,919	4,355	4,465	5,143	5,340
Livestock herds (million tons)	205.4	531.2	597.1	778.9	941.8
Forest area (million hectares)	3,117	2,971	2,980	2,932	2,962

Source: IFs Version 5.47.

both scenarios greatly increase the impact of global human activity on the environment by midcentury, including global carbon emissions from energy use, atmospheric concentrations of CO_2, energy and water demand, and livestock herd size.[17] The table also shows declines in forest area in developing countries.[18] Thus the failure of IFs to represent most of the potential impacts on poverty of these changes in either scenario is significant across all the analytic chapters of this book.

Given the limitations of our present understanding and analytical tools, it is not possible to state precisely what the net effect of more explicitly incorporating the environment would be on the analysis of future poverty levels presented in this volume. This is in line with the general message of much of the poverty and environment literature, which is that from the perspective of poverty reduction, the nature and quality of economic growth is as important as the quantity of that growth (Department for International Development 2002).

Conflict and Poverty

Can poverty reduction lead to a decrease in conflict (even including terrorism)? It is intuitive to think that relative economic prosperity will lead to less strife. What are the implications of success in conflict reduction for the evolution of poverty? What role might the external world have in helping reduce and control internal conflict? These are a few of the questions that motivate this section, in which we review the evidence on the connections between poverty and conflict.

We examine the conflict-poverty relationship for the same reason we examine the environment-poverty relationship, namely that the analysis with IFs largely omitted consideration of it. The IFs model contains a representation of domestic conflict potential across countries and time, using the potential for state failure (see LaFree, Dugan, and Fahey 2008) as the central variable. The model also represents the potential for international conflict, using a wide range of drivers (such as democratization level and economic openness) in the formulation. Since neither formulation is strong enough to form a basis for future projections, in our analysis neither internal nor international conflict affects economic growth

or other variables that shape poverty levels. We need to consider how important such an omission from the analysis might be.

Placing the discussion in an even more general context, the analysis of poverty futures in Chapters 5–8 did not capture unexpected events like the outbreak of conflict. Just as conflicts or plagues can derail even the gradual decreases in poverty resulting from slow and steady growth, growth miracles can bring about decreases in poverty far exceeding those seen during normal times (as in East Asia, China, and India). Therefore, understanding the implications of conflict on the poverty analysis conducted thus far is a useful exercise on robustness.

The World Bank (2005d: 7) provides a succinct summary of the interconnection between conflict and poverty:

> Empirical evidence shows that poorer countries are more likely to experience violent conflict, while conflict-affected countries tend to experience higher levels of poverty. Violent conflict results in the destruction of economic and human capital. A country emerging from conflict is faced with damaged physical infrastructure, scarce employment opportunities, reduced foreign investment, and increased capital flight. … The situation is worsened by weak governing institutions, which are often unable to implement policy and uphold the rule of law.

Viewed from the other direction, although poverty itself is neither a necessary nor a sufficient condition for conflict, poverty factors increase the likelihood of violent conflict in three main ways. First, a combination of poverty and unequal income levels makes it easier for many people, particularly young men, to be easily mobilized and recruited to armed groups. Second, weak and undemocratic governance structures, usually present in poor countries, are often incapable of preventing the onset of violence by peaceful means. Third, if a country with a large population is endowed with significant natural resources, rebel organizations are able to raise finances and galvanize public resentment against perceived or real injustices.

We therefore examine in greater detail how poverty can cause conflict and possibly

A poverty-conflict nexus also involves two-way relationships and links to a wider range of institutional variables.

terrorism, how conflict can cause poverty, and how their mutual influence can result in economic stagnation with prolonged conflicts. Ideally, we want to identify options available for conflict-ridden countries and the external community to break this cycle.

The influence of poverty on conflict

Civil conflicts are much more widely prevalent than wars between countries (Hewitt, Wilkenfeld, and Gurr 2008). In sub-Saharan Africa alone, twenty-nine of forty-three countries suffered civil conflicts in the 1980s and 1990s (Sambanis 2001). Although such conflicts have multiple causes, Paul Collier et al. (2003: 53) note that civil war is concentrated heavily in the poorest countries and emphatically state, "The key root cause for conflict is the failure of economic development." Doubling per capita income is associated with half the risk of rebellion, and an increase in growth by one percentage point is linked to a decrease of one percentage point in risk. Susan E. Rice, Corinne Graff, and Janet Lewis (2006: 5) echo this view.

For years, a debate has raged in academic circles over the principal causes of civil conflict. Is it ethnicity, grievance, rebel greed, topography or venal leadership? Today, an important element of this debate has been resolved: recent academic research on the causes of conflict demonstrates compellingly that countries with low income per capita are at increased risk of civil conflict. Recent statistical research on poverty and conflict suggests that for a country at the fiftieth percentile for income (like Iran today), the risk of experiencing civil conflict within five years is 7–11 percent; for countries at the tenth percentile (like Ghana or Uganda today), the risk rises to 15–18 percent.

According to Paul Collier and Anke Hoeffler (2004), a country with a gross domestic product (GDP) per capita of $250 runs a 15 percent risk of experiencing a civil conflict; this risk drops to 7.5 percent with $600 GDP per capita and 1 percent with $5,000. Political causes and grievances do contribute to the complex phenomenon of conflict, but there is little

dispute over the finding that higher per capita income reduces the risk of conflict. Rice, Graff, and Lewis (2006: 7) provide a useful summary of relevant findings from the literature.[19]

Most studies use per capita income as an explanatory variable rather than direct poverty measures, but the evidence is quite suggestive of poverty giving rise to conflicts. As Collier and his colleagues (2003: 53) state: "Countries with low, stagnant, and unequally distributed per capita incomes that have remained dependent on primary commodities for their exports face dangerously high risks of prolonged conflict. In the absence of economic development neither good political institutions, nor ethnic and religious homogeneity, nor high military spending provide significant defenses against large-scale violence."

In addition to the level of per capita GDP, the *growth rate* of GDP per capita also affects conflict. Collier and Hoeffler (2004) find that a 1 percent increase in the GDP growth rate reduces the risk of conflict by 1 percent. S. Brock Bloomberg, Gregory D. Hess, and Siddharth Thacker (2006) develop a simple theoretical model in which governments consider initiating diversionary conflict in order to increase their chances of staying in power. Societies with selfish leaders and lower gains from capital formation are more likely to be engaged in conflicts, lowering investment and growth.

Edward Miguel, Satyanath Satyanath, and Ernest Sergenti (2004) criticized the way in which the existing literature deals with issues of endogeneity (conflicts affect poverty, rather than the other way around) and omitted variable bias (government institution quality influences both economic outcomes and conflict, for example). To overcome these problems, they use the exogenous variation in rainfall (proportional change in rainfall from the previous year) as an instrument for economic growth in sub-Saharan African countries. Since these economies largely rely on rain-fed agriculture, rainfall is a plausible instrument.

Instead of the commonly used correlates of war conflict data, they use the armed conflict data from the International Peace Research Institute of Oslo and the Uppsala Conflict Database. They find these data to be more transparent in construction than correlates of war and also to include more small conflicts

The correlation between conflict and poverty is indisputable.

(a threshold of twenty-five battle deaths per year, in addition to the standard 1,000-death threshold). Using rainfall as an instrument, they find a strong connection between GDP growth and the incidence of civil wars:

> A five-percentage-point drop in annual economic growth increases the likelihood of a civil conflict (at least 25 deaths per year) in the following year by over 12 percentage points—which amounts to an increase of more than one-half in the likelihood of civil war. Other variables that have gained prominence in the recent literature—per capita GDP level, democracy, ethnic diversity, and oil explorer status—do not display a similarly robust relationship with the incidence of civil wars in sub-Saharan Africa.... The impact of income shocks on civil conflict is not significantly different in richer, more democratic, more ethnically diverse, or more mountainous African countries or in countries with a range of different political institutional characteristics. (727)

They argue that their result is consistent with both channels typically attributed to how low income influences conflict: it reduces the opportunity cost of taking up arms as well as leads to a weak state with poor infrastructure that is unable to quell rebellions. They view these channels as complementary—weak states form the background in which poor individuals choose conflict over other economic activities.

What are the implications of these findings for our analysis? If there is a positive connection between poverty and conflict, a reduction in poverty can reduce the risk of conflicts. Since IFs does not capture the interconnection between poverty and conflict, we may be understating the benefits of reduced poverty. On the flip side, the concentration of poverty in sub-Saharan Africa, even as poverty in other regions of the world decreases, could increase the possibility of conflict and lead to sudden disruptions and setbacks that our analysis cannot fully capture, except perhaps through scenario analysis. What we know to be missing is explicit representation of the relationship in earlier forecasts.

Nonpoverty determinants of conflicts

Complicating the analysis of poverty and conflict, the idea that economic variables such as GDP per capita or income are the primary determinants of conflicts has been contested. Even with respect to economic variables, it is important to emphasize that much more than GDP or income and its growth affect conflict. Among the other economic drivers of conflict are the availability of resources that elites can appropriate and fight over. For instance, if too little income can lead to conflict, so too can wealth in the form of natural resources. Collier and his colleagues (2003) note that natural resource endowments often correlate with conflict, poor governance, and economic decline.[20] Similarly, foreign aid accrues to the government, and a rebel group can access this resource by overthrowing the government. Therefore, economists (for example, Grossman 1992) have hypothesized that aid can be a source of conflict.[21]

Going beyond solely economic variables, the Political Instability Task Force has studied the causes of state failure and domestic conflict more generally since 1994 (Bates et al. 2006; LaFree, Dugan, and Fahey 2008). Among their early and often repeated findings are that democracy level and trade openness (exports and imports relative to GDP) correlate positively with state failure, while infant mortality relative to global averages correlates negatively. Note the absence of GDP or income in this set of findings.

Grievances of various kinds, including ethnic or religious fractionalization, also link to conflict (although poverty may give rise to the definition of such grievances).[22] For instance, Milton Esman (1994) notes: "To argue, for example that the Israeli-Palestinian struggle is basically about economic values, or that the Quiet Revolution is mainly about employment opportunities for educated Quebecois, or that Malays are concerned primarily with closing the economic gap [with the Chinese in Malaysia] utterly trivializes and distorts the meaning and the stakes of these conflicts."

What is the evidence for this alternate ("grievance" perspective) of conflicts? Alan B. Krueger and Jitka Maleckova (2003) go beyond description to systematically examine a variety of evidence connecting education, poverty and a particular type of conflict, namely terrorism.

● *Earlier analysis in this volume did not consider the conflict-reduction value of poverty-reduction initiatives.* ●

● *Much more than poverty underlies conflict, and forecasting of conflict has proven very difficult.* ●

They undertake an analysis that reaches out to the literature on the economics of crime, that looks to survey research of Palestinians, that explores Hezbollah in Lebanon in some detail, and that draws on cross-country evidence across a number of international terrorist events. They conclude: "Any connection between poverty, education and terrorism is indirect, complicated and probably quite weak. Instead of viewing terrorism as a direct response to low market opportunities or ignorance, we suggest it is more accurately viewed as a response to political conditions and long-standing feelings of indignity and frustration that have little to do with economics" (119).

These findings resonate with Jonathan Goodhand's (2001) claim that it is more likely the transiently poor, rather than the chronically poor, who rebel, since the latter group is likely to be the least organized. Relative rather than absolute poverty is likely to be more critical in conflict-inducing grievance. He notes that in Central Asia, the disgruntled middle class, whose expectations have been dashed by the stagnant economy, join the Islamist cause most actively.

How can the above evidence be reconciled with the earlier evidence on poverty and civil conflict? The most plausible explanation is that terrorism is quite different in nature from civil conflicts and is much more likely to be driven by political rather than economic considerations. As Krueger and Maleckova note, terrorism has arisen in countries not embroiled in civil war, and countries undergoing civil war have not always been a breeding ground for terrorism (though they consider the connection between national poverty and terrorism a useful research area for the future).

From the point of view of our analysis, reductions in poverty that occur in our simulations do not necessarily imply a drop in terrorism or any other kind of conflict. Thus again our analysis may underestimate the overall benefits of incremental poverty reduction, because such reduction could reduce conflict, enhance growth, and create a positive feedback loop that furthers poverty reduction. The next subsection explores this closing of the analysis loop.

The influence of conflict on poverty

There is extensive evidence on conflict increasing poverty. As Collier and his colleagues

(2003) succinctly note: "War reverses development." It causes displacement of people; decreases in per capita income, growth, and food production; and an increase in disability and disease, which affects even more people than those killed in the conflict.

Stark, specific examples for precipitous declines in income due to conflicts are readily available—for instance, Rice, Graff, and Lewis (2006) note that Côte d'Ivoire's per capita income dropped from $1,120 in 1980 to $650 in 2000. Collier (1999) finds that during civil war, countries grow around 2.2 percentage points more slowly than during peace. Based on an average civil war duration of seven years, he calculates that incomes would be lower by 15 percent and absolute poverty would be higher by 30 percent. This is in line with the World Bank estimate that conflict in Africa is causing a loss of 2 percent annual economic growth (Department for International Development 2001). Stewart C. Huang, and M. Wang (2001) find that in fourteen countries affected by civil war, the average annual growth rate was –3.3 percent. For most of these countries, per capita income fell, food production declined, external debt increased, and export growth decreased.

Goodhand (2001) surveys the research on poverty and conflicts and concludes, "Chronic internal wars are likely to produce chronic poverty." He notes that chronic poverty is likely to increase due to the higher dependency ratios caused by an increased proportion of the old, disabled, and women in the population left after the conflict.

What are some of the other paths that link conflict to loss of economic growth, increased poverty, and adverse social consequences? During civil conflicts, developing countries spend more on the military—5 percent of GDP—instead of the 2.8 percent of GDP during normal times (Collier et al. 2003). Increased military spending decreases expenditures on infrastructure and health, which has negative consequences for incomes and social indicators. On the income front, according to the simulations in Malcolm Knight, Norman Loayza, and Delano Villanueva (1996), the extra 2.2 percent of GDP spent on the military over the seven years of a typical conflict would result in a permanent loss of 2 percent of GDP. On the health front, Anke Hoeffler and

Marta Reynal-Querol (2003) find that during a five-year war, infant mortality increases by 13 percent, and in the first five years of peace after conflict, the mortality rate remains 11 percent higher than the baseline. Civil wars also increase the incidence of malaria and its transmission across borders. The negative health effects of conflicts result both from the increased exposure of the civilian population to the risk of disease, injury, and death and because the government devotes less of its budget to public health.

Conflicts also result in the flight of already scarce capital. A typical country in civil war held 9 percent of its private wealth abroad prior to the war. By the end of the war that had risen to 20 percent, signifying a flight of more of than a tenth of the private capital stock (Collier et al. 2003). Civil war also leads to a deterioration of political institutions. A typical low-income country neither at war nor in postwar peace has a Polity IV index of 2.11 (on a ten-point democracy scale, higher indicating greater democracy), whereas countries in the first decade of postwar peace average only 1.49.[23]

In summary, conflicts increase poverty, whether narrowly construed (income) or broadly construed (disease, mortality, deterioration of freedom). Since IFs does not capture these interactions, it is possible that sudden conflagrations could derail the march toward a global reduction in poverty reported in our simulations.

What might the possibility for loss in the fight against poverty be in sub-Saharan Africa if greater conflict wracked the continent in the future? Chapter 5 provided a basis for thinking about that. It documented (see Table 5.2) that the economic forecasts for Africa in the IFs base case at PPP are 0.7 percent higher through 2030 than those of a recent *Global Economic Prospects* (World Bank 2007).[24] This economic growth differential is a very large portion of the explanation for the difference in extreme poverty forecasts between the IFs base case and the World Bank (see Table 5.3). Although the IFs base case estimates with its lognormal formulation that 29.4 percent of sub-Saharan Africa will live in extreme poverty in 2015, the World Bank estimates that it will be 31.4 percent. The discussion in this section suggests that lower conflict rates could easily generate

a gain of 0.7 percent in economic growth for the continent (as higher ones could lead to economic loss).

The conflict trap

Given the evidence on poverty causing conflict and conflict causing poverty, it is natural to conjecture that the mutual feedback could cause a "conflict trap"—a stagnant situation in which civil war dramatically slow downs a country's development, and the failure of development creates a greater risk of conflicts.

Indeed, many researchers emphasize this mutual feedback. Frances Stewart and V. Fitzgerald (2001: 4) note: "The very high incidence of wars among low-income countries almost certainly reflects a two-way causality with low income predisposing to conflict and itself being a probable outcome of conflict." Ted Robert Gurr, Monty G. Marshall, and Deepa Khosla (2001: 13) state: "Poor societies are at risk of falling into no-exit cycles of conflict in which ineffective governance, societal welfare, humanitarian crises, and the lack of development perpetually chase one another."

There is little evidence, however, for a true conflict-trap equilibrium.[25] Countries do escape conflict periodically, only to fall back into it. Collier and his colleagues (2003), for instance, note that a conflict further increases the risk of long-term conflict by about 17 percent. Fluctuations between conflict-free and conflict-ridden periods could well be a long-run equilibrium.

What can be done externally?

Policies to reduce the risk of conflict follow naturally from the leading causes—reducing poverty, increasing growth, reducing dependence on natural resources and primary commodities, and reducing corruption and improving governance in general. Since our focus is on poverty rather than conflict per se, we will survey suggested policies only briefly, with the aim of identifying implications for our analysis.

Improving governance is a common (perhaps the most common) contemporary prescription for reducing conflict as well as reducing poverty. (The next section will, in fact, turn to governance and poverty specifically.) Collier and his colleagues (2003) note, for example, that in 1970 both Botswana and Sierra Leone were low-income countries with substantial diamond resources. Diamonds fueled the economic growth of Botswana, but they brought about the downfall of Sierra Leone. Democracy and stability and development of a national plan with clearly targeted public expenditures greatly aided Botswana's cause. That example often bolsters the call for improved governance. The diagnosis underlying the prescription may, however, be simplistic.

The story is more complex. The diamonds in Botswana are concentrated and subject to government control, while those in Sierra Leone are alluvial and difficult for the government to control. In conjunction with fiscal mismanagement and corruption, these conditions set the stage for organized criminals to take over diamond mining. There are many other elements that may underlie improved government capacity and reduced conflict. Botswana benefited, for example, from an unusually cohesive ethnic structure (the Tswana make up nearly 80 percent of the population), whereas ethnicity and religion are more divisive in Sierra Leone. The lesson is that the interaction among governance, natural resources, and conflict is nuanced.

A number of possible activities, many of them with assistance from the international community, can support the emergence of stronger government and less conflict:

- International initiatives such as "publish what you pay." All payments made by multinational corporations, especially those involved in resource extraction, should be made public. This information would aid transparency and assist citizens of resource-rich countries in holding their governments accountable for revenues and their use and distribution.
- International assistance in controlling theft of local commodities that encourages domestic conflict over them. The Kimberley process, initiated in 2002 to eliminate conflict diamonds from shipments of rough diamonds, is an example of such an intervention.
- Further progress in preventing economic shocks from destroying governance capacity. Commodity price crashes often occur without reserve funds in place; natural disasters such

as hurricanes often strike without internal capacity for response or external assistance (although international insurance schemes for natural disasters are improving).
- Timing foreign aid so as to help governments rebound from conflict. Collier and his colleagues (2003) criticize the tendency of donor countries to concentrate aid immediately after a conflict ends and then to decrease flows rapidly. They recommend both larger flows and a more gradual tapering off.
- Use of foreign assistance processes to widen participation in governance and to analyze and target conflict reduction. The World Bank's (2005d) own retrospective analysis of poverty reduction strategies in nine conflict-affected countries concluded that much more could be done along these lines.

The implications of having omitted conflict from the analysis

We have already noted the risk of omitting an explicit treatment of conflict from our analysis: it can lead to more optimistic growth rates in the base case for Africa and therefore more optimistic projections of poverty reduction. At the same time, however, omission of conflict from the analysis means that the opportunity for reducing conflict and thereby accelerating poverty reduction may also be underestimated. In sum, although the base case may risk overestimating poverty reduction, the combined intervention scenario, in particular, may err on the side of underestimating leverage for reducing poverty.

Governance and Poverty

The discussion of conflict and poverty touched upon the relationship between governance and poverty. This section considers that relationship in greater detail. In contrast to the significant omission of conflict from the volume's earlier analysis, and to the very limited treatment of environmental issues in that analysis, governance discussions have been fairly extensive. Yet the topic is important enough to ask, (1) Have the inevitable weaknesses in the empirical analysis led us to any systematic misrepresentations in the projections? and (2) What improvements might be undertaken in future analyses?

This volume has paid substantial attention to the interaction between governance and

External initiatives can help break the vicious cycle of conflict and poverty.

Omission of poverty-conflict linkages means that the combined intervention scenario may underestimate poverty reduction potential.

poverty reduction. Inspired by the World Bank project on governance, in Chapter 7 we explored interventions based on improvements in economic freedom, governance effectiveness, and government corruption, which are part of the "domestic self-help" strategy. Table 7.3 presented the effects of the individual levers on poverty reduction. Chapter 8 explored further the linkages between many dimensions of governance and poverty reduction in specific continents and countries.

The IFs model also captures linkages from poverty reduction to improved governance, based on the strong empirical relationship between the two. Yet, Chapter 7 noted that the analysis does not capture the cost of improvements in governance. Indeed, most of the development literature is silent on the costs of institutional change. Given this, the results in Chapter 7 pertaining to governance are best viewed as "scenario planning" exercises rather than an analysis of poverty reduction based on cost-benefit trade-offs.

More generally, this volume has not considered factors other than economic growth that may bring about better governance. There is much consideration in the global community of how external actors might assist domestic efforts, for instance by tying foreign assistance to governance improvements. No such efforts or linkages affected our analysis, including the intervention that increased aid to at least 0.5 percent of GDP for donor countries.

IFs captures some of the economic effects of aid (such as the Dutch disease), but not the effects of sociopolitical forces (such as diversion of funds). Nor does IFs represent how governance and aid interact (recent research shows differential effects of aid based on the quality of governance and institutions). In particular, can aid be structured so as to improve governance and decrease corruption? Discussing these issues here is clearly in the spirit of checking the robustness of our earlier analysis, especially because the intervention of higher foreign aid outperforms other interventions in reducing the poverty headcount.

Although government efficiency and even specific government policies are arguably as important as corruption, corruption is at the heart of contemporary analysis of governance because it fundamentally affects efficiency and

policy choice. We focus on it here. We survey the literature on the linkage of corruption to poverty and of poverty to corruption only briefly. We then turn to a discussion of external levers to improve governance, the linkages missing from our earlier analysis. Clearly, this discussion complements the one in the previous section, since improvement in governance is also critical for conflict reduction.

Corruption causes poverty

Eric Chetwynd and colleagues (2003) note that existing research examines an indirect relationship between corruption and poverty. "Corruption, by itself, does not produce poverty. Rather, *corruption has direct consequences on economic and governance factors, intermediaries that in turn produce poverty*" (6, italics in original). They distinguish between an "economic model," in which corruption affects poverty via economic factors (reduced investment, distorted markets, and increased inefficiency of doing business) and a "governance model," in which corruption affects poverty via governance factors (decreased institutional capacity to deliver quality public services, increased spending on capital projects more conducive to corruption, and decreased compliance with safety and health regulations).

The economic channel of corruption affects two proximate drivers of poverty—growth and inequality. Several World Bank surveys on corruption have found that corruption hinders economic growth by scuttling the expansion plans of businesses (thereby diminishing domestic investment), hurting entrepreneurship (since small business pay a disproportionate share of their revenues as bribes), and causing evasion of taxes and fees by bribing the appropriate authorities.[26] Even after controlling for the state of economic development, Sanjeev Gupta, Hamid Davoodi, and Rosa Alonso-Terme (2002) find that higher corruption increases inequality of income as well as factor ownership. It also increases inequality by effectively decreasing the progressivity of taxes.

Turning to the governance model, Michael Johnston (2000) studied eighty-three countries and found political competition is correlated with lower corruption (after controlling for GDP), suggesting corruption threatens governance through weaker political institutions and reduced mass participation. Paolo Mauro (2002) finds evidence that corruption affects governance by altering the composition of government spending—corrupt governments spend less on education and health.

The IFs-based analysis in Chapter 7 (see the chapter appendix) accounts, at least partially, for the economic channels discussed above when it considers interventions to reduce corruption (for instance, the 60 percent reduction in the corruption perceptions index over twenty years for Middle Africa and Eastern Europe, and 50 percent for Western Africa). Inasmuch as IFs does not capture other economic and governance channels, however, the analysis could well understate the effect of these interventions on poverty. However, simultaneously ignoring the cost of reducing corruption, which could divert government spending from other priority areas, might overstate the effect of these interventions on poverty, somewhat offsetting the omission.

Poverty causes corruption

Although evidence for corruption causing poverty (i.e., lower income) is widely available in the literature, the evidence for reverse causality is much rarer. Jeffrey Sachs (2005: 312) states: "As a country's income rises, governance improves for two major reasons. First, a more literate and affluent society is better able to keep the government honest by playing a watchdog role over government processes. ... Second, a more affluent society can afford to invest in high-quality governance."

Daniel Treisman (2000) lists additional channels by which development might lower corruption. He notes that economic development draws a clearer line between the public and the private. In traditional societies this distinction is fuzzy and bribery gets confused for tributes, lowering the social stigma of corruption. He uses econometric methods to search for evidence on income affecting governance in general and corruption in particular. The effect is strong: "A tenfold increase in 1990 per capita GDP—say from that of El Salvador to that of Canada—would lead to a drop in the corruption rating of between 4.16 and 4.76 points—which would bring El Salvador up to somewhere around Hong Kong or Ireland. ... Log per capita GDP can by itself explain at least 73 percent of the variation in

each of the 1990 TI [Transparency International] perceived corruption indexes" (430).[27]

The earlier analysis did build on a representation by IFs of the ability of economic growth and corruption to influence each other. The analytical weakness, however, has been in not relating a variety of other interventions to the reduction of corruption. These include the efforts of external actors, to which we turn next.

External involvement and governance

The general debate about whether foreign aid helps recipient countries economically overlaps with the debate about the role of external involvement in influencing governance of recipients. Craig Burnside and David Dollar (2000) conclude that aid positively affects growth for developing countries that have sound fiscal, monetary, and trade policies. Their study has also been influential in providing *criteria* for targeting aid. However, William Easterly (2003) argues that the Burnside-Dollar conclusions are not robust across alternative definitions of aid, policies, and growth. Raghuram G. Rajan and Arvind Subramanian (2005) find that even after correcting for the possible bias that poorer (or stronger) growth might affect aid inflow, there is little robust relationship between aid and growth.

The somewhat narrower debate of interest to us here is whether foreign assistance can be *used* as a lever to reform corrupt countries, or more pessimistically, whether aid causes corruption in the first place. Paul Collier and David Dollar (2001) identify two opposing effects of aid on corruption. If aid is linked to government actions to reduce corruption, there will be a direct, favorable effect. However, aid could exert a negative effect by adding to the government's resources, thereby reducing the need for meeting expenditures through taxation and with it the domestic pressure for accountability.

The empirical debate on this question, too, continues to rage. Stephen Knack (2000) found that in the 1982–1995 timeframe aid actually increased corruption and decreased bureaucratic quality and the rule of law. Alberto Alesina and David Dollar (2000) look at more than a hundred cases of "surges" in finance but find that only in a handful of cases does policy really improve in the following three to five years, and in as many cases policy significantly worsens. Alberto Alesina and Beatrice Weder (2002) use

The potential of foreign assistance to reduce corruption is controversial.

time series data on corruption and find that an increase in aid is associated with an increase in corruption. (See also Jakob Svensson 2000 on ethnically fragmented countries.)

Given such negative findings, it is not surprising that recent debate on aid has also focused on the issue of *conditionality*—should aid be given based on promises of good policy to follow? Collier and Dollar (2001) note that such ex-ante conditionality does not work since promises are seldom kept in practice. Burnside and Dollar (2000) also argue for ex-post rather than ex-ante conditionality.

Are donors targeting recipients based on their governance in practice? Alesina and Weder (2002) examined a cross-section of countries in the 1975–1994 time period and found that, after controlling for other potential determinants of foreign aid (such as income, size, economic policies, political system, and historical links with donors), there is no evidence that bilateral or multilateral aid goes disproportionately to less corrupt governments. The Scandinavian countries and Australia, however, which do not have any colonial links, appear to have greater flexibility in the countries they choose to provide aid to, and give more to less corrupt countries.

There is contrary evidence when studies conceptualize governance more broadly. Eric Neumayer (2003) examines all aspects of governance and finds that democracy, human rights, and regulatory burden, in addition to corruption, influence donors' decisions at the eligibility stage. Human rights and regulatory burden also influence the actual aid flows. Even the Alesina and Dollar (2000) study mentioned earlier finds that developing countries that support civil liberties and political freedom receive more aid. Kamiljon Akramov (2006) finds that lower governance quality reduces the likelihood of receiving foreign aid.

In summary, the available evidence seems to indicate a tendency among donors to select recipients for foreign aid and choose the amount of aid to selected countries based on governance, broadly construed, though not necessarily based on corruption alone. There is also substantial heterogeneity in such targeting across donor countries.

Donor countries also attempt to use levers other than foreign aid on behalf of better governance. They have tied debt cancellation

for heavily indebted poor countries (HIPC) to the preparation and implementation of a Poverty Reduction Strategy Paper (PRSP). PRSP preparation and implementation are linked to three principles relevant to corruption prevention: (1) participation of social actors capable of monitoring, criticizing, or sanctioning the actions of the government and other public institutions; (2) an increase in the transparency of government actions; and (3) accountability by way of a clear definition of which public institutions are responsible for which political measures.

Walter Eberlei and Bettina Fuhrmann (2004) study PRSPs from fifty-four countries and conduct an in-depth analysis of five country case studies. Only nine out of the fifty-four countries studied dealt with corruption in detail in their PRSPs, and even those display weaknesses in the quality of their analysis or formulation of strategies to combat corruption and poverty. Yet the study concludes there is little doubt that the PRSP approach can be effective in the fight against corruption.

Implications for our analysis

Based on the evidence presented in this section, one would have to conclude that the connections among aid, development, and governance are complex; few concrete findings emerge. Although there is evidence that aid increases corruption, there is also evidence that some countries target aid based on governance. The coming years will no doubt see much more research on this important topic. Meanwhile, our approach of treating aid and governance separately in the context of poverty reduction, and not representing any direct relationship between aid and quality of governance, appears consistent with the current state of research findings.

Conclusion

From the outset, this study has attempted to recognize its limitations. This chapter acknowledged inadequacies in our treatment of several key variables or systems and their influence on poverty. In particular, the chapter singled out environmental systems, conflict, and governance, and it looked at possible relationships between external action and all of these. (Were more time and space available, it could also have added attention to infrastructure

Any model for forecasting poverty reduction will unfortunately omit or incorrectly specify much of importance.

and science and technology.) Even though our treatment of these topics has been inadequate, a review of the literatures indicates that great theoretical and empirical uncertainties remain about how they relate to poverty. In some cases it appears that omissions in our study have caused us potentially to overestimate prospects for poverty reduction, and in other cases to underestimate those prospects; in many instances, the direction of impact from omissions is simply not clear.

This analysis is not an attempt to absolve analyses of poverty, including this one, of the responsibility of delving more deeply into this broader set of relationships. Future studies, inside and outside this project, must continue to do so.

---

1 Available at http://www.povertyenvironment.net/ pep/filestore2/download/193/pep policy dialogue report final 28-11.pdf.

2 Available at http://www.unep.org/Documents. Multilingual/Default.asp?ArticleID=5514&Document ID=499&l=en.

3 See, for example, UNEP GC21/15, GC22/10, and GC23/10.

4 A UN Development Programme (UNDP)–European Commission (EC) initiative of the same name (see UNDP/EC 1999a, 1999b) preceded this partnership.

5 See http://www.undp.org/pei and http://www. povertyenvironment.net/pep.

6 Among the first efforts in this vein after from the report of the WCED were those by Leonard (1989), Durning (1989), and Gallopin, Gutman, and Maletta (1989) Duraiappah (1996), Forsyth, Leach, and Scoones (1998), Scherr (2000), and the Poverty-Environment Partnership (2005). These studies provide overviews of the relationships between poverty and the environment. Specific empirical work includes that of Agarwal (1997), Barbier (2000), Carter et al. (2007), Cavendish (1999a and 1999b), Dasgupta et al. 2005), Lufumpa (2005), Narain, Gupta, and Klaas van 't Veld (2005), Scott (2006), and Swinton, Escobar, and Reardon (2003). The relationships between the environment and human well-being have also been central to recent international environmental assessments, including the Millennium Ecosystem Assessment (2003; 2005), and the fourth Global Environment Outlook (United Nations Environment Programme 2007), as well as recent World Resources Institute reports (2000; 2005).

7 Dramatic examples of the importance of these factors are seen in the cases of what are referred to as "resource curses" discussed elsewhere in this chapter and volume.

8 See Duraiappah 1998; Arnold and Bird 1999; Parikh 2002; Jahan and Umana 2003; Nayak 2004; Dasgupta et al. 2005; Lufumpa 2005; Poverty-Environment Partnership 2005a; ADB 2007. A short-lived newsletter aimed at enhancing the poverty-environment dialogue was, in fact, simply titled *Nexus* (http://www.iisd.org/publications/pub. aspx?id=454).

9 It is interesting that Duraiappah (1998) does not also draw direct links from power, wealth, and greed, institutional failure, and market failure directly to poverty, especially because he is careful to distinguish between environmentally induced and nonenvironmentally induced poverty.

10 See for example Duraiappah (1996; 1998; 2004), Forsyth, Leach, and Scoones (1998), and Gangadharan and Valenzuela (2001).

11 See Bass et al. (2006), Narain, Gupta, and van 't Veld (2005), Poverty-Environment Partnership (2005), World Bank (2005), and WRI (2005). WRI , in fact, refers to the environment as the "wealth of the poor."

12 The third volume of this series will address links between health and the environment more thoroughly. Here we focus on its potential impact on economic productivity.

13 See http://www.who.int/quantifying_ehimpacts/en and http://www.who.int/heli/en.

14 See Toman (2003) for a similar approach to that described here.

15 The physical values from the partial equilibrium modules for agriculture and energy, multiplied by initial prices and relative price change over time, enter the broader economic module in value terms and override the simpler production function calculation of the economic module.

16 IFs calculates a measure of mean world temperature from the carbon dioxide levels, but the function is very basic; the model looks to elaborate climate models for leadership on such forecasts.

17 The table hides the fact that emissions peak around 2030 in both scenarios before leveling off and beginning a gradual decline. Because of the cumulative and delayed nature of the impact of emissions on the global climate, though, the atmospheric concentrations and world temperature continue to rise throughout the scenario period.

18 By the end of the scenario period, these declines have leveled off in the combined scenario and are close to leveling off in the base case.

19 Looking at a one-year horizon, Fearon and Laitin (2003) find that at a $579 per capita GDP level, there is a 17.7 percent risk of conflict, at $2,043, a 10.7 percent risk, and at $9,466, less than 1 percent risk. Sambanis (2003) finds that the average GDP per capita for countries that experienced war within five years is $2,176; for those that did not experience war within five years, it is $5,173.

20 They find that the relationship between exports of primary commodities as a fraction of GDP and conflict is nonlinear and peaks with 30 percent resource dependency.

21 Collier and Hoeffler (2002) do not find, however, that aid increases the risk of rebellion. Aid could affect conflict through growth but does not appear to have a direct effect.

22 Although ethnic fractionalization has been often cited as a reason for conflicts, Collier and Hoeffler (2002) suggest that limited ethnic differentiation can actually be a problem—if the largest ethnic group is an absolute majority, the risk of rebellion increases by 50 percent. In such societies, the minorities might fear exclusion from influence despite a democratic political process. Ethnic differentiation could be of greater importance if a country discovers natural resources such as oil, since resources are usually geographically concentrated, and the issue arises of whether the locality or the nation as a whole owns it.

23 The comparable numbers are 4.79 and 5.66 on the seven-point Freedom House scale of political freedoms, on which higher numbers are less free (Collier et al. 2003).

24 The growth rate assumption differential results directly from the use in IFs of higher African growth rates based on the late 1990s to estimate future growth. The higher growth rate in IFs thus in part reflects lower conflict in the last half of the 1990s.

25 Although we are not aware of studies that explicitly seek to test for the existence of *conflict* traps, there are a few that test for the existence of income or poverty traps (McKenzie and Woodruff 2002, Kraay and Raddatz 2005, and Caucutt and Kumar 2006). All these studies conclude that there is scant evidence for the existence of poverty traps as described above.

26 Mauro (1995, 2002) finds in a cross-country sample that a high level of corruption is associated with a lower level of investment as a share of GDP and lower growth of per capita GDP. In another cross-country study, Tanzi and Davodi (1997) find that higher corruption increases (low-productivity) public investment, reduces government revenues, lowers expenditures on operations and maintenance, and reduces the quality of public infrastructure, all of which lower growth. Kauffmann et al (1999) find a strong positive causal connection between governance and per capita income.

27 To shed light on causality, Treisman uses the distance from the equator as an instrumental variable for economic development. Previous research (for instance, Sachs 1997) has suggested that tropical countries grew slower than temperate countries. The correlation between these two variables is high (0.69 for 1990 per capita GDP), and the distance from the equator is unlikely to directly affect corruption other than through economic development, which makes it a useful instrument.

The Future of Global Poverty and Human Development

This volume conveys and explores the most extensive set of forecasts of global poverty ever made. The forecasts are long-term, looking fifty years into the future. They are geographically rich, building up from the country level to continental subregions, continents as wholes, and the world. With India, the study even begins the necessary process of drilling down into countries. Full country details are available in the forecast tables at the end of this volume and accompanying web postings.

The forecasts are also very much contingent; they are scenarios, not predictions. The volume supplements the base case forecast with framing scenarios to provide a sense of the outer boundaries of likely poverty forecasts. It presents intervention scenarios (individual and in packages) to explore the possible leverage that the global community has to incrementally shift the long-term patterns of poverty reduction.

Finally, the study, while focusing very heavily on the specific measure of income poverty now at the center of global attention, namely $1 per day, reaches well beyond that measure. It reports forecasts using other measures of income poverty, especially $2 per day, but also $5 and $10 per day. It provides some information on income poverty gaps and on relative, not just absolute poverty. Although more difficult and even more uncertain than income poverty forecasts, the study provides some information about human capabilities and functioning using the human development index and human poverty index of the UN Development Programme. For purposes of consistency across the analysis and because of limitations of space, the text discusses poverty primarily in terms of the $1 per day measure. Again, however, we invite readers to look at the appendices and supporting analyses for other measures.

What Have We Learned?

With respect to where interacting systems appear to be taking us, other studies have documented the very rapid rate of poverty reduction globally and forecast its continuance. They also made clear that sub-Saharan Africa is all but certain to miss the Millennium Development Goal (MDG) on poverty and to remain, along with South Asia because of its absolute numbers, of greatest global concern. The base case of International Futures (IFs) reinforces those general understandings and adds considerable detail to them in terms of the countries and regions within those two continental regions and the broader globe. It also holds out the hope, however, that progress in sub-Saharan Africa might well prove considerably faster than has often been anticipated.

With respect to framing scenarios and specific interventions, the study repeatedly concludes that it is highly unlikely that goals as broad in geographic scope and as relatively near-term as the first MDG can be realized, because we have limited ability to shift the underlying systems that rapidly. The study simultaneously reinforces the very substantial leverage that conscious and well-judged interventions can have in the longer term. It also is cognizant of the reality that some countries, such as China via its economic liberalization, have accomplished quite dramatic changes in trajectory; the exceptional foundations for that change nonetheless reinforce the more general conclusion.

With respect to specific interventions, no silver bullets emerged across a wide range of candidates examined. Poverty is a complex syndrome of interacting variables and reinforcing dynamics. Domestic and international transfers appear to provide special leverage in the short run because, if well structured to reach intended recipients, they can directly redress inequalities. In the longer run, however, their impact, too, appears quite limited in the absence of other individual initiatives.

Further with respect to interventions, combined packages involving a very wide range of actions appear to present some trade-offs, but even more synergies. The longer-term effects of broad packages of intervention appear reinforcing. This finding is quite striking, because when the study began it seemed at least as likely that significant trade-offs would appear.

Finally, with respect to interventions, specific subregions and countries obviously have their own histories and paths, still another reason that silver bullets do not exist globally.

Chapters 7 and 8 explored some of the specific conditions that surface in subregions and countries, tailoring interventions in Chapter 7 according to the conditions of the subregions. Such "clinical" analysis of local conditions would ideally drill down to the level of subpopulations and geographic subregions within countries, something not possible in this more aggregate study but potentially feasible with the underlying analytic tool and approach.

Procedurally, this book demonstrates the value of studying poverty futures in the context of a system of models. Poverty analysis obviously requires consideration of the interacting dynamics within and across demographic, economic, educational, health, and sociopolitical systems. In addition, Chapter 9 argues the need for greater attention to the environment, conflict, and governance than has been possible here. One could add infrastructure and technological change to the list of key subsystems given inadequate attention.

What Are Our Uncertainties?

Discussion of what we have learned has also indicated many of the weaknesses of this study and our uncertainties about the future of global poverty. We can identify many others. For instance, poverty analysis should attend to the urban-rural dimension, as well as to age and sex and even to important ethnic and rigid class or caste divisions. Current problems with breaking our models down into such categories in no way obviates the need to do so in the future. Chronic poverty pockets will increasingly become the focus of extreme poverty reduction efforts as large portions of most global populations move beyond it. The use in this volume of an alternative, cross-sectionally based formulation for forecasting poverty reduction hints at the possibility that traditional forecasts, treating populations as largely homogeneous across a lognormal or similar distribution, may be inadequate.

Beyond this, we must admit that uncertainties in forecasting with a complex model are legion. Each formulation is a simplification of real-world relationships and each is almost always less understood that we would like. Collectively, the interaction of such formulations quite reasonably leads some to conclude that the task is hopeless and even

Significant poverty reduction requires combined packages of initiatives, tailored to specific conditions.

misleading. This study has repeatedly concurred with the analysis of difficulties. Yet it has also repeatedly argued that policy analysis requires forecasting and that explicit, generally transparent, formal efforts can add value relative to simple extrapolations or assertions from often implicit mental models.

What Next?

No one should have believed that the process of setting and pursuing MDGs, including that for poverty reduction, would end with the target date of 2015. Global pursuit of improvements in the human condition has progressed through many rounds of targets, some met, most not. And even if the poverty MDGs were to be met in 2015, doing so would only cut poverty and hunger by one-half.

There is thus need, increasingly pressing, for several steps. The first is to extend the horizon of global goal setting to at least 2030. This time, however, we should explicitly acknowledge the difficulty of rapid progress and at least frame such goal setting in a still longer perspective. Midcentury seems a reasonable horizon for such framing. Theoretically, the last round of goal setting extended across twenty-five years, from 1990 through 2015, but after the enunciation of the goals, only fifteen years remained. If the global community enunciated a new set of global targets in 2010, perhaps for 2030, the deeper framing analysis should look at least out forty years to 2050.

Second, global goals should not pretend to be appropriate for all regions and countries. Setting of global goals has the benefit of facilitating easy statement and review. It can help draw attention to regions and countries falling short. It can help mobilize resources and even appropriately direct those to the regions and countries furthest from the goals.

Yet nondifferentiated goals also fundamentally condemn some countries and regions to the status of failure from the day of their statement. Sub-Saharan Africa is, of course, the primary victim of such failed expectations. Poverty reduction is not the only example or even the most egregious. The goal of universal completion of primary education by 2015 did not even recognize the different starting positions of countries around the world on the indicator variable. At least the

poverty goal, with its relative statement of the goal in terms of 50 percent reduction, did that, although the poverty goal also failed to recognize the very different contextual conditions and dynamics of countries.

The Poverty Reduction Strategy Paper (PRSP) system offers real hope of more differentiated goal setting within the context of global objectives. It needs, however, to look longer-term as well. And, of course, we still need to set and evaluate country-specific goals in the context of a dynamic analysis of prospects.

Finally, the global development community needs integrated reviews of progress toward the goals, set within an analysis of the potential for future progress. In addition to the PRSP process, the World Bank and United Nations agencies and regional commissions have set up useful monitoring reviews around the MDGs. Studies such as this one can contribute needed analysis of longer-term context.

With respect to the "What Next?" question, this project on Patterns of Potential Human Progress has several plans of its own. The next two volumes will drill down into global education and health. Ones after that will look at infrastructure and governance. Active development will continue on the tools underlying the studies, which will remain publicly and freely available. The analysis will continue to be global, with as much geographic differentiation as possible, and will be long-term. The ultimate goal of the project is better understanding of the global human condition so as to contribute to its improvement.

The setting of global goals and evaluation of progress toward them should involve integrated analysis of human systems and long-term analysis horizons.

Appendix 1
Cross-Sectional and Lognormal Formulations for Poverty

This appendix provides basic information on the two formulations used for forecasting poverty in the IFs model. Appendix 2 elaborates the lognormal approach.

Figure A1.1 Cross-sectional relationship of GDP per capita and extreme poverty

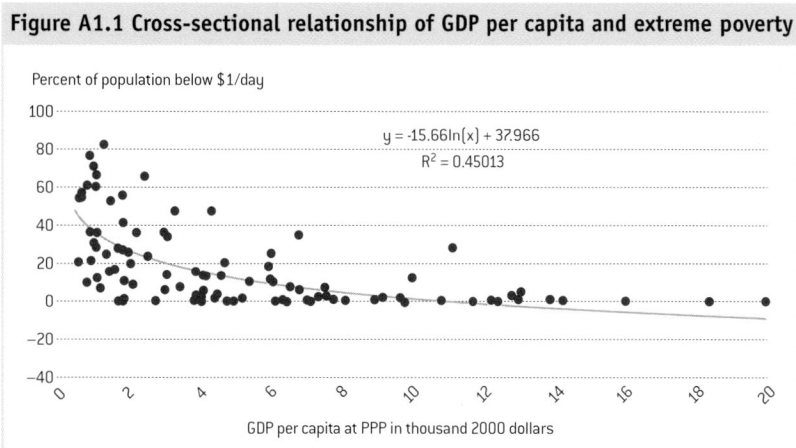

Percent of population below $1/day

$$y = -15.66\ln(x) + 37.966$$
$$R^2 = 0.45013$$

GDP per capita at PPP in thousand 2000 dollars

Source: IFs Version 5.47.

Figure A1.2 Cross-sectional formulations linking GDP per capita to poverty rate

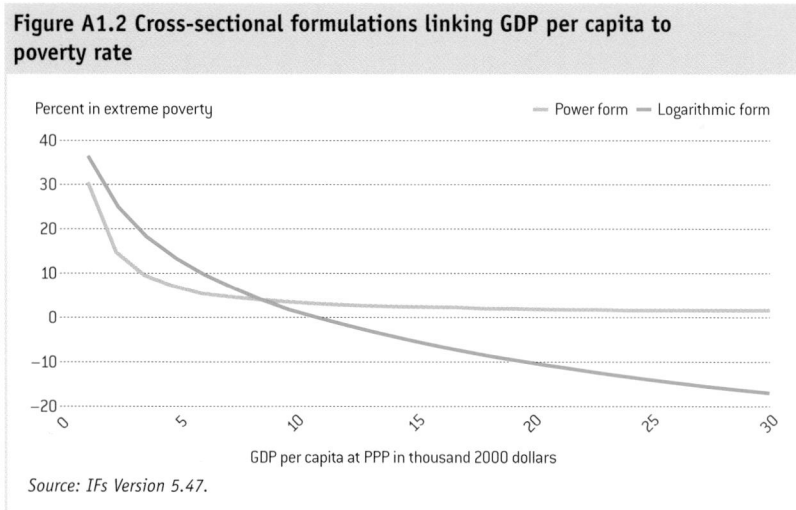

Percent in extreme poverty

— Power form — Logarithmic form

GDP per capita at PPP in thousand 2000 dollars

Source: IFs Version 5.47.

Cross-Sectional Analysis of Change in Poverty

Looking at the simpler and much less heavily used approach first, Figure A1.1 shows a scatterplot of countries for which there are data on which to build a cross-sectional formulation. The logarithmic curve fit to that data suggests that as countries reach about $10,000 per capita at purchasing power parity (PPP), extreme poverty essentially disappears.

The cross-sectional formulation used within International Futures (IFs) to fill holes for countries without surveys uses the logarithmic form of Figure A1.1 (do not confuse using the logarithmic form with the lognormal approach, discussed below), but statistical analysis added the Gini coefficient to the formulation with the expected positive relationship (taking the adjusted R-squared to 0.62).

$$IncomeLTICS_r = 14.514 - 15.196* LN(GDPPCP2000_r) + 56.17* GINI_r$$

where

IncomeLTICS is the percentage living on less than $1

GDPPCP2000 is GDP per capita at PPP in 2000 $

GINI is the Gini coefficient

r is a specific country/region

It should be noted, however, that an exponential or power curve can be fit to the same cross-sectional data with approximately the same R-squared, but it will exhibit slower decline with increasing gross domestic product (GDP) per capita and has a much longer tail of nonzero poverty. Figure A1.2 compares the two quite different functions. When the exponential form is substituted within IFs, the forecasts for poverty reduction are, of course, even less positive. The logarithmic form is normally used in IFs, however, because it appears visually to capture better both the higher levels of poverty at low levels of GDP per capita and to capture the near elimination of extreme poverty by about $10,000 per capita.

In the process of forecasting with the cross-sectionally estimated function, it is necessary to recognize initial differences between the most recent survey-based data for each country and the expected values of the function. These differences could represent a variety of forces, including patterns of government transfers or patterns of social discrimination across ethnic or caste groupings. It is impossible to know if such differences or country-specific shifts relative to the function will persist or not. IFs forecasts assume very slow erosion of the differences for individual countries from the general function over time, thus protecting the country differences (path dependencies) for many years. Specifically, the differences are captured by a multiplicative adjustment factor in the base year of the model.[1]

Lognormal Analysis of Change in Poverty

The use of distributions in forecasting begins with the distinction between a detailed distribution and the simpler parametric representation of such a distribution. By far the most widely used method for detailing distributions of income, wealth, or other quantities is the Lorenz curve (see, again, Figure 3.1 and the discussion of it). Any survey data on income or consumption for a society can be shown in Lorenz curve form with essentially complete accuracy. There is a clear relationship between the Lorenz curve and the expression of shares of income held by quintiles, deciles, or even percentiles of population.

Although it would be possible simply to project forward the quintile or decile shares of a Lorenz curve to specify future income distributions, doing so would have at least two significant weaknesses. First, it would largely freeze those distributions, which can be quite dynamic. Second, it would not directly facilitate the computation of key poverty indexes such as the headcount of those with less than $1 per day.

What we want instead is an analytic representation of the income distribution that can change in form in response to both changing average income levels and changing income distributions, in turn represented by something as simple as the Gini coefficient. Moreover, we want a representational form from which we can conveniently compute specific deciles or quintiles (thereby reconstructing the Lorenz curve) and also compute key poverty measures like the headcount.

Fortunately, there are a number of analytic formulations and estimation techniques that allow us to do exactly that. The most widely used is the lognormal formulation. Chapter 3 discussed it and portrayed it in Figures 3.2–3.3. Although not all national income distributions have lognormal form, something very close to that form is very typical.[2]

A lognormal distribution that fully represents the distribution of income in a society can be specified with only two parameters: average income and the standard deviation of it.[3] Very usefully for forecasting purposes, the Gini coefficient can be used in lieu of the standard deviation. The Lorenz curve and standard poverty measures are then easily computable from the lognormal equation with the two specific parameters.[4]

Given its advantages, the IFs approach to forecasting poverty uses the lognormal formulation, driven by average consumption and the Gini coefficient. More concretely, the procedure in IFs requires specification and use of the general function below.

$IncomeLT1LN_r = f (LogNormalDistribution, CperCap_r,$
$\quad GINI_r, NSNARAT_r)$

where

$NSNARAT_r = (IncomeLT1LN_r^{t=1}, CperCap_r^{t=1}, GINI_r^{t=1})$

where

IncomeLT1LN is the percentage living on less than $1 (lognormal)

CperCap is household consumption per capita in 2000 $ at PPP

GINI is the Gini coefficient

NSNARAT is the ratio of national survey poverty level to household consumption from national account data, computed in the initial model year (2000)

r is a specific country/region

As with the cross-sectional formulation, the computed value of those living on less than $1 per day in the base year (2000) is fit to initial conditions.

Appendix 2
Using Lognormal Income Distributions

Lognormal Distribution of Income

A variable x is said to be lognormally distributed when its log has a normal distribution. To be lognormally distributed, x always has to be positive. Let us assume that income x has a lognormal distribution, such that $y = \ln(x)$ has a normal distribution with mean μ_x and standard deviation σ_x.

The probability density function (PDF) $f_x(x)$ of the lognormal distribution is given by

(1a)
$$f_x(x) = \frac{1}{x\sigma_x\sqrt{2\pi}}e^{-\frac{1}{2}\left[\frac{\ln x - \mu_x}{\sigma_x}\right]^2}$$

Let us denote the lognormal distribution by $\Lambda(\mu_x, \sigma_x)$ and the normal distribution by $N(\mu_x, \sigma_x)$. The PDF of N is given by

(1b)
$$f_y = \frac{1}{\sqrt{2\pi}}e^{-\frac{y^2}{2}}$$

Derivation of the Parameters of Lognormal Distribution from Available Data

J. Aitchison and James Allen C. Brown (1957: 8) note that, the mean, μ of a variable x (e.g., income or consumption), when x has a lognormal distribution, $\Lambda(\mu_x, \sigma_x)$ can be found from the following:

(2)
$$\mu = \exp\left[\mu_x + \frac{1}{2}\sigma_x^2\right]$$

From the Theorem 2.7 of Aitchison and Brown (1957: 13) the Gini coefficient, G for lognormal distribution can be derived as (see Chotikapanich, Valenzuela, and Prasada Rao 1997):

(3)
$$G = 2\Phi\left(\frac{\sigma_x}{\sqrt{2}}\right) - 1$$

where Φ is the standard normal distribution. From the above equation, we can calculate one of the parameters of Λ,

(4)
$$\sigma_x = \sqrt{2}\Phi^{-1}\left(\frac{G+1}{2}\right)$$

Given the mean income, μ, we can use equations (4) and (2) to calculate the other parameter of the lognormal distribution:

(5)
$$\mu_x = \ln(\mu) - \frac{1}{2}\sigma_x^2$$

Calculating Population and Income Shares

Once we find mean μ_x and standard deviation σ_x, we can construct the distribution equation and integrate it for any cutoff of income.

The proportion of the population with incomes less than or equal to a given level x is given by the distribution function:

(6)
$$\pi(x) = \int_0^x f_x(x)dx$$

The integral $\int_0^x f_x(x)dx$, is the lognormal cumulative distribution function (CDF) at x, that is:

Population fraction below income

(7)
$$x = \Lambda(x \mid \mu_x, \sigma_x)$$

The corresponding income shares (at x) can be obtained from the following first moment distribution (Chotikapanich, Valenzuela, and

Prasada Rao 1997; Aitchison and Brown 1957):

(8)
$$\eta(x) = \frac{1}{\mu} \int_0^x x f_x(x) dx$$

and according to the fundamental theorem of the moment distribution (Aitchinson and Brown 1957: 12), the first moment distribution with parameters (μ_x, σ_x) is the same as the lognormal distribution with parameters $(\mu_x + 0.5\,\sigma_x^2, \sigma_x)$, that is, the income fraction held by people earning below income x,

(9) $\eta(x) = \Lambda\,(x \mid \mu_x + 0.5\,\sigma_x^2, \sigma_x)$

Poverty Measure: Poverty Headcount

Replacing x with the poverty line income, z (e.g., $1 PPP a day, or $365 PPP per year) in equation 7, we obtain the percentage of people living below $1 a day (the headcount index, or H/P, where H is the number of poor and P the total population):

(10) Poverty Headcount Index,
$$H/P = \Lambda\,(z \mid \mu_x, \sigma_x)$$

Poverty Measure: Poverty Gap

The poverty gap is obtained from the following generalized class of Foster-Gear-Thorbeck (FGT) poverty measures,

(11)
$$P_\alpha = \int_0^z \left[\frac{z-x}{z} \right]^\alpha f_x(x) dx$$

where, $\alpha, \ge 0$, $f_x(x)$ is the density function at income x and z is the income at the poverty line.

The above equation returns poverty headcount index for $\alpha = 0$. When $\alpha = 1$, we get the poverty gap (PG), which can be interpreted as the shortfall from the poverty line or the depth of poverty below the line. The poverty gap, expressed as a percentage, can be further simplified to:

(12)
$$PG = \int_0^z \left[\frac{z-x}{z} \right] f_x(x) dx$$

(13)
$$PG = \int_0^z f_x(x) dx - \frac{1}{z} \int_0^z x f_x(x) dx$$

(14)
$$PG = \frac{H}{P} - \frac{\mu}{z} \eta(z)$$

where μ is the mean income (or consumption), using equation 8.

(15)
$$PG = \frac{H}{P} - \frac{\mu}{z} \Lambda\left(z \mid \mu_x + 0.5\sigma_x^2, \sigma_x\right)$$

using equation 9 from above.

Reconciliation Between National Accounts and Survey Data

To reconcile the discrepancy between national accounts (NA) and household survey (HS) figures, International Futures converts its NA mean income (GDP per capita in PPP dollars) to an equivalent HS mean consumption. It does so using a reverse calculation of the mean consumption from the available data on Gini index and the population share with consumption below a dollar PPP a day, both calculated (at the source) by using the HS data.

We know (from the definition section on lognormal distribution above),

(16)
$$\Lambda(x \mid \mu_x, \sigma_x) = \Phi\left(\frac{\ln(x) - \mu_x}{\sigma_x} \right)$$

therefore,

(17)
$$\Lambda(365 \mid \mu_x, \sigma_x) = \Phi\left(\frac{\ln(365) - \mu_x}{\sigma_x} \right)$$

or, population fraction below an income of $1 PPP a day, or $365/year, H/P

(18)
$$= \Phi\left(\frac{\ln(365) - \mu_x}{\sigma_x} \right) \quad \text{or,}$$

(19)
$$\Phi^{-1}\left(\frac{H}{P} \right) = \frac{\ln(365) - \mu_x}{\sigma_x} \quad \text{or,}$$

(20)
$$\mu_x = \ln(365) - \Phi^{-1}\left(\frac{H}{P} \right) * \sigma_x$$

In the above equation $\Phi^{-1}\left(\frac{H}{P} \right), \sigma_x$ is available

from World Bank, where it is calculated using HS data on (mostly) consumption. We can calculate μ_x from this equation and obtain a (HS equivalent) mean consumption using equation 2 above.

Appendix 3
Deep Drivers of Economic Growth and Distribution

Deep Drivers of Economic Growth

As noted at the beginning of Chapter 4, extrapolation is a good first step to explore possible future poverty levels. Multivariate formulations involving the key proximate causal drivers, namely average income and income distribution, are the appropriate second step. Yet if we want to analyze the leverage of policy interventions, it is necessary to go further by beginning exploration of the deep drivers of the proximate drivers, ideally with tools that frame the deep drivers in terms relatively close to agent action: government spending and regulation, household behavior, technical and other assistance by nongovernmental organizations, or decisions by firms.

Such richness of specification is, of course, the Holy Grail of poverty (and much other policy) analysis and may be as difficult to find as the religious one. In this book we make do with the structures that have been developed within the IFs model. Because of its special importance, this appendix sketches the drivers of GDP per capita (and household consumption).

Chapter 4 summarily described the economic module of IFs as a general equilibrium-seeking model that uses inventories as buffer stocks to provide price signals, so that the model chases equilibrium over time.[5] Its production function represents GDP as a function of production capital, labor, and multifactor productivity (MFP). MPF is a function of human capital (education and health), social capital, governance quality and policies, physical and natural capital (infrastructure and energy prices), and knowledge development and diffusion (R&D and economic integration with the outside world). The cohort-component demographic model determines the size of the labor force, while domestic and foreign savings help determine capital investment. A social accounting matrix (SAM) envelope ties economic production and consumption to simple interactor financial flows, including government taxation or transfers and domestic and international transfers.

In short, many of the desired agent-based policy levers, such as governmental spending and transfers, are available in the structure. In many other cases, such as the levels of governmental corruption or economic freedom, the variables are also included in the model, even without clear roots running to specific actors and agency.

This brief discussion cannot specify the full model, and sources of detailed model elaboration were listed earlier. We invite the reader to call up a window in IFs called "Development Profile," available for any country or grouping. That window shows, for instance, that in Afghanistan in 2000, those aged twenty-five or older had completed an average of only 1.1 years of education. The expected value, based on a cross-sectionally estimated relationship with GDP per capita, was 1.9. The parameter assigned to translate such deviation into impact on productivity, based on the extensive empirical work that many analysts have done on the drivers of productivity, was 0.1 percent lower productivity per year of "missing" education, suggesting that the weakness of Afghanistan in educational performance would cost it nearly 0.3 percent annual growth.[6] Altogether, underperformance with respect to human capital was estimated to be costing Afghanistan about 0.74 percent per year in growth, and underperformance on social capital and governance might cost another 0.15 percent.

Calculations of the impact of social and governmental performance, in spite of extensive empirical work, are obviously uncertain. It is hard to believe, for instance, that weaknesses in social capital and governance were not costing Afghanistan more than 0.15 percent per year in productivity and growth. Because there were no data for Afghanistan on economic freedom, for example, the computed values were set at the level of the expected ones; surely the level of economic freedom in Afghanistan was considerably below the cross-sectionally estimated value in 2000. Fortunately, data are fairly complete on most drivers of productivity for most countries.[7]

In spite of limitations, the approach that the Development Profile illustrates has some significant advantages for the study. First, there is endogeneity in the model's representation of the various drivers of productivity and growth. To illustrate, education and health spending are affected over time by government revenue and expenditure balances, and foreign aid can supplement revenues and increase that spending, but current account deficits may lead to government retrenchment that restricts them. Second, the user of the model can flexibly intervene with respect to these growth drivers and their expected per unit contributions to growth. That is, a user can direct more government spending to education and can also change the empirically often contentious parametric impact of years of education on productivity.

The focus here has been on the drivers of economic growth related to multifactor productivity, but there are many other leverage points in the model. For instance, changes in fertility patterns will, over longer time horizons, affect labor supply, as will changes in the female participation rate in the shorter term. Savings rates and capital investment can be affected by foreign direct investment or worker remittances. Of considerable relevance to the Millennium Project's proposed plan of action and to the Global Compact of the eighth Millennium Development Goal, foreign aid levels can be changed and will affect current account balances and government revenue and spending patterns and balances. Chapter 7 elaborates the leverage points for analysis in considerably more detail.

Deep Drivers of Distribution

If the forecasting of economic growth is very difficult, the forecasting of income distribution is even harder. For that reason, many users of the IFs model will prefer to specify changes in the Gini coefficient over time exogenously rather than to rely on the endogenous computations of IFs. Nonetheless, the endogenous computations of IFs do begin to tie deep drivers to the income distribution and therefore allow, once again, some capability for analyzing the possible impact of policy-based interventions.

Forecasting of changes in Gini necessarily involves the forecasting of the differential performance of segments within the population. Based on historical data, the means of different deciles could be extrapolated or in some other way forecast, but that would be, once again, unrelated to specific interventions and not add much simply to extrapolating changes in Gini itself.

Ideally, the forecasting of Gini should be tied to an elaboration of household types as is done with a social accounting matrix. SAMs can distinguish multiple categories of urban and rural households and their changing demographic sizes (as a result, for instance, of rural-to-urban migration) and income structures (as a result of structural change in the economy, of changing patterns of government transfers, and of many other factors). For the purposes of studying longer-term change in global poverty levels, the SAM ideal is tarnished by two realities: (1) in spite of efforts via the UN's system of national accounts, there is no standard household classification system for SAMs, so that they vary widely and are generally used in single-country analysis, not global forecasting; and (2) most models built around SAMs are used for rather short-term analysis and even more commonly for comparative static analysis (for example, comparison of income patterns in a society open to agricultural imports to those in one that is not, without much or any consideration of the dynamic path from one to the other).

Nonetheless, the basic rooting of forecasts of Gini in a SAM retains the tremendous advantage of tying those forecasts to changes in interventions that are clearly policy-relevant. And fortunately, the Global Trade Analysis Project (GTAP) has collected key information, such as share taken of value added, for two classes of households, those based respectively on skilled and unskilled labor, across eighty-seven countries and regions and fifty-seven economic sectors. IFs has drawn heavily on the GTAP data, most recently Version 6, in its own economic model specification, and the IFs SAM is built on the basis of the two household categories. The GTAP database has made it possible to develop forecasts of income by type of household as economies, and therefore value-added shares, shift from agriculture to manufacturing and to services. Moreover, IFs has used the GTAP database to simulate changes not just in sector shares but also in more fundamental economic structures, by making the household shares in each sector a function of GDP per capita levels.

For the calculation of Gini it is necessary, however, to know not just the household income shares, but also their sizes. Unfortunately, the GTAP dataset does not provide numbers on labor force size by skill level within sectors.[8] And data from the Organization for Economic Cooperation and Development (OECD) on labor force size by classifications such as professional and administrative, which could be used to estimate numbers of skilled versus unskilled workers, exist only for well-to-do countries. Within IFs, however, the submodel of formal education helps generate future values of education levels in the adult population, which in turn allow estimates of the size of the skilled and unskilled household sets.

Given the income shares accruing to skilled and unskilled shares of the population from GTAP foundations and the sizes of those portions of the population from the IFs educational model, the Gini index is computed from the simple Lorenz curve that those two incomes and population shares create, scaled to the empirically known initial condition.

As stated at the beginning of this subsection, the formulation for forecasting domestic Gini coefficients for each country, relying on only two household types, is very crude. For that reason, most analysis in this study is done with scenarios of distributional change rather than with endogenous forecasts. Nonetheless, the endogenously computed Gini coefficients carry the advantage of being responsive to many interventions in the model, not least being expenditures on education. Thus it is of interest to explore those computations in some of the analysis.

Appendix 4
Countries in UN Regions and Subregions

Africa

Eastern Africa	Middle Africa	Northern Africa	Southern Africa	Western Africa
Burundi	Angola	Algeria	Botswana	Benin
Comoros	Cameroon	Egypt	Lesotho	Burkina Faso
Djibouti	Central African Republic	Libya	Namibia	Cape Verde
Eritrea	Chad	Morocco	South Africa	Côte d'Ivoire
Ethiopia	Congo, Rep. of	Sudan	Swaziland	Gambia
Kenya	Congo, Dem. Rep. of the	Tunisia		Ghana
Madagascar	Equatorial Guinea			Guinea
Malawi	Gabon			Guinea-Bissau
Mauritius	São Tomé and Príncipe			Liberia
Mozambique				Mali
Réunion				Mauritania
Rwanda				Niger
Seychelles				Nigeria
Somalia				St. Helena (UK)
Uganda				Senegal
Tanzania				Sierra Leone
Zambia				Togo
Zimbabwe				

Asia

Eastern Asia	South-Central Asia	South-Eastern Asia	Western Asia	
China	Afghanistan	Brunei	Armenia	Saudi Arabia
Hong Kong	Bangladesh	Cambodia	Azerbaijan	Syria
Korea, Dem. Rep. of	Bhutan	Indonesia	Bahrain	Turkey
Korea, Rep. of	India	Laos	Cyprus	United Arab Emirates
Japan	Iran, Islamic Rep. of	Malaysia	Gaza Strip	Yemen
Macau	Kazakhstan	Myanmar	Georgia	
Mongolia	Kyrgyzstan	Philippines	Iraq	
Taiwan	Maldives	Singapore	Israel	
	Nepal	Thailand	Jordan	
	Pakistan	Timor-Leste	Kuwait	
	Sri Lanka	Vietnam	Lebanon	
	Tajikistan		Oman	
	Turkmenistan		Palestine	
	Uzbekistan		Qatar	

Oceania

Australia-New Zealand	Melanesia	Micronesia	Polynesia
Australia	Fiji	Guam (US)	Samoa
New Zealand	New Caledonia	Kiribati	Cook Islands
	Papua New Guinea	Marshall Islands	French Polynesia
	Solomon Islands	Micronesia	Niue
	Vanuatu	Nauru	Pitcairn (NZ)
		Northern Mariana Islands (US)	Western Samoa
		Palau	Tokelau (NZ)
			Tonga
			Tuvalu (UK)
			Wallis and Futuna Islands (F)

Europe

Eastern Europe	Northern Europe	Southern Europe	Western Europe
Belarus	Channel Islands (UK)	Albania	Austria
Bulgaria	Denmark	Andorra	Belgium
Czech Republic	Estonia	Bosnia and Herzegovina	France
Hungary	Faeroe Islands (DK)	Croatia	Germany
Poland	Finland	Gibraltar (GB)	Liechtenstein
Moldova	Iceland	Greece	Luxembourg
Romania	Ireland	Holy See	Monaco
Russia	Isle of Man (UK)	Italy	Netherlands
Slovak Republic	Latvia	Macedonia	Switzerland
Ukraine	Lithuania	Malta	
	Norway	Portugal	
	Sweden	San Marino	
	United Kingdom	Serbia and Montenegro	
		Slovenia	
		Spain	

Latin America and the Caribbean

Caribbean		Central America	South America
Anguila (UK)	Martinique (F)	Belize	Argentina
Antigua and Barbuda	Monserrat (UK)	Costa Rica	Bolivia
Aruba (NE)	Netherlands Antilles (NE)	El Salvador	Brazil
Bahamas	Puerto Rico	Guatemala	Chile
Barbados	St. Kitts and Nevis	Honduras	Colombia
British Virgin Islands (UK)	St. Lucia	Mexico	Ecuador
Cayman Islands (UK)	St. Vincent & the Grenadines	Nicaragua	Falkland Island (Malvinas) (UK)
Cuba	Trinidad and Tobago	Panama	French Guiana (F)
Dominica	Turks and Caicos Islands (UK)		Guyana
Dominican Republic	US Virgin Islands (US)		Paraguay
Grenada			Peru
Guadeloupe (F)			Suriname
Haiti			Uruguay
Jamaica			Venezuela

Northern America

Northern America
Bermuda (UK)
Canada
Greenland
St. Pierre and Miquelon (F)
United States

Source: http://www.unsystem.org/scn/Publications/4RWNS/Appendix02.pdf.

Appendix 5
Points of Leverage in International Futures (IFs)

Using IFs to explore specific interventions or a strategic package of them (see especially Chapter 7) requires information on the parameters used in the interventions. From the Scenario Tree of IFs, it is possible to use the Parameter Search feature to identify the branch of the tree with a desired parameter. More easily, the specific interventions for this study were packaged with other scenario files, available to the Tree via the Scenario Files/Open/Other and Add Scenario Components menu options. Please look under World Integrated Scenario Sets/HDR Plus 50. In the list below, the parameters used in Chapter 7 have an asterisk. The analyses of the study are replicable with the following parameters.

Parameters that control population

Source/type	Parameter	Definition	Comment
Population	tfrm*, non-OECD	Total fertility rate multiplier	

Parameters that control domestic interventions

Source/type	Parameter	Definition	Comment
Education	gdsm*, education, non-OECD	Education spending multiplier	
Health	gdsm*, health, non-OECD	Health spending multiplier	
Economic freedom	econfreem*, non-OECD	Economic freedom multiplier	
Governance effectiveness	goveffectm*, non-OECD	Governance effectiveness multiplier	
Corruption	govcorruptm*, non-OECD	Corruption multiplier	Higher is less corrupt
Infrastructure	infraroadm* infraelecm*, infratelem*, infranetm*,non-OECD	Infrastructure multipliers: roads, electricity, telecommunications, networking	
Renewable energy	enpm*, other renewable, non-OECD	Energy production multiplier	
R&D	gdsm*, R&D, non-OECD	R&D spending multiplier	
Trade protection	protecm*, non-OECD	Protectionism multiplier	
Female labor	labfemshrm*,non-OECD	Female labor participation rate multiplier	
Investment	invm*, Afr-Subsahar, Asia-SoCent	Investment rate multiplier	
Government transfers	govhhtrnwelm*,unskilled, non-OECD	Government welfare transfers multiplier	

Parameters that control international interventions

Source/type	Parameter	Definition	Comment
High trade	protecm*, non-OECD	Protectionism multiplier	
Export promotion	xshift*, Afr-Subsahar, Asia-SoCent	Export shift/promotion parameter	
FDI flows	xfdistockm*, non-OECD (minus China) xfdiwgrm*	Foreign direct investment inward stocks multiplier; world FDI growth rate	
Portfolio flows	xportfoliom*, non-OECD xportwgrm*	Portfolio inward stocks multiplier; world portfolio investment growth rate	
Remittances	wmigrm*	Global migration multiplier	
Foreign aid	aiddon*, OECD	Aid donations as percent of GDP	
IFI Flows	xwbloanr*, ximfcreditr*	World Bank loan growth rate multiplier; IMF credit growth rate multiplier	
Technology	mfpadd*, non-OECD	Multifactor productivity addition	

1 Normally in IFs, "adjustment shifts" calculated in the first year are allowed to erode back to basic functional specifications over 50 to 100 years. For the analysis of this report, the country-specific poverty shifts were left intact over the forecast horizon.

2 Bourguignon (2003: 7) noted that a lognormal distribution is "a standard approximation of empirical distributions in the applied literature." He further decomposed the growth and distributional change effects in poverty reduction and explored the interaction between them.

3 The lognormal is not the only parameterization possible of the income distribution. Other forms include polynomial functions (used by Dikhanov 2005), a generalized quadratic model (Villasenor and Arnold 1989), and the Beta model (Kakwani 1980). Datt (1991) has derived formulations for computing the common aggregate poverty measures from

multiple parameterizations of the Lorenz curve. In representing income distribution it is also possible to use nonparametric techniques, such as the Gaussian kernel density function (Sala-i-Martin 2002b).

4 Qu and Barney (2002) used the basic procedure for forecasting in the T21 model, and Kemp-Benedict, Heaps, and Raskin (2002) used it in POLESTAR for the computation of malnutrition.

5 Kornai (1971) analyzed the weaknesses of traditional equilibrium models. In addition to allowing much faster computation and representing some of the real world's actual disequilibrium, chasing equilibrium in a recursive structure avoids the artificial assumption that a time path consists of a series of comparative static solutions.

6 Some parameters work with the standard errors and others with the absolute gap between expected and computed values, depending largely on the

preference of the empirical studies from which the parameters came (Hughes 2005 documents the sources of the parameters).

7 A correction factor automatically adjusts the sum of the computed contributions to economic growth so that the adjusted aggregate computed productivity performance matches apparent performance in multifactor productivity of recent years (growth minus the effects of change in labor and capital stock). That means that the model will, all else being equal, calculate growth rates in the forecasts that are comparable to growth rates in the past.

8 The availability only of value-added shares of the two types of labor, not sector-specific labor force sizes, was confirmed via e-mail on December 9, 2005, by Betina Dimaranan, who documents the labor data.

Bibliography

Acemoglu, Daron, and Simon Johnson. 2005. "Unbundling Institutions." *Journal of Political Economy* 113(5), 949–995. http://search.ebscohost.com/login.aspx?direct=true&db=buh&AN=18509302&site=ehost-live.

Adams, Richard H. Jr. 2004. "Economic Growth, Inequality, and Poverty: Estimating the Growth Elasticity of Poverty." *World Development* 32(12), 1989–2014.

———. 2007. "International Remittances and the Household: Analysis and Review of Global Evidence." World Bank Policy Research Working Paper 4116. Forthcoming in *Journal of African Economies*.

Adams, William M., Ros Aveling, Dan Brockington, Barney Dickson, Jo Elliott, Jon Hutton, Dilys Roe, Bhaskar Vira, and William Wolmer. 2004. "Biodiversity Conservation and the Eradication of Poverty." *Science* 306(5699), 1146–1149.

ADB (African Development Bank). 2007. "The Poverty-Environment Nexus in Africa." In African Development Bank, ed., *Gender, Poverty, and Environmental Indicators on African Countries*. Vol. 8, pp. 1–19. Tunis, Tunisia: African Development Bank.

Addison, Douglas, and Quentin Wodon. 2007. "Macroeconomic Volatility, Private Investment, Growth, and Poverty in Nigeria." In Quentin Wodon, ed., *Growth and Poverty Reduction: Case Studies from West Africa*, pp. 121–135. Washington, DC: World Bank.

Adelman, Irma, and Sherman Robinson. 1989. "Income Distribution and Development." In Hollis B. Chenery and T. N. Srinivasan, eds., *Handbook of Development Economics*. Vol. 2. Amsterdam: Elsevier Science.

Agarwal, Bina. 1997. "Gender, Environment, and Poverty Interlinks: Regional Variations and Temporal Shifts in Rural India, 1971–91." *World Development* 25(1), 23–52.

Agarwal, Bina, Jane Humphries, and Ingrid Robeyns. 2005. *Amartya Sen's Work and Ideas: A Gender Perspective*. New York: Routledge. http://www.loc.gov/catdir/enhancements/fy0654/2005050608-d.html.

Agarwal, Rimjhim M. 2006. "Globalization, Local Ecosystems, and the Rural Poor." *World Development* 34(8), 1405–1418.

Aghion, Philippe, and Patrick Bolton. 1997. "A Theory of Trickle-Down Growth and Development." *Review of Economic Studies* 64(2), 151–172. http://links.jstor.org/sici?sici=0034-6527%2819970 4%2964%3A2%3C151%3AATOTGA%3E2.0.CO%3B2-K.

Aghion, Philippe, Eve Caroli, and Cecilia Garcia-Peñalosa. 1999. "Inequality and Economic Growth: The Perspective of the New Growth Theories." *Journal of Economic Literature* 37(4), 1615–1660. http://links.jstor.org/sici?sici=0022-0515%2819991 2%2937%3A4%3C1615%3AIAEGTP%3E2.0.CO%3B2-1.

Aghion, Philippe, and Peter Howitt. 1992. "A Model of Growth Through Creative Destruction." *Econometrica* 60(2), 323–351. http://links.jstor.org/sici?sici=0012-9682%2819920 3%2960%3A2%3C323%3AAMOGTC%3E2.0.CO%3B2-%23.

Aghion, Philippe, Peter Howitt, Maxine Brant-Collett, and Cecilia García-Peñalosa. 1998. *Endogenous Growth theory*. Cambridge, MAasMIT Press.

Ahluwalia, Montek S., Nicholas Carter, and Hollis Chenery. 1979. "Growth and Poverty in Developing Countries." *Journal of Development Economics* 6(2), 299–341. http://planningcommission.nic.in/aboutus/history/spemsabody.htm.

Ahmed, Akhter U., Haider A. Khan, and Rajan K. Sampath. 1991. "Poverty in Bangladesh: Measurement, Decomposition and Intertemporal Comparison." *Journal of Development Studies* 27(4), 48. http://search.ebscohost.com/login.aspx?direct=true&db=aph&AN=7689640&site=ehost-live.

Aitchison, J., and James Allen C. Brown. 1957. *The Lognormal Distribution, with Special Reference to Its Uses in Economics*. Cambridge: Cambridge University Press.

Akramov, Kamiljon T. 2006. "Governance and Foreign Aid Allocation." PhD diss., Pardee RAND Graduate School, Santa Monica, CA.

Alesina, Alberto, and David Dollar. 2000. "Who Gives Foreign Aid to Whom and Why?" *Journal of Economic Growth* 5(1): 33–63.

Alesina, Alberto, and Roberto Perotti. 1996. "Income Distribution, Political Instability, and Investment." *European Economic Review* 40, 1203–1228.

Alesina, Alberto, and Dani Rodrik. 1996. "Distribution, Political Conflict, and Economic Growth: A Simple Theory and Some Empirical Evidence." In Alex Cukierman, Zvi Hercowitz, and Leonardo Leiderman, eds., *Political Economy, Growth, and Business Cycles*. Cambridge: MIT Press.

Alesina, Alberto, and Beatrice Weder. 2002. "Do Corrupt Governments Receive Less Foreign Aid?" *American Economic Review* 92(4): 1126–1137.

Ali, Abdel Gadir. 1997. "Dealing with Poverty and Income Distribution Issues in Developing Countries: Cross-Regional Experiences." Paper presented at the African Economic Research Consortium Bi-Annual Research Workshop, Nairobi, Kenya.

Alkire, Sabina. 2005. *Valuing Freedoms: Sen's Capability Approach and Poverty Reduction*. Oxford: Oxford University Press. http://www.loc.gov/catdir/enhancements/fy0611/2001055463-d.html.

Amiel, Yoram, and Frank Cowell. 1994. "Inequality Changes and Income Growth." In Wolfgang Eichhorn, ed., *Models and Measurements of Welfare and Inequality*. Berlin: Springer-Verlag.

Anand, Sudhir, and S. M. R. Kanbur. 1984. "Inequality and Development: A Reconsideration." In H. P. Nissen, ed., *Towards Income Distribution Policies: From Income Distribution Research to Income Distribution Policy in LDCs*. Padenburg: EADI.

Anand, Sudhir, and Martin Ravallion. 1993. "Human Development in Poor Countries: On the Role of Private Incomes and Public Services." *Journal of Economic Perspectives* 7(1), 133–150. http://links.jstor.org/sici?sici=0895-3309%2819932%2997%3A1%3C133%3AHDIPCO%3E2.0.CO%3B2-G.

Anand, Sudhir, and Amartya Sen. 1997. "Concepts of Human Development and Poverty: A Multidimensional Perspective." In *Background Papers for Human Development Report 1997*. New York: UN Publications.

Arnold, J. E. Mike, and Pippa Bird. 1999. "Forests and the Poverty-Environment Nexus." Paper presented at the UNDP/EC Expert Workshop on Poverty and the Environment.

Arrow, Kenneth J. 1962. "The Economic Implications of Learning by Doing." *Review of Economic Studies* 29(3), 155–173. http://links.jstor.org/sici?sici=0034-6527%2819620%2929%3A3%3C155%3ATEIOLB%3E2.0.CO%3B2-%23.

Aschauer, David A. 1993. *Public Infrastructure Investment: A Bridge to Productivity Growth?* Annandale-on-Hudson, NY: Bard College, Jerome Levy Economic Institute. http://www.levy.org/pubs/ppb/ppb4.pdf.

Asian Development Bank. 2000. "Fighting Poverty in Asia and the Pacific: The Poverty Reduction Strategy." http://www.adb.org/Documents/Policies/Poverty_Reduction/Poverty_Policy.pdf.

———. 2004a. *Asian Development Outlook: ADO*. New York: Oxford University Press.

———. 2004b. "Enhancing the Fight Against Poverty in Asia and the Pacific." http://www.adb.org/Documents/Policies/Poverty_Reduction/2004/prs-2004.pdf.

———. 2004c. *Poverty in Asia: Measurement, Estimates, and Prospects*. Manila: Asian Development Bank, Economics and Research Department.

Aten, Bettina, and Alan Heston. 2003. "Use of Penn World Tables for International Comparisons of Poverty Levels: Potentials and Limitations." Paper presented at the Global Poverty Workshop: Initiative for Policy Dialogue. Columbia University, New York, March 31–April 1. http://webhost.bridgew.edu/baten/papers/PWTPoverty3.pdf.

Atkinson, Anthony B. 1970. "On the Measurement of Inequality." *Journal of Economic Theory* 2(3), 244–263.

———. 1987. "On the Measurement of Poverty." *Econometrica* 55(4), 749–764. http://links.jstor.org/sici?sici=0012-9682%2819870%2955%3A4%3C749%3AOTMOP%3E2.0.CO%3B2-N.

———. 1997. "Bringing Income Distribution in from the Cold." *Economic Journal* 107(441), 297–321. http://links.jstor.org/sici?sici=0013-0133%2819970%29107%3A441%3C297%3ABIDIFT%3E2.0.CO%3B2-%23.

———. 1998. *Poverty in Europe*. Oxford: Blackwell.

Atkinson, Anthony B., and François Bourguignon. 1999. "Poverty and Inclusion from a World Perspective." Paper presented at the Annual Bank Conference on Development Economics.

Atkinson, Anthony B., Lee Rainwater, and Timothy M. Smeeding. 1995. "Income Distribution in OECD Countries: Evidence from the Luxembourg Income Study." OECD. Paris.

Atkinson, Anthony B., and Joseph E. Stiglitz. 1980. *Lectures on Public Economics*. London: McGraw-Hill.

Baldacci, Emanuele, Benedict Clements, Sanjeev Gupta, and Qiang Cui. 2004. "Social Spending, Human Capital, and Growth in Developing Countries: Implications for Achieving the MDGs." IMF Working Paper WP/04/217.

Balisacan, Arsenio M., and Rosemarie Edillon. 2005. "Poverty Targeting in the Philippines." In John Weiss and Asian Development Bank Institute, eds., *Poverty Targeting in Asia*. Cheltenham, UK: Edward Elgar.

Balisacan, Arsenio M., and Ernesto M. Pernia. 2003. "Poverty, Inequality and Growth in the Philippines." In Ernesto M. Pernia and Anil B. Deolalikar, eds., *Poverty, Growth, and Institutions in Developing Asia*. New York: Palgrave Macmillan.

Balisacan, Arsenio M., Ernesto M. Pernia, and Abuzar Asra. 2003. "Revisiting Growth and Poverty Reduction in Indonesia: What Do Subnational Data Show?" *Bulletin of Indonesian Economic Studies* 39(3), 329–351. http://search.ebscohost.com/login.aspx?direct=true&db=buh&AN=11309049&site=ehost-live.

Banerjee, Abhijit V., and Ester Duflo. 2006. "The Economic Lives of the Poor." MIT Department of Economics Working Paper 06-29. http://papers.ssrn.com/sol3/papers.cfm?abstract_id=942062.

Banerjee, Abhijit V., and Andrew F. Newman. 1993. "Occupational Choice and the Process of Development." *Journal of Political Economy* 101(2), 274–298. http://links.jstor.org/sici?sici=0022-3808%28199304%29101%3A2%3C274%3AOCATPO%3E2.0.CO%3B2-B.

Banzhaf, H. Spencer, and V. Kerry Smith. 2002. "Adding Environmental Services to an Economy's Scorecard." Resources for the Future issue brief, Washington DC, http://www.rff.org/Documents/RFF-IB-02-09.pdf.

Barbier, Edward B. 2000. "The Economic Linkages Between Rural Poverty and Land Degradation: Some Evidence from Africa." *Agriculture, Ecosystems, and Environment* 82(1–3), 355–370.

Bardhan, Pranab. 1997. "Corruption and Development: A Review of Issues."

Journal of Economic Literature 35(3), 1320 1346. http://links.jstor.org/sici?sici=0022-0515%28199709%2935%3A3%3C1320%3ACADARO%3E2.0.CO%3B2-6.

Barro, Robert J. 1999a. *Determinants of Economic Growth: A Cross-Country Empirical Study*. Vol. 2. Cambridge, MA: MIT Press.

———. 1999b. "Inequality, Growth, and Investment." New York: National Bureau of Economic Research Working Paper no. 7038.

———. 2001. "Education and Economic Growth." In J. F. Helliwell, ed., *The Contribution of Human and Social Capital to Sustained Economic Growth and Well-Being*. OECT/HDRC.

Barro, Robert J., and Gary S. Becker. 1989. "Fertility Choice in a Model of Economic Growth." *Econometrica* 57(2), 481–501. http://links.jstor.org/sici?sici=0012-9682%28198903%2957%3A2%3C481%3AFCIAMO%3E2.0.CO%3B2-F.

Barro, Robert J., and Jon Wha Lee. 2000. "International Data on Educational Attainment Updates and Implications." *Oxford Economic Papers* 53(3), 541–563.

Barro, Robert. J., and Xavier Sala-i-Martin. 1999. *Economic Growth*. Cambridge: MIT Press.

Bass, Steve, Tom Bigg, Josh Bishop, and Dan Tunstall. 2006. "Sustaining the Environment to Fight Poverty and Achieve the Millennium Development Goals." *Review of European Community and International Environmental Law* 15(1), 39–55.

Bates, Robert H., David L. Epstein, Jack A. Goldstone, Ted Robert Gurr, Barbara Harff, Colin H. Khal, Marc A. Levy, Michael Lustick, Monty G. Marshall, Thomas M. Parris, Jay Ulfelder, and Mark R. Woodward. 2006. "Political Instability Task Force Report: Phase IV Findings." McLean, VA: Science Applications International Corporation.

Baulch, Robert, and Neil McCulloch. 1999. "Tracking Pro-poor Growth." Sussex: Institute of Development Studies: ID21 Insights. http://www.id21.org/insights/insights31/insights-iss31-art03.html.

Becker, Gary S. 1960. "An Economic Analysis of Fertility." National Bureau of Economic Research, ed., *Demographic and Economic Change in Developed Countries: a Conference of the Universities-National Bureau Committee for Economic Research*. Princeton: Princeton University Press.

———. 1964. *Human Capital: A Theoretical and Empirical Analysis, with Special Reference to Education*. New York: National Bureau of Economic Research.

Becker, Gary S., Kevin M. Murphy, and Robert Tamura. 1990. "Human Capital, Fertility, and Economic Growth." *Journal of Political Economy* 98(5), S12–S37. http://links.jstor.org/sici?sici=0022-3808%28199010%2998%3A5%3CS12%3AHCFAEG%3E2.0.CO%3B2-L.

Behrman, Jere. 1993. "The Contribution of Human Capital to Economic Development: Some Selected Issues." World Employment Programme Working Paper no. 36. Geneva: International Labour Organisation.

Benhabib, Jess, and Mark M. Spiegel. 1994. "The Role of human cCpital in eEonomic dDvelopment eEidence from aAgregate cCoss-cCuntry dDta." *Journal of Monetary Economics,* 4(2), 143–173. http://www.sciencedirect.com/science/article/B6VBW-45MFPNH-2/2/13399074d90b2f81076f8cd82df9ff24.

Berrebi, Claude. 2003. *Evidence About the Link Between Education, Poverty and Terrorism Among Palestinians*. Princeton: Industrial Relations Section, Princeton University.

Berry, R. Albert, and William R. Cline. 1979. "Agrarian Structure and Productivity in Developing Countries."

Journal of Comparative Economics 28(1), 172–206.

Berthélemy, Jean-Claude, and Ludvig Soederling. 2001. "Will There Be New Emerging Countries in Africa by the Year 2020?" Paper presented at the Conference on Development Policy in Africa, Oxford University.

Besley, Timothy. 1997. "Political Economy of Alleviating Poverty: Theory and Institutions." *Annual World Bank Conference on Development Economics*, 117–144.

Bhagwati, Jagdish N. 1996. "The 'Miracle' That Did Happen: Understanding East Asia in Comparative Perspective." Keynote Speech at Cornell University Conference in honor of Professors Liu and Tsiang, Ithaca, NY.

Bhalla, Surjit S. 2002. *Imagine There's No Country: Poverty, Inequality, and Growth in the Era of Globalization*. Washington, DC: Institute for International Economics. http://www.loc.gov/catdir/toc/fy036/2002027329.html.

———. 2003. *Crying Wolf on Poverty: Or How the Millennium Development Goal for Poverty Has Already Been Reached*. http://www.iie.com/publications/papers/bhalla0403.pdf.

Biel, Robert. 2006. "The Interplay Between Social and Environmental Degradation in the Development of the International Political Economy." *Journal of World-Systems Research* 12(I), 109–147.

Bils, Mark, and Peter J. Klenow. 2000. "Does Schooling Cause Growth?" *American Economic Review* 90(5), 1160–1183. http://links.jstor.org/sici?sici=0002-8282%28200012%2990%3A5%3C1160%3ADSCG%3E2.0.CO%3B2-5.

Birdsall, Nancy, and Juan Luis Londono. 1997. "Asset Inequality Matters: An Assessment of the World Bank's Approach to Poverty Reduction." *American Economic Review,* 872), 32–37. http://links.jstor.org/sici?sici=0002-

8282%28199705%2987%3A2%3C32%3A AIMAAO%3E2.0.CO%3B2-Z.

Blackburn, McKinley. 1994. "International Comparisons of Poverty." *American Economic Association Papers and Proceedings* 84, 371–374.

Bliss, Christopher, and Nicholas Stern. 1978. "Productivity, Wages, and Nutrition: Some Observations." *Journal of Development Economics* 5(4), 331–362.

Bloom, David E., David Canning, and Jaypee Sevilla. 2003. *The Demographic Dividend: A New Perspective on the Economic Consequences of Population Change*. Santa Monica, CA: RAND Population Matters Project. http://www.rand.org/publications/MR/MR1274.

Bloomberg, S. Brock, Gregory D. Hess, and Siddharth Thacker. 2006. "On the Conflict-Poverty Nexus." *Economics and Politics* 18(3), 237–267.

Bojö, Jan, Julia Bucknall, Kirk Hamilton, Nalin Kishor, Chritiane Kraus, and Poonam Pillai. 2002. "Environment." In Jeni Klugman, ed., *A Sourcebook for Poverty Reduction Strategies*. Vol. 1: *Core Techniques and Cross-Cutting Issues*, pp. 375–401. Washington, DC: World Bank.

Bojö, Jan, and Rama Chandra Reddy. 2003. "Poverty Reduction Strategies and the Millennium Development Goal on Environmental Sustainability." Environment Department Papers, Environmental Economics Series: Washington, DC: World Bank. 59.

Bollin, Johannes C. 2004. "A Trade View on Climate Change Policies: A Multi-Region Multi-Sector Approach." Ph.D. diss., Amsterdam University.

Bonfiglioli, Alessandra. 2005. "Equities and Inequality." HES. Stockholm University. http://www.econ.upf.edu/docs/papers/downloads/947.pdf.

Borensztein, E., J. De Gregorio, and J. W. Lee. 1998. "How Does Foreign

Direct Investment Affect Economic Growth?" *Journal of International Economics* 45(1), 115–135. http://www.sciencedirect.com/science/article/B6V6D-3VSP0RW-6/2/d0f15881addf9e28b143c19e01b6874a.

Bosworth, Barry, and Susan M. Collins. 2003. "The Empirics of Growth: An Update." Economics of Developing Countries Paper. Washington, DC: Brookings Institution.

Bouchet, Michel Henry, Ephraim Clark, and Bertand Groslambert. 2003. *Country Risk Assessment: A Guide to Global Investment Strategy*. Chichester, UK: Wiley.

Bourguignon, François. 1979. "Decomposable Income Inequality Measures." *Econometrica* 47(4), 901–920. http://links.jstor.org/sici?sici=0012-9682%28197907%2947%3A4%3C901%3ADIIM%3E2.0.CO%3B2-T.

———. 2003. "The Poverty-Growth-Inequality Triangle." Conference on Poverty, Inequality, and Growth. Paris: Agence Française de Développement/EU Development Network. http://www.afd.fr/jahia/webdav/site/myjahiasite/users/administrateur/public/eudn2003/Bourguignon-paper.pdf.

Boyd, James, and Spencer Banzhaf. 2006. "What Are Ecosystem Services? The Need for Standardized Environmental Accounting Units." Discussion Paper. Washington, DC: Resources for the Future.

Brockington, Dan, Jim Igoe, and Kai Schmidt-Soltau. 2006. "Conservation, Human Rights, and Poverty Reduction." *Conservation Biology* 20(1), 250–252.

Brocklesby, Mary Ann, and Emily Hinshelwood. 2001. "Poverty and the Environment: What the Poor Say—An Assessment of Poverty-Environment Linkages in Participatory Poverty Assessments." Swansea, UK: Centre for Development Studies, University of Wales Swansea.

Bucknall, Julia, Christiane Kraus, and Poonam Pillai. 2001. "Poverty and

Environment: Background Paper for the World Bank Environment Strategy." Washington, DC: World Bank.

Burnside, Craig, and David Dollar. 2000. "Aid, Policies, and Growth," *American Economic Review* 90(4) (September): 847–868.

Bussolo, Maurizio, Rafael E. DeHoyos, Denis Medvedev, and Dominique van der Mensbrugghe. 2007. "Global Growth and Distribution: Are China and India Reshaping the World?" Paper presented at the World Bank. http://www.anahuac.mx/gof/documentos/China%20India%20%20Global%20Growth%20and%20Distribution.pdf.

Butler, Colin. 2005. "Peering into the Fog: Ecological Change, Human Affairs, and the Future." *EcoHealth* 2(1), 17–21.

Carter, Michael R., Peter D. Little, Tewodaj Mogues, and Workneh Negatu. 2007. "Poverty Traps and Natural Disasters in Ethiopia and Honduras." *World Development* 35(5), 835–856.

Castles, Ian, and David Henderson. 2003. "Economics, Emissions Scenarios, and the World of the IPCC." *Energy and Environment* 14(4), 415–435.

Caucutt, Elizabeth M., and Krishna B. Kumar. 2006a. "Africa: Is Aid an Answer?" University of Western Ontario Working Paper, London, Ontario.

———. 2006b. "Education for All: The Right Course for Africa?" University of Western Ontario Working Paper, London, Ontario.

———. 2006c. "Education Policies to Revive a Stagnant Economy." University of Western Ontario Working Paper, London, Ontario. http://economics.uwo.ca/faculty/caucutt/papers/africa.pdf.

Cavendish, William. 1999a. "Empirical Regularities in the Poverty-Environment Relationship of African Rural Households." Working Paper Series no. 99-21. Oxford: Centre for the Study of African Economies.

———. 1999b. "Poverty, Inequality, and Environmental Resources: Quantitative Analysis of Rural Households." Working Paper Series no. 99-9. Oxford: Centre for the Study of African Economies.

———. 2000. "Empirical Regularities in the Poverty-Environment Relationship of Rural Households: Evidence from Zimbabwe." *World Development* 28(11), 1979–2003.

Chen, Derek Hung Chiat, and Carl Johan Dahlman. 2004. "Knowledge and Development: A Cross-Sectional Approach." World Bank: Washington, D.C. http://www.econ.worldbank.org/view.php?type=5&id=37702.

Chen, Shaohua, and Martin Ravallion. 2000. "How Did the World's Poorest Fare in the 1990s?" Policy Research Working Paper 2409. Washington, DC: World Bank. http://papers.ssrn.com/sol3/papers.cfm?abstract_id=630781.

———. 2004. "How Have the World's Poorest Fared Since the Early 1980s?" World Bank: Development Research Group. http://www.worldbank.org/research/povmonitor/MartinPapers/How_have_the_poorest_fared_since_the_early_1980s.pdf.

Chenery, Hollis B., and Moises Syrquin. 1975. *Patterns of Development 1950–70.* Oxford: Oxford University Press.

Chetwynd, Eric, Frances Chetwynd, and Bertram Spector. 2003. "Corruption and Poverty: A Review of Recent Literature." Washington, D.C.: Management Systems International. Available at http://pdf.dec.org/pdf_docs/PNACW645.pdf.

Chotikapanich, Duangkamon, Rebecca Valenzuela, and D. S. Prasada Rao. 1997. "Global and Regional Inequality in the Distribution of Income: Estimation with Limited and Incomplete Data." *Empirical Economics* 22(4), 533–546. http://search.ebscohost.com/login.aspx?direct=true&db=buh&AN=6756666&site=ehost-live.

Chronic Poverty Research Center. 2005. "Chronic Poverty Report, 2004–2005." Manchester, England: University of Manchester.

Clark, John. 2003. *Worlds Apart: Civil Society and the Battle for Ethical Globalization.* Bloomfield, CT: Kumarian.

Clark, Stephen, Richard Hemming, and David Ulph. 1981. "On Indices for the Measurement of Poverty." *Economic Journal* 91(362), 515–526. http://links.jstor.org/sici?sici=0013-0133%28198106%2991%3A362%3C515%3AOIFTMO%3E2.0.CO%3B2-I.

Clemens, Michael A. 2004. "The Long Walk to School: International Educational Goals in Historical Perspective." Washington, DC: Center for Global Development. Originally prepared as a background paper for the Millennium Project Task Force on Education and Gender Equality. http://ideas.repec.org/p/wpa/wuwpdc/0403007.html.

Cline, William R. 2004. *Trade Policy and Global Poverty.* Washington DC: Center for Global Development and Institute for International Economics.

Coleman, James S. 1988. "Social Capital in the Creation of Human Capital." *American Journal of Sociology* 94, S95-S120. http://links.jstor.org/sici?sici=0002-9602%281988%2994%3CS95%3ASCITCO%3E2.0.CO%3B2-P.

Collier, Paul. 1999. "On the Economic Consequences of Civil War." *Oxford Economic Papers* 51, 168–183.

———. 2006a. *Africa: Geography and Growth.* Oxford: Oxford University, Department of Economics, Centre for the Study of African Economies. http://www.eitransparency.org/UserFiles/File/collier_africa_geography_growth.pdf.

———. 2006b. "African Growth: Why a 'Big Push'?" *Journal of African Economics* 15(2), 188–211.

———. 2007. *The Bottom Billion: Why the Poorest Countries Are Failing and What Can Be Done About It.* Oxford: Oxford University Press.

Collier, Paul, and David Dollar. 2001. "Can the World Cut Poverty in Half? How

Policy Reform and Effective Aid Can Meet International Development Goals." *World Development* 29(11), 1787–1802. http://www.sciencedirect.com/science/article/B6VC6-447D2D9-1/2/1de0c832f6939ce2c396d4d538f8599a.

Collier, Paul, V. L. Elliot, Havard Hegre, Anke Hoeffler, Marta Reyna-Querol, and Nicholas Sambains. 2003. *Breaking the Conflict Trap: Civil War and Development Policy*. Washington, DC: World Bank.

Collier, Paul, and Anke Hoeffler. 2004. "Greed and Grievance in Civil War." *Oxford Economic Papers* 56(4), 563–595.

Collier, Paul, and Stephen A. O'Connell. 2007. "Opportunities and Choices." In *Political Economy of Economic Growth in Africa, 1960–2000,* Vol. 1. Oxford University: Centre for Study of African Economies. http://users.ox.ac.uk/~econpco/research/africa.htm.

Cook, Jess. 2000. *Demographic Trends Alter the National Security Scene*. Santa Monica, CA: RAND.

Coudouel, Aline, Jesko S. Hentschel, and Quentin T. Wodon. 2002. "Poverty Measurement and Analysis." In Jeni Klugman, ed., *A Sourcebook for Poverty Reduction Strategies*. Washington, DC: World Bank.

Cukierman, Alex, Zvi Hercowitz, and Leonardo Leiderman. 1992. *Political Economy, Growth, and Business Cycles*. Cambridge, MA: MIT Press.

Daily, Gretchen C. 1997. *Nature's Services: Societal Dependence on Natural Ecosystems*. Washington, DC: Island.

Dasgupta, Susmita, Uwe Deichmann, Craig Meisner, and David Wheeler. 2005. "Where Is the Poverty-Environment Nexus? Evidence from Cambodia, Laos, PDR, and Vietnam." *World Development* 33(4), 617–638.

Datt, Gaurav. 1991. *Computational Tools for Poverty Measurement and Analysis Using Grouped Data*. Washington, DC: World Bank, Welfare and Human Resources Division.

———. 1998. "Computational Tools for Poverty Measurement and Analysis Using Grouped Data." International Food Policy Research Institute. http://www.ifpri.org/divs/fcnd/dp/papers/dp50.pdf.

Datt, Gaurav, and Martin Ravallion. 1992. "Growth and Redistribution Components of Changes in Poverty Measures: A Decomposition with Applications to Brazil and India in the 1980s." *Journal of Development Economics* 38(2), 275–295. http://www.sciencedirect.com/science/article/B6VBV-45FCJDX-1/2/324c666d3478f6a72782d7d4c26cad22.

De Groot, Rudolf S. 1992. *Functions of Nature: Evaluation of Nature in Environmental Planning, Management, and Decision-making*. Groningen, Netherlands.

de Soto, Hernando. 2000. *The Mystery of Capital: Why Capitalism Triumphs in the West and Fails Everywhere Else*. New York: Basic Books.

Deaton, Angus. 2001. "Counting the World's Poor: Problems and Possible Solutions." *World Bank Research Observer* 16(2), 125–147. http://www.wws.princeton.edu/rpds/downloads/deaton_worlds_poor.pdf.

———. 2002a. "Data for Monitoring the Poverty MDG." Human Development Report Office occasional paper, UN Development Programme.

———. 2002b. "Is World Poverty Falling?" *Finance and Development: A Quarterly Magazine of the IMF* 39(2).

———. 2003. *How to Monitor Poverty for the Millennium Development Goals*. Princeton: Princeton University.

———. 2004. "Measuring Poverty in a Growing World." Princeton University (draft). http://www.wws.princeton.edu/rpds/downloads/deaton_measuringpoverty_204.pdf.

———. 2005. "Measuring Poverty in a Growing World (or Measuring Growth in a Poor World)." *Review of Economic Studies* 1(February), 1–19.

Deininger, Klaus, and Lyn Squire. 1996. "A New Data Set Measuring Income Inequality." *World Bank Economic Review* 10(2), 565–592. http://wber.oxfordjournals.org/cgi/content/abstract/10/3/565.

Delamonica, Enrique, and Santosh Mehrotra. 2006. "A Capability-Centred Approach to Environmental Sustainability: Is Productive Employment the Missing Link between Micro- and Macro Policies?" Working paper no. 13. New York: UN Development Programme, International Poverty Centre.

Department for International Development, United Kingdom (DFID). 2001. "The Causes of Conflict in Africa." Consultation document by the Cabinet Sub-Committee on Conflict Prevention in Africa, London.

Department for International Development, United Kingdom (DFID), European Commission (EC) Directorate General for Development, UN Development Programme, and World Bank. 2002. "Linking Poverty Reduction and Environmental Management: Policy Challenges and Opportunities." Washington, DC: World Bank.

Diamond, Jared M. 1997. *Guns, Germs, and Steel: The Fates of Human Societies*. 1st ed. New York: W. W. Norton.

Dikhanov, Yuri. 2005. *Trends in Global Income Distribution, 1970–2000, and Scenarios for 2015*. New York. http://hdr.undp.org/docs/publications/background_papers/2005/HDR2005_Dikhanov_Yuri_8.pdf.

Dollar, David, and Aart Kraay. 2002a. "Growth *Is* Good for the Poor." *Journal of Economic Growth* (7), 195–225.

———. 2002b. "Spreading the Wealth." *Foreign Affairs* 81(1), 120–133. http://search.ebscohost.com/login.aspx?direct=true&db=aph&AN=5750876&site=ehost-live.

———. 2004. "Trade, Growth, and Poverty." *Economic Journal* 114(493), 22–49.

Drèze, Jean, Peter Lanjouw, and Nicholas Stern. 1992. "Economic Mobility and Agricultural Labour in Rural India: A Case Study." *Indian Economic Review*, 22–54.

Drèze, Jean, and Amartya Kumar Sen. 1995. *India: Economic Development and Social Opportunity*. Delhi: Oxford University Press. http://www.loc.gov/catdir/enhancements/fy0604/96219941-d.html.

Duraiappah, Anantha K. 1996. "Poverty and Environmental Degradation: A Literature Review and Analysis." CREED Working Paper Series no. 8. : London/Amsterdam: International Institute for Environment and Development/Institute for Environmental Studies.

———. 1998. "Poverty and Environmental Degradation: A Review and Analysis of the Nexus." *World Development* 26(12), 2169–2179.

———. 2001. "Poverty and Environment: A Role for UNEP." Nairobi: UN Environment Programme, Division of Policy Development and Law.

———. 2004. "Exploring the Links: Human Well-Being, Poverty and Ecosystem Services." Winnipeg, Canada/Nairobi, Kenya: International Institute for Sustainable Development/UN Development Programme.

Duraiappah, Anantha K., and Arun Abraham. 2004. "Ecological Surety and Capabilities: Normative Issues." Paper presented at the Fourth International Conference on the Capability Approach: Enhancing Human Security.

Durlauf, Steven N., and Marcel Fafchamps. 2005. "Social Capital." In Philippe Agion and Steven N. Durlauf, eds., *Handbook of Economic Growth*. Amsterdam: North-Holland.

Durlauf, Steven, and Danny Quah. 1998. "The New Empirics of Economic Growth." In John Taylor and Michael Woodford, eds., *Handbook of Macroeconomics*. Amsterdam: North-Holland.

Durning, Alan B. 1989. "Poverty and the Environment: Reversing the Downward Spiral." Worldwatch Paper no. 92. Washington, DC: Worldwatch Institute.

Easterly, William Russell. 2001. *The Elusive Quest for Growth: Economists' Adventures and Misadventures in the Tropics*. Cambridge, MA: MIT Press. http://www.loc.gov/catdir/toc/fy02/00068382.html.

Eberlei, Walter, and Bettina Fuhrmann. 2004. "Fighting Poverty and Corruption." Berlin: Ministry for Economic Cooperation and Development.

Edward, Peter. 2006. "The Ethical Poverty Line: A Moral Quantification of Absolute Poverty." *Poverty in Focus* (December): 14–16.

Eichhorn, Wolfgang, and W. Gehrig. 1982. "Measurement of Inequality in Economics." In Bernhard H. Korte, ed., *Modern Applied Mathematics: Optimization and Operations Research*. Amsterdam: North-Holland.

Ekbom, Anders, and Jan Bojö. 1999. "Poverty and Environment: Evidence of Links and Integration into the Country Assistance Strategy Process." Discussion Paper no. 4. Washington, DC: Environment Group, Africa Region, World Bank.

Esman, Milton. 1994. *Ethnic Politics*. Ithaca, NY: Cornell University Press.

Fan, S. 2003. "Public Investment and Poverty Reduction: What Have We Learnt from India and PRC?" Paper presented at the Infrastructure Investment and Poverty Reduction. Retrieved October, 2006, www.adbi.org.

Fearon, James, and David Laitin. 2003. "Ethnicity, Insurgency, and Civil War." *American Political Science Review* 97(01), 75–90.

Ferrantino, Michael. 2006. "Quantifying the Trade and Economic Effects of Non-Tariff Measures." OECD Trade Policy Working Paper 28: TD/TC/WP(2005)26/FINAL.

Fields, Gary S. 1980. *Poverty, Inequality, and Development*. Cambridge: Cambridge University Press.

———. 1989. *A Compendium of Data on Inequality and Poverty for the Developing World*: Ithaca, NY: Cornell University.

———. 1994. "Poverty Changes in Developing Countries." In Rolph van der Hoeven and Richard Anker, eds., *Poverty Monitoring: An International Concern*. New York: St. Martin's.

———. 2001. *Distribution and Development: A New Look at the Developing World*. New York/Cambridge, MA: Russell Sage Foundation/MIT Press.

Firebaugh, Glenn. 2003. *The New Geography of Global Income Inequality*. Cambridge, MA: Harvard University Press.

Forbes, Kristin J. 2000. "A Reassessment of the Relationship Between Inequality and Growth." *American Economic Review* 90(4), 869–887. http://links.jstor.org/sici?sici=0002-8282%28200009%2990%3A4%3C869%3AAROTRB%3E2.0.CO%3B2-L.

Forsyth, Tim, Melissa Leach, and Ian Scoones. 1998. "Poverty and Environment: Priorities for Research and Policy—An Overview Study." Sussex, UK: Institute of Development Studies.

Foster, James, Joel Greer, and Erik Thorbecke. 1984. "A Class of Decomposable Poverty Measures." *Econometrica* 52(3), 761–766. http://links.jstor.org/sici?sici=0012-9682%28198405%2952%3A3%3C761%3AACODPM%3E2.0.CO%3B2-0.

Foster, James, and Amartya Sen. 1997. *On Economic Inequality*: Oxford: Oxford University Press.

Fuchs, Victor R. 1969. "Comment on Measuring the Size of the Low-Income Population." In Lee Soltow, ed., *Six Papers on the Size Distribution of Wealth and Income*, pp. 198–202. New York: National Bureau of Economic Research.

Fuentes, Ricardo. 2005. "Poverty, Pro-Poor Growth, and Simulated Inequality Reduction." Occasional Paper 2005/11. UN Human Development Report Office. http://hdr.undp.org/docs/publications/background_papers/2005/HDR2005_Fuentes_Ricardo_11.pdf.

Fukuda-Parr, Sakiko. 2006. "The Human Poverty Index: A Multidimensional Measure." *Poverty in Focus* (December), 7–9.

Fukuyama, Francis. 1995. *Trust: The Social Virtues and the Creation of Prosperity*. New York: Free Press.

———. 1999. *The Great Disruption: Human Nature and the Reconstitution of Social Order*. New York: Free Press.

Gacitúa-Marió, Estanislao, and Quentin Wodon. 2001. *Measurement and Meaning: Combining Quantitative and Qualitative Methods for the Analysis of Poverty and Social Exclusion in Latin America*. Vol. 518. Washington, DC: World Bank Publications.

Gallopín, Gilberto C. 1994. "Impoverishment and Sustainable Development: A Systems Approach." Winnipeg, Manitoba: International Institute for Sustainable Development.

———. 2003. "A Systems Approach to Sustainability and Sustainable Development." Medio Ambiente y Desarrollo No. 64. Santiago, Chile: Sustainable Development and Human Settlements Division, UN Economic Commission for Latin America and the Caribbean.

Gallopín, Gilberto C., and Koben Christianson. 2000. "Sustainable Development, Society, and the Environment: A Conceptual Framework for Tracking the Linkages." Stockholm: Stockholm Environment Institute.

Gallopín, Gilberto C., and Paul Raskin. 2002. *Global Sustainability: Bending the Curve*. London: Routledge. http://www.loc.gov/catdir/enhancements/fy0650/2004300825-d.html.

Gallopín, Gilberto C., Pablo Gutman, and Hector Maletta. 1989. "Global Impoverishment, Sustainable Development, and the Environment: A Conceptual Approach." *International Social Science Journal* 41(121), 375–397.

Gallup, John Luke, and Jeffrey Sachs. 2001. "The Economic Burden of Malaria." *American Journal of Tropical Medicine and Hygiene* 64(1–2), 85–96.

Galor, Oded, and David N. Weil. 2000. "Population, Technology, and Growth: From Malthusian Stagnation to the Demographic Transition and Beyond." *American Economic Review* 90(4), 806–828. http://links.jstor.org/sici?sici=0002-8282%28200009%2990%3A4%3C806%3APTAGFM%3E2.0.CO%3B2-G.

Galor, Oded, and Joseph Zeira. 1993. "Income Distribution and Macroeconomics." *Review of Economic Studies* 60(1), 35–52. http://links.jstor.org/sici?sici=0034-6527%28199301%2960%3A1%3C35%3AIDAM%3E2.0.CO%3B2-U.

Gangadharan, Lata, and Ma. Rebecca Valenzuela. 2001. "Interrelationships Between Income, Health, and the Environment: Extending the Environmental Kuznets Curve Hypothesis." *Ecological Economics,* 36(3), 513–531.

Glaeser, Edward L., Rafael La Porta, Florencio Lopez de Silanes, and Andrei Shleifer. 2004. "Do Institutions Cause Growth?" *Journal of Economic Growth* 9, 271–304.

Glasmeier, Amy K., and Tracey L. Farrigan. 2003. "Poverty, Sustainability, and the Culture of Despair: Can Sustainable Development Strategies Support Poverty Alleviation in America's Most Environmentally Challenged Communities?" *Annals of the American Academy of Political and Social Science* 590(1), 131–149.

Goldman Sachs. 2003. "Dreaming with BRICs: The Path to 2050." Global Economics Paper no. 99: New York. http://www2.goldmansachs.com/insight/research/reports/99.pdf.

Goodhand, Jonathan. 2001. "Violent Conflict, Poverty, and Chronic Poverty." Working Paper 6. Chronic Poverty Research Centre.

Granja e Barros, Fabio, Augusto F. Mendonça, and Jorge M. Nogueira. 2002. "Poverty and Environmental Degradation: The Kuznets Environmental Curve for the Brazilian Case." Working paper. Brasilia, Brazil: Department of Economics, University of Brasilia.

Gray, Leslie C., and William G. Moseley. 2005. "A Geographical Perspective on Poverty-Environment Interactions." *Geographical Journal* 171(1), 9–23.

Grossman, Gene M., and Elhanan Helpman. 1991a. *Innovation and Growth in the Global Economy*. Cambridge, MA: MIT Press.

———. 1991b. "Quality Ladders and Product Cycles." *Quarterly Journal of Economics* 106(2), 557–586. http://links.jstor.org/sici?sici=0033-5533%28199105%29106%3A2%3C557%3AQLAPC%3E2.0.CO%3B2-%23.

Grossman, Herschel. 1992. "Foreign Aid and Insurrection." *Defense Economics* 3(4), 275–288.

Gupta, Sanjeev, Hamid Davoodi, and Rosa Alonso-Terme. 2002. "Does Corruption Affect Income Inequality and Poverty?" *Economics of Governance* 3(1), 23. http://search.ebscohost.com/login.aspx?direct=true&db=buh&AN=6446767&site=ehost-live.

Gurr, Ted Robert, Monty G. Marshall, and Deepa Khosla. 2001. *Peace and*

Conflict 2001: A Global Survey of Armed Conflicts, Self-Determination Movements, and Democracy. College Park, MD: Center for International Development and Conflict Management.

Gwartney, James D. and Robert Lawson. 2004. "Economic Freedom of the World: 2004 Annual Report." Vancouver, BC: Fraser Institute.

Gwartney, James D., Robert Lawson, and Randall G. Holcombe. 1999. "Economic Freedom and the Environment for Economic Growth." *Journal of Institutional and Theoretical Economics* 155(4), 1–21.

Gwartney, James D., Robert Lawson, and Walter Block. 1996. *Economic Freedom of the World, 1975–1995*. Vancouver, BC: Fraser Institute.

Gwartney, James D., Robert Lawson, Russel S. Sobel, and Peter T. Leeson. 2007. "Economic Freedom of the World: 2007 Annual Report." Vancouver, BC: Fraser Institute.

Gylfason, Thorvaldur. 2001. "Natural Resources, Education, and Economic Development." *European Economic Review, 45*(4–6), 847–859. http://www.sciencedirect.com/science/article/B6V64-430XMS9-S/2/20b69b55103a336156661c818bd13986

Hall, Gillet, and Harry Patrinos. 2005. *Indigenous People, Poverty, and Human Development in Latin America: 1994–2004*. London: Palgrave Macmillan.

Hall, Robert E., and Charles I. Jones. 1999. "Why Do Some Countries Produce So Much More Output per Worker Than Others?" *Quarterly Journal of Economics* 114(1), 83–116. http://links.jstor.org/sici?sici=0033-5533%281999902%29114%3A1%3C83%3AWDSCPS%3E2.0.CO%3B2-S.

Hammond, Allen L. 1998. *Which World? Scenarios for the Twenty-First Century*. Washington, DC: Island. http://www.loc.gov/catdir/enhancements/fy0666/98013589-d.html.

Hanifan, Lyda Judson. 1916. "The Rural School Community Center." *Annals of the American Academy of Political and Social Science* 67, 130–138. http://links.jstor.org/sici?sici=0002-7162%28191609%2967%3C130%3ATRSCC%3E2.0.CO%3B2-0.

———. 1920. *The Community Center*. Boston: Silver.

Hewitt, Joseph, Jonathan Wilkenfeld, and Ted Robert Gurr. 2008. *Peace and Conflict 2008*. Boulder, CO: Paradigm.

Hillebrand, Evan E. 2005. "The Global Distribution of Income in 2050." Paper presented at the Global International Studies Conference, Istanbul, Turkey.

Hodges, James, and James A. Dewar. 1992. *Is It You or Your Model Talking? A Framework for Model Validation*. Santa Monica, CA: RAND.

Hoeffler, Anke, and Marta Reynal-Querol. 2003. "Measuring the Costs of Conflict." Working paper, Oxford University.

Hughes, Barry B. 1997. "Rough Road Ahead: Global Transformations in the Twenty-First Century." *Futures Research Quarterly* 13(2), 83–107.

———. 1999. *International Futures: Choices in the Face of Uncertainty*. Boulder, CO: Westview.

——— 2001. "Global Social Transformation: The Sweet Spot, the Steady Slog, and the Systemic Shift." *Economic Development and Cultural Change* 49(2), 423–458. http://links.jstor.org/sici?sici=0013-0079%2820010 1%2949%3A2%3C423%3AGSTTSS%3E2.0.CO%3B2-0.

———. 2004. "International Futures (IFs): An Overview of Structural Design." International Futures Working Paper, Denver, CO. http://www.ifs.du.edu/reports.htm.

———. 2004a. "Forecasting the Human Development Index." International Futures Working Paper, Denver, CO. http://www.ifs.du.edu/reports.htm.

———. 2004b. "Regimes and Social Transformation." In Arild Underdal and Oran Young, eds., *Regime Consequences: Methodological Challenges and Research Strategies*: Amsterdam: Kluwer.

———. 2004c. "Scenario Analysis with International Futures (IFs)." International Futures Working Paper, Denver, CO. http://www.ifs.du.edu/reports.htm.

———. 2005a. "Forecasting Productivity and Growth with International Futures (IFs)." International Futures Working Paper, Denver, CO. http://www.ifs.du.edu/reports.htm.

———. 2005b. "UNEP GEO-4 Driver Scenarios (Fifth Draft): Using IFs with Pardee." International Futures Working Paper, Denver, CO. http://www.ifs.du.edu/reports.htm.

———. 2006. "Assessing the Credibility of Forecasts Using International Futures (IFs): Verification and Validation." International Futures Working Paper, Denver, CO. http://www.ifs.du.edu/reports.htm.

———. 2007. "International Futures v. 5.34." Denver, CO: University of Denver. http://www.ifs.du.edu/ifs.

Hughes, Barry B., and Evan E. Hillebrand. 2006. *Exploring and Shaping International Futures*. Boulder, CO: Paradigm. http://www.loc.gov/catdir/toc/ecip0519/2005027186.html

Hughes, Barry B., Anwar Hossain, and Mohammod T. Irfan. 2004. "The Structure of IFs." International Futures Working Paper, Denver, CO. http://www.ifs.du.edu/reports.htm.

Hughes, Barry B., and Peter D. Johnston. 2005. "Sustainable Futures: Policies for Global Development." *Futures* 37, 813–831.

IMAGE-Team. 2001. *The IMAGE 2.2 Implementation of the SRES Scenarios. A Comprehensive Analysis of Emissions, Climate Change, and Impacts in the*

Twenty-First Century. Bilthoven, Netherlands: National Institute for Public Health and the Environment.

Initiative for Policy Dialogue. 2003. "Report on Global Poverty Workshop." New York. http://www0.gsb.columbia.edu/ipd/pub/GlobalPovertyWorkshopReport.pdf.

Intergovernmental Panel on Climate Change. 2000. *IPCC Special Report: Emissions Scenarios, Summary for Policymakers*. Geneva, Switzerland: IPCC, World Meteorological Organization/UN Environment Programme.

International Energy Agency. 2006. *World Energy Outlook 2006*. Paris.

———. 2007. *World Energy Outlook 2007*. Paris.

International Forum on Globalization. 2001. "Does Globalization Help the Poor? A Special Report." *International Forum on Globalization, San Francisco*. http://www.thirdworldtraveler.com/Globalization/DoesGlobaliz_HelpPoor.html.

Jahan, Selim, and Alvaro Umana. 2003. "The Environment-Poverty Nexus." *Development Policy Journal* 3, 53–70.

Jalilian, Hossein, and John Weiss. 2006. "Infrastructure and Poverty: Cross-Country Evidence." In Haider Khan, John Weiss, and Asian Development Bank Institute, eds., *Poverty Strategies in Asia: A Growth-Plus Approach*. Cheltenham, UK: Edward Elgar.

James, Jeffery, and Haider Khan. 1993. "Employment Effects of Income Redistribution." *World Development* 21(5), 817–827.

———. 1997. "Technology and Income Redistribution." *World Development* 25(2).

Johnson, Simon, Jonathan D. Ostry, and Arvind Subramanian. 2007. "The Prospects for Sustained Growth in Africa: Benchmarking the Constraints." IMF Working Paper WP/07/52.

Johnston, Michael. 2000. "Party Systems, Competition, and Political Checks Against Corruption," unpublished paper available at http://people.colgate.edu/mjohnston/MJ%20papers%2001/Florence%20revision.pdf.

Kakwani, Nanak. 1980. *Income Inequality and Poverty: Methods of Estimation and Policy Applications*. New York: Published for the World Bank by Oxford University Press.

———. 2004a. "New Global Poverty Counts." *Poverty in Focus* (September), 9–11.

———. 2006. "Poverty and Well-Being." *Poverty in Focus* (December), 20–21.

Kakwani, Nanak, and Ernesto M. Pernia. 2000. "What Is Pro-Poor Growth?" *Asian Development Review* 18, 1–16.

Kaldor, Nicholas. 1957. "A Model of Economic Growth." *Economic Journal* 67(268), 591–624. http://links.jstor.org/sici?sici=0013-0133%2819571%2967%3A268%3C591%3AAMOEG%3E2.0.CO%3B2-M.

Kanbur, Ravi. 1999. "Income Distribution and Development." In Anthony B. Atkinson and Francois Bourguignon, eds., *Handbook of Income Distribution*. Amsterdam: Elseviere Science.

———. 2004. "Economic Policy, Distribution, and Poverty: The Nature of Disagreements." In Anthony F. Shorrocks, Rolph van der Hoeven, and World Institute for Development Economics Research, eds., *Growth, Inequality, and Poverty: Prospects for Pro-poor Economic Development*. Oxford; New York: Oxford University Press.

Kanbur, Ravi, and Lyn Squire. 1999. "The Evolution of Thinking About Poverty: Exploring the Interactions." Cornell University Working Paper, Ithaca, NY. http://people.cornell.edu/pages/sk145/papers/evolution_of_thinking_about_poverty.pdf.

Kant, Immanuel. 1897. *Perpetual Peace: A Philosophic Essay by Immanuel Kant, published in 1795,* trans. Benjamin Franklin Trueblood. Boston: American Peace Society.

Kapteyn, Arie, and Tom Wansbeek. 1985. "The Individual Welfare Function: A Review." *Journal of Economic Psychology* 6(4), 333–363.

Karshenas, Massoud. 2004. "Global Poverty Estimates and the Millennium Goals: Towards a Unified Framework." Employment Strategy Department. Geneva: International Labor Organization: Employment Strategy Papers 2004/5. http://www.ilo.org/public/english/employment/strat/download/esp5.pdf.

Kaufmann, Daniel. 1997. "Corruption: The Facts." *Foreign Policy* (107), 114–131. http://links.jstor.org/sici?sici=0015-7228%28199722%290%3A107%3C114%3ACTF%3E2.0.CO%3B2-D.

Kaufmann, Daniel, Aart Kraay, and Massimo Mastruzzi. 2003. *Governance Matters III: Governance Indicators for 1996–2002*. Washington, DC: World Bank. http://siteresources.worldbank.org/INTWBIGOVANTCOR/Resources/govmatters3.pdf.

Kaufmann, Daniel, Aart Kraay, and Pablo Zoido-Lobatón. 1999. "Governance Matters." Policy Research Department Working Paper no. 2196: Washington DC: World Bank. http://siteresources.worldbank.org/INTWBIGOVANTCOR/Resources/govmatrs.pdf.

Kemp-Benedict, Eric, Charles Heaps, and Paul Raskin. 2002. "Global Scenario Group Futures Technical Notes." Stockholm Environment Institute: SEI Polestar Series Report.

Kessler, Jan Joost, Trudy Rood, Tonnie Tekelenburg, and Michel Bakkenes. "Biodiversity and Socio-Economic Impacts of Export Commodities in Their Production Regions." Unpublished manuscript.

Khan, Haider. 1982. "Energy, Technology, and Income Distribution: A Social Accounting Matrix for Energy Modeling." In Hamid Hamza, ed., *Applied Simulation and Modeling*. Calgary, Canada: ACTA Press.

———. 1983. "Choice of Technology, Energy, and Income Distribution: A Macroeconomic Framework." Ph.D. diss., Cornell University, Ithaca, NY.

———. 1985. "Technology Choice in the Energy and Textiles Sectors in Korea." In Surjit S. Bhalla, ed., *Technology and Employment in Industry: A Case Study Approach*. 3rd ed. Geneva: International Labour Organisation.

———. 1989. "Macroeconomic Effects of Technology Choice: Multiplier and Structural Path Analysis." *Journal of Policy Modeling* 11(1).

———. 1994a. "A Further Extension of Adjustment Models: The Environment and Equity." In George Shepherd and Karamo Sonko, eds., *Economic Justice in Africa: Adjustment and Sustainable Development*. Westport: Greenwood.

———. 1994b. "Poverty in Bangladesh: What Have We Learned?" In Selim Rashid, ed., *Bangladesh Economy*. Dhaka: University Press.

———. 1997a. "Ecology, Inequality, and Poverty." *Asian Development Review* 15(2).

———. 1997b. *Technology, Energy, and Development: The South Korean Transition*. Cheltenham, UK: Edward Elgar.

———. 1998. *Technology, Development, and Democracy: Limits of National Innovation Systems in the Age of Postmodernism*. Cheltenham, UK: Edward Elgar.

———. 1999. "Sectoral Growth and Poverty: A Multiplier Decomposition Analysis for South Africa." *World Development* 27(3), 521–530.

———. 2002. *On Paradigm, Theories, and Models*. Tokyo: University of Tokyo.

———. 2003. "On Paradigm, Theories, and Models Problems." *Del Desarrollo* 134 (July–September), 149–156.

———. 2004. *On Mortality and Poverty*. Tokyo: University of Tokyo, Graduate School of Economics.

———. 2005a. *Governance and Effectiveness of Japanese Aid: Towards Optimality*. CIRJE Discussion Paper no. F 331. Tokyo: University of Tokyo, Graduate School of Economics.

———. 2005b. *Governance, African Debt, and Sustainable Development: Policies for Partnership with Africa*. CIRJE Discussion Paper no. F 334. Tokyo: University of Tokyo, Graduate School of Economics.

———. 2005c. "Macromodeling of Poverty and the Dual-Dual Model." Tokyo: ADBI Research Paper.

Khan, Haider, Erik Thorbecke, and International Labour Organisation. 1988. *Macroeconomic Effects and Diffusion of Alternative Technologies Within a Social Accounting Matrix Framework: The Case of Indonesia*. Aldershot, Hants, England: Gower.

Khan, Haider, and John Weiss, eds. 2006. *Poverty Strategies in Asia: Growth-Plus Approach*. Cheltenham, UK: Edward Elgar.

Kingdon, G. G., and John Knight. 2003. "Well-Being Poverty Versus Income Poverty." *Global Poverty Research Group*. WPS/2003-16.

———. 2004. *Subjective Well-Being Poverty Versus Income Poverty and Capabilities Poverty?* Working Paper Series no. 003. Oxford: Global Poverty Research Group.

Klenow, Peter J., and Andres Rodriguez. 1997a. *Quantifying Variety Gains from Trade Liberalization*. Chicago: University of Chicago, Graduate School of Business.

———, eds. 1997b. *The Neoclassical Revival in Growth Economics: Has It Gone Too Far?* Cambridge, MA: MIT Press.

Knack, Stephen. 2000. *Aid Dependence and the Quality of Governance: A Cross-Country Empirical Analysis*. Washington, DC: World Bank.

Knack, Stephen, and Philip Keefer. 1997. "Does Social Capital Have an Economic Payoff? A Cross-Country Investigation." *Quarterly Journal of Economics* 112(4), 1251–1288. http://links.jstor.org/sici?sici=0033-5533%28199711%29112%3A4%3C1251%3ADSCHAE%3E2.0.CO%3B2-Y.

Knight, John. 1976. "Explaining Income Distribution in Less Developed Countries: A Framework and an Agenda." *Bulletin of the Oxford Institute of Economics and Statistics* 38(3), 161–177.

Knight, Malcolm, Norman Loayza, and Delano Villanueva. 1996. "The Peace Dividend: Military Spending Cuts and Economic Growth." IMF Staff Papers.

Kornai, János. 1971. *Anti-equilibrium: On Economic Systems Theory and the Tasks of Research*. Amsterdam,: North-Holland.

Kraay, Aart. 2004. "When Is Growth Pro-poor? Cross-Country Evidence." IMF Working Paper WP/04/47, New York. http://www.imf.org/external/pubs/ft/wp/2004/wp0447.pdf.

Kraay, Aart, and Claudio Raddatz. 2005. "Poverty Traps, Aid, and Growth." World Bank Working Paper. Washington, DC.

———. 2007. "Poverty Traps, Aid, and Growth." *Journal Development Economics* 82(2), 315–347.

Kravis, Irving B. 1960. "International Differences in the Distribution of Income." *Review of Economics and Statistics* 42(4), 408–416. http://links.jstor.org/sici?sici=0034-6535%2819601 1%2942%3A4%3C408%3AIDITDO%3E2.0.CO%3B2-W.

Kravis, Irving B., Alan W. Heston, and Robert Summers. 1978a. *International Comparisons of Real Product and*

Purchasing Power. Baltimore: Published for the World Bank by the Johns Hopkins University Press.

———. 1978b. "Real GDP per Capita for More Than One Hundred Countries." *Economic Journal* 88(350), 215–242. http://links.jstor.org/sici?sici=0013-0133%28197806%2988%3A350%3C215%3ARGPCFM%3E2.0.CO%3B2-M.

Kremer, Michael, Nazmul Chaudhury, F. Halsey Rogers, Karthik Muralidharan, and Jeffrey Hammer. 2005. "Teacher Absence in India: A Snapshot." *Journal of the European Economic Association* 3(2/3), 658–667. http://search. ebscohost.com/login.aspx?direct=true& db=buh&AN=17644678&site=ehost-live.

Krueger, Alan B., and Jitka Maleckova. 2003. "Education, Poverty, and Terrorism: Is There a Causal Connection?" *Journal of Economic Perspectives* 17(4), 119–144.

Krugman, Paul. 1994. "The Myth of Asia's Miracle." *Foreign Affairs* 73(6), 62–78. http://search.ebscohost.com/login. aspx?direct=true&db=aph&AN=9411180 052&site=ehost-live.

Kumar, Krishna B. 2003. "Education and Technology Adoption in a Small Open Economy: Theory, and Evidence." *Macroeconomic Dynamics* 7, 586–617.

Kumar, Krishna B., and John G. Matsusaka. 2006. "Village Versus Market Social Capital: An Approach to Development." University of Southern California Working Paper. http://www-rcf.usc.edu/~matsusak/Papers/Kumar_ Matsusaka_Social_Capital_2006.pdf.

Kuznets, Simon. 1963. "Quantitative Aspects of the Economic Growth of Nations: Distribution of Income by Size." *Economic Development and Cultural Change* 11(2), 1–80. http:// links.jstor.org/sici?sici=0013-0079%281 96301%2911%3A2%3C1%3AQAOTEG%3E 2.0.CO%3B2-3.

La Porta, Rafael, Florencio Lopez-de-Silanes, Andrei Shleifer, and Robert

W. Vishny. 1997. "Trust in Large Organizations." *American Economic Review* 87(2), 333–338.

Laderchi, Caterina Ruggeri, Ruhi Saith, and Frances Stewart. 2006. "Does the Definition of Poverty Matter? Comparing Four Approaches." *Poverty in Focus* (December), 10–11.

LaFree, Gary, Laura Dugan, and Susan Sahey. 2008. "Global Terrorism and Failed States." In J. Joseph Hewitt, Jonathan Wilkenfeld, and Ted Robert Gurr, eds., *Peace and Conflict 2008*, pp. 39–54. Boulder, CO: Paradigm.

Lee, Ha Yan, Luca Antonio Ricci, and Roberto Rigobon. 2004. "Once Again, Is Openness Good for Growth?" *Journal of Development Economics* 75, 451–472.

Lee, Jong-Wha. 1993. "International Trade, Distortions, and Long-Run Economic Growth." IMF Staff Papers. Washington, DC: International Monetary Fund.

———. 1995. "Capital Goods imports and lLng-run gGrwth." *Journal of Development Economics,* 8(1), 91–110. http://www.sciencedirect.com/ science/article/B6VBV-3YVCYWS-5/2/ ce0ab4d96743c42717cfa40e50afd480.

Lempert, Robert J., Steven W. Popper, and Steven C. Bankes. 2003. *Shaping the Next One Hundred Years: New Methods for Quantitative Long-Term Policy Analysis*. Santa Monica, CA: RAND.

Leonard, Hugh Jeffrey, ed. 1989. *Environment and the Poor: Development Strategies for a Common Agenda*. Washington, DC: Overseas Development Council.

Lopez-Claros, Augusto, Michael E. Porter, and Xavier Sala-i-Martin. 2006. *The Global Competitiveness Report*. New York: World Economic Forum.

Loury, Glenn C. 1981. "Intergenerational Transfers and the Distribution of Earnings." *Econometrica* 49(4), 843–867. http://links.jstor.org/sici?

sici=0012-9682%28198107%2949%3A4% 3C843%3AITATDO%3E2.0.CO%3B2-C.

Lucas, Robert E. 1988. "On the Mechanics of Economic Development." *Journal of Monetary Economics* 22(1), 3–42. http://www.sciencedirect.com/science/ article/B6VBW-47N61RY-3/2/d5af17f23 7229feefc2278ac76c2bc56.

———. 2002. *Lectures on Economic growth*. Cambridge, MAasHarvard University Press.

Lufumpa, Charles Leyeka. 2005. "The Poverty-Environment Nexus in Africa." *African Development Review* 17(3), 366–381.

Lutz, Wolfgang, Warren C. Sanderson, and Sergei Scherbov. 2004. *The End of World Population Growth in the Twenty-First Century: New Challenges for Human Capital Formation and Sustainable Development*. London: Earthscan. http://www.loc.gov/catdir/toc/ ecip0411/2003025468.html.

Mabogunje, Akin L. 2002. "Poverty and Environmental Degradation: Challenges within the Global Economy." *Environment* 44(1), 8–18.

Maddison, Angus. 1995. *Monitoring the World Economy, 1820–1992*. Paris: Development Centre of the Organization for Economic Cooperation and Development, OECD Publications and Information Center (distributor). http://www.h-net.org/review/hrev-a0a6h1-aa.

———. 2001. *The World Economy: A Millennial Perspective*. Paris: Development Centre of the Organization for Economic Co-operation and Development.

Mankiw, N. Gregory, David Romer, and David N. Weil. 1992. "A Contribution to the Empirics of Economic Growth." *Quarterly Journal of Economics* 107(2), 407–437. http://links.jstor.org/ sici?sici=0033-5533%28199205%29107 %3A2%3C407%3AACTTEO%3E2.0.CO% 3B2-5.

Mauro, Paolo. 1995. "Corruption and Growth," *Quarterly Journal of Economics* 110(3), 681–712.

———. 2002. "The Effects of Corruption on Growth and Public Expenditure." In Arnold J. Heidenheimer and Michael Johnston, eds., *Political Corruption: Concepts and Contexts*, 3rd ed. New Brunswick, N.J.: Transaction.

McGillivray, Mark, and Matthew Clarke, eds. 2006. *Understanding Human Well-Being*. Tokyo: UN University Press.

McKenzie, David J., and Christopher Woodruff. 2002. "Is There an Empirical Basis for Poverty Traps in Developing Countries?" Stanford University Working Paper.

McKinley, Terry. 2006. *What Is Poverty? Good Question* (pamphlet). New York: UN Development Programme, International Poverty Centre.

McMichael, Anthony J., and Rosalie E. Woodruff. 2005. "Detecting the Health Effects of Environmental Change: Scientific and Political Challenge." *EcoHealth* 2(1), 1–3.

Mehrotra, Santosh, and Enrique Delamonica. 2007. *Eliminating Human Poverty: Macroeconomic and Social Policies for Equitable Growth*: London: Zed.

Miguel, Edward, Satyanath Satyanath, and Ernest Sergenti. 2004. "Economic Shocks and Civil Conflict: An Instrumental Variables Approach." *Journal of Political Economy* 112(4), 725–753.

Milanovic, Branko. 2002. "True World Income Distribution, 1988 and 1993: First Calculation Based on Household Surveys Alone." *Economic Journal* 112(476), 51–92. http://ejournals. ebsco.com/direct.asp?ArticleID=9RWJP5 NXDRO8FNG3NMCX.

———. 2005. *Worlds Apart: Measuring International and Global Inequality*. Princeton: Princeton University Press. http://www.loc.gov/catdir/ enhancements/fy0704/2004058312- d.html.

Millennium Ecosystem Assessment. 2003. *People and Ecosystems: A Framework for Assessment and Action*. Washington, DC: Island.

———. 2005. *Ecosystems and Human Well-Being: Synthesis*. Washington, DC: Island. http://www.maweb.org/en/ products.global.scenarios.aspx.

Moran, Theodore H., Edward M. Graham, and Magnus Blomström. 2005. *Does Foreign Direct Investment Promote Development?* Washington, DC: Institute for International Economics; Center for Global Development.

Morris, Ellen, and Sudhir Chella Rajan. 1999. "Energy as It Relates to Poverty Alleviation and Environmental Protection." Paper presented at the UNDP/EC Expert Workshop on Poverty and the Environment.

Nakićenović, Nebojša, Arnulf Grübler, and Alan McDonald. 1998. *Global Energy Perspectives*. Cambridge: Cambridge University Press. http://www. worldenergy.org/wec-geis/publications/ reports/etwan/supporting_ publications/annex_2_chap1.asp.

Narain, Urvashi, Shreekant Gupta, and Klaas van 't Veld. 2005. "Poverty and the Environment, Exploring the Relationship Between Household Incomes, Private Assets, and Natural Assets." Discussion Paper no. 05-18. Washington, DC: Resources for the Future.

National Geographic. 2007. "Curse of the Black Gold: Hope and Betrayal in the Niger Delta." Interactive On-Line Edition, available at http://www7. nationalgeographic.com/ngm/0702/ feature3.

Nayak, Purusottam. 2004. "Poverty and Environmental Degradation in Rural India: A Nexus." Paper presented at the Annual Conference of the Northeastern Economic Association.

Neumayer, Eric. 2003. *The Pattern of Aid Giving: The Impact of Good Governance on Development Assistance*. London: Routledge.

Noland, Marcus, and Howard Pack. 2007. *The Arab Countries in a Changing World*. Washington, DC: Peterson Institute for International Economics.

Nordhaus, William. 2005. *Alternative Measures of Output in Global Economic-Environmental Models: Purchasing Power Parity or Market Exchange Rates?* Washington, DC: http://nordhaus.econ. yale.edu/ppp_020805.pdf.

Nunan, Fiona, Ursula Grant, Godfrey Bahiigwa, Telly Muramira, Pushkar Bajracharya, Diana Pritchard, and Mariano Jose Vargas. 2002. "Poverty and the Environment: Measuring the Links—A Study of Poverty-Environment Indicators with Case Studies from Nepal, Nicaragua, and Uganda." Issue Paper no. 2. London: Environment Policy Department, Department for International Development.

Nussbaum, Martha. 2000. *Women and Human Development: The Capabilities Approach*. Cambridge: Cambridge University Press.

Nussbaum, Martha Craven, and Jonathan Glover. 1995. *Women, Culture, and Development: A Study of Human Capabilities*. Oxford and New York: Clarendon Press and Oxford University Press. http://www.loc.gov/catdir/ enhancements/fy0605/94042602- d.html.

Nuxoll, Daniel A. 1994. "Differences in Relative Prices and International Differences in Growth Rates." *American Economic Review* 84(5), 1423–1436. http://links.jstor.org/sici?sici=0002- 8282%28199412%2984%3A5%3C1423%3 ADIRPAI%3E2.0.CO%3B2-Z.

OECD (Organization for Economic Cooperation and Development). 1999. *The Future of the Global Economy: Towards a Long Boom?* Paris.

———. 2001. *Poverty-Environment Gender Links*. Paris.

———. 2006. *Baseline for the Environmental Outlook to 2030*. Paris.

O'Higgins, M., and S. Jenkins. 1990. "Poverty in the EC: Estimates for 1975, 1980, and 1985." In R. Teekens and B. M. S. van Praag, eds., *Analyzing Poverty in the European Community: Policy Issues, Research Options, and Data Sources*, pp. 198–212. Luxembourg: Office of Official Publications of the European Community.

O'Neill, Brian, and Deborah Balk. 2001. "World Population Futures." New York: Population Reference Bureau, Population Bulletin 56.

Orbeta, Aniceto C. Jr. 2005. "Poverty, Vulnerability, and Family Size: Evidence from the Philippines." In Haider A. Khan and John Weiss, eds., *Poverty Strategies in Asia*. Cheltenham, UK: Edward Elgar.

Oxfam. 2002. "Influencing Poverty Reduction Strategies: A Guide." London: Oxfam International. http://www.oxfam.org.uk/what_we_do/issues/democracy_rights/downloads/prsp_guide.pdf.

Parikh, Jyoti. 2002. "Poverty-Environment-Development Nexus." *International Journal of Global Environmental Issues* 2(3/4), 344–365.

Parnell, Susan. 2000. "Environment and Poverty in Southern Africa: Regional Linkages." Cape Town, South Africa: Department of Environmental and Geographical Sciences, University of Cape Town.

Patz, Jonathan A., Diarmid Campbell-Lendrum, Tracey Holloway, and Jonathan A. Foley. 2005. "Impact of Regional Climate Change on Human Health." *Nature* 438(7066), 310–316.

Perrings, Charles. 1989. "An Optimal Path to Extinction? Poverty and Resource Degradation in the Open Agrarian Economy." *Journal of Development Economics* 30(1), 1–24.

Perry, Guillermo. 2006. *Poverty Reduction and Growth: Virtuous and Vicious Circles*. Washington, DC: World Bank.

Persson, Torsten, and Guido Tabellini. 1994. "Is Inequality Harmful for Growth?" *American Economic Review* 84(3), 600–621. http://links.jstor.org/sici?sici=0002-8282%28199406%2984%3A3%3C600%3AIIHFG%3E2.0.CO%3B2-9.

Poddar, Tushar, and Eva Yi. 2007. "India's Rising Growth Potential." *Goldman Sachs Global Economics Paper* 152. https://portal.gs.com.

Pogge, Thomas W., and Sanjay G. Reddy. 2003. "Unknown: The Extent, Distribution,, and Trend of Global Income Poverty." Columbia University Working Paper.

Popper, Steven W., Robert J. Lempert, and Steven C. Bankes. 2005. "Shaping the Future." *Scientific American* 292(4), 66–71.

Porta, Rafael La, Florencio Lopez-de-Silanes, Andrei Shleifer, and Robert W. Vishny. 1997. "Trust in Large Organizations." *American Economic Review* 87(2), 333–338. http://links.jstor.org/sici?sici=0002-8282%2819970 5%2987%3A2%3C333%3ATILO%3E2.0.CO%3B2-7.

Poverty-Environment Initiative. 1999a. "Attacking Poverty While Improving the Environment: Practical Recommendations." New York: UN Development Programme.

———. "Attacking Poverty While Improving the Environment: Towards Win-Win Policy Options." New York: UN Development Programme.

———. 2007. "Mainstreaming Environment for Poverty Reduction and Pro-Poor Growth: Proposal for Scaling-Up the Poverty-Environment Initiative." New York: UN Development Programme.

Poverty-Environment Partnership. 2005a. "Assessing Environment's Contribution to Poverty Reduction." New York: Poverty-Environment Partnership.

———. 2005b. "Investing in Environmental Wealth for Poverty Reduction." New York: Poverty-Environment Partnership.

———. 2005c. "Investing in the Environment to Fight Poverty: The Economic Case, Priorities for Action,, and Implications for the 2005 World Summit and Beyond—Key Messages from a High-Level Policy Dialogue." New York: Poverty-Environment Partnership.

———. 2005d. "Sustaining the Environment to Fight Poverty and Achieve the MDGs: The Economic Case and Priorities for Action." New York: Poverty-Environment Partnership.

Pradhan, Menno, and Martin Ravallion. 1998. "Measuring Poverty Using Qualitative Perceptions of Welfare." World Bank Policy Research Working Paper no. 2011: World Bank, Development Research Group, Poverty and Human Resources.

Prakash, Sanjeev. 1997. "Poverty and Environment Linkages in Mountains and Uplands: Reflections on the 'Poverty Trap' Thesis. CREED Working Paper Series no. 12. London and Amsterdam: International Institute for Environment and Development/Institute for Environmental Studies.

Prescott, Edward C. 1998. "Needed: A Theory of Total Factor Productivity." *International Economic Review* 39, 525–552.

———. 2006. "Nobel Lecture: The Transformation of Macroeconomic Policy and Research." *Journal of Political Economy* 114(2), 203–235. http://search.ebscohost.com/login.aspx?direct=true&db=buh&AN=21101304&site=ehost-live.

Pritchett, Lant, Asep Suryahadi, and Sudarno Sumarto. 2000. "Quantifying

Vulnerability to Poverty: A Proposed Measure, Applied to Indonesia." World Bank Policy Research Working Paper no. 2437.

Prüss-Üstün, Annette, and Carlos Corvalán. 2006. *Preventing Disease Through Healthy Environments: Towards an Estimate of the Environmental Burden of Disease*. Geneva: World Health Organization.

Putnam, Robert D. 1995. "Bowling Alone: America's Declining Social Capital." *Journal of Democracy* 6(1), 65–78.

Qu, Weishuang, and Gerald O. Barney. 2002. "A Model for Evaluating the Policy Impact on Poverty." Arlington, VA: Millennium Institute Paper, http://www.systemdynamics.org/conferences/2002/papers/Qu1.pdf.

Quibria, M. G. 2002. "Growth and Poverty: Lessons from the East Asian Miracle revisited." Tokyo: ADB Institute Research Paper. http://www.adbi.org/files/2002.02.rp33.growth.poverty.eastasia.pdf.

Rajan, Raghuram G., and Arvind Subramanian. 2005. "What Undermines Aid's Impact on Growth?" IMF Working Paper WP/05/126. Available at http://www.imf.org/external/pubs/ft/wp/2005/wp05126.pdf.

Raskin, Paul, Gilberto Gallopín, Pablo Gutman, Al Hammond, and Rob Swart. 1998. *Bending the Curve: Toward Global Sustainability*. Stockholm Environment Institute. www.sei.se.

Raskin, Paul, Tariq Banuri, Gilberto C. Gallopín, Pablo Gutman, Allen L. Hammond, Robert Kates, and Rob Swart. 2002. *Great Transition: The Promise and Lure of the Times Ahead*. Boston: Stockholm Environmental Institute. www.sei.se.

Ravallion, Martin. 1995. "Growth and Poverty: Evidence for Developing Countries in the 1980s." *Economics Letters* 48, 411–417.

———. 2001a. "Comment on Counting the World's Poor." *World Bank Research Observer* 16(2).

———. 2001b. "Growth, Inequality, and Poverty: Looking Beyond Averages." *World Development* 29, 1803–1815.

———. 2001c. "On the Urbanization of Poverty." World Bank Development Research Group paper: Washington, DC: World Bank. http://unpan1.un.org/intradoc/groups/public/documents/APCITY/UNPAN002542.pdf.

———. 2002a. "Have We Already Met the Millennium Development Goal of Poverty?" Washington, DC: World Bank. http://www.iie.com/publications/papers/ravallion0203.pdf.

———. 2002b. "How *Not* to Count the Poor? A Reply to Reddy and Pogge." Working Paper. Washington, DC: World Bank. http://www.columbia.edu/~sr793/wbreply.pdf.

———. 2003. "The Debate on Globalization, Poverty, and Inequality: Why Measurement Matters." *International Affairs* 79(4), 739–753.

———. 2004a. "Monitoring Progress Against Global Poverty." *Poverty in Focus* (September), 12–15.

———. 2004b. *Pro-Poor Growth: A Primer*. Washington, DC: World Bank. http://ideas.repec.org/p/wbk/wbrwps/3242.html.

Ravallion, Martin, and Benu Bidani. 1994. "How Robust Is a Poverty Profile?" *World Bank Economic Review* 8(1), 75.

Ravallion, Martin, and Shaohua Chen. 1997. "What Can New Survey Data Tell Us About Recent Changes in Distribution and Poverty?" *World Bank Economic Review* 11, 357–382.

———. 2003. "Measuring Pro-Poor Growth." *Economics Letters* 78, 93–99.

Ravallion, Martin, Gaurav Datt, and Dominique van de Walle. 1991. "Qualifying Absolute Poverty in the Developing World." *Review of Income and Wealth* 37, 345–361.

Rawls, John. 1971. *A Theory of Justice*. Cambridge, MA: Belknap Press of Harvard University Press.

Reddy, Sanjay G., and Thomas W. Pogge. 2002. "How Not to Count the Poor!—A Reply to Ravallion." http://www.columbia.edu/~sr793/poggereddyreply.pdf.

Reddy, Sanjay, Sujata Visaria, and Muhammad Asali. 2006. "Intercountry Comparisons of Poverty Based on a Capability Approach: An Empirical Exercise." International Poverty Center Working Paper.

Reed, David. 2002. "Poverty and the Environment: Changing Concepts." *Development Bulletin* 58, 9–15.

———. 2004. "Analyzing the Political Economy of Poverty and Ecological Disruption." Washington, DC: World Wide Fund for Nature, Macroeconomics Program Office.

Rice, Susan E., Corinne Graff, and Janet Lewis. 2006. "Poverty and Civil War: What Policymakers Need to Know." Washington, DC: Brookings Institution.

Richels, Richard G., Alan S. Manne, and Tom M. L. Wigley. 2004. "Moving Beyond Concentrations: The Challenges of Limiting Temperature Change." Working paper 04-11: AEI-Brookings Joint Center for Regulatory Studies. http://www.aei-brookings.org/admin/authorpdfs/page.php?id=937.

Rodriguez, Francisco, and Dani Rodik. 2000. *Trade Policy and Economic Growth: A Skeptic's Guide to the Cross-National Evidence*. Cambridge, MA: MIT Press.

Roe, Dilys. 2005. "Poverty-Conservation Linkages: A Conceptual Framework." London: International Institute for Environment and Development, Poverty and Conservation Learning Group.

Romer, Paul M. 1986. "Increasing Returns and Long-Run Growth." *Journal of Political Economy* 94(5), 1002–1037.

———. 1987. "Growth Based on Increasing Returns Due to Specialization." *American Economic Review* 77(2), 56–62. http://links.jstor.org/sici?sici=0002-8282%28198705%2977%3A2%3C56%3AGBOIRD%3E2.0.CO%3B2-Y.

———. 1989. "What Determines the Rate of Growth and Technological Change?" Working Paper WPS279: Washington, DC: World Bank.

———. 1990. "Endogenous Technological Change." *Journal of Political Economy* 98(5), S71-S102. http://links.jstor.org/sici?sici=0022-3808%28199010%2998%3A5%3CS71%3AETC%3E2.0.CO%3B2-8.

———. 1993. "Idea Gaps and object Gaps in Economic Development." *Journal of Monetary Economics* 32(3), 543–573. http://www.sciencedirect.com/science/article/B6VBW-458XPFR-9/2/43d92f456d3a6853def6bf92bc94c786.

Rowntree, B. Seebohm. 1922. *Poverty: A Study of Town Life.* New ed. London: Longmans, Green.

Rubin, Barnett R. 2002. *Blood on the Doorstep: The Politics of Preventive Action.* New York: Century Foundation Press. http://www.loc.gov/catdir/toc/fy035/2002012074.html.

Sachs, Jeffrey. 1995. "Natural Resource Abundance and Economic Growth." National Bureau of Research Working Paper 5398. http://www.earthinstitute.columbia.edu/about/director/documents/NaturalResourceAbundanceandEconomicDevelopmentwithWarner-1997.pdf.

———. 2005. *The End of Poverty: Economic Possibilities for Our Time.* New York: Penguin Press.

Sachs, Jeffrey, and Pia Malaney. 2002. "The Economic and Social Burden of Malaria." *Nature* 415(6872), 680–685.

Sachs, Jeffrey, and Andrew M. Warner. 1997. "Sources of Slow Growth in African Economies." *Journal of African Economies* (6), 335–376.

———. 1999. "Natural Resource Intensity and Economic Growth." In Jorg Mayer, Brian Chambers, and Ayisha Farooq, eds., *Development Policies in Natural Resource Economies.* Cheltenham, UK: Edward Elgar.

Sala-i-Martin, Xavier. 2002a. "The Disturbing 'Rise' in Global Income Inequality." NBER Working Paper 8904. Cambridge, MA. http://www.columbia.edu/~xs23/papers/GlobalIncomeInequality.htm.

———. 2002b. "The World Distribution of Income Estimated from Individual Country Distributions." NBER Working Paper 8933.

Sall, Alioune, ed. 2003. *Africa 2025: What Possible Futures for Sub-Saharan Africa?* Durban: University of South Africa Press; UNDP/African Futures.

Sambanis, Nicholas. 2001. "A Review of Recent Advances and Future Directions in the Quantitative Literature on Civil War." Yale University Working Paper.

———. 2003. "Using Case Studies to Expand the Theory of Civil War." *Perspectives on Politics* 2(2), 259–279.

Sánchez-Triana, Ernesto, Kulsum Ahmed, and Yewande A. Awe, eds. 2007. *Environmental Priorities and Poverty Reduction: A Country Environmental Analysis for Columbia.* Washington, DC: World Bank.

Sanderson, Steven. 2005. "Poverty and Conservation: The New Century's 'Peasant Question?'" *World Development* 33(2), 323–332.

Satterthwaite, David. 2003. "The Links Between Poverty and the Environment in Urban Areas of Africa, Asia, and Latin America." *Annals of the American Academy of Political and Social Science* 590(1), 73–92.

Scherr, Sara J. 1999. "Poverty-Environment Interactions in Agriculture: Key Factors and Policy Implications." Paper presented at the UNDP/EC Expert Workshop on Poverty and the Environment.

———. 2000. "A Downward Spiral? Research Evidence on the Relationship Between Poverty and Natural Resource Degradation." *Food Policy* 25(4), 479–498.

———. 2003. "Hunger, Poverty and Biodiversity in Developing Countries." Paper presented at the Mexico Action Summit, Mexico City.

Schultz, Theodore W. 1963. *The Economic Value of Education.* New York: Columbia University Press.

Scott, Lucy. 2006. "Chronic Poverty and the Environment: A Vulnerability Perspective." Chronic Poverty Research Centre Working Paper no. 62. London: Overseas Development Insitute.

Sedlacek, Guilherme, Nadeem Ilahi, and Emily Gustafsson-Wright. 2000. *Targeted Conditional Transfer Programs in Latin America: An Early Survey.* Washington, DC: World Bank.

Sen, Amartya Kumar. 1976. "Poverty: An Ordinal Approach to Measurement." *Econometrica* 44(2), 219–231. http://links.jstor.org/sici?sici=0012-9682%2819760%2944%3A2%3C219%3APAOATM%3E2.0.CO%3B2-Z.

———. 1984. *Resources, Values, and Development.* Oxford: Blackwell.

———. 1992a. *Inequality Reexamined.* New York; Cambridge, MA: Russell Sage Foundation; Harvard University Press.

———. 1992b. "Missing Women." *British Medical Journal* 304(March), 586–587.

———. 1999. *Development as Freedom.* 1st ed. New York: Knopf.

Sen, Amartya Kumar, and James E. Foster. 1997. *On Economic Inequality.* Oxford: Oxford University Press.

Shell International. 2001. *Energy Needs, Choices, and Possibilities: Scenarios to 2050*. London: Shell International.

Shyamsundar, Priya. 2002. "Poverty-Environment Indicators." Environment Department Papers, Environmental Economics Series: Washington, DC: World Bank.

Silva Leander, Sebastian. 2005. "Multidimensional Poverty Indices: Empirical Issues in the Operationalisation of the Capability Approach." Harvard University Working Paper, Global Equity Initiative, April.

Sobel, Joel. 2002. "Can We Trust Social Capital?" *Journal of Economic Literature* 40(1), 139–154. http://links.jstor.org/sici?sici=0022-0515%28200203%2940%3A1%3C139%3ACWTSC%3E2.0.CO%3B2-C.

Solow, Robert M. 1956. "A Contribution to the Theory of Economic Growth." *Quarterly Journal of Economics* 70(1), 65–94. http://links.jstor.org/sici?sici=0033-5533%28195602%2970%3A1%3C65%3AACTTTO%3E2.0.CO%3B2-M.

———. 1957. "Technical Change and the Aggregate Production Function." *Review of Economics and Statistics*, 393), 312–320. http://links.jstor.org/sici?sici=0034-6535%28195708%2939%3A3%3C312%3ATCATAP%3E2.0.CO%3B2-U.

Srinivasan, T. 2004. "The Unsatisfactory State of Global Poverty Estimation." *Poverty in Focus* (September), 2–5.

Srivastava, Pradeep. 2005. "Poverty Targeting in India." In John Weiss, ed., *Poverty Targeting in Asia*. Cheltenham, UK: Edward Elgar.

Stewart, Frances, and V. Fitzgerald. 2001. *War and Underdevelopment*. Oxford: Oxford University Press.

Stewart, Frances, C. Huang, and M. Wang. 2001. *Internal Wars in Developing Countries: An Empirical Overview of Economic and Social Consequences*. Vol. 1. Oxford: Oxford University Press.

Stifel, David C., and Erik Thorbecke. 2003. "A Dual-Dual Model of an Archetype African Economy: Trade Reform, Migration, and Poverty." *Journal of Policy Modelling* 25, 207–235.

Stokey, Nancy L. 1991. "Human Capital, Product Quality, and Growth." *Quarterly Journal of Economics* 106(2), 587–616. http://links.jstor.org/sici?sici=0033-5533%28199105%29106%3A2%3C587%3AHCPQAG%3E2.0.CO%3B2-G.

———. 1995. "R&D and Economic Growth." *Review of Economic Studies* 62(3), 469–489. http://links.jstor.org/sici?sici=0034-6527%28199507%2962%3A3%3C469%3ARAEG%3E2.0.CO%3B2-S.

———. 1998. "Are There Limits to Growth?" *International Economic Review* 39, 1–32.

Svensson, Jakob. 2000. "Foreign Aid and Rent-Seeking." *Journal of International Economics* 51(2): 437–461.

Swinton, Scott M., Germán Escobar, and Thomas Reardon. 2003. "Poverty and Environment in Latin America: Concepts, Evidence, and Policy Implications." *World Development* 31(11), 1865–1872.

Tamura, Robert. 2001. "Teachers, Growth, and Convergence." *Journal of Political Economy* 109(5), 1021–1059. http://links.jstor.org/sici?sici=0022-3808%28200110%29109%3A5%3C1021%3ATGAC%3E2.0.CO%3B2-U.

Tanzi, Vito, and Hamid Davoodi. 1997. "Corruption, Public Investment, and Growth." IMF Working Paper 97/139.

Tekelenburg, Tonnie, and Jan Joost Kessler. 2005. "How Biodiversity Relates to Poverty, Conceptual Framework Design to Support Policy Making." Paper presented at the FAO-IFSA Global Learning Opportunity.

Tekelenburg, Tonnie, Jan Joost Kessler, and Ben ten Brink. 2005. *Poverty-Biodiversity Relationships: An Investigation Towards a Poverty Module for the GLOBIO Model*. Unpublished manuscript. April 13.

Teschl, Miriam, and Laurent Derobert. 2001. "Capabilities, Networks, and Activity Conference on Justice and Poverty: Examining Sen's Capability Approach." Capabilities, Networks, and Activity' Conference on Justice and Poverty.

Todaro, Michael P., and Stephen C. Smith. 2003. *Economic Development*. 9th ed. Boston: Addison-Wesley.

Toman, Michael. 2003. "The Roles of the Environment and Natural Resources in Economic Growth Analysis." Discussion Paper no. 02-71. Washington, DC: Resources for the Future.

Treisman, Daniel. 2000. "The Causes of Corruption: A Cross-National Study." *Journal of Public Economics* 76(3): 399–457.

UNAIDS. 2007. "AIDS Epidemic Update." Geneva.

UN Development Programme. 2002. *Arab Human Development Report 2002: Creating Opportunities for Future Generations*. New York: UN Development Programme.

UN ECAF (UN Economic Commission for Africa). 2005 (August). The Millennium Development Goals in Africa: Progress and Challenges, ed. Abebe Shimeles, Workie Mitiku, Vanessa Steinmayer, and Reto Thoenen. Addis Ababa, Ethiopia: UN ECAF.

UN ECLAC (UN Economic Commission for Latin America and the Caribbean). 2004. "Social Panorama of Latin America 2002–2003." Santiago: UN ECLAC.

———. 2005. "The Millennium Development Goals: A Latin American and Caribbean Perspective." Ed. Alicia Bárcena, José Luis Machinea, and Arturo León. Santiago: UN ECLAC.

UN Environment Programme. 2003. "Poverty and Ecosystems: A Conceptual Framework—A Synthesis." Nairobi: UN Environment Programme.

———. Division of Early Warning and Assessment. 2002. *Global Environment*

Outlook 3: Past, Present, and Future Perspectives. Nairobi: UN Environment Programme.

——— 2007. "Global Environment Outlook 4: Environment for Development." Nairobi: UN Environment Programme.

UN ESA (UN Department of Economic and Social Affairs). 2004. "World Population Prospects: The 2004 Revision, Volume 3 Analytical Report." New York: UN Population Division. 2006. http://www.un.org/esa/population/publications/WPP2004/WPP2004_Volume3.htm.

UN FAO (UN Food and Agriculture Organization). 2005. "The State of Food Insecurity in the World 2005: Eradicating World Hunger—The Key to Achieving the Millennium Development Goals." Rome: UN FAO. http://www.fao.org/icatalog/inter-e.htm.

United Nations. 1987. *The World Commission on Environment and Development*. Oxford: Oxford University Press.

———. 2003. *Human Development Report 2003: Millennium Development Goals—A Compact Among Nations to End Human Poverty*. New York: United Nations.

———. 2005. *Human Development Report 2005: International Cooperation at a Crossroads: Aid, Trade, and Security in an Unequal World*. New York: United Nations.

———. 2007. *Human Development Report 2007/2008: Fighting Climate Change—Human Solidarity in a Divided World*. New York: United Nations.

UN Millennium Project. 2005a. *Environment and Human Well-Being: A Practical Strategy*. London: Earthscan.

———. 2005b. *Investing in Development: A Practical Plan to Achieve the Millennium Development Goals*. New York: UN Development Programme.

UN Population Division. 2003. "World Population in 2300." New York. http://www.un.org/esa/population/publications/longrange2/Long_range_report.pdf.

———. 2006. "World Population Prospects: The 2004 Revision, Volume 3 Analytical Report." New York. http://www.un.org/esa/population/publications/WPP2004/WPP2004_Volume3.htm.

Uppsala Conflict Data Project. 2006. "UCDP/PRIO Armed Conflicts Dataset." http://new.prio.no/CSCW-Datasets/Data-on-Armed-Conflict/UppsalaPRIO-Armed-Conflicts-Dataset/UppsalaPRIO-Armed-Conflict-Dataset/.

U.S. Census Bureau. 2004. "Global Population Profile 2002." Washington, DC: US Government Printing Office. http://www.census.gov/ipc/prod/wp02/wp-02.pdf.

U.S. Central Intelligence Agency Strategic Assessment Group. 2001. *The Global Economy in the Long Term*. Washington, DC: Strategic Assessment Group.

U.S. Department of Energy. 2006. "International Energy Outlook 2006." Washington, DC: U.S. DOE, Energy Information Administration.

———. 2007. "International Energy Outlook 2007." Washington, DC: U.S. Department of Energy, Energy Information Administration.

Upton, Simon, and Vangelis Vitalis. 2002. "Poverty, Demography, Economics, and Sustainable Development: Perspectives from the Developed and Developing Worlds: What Are the Realistic Prospects for Sustainable Development in the First Decade of the New Millennium?" Paper presented at the annual meeting of the Alliance for Global Sustainability.

van der Mensbrugghe, Dominique. 2001. "Poverty Calculations." Development Prospects Group document.

———. 2005. "Linkage Technical Reference Document." Version 6.0 Linkage Technical Reference Document. Washington, DC: World Bank van Vurren, Detlef P., and Brian C. O'Neil. 2006. "The Consistency of IPCC's SRES

Scenarios to Recent Literature and Recent Projections." *Climatic Change*. http://www.springerlink.com/content/d1357287j8646425.

Villasenor, Jose A., and Barry C. Arnold. 1989. "Elliptical Lorenz Curves." *Journal of Econometrics* 40, 327–338.

Waldman, Linda. 2005. "Environment, Politics, and Poverty: Lessons from a Review of PRSP Stakeholder Perspectives—Synthesis Review." London: Institute for Development Studies.

Wang, Sangui. 2005. "Poverty Targeting in the People's Republic of China." In John Weiss, ed., *Poverty Targeting in Asia*. Cheltenham: Edward Elgar.

Warr, Peter. 2000. "Poverty Reduction and Economic Growth: Evidence from Asia." *Asian Development Review* 18(2).

Weiss, John. 2005. "Experiences with Poverty Targeting in Asia: An Overview." In John Weiss, ed., *Poverty Targeting in Asia*. Cheltenham, UK: Edward Elgar.

Weiss, John, and Heather Montgomery. 2004. "Microfinance and Poverty Reduction in Asia and Latin America." ADB Institute Discussion Paper. http://www.adbi.org/files/2004.09.dp15.micofinance.poverty.asia.latin.pdf.

Weiss, John, Heather Montgomery, and Elvira Kurmanalieva. 2005. "Microfinance and Poverty Reduction in Asia: What Is the Evidence?" In John Weiss, ed., *Poverty Targeting in Asia*. Cheltenham, UK: Edward Elgar.

Weller, Christian E., Robert E. Scott, and Adam S. Hersh. 2001. "The Unremarkable Record of Liberalized Trade." Economic Policy Institute Briefing Paper, Washington, DC. http://www.epinet.org/content.cfm/briefingpapers_sept01inequality.

Wodon, Quentin. 2007. *Growth and Poverty Reduction: Case Studies from West Africa*. Washington, DC: World Bank.

World Bank. N.d.-a. "Detailed LSMS Household Survey Data." Washington,

DC: World Bank. http://www. worldbank.org/lsms.

World Bank. N.d.-b. "DR-CAFTA: Challenges and Opportunities for Central America." Central America Department and Office of the Chief Economist for the Latin America and Caribbean Region, Washington, DC: World Bank. http://siteresources.worldbank. org/LACEXT/Resources/258553-1119648763980/DR_CAFTA_Challenges_ Opport_Final_en.pdf.

World Bank. N.d.-c. "POVCAL." Shaohua Chen, Gaurav Datt, and Martin Ravallion. This program allows calculation of assorted poverty measures from grouped data, such as that in deciles. http://www.worldbank. org/lsms/tools/povcal.

World Bank. N.d.-d. "Project Information Document (PID) Appraisal Stage for Ghana." Washington, DC: World Bank.

———. 1980. *World Development Report 1980: Poverty and Human Development.* New York: Oxford University Press.

———. 1990. *World Development Report 1990: Poverty.* New York: Oxford University Press.

———. 1994. *World Development Report: Infrastructure for Development.* New York: Oxford University Press.

———. 2001a. *World Development Report 2000–2001: Attacking Poverty.* New York: Oxford University Press.

———. 2001b. *Global Economic Prospects and the Developing Countries 2001.* Washington, DC: World Bank.

———. 2002. *Global Economic Prospects 2002: Making Trade Work for the World's Poor.* Washington, DC: World Bank.

———. 2004a. *World Development Report 2004: Making Services Work for Poor People.* Washington, DC: World Bank.

———. 2004b. *Global Economic Prospects 2004: Realizing the Development Promise of the Doha Agenda.* Washington, DC: World Bank.

———. 2005a. *Global Economic Prospects 2005: Trade, Regionalism, and Development.* Washington, DC: World Bank.

———. 2005b. "Project Appraisal Document on a Proposed Loan in the Amount of U.S.$ 100 Million to the People's Republic of China for a Liuzhou Environment Management Project." Washington, DC: World Bank.

———. 2005c. *Pro-Poor Growth in the 1990s: Lessons and Insights from Fourteen Countries.* Washington, DC: World Bank.

———. 2005d. "Toward a Conflict-Sensitive Poverty Reduction Strategy: Lessons from a Retrospective Analysis." Washington, DC: World Bank.

———. 2005e. *Where Is the Wealth of Nations? Measuring Capital for the Twenty-First Century.* Washington, DC: World Bank.

———. 2005f. *World Development Report 2005: A Better Investment Climate for Everyone.* Washington, DC: World Bank.

———. 2005g. "World Development Report." Washington, DC: World Bank.

———. 2006a. *Global Economic Prospects 2006: Economic Implications of Remittances and Migration.* Washington, DC: World Bank.

———. 2006b. "Project Performance Assessment Report for India: States' Road Infrastructure Development Technical Assistance Project." Washington, DC: World Bank.

———. 2006c. *World Development Indicators 2006.* Washington, DC: World Bank.

———. 2007. *Global Economic Prospects 2007: Managing the Next Wave of Globalization.* Washington, DC: World Bank.

———. 2008. *Global Economic Prospects 2008: Technology Diffusion in the Developing World.* Washington, DC: World Bank.

World Commission on Environment and Development. 1987. *Our Common Future: The Report of the World Commission on Environment and Development.* New York: Oxford University Press.

World Energy Conference. Congress and World Energy Conference. 1989. *Global Energy Perspectives, 2000–2020.* London: WEC Committee.

World Health Organization and United Nations Environment Programme. 2005. "Health and Environment: Tools for Effective Decision-Making. The WHO-UNEP Health and Environment Linkages Initiative (HELI)—Review of Initial Findings." Norway: UNEP/GRID Arendal.

World Resources Institute. 2000. *World Resources 2000–2001: People and Ecosystems—The Fraying Web of Life.* Washington, DC: World Resources Institute.

———. 2005. *World Resources 2005: The Wealth of the Poor—Managing Ecosystems to Fight Poverty.* Washington, DC: World Resources Institute.

Wratten, Ellen. 1995. "Conceptualizing Urban Poverty." *Environment and Urbanization,* 7(1), 11–38.

Xie, Danyang. 1991. "Increasing Returns and Increasing Rates of Growth." *Journal of Political Economy* 99(2), 429–435. http://links.jstor.org/sici? sici=0022-3808%281991904%2999%3A2% 3C429%3AIRAIRO%3E2.0.CO%3B2-W.

Yohe, Gary W., Rodel D. Lasco, Nigel Arnell, Stewart J. Cohen, Chris Hope, Anthony C. Janetos, and Rosa T. Perez. 2007. "Perspectives on Climate Change and Sustainability." In Martin L. Parry, Osvaldo F. Canziani, Jean P. Palutikof, Paul J. van der Linden, and Claire E. Hanson, eds., *Climate Change 2007: Impacts, Adaptation and Vulnerability. Contribution of Working Group II to the Fourth Assessment Report of the Intergovernmental Panel on Climate Change,* pp. 811–841. Cambridge: Cambridge University Press.

Forecast Tables:
Introduction and Glossary

Forecasts (or simulation results) from International Futures (IFs) are dynamic calculations of the full modelling system, not extrapolations of series, results of isolated multiple regressions, or representations of the forecasts of others. To understand more about IFs forecasts and the specific formulations for the variables shown in the following tables, see the text of this volume, especially Chapters 4 and 5, and the documentation of the model.

Forecasts for individual countries over a long period of time are very seldom done. There are good reasons for reluctance to provide such forecasts, including:

- Data in any series are seldom available for all countries, particularly for smaller ones or those that have undergone substantial sociopolitical transitions. IFs represents 182 countries and uses estimation procedures to fill data holes as necessary.
- Every country is very much unique. Formulating a large-scale dynamic model to behave reasonably in the face of such complexity is extremely challenging, and structures of the system will never be completely free of poor behavior for many countries, especially under extreme or new circumstances.
- Some variables, such as income distribution (Gini), have especially weak bases for forecasting.

Most longer-term global forecasting reduces the severity of these problems in several ways, including reliance on regional aggregations of countries and significantly limiting the forecast horizon. The tables included here obviously ignore such practical approaches and simply present the numbers the model produces. This volume has repeatedly emphasized that we should never treat any model results as predictions; we should instead use them for thinking about and exploring possible futures. That is the spirit behind these tables. With continuing development of the modeling system, results will change and presumably improve on average. The project will give regular attention, in particular, to results that are extreme relative to other countries or to expectations based on regional expertise or other forecasts.

These forecast tables are organized by geographical, substantive, and temporal attributes. Geographically, the first page of each of eighteen sets begins with global and four-continent totals (Africa, the Americas, Asia with Oceania, and Europe), followed by the UN subregional divisions within each of the continents—see Chapter 7 for definition and discussion of those subregions. The subsequent six pages of each set provide forecasts for each of the country members of the subregional divisions within the four continents.

The eighteen sets cover six substantive issue areas. The first simply provides total population and population density information. The remaining sets of forecasting variables are divided into five categories: poverty (with standard economic variables such as GDP and GDP per capita as well as some demographic ones), health, education, infrastructure, and governance. These five categories correspond to the topics the Patterns of Potential Human Progress series will cover, and forecasts in each category will therefore be developed across volumes.

Temporally, each forecast series contains values for 2005, 2030, and 2055, thereby providing a forecast horizon of fifty years. Additional columns show the cumulative percentage change forecast from 2005 through 2055 and the annualized rate of change over the period. The model is currently initialized in 2000, and it computes annual results recursively from 2000 through the simulation horizon. Thus results in years after 2001 are computations rather than actual values, even when data are available. The only exception is that IFs imposes the actual GDP data from 2001–2005 on the model calculations so as to obtain accurate values for this key series. In the near future the model will be rebased to 2005 and run from that year. That rebasing will change (and improve) all results, although few are likely to change dramatically. We will post new forecast sets on line periodically.

To facilitate reading and interpretation of the hard-copy tables presented here and the electronic copies on the IFs web site (www.ifs. du.edu), we provide the following glossary of the variable names used in the tables, the variable name used in IFs, and some basic comments on the variables, such as the sources of initial conditions and/or the forecast approach.

Variable	IFs Name	Source and Comments
Annual Carbon Emissions	CARANN	Releases to the atmosphere of carbon dioxide from any human activity (such as burning fossil fuels or deforestation).
Calories per Capita	CLPC	Calorie consumption per day from all sources. Initialized with data originally from the UN FAO.
Contraception Use	CONTRUSE	Percentage of women of reproductive age (usually measured as 15–49) using any form of contraception. Initialized from Population Reference Bureau assorted years.
Crop Yield	YL	Agricultural crop production of all kinds summed and divided by land area devoted to the production. Initialized with production and land data originally from UN FAO.
Crude Birth Rate	CBR	Annual births per thousand population. Although the measure shows progress of the demographic transition, total fertility rate (see TFR) is a better measure of fertility.
Crude Death Rate	CDR	Annual deaths per thousand population. Although the measure indicates progress of the demographic transition, life expectancy is a better measure of population health.
Economic Freedom	ECONFREE	Initialized from Fraser International, which defines economic freedom as "the extent to which one can pursue economic activity without interference from government" and builds its index on several measures assessed by experts. See http://www.freetheworld.com.
Economic Integration Index	ECONINTEG	Based on A.T. Kearney/Foreign Policy globalization subindex, tied to trade and foreign direct investment flows. See Hughes 2005, Part II, for IFs specification.
Education: Adults (15+) with Primary Education	EDPRIPER	Percentage of adults aged 15 years or older with a completed primary education. Initialized from the Barro-Lee data set (Barro and Lee 2000).
Education: Adults (15+) with Secondary Education	EDSECPER	Percentage of adults aged 15 years or older with a completed secondary education. Initialized from the Barro-Lee data set (Barro and Lee 2000).
Education: Adults (15+) with Tertiary Education	EDTERPER	Percentage of adults of 15 years or older with a completed tertiary education (any degree). Initialized from the Barro-Lee data set (Barro and Lee 2000). Tertiary education for most countries begins beyond grades 10–12.
Education: Adult (25+ Years of Education)	EDYRSAG25	Average number of years of education of adults 25 years of age or older. Initialized from the Barro-Lee data set (Barro and Lee 2000).

Variable	IFs Name	Source and Comments
Education: Net Primary Education Enrollment	EDPRIENR	The percentage of the relevant age group (based on the International Standard Classification of Education 1997) enrolled in primary education. Contrast this with gross enrollment, which includes those enrolled from other age groups, but maintains the base of the relevant age group and can therefore exceed 100%) . Initialized with UNESCO data.
Education: Primary Education Completion	EDPRICR	The percentage of the relevant age group that completes primary education. Initialized from UNESCO data. Primary education for many countries is the first 5 grades.
Education: Net Secondary Education Enrollment	EDSECENR	The percent of the relevant age group enrolled in secondary education. Initialized with UNESCO data. Secondary education for most countries is approximately grades 6–10. (See net primary enrollment for distinction between gross and net.)
Energy Demand Ratio to GDP	ENRGDP	Sometimes called energy intensity, the units of energy consumed per unit of GDP generally decrease as countries get richer. Initialized mostly using data from British Petroleum. A technology parameter heavily influences forecasts.
Freedom House Index (Inverted)	FREEDOM	Freedom or democracy levels. This variable is initialized from the well-known indicator from the Freedom House Freedom in the World series. Freedom House defines freedom as "the opportunity to act spontaneously in a variety of fields outside the control of government and other centers of potential domination." See www.freedomhouse.org. Coding of countries on separate civil and political liberty scales are done by experts. Inverted from Freedom House so that higher means more free (2–14).
Gini Index	GINI	The Gini index, originally from Corrado Gini, is computed from the Lorenz curve of income or other distribution and varies from 0 to 1 (highest means most unequal); sometimes values are multiplied by 100 and expressed as a percentage. See Figure 3.1 and discussion. Initialized from compiled World Bank sources and IFs data preprocessor to fill holes. Computed in IFs only across two categories of country subpopulation, so that forecasts of this variable are highly problematic.
Globalization Index	GLOBALIZ	Based on A.T. Kearney/Foreign Policy globalization index, built on four subindexes for economic integration, personal contact, technological connectivity, and political engagement. See Hughes 2005, Part II for specification in IFs.
GDP per Capita	GDPPC	GDP per person (of any age) in a population. Computed in IFs economic model.
GDP per Capita at PPP	GDPPCP	See GDPP and GDPPC. See GDPP for explanation of PPP.
Government Corruption Perception	GOVCORRUPT	Based on and initialized from Transparency International's Corruption Perceptions Index. CPI is a composite index that draws on multiple polls and surveys. See www.transparency.org.
Government Effectiveness	GOVEFFECT	Initialized from the World Bank's (Daniel Kaufman, Aart Kraay and others) Governance Matters index, defined as "the quality of public services, the quality of the civil service and the degree of its independence from political pressures, the quality of policy formulation and implementation, and the credibility of the government's commitment to such policies." Rescaled from the original to run from 0–5 (most effective).
Gross Domestic Product	GDP	Gross domestic product is defined as either the sum of value added across all sectors of an economy or as the sum of goods and services delivered to meet final demand of an economy. Initialized from WDI data using 2000$; forecasts use much other data including GTAP series.

Variable	IFs Name	Source and Comments
Gross Domestic Product at PPP	GDPP	See GDP and Box 2.2 on purchasing power parity. In an OECD definition, "Purchasing Power Parities (PPPs) are currency conversion rates that both convert to a common currency and equalize the purchasing power of different currencies. In other words, they eliminate the differences in price levels between countries in the process of conversion." Initialized from WDI data using 2000$ at purchasing power parity; forecasts use much other data including GTAP series.
HIV Infection Rate	Not directly available in model; calculated as infection numbers over population	The percentage of adults (15–49) living with HIV infection at end of the year. Computed from HIVCASES and POP in IFs population model. Initial conditions from UNAIDS and recent downward revisions by that source are not fully reflected.
Human Development Index	HDI	This corresponds very closely to the UNDP's HDI (see http://hdr.undp.org), which is an average of three components: long and healthy life, knowledge (literacy and education), and standard of living (GDP per capita). Computed in IFs population model from nearly identical drivers within IFs (see Hughes 2004c for specifics).
Human Development Index: HDI with Higher Ceilings	HDI21STFIX	An IFs-specific measure. Computed in IFs population model from driver categories within IFs corresponding to the UNDP's HDI, but with maximum values raised to levels that constitute better upper limits for the twenty-first century, notably life expectancy of 120 and GDP per capita of $100,000. It would be good to substitute secondary education completion for literacy rate (see Hughes 2004c).
Infant Mortality	INFMOR	The death rate of infants in the first year of life per 1,000 births. Initialized from WDI.
Infrastructure: Electricity Use	INFRAELEC	Defined as kilowatt hours per capita. Initialized from WDI. Formulations for this and other infrastructure variables in IFs are very simple at this stage.
Infrastructure: Internet Use	Not directly available in model; calculated	The percentage of the population with Internet access. Calculated from the number of networked people (NUMNWP) divided by the population size.
Infrastructure: Road Density	INFRAROAD	Defined as meters of road per hectare. Initialized from WDI. Formulations for this and other infrastructure variables in IFs are very simple at this stage.
Infrastructure: Telephone Density	INFRATELE	Defined as telephone lines per 1,000 people. Initialized from WDI and indirectly from ITU. Formulations for this and other infrastructure variables in IFs are very simple at this stage.
Knowledge Society Index	KNOWSOC	Based on A.T. Kearney/Foreign Policy knowledge subindex. See Hughes 2005, Part II for specification tied to research and development spending and tertiary graduation rate.
Land Area	LANDAREA	Total national land area in 10,000 square kilometers, which equal 1 million hectares. Constant over time.
Life Expectancy at Birth	LIFEXP	The average number of years a newborn is expected to live.
Literacy	LIT	The basic definition is the ability of adults to read and write, but different countries use very different standards. Initialized from WDI data.

Variable	IFs Name	Source and Comments
Malnourished Children	MALNCHP	As defined by the World Bank, "The percentage of children under five whose weight for age is more than two standard deviations below the median reference standard for their age as established by the World Health Organization" and other bodies. Individual countries may look at children at ages 3, 4, or 5. Initialized from WDI data using weight-based malnutrition measure.
Malnourished Population	MALNPOPP	As defined by the World Bank, "Population below minimum level of dietary energy consumption (also referred to as prevalence of undernourishment)" on a continuous basis. Initialized from WDI data.
Polity Democracy Index	DEMOCPOLITY	Democracy level, with attention to autocracy level. Based on and initialized from Polity project data (see http://www.cidcm.umd.edu/polity). Historical values are coded by experts. Computed in IFs as the Polity measure of democracy (1–10 with highest meaning most democratic) minus Polity autocracy (1–10 with highest meaning most authoritarian) plus 10. This combined index measure is fairly widely used. See also FREEDOM.
Pop per Area	No variable name in model; calculated from others	Population per land area
Population	POP	Total number of people within a country. Total initialized from WDI data, with cohort data on age-sex distribution, fertility, and mortality from UN Population Division.
Population Growth Rate	POPR	Annual percentage change. See population.
Population Above 65 Years	POPGT65	The total number of people in this age category, which is generally considered a period of nonparticipation in the labor force.
Population Below 15 Years	POPLE15	The total number of people in this age category, which is generally considered a period of economic dependence on others.
Poverty (below $1 cross-section)	INCOMELT1CS	Population living below $1.08 per day at 1993 international prices (purchasing power parity). Initialized from the World Bank's PovCalNet. See Chapter 4 for details of forecasting formulation, which is based on a cross-sectional (CS) analysis of the relationship of GDP per capita and poverty rates, also responsive to the Gini index of distribution. See Poverty below $1 lognormal for a note on our inability to translate 1993 dollars to more contemporary values.
Poverty (below $1 lognormal)	INCOMELT1LN	Population living below $1.08 per day at 1993 international prices (purchasing power parity). Initialized from the World Bank's PovCalNet. See Chapter 4 for details of forecasting formulation, which is based on an assumption that income in a country is subject to lognormal (LN) distribution, also responsive to the Gini index of distribution. See Chapter 2 for a discussion of the problems with converting values from 1993 dollars to contemporary currency levels; although changes in the global consumer price index suggest that $1.08 in 1993 dollars would be $1.98 in 2000 dollars and $2.82 in 2005 dollars, the problems with converting different countries with different market baskets and inflation patterns preclude such simple translation.
Poverty (below $2 cross-section)	INCOMELT2CS	Population living below $2.15 per day at 1993 international prices (purchasing power parity). See poverty at $1 for information.

Variable	IFs Name	Source and Comments
Poverty (below $2 lognormal)	INCOMELT2LN	Population living below $2.15 per day at 1993 international prices (purchasing power parity). Initialized from the World Bank's PovCalNet. See poverty at $1 for information.
Poverty (below $5 lognormal)	No variable name in model; calculated from others	Population living below $5.40 per day at 1993 international prices (purchasing power parity). See poverty at $1 for interpretation. The forecasts of values at income poverty levels above $2 per day do not use survey data for initial conditions, but rather use the lognormal formulation and survey data for $2 per day to estimate initial conditions.
Poverty (below $10 lognormal)	No variable name in model; calculated from others	Population living below $10.80 per day at 1993 international prices (purchasing power parity). See poverty at $1 for general interpretation and poverty below $5 for a note on initialization.
Poverty (below $20 lognormal)	No variable name in model; calculated from others	Population living below $21.60 per day at 1993 international prices (purchasing power parity). See poverty at $1 for general interpretation and poverty below $5 for a note on initialization.
Research and Development Expenditures	RANDDEXP	The OECD defines research and development to cover basic research, applied research, and experimental development; expenditures can be private or public. Initialized from OECD and WDI data.
Total Fertility Rate	TFR	The average number of children a woman is expected to bear throughout her life. Initialized from WDI data; forecasts initialized with cohort data on fertility from UN Population Division.
Water Use per Capita	WATUSEPC	Annual water withdrawals (all uses) divided by population. Initialized with data from FAO via WRI EarthTrends. Formulation in IFs is very basic and does not include feedback from water supply constraints.
Youth Bulge	YTHBULGE	Although the youth bulge is always an indicator of the portion of a population that is young, specific definitions vary. In IFs the definition is population 15–29 as a percentage of all adults (15 and up). A bulge exists when this ratio is above a specified level, such as 50 percent.

Data Source Organization Abbreviations

FAO: Food and Agriculture Organization of the United Nations

ITU: International Telecommunications Union

OECD: Organization for Economic Cooperation and Development

UNAIDS: The United Nations Program on AIDS

UNDP: UN Development Program

UNESCO: UN Educational, Scientific, and Cultural Organization

WDI: World Development Indicators of the World Bank

WRI: World Resource Institute

Forecast Tables

Measures of Poverty, Health, Education, Infrastructure and Governance

Multination Regional Analysis

Measures of Poverty, Health, Education, Infrastructure and Governance

Population, Land Area and Human Development Index

Base Case
Source: International Futures
Version 5.47 March 2008

	Population (Million People)					Land Area		Population Density					
						Sq Km (000s)	Sq Mi (000s)	Persons per Sq Km			Persons per Sq Mi		
	2005	2030	2055	% Chg	% An Chg			2005	2030	2055	2005	2030	2055
World	6434	8228	9451	46.9%	0.8%	13358	51576.6	48	62	71	125	160	183
Africa	905.3	1522	2190	141.9%	1.8%	3004.3	11599.9	30	51	73	78	131	189
Americas	888	1104	1213	36.6%	0.6%	4007	15471.4	22	28	30	57	71	78
Asia incl Oceania	3914	4904	5425	38.6%	0.7%	4044	15614.3	97	121	134	251	314	347
Europe	726.4	697.8	622.1	-14.4%	-0.3%	2302.7	8891.0	32	30	27	82	78	70
World	6434	8228	9451	46.9%	0.8%	13358	51576.6	48	62	71	125	160	183
Africa-Eastern	285	511.4	747.3	162.2%	1.9%	635.8	2454.9	45	80	118	116	208	304
Africa-Middle	111.4	214.8	362.6	225.5%	2.4%	661.3	2553.3	17	32	55	44	84	142
Africa-Northern	189.4	265.4	313.3	65.4%	1.0%	825.9	3188.9	23	32	38	59	83	98
Africa-Southern	53.87	63.38	67.82	25.9%	0.5%	267.5	1032.8	20	24	25	52	61	66
Africa-Western	265.6	467.3	698.8	163.1%	2.0%	613.8	2369.9	43	76	114	112	197	295
Africa	905.3	1522	2190	141.9%	1.8%	3004.3	11599.9	30	51	73	78	131	189
America-Caribbean	37.96	45.86	50.12	32.0%	0.6%	22.81	88.1	166	201	220	431	521	569
America-Central	40.19	62.69	79.89	98.8%	1.4%	52.16	201.4	77	120	153	200	311	397
America-North	434.1	517.7	557	28.3%	0.5%	2156	8324.6	20	24	26	52	62	67
America-South	375.8	477.4	526.4	40.1%	0.7%	1776	6857.3	21	27	30	55	70	77
Americas	888	1104	1213	36.6%	0.6%	4007	15471.4	22	28	30	57	71	78
Asia-East	1541	1727	1739	12.8%	0.2%	1180	4556.1	131	146	147	338	379	382
Asia-South Central	1581	2141	2516	59.1%	0.9%	1079	4166.1	147	198	233	379	514	604
Asia-South East	550.4	689.4	746.6	35.6%	0.6%	449.5	1735.6	122	153	166	317	397	430
Asia-West	209.4	305.2	375.8	79.5%	1.2%	481.5	1859.1	43	63	78	113	164	202
Oceania	32.1	41.17	47.25	47.2%	0.8%	854.3	3298.5	4	5	6	10	12	14
Asia incl Oceania	3914	4904	5425	38.6%	0.7%	4044.3	15615.5	97	121	134	251	314	347
Europe-East	300.3	274	235.5	-21.6%	-0.5%	1885.7	7280.9	16	15	12	41	38	32
Europe-North	96.61	100.2	96.27	-0.4%	-0.0%	174.6	674.1	55	57	55	143	149	143
Europe-South	143.8	137.5	119.1	-17.2%	-0.4%	131.6	508.1	109	104	91	283	271	234
Europe-West	185.7	186.1	171.2	-7.8%	-0.2%	110.8	427.8	168	168	155	434	435	400
Europe	726.4	697.8	622.1	-14.4%	-0.3%	2302.7	8890.9	32	30	27	82	78	70

Population, Land Area and Human Development Index

Base Case: Countries in Year 2055 Descending Population Sequence	Population (Million People)					Land Area		Population Density					
						Sq Km (000s)	Sq Mi (000s)	Persons per Sq Km			Persons per Sq Mi		
	2005	2030	2055	% Chg	% An Chg			2005	2030	2055	2005	2030	2055
AFRICA													
Ethiopia	72.28	127.7	188.9	161.3%	1.9%	110.4	426.3	65	116	171	170	300	443
Tanzania	39.53	69.92	100.3	153.7%	1.9%	94.51	364.9	42	74	106	108	192	275
Uganda	28.88	61.6	92.96	221.9%	2.4%	24.1	93.1	120	256	386	310	662	999
Kenya	34.86	60.41	80.41	130.7%	1.7%	58.04	224.1	60	104	139	156	270	359
Madagascar	18.51	33.61	51.29	177.1%	2.1%	58.7	226.6	32	57	87	82	148	226
Mozambique	20.19	33.2	44.94	122.6%	1.6%	80.16	309.5	25	41	56	65	107	145
Malawi	13.26	24.53	38.1	187.3%	2.1%	11.85	45.8	112	207	322	290	536	833
Zambia	12.11	22.22	34.53	185.1%	2.1%	75.26	290.6	16	30	46	42	76	119
Zimbabwe	13.76	20.55	26.27	90.9%	1.3%	39.08	150.9	35	53	67	91	136	174
Burundi	7.434	14.61	24.09	224.1%	2.4%	2.783	10.7	267	525	866	692	1360	2242
Rwanda	9.12	16.55	23.89	162.0%	1.9%	2.634	10.2	346	628	907	897	1627	2349
Somalia	8.088	14.73	23.41	189.4%	2.1%	63.77	246.4	13	23	37	33	60	95
Eritrea	4.364	8.386	13.99	220.6%	2.4%	11.76	45.4	37	71	119	96	185	308
Mauritius	1.245	1.447	1.474	18.4%	0.3%	0.204	0.8	610	709	723	1581	1837	1871
Comoros	0.603	1.016	1.429	137.0%	1.7%	0.223	0.9	270	456	641	700	1180	1660
Djibouti	0.775	1.004	1.309	68.9%	1.1%	2.32	9.0	33	43	56	87	112	146
Africa-Eastern	**285.0**	**511.4**	**747.3**	**162.2%**	**1.9%**	**635.8**	**2454.9**	**45**	**80**	**118**	**116**	**208**	**304**
Congo, Dem. Rep. of the	59.16	125.1	225.7	281.5%	2.7%	234.5	905.4	25	53	96	65	138	249
Angola	15.89	29.13	45.94	189.1%	2.1%	124.7	481.5	13	23	37	33	61	95
Cameroon	16.59	25.11	37.47	125.9%	1.6%	47.54	183.6	35	53	79	90	137	204
Chad	9.516	18.19	28.69	201.5%	2.2%	128.4	495.8	7	14	22	19	37	58
Central African Republic	4.2	6.955	10.44	148.6%	1.8%	62.3	240.5	7	11	17	17	29	43
Congo, Rep. of	3.903	6.989	10.25	162.6%	1.9%	34.2	132.0	11	20	30	30	53	78
Gabon	1.427	2.212	2.67	87.1%	1.3%	26.77	103.4	5	8	10	14	21	26
Equatorial Guinea	0.511	0.839	1.044	104.3%	1.4%	2.805	10.8	18	30	37	47	77	96
São Tomé and Príncipe	0.156	0.248	0.323	107.1%	1.5%	0.096	0.4	163	258	336	421	669	871
Africa-Middle	**111.4**	**214.8**	**362.6**	**225.5%**	**2.4%**	**661.3**	**2553.3**	**17**	**32**	**55**	**44**	**84**	**142**
Egypt	74.13	106.4	127.3	71.7%	1.1%	100.1	386.5	74	106	127	192	275	329
Sudan	36.72	56.5	73.08	99.0%	1.4%	250.6	967.6	15	23	29	38	58	76
Algeria	32.76	43.07	47.41	44.7%	0.7%	238.2	919.7	14	18	20	36	47	52
Morocco	29.86	38.84	42.36	41.9%	0.7%	44.65	172.4	67	87	95	173	225	246
Tunisia	10.09	12.44	13.53	34.1%	0.6%	16.36	63.2	62	76	83	160	197	214
Libya	5.837	8.181	9.631	65.0%	1.0%	176	679.6	3	5	5	9	12	14
Africa-Northern	**189.4**	**265.4**	**313.3**	**65.4%**	**1.0%**	**825.9**	**3188.9**	**23**	**32**	**38**	**59**	**83**	**98**

Multination Regional Analysis

Measures of Poverty, Health, Education, Infrastructure and Governance

Population, Land Area and Human Development Index

Base Case: Countries in Year 2055 Descending Population Sequence	Population — Million People					Land Area		Population Density — Persons per Sq Km			Population Density — Persons per Sq Mi		
	2005	2030	2055	% Chg	% An Chg	Sq Km (000s)	Sq Mi (000s)	2005	2030	2055	2005	2030	2055
AFRICA continued													
South Africa	46.81	53.56	56.1	19.8%	0.4%	122.1	471.4	38	44	46	99	114	119
Namibia	2.087	3.09	3.802	82.2%	1.2%	82.43	318.3	3	4	5	7	10	12
Lesotho	1.914	2.555	3.093	61.6%	1.0%	3.035	11.7	63	84	102	163	218	264
Botswana	1.893	2.336	2.582	36.4%	0.6%	58.17	224.6	3	4	4	8	10	11
Swaziland	1.164	1.833	2.236	92.1%	1.3%	1.736	6.7	67	106	129	174	273	334
Africa-Southern	**53.87**	**63.38**	**67.82**	**25.9%**	**0.5%**	**267.5**	**1032.8**	**20**	**24**	**25**	**52**	**61**	**66**
Nigeria	133.6	229.5	336.1	151.6%	1.9%	92.38	356.7	145	248	364	375	643	942
Niger	14.02	30.25	54.47	288.5%	2.8%	126.7	489.2	11	24	43	29	62	111
Ghana	22.1	35.38	48.42	119.1%	1.6%	23.85	92.1	93	148	203	240	384	526
Côte d'Ivoire	18.98	33.26	47.33	149.4%	1.8%	32.25	124.5	59	103	147	152	267	380
Mali	13.48	26.03	41.2	205.6%	2.3%	124	478.8	11	21	33	28	54	86
Burkina Faso	13	25.32	40.51	211.6%	2.3%	27.4	105.8	47	92	148	123	239	383
Senegal	11.67	19.97	27.82	138.4%	1.8%	19.67	75.9	59	102	141	154	263	366
Guinea	9.159	15.94	23.63	158.0%	1.9%	24.59	94.9	37	65	96	96	168	249
Benin	8.234	14.83	22.43	172.4%	2.0%	11.26	43.5	73	132	199	189	341	516
Togo	6.125	11.17	17.21	181.0%	2.1%	5.679	21.9	108	197	303	279	509	785
Liberia	3.58	6.808	11.1	210.1%	2.3%	11.14	43.0	32	61	100	83	158	258
Sierra Leone	5.089	7.095	10.6	108.3%	1.5%	7.174	27.7	71	99	148	184	256	383
Mauritania	3.019	5.31	7.817	158.9%	1.9%	102.6	396.1	3	5	8	8	13	20
Guinea-Bissau	1.59	3.184	5.575	250.6%	2.5%	3.612	13.9	44	88	154	114	228	400
Gambia	1.499	2.51	3.541	136.2%	1.7%	1.13	4.4	133	222	313	344	575	812
Cape Verde	0.506	0.796	0.978	93.3%	1.3%	0.403	1.6	126	198	243	325	512	629
Africa-Western	**265.6**	**467.3**	**698.8**	**163.1%**	**2.0%**	**613.8**	**2369.9**	**43**	**76**	**114**	**112**	**197**	**295**

Multination Regional Analysis

Measures of Poverty, Health, Education, Infrastructure and Governance

Population, Land Area and Human Development Index

Base Case: Countries in Year 2055 Descending Population Sequence	Population (Million People)					Land Area		Population Density					
						Sq Km (000s)	Sq Mi (000s)	Persons per Sq Km			Persons per Sq Mi		
	2005	2030	2055	% Chg	% An Chg			2005	2030	2055	2005	2030	2055
AMERICAS													
Haiti	8.652	12.78	16.84	94.6%	1.3%	2.775	10.7	312	461	607	807	1193	1572
Dominican Republic	8.953	11.29	12.27	37.0%	0.6%	4.873	18.8	184	232	252	476	600	652
Cuba	11.37	11.38	10.21	-10.2%	-0.2%	11.09	42.8	103	103	92	266	266	238
Puerto Rico	3.971	4.579	4.848	22.1%	0.4%	0.895	3.5	444	512	542	1149	1325	1403
Jamaica	2.713	3.231	3.406	25.5%	0.5%	1.099	4.2	247	294	310	639	761	803
Trinidad and Tobago	1.316	1.439	1.354	2.9%	0.1%	0.513	2.0	257	281	264	664	726	684
Bahamas	0.32	0.379	0.399	24.7%	0.4%	1.388	5.4	23	27	29	60	71	74
Barbados	0.274	0.294	0.281	2.6%	0.1%	0.043	0.2	637	684	653	1650	1771	1692
Grenada	0.112	0.158	0.185	65.2%	1.0%	0.034	0.1	329	465	544	853	1204	1409
St. Vincent & the Grenadines	0.124	0.159	0.177	42.7%	0.7%	0.039	0.2	318	408	454	823	1056	1175
St. Lucia	0.159	0.169	0.159	0.0%	0.0%	0.062	0.2	256	273	256	664	706	664
America-Caribbean	**37.96**	**45.86**	**50.12**	**32.0%**	**0.6%**	**22.81**	**88.1**	**166**	**201**	**220**	**431**	**521**	**569**
Guatemala	12.78	22.57	30.94	142.1%	1.8%	10.89	42.0	117	207	284	304	537	736
Honduras	7.214	11.51	14.87	106.1%	1.5%	11.21	43.3	64	103	133	167	266	344
Nicaragua	5.539	9.119	11.9	114.8%	1.5%	13	50.2	43	70	92	110	182	237
El Salvador	6.889	9.442	10.83	57.2%	0.9%	2.104	8.1	327	449	515	848	1162	1333
Costa Rica	4.285	5.559	6.259	46.1%	0.8%	5.11	19.7	84	109	122	217	282	317
Panama	3.199	4.099	4.616	44.3%	0.7%	7.552	29.2	42	54	61	110	141	158
Belize	0.277	0.395	0.47	69.7%	1.1%	2.296	8.9	12	17	20	31	45	53
America-Central	**40.19**	**62.69**	**79.89**	**98.8%**	**1.4%**	**52.16**	**201.4**	**77**	**120**	**153**	**200**	**311**	**397**
United States	296.8	349.9	381	28.4%	0.5%	962.9	3717.9	31	36	40	80	94	102
Mexico	105.2	130.5	136.9	30.1%	0.5%	195.8	756.0	54	67	70	139	173	181
Canada	32.09	37.27	39.17	22.1%	0.4%	997.1	3849.9	3	4	4	8	10	10
America-North	**434.1**	**517.7**	**557**	**28.3%**	**0.5%**	**2156**	**8324.6**	**20**	**24**	**26**	**52**	**62**	**67**
Brazil	186.5	230	247.8	32.9%	0.6%	854.7	3300.1	22	27	29	57	70	75
Colombia	45.78	60.53	68.11	48.8%	0.8%	113.9	439.8	40	53	60	104	138	155
Argentina	39.07	47.31	51.49	31.8%	0.6%	278	1073.4	14	17	19	36	44	48
Peru	28.26	37.79	42.72	51.2%	0.8%	128.5	496.2	22	29	33	57	76	86
Venezuela	26.57	35.46	40.95	54.1%	0.9%	91.21	352.2	29	39	45	75	101	116
Chile	16.25	19.59	20.9	28.6%	0.5%	75.66	292.1	21	26	28	56	67	72
Ecuador	13.46	18.48	20.72	53.9%	0.9%	28.36	109.5	47	65	73	123	169	189
Bolivia	9.175	13.48	16.23	76.9%	1.1%	109.9	424.3	8	12	15	22	32	38
Paraguay	6.024	9.767	12.52	107.8%	1.5%	40.67	157.0	15	24	31	38	62	80
Uruguay	3.455	3.799	3.949	14.3%	0.3%	17.62	68.0	20	22	22	51	56	58
Guyana	0.756	0.7	0.624	-17.5%	-0.4%	21.5	83.0	4	3	3	9	8	8
Suriname	0.451	0.482	0.45	-0.2%	-0.0%	16.33	63.1	3	3	3	7	8	7
America-South	**375.8**	**477.4**	**526.4**	**40.1%**	**0.7%**	**1776**	**6857.3**	**21**	**27**	**30**	**55**	**70**	**77**

Multination Regional Analysis

Measures of Poverty, Health, Education, Infrastructure and Governance

Population, Land Area and Human Development Index

Base Case: Countries in Year 2055 / Descending Population Sequence	Population (Million People) 2005	2030	2055	% Chg	% An Chg	Land Area Sq Km (000s)	Sq Mi (000s)	Population Density Persons per Sq Km 2005	2030	2055	Persons per Sq Mi 2005	2030	2055
ASIA INCL OCEANIA													
China	1308	1492	1529	16.9%	0.3%	959.8	3705.9	136	155	159	353	403	413
Japan	128.4	120.2	99.72	-22.3%	-0.5%	37.78	145.9	340	318	264	880	824	684
Korea, Rep. of	48.7	52.87	47.99	-1.5%	-0.0%	9.926	38.3	491	533	483	1271	1380	1252
Taiwan	23.36	26.5	25.63	9.7%	0.2%	3.598	13.9	649	737	712	1682	1908	1845
Korea, Dem. Rep. of	22.53	24.28	24.19	7.4%	0.1%	12.05	46.5	187	201	201	484	522	520
Hong Kong	7.067	8.422	8.782	24.3%	0.4%	0.107	0.4	6605	7871	8207	17106	20385	21257
Mongolia	2.575	3.41	3.718	44.4%	0.7%	156.6	604.6	2	2	2	4	6	6
Asia-East	**1541**	**1727**	**1739**	**12.8%**	**0.2%**	**1180**	**4556.1**	**131**	**146**	**147**	**338**	**379**	**382**
India	1089	1410	1586	45.6%	0.8%	328.7	1269.1	331	429	483	858	1111	1250
Pakistan	153.4	252.7	347.1	126.3%	1.6%	79.61	307.4	193	317	436	499	822	1129
Bangladesh	140.6	198.5	231.9	64.9%	1.0%	14.4	55.6	976	1378	1610	2529	3570	4171
Iran, Islamic Rep. of	67.34	88.99	101.8	51.2%	0.8%	164.8	636.3	41	54	62	106	140	160
Afghanistan	24.92	50.45	88.45	254.9%	2.6%	65.21	251.8	38	77	136	99	200	351
Nepal	27.01	42.24	57.33	112.3%	1.5%	14.72	56.8	183	287	389	475	743	1009
Uzbekistan	26.55	35.95	39.84	50.1%	0.8%	44.74	172.7	59	80	89	154	208	231
Sri Lanka	20.19	22.52	21.99	8.9%	0.2%	6.561	25.3	308	343	335	797	889	868
Kazakhstan	14.75	15.3	14.11	-4.3%	-0.1%	272.5	1052.2	5	6	5	14	15	13
Tajikistan	6.592	9.723	11.34	72.0%	1.1%	14.31	55.3	46	68	79	119	176	205
Turkmenistan	4.833	6.474	7.369	52.5%	0.8%	48.81	188.5	10	13	15	26	34	39
Kyrgyzstan	5.22	6.665	7.106	36.1%	0.6%	19.99	77.2	26	33	36	68	86	92
Bhutan	0.67	1.047	1.328	98.2%	1.4%	4.7	18.1	14	22	28	37	58	73
Maldives	0.328	0.533	0.676	106.1%	1.5%	0.03	0.1	1093	1777	2253	2832	4601	5836
Asia-South Central	**1581.4**	**2141.1**	**2516.3**	**59.1%**	**0.9%**	**1079**	**4166.1**	**147**	**198**	**233**	**380**	**514**	**604**
Indonesia	219.1	261.6	271.1	23.7%	0.4%	190.5	735.5	115	137	142	298	356	369
Philippines	83.69	121.8	142.8	70.6%	1.1%	30	115.8	279	406	476	723	1052	1233
Vietnam	82.25	99.85	107.2	30.3%	0.5%	33.17	128.1	248	301	323	642	780	837
Thailand	64.14	73.58	76.29	18.9%	0.3%	51.31	198.1	125	143	149	324	371	385
Myanmar	50.44	61.31	65.42	29.7%	0.5%	67.66	261.2	75	91	97	193	235	250
Malaysia	25.19	33.7	38.67	53.5%	0.9%	32.97	127.3	76	102	117	198	265	304
Cambodia	13.98	20.62	24.77	77.2%	1.2%	18.1	69.9	77	114	137	200	295	354
Laos	5.901	9.303	11.58	96.2%	1.4%	23.68	91.4	25	39	49	65	102	127
Singapore	4.373	5.343	5.513	26.1%	0.5%	0.062	0.2	7053	8618	8892	18267	22319	23030
Timor-Leste	0.966	1.813	2.721	181.7%	2.1%	1.487	5.7	65	122	183	168	316	474
Brunei	0.373	0.522	0.61	63.5%	1.0%	0.577	2.2	65	90	106	167	234	274
Asia-South East	**550.4**	**689.4**	**746.6**	**35.6%**	**0.6%**	**449.5**	**1735.6**	**122**	**153**	**166**	**317**	**397**	**430**

Multination Regional Analysis

Measures of Poverty, Health, Education, Infrastructure and Governance

Population, Land Area and Human Development Index

Base Case: Countries in Year 2055 Descending Population Sequence	Population Million People					Land Area		Population Density Persons per Sq Km			Persons per Sq Mi		
	2005	2030	2055	% Chg	% An Chg	Sq Km (000s)	Sq Mi (000s)	2005	2030	2055	2005	2030	2055
ASIA INCL OCEANIA continued													
Turkey	72.65	91.82	102.1	40.5%	0.7%	77.48	299.2	94	119	132	243	307	341
Yemen	20.87	40.91	62.66	200.2%	2.2%	52.8	203.9	40	77	119	102	201	307
Iraq	26.48	44.52	57.95	118.8%	1.6%	43.83	169.2	60	102	132	156	263	0
Saudi Arabia	23.52	36.25	45.12	91.8%	1.3%	215	830.1	11	17	21	28	44	54
Syria	19.06	30.66	38.36	101.3%	1.4%	18.52	71.5	103	166	207	267	429	536
Israel	6.993	9.357	11.02	57.6%	0.9%	2.106	8.1	332	444	523	860	1151	1355
Azerbaijan	8.485	10.05	10.24	20.7%	0.4%	8.66	33.4	98	116	118	254	301	306
Jordan	5.476	8.19	10.18	85.9%	1.2%	8.921	34.4	61	92	114	159	238	296
Palestine	3.469	6.596	9.307	168.3%	2.0%	0.038	0.1	9129	17358	24492	23643	44956	63433
Oman	2.757	4.304	5.268	91.1%	1.3%	30.95	119.5	9	14	17	23	36	44
Lebanon	3.648	4.472	4.97	36.2%	0.6%	1.04	4.0	351	430	478	908	1114	1238
United Arab Emirates	3.572	4.652	4.865	36.2%	0.6%	8.36	32.3	43	56	58	111	144	151
Kuwait	2.478	3.618	4.467	80.3%	1.2%	1.782	6.9	139	203	251	360	526	649
Georgia	4.606	3.854	3.299	-28.4%	-0.7%	6.97	26.9	66	55	47	171	143	123
Armenia	3.163	3.33	3.202	1.2%	0.0%	2.98	11.5	106	112	107	275	289	278
Bahrain	0.743	1.006	1.137	53.0%	0.9%	0.071	0.3	1046	1417	1601	2710	3670	4148
Qatar	0.658	0.823	0.857	30.2%	0.5%	1.1	4.2	60	75	78	155	194	202
Cyprus	0.718	0.793	0.761	6.0%	0.1%	0.925	3.6	78	86	82	201	222	213
Asia-West	**209.4**	**305.2**	**375.8**	**79.5%**	**1.2%**	**481.5**	**1859.1**	**43**	**63**	**78**	**113**	**164**	**202**
Australia	20.22	24.57	27.16	34.3%	0.6%	774.1	2988.9	3	3	4	7	8	9
Papua New Guinea	5.9	9.277	12.21	106.9%	1.5%	46.28	178.7	13	20	26	33	52	68
New Zealand	4.021	4.614	4.721	17.4%	0.3%	27.05	104.4	15	17	17	38	44	45
Solomon Islands	0.475	0.797	1.094	130.3%	1.7%	2.89	11.2	16	28	38	43	71	98
Fiji	0.856	0.964	0.91	6.3%	0.1%	1.827	7.1	47	53	50	121	137	129
Vanuatu	0.216	0.353	0.46	113.0%	1.5%	1.219	4.7	18	29	38	46	75	98
Micronesia	0.121	0.196	0.248	105.0%	1.4%	0.591	2.3	20	33	42	53	86	109
Samoa	0.184	0.223	0.222	20.7%	0.4%	0.284	1.1	65	79	78	168	203	202
Tonga	0.111	0.173	0.221	99.1%	1.4%	0.075	0.3	148	231	295	383	597	763
Oceania	**32.1**	**41.17**	**47.25**	**47.2%**	**0.8%**	**854.3**	**3298.5**	**4**	**5**	**6**	**10**	**12**	**14**

Multination Regional Analysis

Measures of Poverty, Health, Education, Infrastructure and Governance

Population, Land Area and Human Development Index

Base Case: Countries in Year 2055 Descending Population Sequence	Population (Million People)					Land Area		Population Density					
						Sq Km (000s)	Sq Mi (000s)	Persons per Sq Km			Persons per Sq Mi		
	2005	2030	2055	% Chg	% An Chg			2005	2030	2055	2005	2030	2055
EUROPE													
Russia	143.8	133.3	114.8	-20.2%	-0.4%	1708	6594.8	8	8	7	22	20	17
Poland	38.67	37.6	33.16	-14.2%	-0.3%	31.27	120.7	124	120	106	320	311	275
Ukraine	47.57	38.83	31.93	-32.9%	-0.8%	60.37	233.1	79	64	53	204	167	137
Romania	22.37	20.42	17.42	-22.1%	-0.5%	23.84	92.0	94	86	73	243	222	189
Belarus	9.914	9.399	8.775	-11.5%	-0.2%	20.76	80.2	48	45	42	124	117	109
Czech Republic	10.3	9.678	8.209	-20.3%	-0.5%	12.79	49.4	81	76	64	209	196	166
Hungary	10.11	9.19	7.793	-22.9%	-0.5%	9.303	35.9	109	99	84	281	256	217
Bulgaria	7.82	6.378	5.303	-32.2%	-0.8%	11.09	42.8	71	58	48	183	149	124
Slovak Republic	5.455	5.442	4.864	-10.8%	-0.2%	4.901	18.9	111	111	99	288	288	257
Moldova	4.254	3.814	3.213	-24.5%	-0.6%	3.385	13.1	126	113	95	325	292	246
Europe-East	**300.3**	**274**	**235.5**	**-21.6%**	**-0.5%**	**1885.7**	**7280.9**	**16**	**15**	**12**	**41**	**38**	**32**
United Kingdom	60.9	63.5	61.18	0.5%	0.0%	24.29	93.8	251	261	252	649	677	652
Sweden	8.951	8.956	8.212	-8.3%	-0.2%	45	173.7	20	20	18	52	52	47
Denmark	5.46	5.695	5.59	2.4%	0.0%	4.309	16.6	127	132	130	328	342	336
Norway	4.621	5.048	5.142	11.3%	0.2%	32.39	125.1	14	16	16	37	40	41
Ireland	3.986	4.716	5.068	27.1%	0.5%	7.027	27.1	57	67	72	147	174	187
Finland	5.251	5.331	4.937	-6.0%	-0.1%	33.81	130.5	16	16	15	40	41	38
Lithuania	3.497	3.379	3.057	-12.6%	-0.3%	6.52	25.2	54	52	47	139	134	121
Latvia	2.336	2.14	1.838	-21.3%	-0.5%	6.46	24.9	36	33	28	94	86	74
Estonia	1.319	1.102	0.921	-30.2%	-0.7%	4.51	17.4	29	24	20	76	63	53
Iceland	0.292	0.327	0.323	10.6%	0.2%	10.3	39.8	3	3	3	7	8	8
Europe-North	**96.61**	**100.2**	**96.27**	**-0.4%**	**-0.0%**	**174.6**	**674.1**	**55**	**57**	**55**	**143**	**149**	**143**
Italy	57.3	52.95	44.08	-23.1%	-0.5%	30.13	116.3	190	176	146	493	455	379
Spain	40.81	39.54	33.85	-17.1%	-0.4%	50.6	195.4	81	78	67	209	202	173
Greece	11.08	11.07	10.07	-9.1%	-0.2%	13.2	51.0	84	84	76	217	217	198
Portugal	10.36	10.25	9.566	-7.7%	-0.2%	9.198	35.5	113	111	104	292	289	269
Serbia and Montenegro	8.153	7.639	7.023	-13.9%	-0.3%	10.22	39.5	80	75	69	207	194	178
Croatia	4.481	4.13	3.653	-18.5%	-0.4%	5.654	21.8	79	73	65	205	189	167
Bosnia and Herzegovina	4.036	3.915	3.392	-16.0%	-0.3%	5.12	19.8	79	76	66	204	198	172
Albania	3.157	3.489	3.374	6.9%	0.1%	2.875	11.1	110	121	117	284	314	304
Macedonia	2.064	2.151	2.062	-0.1%	-0.0%	2.571	9.9	80	84	80	208	217	208
Slovenia	2.001	1.899	1.592	-20.4%	-0.5%	2.025	7.8	99	94	79	256	243	204
Malta	0.399	0.423	0.4	0.3%	0.0%	0.032	0.1	1247	1322	1250	3229	3424	3237
Europe-South	**143.8**	**137.5**	**119.1**	**-17.2%**	**-0.4%**	**131.6**	**508.1**	**109**	**104**	**91**	**283**	**271**	**234**
Germany	82.9	80.33	71.27	-14.0%	-0.3%	35.7	137.8	232	225	200	601	583	517
France	60.18	62.58	60.09	-0.1%	-0.0%	55.15	212.9	109	113	109	283	294	282
Netherlands	16.42	17.44	16.88	2.8%	0.1%	4.153	16.0	395	420	406	1024	1088	1053
Belgium	10.38	10.4	9.68	-6.7%	-0.1%	3.051	11.8	340	341	317	881	883	822
Austria	8.053	7.609	6.379	-20.8%	-0.5%	8.386	32.4	96	91	76	249	235	197
Switzerland	7.292	7.143	6.19	-15.1%	-0.3%	4.129	15.9	177	173	150	457	448	388
Luxembourg	0.468	0.597	0.736	57.3%	0.9%	0.259	1.0	181	231	284	468	597	736
Europe-West	**185.7**	**186.1**	**171.2**	**-7.8%**	**-0.2%**	**110.8**	**427.8**	**168**	**168**	**155**	**434**	**435**	**400**

Multination Regional Analysis

Measures of Poverty, Health, Education, Infrastructure and Governance

Population, Land Area and Human Development Index

Base Case
Source: International Futures
Version 5.47 March 2008

| | Human Development Index | | | | | HDI with Higher Ceilings | | | | |
| | Index | | | | | Index | | | | |
	2005	2030	2055	% Chg	% An Chg	2005	2030	2055	% Chg	% An Chg
World	0.72	0.816	0.881	22.4%	0.4%	0.605	0.681	0.738	22.0%	0.4%
Africa	0.5	0.643	0.74	48.0%	0.8%	0.431	0.544	0.623	44.5%	0.7%
Americas	0.856	0.924	0.969	13.2%	0.2%	0.72	0.775	0.822	14.2%	0.3%
Asia incl Oceania	0.708	0.825	0.905	27.8%	0.5%	0.593	0.685	0.754	27.2%	0.5%
Europe	0.89	0.958	0.992	11.5%	0.2%	0.75	0.802	0.844	12.5%	0.2%
World	0.72	0.816	0.881	22.4%	0.4%	0.605	0.681	0.738	22.0%	0.4%
Africa-Eastern	0.456	0.637	0.756	65.8%	1.0%	0.399	0.54	0.637	59.6%	0.9%
Africa-Middle	0.443	0.559	0.667	50.6%	0.8%	0.392	0.481	0.568	44.9%	0.7%
Africa-Northern	0.664	0.782	0.895	34.8%	0.6%	0.551	0.651	0.742	34.7%	0.6%
Africa-Southern	0.623	0.811	0.918	47.4%	0.8%	0.558	0.693	0.775	38.9%	0.7%
Africa-Western	0.429	0.587	0.675	57.3%	0.9%	0.371	0.497	0.568	53.1%	0.9%
Africa	0.5	0.643	0.74	48.0%	0.8%	0.431	0.544	0.623	44.5%	0.7%
America-Caribbean	0.712	0.797	0.864	21.3%	0.4%	0.6	0.669	0.725	20.8%	0.4%
America-Central	0.719	0.809	0.897	24.8%	0.4%	0.601	0.678	0.755	25.6%	0.5%
America-North	0.925	0.977	0.993	7.4%	0.1%	0.778	0.819	0.855	9.9%	0.2%
America-South	0.805	0.894	0.963	19.6%	0.4%	0.678	0.751	0.807	19.0%	0.3%
Americas	0.856	0.924	0.969	13.2%	0.2%	0.72	0.775	0.822	14.2%	0.3%
Asia-East	0.807	0.95	0.997	23.5%	0.4%	0.679	0.792	0.845	24.4%	0.4%
Asia-South Central	0.594	0.714	0.834	40.4%	0.7%	0.49	0.587	0.683	39.4%	0.7%
Asia-South East	0.738	0.842	0.917	24.3%	0.4%	0.626	0.709	0.767	22.5%	0.4%
Asia-West	0.743	0.848	0.929	25.0%	0.4%	0.622	0.709	0.779	25.2%	0.5%
Oceania	0.863	0.914	0.943	9.3%	0.2%	0.724	0.767	0.814	12.4%	0.2%
Asia incl Oceania	0.708	0.825	0.905	27.8%	0.5%	0.593	0.685	0.754	27.2%	0.5%
Europe-East	0.826	0.923	0.983	19.0%	0.3%	0.701	0.774	0.819	16.8%	0.3%
Europe-North	0.942	0.992	1	6.2%	0.1%	0.791	0.832	0.869	9.9%	0.2%
Europe-South	0.919	0.964	0.992	7.9%	0.2%	0.771	0.805	0.841	9.1%	0.2%
Europe-West	0.944	0.987	1	5.9%	0.1%	0.793	0.826	0.865	9.1%	0.2%
Europe	0.89	0.958	0.992	11.5%	0.2%	0.75	0.802	0.844	12.5%	0.2%

Poverty

| | Poverty (below $1 CS) | | | | |
| | Million People | | | | |
	2005	2030	2055	% Chg	% An Chg
World	1085	765	526.7	-51.5%	-1.4%
Africa	322.2	437.9	421.8	30.9%	0.5%
Americas	53.35	38.17	17.32	-67.5%	-2.2%
Asia incl Oceania	699.2	287.9	87.54	-87.5%	-4.1%
Europe	10.53	1.012	0.03	-99.7%	-11.1%
World	1085	765	526.7	-51.5%	-1.4%
Africa-Eastern	119	165.8	107.5	-9.7%	-0.2%
Africa-Middle	44.71	74.88	92.13	106.1%	1.5%
Africa-Northern	13.19	11.75	6.846	-48.1%	-1.3%
Africa-Southern	7.051	4.701	0.544	-92.3%	-5.0%
Africa-Western	138.3	180.8	214.7	55.2%	0.9%
Africa	322.2	437.9	421.8	30.9%	0.5%
America-Caribbean	7.682	7.763	7.071	-8.0%	-0.2%
America-Central	6.969	8.959	7.062	1.3%	0.0%
America-North	6.023	1.389	0.001	-100.0%	-16.0%
America-South	32.68	20.05	3.184	-90.3%	-4.6%
Americas	53.35	38.17	17.32	-67.5%	-2.2%
Asia-East	182.8	6.675	3.202	-98.2%	-7.8%
Asia-South Central	446.7	236.1	68.15	-84.7%	-3.7%
Asia-South East	54.66	34.18	12.68	-76.8%	-2.9%
Asia-West	13.18	9.042	1.981	-85.0%	-3.7%
Oceania	1.846	1.912	1.531	-17.1%	-0.4%
Asia incl Oceania	699.2	287.9	87.54	-87.5%	-4.1%
Europe-East	8.1	0.307	0.029	-99.6%	-10.7%
Europe-North	0	0	0		
Europe-South	2.43	0.705	0	-100.0%	
Europe-West	0	0	0		
Europe	10.53	1.012	0.03	-99.7%	-11.1%

Population, Land Area and Human Development Index

Poverty

Base Case: Countries in Year 2055 Descending Population Sequence	Human Development Index — Index					HDI with Higher Ceilings — Index					Poverty (below $1 CS) — Million People				
	2005	2030	2055	% Chg	% An Chg	2005	2030	2055	% Chg	% An Chg	2005	2030	2055	% Chg	% An Chg
AFRICA															
Ethiopia	0.365	0.496	0.623	70.7%	1.1%	0.309	0.407	0.514	66.3%	1.0%	15.12	20.88	13.35	-11.7%	-0.2%
Tanzania	0.511	0.731	0.864	69.1%	1.1%	0.459	0.623	0.727	58.4%	0.9%	21.2	24.05	2.835	-86.6%	-3.9%
Uganda	0.491	0.734	0.867	76.6%	1.1%	0.432	0.623	0.733	69.7%	1.1%	23.38	34.08	8.192	-65.0%	-2.1%
Kenya	0.554	0.75	0.868	56.7%	0.9%	0.488	0.638	0.732	50.0%	0.8%	4.223	5.158	1.129	-73.3%	-2.6%
Madagascar	0.543	0.659	0.756	39.2%	0.7%	0.465	0.568	0.645	38.7%	0.7%	11.81	19.03	23.16	96.1%	1.4%
Mozambique	0.383	0.67	0.834	117.8%	1.6%	0.334	0.568	0.708	112.0%	1.5%	7.537	8.09	4.594	-39.0%	-1.0%
Malawi	0.394	0.581	0.707	79.4%	1.2%	0.355	0.504	0.608	71.3%	1.1%	4.26	6.232	5.847	37.3%	0.6%
Zambia	0.45	0.612	0.728	61.8%	1.0%	0.41	0.525	0.62	51.2%	0.8%	8.37	12.68	11.38	36.0%	0.6%
Zimbabwe	0.553	0.748	0.841	52.1%	0.8%	0.503	0.642	0.713	41.7%	0.7%	7.363	9.414	5.994	-18.6%	-0.4%
Burundi	0.393	0.602	0.709	80.4%	1.2%	0.342	0.514	0.611	78.7%	1.2%	4.099	6.523	6.824	66.5%	1.0%
Rwanda	0.466	0.667	0.757	62.4%	1.0%	0.413	0.578	0.65	57.4%	0.9%	5.374	8.162	7.434	38.3%	0.7%
Somalia	0.39	0.48	0.59	51.3%	0.8%	0.335	0.409	0.506	51.0%	0.8%	4.129	7.451	10.65	157.9%	1.9%
Eritrea	0.423	0.445	0.51	20.6%	0.4%	0.356	0.376	0.425	19.4%	0.4%	1.699	3.447	5.531	225.5%	2.4%
Mauritius	0.813	0.915	0.981	20.7%	0.4%	0.681	0.764	0.817	20.0%	0.4%	0	0	0		
Comoros	0.545	0.592	0.697	27.9%	0.5%	0.45	0.489	0.576	28.0%	0.5%	0.185	0.296	0.322	74.1%	1.1%
Djibouti	0.421	0.479	0.612	45.4%	0.8%	0.37	0.41	0.506	36.8%	0.6%	0.224	0.28	0.288	28.6%	0.5%
Africa-Eastern	**0.456**	**0.637**	**0.756**	**65.8%**	**1.0%**	**0.399**	**0.54**	**0.637**	**59.6%**	**0.9%**	**119**	**165.8**	**107.5**	**-9.7%**	**-0.2%**
Congo, Dem. Rep. of the	0.425	0.541	0.655	54.1%	0.9%	0.377	0.466	0.558	48.0%	0.8%	27.98	51.27	60.18	115.1%	1.5%
Angola	0.462	0.592	0.691	49.6%	0.8%	0.413	0.512	0.589	42.6%	0.7%	4.801	6.436	9.478	97.4%	1.4%
Cameroon	0.479	0.583	0.723	50.9%	0.8%	0.433	0.516	0.62	43.2%	0.7%	3.823	5.64	7.889	106.4%	1.5%
Chad	0.388	0.55	0.612	57.7%	0.9%	0.33	0.459	0.513	55.5%	0.9%	3.81	5.165	6.888	80.8%	1.2%
Central African Republic	0.37	0.403	0.576	55.7%	0.9%	0.325	0.358	0.489	50.5%	0.8%	2.671	4.435	5.701	113.4%	1.5%
Congo, Rep. of	0.552	0.705	0.794	43.8%	0.7%	0.481	0.595	0.67	39.3%	0.7%	1.413	1.758	1.801	27.5%	0.5%
Gabon	0.696	0.826	0.873	25.4%	0.5%	0.601	0.704	0.739	23.0%	0.4%	0.118	0.103	0.085	-28.0%	-0.7%
Equatorial Guinea	0.641	0.787	0.83	29.5%	0.5%	0.567	0.681	0.71	25.2%	0.5%	0.051	0	0	-100.0%	
São Tomé and Príncipe	0.59	0.635	0.668	13.2%	0.2%	0.504	0.548	0.576	14.3%	0.3%	0.045	0.077	0.112	148.9%	1.8%
Africa-Middle	**0.443**	**0.559**	**0.667**	**50.6%**	**0.8%**	**0.392**	**0.481**	**0.568**	**44.9%**	**0.7%**	**44.71**	**74.88**	**92.13**	**106.1%**	**1.5%**
Egypt	0.697	0.807	0.942	35.2%	0.6%	0.58	0.673	0.779	34.3%	0.6%	1.534	0.702	0	-100.0%	
Sudan	0.536	0.723	0.844	57.5%	0.9%	0.454	0.612	0.712	56.8%	0.9%	11.22	10.94	6.827	-39.2%	-1.0%
Algeria	0.721	0.83	0.903	25.2%	0.5%	0.596	0.689	0.748	25.5%	0.5%	0	0	0		
Morocco	0.615	0.674	0.778	26.5%	0.5%	0.498	0.546	0.628	26.1%	0.5%	0.118	0.107	0.019	-83.9%	-3.6%
Tunisia	0.756	0.895	1	32.3%	0.6%	0.626	0.744	0.837	33.7%	0.6%	0.028	0	0	-100.0%	
Libya	0.823	0.94	1	21.5%	0.4%	0.691	0.785	0.829	20.0%	0.4%	0.288	0	0	-100.0%	
Africa-Northern	**0.664**	**0.782**	**0.895**	**34.8%**	**0.6%**	**0.551**	**0.651**	**0.742**	**34.7%**	**0.6%**	**13.19**	**11.75**	**6.846**	**-48.1%**	**-1.3%**

Multination Regional Analysis — Measures of Poverty, Health, Education, Infrastructure and Governance

Population, Land Area and Human Development Index

Poverty

Base Case: Countries in Year 2055 / Descending Population Sequence	Human Development Index (Index)					HDI with Higher Ceilings (Index)					Poverty (below $1 CS) — Million People				
	2005	2030	2055	% Chg	% An Chg	2005	2030	2055	% Chg	% An Chg	2005	2030	2055	% Chg	% An Chg
AFRICA continued															
South Africa	0.63	0.817	0.922	46.3%	0.8%	0.564	0.698	0.779	38.1%	0.6%	5.081	2.927	0	-100.0%	-100.0%
Namibia	0.618	0.788	0.943	52.6%	0.8%	0.547	0.669	0.793	45.0%	0.7%	0.485	0.434	0	-100.0%	-100.0%
Lesotho	0.532	0.696	0.805	51.3%	0.8%	0.482	0.603	0.686	42.3%	0.7%	0.573	0.706	0.544	-5.1%	-0.1%
Botswana	0.588	0.854	0.947	61.1%	1.0%	0.528	0.72	0.797	50.9%	0.8%	0.324	0.037	0	-100.0%	-100.0%
Swaziland	0.578	0.773	0.889	53.8%	0.9%	0.512	0.653	0.749	46.3%	0.8%	0.588	0.596	0	-100.0%	-100.0%
Africa-Southern	**0.623**	**0.811**	**0.918**	**47.4%**	**0.8%**	**0.558**	**0.693**	**0.775**	**38.9%**	**0.7%**	**7.051**	**4.701**	**0.544**	**-92.3%**	**-5.0%**
Nigeria	0.441	0.661	0.744	68.7%	1.1%	0.392	0.57	0.638	62.8%	1.0%	94.21	110.6	132.1	40.2%	0.7%
Niger	0.277	0.366	0.482	74.0%	1.1%	0.224	0.298	0.392	75.0%	1.1%	7.561	14.49	20.14	166.4%	2.0%
Ghana	0.586	0.642	0.71	21.2%	0.4%	0.499	0.545	0.601	20.4%	0.4%	7.519	12.09	14.53	93.2%	1.3%
Côte d'Ivoire	0.441	0.587	0.669	51.7%	0.8%	0.376	0.484	0.554	47.3%	0.8%	2.995	3.983	3.349	11.8%	0.2%
Mali	0.329	0.496	0.627	90.6%	1.3%	0.268	0.413	0.523	95.1%	1.3%	5.465	8.625	9.345	71.0%	1.1%
Burkina Faso	0.324	0.441	0.529	63.3%	1.0%	0.263	0.346	0.418	58.9%	0.9%	4.893	7.754	7.853	60.5%	1.0%
Senegal	0.463	0.564	0.678	46.4%	0.8%	0.378	0.463	0.556	47.1%	0.8%	2.011	2.684	2.035	1.2%	0.0%
Guinea	0.423	0.488	0.555	31.2%	0.5%	0.343	0.39	0.443	29.2%	0.5%	2.537	3.715	4.148	63.5%	1.0%
Benin	0.394	0.519	0.656	66.5%	1.0%	0.33	0.431	0.541	63.9%	1.0%	2.667	4.097	3.793	42.2%	0.7%
Togo	0.505	0.594	0.637	26.1%	0.5%	0.427	0.5	0.54	26.5%	0.5%	2.1	3.654	5.676	170.3%	2.0%
Liberia	0.386	0.41	0.605	56.7%	0.9%	0.343	0.377	0.52	51.6%	0.8%	1.451	2.584	3.679	153.5%	1.9%
Sierra Leone	0.252	0.36	0.568	125.4%	1.6%	0.229	0.322	0.473	106.6%	1.5%	3.006	3.353	3.83	27.4%	0.5%
Mauritania	0.462	0.547	0.636	37.7%	0.6%	0.384	0.459	0.533	38.8%	0.7%	0.768	1.248	1.515	97.3%	1.4%
Guinea-Bissau	0.434	0.521	0.588	35.5%	0.6%	0.38	0.455	0.511	34.5%	0.6%	0.668	1.349	2.226	233.2%	2.4%
Gambia	0.422	0.514	0.608	44.1%	0.7%	0.339	0.416	0.49	44.5%	0.7%	0.39	0.562	0.55	41.0%	0.7%
Cape Verde	0.716	0.823	0.938	31.0%	0.5%	0.596	0.685	0.775	30.0%	0.5%	0.012	0.007	0	-100.0%	-100.0%
Africa-Western	**0.429**	**0.587**	**0.675**	**57.3%**	**0.9%**	**0.371**	**0.497**	**0.568**	**53.1%**	**0.9%**	**138.3**	**180.8**	**214.7**	**55.2%**	**0.9%**

Population, Land Area and Human Development Index / Poverty

Base Case: Countries in Year 2055 / Descending Population Sequence	Human Development Index					HDI with Higher Ceilings					Poverty (below $1 CS) Million People				
	2005	2030	2055	% Chg	% An Chg	2005	2030	2055	% Chg	% An Chg	2005	2030	2055	% Chg	% An Chg
AMERICAS															
Haiti	0.439	0.545	0.64	45.8%	0.8%	0.376	0.457	0.536	42.6%	0.7%	4.635	6.647	7.071	52.6%	0.8%
Dominican Republic	0.764	0.894	0.957	25.3%	0.5%	0.647	0.753	0.799	23.5%	0.4%	0.089	0.033	0	-100.0%	-100.0%
Cuba	0.784	0.857	0.988	26.0%	0.5%	0.656	0.718	0.819	24.8%	0.4%	2.899	1.074	0	-100.0%	
Puerto Rico	0.875	0.992	1	14.3%	0.3%	0.733	0.825	0.884	20.6%	0.4%	0	0	0		
Jamaica	0.755	0.85	0.973	28.9%	0.5%	0.635	0.716	0.808	27.2%	0.5%	0.001	0.001	0	-100.0%	
Trinidad and Tobago	0.862	0.977	1	16.0%	0.3%	0.73	0.815	0.832	14.0%	0.3%	0	0	0		
Bahamas	0.85	0.919	0.977	14.9%	0.3%	0.722	0.775	0.818	13.3%	0.2%	0	0	0		
Barbados	0.894	0.962	1	11.9%	0.2%	0.754	0.803	0.853	13.1%	0.2%	0	0	0		
Grenada	0.806	0.886	0.991	23.0%	0.4%	0.677	0.744	0.823	21.6%	0.4%	0.007	0.002	0	-100.0%	
St. Vincent & the Grenadines	0.779	0.857	0.962	23.5%	0.4%	0.651	0.719	0.8	22.9%	0.4%	0.014	0.006	0	-100.0%	
St. Lucia	0.784	0.908	1	27.6%	0.5%	0.658	0.758	0.847	28.7%	0.5%	0.037	0	0	-100.0%	
America-Caribbean	**0.712**	**0.797**	**0.864**	**21.3%**	**0.4%**	**0.6**	**0.669**	**0.725**	**20.8%**	**0.4%**	**7.682**	**7.763**	**7.071**	**-8.0%**	**-0.2%**
Guatemala	0.68	0.799	0.9	32.4%	0.6%	0.569	0.672	0.754	32.5%	0.6%	1.38	1.92	1.365	-1.1%	-0.0%
Honduras	0.675	0.753	0.86	27.4%	0.5%	0.566	0.635	0.722	27.6%	0.5%	1.372	1.93	1.639	19.5%	0.4%
Nicaragua	0.662	0.714	0.796	20.2%	0.4%	0.547	0.594	0.663	21.2%	0.4%	2.589	3.925	3.699	42.9%	0.7%
El Salvador	0.736	0.839	0.945	28.4%	0.5%	0.616	0.704	0.788	27.9%	0.5%	1.316	1.184	0.359	-72.7%	-2.6%
Costa Rica	0.872	0.961	1	14.7%	0.3%	0.731	0.799	0.862	17.9%	0.3%	0.076	0	0	-100.0%	
Panama	0.823	0.954	1	21.5%	0.4%	0.689	0.794	0.864	25.4%	0.5%	0.21	0	0	-100.0%	
Belize	0.755	0.891	0.998	32.2%	0.6%	0.628	0.737	0.824	31.2%	0.5%	0.025	0	0	-100.0%	
America-Central	**0.719**	**0.809**	**0.897**	**24.8%**	**0.4%**	**0.601**	**0.678**	**0.755**	**25.6%**	**0.5%**	**6.969**	**8.959**	**7.062**	**1.3%**	**0.0%**
United States	0.955	1	1	4.7%	0.1%	0.804	0.839	0.869	8.1%	0.2%	0	0	0		
Mexico	0.833	0.911	0.973	16.8%	0.3%	0.698	0.762	0.809	15.9%	0.3%	6.023	1.389	0.001	-100.0%	-16.0%
Canada	0.954	0.999	1	4.8%	0.1%	0.8	0.835	0.872	9.0%	0.2%	0	0	0		
America-North	**0.925**	**0.977**	**0.993**	**7.4%**	**0.1%**	**0.778**	**0.819**	**0.855**	**9.9%**	**0.2%**	**6.023**	**1.389**	**0.001**	**-100.0%**	**-16.0%**
Brazil	0.792	0.884	0.96	21.2%	0.4%	0.667	0.743	0.801	20.1%	0.4%	14.61	9.052	0.001	-100.0%	-17.5%
Colombia	0.804	0.883	0.973	21.0%	0.4%	0.678	0.742	0.809	19.3%	0.4%	3.614	2.759	0.102	-97.2%	-6.9%
Argentina	0.883	0.975	1	13.3%	0.2%	0.742	0.813	0.857	15.5%	0.3%	1.07	0	0	-100.0%	
Peru	0.773	0.868	0.944	22.1%	0.4%	0.652	0.73	0.787	20.7%	0.4%	4.769	3.002	0	-100.0%	
Venezuela	0.827	0.936	1	20.9%	0.4%	0.695	0.781	0.839	20.7%	0.4%	3.31	0	0.001	-100.0%	-15.0%
Chile	0.874	0.972	1	14.4%	0.3%	0.732	0.809	0.855	16.8%	0.3%	0.056	0	0	-100.0%	
Ecuador	0.777	0.831	0.864	11.2%	0.2%	0.652	0.699	0.725	11.2%	0.2%	1.981	1.865	1.68	-15.2%	-0.3%
Bolivia	0.692	0.814	0.928	34.1%	0.6%	0.59	0.689	0.775	31.4%	0.5%	2.283	2.079	0.565	-75.3%	-2.8%
Paraguay	0.778	0.822	0.903	16.1%	0.3%	0.658	0.695	0.755	14.7%	0.3%	0.931	1.277	0.829	-11.0%	-0.2%
Uruguay	0.872	0.958	1	14.7%	0.3%	0.734	0.799	0.849	15.7%	0.3%	0	0	0		
Guyana	0.728	0.797	0.856	17.6%	0.3%	0.63	0.68	0.723	14.8%	0.3%	0.015	0.01	0.007	-53.3%	-1.5%
Suriname	0.783	0.877	0.965	23.2%	0.4%	0.662	0.738	0.804	21.5%	0.4%	0.036	0.008	0	-100.0%	
America-South	**0.805**	**0.894**	**0.963**	**19.6%**	**0.4%**	**0.678**	**0.751**	**0.807**	**19.0%**	**0.3%**	**32.68**	**20.05**	**3.184**	**-90.3%**	**-4.6%**

Multination Regional Analysis

Measures of Poverty, Health, Education, Infrastructure and Governance

Population, Land Area and Human Development Index

Poverty

Base Case: Countries in Year 2055 Descending Population Sequence	Human Development Index					HDI with Higher Ceilings					Poverty (below $1 CS)				
	Index					Index					Million People				
	2005	2030	2055	% Chg	% An Chg	2005	2030	2055	% Chg	% An Chg	2005	2030	2055	% Chg	% An Chg
ASIA INCL OCEANIA															
China	0.789	0.949	1	26.7%	0.5%	0.665	0.791	0.845	27.1%	0.5%	174.3	0.012	0.013	-100.0%	-17.3%
Japan	0.965	1	1	3.6%	0.1%	0.806	0.837	0.873	8.3%	0.2%	0	0	0		
Korea, Rep. of	0.909	0.996	1	10.0%	0.2%	0.764	0.832	0.867	13.5%	0.3%	0	0	0		
Taiwan	0.936	0.983	1	6.8%	0.1%	0.786	0.821	0.859	9.3%	0.2%	0	0	0		
Korea, Dem. Rep. of	0.566	0.672	0.815	44.0%	0.7%	0.47	0.562	0.68	44.7%	0.7%	8.065	6.232	2.978	-63.1%	-2.0%
Hong Kong	0.97	1	1	3.1%	0.1%	0.811	0.838	0.858	5.8%	0.1%	0	0	0		
Mongolia	0.714	0.764	0.854	19.6%	0.4%	0.612	0.651	0.718	17.3%	0.3%	0.464	0.431	0.212	-54.3%	-1.6%
Asia-East	**0.807**	**0.95**	**0.997**	**23.5%**	**0.4%**	**0.679**	**0.792**	**0.845**	**24.4%**	**0.4%**	**182.8**	**6.675**	**3.202**	**-98.2%**	**-7.8%**
India	0.598	0.732	0.876	46.5%	0.8%	0.493	0.601	0.714	44.8%	0.7%	344.1	133.6	0.025	-100.0%	-17.4%
Pakistan	0.552	0.643	0.759	37.5%	0.6%	0.451	0.527	0.625	38.6%	0.7%	23.02	23.13	8.106	-64.8%	-2.1%
Bangladesh	0.51	0.632	0.737	44.5%	0.7%	0.413	0.515	0.6	45.3%	0.7%	54.35	44.4	15.86	-70.8%	-2.4%
Iran, Islamic Rep. of	0.756	0.919	1	32.3%	0.6%	0.631	0.765	0.831	31.7%	0.6%	0	0	0		
Afghanistan	0.323	0.395	0.501	55.1%	0.9%	0.265	0.327	0.416	57.0%	0.9%	10.88	20.37	30.73	182.4%	2.1%
Nepal	0.49	0.567	0.649	32.4%	0.6%	0.398	0.467	0.537	34.9%	0.6%	7.631	10.96	13.04	70.9%	1.1%
Uzbekistan	0.73	0.79	0.857	17.4%	0.3%	0.622	0.67	0.721	15.9%	0.3%	4.126	2.207	0	-100.0%	
Sri Lanka	0.786	0.858	0.927	17.9%	0.3%	0.66	0.722	0.773	17.1%	0.3%	1.301	0.616	0	-100.0%	
Kazakhstan	0.8	0.966	0.999	24.9%	0.4%	0.681	0.807	0.831	22.0%	0.4%	0.039	0	0	-100.0%	
Tajikistan	0.677	0.734	0.806	19.1%	0.3%	0.582	0.628	0.683	17.4%	0.3%	0.718	0.571	0.3	-58.2%	-1.7%
Turkmenistan	0.762	0.901	0.917	20.3%	0.4%	0.652	0.756	0.766	17.5%	0.3%	0.224	0	0	-100.0%	
Kyrgyzstan	0.728	0.742	0.781	7.3%	0.1%	0.619	0.632	0.663	7.1%	0.1%	0.109	0.109	0.086	-21.1%	-0.5%
Bhutan	0.658	0.818	0.991	50.6%	0.8%	0.555	0.686	0.823	48.3%	0.8%	0.149	0.112	0	-100.0%	
Maldives	0.79	0.881	1	26.6%	0.5%	0.674	0.742	0.831	23.3%	0.4%	0.034	0	0	-100.0%	
Asia-South Central	**0.594**	**0.714**	**0.834**	**40.4%**	**0.7%**	**0.49**	**0.587**	**0.683**	**39.4%**	**0.7%**	**446.7**	**236.1**	**68.15**	**-84.7%**	**-3.7%**
Indonesia	0.727	0.838	0.903	24.2%	0.4%	0.617	0.707	0.756	22.5%	0.4%	14.31	2.834	0.001	-100.0%	-17.4%
Philippines	0.768	0.829	0.911	18.6%	0.3%	0.649	0.698	0.762	17.4%	0.3%	10.96	10.23	3.278	-70.1%	-2.4%
Vietnam	0.741	0.856	0.947	27.8%	0.5%	0.628	0.72	0.788	25.5%	0.5%	2.089	0.517	0	-100.0%	
Thailand	0.808	0.911	0.983	21.7%	0.4%	0.683	0.763	0.817	19.6%	0.4%	1.058	0	0	-100.0%	
Myanmar	0.653	0.751	0.838	28.3%	0.5%	0.563	0.643	0.706	25.4%	0.5%	14.91	13.48	8.916	-40.2%	-1.0%
Malaysia	0.824	0.961	1	21.4%	0.4%	0.692	0.801	0.846	22.3%	0.4%	0	0	0		
Cambodia	0.569	0.754	0.877	54.1%	0.9%	0.485	0.634	0.733	51.1%	0.8%	9.49	5.67	0.001	-100.0%	-16.7%
Laos	0.551	0.721	0.856	55.4%	0.9%	0.469	0.609	0.717	52.9%	0.9%	1.543	0.998	0	-100.0%	
Singapore	0.93	0.999	1	7.5%	0.1%	0.776	0.835	0.854	10.1%	0.2%	0	0	0		
Timor-Leste	0.557	0.638	0.752	35.0%	0.6%	0.477	0.551	0.641	34.4%	0.6%	0.302	0.447	0.487	61.3%	1.0%
Brunei	0.893	0.974	0.995	11.4%	0.2%	0.748	0.812	0.827	10.6%	0.2%	0	0	0		
Asia-South East	**0.738**	**0.842**	**0.917**	**24.3%**	**0.4%**	**0.626**	**0.709**	**0.767**	**22.5%**	**0.4%**	**54.66**	**34.18**	**12.68**	**-76.8%**	**-2.9%**

Multination Regional Analysis

Population, Land Area and Human Development Index   **Measures of Poverty, Health, Education, Infrastructure and Governance**

Poverty

Base Case: Countries in Year 2055 Descending Population Sequence	Human Development Index — Index					HDI with Higher Ceilings — Index					Poverty (below $1 CS) — Million People				
	2005	2030	2055	% Chg	% An Chg	2005	2030	2055	% Chg	% An Chg	2005	2030	2055	% Chg	% An Chg
ASIA INCL OCEANIA continued															
Turkey	0.8	0.924	1	25.0%	0.4%	0.671	0.773	0.842	25.5%	0.5%	0.442	0	0	-100.0%	
Yemen	0.481	0.641	0.776	61.3%	1.0%	0.394	0.534	0.644	63.5%	1.0%	1.682	2.093	1.46	-13.2%	-0.3%
Iraq	33	128	0	280	1082	0.545	0.669	0.759	39.3%	0.7%	5.602	2.102	0.001	-100.0%	-15.9%
Saudi Arabia	0.796	0.903	0.976	22.6%	0.4%	0.663	0.747	0.807	21.7%	0.4%	0	0	0		
Syria	0.715	0.793	0.901	26.0%	0.5%	0.593	0.662	0.747	26.0%	0.5%	3.765	3.971	0.506	-86.6%	-3.9%
Israel	0.928	1	1	7.8%	0.1%	0.776	0.842	0.881	13.5%	0.3%	0	0	0		
Azerbaijan	0.789	0.878	0.952	20.7%	0.4%	0.667	0.737	0.792	18.7%	0.3%	0.329	0	0	-100.0%	
Jordan	0.779	0.907	1	28.4%	0.5%	0.657	0.758	0.857	30.4%	0.5%	0.011	0	0	-100.0%	
Palestine	0.789	0.826	0.909	15.2%	0.3%	0.666	0.697	0.76	14.1%	0.3%	0.629	0.821	0	-100.0%	
Oman	0.786	0.877	0.937	19.2%	0.4%	0.65	0.721	0.77	18.5%	0.3%	0	0	0		
Lebanon	0.754	0.906	1	32.6%	0.6%	0.629	0.752	0.852	35.5%	0.6%	0.461	0	0	-100.0%	
United Arab Emirates	0.925	1	1	8.1%	0.2%	0.773	0.842	0.865	11.9%	0.2%	0	0	0		
Kuwait	0.875	0.961	1	14.3%	0.3%	0.726	0.797	0.849	16.9%	0.3%	0	0	0		
Georgia	0.679	0.77	0.858	26.4%	0.5%	0.562	0.642	0.714	27.0%	0.5%	0.113	0.049	0.014	-87.6%	-4.1%
Armenia	0.793	0.876	0.946	19.3%	0.4%	0.67	0.735	0.788	17.6%	0.3%	0.146	0.006	0	-100.0%	
Bahrain	0.863	0.962	1	15.9%	0.3%	0.722	0.8	0.85	17.7%	0.3%	0	0	0		
Qatar	0.874	0.96	1	14.4%	0.3%	0.734	0.803	0.836	13.9%	0.3%	0	0	0		
Cyprus	0.925	0.989	1	8.1%	0.2%	0.775	0.824	0.858	10.7%	0.2%	0	0	0		
Asia-West	**0.743**	**0.848**	**0.929**	**25.0%**	**0.4%**	**0.622**	**0.709**	**0.779**	**25.2%**	**0.5%**	**13.18**	**9.042**	**1.981**	**-85.0%**	**-3.7%**
Australia	0.954	1	1	4.8%	0.1%	0.799	0.839	0.873	9.3%	0.2%	0	0	0		
Papua New Guinea	0.545	0.68	0.806	47.9%	0.8%	0.46	0.574	0.68	47.8%	0.8%	1.513	1.613	1.36	-10.1%	-0.2%
New Zealand	0.936	0.991	1	6.8%	0.1%	0.784	0.826	0.871	11.1%	0.2%	0	0	0		
Solomon Islands	0.622	0.713	0.831	33.6%	0.6%	0.524	0.603	0.698	33.2%	0.6%	0.135	0.17	0.123	-8.9%	-0.2%
Fiji	0.775	0.865	0.959	23.7%	0.4%	0.658	0.729	0.799	21.4%	0.4%	0.111	0.033	0	-100.0%	
Vanuatu	0.683	0.764	0.877	28.4%	0.5%	0.57	0.64	0.73	28.1%	0.5%	0.046	0.053	0.025	-45.7%	-1.2%
Micronesia	0.76	0.812	0.872	14.7%	0.3%	0.644	0.692	0.735	14.1%	0.3%	0.011	0.016	0.016	45.5%	0.8%
Samoa	0.8	0.857	0.952	19.0%	0.3%	0.68	0.722	0.793	16.6%	0.3%	0.023	0.016	0	-100.0%	
Tonga	0.825	0.836	0.873	5.8%	0.1%	0.698	0.707	0.734	5.2%	0.1%	0.008	0.01	0.008	0.0%	0.0%
Oceania	**0.863**	**0.914**	**0.943**	**9.3%**	**0.2%**	**0.724**	**0.767**	**0.814**	**12.4%**	**0.2%**	**1.846**	**1.912**	**1.531**	**-17.1%**	**-0.4%**

Population, Land Area and Human Development Index

Poverty

Base Case: Countries in Year 2055 Descending Population Sequence	Human Development Index					HDI with Higher Ceilings					Poverty (below $1 C$) Million People				
	Index					Index									
	2005	2030	2055	% Chg	% An Chg	2005	2030	2055	% Chg	% An Chg	2005	2030	2055	% Chg	% An Chg
EUROPE															
Russia	0.821	0.933	0.982	19.6%	0.4%	0.7	0.783	0.818	16.9%	0.3%	6.634	0.001	0.001	-100.0%	-16.1%
Poland	0.852	0.939	1	17.4%	0.3%	0.716	0.785	0.834	16.5%	0.3%	0.002	0.002	0.001	-50.0%	-1.4%
Ukraine	0.797	0.896	0.988	24.0%	0.4%	0.678	0.752	0.82	20.9%	0.4%	0.663	0	0	-100.0%	
Romania	0.83	0.894	0.95	14.5%	0.3%	0.702	0.75	0.792	12.8%	0.2%	0.179	0	0	-100.0%	
Belarus	0.81	0.918	1	23.5%	0.4%	0.688	0.77	0.849	23.4%	0.4%	0	0	0		
Czech Republic	0.9	0.951	0.997	10.8%	0.2%	0.757	0.796	0.83	9.6%	0.2%	0	0	0		
Hungary	0.877	0.938	0.988	12.7%	0.2%	0.742	0.787	0.824	11.1%	0.2%	0	0	0		
Bulgaria	0.835	0.909	0.991	18.7%	0.3%	0.706	0.762	0.823	16.6%	0.3%	0.066	0	0	-100.0%	
Slovak Republic	0.88	0.932	0.991	12.6%	0.2%	0.743	0.78	0.824	10.9%	0.2%	0	0	0		
Moldova	0.727	0.779	0.88	21.0%	0.4%	0.618	0.661	0.738	19.4%	0.4%	0.557	0.304	0.027	-95.2%	-5.9%
Europe-East	**0.826**	**0.923**	**0.983**	**19.0%**	**0.3%**	**0.701**	**0.774**	**0.819**	**16.8%**	**0.3%**	**8.1**	**0.307**	**0.029**	**-99.6%**	**-10.7%**
United Kingdom	0.946	0.995	1	5.7%	0.1%	0.795	0.832	0.869	9.3%	0.2%	0	0	0		
Sweden	0.957	1	1	4.5%	0.1%	0.801	0.845	0.88	9.9%	0.2%	0	0	0		
Denmark	0.942	0.99	1	6.2%	0.1%	0.792	0.83	0.871	10.0%	0.2%	0	0	0		
Norway	0.963	1	1	3.8%	0.1%	0.809	0.84	0.871	7.7%	0.1%	0	0	0		
Ireland	0.949	0.996	1	5.4%	0.1%	0.799	0.836	0.855	7.0%	0.1%	0	0	0		
Finland	0.945	0.989	1	5.8%	0.1%	0.793	0.827	0.866	9.2%	0.2%	0	0	0		
Lithuania	0.866	0.952	1	15.5%	0.3%	0.732	0.795	0.852	16.4%	0.3%	0	0	0		
Latvia	0.859	0.96	1	16.4%	0.3%	0.727	0.802	0.853	17.3%	0.3%	0	0	0		
Estonia	0.874	0.979	1	14.4%	0.3%	0.738	0.817	0.868	17.6%	0.3%	0	0	0		
Iceland	0.96	1	1	4.2%	0.1%	0.805	0.841	0.875	8.7%	0.2%	0	0	0		
Europe-North	**0.942**	**0.992**	**1**	**6.2%**	**0.1%**	**0.791**	**0.832**	**0.869**	**9.9%**	**0.2%**	**0**	**0**	**0**		
Italy	0.947	0.978	1	5.6%	0.1%	0.794	0.816	0.843	6.2%	0.1%	0	0	0		
Spain	0.945	0.991	1	5.8%	0.1%	0.792	0.826	0.856	8.1%	0.2%	0	0	0		
Greece	0.924	0.991	1	8.2%	0.2%	0.773	0.825	0.865	11.9%	0.2%	0	0	0		
Portugal	0.899	0.965	1	11.2%	0.2%	0.754	0.806	0.846	12.2%	0.2%	0	0	0		
Serbia and Montenegro	0.769	0.82	0.952	23.8%	0.4%	0.648	0.692	0.792	22.2%	0.4%	1.902	0.573	0	-100.0%	
Croatia	0.87	0.937	1	14.9%	0.3%	0.733	0.783	0.851	16.1%	0.3%	0	0	0		
Bosnia and Herzegovina	0.822	0.866	0.927	12.8%	0.2%	0.692	0.728	0.774	11.8%	0.2%	0.485	0.111	0	-100.0%	
Albania	0.779	0.87	0.935	20.0%	0.4%	0.649	0.731	0.78	20.2%	0.4%	0.01	0.003	0	-100.0%	
Macedonia	0.828	0.857	0.922	11.4%	0.2%	0.699	0.722	0.77	10.2%	0.2%	0.033	0.019	0	-100.0%	
Slovenia	0.915	0.972	1	9.3%	0.2%	0.769	0.811	0.854	11.1%	0.2%	0	0	0		
Malta	0.896	0.973	1	11.6%	0.2%	0.748	0.81	0.855	14.3%	0.3%	0	0	0		
Europe-South	**0.919**	**0.964**	**0.992**	**7.9%**	**0.2%**	**0.771**	**0.805**	**0.841**	**9.1%**	**0.2%**	**2.43**	**0.705**	**0**	**-100.0%**	
Germany	0.939	0.986	1	6.5%	0.1%	0.789	0.825	0.867	9.9%	0.2%	0	0	0		
France	0.948	0.991	1	5.5%	0.1%	0.795	0.828	0.869	9.3%	0.2%	0	0	0		
Netherlands	0.945	0.984	1	5.8%	0.1%	0.794	0.824	0.859	8.2%	0.2%	0	0	0		
Belgium	0.944	0.967	1	5.9%	0.1%	0.793	0.809	0.839	5.8%	0.1%	0	0	0		
Austria	0.95	0.988	1	5.3%	0.1%	0.797	0.827	0.859	7.8%	0.1%	0	0	0		
Switzerland	0.962	0.999	1	4.0%	0.1%	0.806	0.836	0.869	7.8%	0.2%	0	0	0		
Luxembourg	0.977	1	1	2.4%	0.0%	0.822	0.849	0.863	5.0%	0.1%	0	0	0		
Europe-West	**0.944**	**0.987**	**1**	**5.9%**	**0.1%**	**0.793**	**0.826**	**0.865**	**9.1%**	**0.2%**	**0**	**0**	**0**		

Poverty

Base Case
Source: International Futures
Version 5.47 March 2008

	Poverty (below $1 LN) Million People					Poverty (below $2 CS) Million People					Poverty (below $2 LN) Million People				
	2005	2030	2055	% Chg	% An Chg	2005	2030	2055	% Chg	% An Chg	2005	2030	2055	% Chg	% An Chg
World	956.3	442.2	314	-67.2%	-2.2%	2728	2003	1224	-55.1%	-1.6%	2615	1539	963.5	-63.2%	-2.0%
Africa	287.7	269.9	231.8	-19.4%	-0.4%	596.6	820.9	818	37.1%	0.6%	581.1	678.4	681	17.2%	0.3%
Americas	52.03	32.91	17.2	-66.9%	-2.2%	136.1	100.8	41.03	-69.9%	-2.4%	134.3	92.88	48.58	-63.8%	-2.0%
Asia incl Oceania	611.7	138.1	64.61	-89.4%	-4.4%	1957	1075	364.3	-81.4%	-3.3%	1878	763.1	232.8	-87.6%	-4.1%
Europe	4.946	1.273	0.33	-93.3%	-5.3%	38.85	6.112	0.786	-98.0%	-7.5%	21.55	4.565	1.063	-95.1%	-5.8%
World	956.3	442.2	314	-67.2%	-2.2%	2728	2003	1224	-55.1%	-1.6%	2615	1539	963.5	-63.2%	-2.0%
Africa-Eastern	109	125.9	62.56	-42.6%	-1.1%	215.3	306	244.3	13.5%	0.3%	208.4	259.2	133.3	-36.0%	-0.9%
Africa-Middle	35.73	48.72	44.74	25.2%	0.5%	85.29	144.4	187.5	119.8%	1.6%	76.71	125	166.9	117.6%	1.6%
Africa-Northern	11.61	3.99	1.669	-85.6%	-3.8%	62.33	53.99	20.47	-67.2%	-2.2%	59.93	35.33	9.362	-84.4%	-3.6%
Africa-Southern	6.33	4.247	1.12	-82.3%	-3.4%	17.31	12.86	0.997	-94.2%	-5.5%	16.63	13.11	4.449	-73.2%	-2.6%
Africa-Western	125	87.12	121.8	-2.6%	-0.1%	216.3	303.6	364.7	68.6%	1.1%	219.4	245.7	366.9	67.2%	1.0%
Africa	287.7	269.9	231.8	-19.4%	-0.4%	596.6	820.9	818	37.1%	0.6%	581.1	678.4	681	17.2%	0.3%
America-Caribbean	7.875	6.863	5.773	-26.7%	-0.6%	15.09	13.75	10.56	-30.0%	-0.7%	15.67	12.66	10.62	-32.2%	-0.8%
America-Central	7.273	9.34	6.965	-4.2%	-0.1%	15.51	19.49	15.41	-0.6%	-0.0%	15.89	20.27	16.72	5.2%	0.1%
America-North	6.071	2.393	0.768	-87.3%	-4.1%	21.32	11.54	0.001	-100.0%	-18.1%	21.46	12.26	5.168	-75.9%	-2.8%
America-South	30.81	14.32	3.696	-88.0%	-4.2%	84.23	56.05	15.07	-82.1%	-3.4%	81.31	47.69	16.08	-80.2%	-3.2%
Americas	52.03	32.91	17.2	-66.9%	-2.2%	136.1	100.8	41.03	-69.9%	-2.4%	134.3	92.88	48.58	-63.8%	-2.0%
Asia-East	154.6	9.136	0.702	-99.5%	-10.2%	557.4	51.51	8.288	-98.5%	-8.1%	530.5	70.82	11.95	-97.7%	-7.3%
Asia-South Central	399.7	101.8	56.14	-86.0%	-3.8%	1092	813.7	269.3	-75.3%	-2.8%	1080	584.4	182.9	-83.1%	-3.5%
Asia-South East	47.03	20.02	6.009	-87.2%	-4.0%	253.8	169.6	66.87	-73.7%	-2.6%	223.7	86.31	31.25	-86.0%	-3.9%
Asia-West	8.636	5.788	1.334	-84.6%	-3.7%	49.01	36.01	16.26	-66.8%	-2.2%	39.65	17.84	5.089	-87.2%	-4.0%
Oceania	1.714	1.322	0.424	-75.3%	-2.8%	3.912	4.382	3.611	-7.7%	-0.2%	3.696	3.773	1.623	-56.1%	-1.6%
Asia incl Oceania	611.7	138.1	64.61	-89.4%	-4.4%	1957	1075	364.3	-81.4%	-3.3%	1878	763.1	232.8	-87.6%	-4.1%
Europe-East	2.708	0.137	0.024	-99.1%	-9.0%	32.37	2.831	0.503	-98.4%	-8.0%	15.36	2.012	0.411	-97.3%	-7.0%
Europe-North	0.019	0	0	-100.0%		0.573	0	0	-100.0%		0.605	0.025	0	-100.0%	
Europe-South	2.219	1.135	0.306	-86.2%	-3.9%	5.904	3.281	0.283	-95.2%	-5.9%	5.579	2.527	0.652	-88.3%	-4.2%
Europe-West	0	0	0			0	0	0			0	0	0		
Europe	4.946	1.273	0.33	-93.3%	-5.3%	38.85	6.112	0.786	-98.0%	-7.5%	21.55	4.565	1.063	-95.1%	-5.8%

Poverty

Base Case: Countries in Year 2055 Descending Population Sequence	Poverty (below $1 LN) Million People					Poverty (below $2 CS) Million People					Poverty (below $2 LN) Million People				
	2005	2030	2055	% Chg	% An Chg	2005	2030	2055	% Chg	% An Chg	2005	2030	2055	% Chg	% An Chg
AFRICA															
Ethiopia	12.84	10.83	0.099	-99.2%	-9.3%	54.48	79.77	68.21	25.2%	0.5%	51.7	70.84	7.599	-85.3%	-3.8%
Tanzania	17.78	3.446	0.005	-100.0%	-15.1%	33.53	40.47	16.77	-50.0%	-1.4%	32.53	17.33	0.225	-99.3%	-9.5%
Uganda	23.36	35.81	7.711	-67.0%	-2.2%	20.23	30.27	12.98	-35.8%	-0.9%	19.35	26.21	3.537	-81.7%	-3.3%
Kenya	4.345	1.312	0.01	-99.8%	-11.4%	19.85	25.3	10.65	-46.3%	-1.2%	20.42	14.32	0.781	-96.2%	-6.3%
Madagascar	10.99	17.68	15.44	40.5%	0.7%	15.83	25.5	30.23	91.0%	1.3%	15.31	25.89	26.9	75.7%	1.1%
Mozambique	5.44	1.937	0.693	-87.3%	-4.0%	13.4	14.6	9.595	-28.4%	-0.7%	11.32	6.349	3.269	-71.1%	-2.5%
Malawi	3.882	5.364	0.327	-91.6%	-4.8%	9.792	15.2	15.51	58.4%	0.9%	9.536	16.92	4.108	-56.9%	-1.7%
Zambia	8.001	12.38	5.214	-34.8%	-0.9%	11.31	17.51	16.66	47.3%	0.8%	11.6	20.46	19.7	69.8%	1.1%
Zimbabwe	7.316	9.527	4.674	-36.1%	-0.9%	10.93	14.11	9.614	-12.0%	-0.3%	11.02	15.37	11.26	2.2%	0.0%
Burundi	3.961	7.384	3.84	-3.1%	-0.1%	6.59	11.13	12.95	96.5%	1.4%	6.501	12.95	13.33	105.0%	1.4%
Rwanda	5.172	9.208	4.654	-10.0%	-0.2%	7.439	11.37	10.79	45.0%	0.7%	7.376	13.1	9.837	33.4%	0.6%
Somalia	3.605	4.657	10.86	201.2%	2.2%	7.684	13	18.65	142.7%	1.8%	7.334	10.5	19.4	164.5%	2.0%
Eritrea	1.873	5.631	8.519	354.8%	3.1%	3.316	6.628	10.48	216.0%	2.3%	3.455	7.706	12.24	254.3%	2.6%
Mauritius	0.01	0.002	0.001	-90.0%	-4.5%	0.137	0	0	-100.0%		0.114	0.032	0.015	-86.8%	-4.0%
Comoros	0.2	0.366	0.268	34.0%	0.6%	0.371	0.587	0.637	71.7%	1.1%	0.384	0.654	0.581	51.3%	0.8%
Djibouti	0.231	0.324	0.242	4.8%	0.1%	0.451	0.562	0.593	31.5%	0.5%	0.454	0.607	0.551	21.4%	0.4%
Africa-Eastern	**109**	**125.9**	**62.56**	**-42.6%**	**-1.1%**	**215.3**	**306**	**244.3**	**13.5%**	**0.3%**	**208.4**	**259.2**	**133.3**	**-36.0%**	**-0.9%**
Congo, Dem. Rep. of the	25.18	35.65	34.5	37.0%	0.6%	52.98	97.8	124.7	135.4%	1.7%	51.83	95.55	144.9	179.6%	2.1%
Angola	1.762	0.395	0.136	-92.3%	-5.0%	9.708	13.85	19.93	105.3%	1.4%	5.609	2.571	1.102	-80.4%	-3.2%
Cameroon	3.428	6.184	3.551	3.6%	0.1%	8.581	12.66	16.92	97.2%	1.4%	7.992	13.32	9.455	18.3%	0.3%
Chad	1.755	1.36	0.244	-86.1%	-3.9%	7.343	10.42	14.41	96.2%	1.4%	5.452	6.461	2.803	-48.6%	-1.3%
Central African Republic	2.699	4.823	6.061	124.6%	1.6%	3.337	5.54	7.163	114.7%	1.5%	3.349	5.804	7.814	133.3%	1.7%
Congo, Rep. of	0.815	0.175	0.063	-92.3%	-5.0%	2.76	3.614	3.88	40.6%	0.7%	2.149	1.045	0.522	-75.7%	-2.8%
Gabon	0.058	0.006	0.014	-75.9%	-2.8%	0.353	0.325	0.284	-19.5%	-0.4%	0.225	0.043	0.094	-58.2%	-1.7%
Equatorial Guinea	0.006	0	0	-100.0%		0.14	0.041	0.048	-65.7%	-2.1%	0.027	0.002	0.002	-92.6%	-5.1%
São Tomé and Príncipe	0.035	0.131	0.171	388.6%	3.2%	0.091	0.153	0.206	126.4%	1.6%	0.08	0.195	0.242	202.5%	2.2%
Africa-Middle	**35.73**	**48.72**	**44.74**	**25.2%**	**0.5%**	**85.29**	**144.4**	**187.5**	**119.8%**	**1.6%**	**76.71**	**125**	**166.9**	**117.6%**	**1.6%**
Egypt	1.571	0.455	0.002	-99.9%	-12.5%	30.86	24.44	0.001	-100.0%	-18.7%	32.62	20.66	0.891	-97.3%	-6.9%
Sudan	9.711	3.466	1.652	-83.0%	-3.5%	22.56	23.55	18.44	-18.3%	-0.4%	21.07	11.94	7.49	-64.5%	-2.0%
Algeria	0	0	0			3.19	1.927	0.353	-88.9%	-4.3%	1.38	0.009	0.163	-88.2%	-4.2%
Morocco	0.097	0.066	0.016	-83.5%	-3.5%	3.986	3.923	1.682	-57.8%	-1.7%	3.485	2.602	0.806	-76.9%	-2.9%
Tunisia	0.026	0.002	0	-100.0%		0.617	0.147	0	-100.0%		0.558	0.098	0.012	-97.8%	-7.4%
Libya	0.206	0.001	0	-100.0%		1.121	0	0	-100.0%		0.825	0.025	0	-100.0%	
Africa-Northern	**11.61**	**3.99**	**1.669**	**-85.6%**	**-3.8%**	**62.33**	**53.99**	**20.47**	**-67.2%**	**-2.2%**	**59.93**	**35.33**	**9.362**	**-84.4%**	**-3.6%**

Multination Regional Analysis

Measures of Poverty, Health, Education, Infrastructure and Governance

Poverty

Base Case: Countries in Year 2055 Descending Population Sequence	Poverty (below $1 LN) Million People					Poverty (below $2 CS) Million People					Poverty (below $2 LN) Million People				
	2005	2030	2055	% Chg	% An Chg	2005	2030	2055	% Chg	% An Chg	2005	2030	2055	% Chg	% An Chg
AFRICA continued															
South Africa	4.703	2.769	0.593	-87.4%	-4.1%	14.5	10.32	0.001	-100.0%	-17.4%	14.17	10.89	3.528	-75.1%	-2.7%
Namibia	0.332	0.222	0.031	-90.7%	-4.6%	0.863	0.81	0	-100.0%		0.719	0.598	0.134	-81.4%	-3.3%
Lesotho	0.526	0.624	0.303	-42.4%	-1.1%	0.892	1.105	0.875	-1.9%	-0.0%	0.851	1.043	0.626	-26.4%	-0.6%
Botswana	0.202	0.053	0.016	-92.1%	-4.9%	0.614	0.142	0	-100.0%		0.444	0.162	0.06	-86.5%	-3.9%
Swaziland	0.567	0.579	0.176	-69.0%	-2.3%	0.443	0.483	0.121	-72.7%	-2.6%	0.442	0.414	0.101	-77.1%	-2.9%
Africa-Southern	**6.33**	**4.247**	**1.12**	**-82.3%**	**-3.4%**	**17.31**	**12.86**	**0.997**	**-94.2%**	**-5.5%**	**16.63**	**13.11**	**4.449**	**-73.2%**	**-2.6%**
Nigeria	82.51	13.55	62.19	-24.6%	-0.6%	124.1	156.3	192.3	55.0%	0.9%	128.5	96.63	222.3	73.0%	1.1%
Niger	7.502	16.38	15.68	109.0%	1.5%	11.88	23.18	32.46	173.2%	2.0%	11.84	25.91	34.49	191.3%	2.2%
Ghana	7.396	18.1	15.66	111.7%	1.5%	16.63	26.5	30.78	85.1%	1.2%	16.57	30.56	32.44	95.8%	1.4%
Côte d'Ivoire	2.779	1.549	0.456	-83.6%	-3.6%	9.2	12.68	11.88	29.1%	0.5%	8.797	7.602	3.733	-57.6%	-1.7%
Mali	4.855	5.469	2.585	-46.8%	-1.3%	10.93	17.65	20.11	84.0%	1.2%	10.56	16.12	12.95	22.6%	0.4%
Burkina Faso	4.614	8.504	2.223	-51.8%	-1.4%	9.663	15.87	16.93	75.2%	1.1%	9.46	18.04	9.381	-0.8%	-0.0%
Senegal	1.93	1.109	0.262	-86.4%	-3.9%	6.552	9.022	7.895	20.5%	0.4%	6.426	5.879	2.685	-58.2%	-1.7%
Guinea	2.451	3.463	2.688	9.7%	0.2%	5.207	7.777	9.093	74.6%	1.1%	5.101	7.566	7.038	38.0%	0.6%
Benin	2.641	3.426	0.931	-64.7%	-2.1%	6.256	9.786	9.76	56.0%	0.9%	6.265	9.627	5.245	-16.3%	-0.4%
Togo	2.314	5.956	8.826	281.4%	2.7%	4.166	7.346	10.94	162.6%	1.9%	4.361	9.336	13.53	210.2%	2.3%
Liberia	1.366	3.887	3.496	155.9%	1.9%	2.805	5.108	7.181	156.0%	1.9%	2.739	6.115	7.562	176.1%	2.1%
Sierra Leone	2.718	2.363	2.046	-24.7%	-0.6%	4.358	4.896	5.655	29.8%	0.5%	4.161	4.624	5.107	22.7%	0.4%
Mauritania	0.879	1.332	2.003	127.9%	1.7%	1.874	3.033	3.755	100.4%	1.4%	2.007	3.156	4.529	125.7%	1.6%
Guinea-Bissau	0.685	1.636	2.511	266.6%	2.6%	1.29	2.6	4.277	231.6%	2.4%	1.297	2.757	4.55	250.8%	2.5%
Gambia	0.358	0.396	0.187	-47.8%	-1.3%	1.185	1.715	1.736	46.5%	0.8%	1.166	1.644	1.388	19.0%	0.3%
Cape Verde	0.012	0.008	0.001	-91.7%	-4.8%	0.17	0.139	0	-100.0%		0.166	0.138	0.031	-81.3%	-3.3%
Africa-Western	**125**	**87.12**	**121.8**	**-2.6%**	**-0.1%**	**216.3**	**303.6**	**364.7**	**68.6%**	**1.1%**	**219.4**	**245.7**	**366.9**	**67.2%**	**1.0%**

Poverty

Poverty

Base Case: Countries in Year 2055 / Descending Population Sequence	Poverty (below $1 LN) Million People					Poverty (below $2 CS) Million People					Poverty (below $2 LN) Million People				
	2005	2030	2055	% Chg	% An Chg	2005	2030	2055	% Chg	% An Chg	2005	2030	2055	% Chg	% An Chg
AMERICAS															
Haiti	4.689	6.326	5.759	22.8%	0.4%	6.848	9.777	10.48	53.0%	0.9%	6.843	9.597	10.26	49.9%	0.8%
Dominican Republic	0.096	0.028	0.012	-87.5%	-4.1%	1.145	0.611	0.076	-93.4%	-5.3%	1.21	0.555	0.291	-76.0%	-2.8%
Cuba	3.023	0.49	0.001	-100.0%	-14.8%	6.091	3.037	0	-100.0%		6.473	2.117	0.016	-99.8%	-11.3%
Puerto Rico	0.003	0	0	-100.0%		0.333	0	0	-100.0%		0.467	0.091	0.003	-99.4%	-9.6%
Jamaica	0.007	0	0	-100.0%		0.344	0.27	0.002	-99.4%	-9.8%	0.378	0.25	0.032	-91.5%	-4.8%
Trinidad and Tobago	0	0	0			0.228	0	0	-100.0%		0.191	0.001	0.017	-91.1%	-4.7%
Bahamas	0	0	0			0	0	0			0	0	0		
Barbados	0	0	0			0.002	0	0	-100.0%		0.002	0	0	-100.0%	
Grenada	0.009	0.007	0.001	-88.9%	-4.3%	0.023	0.018	0	-100.0%		0.028	0.024	0.003	-89.3%	-4.4%
St. Vincent & the Grenadines	0.012	0.004	0	-100.0%		0.037	0.028	0	-100.0%		0.033	0.017	0.001	-97.0%	-6.8%
St. Lucia	0.037	0.008	0	-100.0%		0.041	0.009	0	-100.0%		0.042	0.01	0	-100.0%	
America-Caribbean	**7.875**	**6.863**	**5.773**	**-26.7%**	**-0.6%**	**15.09**	**13.75**	**10.56**	**-30.0%**	**-0.7%**	**15.67**	**12.66**	**10.62**	**-32.2%**	**-0.8%**
Guatemala	1.536	1.775	1.039	-32.4%	-0.8%	4.226	5.823	4.38	3.6%	0.1%	4.494	5.632	4.106	-8.6%	-0.2%
Honduras	1.451	2.195	1.297	-10.6%	-0.2%	3.06	4.239	3.651	19.3%	0.4%	3.154	4.66	3.368	6.8%	0.1%
Nicaragua	2.658	4.174	4.066	53.0%	0.9%	4.467	6.659	6.331	41.7%	0.7%	4.512	7.076	7.639	69.3%	1.1%
El Salvador	1.345	1.175	0.563	-58.1%	-1.7%	2.89	2.658	1.045	-63.8%	-2.0%	2.919	2.794	1.6	-45.2%	-1.2%
Costa Rica	0.086	0.003	0	-100.0%		0.281	0	0	-100.0%		0.303	0.022	0	-100.0%	
Panama	0.167	0.012	0	-100.0%		0.512	0.099	0	-100.0%		0.431	0.055	0.001	-99.8%	-11.4%
Belize	0.031	0.007	0	-100.0%		0.071	0.013	0	-100.0%		0.081	0.028	0.003	-96.3%	-6.4%
America-Central	**7.273**	**9.34**	**6.965**	**-4.2%**	**-0.1%**	**15.51**	**19.49**	**15.41**	**-0.6%**	**-0.0%**	**15.89**	**20.27**	**16.72**	**5.2%**	**0.1%**
United States	0	0	0			0	0	0			0	0	0		
Mexico	6.071	2.393	0.768	-87.3%	-4.1%	21.32	11.54	0.001	-100.0%	-18.1%	21.46	12.26	5.168	-75.9%	-2.8%
Canada	0	0	0			0	0	0			0	0	0		
America-North	**6.071**	**2.393**	**0.768**	**-87.3%**	**-4.1%**	**21.32**	**11.54**	**0.001**	**-100.0%**	**-18.1%**	**21.46**	**12.26**	**5.168**	**-75.9%**	**-2.8%**
Brazil	13.85	6.255	1.932	-86.1%	-3.9%	41.36	30.13	3.881	-90.6%	-4.6%	40.07	24.5	9.791	-75.6%	-2.8%
Colombia	3.389	2.27	0.371	-89.1%	-4.3%	8.879	7.282	1.269	-85.7%	-3.8%	8.563	6.696	1.505	-82.4%	-3.4%
Argentina	1.416	0.183	0.008	-99.4%	-9.8%	6.609	0.001	0.001	-100.0%	-16.1%	7.396	2.133	0.216	-97.1%	-6.8%
Peru	4.545	1.852	0.522	-88.5%	-4.2%	8.907	6.778	2.19	-75.4%	-2.8%	8.624	4.535	1.576	-81.7%	-3.3%
Venezuela	2.75	0.104	0.002	-99.9%	-13.5%	6.226	0.397	0	-100.0%		5.167	0.363	0.01	-99.8%	-11.7%
Chile	0.047	0.002	0	-100.0%		1.397	0.019	0	-100.0%		1.296	0.24	0.039	-97.0%	-6.8%
Ecuador	1.621	1.309	0.213	-86.9%	-4.0%	4.694	4.869	4.402	-6.2%	-0.1%	4.082	3.881	0.89	-78.2%	-3.0%
Bolivia	2.123	0.903	0.175	-91.8%	-4.9%	3.891	3.73	1.399	-64.0%	-2.0%	3.712	2.197	0.625	-83.2%	-3.5%
Paraguay	1.005	1.405	0.46	-54.2%	-1.6%	2.007	2.75	1.907	-5.0%	-0.1%	2.113	3.027	1.383	-34.5%	-0.8%
Uruguay	0	0	0			0.111	0	0	-100.0%		0.107	0.008	0	-100.0%	
Guyana	0.014	0.015	0.01	-28.6%	-0.7%	0.041	0.03	0.02	-51.2%	-1.4%	0.039	0.039	0.024	-38.5%	-1.0%
Suriname	0.055	0.019	0.003	-94.5%	-5.7%	0.11	0.063	0	-100.0%		0.146	0.068	0.016	-89.0%	-4.3%
America-South	**30.81**	**14.32**	**3.696**	**-88.0%**	**-4.2%**	**84.23**	**56.05**	**15.07**	**-82.1%**	**-3.4%**	**81.31**	**47.69**	**16.08**	**-80.2%**	**-3.2%**

Poverty

Base Case: Countries in Year 2055 Descending Population Sequence	Poverty (below $1 LN) Million People					Poverty (below $2 CS) Million People					Poverty (below $2 LN) Million People				
	2005	2030	2055	% Chg	% An Chg	2005	2030	2055	% Chg	% An Chg	2005	2030	2055	% Chg	% An Chg
ASIA INCL OCEANIA															
China	147.2	4.875	0.467	-99.7%	-10.9%	539.6	36.93	0.018	-100.0%	-18.6%	513.3	57.79	9.804	-98.1%	-7.6%
Japan	0	0	0			0	0	0			0	0	0		
Korea, Rep. of	0	0	0			0	0	0			0	0	0		
Taiwan	0	0	0			0	0	0			0	0	0		
Korea, Dem. Rep. of	7.043	4.17	0.18	-97.4%	-7.1%	15.94	12.78	7.152	-55.1%	-1.6%	15.65	12.09	1.555	-90.1%	-4.5%
Hong Kong	0	0				0	0				0	0			
Mongolia	0.295	0.091	0.055	-81.4%	-3.3%	1.795	1.797	1.119	-37.7%	-0.9%	1.524	0.942	0.595	-61.0%	-1.9%
Asia-East	**154.6**	**9.136**	**0.702**	**-99.5%**	**-10.2%**	**557.4**	**51.51**	**8.288**	**-98.5%**	**-8.1%**	**530.5**	**70.82**	**11.95**	**-97.7%**	**-7.3%**
India	307.2	43.34	0.712	-99.8%	-11.4%	796.3	488.9	0.025	-100.0%	-18.7%	795.7	330.7	24.6	-96.9%	-6.7%
Pakistan	22.11	6.048	0.427	-98.1%	-7.6%	109.1	131.1	101.4	-7.1%	-0.1%	111.3	96.46	29.94	-73.1%	-2.6%
Bangladesh	48.65	17.66	2.294	-95.3%	-5.9%	110.5	104.8	64.61	-41.5%	-1.1%	109.2	80.62	23.14	-78.8%	-3.1%
Iran, Islamic Rep. of	0	0	0			3.999	0.244	0	-100.0%		2.143	0.017	0.007	-99.7%	-10.8%
Afghanistan	11.05	23.04	43.08	289.9%	2.8%	20.79	39.78	60.53	191.1%	2.2%	20.97	43.67	76.74	266.0%	2.6%
Nepal	7.83	11.2	9.51	21.5%	0.4%	18.37	26.1	30.48	65.9%	1.0%	18.62	26.75	26.45	42.1%	0.7%
Uzbekistan	1.179	0	0	-100.0%		15.86	12.54	6.594	-58.4%	-1.7%	9.881	0.007	0.086	-99.1%	-9.1%
Sri Lanka	1.164	0.337	0.088	-92.4%	-5.0%	8.037	5.112	1.718	-78.6%	-3.0%	7.733	3.909	1.405	-81.8%	-3.4%
Kazakhstan	0.001	0	0	-100.0%		2.912	0	0	-100.0%		0.332	0	0	-100.0%	
Tajikistan	0.267	0.006	0	-100.0%		3.102	3.045	2.213	-28.7%	-0.7%	1.888	0.339	0.031	-98.4%	-7.9%
Turkmenistan	0.058	0	0	-100.0%		1.825	0.368	0.561	-69.3%	-2.3%	0.984	0.005	0.001	-99.9%	-12.9%
Kyrgyzstan	0.085	0.128	0.025	-70.6%	-2.4%	1.262	1.373	1.154	-8.6%	-0.2%	1.04	1.627	0.489	-53.0%	-1.5%
Bhutan	0.133	0.07	0.007	-94.7%	-5.7%	0.317	0.265	0	-100.0%		0.299	0.197	0.03	-90.0%	-4.5%
Maldives	0.015	0.003	0	-100.0%		0.092	0.053	0	-100.0%		0.052	0.015	0	-100.0%	
Asia-South Central	**399.7**	**101.8**	**56.14**	**-86.0%**	**-3.8%**	**1092**	**813.7**	**269.3**	**-75.3%**	**-2.8%**	**1080**	**584.4**	**182.9**	**-83.1%**	**-3.5%**
Indonesia	9.127	0.203	0.005	-99.9%	-13.9%	110	65.29	20.52	-81.3%	-3.3%	91.82	14.45	1.11	-98.8%	-8.5%
Philippines	9.881	6.875	2.38	-75.9%	-2.8%	38.44	39.74	21.53	-44.0%	-1.2%	36.4	34.27	17.8	-51.1%	-1.4%
Vietnam	1.346	0.021	0	-100.0%		42.86	21.11	0.001	-100.0%	-19.2%	35.78	5.44	0.234	-99.3%	-9.6%
Thailand	0.724	0.021	0.001	-99.9%	-12.3%	16.06	3.302	0.001	-100.0%	-17.6%	13.27	2.449	0.382	-97.1%	-6.8%
Myanmar	15.79	8.465	2.633	-83.3%	-3.5%	30.33	28.5	20.21	-33.4%	-0.8%	32.08	23.59	10.14	-68.4%	-2.3%
Malaysia	0	0	0			1.717	0	0	-100.0%		1.189	0.078	0.01	-99.2%	-9.1%
Cambodia	8.76	3.83	0.708	-91.9%	-4.9%	9.377	7.006	2.435	-74.0%	-2.7%	8.679	3.745	0.683	-92.1%	-5.0%
Laos	1.181	0.08	0.001	-99.9%	-13.2%	4.358	3.654	1.134	-74.0%	-2.7%	3.954	1.178	0.091	-97.7%	-7.3%
Singapore	0	0	0			0	0	0			0	0	0		
Timor-Leste	0.218	0.522	0.28	28.4%	0.5%	0.606	0.946	1.038	71.3%	1.1%	0.503	1.106	0.796	58.3%	0.9%
Brunei	0	0	0			0	0				0	0			
Asia-South East	**47.03**	**20.02**	**6.009**	**-87.2%**	**-4.0%**	**253.8**	**169.6**	**66.87**	**-73.7%**	**-2.6%**	**223.7**	**86.31**	**31.25**	**-86.0%**	**-3.9%**

Multination Regional Analysis — Measures of Poverty, Health, Education, Infrastructure and Governance

Poverty

Base Case: Countries in Year 2055 Descending Population Sequence	Poverty (below $1 LN) Million People					Poverty (below $2 CS) Million People					Poverty (below $2 LN) Million People				
	2005	2030	2055	% Chg	% An Chg	2005	2030	2055	% Chg	% An Chg	2005	2030	2055	% Chg	% An Chg
ASIA INCL. OCEANIA continued															
Turkey	0.407	0.041	0.002	-99.5%	-10.1%	12.72	2.264	0.001	-100.0%	-17.2%	12.45	3.191	0.342	-97.3%	-6.9%
Yemen	1.069	0.115	0.024	-97.8%	-7.3%	8.589	11.41	10.09	17.5%	0.3%	6.374	1.592	0.554	-91.3%	-4.8%
Iraq	2.629	0.001	0	-100.0%		12.29	9.316	1.079	-91.2%	-4.7%	7.699	0.018	0	-100.0%	
Saudi Arabia	0	0	0			0.834	0	0	-100.0%		0.387	0.019	0	-100.0%	
Syria	3.104	4.071	0.62	-80.0%	-3.2%	8.272	9.289	3.802	-54.0%	-1.5%	7.264	9.55	2.392	-67.1%	-2.2%
Israel	0	0	0			0	0	0			0.001	0	0	-100.0%	
Azerbaijan	0.052	0	0	-100.0%		0.59	0.207	0	-100.0%		0.105	0	0	-100.0%	
Jordan	0.01	0	0	-100.0%		0.48	0.161	0	-100.0%		0.491	0.037	0	-100.0%	
Palestine	0.729	1.512	0.685	-6.0%	-0.1%	1.387	2.015	0.958	-30.9%	-0.7%	1.512	2.886	1.666	10.2%	0.2%
Oman	0	0	0			0.141	0	0	-100.0%		0.092	0.001	0.002	-97.8%	-7.4%
Lebanon	0.454	0.04	0.001	-99.8%	-11.5%	1.169	0.197	0	-100.0%		1.168	0.201	0.01	-99.1%	-9.1%
United Arab Emirates	0	0	0			0	0	0			0	0	0		
Kuwait	0	0	0			0	0	0			0	0	0		
Georgia	0.078	0.005	0.002	-97.4%	-7.1%	1.397	0.732	0.327	-76.6%	-2.9%	1.175	0.25	0.097	-91.7%	-4.9%
Armenia	0.104	0.002	0	-100.0%		1.13	0.41	0	-100.0%		0.929	0.091	0.025	-97.3%	-7.0%
Bahrain	0	0	0			0	0	0			0	0	0		
Qatar	0	0	0			0	0	0			0	0	0		
Cyprus	0	0	0			0	0	0			0	0	0		
Asia-West	**8.636**	**5.788**	**1.334**	**-84.6%**	**-3.7%**	**49.01**	**36.01**	**16.26**	**-66.8%**	**-2.2%**	**39.65**	**17.84**	**5.089**	**-87.2%**	**-4.0%**
Australia	0	0	0			0	0	0			0	0	0		
Papua New Guinea	1.423	1.103	0.301	-78.8%	-3.1%	3.153	3.617	3.151	-0.1%	-0.0%	3.006	3.152	1.25	-58.4%	-1.7%
New Zealand	0	0	0			0	0	0			0	0	0		
Solomon Islands	0.112	0.092	0.041	-63.4%	-2.0%	0.273	0.364	0.303	11.0%	0.2%	0.243	0.261	0.159	-34.6%	-0.8%
Fiji	0.1	0.026	0.002	-98.0%	-7.5%	0.273	0.152	0	-100.0%		0.252	0.1	0.011	-95.6%	-6.1%
Vanuatu	0.041	0.043	0.016	-61.0%	-1.9%	0.098	0.12	0.074	-24.5%	-0.6%	0.089	0.103	0.05	-43.8%	-1.1%
Micronesia	0.006	0.017	0.023	283.3%	2.7%	0.031	0.046	0.042	35.5%	0.6%	0.022	0.045	0.053	140.9%	1.8%
Samoa	0.021	0.02	0.005	-76.2%	-2.8%	0.058	0.046	0.007	-87.9%	-4.1%	0.053	0.051	0.017	-67.9%	-2.2%
Tonga	0.01	0.022	0.035	250.0%	2.5%	0.026	0.037	0.035	34.6%	0.6%	0.031	0.061	0.083	167.7%	2.0%
Oceania	**1.714**	**1.322**	**0.424**	**-75.3%**	**-2.8%**	**3.912**	**4.382**	**3.611**	**-7.7%**	**-0.2%**	**3.696**	**3.773**	**1.623**	**-56.1%**	**-1.6%**

Poverty

Base Case: Countries in Year 2055 / Descending Population Sequence	Poverty (below $1 LN) Million People					Poverty (below $2 CS) Million People					Poverty (below $2 LN) Million People				
	2005	2030	2055	% Chg	% An Chg	2005	2030	2055	% Chg	% An Chg	2005	2030	2055	% Chg	% An Chg
EUROPE															
Russia	1.681	0	0.007	-99.6%	-10.4%	18.85	0.001	0.001	-100.0%	-17.9%	6.005	0.001	0.055	-99.1%	-9.0%
Poland	0.028	0.002	0	-100.0%		1.197	0	0	-100.0%		1.119	0.155	0.028	-97.5%	-7.1%
Ukraine	0.181	0	0	-100.0%		5.091	0.291	0	-100.0%		1.777	0.001	0	-100.0%	
Romania	0.226	0.043	0.016	-92.9%	-5.2%	3.484	0.949	0	-100.0%		2.838	0.753	0.256	-91.0%	-4.7%
Belarus	0	0	0			0.468	0	0	-100.0%		0.345	0.005	0	-100.0%	
Czech Republic	0	0	0			0	0	0			0	0	0		
Hungary	0	0	0			0.764	0.022	0	-100.0%		0.234	0.062	0.03	-87.2%	-4.0%
Bulgaria	0.102	0.004	0	-100.0%		0	0	0			0.595	0.046	0.001	-99.8%	-12.0%
Slovak Republic	0	0	0			0	0	0			0	0	0		
Moldova	0.49	0.088	0.001	-99.8%	-11.7%	2.519	1.567	0.501	-80.1%	-3.2%	2.45	0.989	0.04	-98.4%	-7.9%
Europe-East	**2.708**	**0.137**	**0.024**	**-99.1%**	**-9.0%**	**32.37**	**2.831**	**0.503**	**-98.4%**	**-8.0%**	**15.36**	**2.012**	**0.411**	**-97.3%**	**-7.0%**
United Kingdom	0	0	0			0	0	0			0	0	0		
Sweden	0	0	0			0	0	0			0	0	0		
Denmark	0	0	0			0	0	0			0	0	0		
Norway	0	0	0			0	0	0			0	0	0		
Ireland	0	0	0			0	0	0			0	0	0		
Finland	0	0	0			0	0	0			0	0	0		
Lithuania	0.006	0	0	-100.0%		0.294	0	0	-100.0%		0.306	0.01	0	-100.0%	
Latvia	0.011	0	0	-100.0%		0.183	0	0	-100.0%		0.182	0.01	0	-100.0%	
Estonia	0.002	0	0	-100.0%		0.096	0	0	-100.0%		0.117	0.004	0	-100.0%	
Iceland	0	0	0			0	0	0			0	0	0		
Europe-North	**0.019**	**0**	**0**	**-100.0%**		**0.573**	**0**	**0**	**-100.0%**		**0.605**	**0.025**	**0**	**-100.0%**	
Italy	0	0	0			0	0	0			0	0	0.001		
Spain	0	0	0			0	0	0			0	0	0		
Greece	0	0	0			0	0	0			0	0	0		
Portugal	0	0	0			0	0	0			0.001	0.002	0	-100.0%	
Serbia and Montenegro	1.411	0.084	0	-100.0%		4.143	2.222	0	-100.0%		3.532	0.562	0.001	-100.0%	-15.1%
Croatia	0.067	0.008	0	-100.0%		0.095	0	0	-100.0%		0.101	0.014	0	-100.0%	
Bosnia and Herzegovina	0.696	1.009	0.297	-57.3%	-1.7%	1.154	0.749	0.215	-81.4%	-3.3%	1.46	1.727	0.581	-60.2%	-1.8%
Albania	0.01	0.004	0.001	-90.0%	-4.5%	0.453	0.265	0.053	-88.3%	-4.2%	0.422	0.173	0.055	-87.0%	-4.0%
Macedonia	0.036	0.029	0.008	-77.8%	-3.0%	0.058	0.045	0.015	-74.1%	-2.7%	0.062	0.051	0.014	-77.4%	-2.9%
Slovenia	0	0	0			0	0	0			0	0	0		
Malta	0	0	0			0	0	0			0	0	0		
Europe-South	**2.219**	**1.135**	**0.306**	**-86.2%**	**-3.9%**	**5.904**	**3.281**	**0.283**	**-95.2%**	**-5.9%**	**5.579**	**2.527**	**0.652**	**-88.3%**	**-4.2%**
Germany	0	0	0			0	0	0			0	0	0		
France	0	0	0			0	0	0			0	0	0		
Netherlands	0	0	0			0	0	0			0	0	0		
Belgium	0	0	0			0	0	0			0	0	0		
Austria	0	0	0			0	0	0			0	0	0		
Switzerland	0	0	0			0	0	0			0	0	0		
Luxembourg	0	0	0			0	0	0			0	0	0		
Europe-West	**0**	**0**	**0**			**0**	**0**	**0**			**0**	**0**	**0**		

Multination Regional Analysis

Measures of Poverty, Health, Education, Infrastructure and Governance

Poverty

Base Case
Source: International Futures
Version 5.47 March 2008

	Poverty (below $5 LN)						Poverty (below $10 LN)						Poverty (below $20 LN)					
	Mil People			Percent			Mil People			Percent			Mil People			Percent		
	2005	2030	2055	2005	2030	2055	2005	2030	2055	2005	2030	2055	2005	2030	2055	2005	2030	2055
World	4366	3808	2524	67.9%	46.3%	26.7%	5086	5387	4483	79.1%	65.5%	47.4%	5519	6455	6434	85.8%	78.4%	68.1%
Africa	800.8	1169	1246	88.5%	76.8%	56.9%	868.6	1374	1673	95.9%	90.3%	76.4%	890.9	1463	1975	98.4%	96.1%	90.2%
Americas	309.6	263.9	153.3	34.9%	23.9%	12.6%	440.9	441.6	303.2	49.7%	40.0%	25.0%	551.9	602.5	490.4	62.2%	54.6%	40.4%
Asia incl Oceania	3086.9	2321.3	1108	78.9%	47.3%	20.4%	3478	3433.8	2443.4	88.9%	70.0%	45.0%	3649.3	4139.1	3807.7	93.2%	84.4%	70.2%
Europe	168.2	53.97	16.42	23.2%	7.7%	2.6%	298.7	137.1	63.27	41.1%	19.6%	10.2%	426.6	250.1	161.2	58.7%	35.8%	25.9%
World	4365.5	3808.2	2523.7	67.9%	46.3%	26.7%	5086.2	5386.5	4482.9	79.1%	65.5%	47.4%	5518.7	6454.7	6434.3	85.8%	78.4%	68.1%
Africa-Eastern	273.3	429.5	326.8	95.9%	84.0%	43.7%	281.5	485	520	98.8%	94.8%	69.6%	282.2	503	656.2	99.0%	98.4%	87.8%
Africa-Middle	101.8	179.3	266.8	91.4%	83.5%	73.6%	108.4	200.6	313.3	97.3%	93.4%	86.4%	110	209	340.9	98.7%	97.3%	94.0%
Africa-Northern	135.5	126.9	60.29	71.5%	47.8%	19.2%	171.9	190.4	151	90.8%	71.7%	48.2%	185.2	231.2	245.1	97.8%	87.1%	78.2%
Africa-Southern	33.66	32.35	16.53	62.5%	51.0%	24.4%	44.46	47.29	31.88	82.5%	74.6%	47.0%	50.63	57.15	47.92	94.0%	90.2%	70.7%
Africa-Western	256.5	400.6	575.5	96.6%	85.7%	82.4%	262.4	451.2	656.5	98.8%	96.6%	93.9%	263	462.1	684.4	99.0%	98.9%	97.9%
Africa	800.8	1169	1246	88.5%	76.8%	56.9%	868.6	1374	1673	95.9%	90.3%	76.4%	890.9	1463	1975	98.4%	96.1%	90.2%
America-Caribbean	26.36	23.43	16.92	69.4%	51.1%	33.8%	32.48	32.33	24.11	85.6%	70.5%	48.1%	35.8	39.23	33.84	94.3%	85.5%	67.5%
America-Central	27.74	36.04	33.96	69.0%	57.5%	42.5%	34.53	46.83	48.05	85.9%	74.7%	60.1%	38.27	54.95	60.01	95.2%	87.7%	75.1%
America-North	56.87	46.7	27.33	13.1%	9.0%	4.9%	88.14	84.34	61.24	20.3%	16.3%	11.0%	136.6	124	101.6	31.5%	24.0%	18.2%
America-South	198.6	157.8	75.13	52.8%	33.1%	14.3%	285.8	278.1	169.8	76.1%	58.3%	32.3%	341.2	384.3	294.9	90.8%	80.5%	56.0%
Americas	309.6	263.9	153.3	34.9%	23.9%	12.6%	440.9	441.6	303.2	49.7%	40.0%	25.0%	551.9	602.5	490.4	62.2%	54.6%	40.4%
Asia-East	1035	370.6	118.1	67.2%	21.5%	6.8%	1254	804.8	388.6	81.4%	46.6%	22.3%	1354	1226	833.6	87.9%	71.0%	47.9%
Asia-South Central	1472.1	1521.5	794.7	93.1%	71.1%	31.6%	1530.2	1910.5	1569.5	96.8%	89.2%	62.4%	1553.9	2028.8	2177.2	98.3%	94.8%	86.5%
Asia-South East	454.8	349.5	156.8	82.6%	50.7%	21.0%	516.9	561	385.5	93.9%	81.4%	51.6%	534.6	644.5	602.9	97.1%	93.5%	80.8%
Asia-West	118.5	71.44	32.81	56.6%	23.4%	8.7%	168.7	146.6	90.22	80.6%	48.0%	24.0%	194	226.2	180.8	92.6%	74.1%	48.1%
Oceania	6.442	8.326	5.543	20.1%	20.2%	11.7%	8.217	10.88	9.622	25.6%	26.4%	20.4%	12.76	13.53	13.2	39.8%	32.9%	27.9%
Asia incl Oceania	3086.9	2321.3	1108.0	78.9%	47.3%	20.4%	3478.0	3433.8	2443.4	88.9%	70.0%	45.0%	3649.3	4139.1	3807.7	93.2%	84.4%	70.2%
Europe-East	105.8	19.81	7.554	35.2%	7.2%	3.2%	202.7	60.43	31.34	67.5%	22.1%	13.3%	263.9	117.6	80.97	87.9%	42.9%	34.4%
Europe-North	3.92	0.83	0.046	4.1%	0.8%	0.0%	7.634	3.48	0.557	7.9%	3.5%	0.6%	18.97	8.733	2.897	19.6%	8.7%	3.0%
Europe-South	16.28	11.28	3.041	11.3%	8.2%	2.6%	25.72	20.78	8.469	17.9%	15.1%	7.1%	52.36	39.21	22.82	36.4%	28.5%	19.2%
Europe-West	0.061	0.02	0.003	0.0%	0.0%	0.0%	2.223	0.684	0.104	1.2%	0.4%	0.1%	27.21	10.27	1.883	14.7%	5.5%	1.1%
Europe	168.2	53.97	16.42	23.2%	7.7%	2.6%	298.7	137.1	63.27	41.1%	19.6%	10.2%	426.6	250.1	161.2	58.7%	35.8%	25.9%

Poverty

Base Case: Countries in Year 2055 Descending Population Sequence	Poverty (below $5 LN) Mil People 2005	2030	2055	Percent 2005	2030	2055	Poverty (below $10 LN) Mil People 2005	2030	2055	Percent 2005	2030	2055	Poverty (below $20 LN) Mil People 2005	2030	2055	Percent 2005	2030	2055
AFRICA																		
Ethiopia	71.25	122.8	87.74	98.6%	96.2%	46.4%	71.56	126.4	165.9	99.0%	99.0%	87.8%	71.56	126.4	187	99.0%	99.0%	99.0%
Tanzania	39.12	50.55	7.064	99.0%	72.3%	7.0%	39.14	65.72	33.19	99.0%	94.0%	33.1%	39.14	69.22	72.71	99.0%	99.0%	72.5%
Uganda	27.1	48.74	20.04	93.8%	79.1%	21.6%	28.59	57.99	44.96	99.0%	94.1%	48.4%	28.59	60.97	70.62	99.0%	99.0%	76.0%
Kenya	31.92	39.33	9.017	91.6%	65.1%	11.2%	34.44	53.73	28.71	98.8%	88.9%	35.7%	34.51	59.22	55.1	99.0%	98.0%	68.5%
Madagascar	17.97	31.96	41.17	97.1%	95.1%	80.3%	18.32	33.27	47.5	99.0%	99.0%	92.6%	18.32	33.27	50.24	99.0%	99.0%	98.0%
Mozambique	17.58	16.78	12.96	87.1%	50.5%	28.8%	19.57	25.01	24.64	96.9%	75.3%	54.8%	19.99	30.29	35.42	99.0%	91.2%	78.8%
Malawi	12.84	23.88	19.95	96.8%	97.4%	52.4%	13.13	24.28	32.42	99.0%	99.0%	85.1%	13.13	24.28	37.28	99.0%	99.0%	97.8%
Zambia	11.99	21.99	29.79	99.0%	99.0%	86.3%	11.99	22	33.27	99.0%	99.0%	96.4%	11.99	22	34.18	99.0%	99.0%	99.0%
Zimbabwe	13.12	19.17	19.35	95.3%	93.3%	73.7%	13.62	20.21	23.48	99.0%	98.3%	89.4%	13.62	20.35	25.45	99.0%	99.0%	96.9%
Burundi	7.36	14.46	23.14	99.0%	99.0%	96.1%	7.36	14.46	23.85	99.0%	99.0%	99.0%	7.36	14.46	23.85	99.0%	99.0%	99.0%
Rwanda	8.849	15.92	18.05	97.0%	96.2%	75.6%	9.029	16.38	21.91	99.0%	99.0%	91.7%	9.029	16.38	23.44	99.0%	99.0%	98.1%
Somalia	8.008	13.39	22.41	99.0%	90.9%	95.7%	8.008	14.32	23.16	99.0%	97.2%	98.9%	8.008	14.59	23.18	99.0%	99.0%	99.0%
Eritrea	4.255	8.303	13.78	97.5%	99.0%	98.5%	4.32	8.303	13.85	99.0%	99.0%	99.0%	4.32	8.303	13.85	99.0%	99.0%	99.0%
Mauritius	0.637	0.363	0.202	51.2%	25.1%	13.7%	1.064	0.919	0.64	85.5%	63.5%	43.4%	1.222	1.322	1.145	98.2%	91.4%	77.7%
Comoros	0.56	0.934	1.078	92.9%	91.9%	75.4%	0.597	1.001	1.311	99.0%	98.5%	91.7%	0.597	1.006	1.403	99.0%	99.0%	98.2%
Djibouti	0.7	0.91	1.038	90.3%	90.6%	79.3%	0.762	0.987	1.235	98.3%	98.3%	94.3%	0.768	0.994	1.296	99.1%	99.0%	99.0%
Africa-Eastern	**273.3**	**429.5**	**326.8**	**95.9%**	**84.0%**	**43.7%**	**281.5**	**485**	**520**	**98.8%**	**94.8%**	**69.6%**	**282.2**	**503**	**656.2**	**99.0%**	**98.4%**	**87.8%**
Congo, Dem. Rep. of the	58.48	120.5	211.2	98.9%	96.3%	93.6%	58.57	123.9	223.5	99.0%	99.0%	99.0%	58.57	123.9	223.5	99.0%	99.0%	99.0%
Angola	12.3	12.29	8.012	77.6%	42.2%	17.4%	15.05	21.86	20.24	94.7%	75.0%	44.1%	15.73	27.36	33.91	99.0%	93.9%	73.8%
Cameroon	14.04	21.86	22.03	84.6%	87.1%	58.8%	16.03	24.43	30.53	96.6%	97.3%	81.5%	16.43	24.86	35.28	99.0%	99.0%	94.2%
Chad	8.578	13.91	12.3	90.1%	76.5%	42.9%	9.357	17.08	21.43	98.3%	93.9%	74.7%	9.421	18.01	26.81	99.0%	99.0%	93.4%
Central African Republic	3.971	6.672	9.655	94.5%	95.9%	92.5%	4.139	6.885	10.21	98.5%	99.0%	97.8%	4.158	6.885	10.33	99.0%	99.0%	98.9%
Congo, Rep. of	3.477	3.623	2.76	89.1%	51.8%	26.9%	3.827	5.64	5.764	98.1%	80.7%	56.2%	3.864	6.669	8.44	99.0%	95.4%	82.3%
Gabon	0.581	0.215	0.399	40.7%	9.7%	14.9%	0.908	0.525	0.864	63.6%	23.7%	32.4%	1.176	0.989	1.468	82.4%	44.7%	55.0%
Equatorial Guinea	0.174	0	0.101	34.1%	0.0%	9.7%	0.353	0.012	0.477	69.1%	1.4%	45.7%	0.47	0.119	0.899	92.0%	14.2%	86.1%
São Tomé and Príncipe	0.137	0.24	0.302	87.8%	96.8%	93.5%	0.152	0.246	0.318	97.4%	99.2%	98.5%	0.154	0.246	0.32	98.7%	99.2%	99.1%
Africa-Middle	**101.8**	**179.3**	**266.8**	**91.4%**	**83.5%**	**73.6%**	**108.4**	**200.6**	**313.3**	**97.3%**	**93.4%**	**86.4%**	**110**	**209**	**340.9**	**98.7%**	**97.3%**	**94.0%**
Egypt	67.3	74.61	17.84	90.8%	70.1%	14.0%	73.39	100.3	61.73	99.0%	94.3%	48.5%	73.39	105.3	107.2	99.0%	99.0%	84.2%
Sudan	33.94	35.65	32.45	92.4%	63.1%	44.4%	36.35	49.93	55.66	99.0%	88.4%	76.2%	36.35	55.37	68.77	99.0%	98.0%	94.1%
Algeria	12	0.4	3.248	36.6%	0.9%	6.9%	25	5.315	14.37	76.3%	12.3%	30.3%	31.35	19.71	31.65	95.7%	45.8%	66.8%
Morocco	15.39	14.14	6.442	51.5%	36.4%	15.2%	24.89	27.17	17.23	83.4%	70.0%	40.7%	29	35.67	30.11	97.1%	91.8%	71.1%
Tunisia	3.578	1.329	0.275	35.5%	10.7%	2.0%	7.161	4.481	1.492	71.0%	36.0%	11.0%	9.388	8.722	4.646	93.0%	70.1%	34.3%
Libya	3.325	0.741	0.045	57.0%	9.1%	0.5%	5.071	3.214	0.539	86.9%	39.3%	5.6%	5.724	6.432	2.719	98.1%	78.6%	28.2%
Africa-Northern	**135.5**	**126.9**	**60.29**	**71.5%**	**47.8%**	**19.2%**	**171.9**	**190.4**	**151**	**90.8%**	**71.7%**	**48.2%**	**185.2**	**231.2**	**245.1**	**97.8%**	**87.1%**	**78.2%**

Poverty

Base Case: Countries in Year 2055 Descending Population Sequence	Poverty (below $5 LN) Mil People 2005	2030	2055	Percent 2005	2030	2055	Poverty (below $10 LN) Mil People 2005	2030	2055	Percent 2005	2030	2055	Poverty (below $20 LN) Mil People 2005	2030	2055	Percent 2005	2030	2055
AFRICA																		
South Africa	29.07	27.53	13.69	62.1%	51.4%	24.4%	38.59	40.42	26.71	82.4%	75.5%	47.6%	44.01	48.76	40.22	94.0%	91.0%	71.7%
Namibia	1.345	1.428	0.569	64.4%	46.2%	15.0%	1.731	2.123	1.234	82.9%	68.7%	32.5%	1.956	2.65	2.093	93.7%	85.8%	55.0%
Lesotho	1.408	1.8	1.469	73.6%	70.5%	47.5%	1.698	2.219	2.16	88.7%	86.8%	69.8%	1.844	2.441	2.675	96.3%	95.5%	86.5%
Botswana	0.981	0.557	0.287	51.8%	23.8%	11.1%	1.391	1.048	0.675	73.5%	44.9%	26.1%	1.679	1.576	1.233	88.7%	67.5%	47.8%
Swaziland	0.852	1.039	0.511	73.2%	56.7%	22.9%	1.055	1.479	1.097	90.6%	80.7%	49.1%	1.139	1.725	1.693	97.9%	94.1%	75.7%
Africa-Southern	**33.66**	**32.35**	**16.53**	**62.5%**	**51.0%**	**24.4%**	**44.46**	**47.29**	**31.88**	**82.5%**	**74.6%**	**47.0%**	**50.63**	**57.15**	**47.92**	**94.0%**	**90.2%**	**70.7%**
Nigeria	132.2	189.5	314.7	99.0%	82.6%	93.6%	132.2	221.6	332.8	99.0%	96.6%	99.0%	132.2	227.2	332.8	99.0%	99.0%	99.0%
Niger	13.66	29.63	48.76	97.4%	98.0%	89.5%	13.88	29.95	53.06	99.0%	99.0%	97.4%	13.88	29.95	53.93	99.0%	99.0%	99.0%
Ghana	21.45	34.97	44.7	97.1%	98.8%	92.3%	21.88	35.03	47.7	99.0%	99.0%	98.5%	21.88	35.03	47.93	99.0%	99.0%	99.0%
Côte d'Ivoire	15.98	20.83	17.08	84.2%	62.6%	36.1%	18.34	28.95	31.77	96.6%	87.0%	67.1%	18.79	32.38	42.27	99.0%	97.4%	89.3%
Mali	13.16	24.18	30.14	97.6%	92.9%	73.2%	13.34	25.77	38.17	99.0%	99.0%	92.6%	13.34	25.77	40.74	99.0%	99.0%	98.9%
Burkina Faso	12.57	24.41	25.84	96.7%	96.4%	63.8%	12.87	25.07	35.65	99.0%	99.0%	88.0%	12.87	25.07	39.58	99.0%	99.0%	97.7%
Senegal	10.53	14.36	11.83	90.2%	71.9%	42.5%	11.5	18.44	20.68	98.5%	92.3%	74.3%	11.55	19.75	25.95	99.0%	98.9%	93.3%
Guinea	8.442	13.9	17.13	92.2%	87.2%	72.5%	9.067	15.61	21.89	99.0%	97.9%	92.6%	9.067	15.78	23.38	99.0%	99.0%	98.9%
Benin	8.069	14.12	14.91	98.0%	95.2%	66.5%	8.151	14.69	20.25	99.0%	99.1%	90.3%	8.151	14.69	22.09	99.0%	99.1%	98.5%
Togo	5.851	11	16.58	95.5%	98.5%	96.3%	6.064	11.06	17.04	99.0%	99.0%	99.0%	6.064	11.06	17.04	99.0%	99.0%	99.0%
Liberia	3.465	6.74	10.39	96.8%	99.0%	93.6%	3.544	6.74	10.98	99.0%	99.0%	98.9%	3.544	6.74	10.99	99.0%	99.0%	99.0%
Sierra Leone	4.851	6.222	8.114	95.3%	87.7%	76.5%	5.029	6.806	9.584	98.8%	95.9%	90.4%	5.038	7.024	10.29	99.0%	97.4%	97.1%
Mauritania	2.882	4.896	7.073	95.5%	92.2%	90.5%	2.989	5.255	7.693	99.0%	99.0%	98.4%	2.989	5.257	7.739	99.0%	99.0%	99.0%
Guinea-Bissau	1.549	3.134	5.415	97.4%	98.4%	97.1%	1.574	3.153	5.52	99.0%	99.0%	99.0%	1.574	3.153	5.52	99.0%	99.0%	99.0%
Gambia	1.441	2.289	2.615	96.1%	91.2%	73.8%	1.484	2.462	3.216	99.0%	98.1%	90.8%	1.484	2.485	3.464	99.0%	99.0%	97.8%
Cape Verde	0.384	0.429	0.203	75.9%	53.9%	20.8%	0.476	0.645	0.477	94.1%	81.0%	48.8%	0.501	0.757	0.757	99.0%	95.1%	77.4%
Africa-Western	**256.5**	**400.6**	**575.5**	**96.6%**	**85.7%**	**82.4%**	**262.4**	**451.2**	**656.5**	**98.8%**	**96.6%**	**93.9%**	**263**	**462.1**	**684.4**	**99.0%**	**98.9%**	**97.9%**

Poverty

Base Case: Countries in Year 2055 Descending Population Sequence	Poverty (below $5 LN) Mil People 2005	2030	2055	Percent 2005	2030	2055	Poverty (below $10 LN) Mil People 2005	2030	2055	Percent 2005	2030	2055	Poverty (below $20 LN) Mil People 2005	2030	2055	Percent 2005	2030	2055
AMERICAS																		
Haiti	8.18	11.85	14.35	94.5%	92.7%	85.2%	8.532	12.52	15.97	98.6%	98.0%	94.8%	8.565	12.66	16.61	99.0%	99.1%	98.6%
Dominican Republic	3.826	2.511	1.569	42.7%	22.2%	12.8%	6.228	5.23	3.801	69.6%	46.3%	31.0%	7.935	8.116	6.836	88.6%	71.9%	55.7%
Cuba	10.35	7.08	0.482	91.0%	62.2%	4.7%	11.22	10.12	2.47	98.7%	88.9%	24.2%	11.25	11.2	6.199	98.9%	98.4%	60.7%
Puerto Rico	1.593	0.631	0.044	40.1%	13.8%	0.9%	2.692	1.663	0.295	67.8%	36.3%	6.1%	3.49	2.979	1.046	87.9%	65.1%	21.6%
Jamaica	1.37	1.082	0.213	50.5%	33.5%	6.3%	2.18	2.074	0.755	80.4%	64.2%	22.2%	2.56	2.803	1.633	94.4%	86.8%	47.9%
Trinidad and Tobago	0.734	0.046	0.214	55.8%	3.2%	15.8%	1.124	0.27	0.646	85.4%	18.8%	47.7%	1.283	0.765	1.1	97.5%	53.2%	81.2%
Bahamas	0.002	0.001	0	0.6%	0.3%	0.0%	0.021	0.011	0.003	6.6%	2.9%	0.8%	0.106	0.078	0.03	33.1%	20.6%	7.5%
Barbados	0.035	0.013	0.001	12.8%	4.4%	0.4%	0.121	0.069	0.01	44.2%	23.5%	3.6%	0.218	0.177	0.055	79.6%	60.2%	19.6%
Grenada	0.079	0.087	0.028	70.5%	55.1%	15.1%	0.104	0.133	0.077	92.9%	84.2%	41.6%	0.111	0.153	0.135	99.1%	96.8%	73.0%
St. Vincent & the Grenadines	0.088	0.079	0.016	71.0%	49.7%	9.0%	0.115	0.13	0.061	92.7%	81.8%	34.5%	0.123	0.154	0.124	99.2%	96.9%	70.1%
St. Lucia	0.108	0.057	0.004	67.9%	33.7%	2.5%	0.143	0.114	0.025	89.9%	67.5%	15.7%	0.157	0.153	0.073	98.7%	90.5%	45.9%
America-Caribbean	**26.36**	**23.43**	**16.92**	**69.4%**	**51.1%**	**33.8%**	**32.48**	**32.33**	**24.11**	**85.6%**	**70.5%**	**48.1%**	**35.8**	**39.23**	**33.84**	**94.3%**	**85.5%**	**67.5%**
Guatemala	8.706	12.34	11.31	68.1%	54.7%	36.6%	11.09	17.23	18.39	86.8%	76.3%	59.4%	12.28	20.45	24.57	96.1%	90.6%	79.4%
Honduras	5.474	8.211	7.549	75.9%	71.3%	50.8%	6.58	10.12	10.8	91.2%	87.9%	72.6%	7.052	11.08	13.11	97.8%	96.3%	88.2%
Nicaragua	5.419	8.783	10.71	97.8%	96.3%	90.0%	5.484	9.028	11.62	99.0%	99.0%	97.6%	5.484	9.028	11.78	99.0%	99.0%	99.0%
El Salvador	5.253	5.844	4.32	76.3%	61.9%	39.9%	6.334	7.796	6.86	91.9%	82.6%	63.3%	6.762	8.894	8.946	98.2%	94.2%	82.6%
Costa Rica	1.427	0.346	0.012	33.3%	6.2%	0.2%	2.735	1.359	0.14	63.8%	24.4%	2.2%	3.74	3.115	0.827	87.3%	56.0%	13.2%
Panama	1.258	0.372	0.02	39.3%	9.1%	0.4%	2.047	1.025	0.125	64.0%	25.0%	2.7%	2.682	2.031	0.501	83.8%	49.5%	10.9%
Belize	0.204	0.143	0.036	73.6%	36.2%	7.7%	0.259	0.271	0.127	93.5%	68.6%	27.0%	0.274	0.358	0.271	98.9%	90.6%	57.7%
America-Central	**27.74**	**36.04**	**33.96**	**69.0%**	**57.5%**	**42.5%**	**34.53**	**46.83**	**48.05**	**85.9%**	**74.7%**	**60.1%**	**38.27**	**54.95**	**60.01**	**95.2%**	**87.7%**	**75.1%**
United States	0.37	0.038	0.007	0.1%	0.0%	0.0%	5.115	0.944	0.223	1.7%	0.3%	0.1%	33.84	10.82	3.565	11.4%	3.1%	0.9%
Mexico	56.49	46.66	27.32	53.7%	35.8%	20.0%	82.57	83.35	61.02	78.5%	63.9%	44.6%	97.96	112.1	97.98	93.1%	85.9%	71.6%
Canada	0.013	0	0	0.0%	0.0%	0.0%	0.452	0.043	0.001	1.4%	0.1%	0.0%	4.772	1.081	0.061	14.9%	2.9%	0.2%
America-North	**56.87**	**46.7**	**27.33**	**13.1%**	**9.0%**	**4.9%**	**88.14**	**84.34**	**61.24**	**20.3%**	**16.3%**	**11.0%**	**136.6**	**124**	**101.6**	**31.5%**	**24.0%**	**18.2%**
Brazil	96.04	80.23	44.26	51.5%	34.9%	17.9%	139.2	138.6	95.78	74.6%	60.3%	38.7%	168.1	188.2	157.2	90.1%	81.8%	63.4%
Colombia	21.35	20.42	7.291	46.6%	33.7%	10.7%	32.04	34.79	17.34	70.0%	57.5%	25.5%	39.89	47.65	31.95	87.1%	78.7%	46.9%
Argentina	20.3	11.3	2.501	52.0%	23.9%	4.9%	30.25	24.31	9.203	77.4%	51.4%	17.9%	36.23	37	22.04	92.7%	78.2%	42.8%
Peru	19.04	15.63	8.247	67.4%	41.4%	19.3%	24.87	26.2	18.48	88.0%	69.3%	43.3%	27.45	33.65	29.94	97.1%	89.0%	70.1%
Venezuela	16.04	4.874	0.422	60.4%	13.7%	1.0%	23.04	15.41	3.083	86.7%	43.5%	7.5%	25.91	27.56	11.79	97.5%	77.7%	28.8%
Chile	4.467	1.571	0.417	27.5%	8.0%	2.0%	8.213	4.358	1.648	50.5%	22.2%	7.9%	11.93	8.828	4.603	73.4%	45.1%	22.0%
Ecuador	9.654	11.37	4.849	71.7%	61.5%	23.4%	12.37	16.07	10.56	91.9%	87.0%	51.0%	13.28	18.01	16.18	98.7%	97.5%	78.1%
Bolivia	6.435	5.799	2.815	70.1%	43.0%	17.3%	7.951	9.003	6.112	86.7%	66.8%	37.7%	8.76	11.48	10.1	95.5%	85.2%	62.2%
Paraguay	3.972	5.943	4.066	65.9%	60.8%	32.5%	5.085	7.861	6.898	84.4%	80.5%	55.1%	5.702	9.039	9.531	94.7%	92.5%	76.1%
Uruguay	0.759	0.149	0.014	22.0%	3.9%	0.4%	1.806	0.706	0.156	52.3%	18.6%	4.0%	2.805	1.847	0.742	81.2%	48.6%	18.8%
Guyana	0.24	0.215	0.121	31.7%	30.7%	19.4%	0.495	0.436	0.268	65.5%	62.3%	42.9%	0.679	0.61	0.434	89.6%	87.1%	69.6%
Suriname	0.353	0.264	0.124	78.3%	54.8%	27.6%	0.431	0.408	0.28	95.6%	84.6%	62.2%	0.446	0.469	0.4	98.9%	97.3%	88.9%
America-South	**198.6**	**157.8**	**75.13**	**52.8%**	**33.1%**	**14.3%**	**285.8**	**278.1**	**169.8**	**76.1%**	**58.3%**	**32.3%**	**341.2**	**384.3**	**294.9**	**90.8%**	**80.5%**	**56.0%**

Multination Regional Analysis — Measures of Poverty, Health, Education, Infrastructure and Governance

Poverty

Base Case: Countries in Year 2055 Descending Population Sequence	Poverty (below $5 LN) Mil People			Poverty (below $5 LN) Percent			Poverty (below $10 LN) Mil People			Poverty (below $10 LN) Percent			Poverty (below $20 LN) Mil People			Poverty (below $20 LN) Percent		
	2005	2030	2055	2005	2030	2055	2005	2030	2055	2005	2030	2055	2005	2030	2055	2005	2030	2055
ASIA INCL OCEANIA																		
China	1011	347	108.1	77.3%	23.3%	7.1%	1224	777.4	369.9	93.6%	52.1%	24.2%	1294	1191	807.3	98.9%	79.8%	52.8%
Japan	0	0	0	0.0%	0.0%	0.0%	0.173	0.008	0	0.1%	0.0%	0.0%	9.637	1.263	0.051	7.5%	1.1%	0.1%
Korea, Rep. of	0.165	0.002	0	0.3%	0.0%	0.0%	3.098	0.141	0.012	6.4%	0.3%	0.0%	17.8	2.86	0.43	36.6%	5.4%	0.9%
Taiwan	0.048	0.006	0	0.2%	0.0%	0.0%	0.97	0.26	0.029	4.2%	1.0%	0.1%	6.428	3.198	0.596	27.5%	12.1%	2.3%
Korea, Dem. Rep. of	21.45	20.9	7.806	95.2%	86.1%	32.3%	22.31	23.6	15.33	99.0%	97.2%	63.4%	22.31	24.04	21.13	99.0%	99.0%	87.4%
Hong Kong	0.049	0.006	0.005	0.7%	0.1%	0.1%	0.378	0.094	0.065	5.3%	1.1%	0.7%	1.574	0.676	0.454	22.3%	8.0%	5.2%
Mongolia	2.46	2.66	2.175	95.5%	78.0%	58.5%	2.55	3.289	3.237	99.0%	96.5%	87.1%	2.55	3.376	3.642	99.0%	99.0%	98.0%
Asia-East	**1035**	**370.6**	**118.1**	**67.2%**	**21.5%**	**6.8%**	**1254**	**804.8**	**388.6**	**81.4%**	**46.6%**	**22.3%**	**1354**	**1226**	**833.6**	**87.9%**	**71.0%**	**47.9%**
India	1060	1001	309.2	97.3%	71.0%	19.5%	1078	1319	869.5	99.0%	93.5%	54.8%	1078	1396	1372	99.0%	99.0%	86.5%
Pakistan	151.5	231	213.1	98.8%	91.4%	61.4%	151.9	250.2	325.7	99.0%	99.0%	93.8%	151.9	250.2	343.7	99.0%	99.0%	99.0%
Bangladesh	138.9	175.3	122	98.8%	88.3%	52.6%	139.2	196.2	199.7	99.0%	98.8%	86.1%	139.2	196.5	227.8	99.0%	99.0%	98.2%
Iran, Islamic Rep. of	14.62	0	0	21.7%	0.0%	0.0%	36.41	4.223	1.345	54.1%	4.7%	1.3%	55.57	21.5	12.35	82.5%	24.2%	12.1%
Afghanistan	24.49	49.9	87.33	98.3%	98.9%	98.7%	24.67	49.95	87.56	99.0%	99.0%	99.0%	24.67	49.95	87.56	99.0%	99.0%	99.0%
Nepal	25.28	38.08	44.51	93.6%	90.2%	77.6%	26.72	41.3	52.77	98.9%	97.8%	92.0%	26.74	41.81	56.19	99.0%	99.0%	98.0%
Uzbekistan	22.88	1.41	6.028	86.2%	3.9%	15.1%	26.14	12.16	25.35	98.5%	33.8%	63.6%	26.28	29.57	38.17	99.0%	82.3%	95.8%
Sri Lanka	16.61	13.39	7.241	82.3%	59.5%	32.9%	19.55	19.61	14.22	96.8%	87.1%	64.7%	19.99	22.04	19.43	99.0%	97.9%	88.4%
Kazakhstan	4.429	0	0	30.0%	0.0%	0.0%	10.69	0	0	72.5%	0.0%	0.0%	14.12	0.012	0.054	95.7%	0.1%	0.4%
Tajikistan	5.446	4.882	1.496	82.6%	50.2%	13.2%	6.467	8.91	6.313	98.1%	91.6%	55.7%	6.526	9.626	10.43	99.0%	99.0%	92.0%
Turkmenistan	3.169	0.204	0.039	65.6%	3.2%	0.5%	4.39	1.263	0.337	90.8%	19.5%	4.6%	4.776	3.596	1.526	98.8%	55.5%	20.7%
Kyrgyzstan	4.049	5.625	3.593	77.6%	84.4%	50.6%	5.092	6.593	6.214	97.5%	98.9%	87.4%	5.168	6.598	7.026	99.0%	98.9%	98.9%
Bhutan	0.561	0.561	0.18	83.7%	53.6%	13.6%	0.647	0.833	0.451	96.6%	79.6%	34.0%	0.663	0.985	0.806	99.0%	94.1%	60.7%
Maldives	0.191	0.127	0.001	58.2%	23.8%	0.1%	0.285	0.304	0.019	86.9%	57.0%	2.8%	0.322	0.458	0.117	98.2%	85.9%	17.3%
Asia-South Central	**1472.1**	**1521.5**	**794.7**	**93.1%**	**71.1%**	**31.6%**	**1530.2**	**1910.5**	**1589.5**	**96.8%**	**89.2%**	**63.2%**	**1553.9**	**2028.8**	**2177.2**	**98.3%**	**94.8%**	**86.5%**
Indonesia	202.5	139.7	39.74	92.4%	53.4%	14.7%	216.9	238.8	152.1	99.0%	91.3%	56.1%	216.9	259	247.5	99.0%	99.0%	91.3%
Philippines	67.68	81.78	62.31	80.9%	67.1%	43.6%	79.61	108.2	103.2	95.1%	88.8%	72.3%	82.85	119	129.9	99.0%	97.7%	91.0%
Vietnam	73.02	39.83	6.874	88.8%	39.9%	6.4%	81.26	77.6	32.5	98.8%	77.7%	30.3%	81.42	96.12	73.74	99.0%	96.3%	68.8%
Thailand	39.76	20.13	6.438	62.0%	27.4%	8.4%	56.17	46.31	24.38	87.6%	62.9%	32.0%	62.69	65.98	51.07	97.7%	89.7%	66.9%
Myanmar	47.03	48.31	32.43	93.2%	78.8%	49.6%	49.93	58.12	50.59	99.0%	94.8%	77.3%	49.93	60.69	61.13	99.0%	99.0%	93.4%
Malaysia	5.342	0.637	0	21.2%	1.9%	0.0%	11.86	4.212	1.201	47.1%	12.5%	3.1%	18.48	12	6.095	73.4%	35.6%	15.8%
Cambodia	12.9	12.03	5.532	92.3%	58.3%	22.3%	13.82	17.63	13.51	98.9%	85.5%	54.5%	13.84	20.04	20.78	99.0%	97.2%	83.9%
Laos	5.702	5.4	1.656	96.6%	58.0%	14.3%	5.842	8.27	5.57	99.0%	88.9%	48.1%	5.842	9.186	9.66	99.0%	98.7%	83.4%
Singapore	0.084	0.007	0.002	1.9%	0.1%	0.0%	0.471	0.109	0.038	10.8%	2.0%	0.7%	1.496	0.733	0.302	34.2%	13.7%	5.5%
Timor-Leste	0.85	1.681	1.843	88.0%	92.7%	67.7%	0.946	1.795	2.419	97.9%	99.0%	88.9%	0.957	1.795	2.656	99.1%	99.0%	97.6%
Brunei	0.006	0	0	1.6%	0.0%	0.0%	0.054	0.008	0.002	14.5%	1.5%	0.3%	0.188	0.08	0.031	50.4%	15.3%	5.1%
Asia-South East	**454.8**	**349.5**	**156.8**	**82.6%**	**50.7%**	**21.0%**	**516.9**	**561**	**385.5**	**93.9%**	**81.4%**	**51.6%**	**534.6**	**644.5**	**602.9**	**97.1%**	**93.5%**	**80.8%**

Poverty

Base Case: Countries in Year 2055 Descending Population Sequence	Poverty (below $5 LN) Mil People 2005	2030	2055	Percent 2005	2030	2055	Poverty (below $10 LN) Mil People 2005	2030	2055	Percent 2005	2030	2055	Poverty (below $20 LN) Mil People 2005	2030	2055	Percent 2005	2030	2055
ASIA INCL OCEANIA																		
Turkey	44.87	24.2	5.663	61.8%	26.4%	5.5%	64.88	55.4	23.17	89.3%	60.3%	22.7%	71.61	80.46	54.96	98.6%	87.6%	53.8%
Yemen	17.08	12.71	8.31	81.8%	31.1%	13.3%	20.38	27.79	27.28	97.7%	67.9%	43.5%	20.67	37.76	49.18	99.0%	92.3%	78.5%
Iraq	19.52	1.215	0.124	73.7%	2.7%	0.2%	24.82	8.843	2.557	93.7%	19.9%	4.4%	26.22	26.3	16.83	99.0%	59.1%	29.0%
Saudi Arabia	4.976	1.137	0.017	21.2%	3.1%	0.0%	13.7	7.86	0.651	58.2%	21.7%	1.4%	20.88	22.28	5.673	88.8%	61.5%	12.6%
Syria	15.2	21.69	11.49	79.7%	70.7%	30.0%	18.19	27.85	22.79	95.4%	90.8%	59.4%	18.87	30.13	32.29	99.0%	98.3%	84.2%
Israel	0.114	0.008	0	1.6%	0.1%	0.0%	0.831	0.135	0.011	11.9%	1.4%	0.1%	2.871	1.017	0.171	41.1%	10.9%	1.6%
Azerbaijan	1.551	0.015	0	18.3%	0.1%	0.0%	4.607	0.354	0.001	54.3%	3.5%	0.0%	7.372	2.573	0.066	86.9%	25.6%	0.6%
Jordan	2.621	0.868	0.002	47.9%	10.6%	0.0%	4.5	3.399	0.076	82.2%	41.5%	0.7%	5.318	6.5	1.022	97.1%	79.4%	10.0%
Palestine	3.122	5.772	5.634	90.0%	87.5%	60.5%	3.435	6.489	8.171	99.0%	98.4%	87.8%	3.435	6.53	9.124	99.0%	99.0%	98.0%
Oman	0.856	0.049	0.138	31.0%	1.1%	2.6%	1.925	0.448	1.069	69.8%	10.4%	20.3%	2.585	1.744	3.207	93.8%	40.5%	60.9%
Lebanon	2.802	1.335	0.241	76.8%	29.9%	4.8%	3.464	2.855	1.138	95.0%	63.8%	22.9%	3.612	3.989	2.831	99.0%	89.2%	57.0%
United Arab Emirates	0.01	0	0	0.3%	0.0%	0.0%	0.182	0.001	0	5.1%	0.0%	0.0%	1.087	0.035	0.004	30.4%	0.8%	0.1%
Kuwait	0.011	0	0	0.4%	0.0%	0.0%	0.165	0	0	6.7%	0.0%	0.0%	0.875	0.026	0	35.3%	0.7%	0.0%
Georgia	3.238	1.462	0.716	70.3%	37.9%	21.7%	4.258	2.807	1.722	92.4%	72.8%	52.2%	4.56	3.608	2.685	99.0%	93.6%	81.4%
Armenia	2.531	0.984	0.467	80.0%	29.5%	14.6%	3.07	2.313	1.573	97.1%	69.5%	49.1%	3.131	3.13	2.702	99.0%	94.0%	84.4%
Bahrain	0.019	0	0	2.6%	0.0%	0.0%	0.135	0.006	0	18.2%	0.6%	0.0%	0.408	0.082	0.008	54.9%	8.2%	0.7%
Qatar	0.008	0	0	1.2%	0.0%	0.0%	0.096	0	0	14.6%	0.0%	0.0%	0.367	0.001	0	55.8%	0.1%	0.0%
Cyprus	0.002	0	0	0.3%	0.0%	0.0%	0.031	0.008	0.001	4.3%	1.0%	0.1%	0.187	0.083	0.014	26.0%	10.5%	1.8%
Asia-West	**118.5**	**71.44**	**32.81**	**56.6%**	**23.4%**	**8.7%**	**168.7**	**146.6**	**90.22**	**80.6%**	**48.0%**	**24.0%**	**194**	**226.2**	**180.8**	**92.6%**	**74.1%**	**48.1%**
Australia	0.025	0.001	0	0.1%	0.0%	0.0%	0.505	0.073	0.007	2.5%	0.3%	0.0%	3.771	1.253	0.219	18.6%	5.1%	0.8%
Papua New Guinea	4.892	6.629	4.306	82.9%	71.5%	35.3%	5.609	8.391	7.523	95.1%	90.4%	61.6%	5.841	9.089	10.18	99.0%	98.0%	83.4%
New Zealand	0.023	0.003	0	0.6%	0.1%	0.0%	0.253	0.062	0.002	6.3%	1.3%	0.0%	1.203	0.554	0.051	29.9%	12.0%	1.1%
Solomon Islands	0.414	0.594	0.548	87.2%	74.5%	50.1%	0.463	0.744	0.863	97.5%	93.4%	78.9%	0.47	0.79	1.035	98.9%	99.1%	94.6%
Fiji	0.623	0.451	0.126	72.8%	46.8%	13.8%	0.796	0.764	0.378	93.0%	79.3%	41.5%	0.848	0.922	0.679	99.1%	95.6%	74.6%
Vanuatu	0.175	0.242	0.18	81.0%	68.6%	39.1%	0.206	0.316	0.311	95.4%	89.5%	67.6%	0.214	0.346	0.406	99.1%	98.0%	88.3%
Micronesia	0.075	0.126	0.136	62.0%	64.3%	54.8%	0.108	0.173	0.196	89.3%	88.3%	79.0%	0.119	0.192	0.231	98.3%	98.0%	93.1%
Samoa	0.134	0.139	0.069	72.8%	62.3%	31.1%	0.171	0.194	0.129	92.9%	87.0%	58.1%	0.182	0.217	0.182	98.9%	97.3%	82.0%
Tonga	0.083	0.142	0.178	74.8%	82.1%	80.5%	0.105	0.168	0.212	94.6%	97.1%	95.9%	0.11	0.171	0.219	99.1%	98.8%	99.1%
Oceania	**6.442**	**8.326**	**5.543**	**20.1%**	**20.2%**	**11.7%**	**8.217**	**10.88**	**9.622**	**25.6%**	**26.4%**	**20.4%**	**12.76**	**13.53**	**13.2**	**39.8%**	**32.9%**	**27.9%**

Multination Regional Analysis

Measures of Poverty, Health, Education, Infrastructure and Governance

Poverty

Base Case: Countries in Year 2055 Descending Population Sequence	Poverty (below $5 LN) Mil People 2005	2030	2055	Percent 2005	2030	2055	Poverty (below $10 LN) Mil People 2005	2030	2055	Percent 2005	2030	2055	Poverty (below $20 LN) Mil People 2005	2030	2055	Percent 2005	2030	2055
EUROPE																		
Russia	35.6	0.095	1.38	24.8%	0.1%	1.2%	78.25	1.246	8.19	54.4%	0.9%	7.1%	117.5	8.682	28.67	81.7%	6.5%	25.0%
Poland	13.06	4.355	1.113	33.8%	11.6%	3.4%	29.31	17.26	6.653	75.8%	45.9%	20.1%	37.33	31.55	18.58	96.5%	83.9%	56.0%
Ukraine	23.65	0.511	0.001	49.7%	1.3%	0.0%	43.25	7.906	0.152	90.9%	20.4%	0.5%	47.09	27.71	3.331	99.0%	71.4%	10.4%
Romania	15.8	8.099	3.517	70.6%	39.7%	20.2%	21.6	16.62	9.964	96.6%	81.4%	57.2%	22.15	20.01	15.41	99.0%	98.0%	88.5%
Belarus	4.21	0.388	0.003	42.5%	4.1%	0.0%	8.433	2.629	0.138	85.1%	28.0%	1.6%	9.797	6.714	1.273	98.8%	71.4%	14.5%
Czech Republic	0.006	0.001	0	0.1%	0.0%	0.0%	0.47	0.133	0.03	4.6%	1.4%	0.4%	4.53	2.051	0.537	44.0%	21.2%	6.5%
Hungary	4.678	2.053	0.828	46.3%	22.3%	10.6%	9.207	6.459	3.344	91.1%	70.3%	42.9%	10.01	8.878	6.338	99.0%	96.6%	81.3%
Bulgaria	4.717	1.331	0.127	60.3%	20.9%	2.4%	7.34	4.245	1.061	93.9%	66.6%	20.0%	7.742	6.073	3.269	99.0%	95.2%	61.6%
Slovak Republic	0.02	0.004	0.002	0.4%	0.1%	0.0%	0.686	0.242	0.068	12.6%	4.4%	1.4%	3.557	2.18	0.771	65.2%	40.1%	15.9%
Moldova	4.043	2.969	0.584	95.0%	77.8%	18.2%	4.211	3.687	1.738	99.0%	96.7%	54.1%	4.211	3.776	2.787	99.0%	99.0%	86.7%
Europe-East	**105.8**	**19.81**	**7.554**	**35.2%**	**7.2%**	**3.2%**	**202.7**	**60.43**	**31.34**	**67.5%**	**22.1%**	**13.3%**	**263.9**	**117.6**	**80.97**	**87.9%**	**42.9%**	**34.4%**
United Kingdom	0.062	0.004	0	0.1%	0.0%	0.0%	1.234	0.176	0.016	2.0%	0.3%	0.0%	9.489	2.678	0.417	15.6%	4.2%	0.7%
Sweden	0	0	0	0.0%	0.0%	0.0%	0.019	0	0	0.2%	0.0%	0.0%	0.796	0.019	0	8.9%	0.2%	0.0%
Denmark	0	0	0	0.0%	0.0%	0.0%	0.008	0	0	0.1%	0.0%	0.0%	0.425	0.035	0.001	7.8%	0.6%	0.0%
Norway	0	0	0	0.0%	0.0%	0.0%	0.002	0.002	0.002	0.0%	0.0%	0.0%	0.145	0.095	0.016	3.1%	1.9%	0.3%
Ireland	0.001	0	0	0.0%	0.0%	0.0%	0.039	0.001	0	1.0%	0.1%	0.0%	0.436	0.046	0.049	10.9%	1.0%	1.0%
Finland	0	0	0	0.0%	0.0%	0.0%	0.029	0.004	0	0.6%	0.0%	0.0%	0.619	0.151	0.018	11.8%	2.8%	0.4%
Lithuania	2.087	0.483	0.018	59.7%	14.3%	0.6%	3.243	1.958	0.295	92.7%	57.9%	9.6%	3.462	3.139	1.427	99.0%	92.9%	46.7%
Latvia	1.09	0.233	0.023	46.7%	10.9%	1.3%	1.922	0.891	0.189	82.3%	41.6%	10.3%	2.274	1.693	0.707	97.3%	79.1%	38.5%
Estonia	0.679	0.11	0.005	51.5%	10.0%	0.5%	1.136	0.448	0.054	86.1%	40.7%	5.9%	1.297	0.872	0.263	98.3%	79.1%	28.6%
Iceland	0	0	0	0.0%	0.0%	0.0%	0.002	0	0	0.7%	0.0%	0.0%	0.028	0.006	0	9.6%	1.8%	0.0%
Europe-North	**3.92**	**0.83**	**0.046**	**4.1%**	**0.8%**	**0.0%**	**7.634**	**3.48**	**0.557**	**7.9%**	**3.5%**	**0.6%**	**18.97**	**8.733**	**2.897**	**19.6%**	**8.7%**	**3.0%**
Italy	0.098	0.085	0.083	0.2%	0.2%	0.2%	1.782	1.315	0.925	3.1%	2.5%	2.1%	12.09	8.66	5.322	21.1%	16.4%	12.1%
Spain	0.092	0.022	0.008	0.2%	0.1%	0.0%	1.643	0.515	0.18	4.0%	1.3%	0.5%	10.44	4.639	1.792	25.6%	11.7%	5.3%
Greece	0.029	0.011	0.002	0.3%	0.1%	0.0%	0.451	0.188	0.036	4.1%	1.7%	0.4%	2.711	1.382	0.378	24.5%	12.5%	3.8%
Portugal	0.197	0.15	0.058	1.9%	1.5%	0.6%	1.428	1.016	0.409	13.8%	9.9%	4.3%	4.744	3.561	1.69	45.8%	34.7%	17.7%
Serbia and Montenegro	7.638	4.984	0.129	93.7%	65.2%	1.8%	8.072	7.356	1.471	99.0%	96.3%	20.9%	8.072	7.563	4.788	99.0%	99.0%	68.2%
Croatia	1.866	0.648	0.017	41.6%	15.7%	0.5%	3.917	2.534	0.285	87.4%	61.4%	7.8%	4.437	3.897	1.48	99.0%	94.4%	40.5%
Bosnia and Herzegovina	3.676	3.532	1.996	91.1%	90.2%	58.8%	3.996	3.875	2.939	99.0%	99.0%	86.6%	3.996	3.875	3.314	99.0%	99.0%	97.7%
Albania	2.121	1.349	0.564	67.2%	38.7%	16.7%	2.991	2.69	1.576	94.7%	77.1%	46.7%	3.126	3.356	2.66	99.0%	96.2%	78.8%
Macedonia	0.557	0.492	0.185	27.0%	22.9%	9.0%	1.311	1.242	0.641	63.5%	57.7%	31.1%	1.866	1.875	1.316	90.4%	87.2%	63.8%
Slovenia	0.002	0	0	0.1%	0.0%	0.0%	0.078	0.023	0.003	3.9%	1.2%	0.2%	0.681	0.289	0.053	34.0%	15.2%	3.3%
Malta	0.005	0.002	0	1.3%	0.5%	0.0%	0.052	0.022	0.003	13.0%	5.2%	0.8%	0.191	0.114	0.029	47.9%	27.0%	7.3%
Europe-South	**16.28**	**11.28**	**3.041**	**11.3%**	**8.2%**	**2.6%**	**25.72**	**20.78**	**8.469**	**17.9%**	**15.1%**	**7.1%**	**52.36**	**39.21**	**22.82**	**36.4%**	**28.5%**	**19.2%**
Germany	0.003	0	0	0.0%	0.0%	0.0%	0.438	0.053	0.001	0.5%	0.1%	0.0%	9.859	2.453	0.134	11.9%	3.1%	0.2%
France	0.05	0.018	0.002	0.1%	0.0%	0.0%	1.418	0.54	0.074	2.4%	0.9%	0.1%	12.26	5.828	1.15	20.4%	9.3%	1.9%
Netherlands	0.004	0.001	0	0.0%	0.0%	0.0%	0.194	0.05	0.009	1.2%	0.3%	0.1%	2.535	1.03	0.229	15.4%	5.9%	1.4%
Belgium	0.002	0	0	0.0%	0.0%	0.0%	0.09	0.028	0.018	0.9%	0.3%	0.2%	1.134	0.574	0.292	10.9%	5.5%	3.0%
Austria	0	0	0	0.0%	0.0%	0.0%	0.035	0.008	0.002	0.4%	0.1%	0.0%	0.758	0.25	0.057	9.4%	3.3%	0.9%
Switzerland	0.001	0	0	0.0%	0.0%	0.0%	0.048	0.004	0	0.7%	0.1%	0.0%	0.648	0.131	0.017	8.9%	1.8%	0.3%
Luxembourg	0	0	0	0.0%	0.0%	0.0%	0	0	0	0.0%	0.0%	0.0%	0.011	0.002	0.003	2.4%	0.3%	0.4%
Europe-West	**0.061**	**0.02**	**0.003**	**0.0%**	**0.0%**	**0.0%**	**2.223**	**0.684**	**0.104**	**1.2%**	**0.4%**	**0.1%**	**27.21**	**10.27**	**1.883**	**14.7%**	**5.5%**	**1.1%**

Poverty

Base Case

Source: International Futures Version 5.47 March 2008

	GDP per Capita at PPP (Thousand Year 2000 $)					Gini Index (Index)					Population Growth Rate (Percent)				
	2005	2030	2055	% Chg	% An Chg	2005	2030	2055	% Chg	% An Chg	2005	2030	2055	% Chg	% An Chg
World	8.135	15.09	26.65	227.6%	2.4%	0.411	0.413	0.424	3.2%	0.1%	1.169	0.746	0.309	-73.6%	-2.6%
Africa	2.198	3.379	6.957	216.5%	2.3%	0.422	0.429	0.439	4.0%	0.1%	2.329	1.801	1.056	-54.7%	-1.6%
Americas	18.19	30.21	49.69	173.2%	2.0%	0.485	0.481	0.493	1.6%	0.0%	1.215	0.602	0.202	-83.4%	-3.5%
Asia incl Oceania	5.34	12.94	25.9	385.0%	3.2%	0.403	0.402	0.407	1.0%	0.0%	1.105	0.601	0.138	-87.5%	-4.1%
Europe	18.3	31.77	57.48	214.1%	2.3%	0.347	0.352	0.382	10.1%	0.2%	0.015	-0.308	-0.618	-4220.0%	-2.6%
World	8.135	15.09	26.65	227.6%	2.4%	0.411	0.413	0.424	3.2%	0.1%	1.169	0.746	0.309	-73.6%	-2.6%
Africa-Eastern	1.037	2.001	6.402	517.4%	3.7%	0.407	0.423	0.426	4.7%	0.1%	2.559	1.992	1.004	-60.8%	-1.9%
Africa-Middle	1.153	1.692	2.734	137.1%	1.7%	0.448	0.457	0.45	0.4%	0.0%	2.867	2.465	1.657	-42.2%	-1.1%
Africa-Northern	4.059	7.604	16.79	313.6%	2.9%	0.368	0.388	0.402	9.2%	0.2%	1.75	0.905	0.399	-77.2%	-2.9%
Africa-Southern	8.959	12.66	27.49	206.8%	2.3%	0.57	0.552	0.564	-1.1%	-0.0%	1.042	0.448	0.051	-95.1%	-5.9%
Africa-Western	1.183	2.005	3.34	182.3%	2.1%	0.436	0.43	0.453	3.9%	0.1%	2.53	1.979	1.193	-52.8%	-1.5%
Africa	2.198	3.379	6.957	216.5%	2.3%	0.422	0.429	0.439	4.0%	0.1%	2.329	1.801	1.056	-54.7%	-1.6%
America-Caribbean	5.054	10.89	24.46	384.0%	3.2%	0.49	0.504	0.519	5.9%	0.1%	1.008	0.512	0.154	-84.7%	-3.7%
America-Central	4.562	8.136	17.58	285.4%	2.7%	0.522	0.547	0.567	8.6%	0.2%	2.19	1.347	0.54	-75.3%	-2.8%
America-North	29.8	49.96	77.9	161.4%	1.9%	0.43	0.426	0.434	0.9%	0.0%	1.001	0.498	0.189	-81.1%	-3.3%
America-South	7.56	13.54	27.11	258.6%	2.6%	0.544	0.53	0.542	-0.4%	-0.0%	1.378	0.624	0.168	-87.8%	-4.1%
Americas	18.19	30.21	49.69	173.2%	2.0%	0.485	0.481	0.493	1.6%	0.0%	1.215	0.602	0.202	-83.4%	-3.5%
Asia-East	7.851	21.42	42.43	440.4%	3.4%	0.448	0.446	0.458	2.2%	0.0%	0.569	0.249	-0.327	-157.5%	-2.5%
Asia-South Central	2.772	6.81	16.05	479.0%	3.6%	0.369	0.376	0.377	2.2%	0.0%	1.475	0.816	0.424	-71.3%	-2.5%
Asia-South East	4.039	8.545	15.97	295.4%	2.8%	0.381	0.38	0.396	3.9%	0.1%	1.219	0.565	0.055	-95.5%	-6.0%
Asia-West	7.341	14.87	30.56	316.3%	2.9%	0.39	0.39	0.395	1.3%	0.0%	1.942	1.139	0.501	-74.2%	-2.7%
Oceania	20.51	35.56	61.92	201.9%	2.2%	0.39	0.382	0.409	4.9%	0.1%	1.215	0.782	0.39	-67.9%	-2.2%
Asia incl Oceania	5.34	12.94	25.9	385.0%	3.2%	0.403	0.402	0.407	1.0%	0.0%	1.105	0.601	0.138	-87.5%	-4.1%
Europe-East	8.612	19.13	30.87	258.5%	2.6%	0.378	0.374	0.401	6.1%	0.1%	-0.258	-0.475	-0.842	-226.4%	-2.5%
Europe-North	27.78	49.65	88.93	220.1%	2.4%	0.335	0.334	0.353	5.4%	0.1%	0.299	-0.011	-0.228	-176.3%	
Europe-South	20.98	30.01	49.37	135.3%	1.7%	0.347	0.369	0.41	18.2%	0.3%	0.139	-0.38	-0.788	-666.9%	
Europe-West	26.97	42.05	82.04	204.2%	2.2%	0.303	0.317	0.352	16.2%	0.3%	0.211	-0.168	-0.411	-294.8%	
Europe	18.3	31.77	57.48	214.1%	2.3%	0.347	0.352	0.382	10.1%	0.2%	0.015	-0.308	-0.618	-4220.0%	-2.6%

Poverty

Base Case: Countries in Year 2055 Descending Population Sequence	GDP per Capita at PPP (Thousand Year 2000 $)					Gini Index					Population Growth Rate (Percent)				
	2005	2030	2055	% Chg	% An Chg	2005	2030	2055	% Chg	% An Chg	2005	2030	2055	% Chg	% An Chg
AFRICA															
Ethiopia	0.911	1.453	3.805	317.7%	2.9%	0.311	0.307	0.304	-2.3%	-0.0%	2.37	1.953	1.131	-52.3%	-1.5%
Tanzania	0.656	1.926	8.652	1218.9%	5.3%	0.361	0.389	0.364	0.8%	0.0%	2.501	1.96	0.888	-64.5%	-2.0%
Uganda	1.215	3.013	12.19	903.3%	4.7%	0.443	0.484	0.489	10.4%	0.2%	3.442	2.462	0.82	-76.2%	-2.8%
Kenya	1.113	2.433	9.856	785.5%	4.5%	0.424	0.443	0.436	2.8%	0.1%	2.552	1.728	0.631	-75.3%	-2.8%
Madagascar	0.924	1.375	2.951	219.4%	2.3%	0.503	0.522	0.588	16.9%	0.3%	2.653	2.045	1.31	-50.6%	-1.4%
Mozambique	0.996	3.06	8.599	763.4%	4.4%	0.492	0.535	0.53	7.7%	0.1%	2.261	1.658	0.714	-68.4%	-2.3%
Malawi	0.611	0.957	2.694	340.9%	3.0%	0.388	0.347	0.382	-1.5%	-0.0%	2.653	2.22	1.206	-54.5%	-1.6%
Zambia	0.888	1.433	4.216	374.8%	3.2%	0.518	0.507	0.517	-0.2%	-0.0%	2.428	2.262	1.156	-52.4%	-1.5%
Zimbabwe	2.585	3.534	8.959	246.6%	2.5%	0.562	0.565	0.575	2.3%	0.0%	1.732	1.426	0.468	-73.0%	-2.6%
Burundi	0.624	0.911	2.108	237.8%	2.5%	0.328	0.294	0.31	-5.5%	-0.1%	2.842	2.373	1.505	-47.0%	-1.3%
Rwanda	1.03	1.729	4.3	317.5%	2.9%	0.478	0.5	0.521	9.0%	0.2%	2.642	1.908	0.935	-64.6%	-2.1%
Somalia	0.516	0.918	1.273	146.7%	1.8%	0.452	0.6	0.6	32.7%	0.6%	2.801	2.126	1.59	-43.2%	-1.1%
Eritrea	0.988	0.906	1.145	15.9%	0.3%	0.427	0.442	0.478	11.9%	0.2%	3.724	2.099	1.803	-51.6%	-1.4%
Mauritius	10.57	18.94	28.04	165.3%	2.0%	0.366	0.37	0.402	9.8%	0.2%	0.839	0.332	-0.157	-118.7%	
Comoros	1.721	2.125	3.927	128.2%	1.7%	0.439	0.47	0.517	17.8%	0.3%	2.288	1.703	1.017	-55.6%	-1.6%
Djibouti	1.991	2.222	3.493	75.4%	1.1%	0.45	0.461	0.476	5.8%	0.1%	1.28	1.138	0.722	-43.6%	-1.1%
Africa-Eastern	**1.037**	**2.001**	**6.402**	**517.4%**	**3.7%**	**0.407**	**0.423**	**0.426**	**4.7%**	**0.1%**	**2.559**	**1.992**	**1.004**	**-60.8%**	**-1.9%**
Congo, Dem. Rep. of the	0.618	0.991	2.236	261.8%	2.6%	0.438	0.455	0.425	-3.0%	-0.1%	3.258	2.801	1.876	-42.4%	-1.1%
Angola	1.74	2.908	3.729	114.3%	1.5%	0.432	0.425	0.466	7.9%	0.2%	2.681	2.181	1.404	-47.6%	-1.3%
Cameroon	1.996	2.139	3.136	57.1%	0.9%	0.457	0.462	0.534	16.8%	0.3%	1.964	1.798	1.195	-39.2%	-1.0%
Chad	0.988	2.141	2.764	179.8%	2.1%	0.442	0.447	0.439	-0.7%	-0.0%	2.899	2.216	1.417	-51.1%	-1.4%
Central African Republic	1.145	1.135	1.757	53.4%	0.9%	0.6	0.6	0.6	0.0%	0.0%	2.134	1.784	1.401	-34.3%	-0.8%
Congo, Rep. of	1.249	2.641	4.75	280.3%	2.7%	0.443	0.45	0.474	7.0%	0.1%	2.532	1.96	1.055	-58.3%	-1.7%
Gabon	6.103	11.12	14.18	132.3%	1.7%	0.6	0.6	0.6	0.0%	0.0%	2.278	1.161	0.432	-81.0%	-3.3%
Equatorial Guinea	5.838	12.66	12.29	110.5%	1.5%	0.41	0.339	0.319	-22.2%	-0.5%	2.482	1.302	0.428	-82.8%	-3.5%
São Tomé and Príncipe	1.879	1.811	1.975	5.1%	0.1%	0.431	0.464	0.552	28.1%	0.5%	2.243	1.402	0.633	-71.8%	-2.5%
Africa-Middle	**1.153**	**1.692**	**2.734**	**137.1%**	**1.7%**	**0.448**	**0.457**	**0.45**	**0.4%**	**0.0%**	**2.867**	**2.465**	**1.657**	**-42.2%**	**-1.1%**
Egypt	3.764	7.388	20.9	455.3%	3.5%	0.339	0.359	0.362	6.8%	0.1%	1.928	0.932	0.524	-72.8%	-2.6%
Sudan	1.736	3.924	7.327	322.1%	2.9%	0.396	0.431	0.435	9.8%	0.2%	2.12	1.377	0.629	-70.3%	-2.4%
Algeria	5.937	10.31	16.1	171.2%	2.0%	0.355	0.363	0.395	11.3%	0.2%	1.459	0.63	0.05	-96.6%	-6.5%
Morocco	3.895	5.927	12.82	229.1%	2.4%	0.402	0.426	0.464	15.4%	0.3%	1.386	0.588	0.147	-89.4%	-4.4%
Tunisia	6.895	15.26	35.15	409.8%	3.3%	0.404	0.42	0.449	11.1%	0.2%	1.031	0.52	0.031	-97.0%	-6.8%
Libya	7.803	17.91	29.51	278.2%	2.7%	0.396	0.355	0.371	-6.3%	-0.1%	1.917	0.848	0.352	-81.6%	-3.3%
Africa-Northern	**4.059**	**7.604**	**16.79**	**313.6%**	**2.9%**	**0.368**	**0.388**	**0.402**	**9.2%**	**0.2%**	**1.75**	**0.905**	**0.399**	**-77.2%**	**-2.9%**

Poverty

Base Case: Countries in Year 2055 Descending Population Sequence	GDP per Capita at PPP (Thousand Year 2000 $)					Gini Index					Population Growth Rate (Percent)				
	2005	2030	2055	% Chg	% An Chg	2005	2030	2055	% Chg	% An Chg	2005	2030	2055	% Chg	% An Chg
AFRICA continued															
South Africa	9.457	13.04	27.62	192.1%	2.2%	0.568	0.546	0.561	-1.2%	-0.0%	0.963	0.34	-0.011	-101.1%	-1.6%
Namibia	6.217	10.59	36.06	480.0%	3.6%	0.6	0.6	0.6	0.0%	0.0%	1.767	1.18	0.66	-62.6%	-2.0%
Lesotho	2.585	3.064	6.472	150.4%	1.9%	0.6	0.6	0.6	0.0%	0.0%	1.254	1.061	0.213	-83.0%	-3.5%
Botswana	9.161	21.83	46.29	405.3%	3.3%	0.6	0.6	0.6	0.0%	0.0%	1.29	0.6	0.036	-97.2%	-6.9%
Swaziland	3.989	6.811	17.08	328.2%	3.0%	0.516	0.518	0.504	-2.3%	-0.0%	2.174	1.294	0.386	-82.2%	-3.4%
Africa-Southern	**8.959**	**12.66**	**27.49**	**206.8%**	**2.3%**	**0.57**	**0.552**	**0.564**	**-1.1%**	**-0.0%**	**1.042**	**0.448**	**0.051**	**-95.1%**	**-5.9%**
Nigeria	0.988	2.094	3.044	208.1%	2.3%	0.44	0.421	0.434	-1.4%	-0.0%	2.47	1.906	1.101	-55.4%	-1.6%
Niger	0.69	0.93	1.98	187.0%	2.1%	0.51	0.494	0.522	2.4%	0.0%	3.445	2.777	1.942	-43.6%	-1.1%
Ghana	2.076	2.149	3.432	65.3%	1.0%	0.408	0.419	0.488	19.6%	0.4%	2.118	1.566	0.919	-56.6%	-1.7%
Côte d'Ivoire	1.553	2.721	5.396	247.5%	2.5%	0.446	0.457	0.46	3.1%	0.1%	2.569	1.862	0.913	-64.5%	-2.0%
Mali	0.864	1.453	3.095	258.2%	2.6%	0.411	0.422	0.444	8.0%	0.2%	2.904	2.265	1.362	-53.1%	-1.5%
Burkina Faso	1.06	1.639	4.003	277.6%	2.7%	0.402	0.4	0.449	11.7%	0.2%	2.845	2.338	1.36	-52.2%	-1.5%
Senegal	1.559	2.615	5.488	252.0%	2.5%	0.42	0.437	0.439	4.5%	0.1%	2.436	1.701	0.892	-63.4%	-2.0%
Guinea	2.017	2.862	4.426	119.4%	1.6%	0.389	0.411	0.434	11.6%	0.2%	1.909	1.949	1.174	-38.5%	-1.0%
Benin	1.042	1.554	3.813	265.9%	2.6%	0.37	0.388	0.426	15.1%	0.3%	2.654	2.047	1.208	-54.5%	-1.6%
Togo	1.332	1.426	1.776	33.3%	0.6%	0.431	0.421	0.485	12.5%	0.2%	2.662	2.08	1.35	-49.3%	-1.3%
Liberia	0.92	0.994	1.653	79.7%	1.2%	0.434	0.409	0.462	6.5%	0.1%	2.994	2.082	1.64	-45.2%	-1.2%
Sierra Leone	0.599	1.251	2.504	318.0%	2.9%	0.6	0.6	0.6	0.0%	0.0%	1.92	1.612	1.32	-31.3%	-0.7%
Mauritania	1.967	2.468	3.564	81.2%	1.2%	0.391	0.417	0.441	12.8%	0.2%	2.584	1.912	1.18	-54.3%	-1.6%
Guinea-Bissau	0.822	0.804	1.016	23.6%	0.4%	0.465	0.465	0.484	4.1%	0.1%	2.994	2.579	1.91	-36.2%	-0.9%
Gambia	1.721	2.528	4.828	180.5%	2.1%	0.482	0.503	0.522	8.3%	0.2%	2.5	1.709	1.025	-59.0%	-1.8%
Cape Verde	4.752	9.957	23.01	384.2%	3.2%	0.429	0.468	0.468	9.1%	0.2%	2.32	1.16	0.521	-77.5%	-2.9%
Africa-Western	**1.183**	**2.005**	**3.34**	**182.3%**	**2.1%**	**0.436**	**0.43**	**0.453**	**3.9%**	**0.1%**	**2.53**	**1.979**	**1.193**	**-52.8%**	**-1.5%**

Poverty

Base Case: Countries in Year 2055 Descending Population Sequence	GDP per Capita at PPP (Thousand Year 2000 $)					Gini Index (Index)					Population Growth Rate (Percent)				
	2005	2030	2055	% Chg	% An Chg	2005	2030	2055	% Chg	% An Chg	2005	2030	2055	% Chg	% An Chg
AMERICAS															
Haiti	1.527	1.715	2.877	88.4%	1.3%	0.586	0.596	0.6	2.4%	0.0%	1.712	1.324	0.726	-57.6%	-1.7%
Dominican Republic	7.347	14.47	23.05	213.7%	2.3%	0.519	0.534	0.556	7.1%	0.1%	1.453	0.592	0.01	-99.3%	-9.5%
Cuba	2.245	6.301	24.11	973.9%	4.9%	0.421	0.41	0.386	-8.3%	-0.2%	0.312	-0.329	-0.399	-227.9%	
Puerto Rico	12.32	33.21	98.18	696.9%	4.2%	0.508	0.494	0.486	-4.3%	-0.1%	0.728	0.477	0.025	-96.6%	-6.5%
Jamaica	3.855	7.123	22.19	475.6%	3.6%	0.428	0.465	0.515	20.3%	0.4%	0.902	0.306	0.042	-95.3%	-5.9%
Trinidad and Tobago	11.84	31.42	37.51	216.8%	2.3%	0.41	0.388	0.396	-3.4%	-0.1%	0.494	0.032	-0.522	-205.7%	
Bahamas	17.38	23.13	37.57	116.2%	1.6%	0.356	0.358	0.378	6.2%	0.1%	1.057	0.429	-0.025	-102.4%	
Barbados	15.53	25.77	56.57	264.3%	2.6%	0.382	0.384	0.395	3.4%	0.1%	0.47	0.109	-0.519	-210.4%	
Grenada	7.374	11.36	28.55	287.2%	2.7%	0.404	0.428	0.454	12.4%	0.2%	1.96	0.792	0.496	-74.7%	-2.7%
St. Vincent & the Grenadines	5.476	8.648	19.97	264.7%	2.6%	0.42	0.403	0.403	-4.0%	-0.1%	1.344	0.635	0.216	-83.9%	-3.6%
St. Lucia	6.493	14.7	42.7	557.6%	3.8%	0.447	0.429	0.411	-8.1%	-0.2%	0.316	-0.104	-0.51	-261.4%	
America-Caribbean	**5.054**	**10.89**	**24.46**	**384.0%**	**3.2%**	**0.49**	**0.504**	**0.519**	**5.9%**	**0.1%**	**1.008**	**0.512**	**0.154**	**-84.7%**	**-3.7%**
Guatemala	4.023	6.388	12.38	207.7%	2.3%	0.553	0.586	0.6	8.5%	0.2%	2.699	1.75	0.747	-72.3%	-2.5%
Honduras	2.993	4.204	8.002	167.4%	2.0%	0.548	0.58	0.6	9.5%	0.2%	2.268	1.416	0.556	-75.5%	-2.8%
Nicaragua	3.151	4.021	6.917	119.5%	1.6%	0.435	0.471	0.519	19.3%	0.4%	2.39	1.489	0.61	-74.5%	-2.7%
El Salvador	4.643	8.43	18.05	288.8%	2.8%	0.525	0.56	0.588	12.0%	0.2%	1.74	0.786	0.309	-82.2%	-3.4%
Costa Rica	8.796	20.75	54.64	521.2%	3.7%	0.467	0.438	0.418	-10.5%	-0.2%	1.572	0.751	0.099	-93.7%	-5.4%
Panama	6.698	19.36	56.94	750.1%	4.4%	0.564	0.541	0.521	-7.6%	-0.2%	1.456	0.765	0.083	-94.3%	-5.6%
Belize	6.33	16.63	41.87	561.5%	3.9%	0.417	0.439	0.456	9.4%	0.2%	1.963	0.908	0.27	-86.2%	-3.9%
America-Central	**4.562**	**8.136**	**17.58**	**285.4%**	**2.7%**	**0.522**	**0.547**	**0.567**	**8.6%**	**0.2%**	**2.19**	**1.347**	**0.54**	**-75.3%**	**-2.8%**
United States	37.15	63.06	95.88	158.1%	1.9%	0.41	0.408	0.416	1.5%	0.0%	0.913	0.522	0.308	-66.3%	-2.1%
Mexico	9.344	14.87	24.07	157.6%	1.9%	0.519	0.504	0.512	-1.3%	-0.0%	1.306	0.464	-0.137	-110.5%	
Canada	28.88	49.82	91.13	215.5%	2.3%	0.329	0.329	0.333	1.2%	0.0%	0.825	0.388	0.173	-79.0%	-3.1%
America-North	**29.8**	**49.96**	**77.9**	**161.4%**	**1.9%**	**0.43**	**0.426**	**0.434**	**0.9%**	**0.0%**	**1.001**	**0.498**	**0.189**	**-81.1%**	**-3.3%**
Brazil	7.353	11.71	22.6	207.4%	2.3%	0.567	0.551	0.562	-0.9%	-0.0%	1.313	0.516	0.091	-93.1%	-5.2%
Colombia	6.266	10.7	23.31	272.0%	2.7%	0.579	0.58	0.6	3.6%	0.1%	1.559	0.667	0.294	-81.1%	-3.3%
Argentina	14.14	28.94	60.37	326.9%	2.9%	0.514	0.49	0.493	-4.1%	-0.1%	1.028	0.608	0.092	-91.1%	-4.7%
Peru	5.167	9.614	17.81	244.7%	2.5%	0.5	0.502	0.518	3.6%	0.1%	1.608	0.689	0.241	-85.0%	-3.7%
Venezuela	6.818	16.82	35.03	413.8%	3.3%	0.436	0.403	0.423	-3.0%	-0.1%	1.647	0.842	0.304	-81.5%	-3.3%
Chile	10.16	24.1	49.12	383.5%	3.2%	0.577	0.556	0.555	-3.8%	-0.1%	0.934	0.528	-0.074	-107.9%	
Ecuador	3.649	5.456	7.601	108.3%	1.5%	0.448	0.445	0.486	8.5%	0.2%	1.712	0.823	0.144	-91.6%	-4.8%
Bolivia	2.509	5.45	15.38	513.0%	3.7%	0.6	0.578	0.566	-5.7%	-0.1%	1.92	1.029	0.565	-70.6%	-2.4%
Paraguay	4.079	5.587	11.47	181.2%	2.1%	0.586	0.599	0.6	2.4%	0.0%	2.358	1.432	0.679	-71.2%	-2.5%
Uruguay	10.18	22.59	47.2	363.7%	3.1%	0.446	0.433	0.431	-3.4%	-0.1%	0.533	0.327	-0.111	-120.8%	
Guyana	4.065	5.843	9.309	129.0%	1.7%	0.425	0.45	0.524	23.3%	0.4%	0.027	-0.503	-0.493	-1925.9%	
Suriname	6.406	10.53	22.49	251.1%	2.5%	0.4	0.413	0.412	3.0%	0.1%	0.592	-0.125	-0.478	-180.7%	
America-South	**7.56**	**13.54**	**27.11**	**258.6%**	**2.6%**	**0.544**	**0.53**	**0.542**	**-0.4%**	**-0.0%**	**1.378**	**0.624**	**0.168**	**-87.8%**	**-4.1%**

Multination Regional Analysis Measures of Poverty, Health, Education, Infrastructure and Governance

Poverty

Base Case: Countries in Year 2055 Descending Population Sequence	GDP per Capita at PPP (Thousand Year 2000 $)					Gini Index (Index)					Population Growth Rate (Percent)				
	2005	2030	2055	% Chg	% An Chg	2005	2030	2055	% Chg	% An Chg	2005	2030	2055	% Chg	% An Chg
ASIA INCL OCEANIA															
China	5.195	18.66	38.74	645.7%	4.1%	0.475	0.469	0.475	0.0%	0.0%	0.596	0.33	-0.287	-148.2%	
Japan	28.34	45.83	84.77	199.1%	2.2%	0.246	0.255	0.276	12.2%	0.2%	0.182	-0.598	-0.816	-548.4%	
Korea, Rep. of	18.11	43.09	77.13	325.9%	2.9%	0.322	0.322	0.341	5.9%	0.1%	0.622	-0.039	-0.742	-219.3%	
Taiwan	22.91	34.68	66.22	189.0%	2.1%	0.334	0.327	0.355	6.3%	0.1%	0.938	0.181	-0.457	-148.7%	
Korea, Dem. Rep. of	1.208	2.541	6.345	425.3%	3.4%	0.426	0.448	0.459	7.7%	0.1%	0.398	0.074	-0.028	-107.0%	
Hong Kong	30.15	46.81	60.25	99.8%	1.4%	0.436	0.422	0.454	4.1%	0.1%	1.137	0.474	0.015	-98.7%	-8.3%
Mongolia	1.748	3.129	6.957	298.0%	2.8%	0.341	0.365	0.408	19.6%	0.4%	1.458	0.626	0.067	-95.4%	-6.0%
Asia-East	**7.851**	**21.42**	**42.43**	**440.4%**	**3.4%**	**0.448**	**0.446**	**0.458**	**2.2%**	**0.0%**	**0.569**	**0.249**	**-0.327**	**-157.5%**	
India	2.822	7.384	19.89	604.8%	4.0%	0.374	0.388	0.383	2.4%	0.0%	1.347	0.6	0.292	-78.3%	-3.0%
Pakistan	2.081	3.489	6.498	212.3%	2.3%	0.305	0.302	0.305	0.0%	0.0%	2.16	1.592	0.872	-59.6%	-1.8%
Bangladesh	1.743	3.658	7.604	336.3%	3.0%	0.337	0.35	0.369	9.5%	0.2%	1.704	0.967	0.279	-83.6%	-3.6%
Iran, Islamic Rep. of	6.541	17.66	31.18	376.7%	3.2%	0.428	0.426	0.452	5.6%	0.1%	1.263	0.765	0.218	-82.7%	-3.5%
Afghanistan	0.774	0.877	1.369	76.9%	1.1%	0.438	0.415	0.436	-0.5%	-0.0%	3.069	2.589	1.902	-38.0%	-1.0%
Nepal	1.338	1.841	2.863	114.0%	1.5%	0.472	0.505	0.55	16.5%	0.3%	1.998	1.467	0.935	-53.2%	-1.5%
Uzbekistan	1.757	3.812	7.377	319.9%	2.9%	0.353	0.285	0.278	-21.2%	-0.5%	1.495	0.689	0.076	-94.9%	-5.8%
Sri Lanka	3.822	7.599	14.46	278.3%	2.7%	0.404	0.417	0.451	11.6%	0.2%	0.743	0.079	-0.292	-139.3%	
Kazakhstan	5.963	27.51	37.3	525.5%	3.7%	0.338	0.275	0.274	-18.9%	-0.4%	-0.068	-0.104	-0.489	-619.1%	
Tajikistan	1.066	2.313	4.746	345.2%	3.0%	0.334	0.278	0.303	-9.3%	-0.2%	1.502	0.997	0.158	-89.5%	-4.4%
Turkmenistan	3.995	13.36	13.75	244.2%	2.5%	0.402	0.376	0.426	6.0%	0.1%	1.45	0.784	0.068	-95.3%	-5.9%
Kyrgyzstan	1.591	2.128	3.443	116.4%	1.6%	0.314	0.296	0.335	6.7%	0.1%	1.224	0.509	-0.036	-102.9%	
Bhutan	2.931	7.857	28.45	870.7%	4.7%	0.437	0.494	0.525	20.1%	0.4%	2.109	1.226	0.825	-60.9%	-1.9%
Maldives	5.678	12.13	36.55	543.7%	3.8%	0.409	0.416	0.39	-4.6%	-0.1%	2.478	1.223	0.705	-71.5%	-2.5%
Asia-South Central	**2.772**	**6.81**	**16.05**	**479.0%**	**3.6%**	**0.369**	**0.376**	**0.377**	**2.2%**	**0.0%**	**1.475**	**0.816**	**0.424**	**-71.3%**	**-2.5%**
Indonesia	3.237	6.765	11.74	262.7%	2.6%	0.308	0.3	0.316	2.6%	0.1%	1.114	0.381	-0.139	-112.5%	
Philippines	4.311	6.829	12.67	193.9%	2.2%	0.468	0.474	0.487	4.1%	0.1%	1.906	1.007	0.326	-82.9%	-3.5%
Vietnam	2.466	7.674	17.34	603.2%	4.0%	0.362	0.37	0.374	3.3%	0.1%	0.899	0.437	0.031	-96.6%	-6.5%
Thailand	7.129	14.76	27.25	282.2%	2.7%	0.436	0.401	0.411	-5.7%	-0.1%	0.736	0.327	-0.042	-105.7%	
Myanmar	1.788	3.163	6.236	248.8%	2.5%	0.428	0.447	0.481	12.4%	0.2%	1.057	0.47	0.041	-96.1%	-6.3%
Malaysia	9.274	23.52	44.95	384.7%	3.2%	0.51	0.485	0.482	-5.5%	-0.1%	1.686	0.903	0.198	-88.3%	-4.2%
Cambodia	2.121	6.235	13.39	531.3%	3.8%	0.439	0.437	0.425	-3.2%	-0.1%	1.885	1.052	0.481	-74.5%	-2.7%
Laos	1.666	4.93	12.18	631.1%	4.1%	0.359	0.37	0.369	2.8%	0.1%	2.213	1.313	0.528	-76.1%	-2.8%
Singapore	27.83	48.08	61.63	121.5%	1.6%	0.444	0.393	0.429	-3.4%	-0.1%	1.431	0.455	0.011	-99.2%	-9.3%
Timor-Leste	1.637	2.38	4.688	186.4%	2.1%	0.436	0.418	0.48	10.1%	0.2%	3.903	1.78	1.196	-69.4%	-2.3%
Brunei	17.39	28.8	33.04	90.0%	1.3%	0.352	0.326	0.355	0.9%	0.0%	2.021	1.075	0.308	-84.8%	-3.7%
Asia-South East	**4.039**	**8.545**	**15.97**	**295.4%**	**2.8%**	**0.381**	**0.38**	**0.396**	**3.9%**	**0.1%**	**1.219**	**0.565**	**0.055**	**-95.5%**	**-6.0%**

Multination Regional Analysis

Measures of Poverty, Health, Education, Infrastructure and Governance

Poverty

Base Case: Countries in Year 2055 Descending Population Sequence	GDP per Capita at PPP (Thousand Year 2000 $)					Gini Index					Population Growth Rate (Percent)				
	2005	2030	2055	% Chg	% An Chg	2005	2030	2055	% Chg	% An Chg	2005	2030	2055	% Chg	% An Chg
ASIA INCL OCEANIA continued															
Turkey	7.567	16.15	40.02	428.9%	3.4%	0.396	0.416	0.438	10.6%	0.2%	1.371	0.658	0.093	-93.2%	-5.2%
Yemen	0.888	2.433	5.6	530.6%	3.8%	0.352	0.39	0.394	11.9%	0.2%	3.098	2.19	1.195	-61.4%	-1.9%
Iraq	2.878	6.915	14.06	388.5%	3.2%	0.415	0.351	0.329	-20.7%	-0.5%	2.581	1.549	0.694	-73.1%	-2.6%
Saudi Arabia	13.87	27.55	54.59	293.6%	2.8%	0.373	0.352	0.365	-2.1%	-0.0%	2.441	1.161	0.485	-80.1%	-3.2%
Syria	3.321	6.04	13.94	319.8%	2.9%	0.432	0.468	0.479	10.9%	0.2%	2.523	1.264	0.622	-75.3%	-2.8%
Israel	23.49	52.24	100.6	328.3%	3.0%	0.392	0.393	0.399	1.8%	0.0%	1.888	0.964	0.454	-76.0%	-2.8%
Azerbaijan	3.351	9.432	17.97	436.3%	3.4%	0.372	0.329	0.331	-11.0%	-0.2%	0.965	0.294	-0.217	-122.5%	
Jordan	4.688	12.23	46.86	899.6%	4.7%	0.385	0.365	0.328	-14.8%	-0.3%	2.273	1.005	0.506	-77.7%	-3.0%
Palestine	3.817	5.709	12.59	229.8%	2.4%	0.347	0.38	0.415	19.6%	0.4%	3.082	1.972	0.995	-67.7%	-2.2%
Oman	12.89	23.36	34.78	169.8%	2.0%	0.371	0.37	0.342	-7.8%	-0.2%	2.427	1.026	0.444	-81.7%	-3.3%
Lebanon	4.907	15.34	47.31	864.1%	4.6%	0.411	0.421	0.407	-1.0%	-0.0%	1.254	0.642	0.078	-93.8%	-5.4%
United Arab Emirates	26.53	55.55	75	182.7%	2.1%	0.337	0.312	0.343	1.8%	0.0%	1.678	0.688	-0.247	-114.7%	
Kuwait	22.75	43.13	68.53	201.2%	2.2%	0.337	0.275	0.263	-22.0%	-0.5%	2.173	1.283	0.617	-71.6%	-2.5%
Georgia	2.597	5.299	10.15	290.8%	2.8%	0.413	0.408	0.442	7.0%	0.1%	-0.64	-0.536	-0.655	-2.3%	
Armenia	3.411	9.454	17.69	418.6%	3.3%	0.36	0.361	0.365	1.4%	0.0%	0.519	-0.007	-0.421	-181.1%	
Bahrain	17.81	38.25	66.73	274.7%	2.7%	0.365	0.345	0.337	-7.7%	-0.2%	1.766	0.95	0.187	-89.4%	-4.4%
Qatar	24.27	49.18	53.91	122.1%	1.6%	0.317	0.263	0.299	-5.7%	-0.1%	1.442	0.582	-0.052	-103.6%	
Cyprus	20.6	35.11	61.27	197.4%	2.2%	0.353	0.359	0.378	7.1%	0.1%	0.61	0.075	-0.392	-164.3%	
Asia-West	**7.341**	**14.87**	**30.56**	**316.3%**	**2.9%**	**0.39**	**0.39**	**0.395**	**1.3%**	**0.0%**	**1.942**	**1.139**	**0.501**	**-74.2%**	**-2.7%**
Australia	27.21	50.51	88.73	226.1%	2.4%	0.353	0.339	0.352	-0.3%	-0.0%	1.031	0.589	0.346	-66.4%	-2.2%
Papua New Guinea	2.283	4.023	7.711	237.8%	2.5%	0.515	0.492	0.533	3.5%	0.1%	2.083	1.482	0.681	-67.3%	-2.2%
New Zealand	21.5	36.24	80.59	274.8%	2.7%	0.374	0.363	0.375	0.3%	0.0%	0.679	0.347	-0.054	-108.0%	
Solomon Islands	2.021	3.209	6.714	232.2%	2.4%	0.444	0.442	0.459	3.4%	0.1%	2.488	1.668	0.838	-66.3%	-2.2%
Fiji	5.066	9.53	21.24	319.3%	2.9%	0.429	0.417	0.424	-1.2%	-0.0%	0.934	-0.074	-0.477	-151.1%	
Vanuatu	3.17	5.283	11.37	258.7%	2.6%	0.446	0.472	0.499	11.9%	0.2%	2.357	1.5	0.666	-71.7%	-2.5%
Micronesia	6.078	7.239	11.22	84.6%	1.2%	0.403	0.443	0.521	29.3%	0.5%	2.481	1.353	0.552	-77.8%	-3.0%
Samoa	5.149	8.625	19.69	282.4%	2.7%	0.424	0.459	0.512	20.8%	0.4%	0.631	0.348	-0.36	-157.1%	
Tonga	6.493	6.983	9.423	45.1%	0.7%	0.393	0.383	0.418	6.4%	0.1%	2.077	1.34	0.557	-73.2%	-2.6%
Oceania	**20.51**	**35.56**	**61.92**	**201.9%**	**2.2%**	**0.39**	**0.382**	**0.409**	**4.9%**	**0.1%**	**1.215**	**0.782**	**0.39**	**-67.9%**	**-2.2%**

Poverty

Base Case: Countries in Year 2055 / Descending Population Sequence	GDP per Capita at PPP (Thousand Year 2000 $)					Gini Index (Index)					Population Growth Rate (Percent)				
	2005	2030	2055	% Chg	% An Chg	2005	2030	2055	% Chg	% An Chg	2005	2030	2055	% Chg	% An Chg
EUROPE															
Russia	8.553	21.96	30.37	255.1%	2.6%	0.463	0.441	0.465	0.4%	0.0%	-0.251	-0.427	-0.897	-257.4%	
Poland	11.45	20.45	36.62	219.8%	2.4%	0.339	0.346	0.379	11.8%	0.2%	0.099	-0.362	-0.722	-829.3%	
Ukraine	5.037	12.59	27.6	447.9%	3.5%	0.285	0.275	0.286	0.4%	0.0%	-0.725	-0.755	-0.908	-25.2%	
Romania	7.031	12.25	19.46	176.8%	2.1%	0.3	0.329	0.37	23.3%	0.4%	-0.122	-0.502	-0.831	-581.1%	
Belarus	6.108	16.36	49.27	706.6%	4.3%	0.31	0.33	0.348	12.3%	0.2%	-0.144	-0.224	-0.558	-287.5%	
Czech Republic	16.98	23.99	36.52	115.1%	1.5%	0.25	0.273	0.323	29.2%	0.5%	0.034	-0.487	-0.847	-2591.2%	
Hungary	14.56	23.42	36.64	151.6%	1.9%	0.267	0.295	0.354	32.6%	0.6%	-0.206	-0.532	-0.821	-298.5%	
Bulgaria	7.205	14.12	28.32	293.1%	2.8%	0.298	0.308	0.333	11.7%	0.2%	-0.71	-0.7	-0.811	-14.2%	
Slovak Republic	12.84	19.08	30.87	140.4%	1.8%	0.25	0.265	0.318	27.2%	0.5%	0.255	-0.272	-0.636	-349.4%	
Moldova	1.682	3.399	9.208	447.4%	3.5%	0.343	0.354	0.372	8.5%	0.2%	-0.143	-0.633	-0.673	-370.6%	
Europe-East	**8.612**	**19.13**	**30.87**	**258.5%**	**2.6%**	**0.378**	**0.374**	**0.401**	**6.1%**	**0.1%**	**-0.258**	**-0.475**	**-0.842**	**-226.4%**	
United Kingdom	28.31	49.53	89.54	216.3%	2.3%	0.364	0.36	0.376	3.3%	0.1%	0.327	0.007	-0.219	-167.0%	
Sweden	28.37	58.74	104.1	266.9%	2.6%	0.254	0.249	0.263	3.5%	0.1%	0.137	-0.204	-0.381	-378.1%	
Denmark	29.49	51.97	99.87	238.7%	2.5%	0.249	0.25	0.273	9.6%	0.2%	0.371	0.071	-0.058	-115.6%	
Norway	37.02	59.1	95.63	158.3%	1.9%	0.258	0.291	0.333	29.1%	0.5%	0.483	0.249	0.043	-91.1%	-4.7%
Ireland	34.59	60.33	74.23	114.6%	1.5%	0.342	0.33	0.356	4.1%	0.1%	0.925	0.454	0.145	-84.3%	-3.6%
Finland	27.91	44.71	86.18	208.8%	2.3%	0.281	0.296	0.329	17.1%	0.3%	0.248	-0.186	-0.291	-217.3%	
Lithuania	11.09	23.04	54.87	394.8%	3.2%	0.314	0.301	0.313	-0.3%	-0.0%	-0.029	-0.479	-0.669	-2206.9%	
Latvia	10.6	25.62	56.68	434.7%	3.4%	0.372	0.369	0.386	3.8%	0.1%	-0.25	-0.479	-0.89	-256.0%	
Estonia	12.47	31.7	79.2	535.1%	3.8%	0.36	0.36	0.377	4.7%	0.1%	-0.759	-0.535	-0.956	-26.0%	
Iceland	33.43	58.05	98.42	194.4%	2.2%	0.312	0.315	0.339	8.7%	0.2%	0.632	0.205	-0.216	-134.2%	
Europe-North	**27.78**	**49.65**	**88.93**	**220.1%**	**2.4%**	**0.335**	**0.334**	**0.353**	**5.4%**	**0.1%**	**0.299**	**-0.011**	**-0.228**	**-176.3%**	
Italy	25.46	32.14	48.03	88.6%	1.3%	0.356	0.382	0.43	20.8%	0.4%	0.018	-0.514	-0.929	-5261.1%	
Spain	24.33	38.13	60.32	147.9%	1.8%	0.347	0.364	0.399	15.0%	0.3%	0.225	-0.362	-0.96	-526.7%	
Greece	19.42	33.51	66.86	244.3%	2.5%	0.359	0.387	0.408	13.6%	0.3%	0.269	-0.156	-0.611	-327.1%	
Portugal	18.21	27.18	51.05	180.3%	2.1%	0.381	0.416	0.464	21.8%	0.4%	0.18	-0.101	-0.493	-373.9%	
Serbia and Montenegro	2.452	4.952	17.77	624.7%	4.0%	0.297	0.275	0.298	0.3%	0.0%	-0.02	-0.442	-0.191	-855.0%	
Croatia	10.66	18.87	49.1	360.6%	3.1%	0.282	0.295	0.323	14.5%	0.3%	-0.155	-0.434	-0.714	-360.6%	
Bosnia and Herzegovina	5.936	8.776	15.09	154.2%	1.9%	0.297	0.347	0.42	41.4%	0.7%	0.661	-0.483	-0.622	-194.1%	
Albania	4.353	8.503	16.02	268.0%	2.6%	0.323	0.366	0.421	30.3%	0.5%	0.571	0.026	-0.353	-161.8%	
Macedonia	6.365	8.345	14.64	130.0%	1.7%	0.391	0.398	0.437	11.8%	0.2%	0.484	-0.099	-0.25	-151.7%	
Slovenia	18.7	29.32	59.93	220.5%	2.4%	0.283	0.311	0.356	25.8%	0.5%	0.084	-0.438	-0.974	-1259.5%	
Malta	17.68	28.55	56.42	219.1%	2.3%	0.351	0.371	0.404	15.1%	0.3%	0.424	-0.022	-0.382	-190.1%	
Europe-South	**20.98**	**30.01**	**49.37**	**135.3%**	**1.7%**	**0.347**	**0.369**	**0.41**	**18.2%**	**0.3%**	**0.139**	**-0.38**	**-0.788**	**-666.9%**	
Germany	25.78	41.58	86.05	233.8%	2.4%	0.278	0.286	0.315	13.3%	0.3%	0.083	-0.317	-0.564	-779.5%	
France	26.74	42.4	84.76	217.0%	2.3%	0.328	0.356	0.392	19.5%	0.4%	0.337	-0.002	-0.247	-173.3%	
Netherlands	28.48	42.71	74.81	162.7%	2.0%	0.306	0.317	0.354	15.7%	0.3%	0.482	0.072	-0.168	-134.9%	
Belgium	28.21	31.77	49.77	76.4%	1.1%	0.33	0.32	0.366	10.9%	0.2%	0.191	-0.138	-0.347	-281.7%	
Austria	29.8	45.51	74.58	150.3%	1.9%	0.293	0.313	0.353	20.5%	0.4%	0.025	-0.466	-0.876	-3604.0%	
Switzerland	32.49	51.21	87.31	168.7%	2.0%	0.334	0.331	0.36	7.8%	0.2%	0.178	-0.35	-0.676	-479.8%	
Luxembourg	51.8	74.91	82.53	59.3%	0.9%	0.31	0.328	0.365	17.7%	0.3%	1.245	0.984	0.916	-26.4%	-0.6%
Europe-West	**26.97**	**42.05**	**82.04**	**204.2%**	**2.2%**	**0.303**	**0.317**	**0.352**	**16.2%**	**0.3%**	**0.211**	**-0.168**	**-0.411**	**-294.8%**	

Multination Regional Analysis

Measures of Poverty, Health, Education, Infrastructure and Governance

Poverty

Base Case
Source: International Futures
Version 5.47 March 2008

	Population Below 15 Years (Million People)					Population Above 65 Years (Million People)					Gross Domestic Product (Billion Year 2000 $)				
	2005	2030	2055	% Chg	% An Chg	2005	2030	2055	% Chg	% An Chg	2005	2030	2055	% Chg	% An Chg
World	1798	1877	1790	-0.4%	-0.0%	488.9	1066	1932	295.2%	2.8%	36460	91503	212264	482.2%	3.6%
Africa	372.2	537.4	607	63.1%	1.0%	32.68	78.13	193.8	493.0%	3.6%	719.3	2380	9584	1232.4%	5.3%
Americas	233.3	217.7	198.2	-15.0%	-0.3%	76.89	168.3	273.7	256.0%	2.6%	14226	30658	57747	305.9%	2.8%
Asia incl Oceania	1078	1031	908.3	-15.7%	-0.3%	259.3	641.6	1254	383.6%	3.2%	11470	39687	111817	874.9%	4.7%
Europe	114.2	90.25	76.21	-33.3%	-0.8%	120	177.8	210.3	75.3%	1.1%	10045	18777	33116	229.7%	2.4%
World	1798	1877	1790	-0.4%	-0.0%	488.9	1066	1932	295.2%	2.8%	36460	91503	212264	482.2%	3.6%
Africa-Eastern	125	192	205.5	64.4%	1.0%	9.089	21.93	58.09	539.1%	3.8%	81.83	374.4	2876	3414.6%	7.4%
Africa-Middle	51.38	89.75	125	143.3%	1.8%	3.498	7.142	17.83	409.7%	3.3%	44.31	138	369.6	734.1%	4.3%
Africa-Northern	61.95	65.56	57.43	-7.3%	-0.2%	8.909	22.28	57.11	541.0%	3.8%	315.5	1105	3942	1149.4%	5.2%
Africa-Southern	17.89	14.98	12.39	-30.7%	-0.7%	2.464	7.029	11.58	370.0%	3.1%	174.4	388.9	1390	697.0%	4.2%
Africa-Western	116	175.1	206.7	78.2%	1.2%	8.724	19.74	49.19	463.8%	3.5%	103.3	373.9	1006	873.9%	4.7%
Africa	372.2	537.4	607	63.1%	1.0%	32.68	78.13	193.8	493.0%	3.6%	719.3	2380	9584	1232.4%	5.3%
America-Caribbean	10.52	10.33	9.674	-8.0%	-0.2%	2.862	5.922	10.31	260.2%	2.6%	162.2	484.6	1341	726.8%	4.3%
America-Central	15.08	18.39	16.56	9.8%	0.2%	1.846	4.424	11.07	499.7%	3.6%	82.72	312.8	1103	1233.4%	5.3%
America-North	98.91	91.7	87.14	-11.9%	-0.3%	47.87	97.35	134.7	181.4%	2.1%	12469	25329	43001	244.9%	2.5%
America-South	108.7	97.28	84.8	-22.0%	-0.5%	24.32	60.57	117.6	383.6%	3.2%	1512	4532	12302	713.6%	4.3%
Americas	233.3	217.7	198.2	-15.0%	-0.3%	76.89	168.3	273.7	256.0%	2.6%	14226	30658	57747	305.9%	2.8%
Asia-East	324.2	273.1	236.4	-27.1%	-0.6%	135.2	336.2	568.3	320.3%	2.9%	8118	25888	64319	692.3%	4.2%
Asia-South Central	514.3	525.3	470	-8.6%	-0.2%	80.69	195.2	451.4	459.4%	3.5%	1018	5794	26126	2466.4%	6.7%
Asia-South East	161.3	148.1	123.5	-23.4%	-0.5%	29.95	74.96	157.3	425.2%	3.4%	834.6	3048	8205	883.1%	4.7%
Asia-West	70.64	76.26	70.07	-0.8%	-0.0%	10.04	28.04	66.91	566.4%	3.9%	962	3610	10405	981.6%	4.9%
Oceania	7.915	8.573	8.396	6.1%	0.1%	3.395	7.144	9.859	190.4%	2.2%	537	1346	2761	414.2%	3.3%
Asia incl Oceania	1078	1031	908.3	-15.7%	-0.3%	259.3	641.6	1254	383.6%	3.2%	11470	39687	111817	874.9%	4.7%
Europe-East	45.44	32.67	25.52	-43.8%	-1.1%	44.83	66.52	88.68	97.8%	1.4%	829.9	2730	5334	542.7%	3.8%
Europe-North	17.19	15.2	13.67	-20.5%	-0.5%	15.89	24.37	27.48	72.9%	1.1%	2530	4896	8524	236.9%	2.5%
Europe-South	21.56	16.31	13.66	-36.6%	-0.9%	26.15	36.99	42.51	62.6%	1.0%	2146	3560	5410	152.1%	1.9%
Europe-West	29.97	26.08	23.35	-22.1%	-0.5%	33.15	49.92	51.68	55.9%	0.9%	4540	7591	13849	205.0%	2.3%
Europe	114.2	90.25	76.21	-33.3%	-0.8%	120	177.8	210.3	75.3%	1.1%	10045	18777	33116	229.7%	2.4%

Poverty

Base Case: Countries in Year 2055 / Descending Population Sequence	Population Below 15 Years (Million People)					Population Above 65 Years (Million People)					Gross Domestic Product (Billion Year 2000 $)				
	2005	2030	2055	% Chg	% An Chg	2005	2030	2055	% Chg	% An Chg	2005	2030	2055	% Chg	% An Chg
AFRICA															
Ethiopia	31.44	47.79	55.38	76.1%	1.1%	2.291	5.585	14.13	516.8%	3.7%	10.32	38.49	246.2	2285.7%	6.5%
Tanzania	17	25.55	24.78	45.8%	0.8%	1.355	3.243	8.662	539.3%	3.8%	12.71	75.11	705	5446.8%	8.4%
Uganda	14.44	25.55	23.81	64.9%	1.0%	0.782	1.85	6.143	685.5%	4.2%	7.562	61.11	708.2	9265.2%	9.5%
Kenya	14.68	20.84	17.74	20.8%	0.4%	1.05	2.916	8.322	692.6%	4.2%	15.13	68.65	571.3	3675.9%	7.5%
Madagascar	8.043	12.66	15.49	92.6%	1.3%	0.613	1.444	3.471	466.2%	3.5%	4.92	14.16	59.47	1108.7%	5.1%
Mozambique	8.685	11.56	11.02	26.9%	0.5%	0.719	1.635	4.097	469.8%	3.5%	5.723	44.29	248.8	4247.4%	7.8%
Malawi	6.181	9.986	12.04	94.8%	1.3%	0.427	0.932	2.147	402.8%	3.3%	2.08	6.382	39.85	1815.9%	6.1%
Zambia	5.5	8.952	10.45	90.0%	1.3%	0.387	0.807	2.207	470.3%	3.5%	4.098	12.16	76.12	1757.5%	6.0%
Zimbabwe	5.404	6.767	5.822	7.7%	0.1%	0.527	1.139	2.986	466.6%	3.5%	8.658	21.71	116.6	1246.7%	5.3%
Burundi	3.356	6.002	8.097	141.3%	1.8%	0.224	0.558	1.46	551.8%	3.8%	0.781	2.582	14.5	1756.6%	6.0%
Rwanda	3.993	6.316	6.866	72.0%	1.1%	0.243	0.661	1.951	702.9%	4.3%	2.338	8.578	44.69	1811.5%	6.1%
Somalia	3.547	5.741	7.955	124.3%	1.6%	0.23	0.575	1.335	480.4%	3.6%	0.422	1.945	5.48	1198.6%	5.3%
Eritrea	1.882	3.341	5.048	168.2%	2.0%	0.113	0.245	0.588	420.4%	3.4%	0.757	1.304	3.152	316.4%	2.9%
Mauritius	0.304	0.258	0.221	-27.3%	-0.6%	0.087	0.253	0.393	351.7%	3.1%	5.464	16.49	33.14	506.5%	3.7%
Comoros	0.242	0.343	0.381	57.4%	0.9%	0.017	0.044	0.124	629.4%	4.1%	0.228	0.543	1.966	762.3%	4.4%
Djibouti	0.323	0.375	0.398	23.2%	0.4%	0.024	0.044	0.073	204.2%	2.2%	0.638	0.865	1.95	205.6%	2.3%
Africa-Eastern	**125**	**192**	**205.5**	**64.4%**	**1.0%**	**9.089**	**21.93**	**58.09**	**539.1%**	**3.8%**	**81.83**	**374.4**	**2876**	**3414.6%**	**7.4%**
Congo, Dem. Rep. of the	28.37	55.51	82.94	192.4%	2.2%	1.698	3.593	8.98	428.9%	3.4%	5.309	23	140.4	2544.6%	6.8%
Angola	7.352	11.53	14.62	98.9%	1.4%	0.43	1.069	2.69	525.6%	3.7%	12.61	41.87	80.72	540.1%	3.8%
Cameroon	6.89	9.468	11.28	63.7%	1.0%	0.648	0.955	2.376	266.7%	2.6%	12.07	18.58	45.06	273.3%	2.7%
Chad	4.407	7.17	9.126	107.1%	1.5%	0.32	0.692	1.73	440.6%	3.4%	2.165	12.37	27.12	1152.7%	5.2%
Central African Republic	1.781	2.578	3.446	93.5%	1.3%	0.181	0.334	0.701	287.3%	2.7%	0.983	1.616	4.633	371.3%	3.1%
Congo, Rep. of	1.737	2.513	2.761	59.0%	0.9%	0.129	0.313	0.896	594.6%	4.0%	3.955	13.42	32.41	719.5%	4.3%
Gabon	0.565	0.632	0.501	-11.3%	-0.2%	0.064	0.132	0.334	421.9%	3.4%	5.363	18.53	29.66	453.0%	3.5%
Equatorial Guinea	0.222	0.28	0.23	3.6%	0.1%	0.022	0.044	0.098	345.5%	3.0%	1.793	8.523	9.48	428.7%	3.4%
São Tomé and Príncipe	0.06	0.077	0.085	41.7%	0.7%	0.006	0.009	0.027	350.0%	3.1%	0.056	0.092	0.147	162.5%	1.9%
Africa-Middle	**51.38**	**89.75**	**125**	**143.3%**	**1.8%**	**3.498**	**7.142**	**17.83**	**409.7%**	**3.3%**	**44.31**	**138**	**369.6**	**734.1%**	**4.3%**
Egypt	24.7	26.41	22.44	-9.1%	-0.2%	3.624	8.876	22.94	533.0%	3.8%	119.9	446.2	2149	1692.3%	5.9%
Sudan	14.24	17.6	16.6	16.6%	0.3%	1.39	3.347	8.142	485.8%	3.6%	16.78	86.02	276.4	1547.2%	5.8%
Algeria	9.667	8.775	7.627	-21.2%	-0.5%	1.522	4.148	11.24	638.5%	4.1%	69.83	223	500.2	616.3%	4.0%
Morocco	8.984	8.738	7.166	-20.2%	-0.5%	1.474	3.504	8.561	480.8%	3.6%	40.97	100.5	347.3	747.7%	4.4%
Tunisia	2.615	2.377	2.014	-23.0%	-0.5%	0.65	1.601	3.907	501.1%	3.7%	24.15	104.5	385.8	1497.5%	5.7%
Libya	1.744	1.657	1.578	-9.5%	-0.2%	0.248	0.805	2.319	835.1%	4.6%	43.8	144.9	283.3	546.8%	3.8%
Africa-Northern	**61.95**	**65.56**	**57.43**	**-7.3%**	**-0.2%**	**8.909**	**22.28**	**57.11**	**541.0%**	**3.8%**	**315.5**	**1105**	**3942**	**1149.4%**	**5.2%**

Poverty

Base Case: Countries in Year 2055 Descending Population Sequence	Population Below 15 Years (Million People)					Population Above 65 Years (Million People)					Gross Domestic Product (Billion Year 2000 $)				
	2005	2030	2055	% Chg	% An Chg	2005	2030	2055	% Chg	% An Chg	2005	2030	2055	% Chg	% An Chg
AFRICA continued															
South Africa	15.15	11.98	9.974	-34.2%	-0.8%	2.176	6.397	10.1	364.2%	3.1%	159.9	331.4	1147	617.3%	4.0%
Namibia	0.856	0.955	0.739	-13.7%	-0.3%	0.073	0.171	0.438	500.0%	3.6%	4.228	14.99	102.9	2333.8%	6.6%
Lesotho	0.722	0.861	0.747	3.5%	0.1%	0.106	0.149	0.329	210.4%	2.3%	0.959	1.812	7.465	678.4%	4.2%
Botswana	0.693	0.572	0.466	-32.8%	-0.8%	0.067	0.206	0.442	559.7%	3.8%	7.886	35.33	106.5	1250.5%	5.3%
Swaziland	0.47	0.604	0.461	-1.9%	-0.0%	0.043	0.105	0.275	539.5%	3.8%	1.499	5.327	26.35	1657.8%	5.9%
Africa-Southern	**17.89**	**14.98**	**12.39**	**-30.7%**	**-0.7%**	**2.464**	**7.029**	**11.58**	**370.0%**	**3.1%**	**174.4**	**388.9**	**1390**	**697.0%**	**4.2%**
Nigeria	58.55	84.62	96	64.0%	1.0%	4.404	10.17	24.82	463.6%	3.5%	59.4	237.6	476.8	702.7%	4.3%
Niger	6.797	13.18	19.82	191.6%	2.2%	0.307	0.867	2.356	667.4%	4.2%	2.158	6.597	33.38	1446.8%	5.6%
Ghana	8.571	11.87	13.34	55.6%	0.9%	0.848	1.909	4.358	413.9%	3.3%	6.366	12.66	40.85	541.7%	3.8%
Côte d'Ivoire	7.828	11.84	12.61	61.1%	1.0%	0.664	1.595	4.04	508.4%	3.7%	11.2	39.02	135.1	1106.3%	5.1%
Mali	6.408	10.67	13.39	109.0%	1.5%	0.399	0.734	2.236	460.4%	3.5%	3.155	11.65	50.63	1504.8%	5.7%
Burkina Faso	6.046	10.18	12.77	111.2%	1.5%	0.399	0.8	2.509	528.8%	3.7%	3.301	11.63	66.39	1911.2%	6.2%
Senegal	4.904	7.045	7.382	50.5%	0.8%	0.385	0.852	2.396	522.3%	3.7%	5.522	19.08	74.57	1250.4%	5.3%
Guinea	3.946	5.838	6.806	72.5%	1.1%	0.35	0.713	1.666	376.0%	3.2%	3.58	11.31	34.91	875.1%	4.7%
Benin	3.619	5.648	6.531	80.5%	1.2%	0.24	0.593	1.476	515.0%	3.7%	2.751	7.748	38.76	1308.9%	5.4%
Togo	2.627	4.168	5.403	105.7%	1.5%	0.201	0.469	1.139	466.7%	3.5%	1.499	3.182	7.116	374.7%	3.2%
Liberia	1.665	2.793	3.908	134.7%	1.7%	0.088	0.211	0.52	490.9%	3.6%	0.645	1.373	4.661	622.6%	4.0%
Sierra Leone	2.171	2.791	3.216	48.1%	0.8%	0.194	0.319	0.444	128.9%	1.7%	0.97	3.204	10.87	1020.6%	5.0%
Mauritania	1.289	1.973	2.323	80.2%	1.2%	0.111	0.225	0.534	381.1%	3.2%	1.314	3.41	9.082	591.2%	3.9%
Guinea-Bissau	0.747	1.371	2.08	178.4%	2.1%	0.053	0.104	0.241	354.7%	3.1%	0.233	0.453	1.116	379.0%	3.2%
Gambia	0.597	0.854	0.939	57.3%	0.9%	0.06	0.142	0.302	403.3%	3.3%	0.524	1.64	6.369	1115.5%	5.1%
Cape Verde	0.198	0.225	0.182	-8.1%	-0.2%	0.022	0.044	0.154	600.0%	4.0%	0.658	3.372	15.76	2295.1%	6.6%
Africa-Western	**116**	**175.1**	**206.7**	**78.2%**	**1.2%**	**8.724**	**19.74**	**49.19**	**463.8%**	**3.5%**	**103.3**	**373.9**	**1006**	**873.9%**	**4.7%**

Poverty

Base Case: Countries in Year 2055 Descending Population Sequence	Population Below 15 Years (Million People)					Population Above 65 Years (Million People)					Gross Domestic Product (Billion Year 2000 $)				
	2005	2030	2055	% Chg	% An Chg	2005	2030	2055	% Chg	% An Chg	2005	2030	2055	% Chg	% An Chg
AMERICAS															
Haiti	3.235	4.381	4.753	46.9%	0.8%	0.366	0.635	1.532	318.6%	2.9%	3.769	6.264	16.87	347.6%	3.0%
Dominican Republic	2.89	2.354	1.968	-31.9%	-0.8%	0.378	1.144	2.607	589.7%	3.9%	24.74	93.11	215.7	771.9%	4.4%
Cuba	2.145	1.643	1.299	-39.4%	-1.0%	1.245	2.41	3.355	169.5%	2.0%	30.75	82.87	347.1	1028.8%	5.0%
Puerto Rico	0.87	0.791	0.725	-16.7%	-0.4%	0.495	0.922	1.342	171.1%	2.0%	72.86	221.9	595.5	717.3%	4.3%
Jamaica	0.838	0.708	0.561	-33.1%	-0.8%	0.204	0.368	0.721	253.4%	2.6%	8.723	19.77	72.17	727.4%	4.3%
Trinidad and Tobago	0.281	0.234	0.182	-35.2%	-0.9%	0.099	0.269	0.45	354.5%	3.1%	11.64	41.32	49.5	325.3%	2.9%
Bahamas	0.091	0.074	0.064	-29.7%	-0.7%	0.021	0.054	0.088	319.0%	2.9%	5.367	8.664	14.92	178.0%	2.1%
Barbados	0.054	0.046	0.039	-27.8%	-0.6%	0.028	0.065	0.089	217.9%	2.3%	2.748	6.346	15.06	448.0%	3.5%
Grenada	0.036	0.037	0.032	-11.1%	-0.2%	0.006	0.016	0.035	483.3%	3.6%	0.466	1.187	4.603	887.8%	4.7%
St. Vincent & the Grenadines	0.035	0.031	0.028	-20.0%	-0.4%	0.008	0.016	0.043	437.5%	3.4%	0.377	0.888	2.988	692.6%	4.2%
St. Lucia	0.044	0.033	0.022	-50.0%	-1.4%	0.012	0.023	0.049	308.3%	2.9%	0.781	2.248	6.593	744.2%	4.4%
America-Caribbean	**10.52**	**10.33**	**9.674**	**-8.0%**	**-0.2%**	**2.862**	**5.922**	**10.31**	**260.2%**	**2.6%**	**162.2**	**484.6**	**1341**	**726.8%**	**4.3%**
Guatemala	5.46	7.728	7.001	28.2%	0.5%	0.544	1.109	3.074	465.1%	3.5%	21.79	73.74	261.1	1098.3%	5.1%
Honduras	2.833	3.615	3.295	16.3%	0.3%	0.28	0.697	1.714	512.1%	3.7%	7.094	18.74	62.65	783.1%	4.5%
Nicaragua	2.154	2.811	2.673	24.1%	0.4%	0.186	0.486	1.355	628.5%	4.1%	4.568	11.52	35.78	683.3%	4.2%
El Salvador	2.348	2.302	1.89	-19.5%	-0.4%	0.373	0.761	1.966	427.1%	3.4%	14.58	46.59	158.1	984.4%	4.9%
Costa Rica	1.213	1.05	0.93	-23.3%	-0.5%	0.256	0.802	1.691	560.5%	3.8%	19.4	87.96	314.7	1522.2%	5.7%
Panama	0.968	0.797	0.693	-28.4%	-0.7%	0.195	0.537	1.175	502.6%	3.7%	14.21	68.84	252.2	1674.8%	5.9%
Belize	0.102	0.092	0.078	-23.5%	-0.5%	0.012	0.032	0.097	708.3%	4.3%	1.079	5.405	18.57	1621.0%	5.9%
America-Central	**15.08**	**18.39**	**16.56**	**9.8%**	**0.2%**	**1.846**	**4.424**	**11.07**	**499.7%**	**3.6%**	**82.72**	**312.8**	**1103**	**1233.4%**	**5.3%**
United States	60.89	60.25	60.61	-0.5%	-0.0%	37.87	73.33	90.61	139.3%	1.8%	11027	22066	36530	231.3%	2.4%
Mexico	32.47	26.06	21.06	-35.1%	-0.9%	5.636	14.83	33.21	489.2%	3.6%	634.3	1507	3027	377.2%	3.2%
Canada	5.54	5.396	5.477	-1.1%	-0.0%	4.362	9.188	10.89	149.7%	1.8%	807.9	1756	3443	326.2%	2.9%
America-North	**98.91**	**91.7**	**87.14**	**-11.9%**	**-0.3%**	**47.87**	**97.35**	**134.7**	**181.4%**	**2.1%**	**12469**	**25329**	**43001**	**244.9%**	**2.5%**
Brazil	51.69	44.69	39.29	-24.0%	-0.5%	11.67	30.1	57.18	390.0%	3.2%	669.5	1656	4626	591.0%	3.9%
Colombia	14.17	12.93	11.24	-20.7%	-0.5%	2.385	7.047	14.21	495.8%	3.6%	99.16	313.8	1143	1052.7%	5.0%
Argentina	10.31	8.877	7.83	-24.1%	-0.5%	4.084	7.467	13.05	219.5%	2.4%	367.2	1201	2992	714.8%	4.3%
Peru	9.097	8.288	7.122	-21.7%	-0.5%	1.506	3.767	8.529	466.3%	3.5%	65.32	217.8	601.2	820.4%	4.5%
Venezuela	8.268	7.126	6.389	-22.7%	-0.5%	1.375	4.318	9.612	599.1%	4.0%	151.9	566.2	1413	830.2%	4.6%
Chile	4.05	3.526	3.053	-24.6%	-0.6%	1.339	3.585	5.983	346.8%	3.0%	92.82	383.3	964.4	939.0%	4.8%
Ecuador	4.295	4.371	3.668	-14.6%	-0.3%	0.769	1.864	3.683	378.9%	3.2%	20.55	49.46	86.7	321.9%	2.9%
Bolivia	3.446	3.655	2.966	-13.9%	-0.3%	0.424	0.934	2.408	467.9%	3.5%	9.723	40.85	200.3	1960.1%	6.2%
Paraguay	2.252	2.888	2.487	10.4%	0.2%	0.228	0.656	1.601	602.2%	4.0%	8.012	21.5	83.2	938.4%	4.8%
Uruguay	0.817	0.681	0.578	-29.3%	-0.7%	0.473	0.687	1.093	131.1%	1.7%	25.46	77.62	181.1	611.3%	4.0%
Guyana	0.225	0.147	0.103	-54.2%	-1.6%	0.039	0.08	0.127	225.6%	2.4%	0.781	1.369	2.683	243.5%	2.5%
Suriname	0.136	0.1	0.07	-48.5%	-1.3%	0.029	0.06	0.11	279.3%	2.7%	1.151	2.714	7.863	583.1%	3.9%
America-South	**108.7**	**97.28**	**84.8**	**-22.0%**	**-0.5%**	**24.32**	**60.57**	**117.6**	**383.6%**	**3.2%**	**1512**	**4532**	**12302**	**713.6%**	**4.3%**

Poverty

Base Case: Countries in Year 2055 Descending Population Sequence	Population Below 15 Years (Million People)					Population Above 65 Years (Million People)					Gross Domestic Product (Billion Year 2000 $)				
	2005	2030	2055	% Chg	% An Chg	2005	2030	2055	% Chg	% An Chg	2005	2030	2055	% Chg	% An Chg
ASIA INCL OCEANIA															
China	284.4	241.5	209.8	-26.2%	-0.6%	100.2	275.9	499.4	398.4%	3.3%	1899	15728	48828	2471.2%	6.7%
Japan	18.13	13.76	11.42	-37.0%	-0.9%	25.64	36.36	36.22	41.3%	0.7%	4992	6874	9680	93.9%	1.3%
Korea, Rep. of	9.465	7.131	5.811	-38.6%	-1.0%	4.616	12.57	16.6	259.6%	2.6%	635.5	2054	3593	465.4%	3.5%
Taiwan	4.755	4.013	3.612	-24.0%	-0.5%	2.233	5.978	7.816	250.0%	2.5%	359.5	790.6	1557	333.1%	3.0%
Korea, Dem. Rep. of	5.636	5.036	4.207	-25.4%	-0.6%	1.609	2.843	4.612	186.6%	2.1%	24.13	46.44	119.8	396.5%	3.3%
Hong Kong	1.049	0.936	0.994	-5.2%	-0.1%	0.869	2.275	2.906	234.4%	2.4%	207.5	391.3	528.1	154.5%	1.9%
Mongolia	0.79	0.766	0.622	-21.3%	-0.5%	0.103	0.269	0.693	572.8%	3.9%	1.219	3.78	13.17	980.4%	4.9%
Asia-East	**324.2**	**273.1**	**236.4**	**-27.1%**	**-0.6%**	**135.2**	**336.2**	**568.3**	**320.3%**	**2.9%**	**8118**	**25888**	**64319**	**692.3%**	**4.2%**
India	342.8	316.4	260.3	-24.1%	-0.5%	59.37	142.8	322	442.4%	3.4%	645.7	3877	20578	3086.9%	7.2%
Pakistan	58.26	81.97	85.34	46.5%	0.8%	6.046	14.11	37.01	512.1%	3.7%	92.78	327.3	1108	1094.2%	5.1%
Bangladesh	49.14	52.56	43.51	-11.5%	-0.2%	5.325	14.28	34.28	543.8%	3.8%	61.36	260.7	901.1	1368.5%	5.5%
Iran, Islamic Rep. of	19.45	17.68	15.42	-20.7%	-0.5%	3.148	9.065	27.67	779.0%	4.4%	132.4	843.7	2510	1795.8%	6.1%
Afghanistan	11.49	21.27	31.92	177.8%	2.1%	0.743	1.669	4.061	446.6%	3.5%	3.393	8.09	27.4	707.5%	4.3%
Nepal	10.47	13.87	15.74	50.3%	0.8%	1.029	2.196	4.821	368.5%	3.1%	6.295	16.71	46.59	640.1%	4.1%
Uzbekistan	8.598	8.585	7.082	-17.6%	-0.4%	1.304	3.02	6.908	429.8%	3.4%	17.93	68.27	178.9	897.8%	4.7%
Sri Lanka	4.791	4.095	3.384	-29.4%	-0.7%	1.505	3.314	5.696	278.5%	2.7%	20.23	68.18	187.5	826.8%	4.6%
Kazakhstan	3.364	2.681	2.026	-39.8%	-1.0%	1.354	2.879	4.488	231.5%	2.4%	29.19	270	455.9	1461.8%	5.7%
Tajikistan	2.496	2.775	2.251	-9.8%	-0.2%	0.253	0.578	1.455	475.1%	3.6%	1.558	7.056	23.15	1385.9%	5.5%
Turkmenistan	1.523	1.383	1.217	-20.1%	-0.4%	0.235	0.633	1.58	572.3%	3.9%	4.085	35.59	50.5	1136.2%	5.2%
Kyrgyzstan	1.576	1.562	1.387	-12.0%	-0.3%	0.333	0.62	1.131	239.6%	2.5%	1.643	3.352	7.718	369.8%	3.1%
Bhutan	0.255	0.305	0.249	-2.4%	-0.0%	0.032	0.067	0.2	525.0%	3.7%	0.64	4.293	30.1	4603.1%	8.0%
Maldives	0.133	0.149	0.123	-7.5%	-0.2%	0.012	0.031	0.103	758.3%	4.4%	0.842	4.153	21.37	2438.0%	6.7%
Asia-South Central	**514.3**	**525.3**	**470**	**-8.6%**	**-0.2%**	**80.69**	**195.2**	**451.4**	**459.4%**	**3.5%**	**1018**	**5794**	**26126**	**2466.4%**	**6.7%**
Indonesia	61.54	50.76	42.72	-30.6%	-0.7%	12.45	28.94	60.53	386.2%	3.2%	207.4	766.8	1869	801.2%	4.5%
Philippines	29.67	33.29	26.63	-10.2%	-0.2%	3.313	9.035	21.89	560.7%	3.8%	93.76	299.2	967.3	931.7%	4.8%
Vietnam	23.1	19.8	16.67	-27.8%	-0.7%	4.621	10.96	26.99	484.1%	3.6%	44.65	313.8	1217	2625.6%	6.8%
Thailand	15.16	13.18	11.53	-23.9%	-0.5%	4.622	12.36	20.38	340.9%	3.0%	156.7	578.7	1612	928.7%	4.8%
Myanmar	14.89	14.13	11.44	-23.2%	-0.5%	2.578	5.904	11.77	356.6%	3.1%	85.8	153.7	306.7	257.5%	2.6%
Malaysia	8.169	6.661	5.957	-27.1%	-0.6%	1.218	4.354	8.909	631.4%	4.1%	113.3	603	1599	1311.3%	5.4%
Cambodia	5.093	5.811	4.562	-10.4%	-0.2%	0.499	1.424	3.601	621.6%	4.0%	5.491	44.3	182.7	3227.3%	7.3%
Laos	2.381	2.904	2.292	-3.7%	-0.1%	0.23	0.514	1.361	491.7%	3.6%	2.289	18.11	87.54	3724.4%	7.6%
Singapore	0.865	0.77	0.738	-14.7%	-0.3%	0.372	1.309	1.573	322.8%	2.9%	119.7	255.7	339.4	183.5%	2.1%
Timor-Leste	0.362	0.686	0.833	130.1%	1.7%	0.033	0.083	0.186	463.6%	3.5%	0.402	1.272	5.199	1193.3%	5.3%
Brunei	0.113	0.096	0.093	-17.7%	-0.4%	0.012	0.071	0.145	1108.3%	5.1%	4.968	13.76	19.5	292.5%	2.8%
Asia-South East	**161.3**	**148.1**	**123.5**	**-23.4%**	**-0.5%**	**29.95**	**74.96**	**157.3**	**425.2%**	**3.4%**	**834.6**	**3048**	**8205**	**883.1%**	**4.7%**

Poverty

Base Case: Countries in Year 2055 / Descending Population Sequence	Population Below 15 Years (Million People)					Population Above 65 Years (Million People)					Gross Domestic Product (Billion Year 2000 $)				
	2005	2030	2055	% Chg	% An Chg	2005	2030	2055	% Chg	% An Chg	2005	2030	2055	% Chg	% An Chg
ASIA INCL OCEANIA continued															
Turkey	21.16	17.73	15.49	-26.8%	-0.6%	4.169	11.5	25.93	522.0%	3.7%	267.1	1059	3678	1277.0%	5.4%
Yemen	9.55	15.47	16.9	77.0%	1.1%	0.505	1.418	4.587	808.3%	4.5%	11.09	63.2	240.9	2072.2%	6.4%
Iraq	10.87	14.04	11.55	6.3%	0.1%	0.773	2.149	6.634	758.2%	4.4%	32.18	181.7	630	1857.7%	6.1%
Saudi Arabia	8.845	8.229	7.807	-11.7%	-0.2%	0.705	3.125	8.136	1054.0%	5.0%	229.1	887.1	2380	938.8%	4.8%
Syria	7.015	8.289	7.09	1.1%	0.0%	0.615	1.77	5.957	868.6%	4.6%	22.31	86.77	371.5	1565.2%	5.8%
Israel	1.942	1.73	1.726	-11.1%	-0.2%	0.702	1.437	2.486	254.1%	2.6%	132.4	457.8	1079	715.0%	4.3%
Azerbaijan	2.196	1.797	1.48	-32.6%	-0.8%	0.626	1.513	2.773	343.0%	3.0%	8.566	49.42	134.7	1472.5%	5.7%
Jordan	2.052	1.957	1.735	-15.4%	-0.3%	0.182	0.564	2.014	1006.6%	4.9%	11.42	66.67	418.8	3567.3%	7.5%
Palestine	1.531	2.217	1.961	28.1%	0.5%	0.113	0.294	0.912	707.1%	4.3%	4.925	16.89	76.58	1454.9%	5.6%
Oman	0.952	1.046	0.926	-2.7%	-0.1%	0.07	0.371	1.025	1364.3%	5.5%	23.5	84.7	174.2	641.3%	4.1%
Lebanon	1.042	0.863	0.739	-29.1%	-0.7%	0.273	0.574	1.319	383.2%	3.2%	20.19	94.23	303.9	1405.2%	5.6%
United Arab Emirates	0.819	0.731	0.69	-15.8%	-0.3%	0.056	0.837	1.46	2507.1%	6.7%	103.4	280.8	384.4	271.8%	2.7%
Kuwait	0.623	0.619	0.687	10.3%	0.2%	0.054	0.588	1.105	1946.3%	6.2%	50.27	151	303.3	503.3%	3.7%
Georgia	0.851	0.553	0.438	-48.5%	-1.3%	0.682	0.801	0.916	34.3%	0.6%	4.248	10.01	21.32	401.9%	3.3%
Armenia	0.678	0.547	0.445	-34.4%	-0.8%	0.385	0.59	0.92	139.0%	1.8%	3.216	16.2	40.78	1168.0%	5.2%
Bahrain	0.2	0.17	0.17	-15.0%	-0.3%	0.023	0.157	0.289	1156.5%	5.2%	10.6	35.99	74.45	602.4%	4.0%
Qatar	0.167	0.141	0.131	-21.6%	-0.5%	0.014	0.161	0.204	1357.1%	5.5%	16.79	43.63	48.43	188.4%	2.1%
Cyprus	0.144	0.124	0.105	-27.1%	-0.6%	0.089	0.184	0.236	165.2%	2.0%	10.63	24.94	44.51	318.7%	2.9%
Asia-West	**70.64**	**76.26**	**70.07**	**-0.8%**	**-0.0%**	**10.04**	**28.04**	**66.91**	**566.4%**	**3.9%**	**962**	**3610**	**10405**	**981.6%**	**4.9%**
Australia	3.982	4.051	4.172	4.8%	0.1%	2.65	5.446	7.002	164.2%	2.0%	467.4	1173	2324	397.2%	3.3%
Papua New Guinea	2.376	2.982	2.871	20.8%	0.4%	0.155	0.439	1.125	625.8%	4.0%	3.755	13.78	47.89	1175.4%	5.2%
New Zealand	0.846	0.775	0.706	-16.5%	-0.4%	0.517	1.066	1.297	150.9%	1.9%	62.74	150.5	361.4	476.0%	3.6%
Solomon Islands	0.192	0.262	0.263	37.0%	0.6%	0.012	0.03	0.1	733.3%	4.3%	0.361	1.095	4.101	1036.0%	5.0%
Fiji	0.277	0.221	0.15	-45.8%	-1.2%	0.035	0.105	0.193	451.4%	3.5%	1.823	5.179	15.5	750.2%	4.4%
Vanuatu	0.085	0.109	0.096	12.9%	0.2%	0.007	0.02	0.054	671.4%	4.2%	0.28	0.919	3.537	1163.2%	5.2%
Micronesia	0.045	0.059	0.051	13.3%	0.3%	0.004	0.011	0.028	600.0%	4.0%	0.233	0.525	1.406	503.4%	3.7%
Samoa	0.073	0.065	0.04	-45.2%	-1.2%	0.009	0.017	0.033	266.7%	2.6%	0.285	0.811	2.941	931.9%	4.8%
Tonga	0.039	0.05	0.047	20.5%	0.4%	0.007	0.011	0.028	300.0%	2.8%	0.166	0.339	0.809	387.3%	3.2%
Oceania	**7.915**	**8.573**	**8.396**	**6.1%**	**0.1%**	**3.395**	**7.144**	**9.859**	**190.4%**	**2.2%**	**537**	**1346**	**2761**	**414.2%**	**3.3%**

Poverty

Base Case: Countries in Year 2055 / Descending Population Sequence	Population Below 15 Years (Million People)					Population Above 65 Years (Million People)					Gross Domestic Product (Billion Year 2000 $)				
	2005	2030	2055	% Chg	% An Chg	2005	2030	2055	% Chg	% An Chg	2005	2030	2055	% Chg	% An Chg
EUROPE															
Russia	21.28	15.86	12.5	-41.3%	-1.1%	20.94	32.72	43.52	107.8%	1.5%	351.3	1528	2494	609.9%	4.0%
Poland	6.395	4.828	3.791	-40.7%	-1.0%	5.197	9.098	12.19	134.6%	1.7%	198.2	492.9	1046	427.7%	3.4%
Ukraine	6.903	4.167	3.064	-55.6%	-1.6%	8.104	9.94	12.83	58.3%	0.9%	44.1	165.6	533.9	1110.7%	5.1%
Romania	3.465	2.508	1.932	-44.2%	-1.2%	3.43	4.267	6.297	83.6%	1.2%	48.94	114	216.3	342.0%	3.0%
Belarus	1.512	1.172	0.995	-34.2%	-0.8%	1.515	2.165	3.215	112.2%	1.5%	18.04	82.77	349.2	1835.7%	6.1%
Czech Republic	1.496	1.054	0.837	-44.1%	-1.2%	1.528	2.516	3.174	107.7%	1.5%	67.89	125.3	228.5	238.0%	2.5%
Hungary	1.593	1.155	0.905	-43.2%	-1.1%	1.608	2.225	2.692	67.4%	1.0%	57.76	122.6	228.1	294.9%	2.8%
Bulgaria	1.081	0.708	0.553	-48.8%	-1.3%	1.38	1.678	2.08	50.7%	0.8%	16.07	40.7	108	572.1%	3.9%
Slovak Republic	0.927	0.689	0.548	-40.9%	-1.0%	0.671	1.24	1.743	159.8%	1.9%	25.71	53.74	112.2	336.4%	3.0%
Moldova	0.785	0.527	0.394	-49.8%	-1.4%	0.457	0.665	0.942	106.1%	1.5%	1.817	4.656	16.93	831.8%	4.6%
Europe-East	**45.44**	**32.67**	**25.52**	**-43.8%**	**-1.1%**	**44.83**	**66.52**	**88.68**	**97.8%**	**1.4%**	**829.9**	**2730**	**5334**	**542.7%**	**3.8%**
United Kingdom	10.86	9.651	8.69	-20.0%	-0.4%	10.15	15.46	17.35	70.9%	1.1%	1600	3079	5434	239.6%	2.5%
Sweden	1.506	1.286	1.099	-27.0%	-0.6%	1.623	2.382	2.52	55.3%	0.9%	270.1	552.5	881.4	226.3%	2.4%
Denmark	1.016	0.906	0.844	-16.9%	-0.4%	0.857	1.357	1.421	65.8%	1.0%	169	306.6	570.9	237.8%	2.5%
Norway	0.896	0.834	0.79	-11.8%	-0.3%	0.712	1.144	1.311	84.1%	1.2%	184.6	315.3	509.2	175.8%	2.1%
Ireland	0.811	0.805	0.798	-1.6%	-0.0%	0.468	0.849	1.281	173.7%	2.0%	124.2	270.8	364.4	193.4%	2.2%
Finland	0.904	0.818	0.729	-19.4%	-0.4%	0.854	1.415	1.376	61.1%	1.0%	124.8	232.7	422	213.1%	2.3%
Lithuania	0.59	0.455	0.367	-37.8%	-0.9%	0.553	0.817	1.074	94.2%	1.3%	16.42	51.81	147.2	796.5%	4.5%
Latvia	0.339	0.257	0.202	-40.4%	-1.0%	0.409	0.556	0.708	73.1%	1.1%	11.61	40.64	94.98	718.1%	4.3%
Estonia	0.195	0.129	0.107	-45.1%	-1.2%	0.235	0.322	0.35	48.9%	0.8%	7.94	26.74	66.59	738.7%	4.3%
Iceland	0.064	0.056	0.049	-23.4%	-0.5%	0.035	0.069	0.087	148.6%	1.8%	10.52	20.01	32.93	213.0%	2.3%
Europe-North	**17.19**	**15.2**	**13.67**	**-20.5%**	**-0.5%**	**15.89**	**24.37**	**27.48**	**72.9%**	**1.1%**	**2530**	**4896**	**8524**	**236.9%**	**2.5%**
Italy	7.977	5.807	4.798	-39.9%	-1.0%	11.67	15.78	16.21	38.9%	0.7%	1132	1541	2003	76.9%	1.1%
Spain	5.841	4.306	3.627	-37.9%	-0.9%	7.168	10.8	13.02	81.6%	1.2%	677.7	1315	1867	175.5%	2.0%
Greece	1.599	1.274	1.131	-29.3%	-0.7%	2.089	3.005	3.732	78.7%	1.2%	142.3	316.6	632	344.1%	3.0%
Portugal	1.684	1.376	1.222	-27.4%	-0.6%	1.797	2.507	3.125	73.9%	1.1%	117.2	221	451.9	285.6%	2.7%
Serbia and Montenegro	1.487	1.213	1.004	-32.5%	-0.8%	1.19	1.427	1.935	62.6%	1.0%	10.92	24.22	106.5	875.3%	4.7%
Croatia	0.697	0.531	0.426	-38.9%	-1.0%	0.796	1.087	1.318	65.6%	1.0%	23.21	53.22	158.9	584.6%	3.9%
Bosnia and Herzegovina	0.665	0.5	0.4	-39.8%	-1.0%	0.563	0.842	1.08	91.8%	1.3%	6.454	12.77	28.02	334.1%	3.0%
Albania	0.838	0.663	0.516	-38.4%	-1.0%	0.267	0.524	0.83	210.9%	2.3%	4.805	14.79	37.59	682.3%	4.2%
Macedonia	0.418	0.358	0.309	-26.1%	-0.6%	0.233	0.37	0.525	125.3%	1.6%	4.019	6.991	17.14	326.5%	2.9%
Slovenia	0.281	0.213	0.174	-38.1%	-1.0%	0.323	0.539	0.61	88.9%	1.3%	22.88	45.1	87.88	284.1%	2.7%
Malta	0.072	0.065	0.057	-20.8%	-0.5%	0.055	0.107	0.124	125.5%	1.6%	4.149	9.386	20.48	393.6%	3.2%
Europe-South	**21.56**	**16.31**	**13.66**	**-36.6%**	**-0.9%**	**26.15**	**36.99**	**42.51**	**62.6%**	**1.0%**	**2146**	**3560**	**5410**	**152.1%**	**1.9%**
Germany	11.89	10.04	8.895	-25.2%	-0.6%	16.02	23.02	23.11	44.3%	0.7%	1969	3261	6092	209.4%	2.3%
France	10.84	9.831	8.93	-17.6%	-0.4%	10.23	15.57	16.93	65.5%	1.0%	1429	2561	5000	249.9%	2.5%
Netherlands	2.973	2.668	2.472	-16.9%	-0.4%	2.393	4.346	4.57	91.0%	1.3%	401.9	700.3	1214	202.1%	2.2%
Belgium	1.744	1.535	1.377	-21.0%	-0.5%	1.859	2.681	2.773	49.2%	0.8%	249.2	310.3	463.7	86.1%	1.2%
Austria	1.239	0.946	0.761	-38.6%	-1.0%	1.383	2.137	2.168	56.8%	0.9%	208.4	324.8	456.4	119.0%	1.6%
Switzerland	1.204	0.962	0.797	-33.8%	-0.8%	1.198	2.041	1.957	63.4%	1.0%	258.4	389.5	562.3	117.6%	1.6%
Luxembourg	0.088	0.1	0.12	36.4%	0.6%	0.068	0.124	0.16	135.3%	1.7%	23.66	43.88	60	153.6%	1.9%
Europe-West	**29.97**	**26.08**	**23.35**	**-22.1%**	**-0.5%**	**33.15**	**49.92**	**51.68**	**55.9%**	**0.9%**	**4540**	**7591**	**13849**	**205.0%**	**2.3%**

Multination Regional Analysis

Measures of Poverty, Health, Education, Infrastructure and Governance

Base Case
Source: International Futures
Version 5.47 March 2008

Poverty

	GDP at PPP (Billion Year 2000 $)				
	2005	2030	2055	% Chg	% An Chg
World	52340	124123	251825	381.1%	3.2%
Africa	1990	5144	15234	665.5%	4.2%
Americas	16153	33338	60295	273.3%	2.7%
Asia incl Oceania	20900	63473	140539	572.4%	3.9%
Europe	13297	22167	35757	168.9%	2.0%
World	52340	124123	251825	381.1%	3.2%
Africa-Eastern	295.6	1023	4784	1518.4%	5.7%
Africa-Middle	128.4	363.4	991.2	672.0%	4.2%
Africa-Northern	768.7	2018	5261	584.4%	3.9%
Africa-Southern	482.6	802.6	1864	286.2%	2.7%
Africa-Western	314.4	936.8	2334	642.4%	4.1%
Africa	1990	5144	15234	665.5%	4.2%
America-Caribbean	191.9	499.2	1226	538.9%	3.8%
America-Central	183.3	510.1	1404	666.0%	4.2%
America-North	12937	25862	43394	235.4%	2.4%
America-South	2841	6466	14271	402.3%	3.3%
Americas	16153	33338	60295	273.3%	2.7%
Asia-East	12098	37001	73809	510.1%	3.7%
Asia-South Central	4383	14580	40399	821.7%	4.5%
Asia-South East	2223	5891	11921	436.3%	3.4%
Asia-West	1537	4538	11485	647.2%	4.1%
Oceania	658.6	1464	2926	344.3%	3.0%
Asia incl Oceania	20900	63473	140539	572.4%	3.9%
Europe-East	2586	5243	7269	181.1%	2.1%
Europe-North	2684	4974	8561	219.0%	2.3%
Europe-South	3018	4125	5879	94.8%	1.3%
Europe-West	5008	7826	14048	180.5%	2.1%
Europe	13297	22167	35757	168.9%	2.0%

Health

	Life Expectancy at Birth (Years)					Infant Mortality (Per Thousand)				
	2005	2030	2055	% Chg	% An Chg	2005	2030	2055	% Chg	% An Chg
World	67.06	74.52	80.13	19.5%	0.4%	46.72	32.4	20.63	-55.8%	-1.6%
Africa	48.72	61.74	68.24	40.1%	0.7%	85.64	70.38	50.49	-41.0%	-1.1%
Americas	73.89	78.54	83.53	13.0%	0.2%	21.51	14.66	7.152	-66.8%	-2.2%
Asia incl Oceania	68.25	76.66	83.63	22.5%	0.4%	50.42	28.36	13.51	-73.2%	-2.6%
Europe	75.22	80.97	84.79	12.7%	0.2%	9.149	5.932	3.991	-56.4%	-1.6%
World	67.06	74.52	80.13	19.5%	0.4%	46.72	32.4	20.63	-55.8%	-1.6%
Africa-Eastern	44.48	61.95	68.68	54.4%	0.9%	93.58	75.4	48.14	-48.6%	-1.3%
Africa-Middle	41.43	53.2	61.55	48.6%	0.8%	90.19	73.72	55.82	-38.1%	-1.0%
Africa-Northern	67.19	73.72	81.9	21.9%	0.4%	49.2	32.85	14.48	-70.6%	-2.4%
Africa-Southern	40.56	65.48	74.59	83.9%	1.2%	38.12	29.41	17.56	-53.9%	-1.5%
Africa-Western	44.81	58.11	64.5	43.9%	0.7%	110.8	90.22	69.59	-37.2%	-0.9%
Africa	48.72	61.74	68.24	40.1%	0.7%	85.64	70.38	50.49	-41.0%	-1.1%
America-Caribbean	66.48	72.53	78.12	17.5%	0.3%	30.29	26.27	19.77	-34.7%	-0.8%
America-Central	69.15	73.62	79.75	15.3%	0.3%	34.44	26.7	15.56	-54.8%	-1.6%
America-North	77	80.4	83.87	8.9%	0.2%	11.76	8.146	4.522	-61.5%	-1.9%
America-South	71.55	77.73	84.26	17.8%	0.3%	30.49	19.04	7.457	-75.5%	-2.8%
Americas	73.89	78.54	83.53	13.0%	0.2%	21.51	14.66	7.152	-66.8%	-2.2%
Asia-East	72.67	83.21	88.44	21.7%	0.4%	34.11	9.066	3.552	-89.6%	-4.4%
Asia-South Central	64.01	72.24	81.3	27.0%	0.5%	70.31	44.19	19.77	-71.9%	-2.5%
Asia-South East	67.06	74.09	80.9	20.6%	0.4%	42.71	28.11	15.1	-64.6%	-2.1%
Asia-West	69.77	76.24	82.65	18.5%	0.3%	45.11	28.68	14.53	-67.8%	-2.2%
Oceania	74.93	78.15	81.42	8.7%	0.2%	19.99	17.1	12.8	-36.0%	-0.9%
Asia incl Oceania	68.25	76.66	83.63	22.5%	0.4%	50.42	28.36	13.51	-73.2%	-2.6%
Europe-East	70.18	79.05	85.02	21.1%	0.4%	14.03	7.838	4.296	-69.4%	-2.3%
Europe-North	78.46	81.87	84.27	7.4%	0.1%	5.751	4.548	3.818	-33.6%	-0.8%
Europe-South	78.77	82.42	85.37	8.4%	0.2%	6.952	5.635	3.998	-42.5%	-1.1%
Europe-West	78.93	82.24	84.35	6.9%	0.1%	4.733	4.091	3.664	-22.6%	-0.5%
Europe	75.22	80.97	84.79	12.7%	0.2%	9.149	5.932	3.991	-56.4%	-1.6%

Multination Regional Analysis

Measures of Poverty, Health, Education, Infrastructure and Governance

Poverty

Health

Base Case: Countries in Year 2055 Descending Population Sequence	GDP at PPP Billion Year 2000 $					Life Expectancy at Birth Years					Infant Mortality Per Thousand				
	2005	2030	2055	% Chg	% An Chg	2005	2030	2055	% Chg	% An Chg	2005	2030	2055	% Chg	% An Chg
AFRICA															
Ethiopia	65.88	185.5	718.7	990.9%	4.9%	44.35	58.39	65.37	47.4%	0.8%	103.1	84.86	55.72	-46.0%	-1.2%
Tanzania	25.93	134.6	867.4	3245.2%	7.3%	43.25	66.96	75.83	75.3%	1.1%	99.63	70.85	32.44	-67.4%	-2.2%
Uganda	35.1	185.6	1133	3127.9%	7.2%	44.99	67.32	72.96	62.2%	1.0%	83.8	64.2	33.25	-60.3%	-1.8%
Kenya	38.79	147	792.5	1943.1%	6.2%	48.87	68.07	75.36	54.2%	0.9%	63.34	47.89	23.48	-62.9%	-2.0%
Madagascar	17.09	46.22	151.4	785.9%	4.5%	55.11	59.8	67.16	21.9%	0.4%	84.89	74.02	52.99	-37.6%	-0.9%
Mozambique	20.1	101.6	386.5	1822.9%	6.1%	40.8	62.67	70.55	72.9%	1.1%	108.3	77.14	46.63	-56.9%	-1.7%
Malawi	8.097	23.48	102.7	1168.4%	5.2%	37.92	54.56	61.54	62.3%	1.0%	117.7	106	76.02	-35.4%	-0.9%
Zambia	10.76	31.85	145.6	1253.2%	5.3%	36.43	57.82	64.38	76.7%	1.1%	96.18	83.47	57.78	-39.9%	-1.0%
Zimbabwe	35.57	72.64	235.4	561.8%	3.9%	37.66	64.01	71.43	89.7%	1.3%	55.7	45.7	29.47	-47.1%	-1.3%
Burundi	4.641	13.3	50.79	994.4%	4.9%	43.23	59.95	62.11	43.7%	0.7%	111.6	98.63	73.67	-34.0%	-0.8%
Rwanda	9.392	28.61	102.7	993.5%	4.9%	42.58	58.43	63.6	49.4%	0.8%	112.6	94.89	66.53	-40.9%	-1.0%
Somalia	4.17	13.53	29.8	614.6%	4.0%	45.63	51.84	57.1	25.1%	0.4%	137.1	117.1	99.97	-27.1%	-0.6%
Eritrea	4.309	7.6	16.02	271.8%	2.7%	49.58	50.67	57.81	16.6%	0.3%	69.2	69.47	62.67	-9.4%	-0.2%
Mauritius	13.16	27.4	41.32	214.0%	2.3%	72.79	79.82	85.22	17.1%	0.3%	16.68	9.458	4.312	-74.1%	-2.7%
Comoros	1.039	2.159	5.613	440.2%	3.4%	60.93	64.13	70.74	16.1%	0.3%	67.1	58.08	40.57	-39.5%	-1.0%
Djibouti	1.543	2.23	4.572	196.3%	2.2%	39.07	47.31	64.15	64.2%	1.0%	98.39	89.9	68.81	-30.1%	-0.7%
Africa-Eastern	**295.6**	**1023**	**4784**	**1518.4%**	**5.7%**	**44.48**	**61.95**	**68.68**	**54.4%**	**0.9%**	**93.58**	**75.4**	**48.14**	**-48.6%**	**-1.3%**
Congo, Dem. Rep. of the	36.56	124	504.8	1280.7%	5.4%	42.01	53.77	61.05	45.3%	0.8%	71.82	61.28	45.63	-36.5%	-0.9%
Angola	27.66	84.69	171.3	519.3%	3.7%	38.75	52.13	61.45	58.6%	0.9%	138.2	108.1	84.83	-38.6%	-1.0%
Cameroon	33.12	53.71	117.5	254.8%	2.6%	36.98	46.51	62.53	69.1%	1.1%	90.75	79.28	62.49	-31.1%	-0.7%
Chad	9.4	38.95	79.3	743.6%	4.4%	45.06	58.47	61.24	35.9%	0.6%	109.9	87.76	74.09	-32.6%	-0.8%
Central African Republic	4.808	7.895	18.34	281.4%	2.7%	37.84	38.24	57.04	50.7%	0.8%	98.35	89.99	73.46	-25.3%	-0.6%
Congo, Rep. of	4.873	18.45	48.67	898.8%	4.7%	50.64	67.31	71.6	41.4%	0.7%	125.4	91.04	63.21	-49.6%	-1.4%
Gabon	8.709	24.61	37.85	334.6%	3.0%	56.26	67.71	72.51	28.9%	0.5%	54.26	38.5	27.39	-49.5%	-1.4%
Equatorial Guinea	2.983	10.62	12.84	330.4%	3.0%	46.6	59.47	66.27	42.2%	0.7%	103.5	72.38	54.76	-47.1%	-1.3%
São Tomé and Príncipe	0.292	0.45	0.637	118.2%	1.6%	56.54	57	59.12	4.6%	0.1%	92.57	89.92	86.46	-6.6%	-0.1%
Africa-Middle	**128.4**	**363.4**	**991.2**	**672.0%**	**4.2%**	**41.43**	**53.2**	**61.55**	**48.6%**	**0.8%**	**90.19**	**73.72**	**55.82**	**-38.1%**	**-1.0%**
Egypt	279	785.9	2660	853.4%	4.6%	69.19	75.13	85.55	23.6%	0.4%	45.9	29.24	5.532	-87.9%	-4.1%
Sudan	63.73	221.7	535.4	740.1%	4.3%	55	66.12	73.84	34.3%	0.6%	75.77	52.61	34.24	-54.8%	-1.6%
Algeria	194.5	443.9	763.1	292.3%	2.8%	71.36	77.31	82.43	15.5%	0.3%	42.7	25.74	12.49	-70.7%	-2.4%
Morocco	116.3	230.2	542.9	366.8%	3.1%	69.28	72.87	80.82	16.7%	0.3%	45.83	34.32	15.67	-65.8%	-2.1%
Tunisia	69.59	189.9	475.6	583.4%	3.9%	73.14	80.77	88.22	20.6%	0.4%	24.79	10.75	3.273	-86.8%	-4.0%
Libya	45.55	146.5	284.2	523.9%	3.7%	73.94	82.27	88.13	19.2%	0.4%	19.89	7.446	3.209	-83.9%	-3.6%
Africa-Northern	**768.7**	**2018**	**5261**	**584.4%**	**3.9%**	**67.19**	**73.72**	**81.9**	**21.9%**	**0.4%**	**49.2**	**32.85**	**14.48**	**-70.6%**	**-2.4%**

Poverty | **Health**

Base Case: Countries in Year 2055 / Descending Population Sequence	GDP at PPP (Billion Year 2000 $)					Life Expectancy at Birth (Years)					Infant Mortality (Per Thousand)				
	2005	2030	2055	% Chg	% An Chg	2005	2030	2055	% Chg	% An Chg	2005	2030	2055	% Chg	% An Chg
AFRICA continued															
South Africa	442.7	698.6	1549	249.9%	2.5%	40.51	65.42	74.64	84.3%	1.2%	35.73	27.14	16	-55.2%	-1.6%
Namibia	12.97	32.73	137.1	957.1%	4.8%	45.16	66.25	77.42	71.4%	1.1%	47.18	34.28	15.84	-66.4%	-2.2%
Lesotho	4.947	7.827	20.02	304.7%	2.8%	37.44	58.49	68.14	82.0%	1.2%	61.8	53.38	36.81	-40.4%	-1.0%
Botswana	17.35	51	119.5	588.8%	3.9%	38.12	71.3	76.42	100.5%	1.4%	42.44	28.85	18.63	-56.1%	-1.6%
Swaziland	4.642	12.48	38.19	722.7%	4.3%	43.59	68.46	75.28	72.7%	1.1%	72.04	54.8	31.89	-55.7%	-1.6%
Africa-Southern	**482.6**	**802.6**	**1864**	**286.2%**	**2.7%**	**40.56**	**65.48**	**74.59**	**83.9%**	**1.2%**	**38.12**	**29.41**	**17.56**	**-53.9%**	**-1.5%**
Nigeria	132	480.4	1023	675.0%	4.2%	40.58	58.58	64.74	59.5%	0.9%	110.8	82.56	64.92	-41.4%	-1.1%
Niger	9.674	28.13	107.9	1015.4%	4.9%	43.73	49.85	58.32	33.4%	0.6%	159.1	143.3	108.7	-31.7%	-0.8%
Ghana	45.89	76.02	166.2	262.2%	2.6%	56.22	61.38	65.75	17.0%	0.3%	63.94	60.57	47.89	-25.1%	-0.6%
Côte d'Ivoire	29.47	90.5	255.4	766.6%	4.4%	46.63	63.28	66.75	43.1%	0.7%	111.7	89.82	63.04	-43.6%	-1.1%
Mali	11.64	37.83	127.5	995.4%	4.9%	46.81	56.38	63.7	36.1%	0.6%	133.4	113.1	82.11	-38.4%	-1.0%
Burkina Faso	13.78	41.51	162.1	1076.3%	5.1%	46.41	61.54	66.06	42.3%	0.7%	120.3	102.6	70.29	-41.6%	-1.1%
Senegal	18.19	52.23	152.6	738.9%	4.3%	56.65	62.63	70.39	24.3%	0.4%	84.08	68.23	45.43	-46.0%	-1.2%
Guinea	18.47	45.62	104.6	466.3%	3.5%	53.37	60.5	65.86	23.4%	0.4%	115.1	96.77	73.75	-35.9%	-0.9%
Benin	8.579	23.06	85.53	897.0%	4.7%	47.85	58.27	68.36	42.9%	0.7%	107.1	92.08	60.99	-43.1%	-1.1%
Togo	8.161	15.93	30.58	274.7%	2.7%	53.74	61.15	61.98	15.3%	0.3%	95.29	89.35	78.31	-17.8%	-0.4%
Liberia	3.294	6.766	18.34	456.8%	3.5%	38.35	32.68	56.34	46.9%	0.8%	149.1	134	107.6	-27.8%	-0.7%
Sierra Leone	3.046	8.876	26.53	771.0%	4.4%	29.77	34.63	59.61	100.2%	1.4%	160.8	136.2	104.1	-35.3%	-0.9%
Mauritania	5.938	13.11	27.86	369.2%	3.1%	52.2	56.68	62.56	19.8%	0.4%	103.2	91.34	72.95	-29.3%	-0.7%
Guinea-Bissau	1.308	2.56	5.666	333.2%	3.0%	43.85	50.02	54.48	24.2%	0.4%	127.2	118.7	103.2	-18.9%	-0.4%
Gambia	2.581	6.345	17.09	562.1%	3.9%	55.23	61.27	68.27	23.6%	0.4%	86.51	73.39	51.5	-40.5%	-1.0%
Cape Verde	2.403	7.923	22.5	836.3%	4.6%	69.52	76.07	85.06	22.4%	0.4%	35	19.96	3.666	-89.5%	-4.4%
Africa-Western	**314.4**	**936.8**	**2334**	**642.4%**	**4.1%**	**44.81**	**58.11**	**64.5**	**43.9%**	**0.7%**	**110.8**	**90.22**	**69.59**	**-37.2%**	**-0.9%**

Poverty

Base Case: Countries in Year 2055 Descending Population Sequence	GDP at PPP Billion Year 2000 $				
	2005	2030	2055	% Chg	% An Chg
AMERICAS					
Haiti	13.21	21.93	48.44	266.7%	2.6%
Dominican Republic	65.78	163.3	282.7	329.8%	3.0%
Cuba	25.52	71.73	246.2	864.7%	4.6%
Puerto Rico	48.94	152.1	476	872.6%	4.7%
Jamaica	10.46	23.01	75.58	622.6%	4.0%
Trinidad and Tobago	15.58	45.2	50.79	226.0%	2.4%
Bahamas	5.57	8.769	14.97	168.8%	2.0%
Barbados	4.253	7.582	15.88	273.4%	2.7%
Grenada	0.829	1.79	5.292	538.4%	3.8%
St. Vincent & the Grenadines	0.679	1.373	3.527	419.4%	3.4%
St. Lucia	1.034	2.477	6.779	555.6%	3.8%
America-Caribbean	**191.9**	**499.2**	**1226**	**538.9%**	**3.8%**
Guatemala	51.42	144.2	383	644.8%	4.1%
Honduras	21.6	48.39	119	450.9%	3.5%
Nicaragua	17.45	36.66	82.34	371.9%	3.2%
El Salvador	31.98	79.59	195.5	511.3%	3.7%
Costa Rica	37.69	115.4	342	807.4%	4.5%
Panama	21.43	79.33	262.8	1126.3%	5.1%
Belize	1.752	6.559	19.67	1022.7%	5.0%
America-Central	**183.3**	**510.1**	**1404**	**666.0%**	**4.2%**
United States	11027	22066	36530	231.3%	2.4%
Mexico	982.9	1940	3295	235.2%	2.4%
Canada	926.7	1857	3570	285.2%	2.7%
America-North	**12937**	**25862**	**43394**	**235.4%**	**2.4%**
Brazil	1372	2694	5599	308.1%	2.9%
Colombia	286.8	647.6	1588	453.7%	3.5%
Argentina	552.5	1369	3109	462.7%	3.5%
Peru	146	363.3	760.9	421.2%	3.4%
Venezuela	181.2	596.4	1434	691.4%	4.2%
Chile	165.1	472.3	1026	521.4%	3.7%
Ecuador	49.11	100.8	157.5	220.7%	2.4%
Bolivia	23.02	73.45	249.6	984.3%	4.9%
Paraguay	24.57	54.56	143.6	484.5%	3.6%
Uruguay	35.16	85.82	186.4	430.1%	3.4%
Guyana	3.072	4.089	5.809	89.1%	1.3%
Suriname	2.888	5.076	10.13	250.8%	2.5%
America-South	**2841**	**6466**	**14271**	**402.3%**	**3.3%**

Health

	Life Expectancy at Birth (Years)					Infant Mortality (Per Thousand)				
	2005	2030	2055	% Chg	% An Chg	2005	2030	2055	% Chg	% An Chg
Haiti	45.63	57.76	63.52	39.2%	0.7%	68.11	61.34	47.29	-30.6%	-0.7%
Dominican Republic	66.9	76.1	82.8	23.8%	0.4%	37.79	22	10.28	-72.8%	-2.6%
Cuba	76.11	77.7	87.88	15.5%	0.3%	9.455	8.467	2.888	-69.5%	-2.3%
Puerto Rico	77.05	85.34	87.06	13.0%	0.2%	9.785	3.465	3.266	-66.6%	-2.2%
Jamaica	70.85	75.27	86.01	21.4%	0.4%	15.56	12.19	3.573	-77.0%	-2.9%
Trinidad and Tobago	72.29	83.32	85.74	18.6%	0.3%	12.93	5.334	3.881	-70.0%	-2.4%
Bahamas	69.01	75.96	81.53	18.1%	0.3%	15.71	11.19	6.951	-55.8%	-1.6%
Barbados	75.44	82.51	86.04	14.1%	0.3%	11.97	6.362	3.678	-69.3%	-2.3%
Grenada	72.76	77.02	86.79	19.3%	0.4%	20.12	13.76	3.29	-83.6%	-3.6%
St. Vincent & the Grenadines	73.16	76.33	85.17	16.4%	0.3%	28.2	21	5.653	-80.0%	-3.2%
St. Lucia	71.71	80.03	88.05	22.8%	0.4%	15.74	7.83	3.163	-79.9%	-3.2%
America-Caribbean	**66.48**	**72.53**	**78.12**	**17.5%**	**0.3%**	**30.29**	**26.27**	**19.77**	**-34.7%**	**-0.8%**
Guatemala	66.33	71.92	78.71	18.7%	0.3%	45.39	33.42	17.83	-60.7%	-1.9%
Honduras	65.95	69.25	76.2	15.5%	0.3%	35.64	30.88	19.77	-44.5%	-1.2%
Nicaragua	68.62	70.09	74.99	9.3%	0.2%	34.88	33.77	23.6	-32.3%	-0.8%
El Salvador	70.01	75.21	83.14	18.8%	0.3%	31.78	20.66	7.425	-76.6%	-2.9%
Costa Rica	77.75	84.47	88.95	14.4%	0.3%	11.76	5.033	3.226	-72.6%	-2.6%
Panama	74.91	83.97	89.09	18.9%	0.3%	23.58	7.153	3.19	-86.5%	-3.9%
Belize	72.11	81.74	88.44	22.6%	0.4%	30.89	10.88	3.261	-89.4%	-4.4%
America-Central	**69.15**	**73.62**	**79.75**	**15.3%**	**0.3%**	**34.44**	**26.7**	**15.56**	**-54.8%**	**-1.6%**
United States	77.63	80.47	83.33	7.3%	0.1%	7.129	5.815	4.582	-35.7%	-0.9%
Mexico	74.32	79.58	85.14	14.6%	0.3%	26.84	15.47	4.576	-83.0%	-3.5%
Canada	80.05	82.64	84.71	5.8%	0.1%	5.209	4.389	3.753	-28.0%	-0.7%
America-North	**77**	**80.4**	**83.87**	**8.9%**	**0.2%**	**11.76**	**8.146**	**4.522**	**-61.5%**	**-1.9%**
Brazil	70.29	76.37	83.6	18.9%	0.3%	33.09	21.56	7.747	-76.6%	-2.9%
Colombia	71.96	77.14	85.57	18.9%	0.3%	28.74	17.23	3.211	-88.8%	-4.3%
Argentina	75.59	83.71	86.18	14.0%	0.3%	19.1	6.477	3.608	-81.1%	-3.3%
Peru	69.65	76.29	82.97	19.1%	0.4%	39.76	23.89	9.091	-77.1%	-2.9%
Venezuela	74.16	82.15	88.67	19.6%	0.4%	20.09	7.857	3.22	-84.0%	-3.6%
Chile	77.51	85	88.38	14.0%	0.3%	11.34	3.684	3.237	-71.5%	-2.5%
Ecuador	73.21	74.6	77.15	5.4%	0.1%	32.98	31.37	26.12	-20.8%	-0.5%
Bolivia	63.4	71.47	81.61	28.7%	0.5%	65.06	41.74	13.88	-78.7%	-3.0%
Paraguay	70.3	72.71	80.07	13.9%	0.3%	38.97	33.36	17.04	-56.3%	-1.6%
Uruguay	75.79	83.2	87.24	15.1%	0.3%	15.52	4.617	3.279	-78.9%	-3.1%
Guyana	59.59	67.75	73.75	23.8%	0.4%	54.98	44.06	30.14	-45.2%	-1.2%
Suriname	69.29	76.3	84.53	22.0%	0.4%	27.01	17.51	5.464	-79.8%	-3.1%
America-South	**71.55**	**77.73**	**84.26**	**17.8%**	**0.3%**	**30.49**	**19.04**	**7.457**	**-75.5%**	**-2.8%**

Poverty

Health

Base Case: Countries in Year 2055 Descending Population Sequence	GDP at PPP (Billion Year 2000 $)					Life Expectancy at Birth (Years)					Infant Mortality (Per Thousand)				
	2005	2030	2055	% Chg	% An Chg	2005	2030	2055	% Chg	% An Chg	2005	2030	2055	% Chg	% An Chg
ASIA INCL OCEANIA															
China	6797	27829	59249	771.7%	4.4%	71.58	83.39	88.96	24.3%	0.4%	38.53	9.227	3.209	-91.7%	-4.8%
Japan	3640	5508	8453	132.2%	1.7%	82.14	84.32	86.07	4.8%	0.1%	3.731	3.58	3.456	-7.4%	-0.2%
Korea, Rep. of	881.7	2278	3702	319.9%	2.9%	77.2	83.62	85.8	11.1%	0.2%	6.605	4.212	3.5	-47.0%	-1.3%
Taiwan	535.1	919.2	1697	217.1%	2.3%	79.15	83.45	85.52	8.0%	0.2%	6.702	4.549	3.657	-45.4%	-1.2%
Korea, Dem. Rep. of	27.21	61.7	153.5	464.1%	3.5%	63.08	67.08	76.03	20.5%	0.4%	44.48	37.1	21.29	-52.1%	-1.5%
Hong Kong	213.1	394.2	529.1	148.3%	1.8%	82.49	84.39	86.36	4.7%	0.1%	3.921	3.616	3.343	-14.7%	-0.3%
Mongolia	4.502	10.67	25.87	474.6%	3.6%	64.95	68.06	76.29	17.5%	0.3%	65.4	56.31	32.1	-50.9%	-1.4%
Asia-East	**12098**	**37001**	**73809**	**510.1%**	**3.7%**	**72.67**	**83.21**	**88.44**	**21.7%**	**0.4%**	**34.11**	**9.066**	**3.552**	**-89.6%**	**-4.4%**
India	3073	10412	31540	926.4%	4.8%	64.07	73.69	84.99	32.7%	0.6%	70.35	38.61	8.204	-88.3%	-4.2%
Pakistan	319.2	881.6	2256	606.8%	4.0%	63.46	68.62	75.33	18.7%	0.3%	82.89	63.34	40.96	-50.6%	-1.4%
Bangladesh	245	725.9	1763	619.6%	4.0%	62.14	69.16	76.13	22.5%	0.4%	68.92	48.91	29.4	-57.3%	-1.7%
Iran, Islamic Rep. of	440.5	1571	3174	620.5%	4.0%	70.97	81.6	87.93	23.9%	0.4%	38.35	13.46	3.127	-91.8%	-4.9%
Afghanistan	19.29	44.24	121.1	527.8%	3.7%	45.59	45.59	57	25.0%	0.4%	147.2	132.9	109.1	-25.9%	-0.6%
Nepal	36.15	77.78	164.2	354.2%	3.1%	60.48	63.21	67.6	11.8%	0.2%	72.55	65.25	52.51	-27.6%	-0.6%
Uzbekistan	46.65	137.1	293.9	530.0%	3.7%	67.76	70.78	76.27	12.6%	0.2%	57.49	51.83	32.24	-43.9%	-1.2%
Sri Lanka	77.18	171.1	318.1	312.2%	2.9%	73.42	76.09	81.98	11.7%	0.2%	19.02	16.53	8.388	-55.9%	-1.6%
Kazakhstan	87.96	420.9	526.5	498.6%	3.6%	68	82.7	85.48	25.7%	0.5%	52.39	8.976	3.311	-93.7%	-5.4%
Tajikistan	7.027	22.49	53.82	665.9%	4.2%	63.24	65.66	71.45	13.0%	0.2%	89.61	83.81	57.76	-35.5%	-0.9%
Turkmenistan	19.31	86.49	101.3	424.6%	3.4%	65.18	78.23	80.73	23.9%	0.4%	67.53	26.4	20.31	-69.9%	-2.4%
Kyrgyzstan	8.307	14.18	24.47	194.6%	2.2%	68.33	67.97	70.17	2.7%	0.1%	59.6	57.82	55.5	-6.9%	-0.1%
Bhutan	1.963	8.226	37.78	1824.6%	6.1%	63.2	73.62	86.8	37.3%	0.6%	61.96	34.71	3.172	-94.9%	-5.8%
Maldives	1.864	6.465	24.7	1225.1%	5.3%	66.68	75.53	85.82	28.7%	0.5%	49.24	27.69	5.214	-89.4%	-4.4%
Asia-South Central	**4383**	**14580**	**40399**	**821.7%**	**4.5%**	**64.01**	**72.24**	**81.3**	**27.0%**	**0.5%**	**70.31**	**44.19**	**19.77**	**-71.9%**	**-2.5%**
Indonesia	709.3	1770	3183	348.8%	3.0%	66.48	73.65	79.81	20.1%	0.4%	46.79	29.18	16.5	-64.7%	-2.1%
Philippines	360.8	831.7	1809	401.4%	3.3%	69.92	74.07	80.58	15.2%	0.3%	33.93	24.45	12.97	-61.8%	-1.9%
Vietnam	202.8	766.3	1859	816.7%	4.5%	68.97	75.55	83.78	21.5%	0.4%	34.56	22.25	8.017	-76.8%	-2.9%
Thailand	457.2	1086	2079	354.7%	3.1%	70.36	78.9	85.76	21.9%	0.4%	21.51	11.66	3.638	-83.1%	-3.5%
Myanmar	90.18	193.9	407.9	352.3%	3.1%	58.22	65.61	74.45	27.9%	0.5%	77.72	57.54	35.88	-53.8%	-1.5%
Malaysia	233.6	792.6	1738	644.0%	4.1%	73.55	83.29	87.07	18.4%	0.3%	10.96	4.93	3.301	-69.9%	-2.4%
Cambodia	29.66	128.6	331.8	1018.7%	4.9%	54.67	68.82	77.79	42.3%	0.7%	95.23	58.79	30.36	-68.1%	-2.3%
Laos	9.828	45.86	141	1334.7%	5.5%	54.91	65.38	75.54	37.6%	0.6%	92.79	62.1	32.78	-64.7%	-2.1%
Singapore	121.7	256.9	339.8	179.2%	2.1%	79.87	82.94	85.18	6.6%	0.1%	3.562	3.422	3.281	-7.9%	-0.2%
Timor-Leste	1.582	4.316	12.76	706.6%	4.3%	53.82	56.07	65.4	21.5%	0.4%	107.2	100.4	69.24	-35.4%	-0.9%
Brunei	6.484	15.04	20.15	210.8%	2.3%	77.33	83.62	85.96	11.2%	0.2%	6.438	4.227	3.466	-46.2%	-1.2%
Asia-South East	**2223**	**5891**	**11921**	**436.3%**	**3.4%**	**67.06**	**74.09**	**80.9**	**20.6%**	**0.4%**	**42.71**	**28.11**	**15.1**	**-64.6%**	**-2.1%**

Multination Regional Analysis

Measures of Poverty, Health, Education, Infrastructure and Governance

Poverty

Health

Base Case: Countries in Year 2055 Descending Population Sequence	GDP at PPP (Billion Year 2000 $)					Life Expectancy at Birth (Years)					Infant Mortality (Per Thousand)				
	2005	2030	2055	% Chg	% An Chg	2005	2030	2055	% Chg	% An Chg	2005	2030	2055	% Chg	% An Chg
ASIA INCL OCEANIA continued															
Turkey	549.8	1483	4086	643.2%	4.1%	72.07	80.46	87.66	21.6%	0.4%	40.32	17.41	3.125	-92.2%	-5.0%
Yemen	18.54	99.53	350.9	1792.7%	6.1%	59.27	66.07	74.64	25.9%	0.5%	80.44	59.94	36.48	-54.6%	-1.6%
Iraq	76.22	307.8	814.8	969.0%	4.9%	60.11	69.62	78.19	30.1%	0.5%	89.4	56.24	29.24	-67.3%	-2.2%
Saudi Arabia	326.1	998.8	2463	655.3%	4.1%	72.28	81.06	84.72	17.2%	0.3%	24.31	10.97	6.285	-74.1%	-2.7%
Syria	63.28	185.2	534.9	745.3%	4.4%	72.37	74.43	82.15	13.5%	0.3%	23.01	20.98	9.134	-60.3%	-1.8%
Israel	164.3	488.8	1109	575.0%	3.9%	79.5	83.89	85.93	8.1%	0.2%	5.687	4.091	3.428	-39.7%	-1.0%
Azerbaijan	28.44	94.77	183.9	546.6%	3.8%	71.82	77.46	84.3	17.4%	0.3%	77.53	48.39	15.22	-80.4%	-3.2%
Jordan	25.67	100.1	477.1	1758.6%	6.0%	71.2	80.05	89.58	25.8%	0.5%	27.99	13.05	3.057	-89.1%	-4.3%
Palestine	13.24	37.66	117.1	784.4%	4.5%	71.83	73.15	80.21	11.7%	0.2%	25.04	24.33	12.23	-51.2%	-1.4%
Oman	35.54	100.5	183.2	415.5%	3.3%	74.08	81.42	85.88	15.9%	0.3%	18.43	9.127	4.153	-77.5%	-2.9%
Lebanon	17.9	68.61	235.1	1213.4%	5.3%	71.94	81.76	89.37	24.2%	0.4%	26.78	9.908	3.109	-88.4%	-4.2%
United Arab Emirates	94.78	258.4	364.9	285.0%	2.7%	79.35	83.07	85.51	7.8%	0.1%	8.809	5.913	4.262	-51.6%	-1.4%
Kuwait	56.38	156.1	306.1	442.9%	3.4%	78.25	83.38	85.87	9.7%	0.2%	10.08	5.799	4.088	-59.4%	-1.8%
Georgia	11.96	20.42	33.49	180.0%	2.1%	70.35	73.17	78.49	11.6%	0.2%	40.11	36.43	21.1	-47.4%	-1.3%
Armenia	10.79	31.48	56.64	424.9%	3.4%	72.4	77.05	83.53	15.4%	0.3%	33.91	23.57	9.317	-72.5%	-2.6%
Bahrain	13.23	38.46	75.87	473.5%	3.6%	75.36	82.47	85.03	12.8%	0.2%	14.08	6.986	4.824	-65.7%	-2.1%
Qatar	15.98	40.49	46.2	189.1%	2.1%	73.48	79.09	83.11	13.1%	0.2%	12.7	8.527	5.947	-53.2%	-1.5%
Cyprus	14.8	27.84	46.6	214.9%	2.3%	79.06	84.3	86.39	9.3%	0.2%	6.092	4.021	3.309	-45.7%	-1.2%
Asia-West	**1537**	**4538**	**11485**	**647.2%**	**4.1%**	**69.77**	**76.24**	**82.65**	**18.5%**	**0.3%**	**45.11**	**28.68**	**14.53**	**-67.8%**	**-2.2%**
Australia	550.3	1241	2410	337.9%	3.0%	80.59	83.43	85.47	6.1%	0.1%	5.837	4.479	3.646	-37.5%	-0.9%
Papua New Guinea	13.47	37.32	94.16	599.0%	4.0%	55.02	63.08	71.18	29.4%	0.5%	74.27	54.87	36.48	-50.9%	-1.4%
New Zealand	86.45	167.2	380.4	340.0%	3.0%	79.68	84.41	86.34	8.4%	0.2%	6.497	4.118	3.359	-48.3%	-1.3%
Solomon Islands	0.96	2.559	7.349	665.5%	4.2%	61.95	66.08	74.53	20.3%	0.4%	36.52	30.37	18.64	-49.0%	-1.3%
Fiji	4.338	9.188	19.34	345.8%	3.0%	67.88	75.05	83.98	23.7%	0.4%	23.68	15.44	5.921	-75.0%	-2.7%
Vanuatu	0.685	1.866	5.228	663.2%	4.1%	67.58	71.43	79.83	18.1%	0.3%	42.14	32.75	16.48	-60.9%	-1.9%
Micronesia	0.736	1.417	2.777	277.3%	2.7%	66.87	68.32	74.69	11.7%	0.2%	40.24	38	24.96	-38.0%	-1.0%
Samoa	0.949	1.926	4.363	359.7%	3.1%	69.5	74.56	83.45	20.1%	0.4%	28.26	19.35	6.115	-78.4%	-3.0%
Tonga	0.719	1.208	2.084	189.8%	2.2%	71.62	72.98	76.56	6.9%	0.1%	23.1	21.18	16.06	-30.5%	-0.7%
Oceania	**658.6**	**1464**	**2926**	**344.3%**	**3.0%**	**74.93**	**78.15**	**81.42**	**8.7%**	**0.2%**	**19.99**	**17.1**	**12.8**	**-36.0%**	**-0.9%**

Poverty · Health

Base Case: Countries in Year 2055 / Descending Population Sequence	GDP at PPP (Billion Year 2000 $)					Life Expectancy at Birth (Years)					Infant Mortality (Per Thousand)				
	2005	2030	2055	% Chg	% An Chg	2005	2030	2055	% Chg	% An Chg	2005	2030	2055	% Chg	% An Chg
EUROPE															
Russia	1230	2927	3487	183.5%	2.1%	68.19	79	84.46	23.9%	0.4%	15.02	7.917	4.651	-69.0%	-2.3%
Poland	442.8	768.9	1214	174.2%	2.0%	74.47	81.24	86.47	16.1%	0.3%	9.533	5.696	3.296	-65.4%	-2.1%
Ukraine	239.6	488.9	881.4	267.9%	2.6%	69.27	77.88	86.53	24.9%	0.4%	14.41	7.42	3.13	-78.3%	-3.0%
Romania	157.3	250.3	339	115.5%	1.5%	72.1	77.72	83.21	15.4%	0.3%	19.99	12.2	5.734	-71.3%	-2.5%
Belarus	60.56	153.7	432.3	613.8%	4.0%	69.66	79.28	86.68	24.4%	0.4%	13.28	6.361	3.139	-76.4%	-2.8%
Czech Republic	174.9	232.2	299.8	71.4%	1.1%	76.35	81.36	85.36	11.8%	0.2%	6.442	4.832	3.584	-44.4%	-1.2%
Hungary	147.3	215.2	285.5	93.8%	1.3%	72.94	79.24	83.77	14.8%	0.3%	8.808	6.095	4.211	-52.2%	-1.5%
Bulgaria	56.35	90.07	150.2	166.5%	2.0%	72.65	79.12	86.88	19.6%	0.4%	13.43	7.55	3.275	-75.6%	-2.8%
Slovak Republic	70.06	103.9	150.1	114.2%	1.5%	74.87	80.17	86.02	14.9%	0.3%	7.891	5.673	3.392	-57.0%	-1.7%
Moldova	7.154	12.96	29.58	313.5%	2.9%	67.94	69.93	78.06	14.9%	0.3%	27.28	26.14	13.96	-48.8%	-1.3%
Europe-East	**2586**	**5243**	**7269**	**181.1%**	**2.1%**	**70.18**	**79.05**	**85.02**	**21.1%**	**0.4%**	**14.03**	**7.838**	**4.296**	**-69.4%**	**-2.3%**
United Kingdom	1724	3145	5478	217.7%	2.3%	78.8	81.89	84.22	6.9%	0.1%	5.535	4.583	3.867	-30.1%	-0.7%
Sweden	253.9	526	854.5	236.5%	2.5%	80.67	83.28	85.3	5.7%	0.1%	4.24	3.791	3.463	-18.3%	-0.4%
Denmark	161	296	558.3	246.8%	2.5%	77.53	80.51	83.28	7.4%	0.1%	5.711	4.839	4.087	-28.4%	-0.7%
Norway	171.1	298.3	491.7	187.4%	2.1%	79.17	81.68	83.97	6.1%	0.1%	5.495	4.7	3.962	-27.9%	-0.7%
Ireland	137.9	284.5	376.2	172.8%	2.0%	77.36	80.09	82.86	7.1%	0.1%	5.985	5.101	4.279	-28.5%	-0.7%
Finland	146.6	238.3	425.4	190.2%	2.2%	78.65	81.83	84	6.8%	0.1%	4.254	3.847	3.544	-16.7%	-0.4%
Lithuania	38.8	77.84	167.8	332.5%	3.0%	73.74	81.88	86.2	16.9%	0.3%	10.46	5.256	3.237	-69.1%	-2.3%
Latvia	24.77	54.81	104.2	320.7%	2.9%	72.93	82.31	85.8	17.6%	0.3%	11.97	5.23	3.246	-72.9%	-2.6%
Estonia	16.45	34.94	72.92	343.3%	3.0%	73.92	83.59	85.6	15.8%	0.3%	9.282	4.398	3.472	-62.6%	-1.9%
Iceland	9.776	18.96	31.83	225.6%	2.4%	79.62	82.14	84.46	6.1%	0.1%	3.545	3.465	3.39	-4.4%	-0.1%
Europe-North	**2684**	**4974**	**8561**	**219.0%**	**2.3%**	**78.46**	**81.87**	**84.27**	**7.4%**	**0.1%**	**5.751**	**4.548**	**3.818**	**-33.6%**	**-0.8%**
Italy	1459	1702	2117	45.1%	0.7%	80.03	83.26	85.35	6.6%	0.1%	5.455	4.286	3.609	-33.8%	-0.8%
Spain	992.9	1508	2042	105.7%	1.5%	80.1	83.79	85.79	7.1%	0.1%	4.794	3.903	3.454	-28.0%	-0.7%
Greece	215.1	370.9	673.6	213.2%	2.3%	79.46	85.14	87	9.5%	0.2%	6.088	3.74	3.257	-46.5%	-1.2%
Portugal	188.6	278.5	488.3	158.9%	1.9%	77.1	82.57	85.47	10.9%	0.2%	6.187	4.477	3.541	-42.8%	-1.1%
Serbia and Montenegro	19.99	37.83	124.8	524.3%	3.7%	72.3	73.53	84.46	16.8%	0.3%	14.68	13.79	5.065	-65.5%	-2.1%
Croatia	47.76	77.93	179.4	275.6%	2.7%	74.76	81.21	87.22	16.7%	0.3%	8.699	5.269	3.203	-63.2%	-2.0%
Bosnia and Herzegovina	23.96	34.36	51.19	113.6%	1.5%	74.09	75.99	81.6	10.1%	0.2%	14.97	12.71	7.325	-51.1%	-1.4%
Albania	13.75	29.66	54.05	293.1%	2.8%	74.62	77.12	82.5	10.6%	0.2%	28.05	25	10.96	-60.9%	-1.9%
Macedonia	13.14	17.95	30.19	129.8%	1.7%	73.09	75.01	80.96	10.8%	0.2%	18.43	14.97	8.358	-54.7%	-1.6%
Slovenia	37.42	55.67	95.43	155.0%	1.9%	77.22	83.14	85.43	10.6%	0.2%	5.737	4.155	3.538	-38.3%	-1.0%
Malta	7.055	12.07	22.58	220.1%	2.4%	78.65	84.32	86.48	10.0%	0.2%	7.501	4.269	3.402	-54.6%	-1.6%
Europe-South	**3018**	**4125**	**5879**	**94.8%**	**1.3%**	**78.77**	**82.42**	**85.37**	**8.4%**	**0.2%**	**6.952**	**5.635**	**3.998**	**-42.5%**	**-1.1%**
Germany	2138	3340	6133	186.9%	2.1%	78.47	82.11	84.12	7.2%	0.1%	4.838	4.145	3.736	-22.8%	-0.5%
France	1609	2653	5093	216.5%	2.3%	79.64	82.85	84.92	6.6%	0.1%	4.617	3.971	3.553	-23.0%	-0.5%
Netherlands	467.6	744.8	1263	170.1%	2.0%	78.43	81.46	83.88	6.9%	0.1%	4.524	4.035	3.645	-19.4%	-0.4%
Belgium	293	330.5	481.8	64.4%	1.0%	78.44	81.36	83.76	6.8%	0.1%	4.337	3.971	3.621	-16.5%	-0.4%
Austria	240	346.3	475.7	98.2%	1.4%	78.92	81.53	83.86	6.3%	0.1%	5.501	4.688	3.96	-28.0%	-0.7%
Switzerland	236.9	365.8	540.4	128.1%	1.7%	80.19	82.38	84.44	5.3%	0.1%	4.609	4.135	3.68	-20.2%	-0.4%
Luxembourg	24.26	44.69	60.71	150.2%	1.9%	78.31	80.96	83.46	6.6%	0.1%	5.688	4.907	4.125	-27.5%	-0.6%
Europe-West	**5008**	**7826**	**14048**	**180.5%**	**2.1%**	**78.93**	**82.24**	**84.35**	**6.9%**	**0.1%**	**4.733**	**4.091**	**3.664**	**-22.6%**	**-0.5%**

Multination Regional Analysis

Measures of Poverty, Health, Education, Infrastructure and Governance

Health

Base Case
Source: International Futures
Version 5.47 March 2008

	HIV Infection Rate (Percent)					Calories per Capita (Per Capita/Day)					Malnourished Children (Percent)				
	2005	2030	2055	% Chg	% An Chg	2005	2030	2055	% Chg	% An Chg	2005	2030	2055	% Chg	% An Chg
World	0.95	0.44	0.028	-97.1%	-6.8%	2857	3162	3442	20.5%	0.4%	15.33	5.587	1.337	-91.3%	-4.8%
Africa	4.411	1.126	0.037	-99.2%	-9.1%	2450	2690	3051	24.5%	0.4%	23.13	13.81	4.606	-80.1%	-3.2%
Americas	0.447	0.18	0.012	-97.3%	-7.0%	3215	3395	3618	12.5%	0.2%	4.645	1.861	0.125	-97.3%	-7.0%
Asia incl Oceania	0.484	0.345	0.03	-93.8%	-5.4%	2784	3196	3525	26.6%	0.5%	18.62	4.664	0.441	-97.6%	-7.2%
Europe	0.464	0.141	0.006	-98.7%	-8.3%	3320	3579	3746	12.8%	0.2%	0.966	0.03	0	-100.0%	
World	0.95	0.44	0.028	-97.1%	-6.8%	2857	3162	3442	20.5%	0.4%	15.33	5.587	1.337	-91.3%	-4.8%
Africa-Eastern	5.863	1.427	0.043	-99.3%	-9.4%	2048	2430	3014	47.2%	0.8%	28.42	18.17	4.637	-83.7%	-3.6%
Africa-Middle	4.563	1.169	0.037	-99.2%	-9.2%	1937	2239	2703	39.5%	0.7%	27.73	21.07	9.959	-64.1%	-2.0%
Africa-Northern	0.498	0.17	0.008	-98.4%	-7.9%	3049	3287	3560	16.8%	0.3%	12.39	4.246	0	-100.0%	
Africa-Southern	16.77	4.297	0.133	-99.2%	-9.2%	2874	3132	3551	23.6%	0.4%	9.643	1.144	0	-100.0%	
Africa-Western	3.147	0.92	0.033	-99.0%	-8.7%	2585	2783	2995	15.9%	0.3%	25.9	12.85	4.309	-83.4%	-3.5%
Africa	4.411	1.126	0.037	-99.2%	-9.1%	2450	2690	3051	24.5%	0.4%	23.13	13.81	4.606	-80.1%	-3.2%
America-Caribbean	1.174	0.382	0.015	-98.7%	-8.4%	2611	2942	3310	26.8%	0.5%	7.227	5.32	2.738	-62.1%	-1.9%
America-Central	0.746	0.299	0.016	-97.9%	-7.4%	2403	2778	3270	36.1%	0.6%	14.6	7.923	0.178	-98.8%	-8.4%
America-North	0.383	0.206	0.018	-95.3%	-5.9%	3633	3697	3755	3.4%	0.1%	2.704	1.278	0	-100.0%	
America-South	0.419	0.121	0.005	-98.8%	-8.5%	2880	3193	3556	23.5%	0.4%	5.561	1.366	0	-100.0%	
Americas	0.447	0.18	0.012	-97.3%	-7.0%	3215	3395	3618	12.5%	0.2%	4.645	1.861	0.125	-97.3%	-7.0%
Asia-East	0.243	0.174	0.014	-94.2%	-5.5%	3061	3551	3782	23.6%	0.4%	2.605	0.191	0.003	-99.9%	-12.7%
Asia-South Central	0.808	0.594	0.051	-93.7%	-5.4%	2498	2930	3373	35.0%	0.6%	34.44	8.987	0.905	-97.4%	-7.0%
Asia-South East	0.499	0.152	0.007	-98.6%	-8.2%	2748	3102	3427	24.7%	0.4%	21.83	3.09	0	-100.0%	
Asia-West	0.027	0.008	0	-100.0%		2960	3261	3545	19.8%	0.4%	10.53	3.362	0.281	-97.3%	-7.0%
Oceania	0.302	0.142	0.008	-97.4%	-7.0%	2966	3271	3567	20.3%	0.4%	5.684	3.544	0.152	-97.3%	-7.0%
Asia incl Oceania	0.484	0.345	0.03	-93.8%	-5.4%	2784	3196	3525	26.6%	0.5%	18.62	4.664	0.441	-97.6%	-7.2%
Europe-East	0.797	0.244	0.011	-98.6%	-8.2%	3109	3464	3679	18.3%	0.3%	2.087	0.021	0	-100.0%	
Europe-North	0.16	0.054	0.002	-98.8%	-8.4%	3369	3641	3795	12.6%	0.2%	0.046	0	0	-100.0%	
Europe-South	0.316	0.096	0.005	-98.4%	-8.0%	3470	3609	3759	8.3%	0.2%	0.493	0.113	0	-100.0%	
Europe-West	0.168	0.059	0.003	-98.2%	-7.7%	3521	3695	3800	7.9%	0.2%	0	0	0		
Europe	0.464	0.141	0.006	-98.7%	-8.3%	3320	3579	3746	12.8%	0.2%	0.966	0.03	0	-100.0%	

Health

Base Case: Countries in Year 2055 Descending Population Sequence	HIV Infection Rate (Percent)					Calories per Capita (Per Capita/Day)					Malnourished Children (Percent)				
	2005	2030	2055	% Chg	% An Chg	2005	2030	2055	% Chg	% An Chg	2005	2030	2055	% Chg	% An Chg
AFRICA															
Ethiopia	3.316	0.813	0.024	-99.3%	-9.4%	1887	2247	2836	50.3%	0.8%	40.24	26.25	7.635	-81.0%	-3.3%
Tanzania	5.261	1.301	0.039	-99.3%	-9.3%	2044	2550	3240	58.5%	0.9%	24.13	12.72	0	-100.0%	
Uganda	5.494	1.375	0.041	-99.3%	-9.3%	2359	2784	3406	44.4%	0.7%	22.28	9.111	0	-100.0%	
Kenya	5.068	1.212	0.036	-99.3%	-9.4%	2171	2586	3258	50.1%	0.8%	20.17	11.65	0	-100.0%	
Madagascar	0.424	0.154	0.007	-98.3%	-7.9%	2188	2439	2852	30.3%	0.5%	35.4	23.26	8.026	-77.3%	-2.9%
Mozambique	13.03	3.186	0.094	-99.3%	-9.4%	2097	2643	3202	52.7%	0.9%	22.8	10.51	0	-100.0%	
Malawi	11.47	2.854	0.086	-99.3%	-9.3%	2181	2411	2874	31.8%	0.6%	23.87	18.08	6.063	-74.6%	-2.7%
Zambia	13.95	3.457	0.104	-99.3%	-9.3%	1970	2307	2906	47.5%	0.8%	23.77	17.84	4.746	-80.0%	-3.2%
Zimbabwe	16.61	4.063	0.118	-99.3%	-9.4%	2119	2477	3103	46.4%	0.8%	14.77	11.36	0.353	-97.6%	-7.2%
Burundi	2.678	0.673	0.02	-99.3%	-9.3%	1668	1867	2592	55.4%	0.9%	43.82	37.23	13.94	-68.2%	-2.3%
Rwanda	2.557	0.624	0.019	-99.3%	-9.3%	2092	2426	2944	40.7%	0.7%	23.52	16.2	4.071	-82.7%	-3.4%
Somalia	0.77	0.275	0.013	-98.3%	-7.8%	1595	2010	2404	50.7%	0.8%	26.56	22.09	15.86	-40.3%	-1.0%
Eritrea	2.683	0.839	0.034	-98.7%	-8.4%	1589	1458	2107	32.6%	0.6%	39.22	48.54	27.3	-30.4%	-0.7%
Mauritius	0.483	0.157	0.007	-98.6%	-8.1%	3010	3331	3590	19.3%	0.4%	6.4	0	0	-100.0%	
Comoros	0.086	0.03	0.001	-98.8%	-8.5%	1829	2196	2762	51.0%	0.8%	25.94	19.96	7.946	-69.4%	-2.3%
Djibouti	6.341	2.027	0.076	-98.8%	-8.5%	2247	2464	2843	26.5%	0.5%	22.17	16.69	6.891	-68.9%	-2.3%
Africa-Eastern	**5.863**	**1.427**	**0.043**	**-99.3%**	**-9.4%**	**2048**	**2430**	**3014**	**47.2%**	**0.8%**	**28.42**	**18.17**	**4.637**	**-83.7%**	**-3.6%**
Congo, Dem. Rep. of the	2.609	0.658	0.02	-99.2%	-9.3%	1708	2078	2628	53.9%	0.9%	30.98	23.95	11.41	-63.2%	-2.0%
Angola	5.181	1.627	0.063	-98.8%	-8.4%	2098	2484	2830	34.9%	0.6%	31.14	17.98	7.743	-75.1%	-2.7%
Cameroon	10.18	3.016	0.105	-99.0%	-8.7%	2307	2491	2822	22.3%	0.4%	17.97	14.62	7.072	-60.6%	-1.8%
Chad	2.832	0.705	0.021	-99.3%	-9.3%	2193	2588	2819	28.5%	0.5%	30.23	15.75	8.395	-72.2%	-2.5%
Central African Republic	8.608	2.153	0.065	-99.2%	-9.3%	1996	1621	2571	28.8%	0.5%	24.32	40.02	13.12	-46.1%	-1.2%
Congo, Rep. of	4.302	1.052	0.031	-99.3%	-9.4%	2090	2524	2951	41.2%	0.7%	12.09	9.181	3.155	-73.9%	-2.7%
Gabon	6.369	1.541	0.044	-99.3%	-9.5%	2616	3019	3330	27.3%	0.5%	11.2	2.265	0	-100.0%	
Equatorial Guinea	3.64	1.258	0.051	-98.6%	-8.2%	2857	3247	3356	17.5%	0.3%	13.87	0	0	-100.0%	
São Tomé and Príncipe	0.009	0.003	0	-100.0%		2357	2479	2675	13.5%	0.3%	12.67	12.5	9.784	-22.8%	-0.5%
Africa-Middle	**4.563**	**1.169**	**0.037**	**-99.2%**	**-9.2%**	**1937**	**2239**	**2703**	**39.5%**	**0.7%**	**27.73**	**21.07**	**9.959**	**-64.1%**	**-2.0%**
Egypt	0.082	0.029	0.001	-98.8%	-8.4%	3342	3520	3788	13.3%	0.3%	8.578	3.577	0	-100.0%	
Sudan	2.422	0.736	0.028	-98.8%	-8.5%	2358	2779	3162	34.1%	0.6%	35.43	13.21	0	-100.0%	
Algeria	0.086	0.028	0.001	-98.8%	-8.5%	3001	3272	3500	16.6%	0.3%	6.044	0	0	-100.0%	
Morocco	0.085	0.028	0.001	-98.8%	-8.5%	3060	3217	3505	14.5%	0.3%	5.977	0	0	-100.0%	
Tunisia	0.084	0.027	0.001	-98.8%	-8.5%	3337	3616	3800	13.9%	0.3%	3.368	0	0	-100.0%	
Libya	0.042	0.014	0.001	-97.6%	-7.2%	3379	3666	3777	11.8%	0.2%	0	0	0		
Africa-Northern	**0.498**	**0.17**	**0.008**	**-98.4%**	**-7.9%**	**3049**	**3287**	**3560**	**16.8%**	**0.3%**	**12.39**	**4.246**	**0**	**-100.0%**	

Multination Regional Analysis

Measures of Poverty, Health, Education, Infrastructure and Governance

Health

Base Case: Countries in Year 2055 Descending Population Sequence	HIV Infection Rate (Percent)					Calories per Capita (Per Capita/Day)					Malnourished Children (Percent)				
	2005	2030	2055	% Chg	% An Chg	2005	2030	2055	% Chg	% An Chg	2005	2030	2055	% Chg	% An Chg
AFRICA continued															
South Africa	16.36	4.176	0.13	-99.2%	-9.2%	2945	3191	3583	21.7%	0.4%	8.713	0	0	-100.0%	
Namibia	15.94	3.849	0.11	-99.3%	-9.5%	2345	2806	3539	50.9%	0.8%	21.36	8.083	0	-100.0%	
Lesotho	18.87	4.797	0.139	-99.3%	-9.4%	2611	2764	3155	20.8%	0.4%	17.08	11.1	0	-100.0%	
Botswana	20.4	5.302	0.158	-99.2%	-9.3%	2256	2876	3514	55.8%	0.9%	11.73	3.892	0	-100.0%	
Swaziland	27.14	6.79	0.197	-99.3%	-9.4%	2400	2797	3368	40.3%	0.7%	10.42	5.508	0	-100.0%	
Africa-Southern	**16.77**	**4.297**	**0.133**	**-99.2%**	**-9.2%**	**2874**	**3132**	**3551**	**23.6%**	**0.4%**	**9.643**	**1.144**	**0**	**-100.0%**	
Nigeria	3.816	1.203	0.046	-98.8%	-8.5%	2756	3003	3061	11.1%	0.2%	25.81	6.72	2.714	-89.5%	-4.4%
Niger	0.87	0.317	0.015	-98.3%	-7.8%	2159	2349	2731	26.5%	0.5%	41.29	29.35	12.64	-69.4%	-2.3%
Ghana	1.853	0.449	0.014	-99.2%	-9.3%	2622	2694	2955	12.7%	0.2%	21.44	16.39	5.482	-74.4%	-2.7%
Côte d'Ivoire	5.7	1.413	0.042	-99.3%	-9.4%	2608	2857	3158	21.1%	0.4%	19.51	8.932	0	-100.0%	
Mali	1.397	0.344	0.01	-99.3%	-9.4%	2261	2530	2903	28.4%	0.5%	28.54	18.08	6.072	-78.7%	-3.0%
Burkina Faso	1.639	0.403	0.012	-99.3%	-9.4%	2404	2622	3024	25.8%	0.5%	32.77	19.74	3.214	-90.2%	-4.5%
Senegal	0.527	0.19	0.009	-98.3%	-7.8%	2335	2643	3063	31.2%	0.5%	20.84	12.28	1.427	-93.2%	-5.2%
Guinea	1.195	0.298	0.009	-99.2%	-9.3%	2381	2644	2971	24.8%	0.4%	26.36	15.38	4.334	-83.6%	-3.5%
Benin	2.962	0.796	0.026	-99.1%	-9.0%	2545	2707	3064	20.4%	0.4%	25.98	16.32	1.897	-92.7%	-5.1%
Togo	2.595	0.634	0.019	-99.3%	-9.4%	2281	2223	2651	16.2%	0.3%	21.52	24.28	12.16	-43.5%	-1.1%
Liberia	6.122	1.931	0.075	-98.8%	-8.4%	2166	1406	2630	21.4%	0.4%	25.89	58.37	12.93	-50.1%	-1.4%
Sierra Leone	6.691	2.246	0.083	-98.8%	-8.4%	2038	2412	2795	37.1%	0.6%	24.53	16.33	7.634	-68.9%	-2.3%
Mauritania	0.59	0.213	0.01	-98.3%	-7.8%	2790	2877	3026	8.5%	0.2%	26.97	16.13	4.791	-82.2%	-3.4%
Guinea-Bissau	2.509	0.795	0.032	-98.7%	-8.4%	2164	2078	2460	13.7%	0.3%	25.13	29.1	17.7	-29.6%	-0.7%
Gambia	1.896	0.467	0.014	-99.3%	-9.4%	2301	2582	2994	30.1%	0.5%	16.5	11.54	2.818	-82.9%	-3.5%
Cape Verde	0.009	0.003	0	-100.0%		3201	3466	3720	16.2%	0.3%	9.249	4.299	0	-100.0%	
Africa-Western	**3.147**	**0.92**	**0.033**	**-99.0%**	**-8.7%**	**2585**	**2783**	**2995**	**15.9%**	**0.3%**	**25.9**	**12.85**	**4.309**	**-83.4%**	**-3.5%**

Health

Base Case: Countries in Year 2055 Descending Population Sequence	HIV Infection Rate (Percent)					Calories per Capita (Per Capita/Day)					Malnourished Children (Percent)				
	2005	2030	2055	% Chg	% An Chg	2005	2030	2055	% Chg	% An Chg	2005	2030	2055	% Chg	% An Chg
AMERICAS															
Haiti	3.098	0.758	0.023	-99.3%	-9.3%	2104	2338	2754	30.9%	0.5%	19.24	16.46	8.152	-57.6%	-1.7%
Dominican Republic	1.325	0.445	0.019	-98.6%	-8.1%	2405	2908	3376	40.4%	0.7%	5.452	2.586	0	-100.0%	
Cuba	0.078	0.024	0.001	-98.7%	-8.3%	2903	3296	3754	29.3%	0.5%	3.057	0	0	-100.0%	
Puerto Rico	0.007	0.003	0	-100.0%		3130	3568	3800	21.4%	0.4%	0	0	0		
Jamaica	1.253	0.427	0.018	-98.6%	-8.1%	2717	3047	3574	31.5%	0.5%	4.559	1.093	0	-100.0%	
Trinidad and Tobago	2.309	0.697	0.03	-98.7%	-8.3%	2834	3338	3577	26.2%	0.5%	4.152	0	0	-100.0%	
Bahamas	2.593	0.589	0.017	-99.3%	-9.6%	2805	3129	3543	26.3%	0.5%	8.496	0	0	-100.0%	
Barbados	1.198	0.371	0.018	-98.5%	-8.1%	3059	3364	3773	23.3%	0.4%	1.607	0	0	-100.0%	
Grenada	0.008	0.003	0	-100.0%		2855	3147	3612	26.5%	0.5%	7.074	0	0	-100.0%	
St. Vincent & the Grenadines	0.009	0.003	0	-100.0%		2535	2900	3427	35.2%	0.6%	15.47	5.556	0	-100.0%	
St. Lucia	0.008	0.003	0	-100.0%		2970	3352	3795	27.8%	0.5%	3.952	0	0	-100.0%	
America-Caribbean	**1.174**	**0.382**	**0.015**	**-98.7%**	**-8.4%**	**2611**	**2942**	**3310**	**26.8%**	**0.5%**	**7.227**	**5.32**	**2.738**	**-62.1%**	**-1.9%**
Guatemala	0.689	0.254	0.011	-98.4%	-7.9%	2209	2639	3196	44.7%	0.7%	22.19	11.45	0	-100.0%	
Honduras	1.693	0.765	0.045	-97.3%	-7.0%	2406	2701	3144	30.7%	0.5%	17.69	10.26	0	-100.0%	
Nicaragua	0.172	0.06	0.003	-98.3%	-7.8%	2321	2616	3059	31.8%	0.6%	10.64	8.391	1.192	-88.8%	-4.3%
El Salvador	0.757	0.256	0.011	-98.5%	-8.1%	2543	2937	3413	34.2%	0.6%	10.34	3.544	0	-100.0%	
Costa Rica	0.248	0.083	0.004	-98.4%	-7.9%	2894	3329	3788	30.9%	0.5%	3.798	0	0	-100.0%	
Panama	0.51	0.17	0.007	-98.6%	-8.2%	2309	2947	3626	57.0%	0.9%	9.062	2.485	0	-100.0%	
Belize	1.873	0.544	0.019	-99.0%	-8.8%	2898	3352	3778	30.4%	0.5%	0.743	0	0	-100.0%	
America-Central	**0.746**	**0.299**	**0.016**	**-97.9%**	**-7.4%**	**2403**	**2778**	**3270**	**36.1%**	**0.6%**	**14.6**	**7.923**	**0.178**	**-98.8%**	**-8.4%**
United States	0.446	0.27	0.025	-94.4%	-5.6%	3800	3800	3800	0.0%	0.0%	0.519	0	0	-100.0%	
Mexico	0.251	0.083	0.004	-98.4%	-7.9%	3180	3401	3615	13.7%	0.3%	9.693	5.07	0	-100.0%	
Canada	0.221	0.076	0.004	-98.2%	-7.7%	3568	3768	3800	6.5%	0.1%	0	0	0		
America-North	**0.383**	**0.206**	**0.018**	**-95.3%**	**-5.9%**	**3633**	**3697**	**3755**	**3.4%**	**0.1%**	**2.704**	**1.278**	**0**	**-100.0%**	
Brazil	0.393	0.089	0.003	-99.2%	-9.3%	3009	3265	3587	19.2%	0.4%	3.901	0	0	-100.0%	
Colombia	0.496	0.167	0.007	-98.6%	-8.2%	2636	3012	3489	32.4%	0.6%	6.986	1.831	0	-100.0%	
Argentina	0.468	0.164	0.007	-98.5%	-8.1%	3254	3566	3800	16.8%	0.3%	11.46	5.28	0	-100.0%	
Peru	0.498	0.17	0.007	-98.6%	-8.2%	2600	2997	3418	31.5%	0.5%	6.363	1.898	0	-100.0%	
Venezuela	0.575	0.197	0.009	-98.4%	-8.0%	2460	3011	3539	43.9%	0.7%	4.784	1.292	0	-100.0%	
Chile	0.239	0.08	0.004	-98.3%	-7.9%	2899	3345	3743	29.1%	0.5%	0.91	0	0	-100.0%	
Ecuador	0.249	0.086	0.004	-98.4%	-7.9%	2766	2996	3220	16.4%	0.3%	10.47	3.467	0	-100.0%	
Bolivia	0.083	0.03	0.001	-98.8%	-8.5%	2296	2755	3350	45.9%	0.8%	8.982	5.316	0	-100.0%	
Paraguay	0.336	0.119	0.005	-98.5%	-8.1%	2601	2864	3311	27.3%	0.5%	5.08	3.576	0	-100.0%	
Uruguay	0.374	0.129	0.006	-98.4%	-7.9%	2922	3341	3742	28.1%	0.5%	1.739	0	0	-100.0%	
Guyana	2.301	0.629	0.024	-99.0%	-8.7%	2767	2995	3285	18.7%	0.3%	10.92	3.618	0	-100.0%	
Suriname	1.6	0.541	0.023	-98.6%	-8.1%	2711	3055	3506	29.3%	0.5%	10.69	1.638	0	-100.0%	
America-South	**0.419**	**0.121**	**0.005**	**-98.8%**	**-8.5%**	**2880**	**3193**	**3556**	**23.5%**	**0.4%**	**5.561**	**1.366**	**0**	**-100.0%**	

Health

Base Case: Countries in Year 2055 Descending Population Sequence	HIV Infection Rate (Percent)					Calories per Capita (Per Capita/Day)					Malnourished Children (Percent)				
	2005	2030	2055	% Chg	% An Chg	2005	2030	2055	% Chg	% An Chg	2005	2030	2055	% Chg	% An Chg
ASIA INCL OCEANIA															
China	0.274	0.196	0.016	-94.2%	-5.5%	3085	3589	3800	23.2%	0.4%	2.033	0	0	-100.0%	
Japan	0.068	0.023	0.001	-98.5%	-8.1%	2885	3284	3682	27.6%	0.5%	6.243	0	0	-100.0%	
Korea, Rep. of	0.079	0.024	0.001	-98.7%	-8.4%	3134	3548	3800	21.3%	0.4%	0	0	0		
Taiwan	0.008	0.002	0	-100.0%		3352	3559	3800	13.4%	0.3%	0	0	0		
Korea, Dem. Rep. of	0.008	0.003	0	-100.0%		2224	2620	3113	40.0%	0.7%	23.18	12.49	0.199	-99.1%	-9.1%
Hong Kong	0.077	0.024	0.001	-98.7%	-8.3%	3307	3557	3757	13.6%	0.3%	0	0	0		
Mongolia	0.087	0.028	0.001	-98.9%	-8.5%	2327	2671	3126	34.3%	0.6%	12.05	7.992	0	-100.0%	
Asia-East	**0.243**	**0.174**	**0.014**	**-94.2%**	**-5.5%**	**3061**	**3551**	**3782**	**23.6%**	**0.4%**	**2.605**	**0.191**	**0.003**	**-99.9%**	**-12.7%**
India	1.108	0.867	0.08	-92.8%	-5.1%	2509	2993	3510	39.9%	0.7%	36.17	5.994	0	-100.0%	
Pakistan	0.084	0.03	0.001	-98.8%	-8.5%	2507	2797	3147	25.5%	0.5%	31.91	14.06	0	-100.0%	
Bangladesh	0.085	0.029	0.001	-98.8%	-8.5%	2245	2676	3138	39.8%	0.7%	47.89	19.67	0	-100.0%	
Iran, Islamic Rep. of	0.17	0.057	0.002	-98.8%	-8.5%	3127	3531	3737	19.5%	0.4%	0	0	0		
Afghanistan	0.084	0.031	0.001	-98.8%	-8.5%	1813	2060	2463	35.9%	0.6%	41.37	31.99	18.46	-55.4%	-1.6%
Nepal	0.418	0.151	0.007	-98.3%	-7.9%	2450	2634	2884	17.7%	0.3%	44.74	26.57	10.19	-77.2%	-2.9%
Uzbekistan	0.173	0.058	0.003	-98.3%	-7.8%	2415	2808	3182	31.8%	0.6%	10.76	5.496	0	-100.0%	
Sri Lanka	0.081	0.026	0.001	-98.8%	-8.4%	2456	2885	3337	35.9%	0.6%	26.61	8.065	0	-100.0%	
Kazakhstan	0.082	0.027	0.001	-98.8%	-8.4%	2542	3259	3576	40.7%	0.7%	3.273	0	0	-100.0%	
Tajikistan	0.088	0.03	0.001	-98.9%	-8.6%	2022	2468	2947	45.7%	0.8%	34.48	18.66	4.564	-86.8%	-4.0%
Turkmenistan	0.086	0.029	0.001	-98.8%	-8.5%	2790	3323	3415	22.4%	0.4%	9.516	0	0	-100.0%	
Kyrgyzstan	0.085	0.029	0.001	-98.8%	-8.5%	2914	2965	3084	5.8%	0.1%	7.74	5.333	1.152	-85.1%	-3.7%
Bhutan	0.083	0.03	0.001	-98.8%	-8.5%	2602	3075	3651	40.3%	0.7%	14.25	1.176	0	-100.0%	
Maldives	0.009	0.003	0	-100.0%		2602	3055	3640	39.9%	0.7%	29.36	2.996	0	-100.0%	
Asia-South Central	**0.808**	**0.594**	**0.051**	**-93.7%**	**-5.4%**	**2498**	**2930**	**3373**	**35.0%**	**0.6%**	**34.44**	**8.987**	**0.905**	**-97.4%**	**-7.0%**
Indonesia	0.083	0.027	0.001	-98.8%	-8.5%	2965	3257	3463	16.8%	0.3%	20.34	0	0	-100.0%	
Philippines	0.084	0.029	0.001	-98.8%	-8.5%	2445	2812	3277	34.0%	0.6%	25.95	10.36	0	-100.0%	
Vietnam	0.426	0.137	0.006	-98.6%	-8.2%	2596	3109	3502	34.9%	0.6%	27.84	0.537	0	-100.0%	
Thailand	1.07	0.237	0.007	-99.3%	-9.6%	2529	3010	3483	37.7%	0.6%	10.71	2.115	0	-100.0%	
Myanmar	2.175	0.793	0.04	-98.2%	-7.7%	2874	3066	3285	14.3%	0.3%	27.13	4.708	0	-100.0%	
Malaysia	0.409	0.141	0.006	-98.5%	-8.1%	2957	3401	3734	26.3%	0.5%	10.58	0	0	-100.0%	
Cambodia	1.525	0.48	0.017	-98.9%	-8.6%	2187	2761	3283	50.1%	0.8%	37.14	12	0	-100.0%	
Laos	0.085	0.03	0.001	-98.8%	-8.5%	2331	2854	3343	43.4%	0.7%	35.74	9.944	0	-100.0%	
Singapore	0.227	0.075	0.004	-98.2%	-7.8%	3423	3665	3800	11.0%	0.2%	2.756	0	0	-100.0%	
Timor-Leste	0.008	0.003	0	-100.0%		2793	2919	3162	13.2%	0.2%	35.2	16.98	0	-100.0%	
Brunei	0.085	0.026	0.001	-98.8%	-8.5%	2902	3261	3520	21.3%	0.4%	5.775	0	0	-100.0%	
Asia-South East	**0.499**	**0.152**	**0.007**	**-98.6%**	**-8.2%**	**2748**	**3102**	**3427**	**24.7%**	**0.4%**	**21.83**	**3.09**	**0**	**-100.0%**	

Health

Base Case: Countries in Year 2055 Descending Population Sequence	HIV Infection Rate (Percent)					Calories per Capita (Per Capita/Day)					Malnourished Children (Percent)				
	2005	2030	2055	% Chg	% An Chg	2005	2030	2055	% Chg	% An Chg	2005	2030	2055	% Chg	% An Chg
ASIA INCL OCEANIA continued															
Turkey	0.008	0.003	0	-100.0%		3429	3675	3800	10.8%	0.2%	5.52	0.36	0	-100.0%	
Yemen	0.009	0.003	0	-100.0%		2108	2600	3064	45.4%	0.8%	40.79	17.8	1.683	-95.9%	-6.2%
Iraq	0.009	0.003	0	-100.0%		2501	2958	3384	35.3%	0.6%	17.4	4.236	0	-100.0%	
Saudi Arabia	0.009	0.003	0	-100.0%		2900	3307	3737	28.9%	0.5%	9.145	0	0	-100.0%	
Syria	0.009	0.003	0	-100.0%		3050	3265	3554	16.5%	0.3%	5.736	0	0	-100.0%	
Israel	0.062	0.022	0.001	-98.4%	-7.9%	3611	3800	3800	5.2%	0.1%	0	0	0		
Azerbaijan	0.085	0.028	0.001	-98.8%	-8.5%	2533	3052	3450	36.2%	0.6%	9.29	1.207	0	-100.0%	
Jordan	0.087	0.029	0.001	-98.9%	-8.5%	2719	3194	3799	39.7%	0.7%	4.433	0	0	-100.0%	
Palestine	0.009	0.003	0	-100.0%		2209	2614	3211	45.4%	0.8%	5.536	5.831	0	-100.0%	
Oman	0.085	0.027	0.001	-98.8%	-8.5%	3145	3443	3667	16.6%	0.3%	0	0	0		
Lebanon	0.082	0.027	0.001	-98.8%	-8.4%	3230	3649	3800	17.6%	0.3%	3.08	0	0	-100.0%	
United Arab Emirates	0.12	0.031	0.002	-98.3%	-7.9%	3269	3626	3800	16.2%	0.3%	0	0	0		
Kuwait	0.096	0.027	0.001	-99.0%	-8.7%	3168	3511	3792	19.7%	0.4%	0	0	0		
Georgia	0.156	0.052	0.002	-98.7%	-8.3%	2314	2752	3222	39.2%	0.7%	2.38	3.396	0	-100.0%	
Armenia	0.081	0.028	0.001	-98.8%	-8.4%	2255	2839	3346	48.4%	0.8%	3.762	2.812	0	-100.0%	
Bahrain	0.086	0.025	0.001	-98.8%	-8.5%	3262	3598	3800	16.5%	0.3%	9.142	3.364	0	-100.0%	
Qatar	0.075	0.023	0.001	-98.7%	-8.3%	3374	3679	3772	11.8%	0.2%	4.798	0	0	-100.0%	
Cyprus	0.075	0.026	0.001	-98.7%	-8.3%	3292	3554	3800	15.4%	0.3%	0	0	0		
Asia-West	**0.027**	**0.008**	**0**	**-100.0%**		**2960**	**3261**	**3545**	**19.8%**	**0.4%**	**10.53**	**3.362**	**0.281**	**-97.3%**	**-7.0%**
Australia	0.061	0.022	0.001	-98.4%	-7.9%	3144	3499	3762	19.7%	0.4%	0	0	0		
Papua New Guinea	1.545	0.545	0.025	-98.4%	-7.9%	2223	2621	3102	39.5%	0.7%	28.38	14.43	0.516	-98.2%	-7.7%
New Zealand	0.074	0.026	0.001	-98.6%	-8.2%	3278	3542	3800	15.9%	0.3%	0	0	0		
Solomon Islands	0.009	0.003	0	-100.0%		2271	2606	3086	35.9%	0.6%	19.76	12.04	0.82	-95.9%	-6.2%
Fiji	0.083	0.029	0.001	-98.8%	-8.5%	2914	3224	3588	23.1%	0.4%	1.886	0	0	-100.0%	
Vanuatu	0.008	0.003	0	-100.0%		2593	2900	3328	28.3%	0.5%	10.77	4.677	0	-100.0%	
Micronesia	0.008	0.003	0	-100.0%		2871	3043	3334	16.1%	0.3%	6.645	2.021	0	-100.0%	
Samoa	0.009	0.003	0	-100.0%		2901	3172	3555	22.5%	0.4%	1.296	0	0	-100.0%	
Tonga	0.008	0.003	0	-100.0%		2895	3030	3272	13.0%	0.2%	5.97	2.363	0	-100.0%	
Oceania	**0.302**	**0.142**	**0.008**	**-97.4%**	**-7.0%**	**2966**	**3271**	**3567**	**20.3%**	**0.4%**	**5.684**	**3.544**	**0.152**	**-97.3%**	**-7.0%**

Health   Measures of Poverty, Health, Education, Infrastructure and Governance

Base Case: Countries in Year 2055 Descending Population Sequence	HIV Infection Rate (Percent)					Calories per Capita (Per Capita/Day)					Malnourished Children (Percent)			
	2005	2030	2055	% Chg	% An Chg	2005	2030	2055	% Chg	% An Chg	2005	2030	2055	% Chg
EUROPE														
Russia	1.232	0.376	0.016	-98.7%	-8.3%	3014	3443	3639	20.7%	0.4%	2.697	0	0	-100.0%
Poland	0.075	0.025	0.001	-98.7%	-8.3%	3416	3621	3800	11.2%	0.2%	0	0	0	
Ukraine	1.056	0.349	0.016	-98.5%	-8.0%	2996	3390	3705	23.7%	0.4%	1.848	0	0	-100.0%
Romania	0.076	0.024	0.001	-98.7%	-8.3%	3426	3588	3680	7.4%	0.1%	2.623	0	0	-100.0%
Belarus	0.142	0.047	0.002	-98.6%	-8.2%	3093	3501	3800	22.9%	0.4%	0.729	0	0	-100.0%
Czech Republic	0.071	0.023	0.001	-98.6%	-8.2%	3132	3368	3641	16.3%	0.3%	0	0	0	
Hungary	0.072	0.024	0.001	-98.6%	-8.2%	3534	3677	3791	7.3%	0.1%	0	0	0	
Bulgaria	0.072	0.024	0.001	-98.6%	-8.2%	2893	3255	3619	25.1%	0.4%	6.023	0	0	-100.0%
Slovak Republic	0.076	0.025	0.001	-98.7%	-8.3%	2956	3244	3570	20.8%	0.4%	4.319	0	0	-100.0%
Moldova	0.623	0.213	0.009	-98.6%	-8.1%	2721	3004	3396	24.8%	0.4%	3.342	1.489	0	-100.0%
Europe-East	**0.797**	**0.244**	**0.011**	**-98.6%**	**-8.2%**	**3109**	**3464**	**3679**	**18.3%**	**0.3%**	**2.087**	**0.021**	**0**	**-100.0%**
United Kingdom	0.145	0.05	0.002	-98.6%	-8.2%	3398	3657	3800	11.8%	0.2%	0	0	0	
Sweden	0.139	0.05	0.002	-98.6%	-8.1%	3151	3544	3761	19.4%	0.4%	0	0	0	
Denmark	0.14	0.05	0.002	-98.6%	-8.1%	3416	3675	3800	11.2%	0.2%	0	0	0	
Norway	0.072	0.025	0.001	-98.6%	-8.2%	3412	3650	3800	11.4%	0.2%	0	0	0	
Ireland	0.153	0.052	0.002	-98.7%	-8.3%	3757	3800	3800	1.1%	0.0%	0	0	0	
Finland	0.069	0.026	0.001	-98.6%	-8.1%	3173	3474	3773	18.9%	0.3%	0	0	0	
Lithuania	0.151	0.051	0.002	-98.7%	-8.3%	3451	3700	3800	10.1%	0.2%	0	0	0	
Latvia	0.595	0.201	0.009	-98.5%	-8.0%	3051	3464	3800	24.5%	0.4%	1.813	0	0	-100.0%
Estonia	0.961	0.322	0.016	-98.3%	-7.9%	3114	3537	3800	22.0%	0.4%	0.187	0	0	-100.0%
Iceland	0.152	0.052	0.002	-98.7%	-8.3%	3290	3592	3786	15.1%	0.3%	0	0	0	
Europe-North	**0.16**	**0.054**	**0.002**	**-98.8%**	**-8.4%**	**3369**	**3641**	**3795**	**12.6%**	**0.2%**	**0.046**	**0**	**0**	**-100.0%**
Italy	0.361	0.113	0.006	-98.3%	-7.9%	3695	3734	3800	2.8%	0.1%	0	0	0	
Spain	0.456	0.134	0.007	-98.5%	-8.0%	3415	3621	3800	11.3%	0.2%	0	0	0	
Greece	0.149	0.047	0.002	-98.7%	-8.3%	3689	3800	3800	3.0%	0.1%	0	0	0	
Portugal	0.223	0.072	0.004	-98.2%	-7.7%	3734	3800	3800	1.8%	0.0%	0	0	0	
Serbia and Montenegro	0.148	0.052	0.002	-98.6%	-8.2%	2770	3076	3599	29.9%	0.5%	1.97	0.489	0	-100.0%
Croatia	0.073	0.025	0.001	-98.6%	-8.2%	2805	3187	3723	32.7%	0.6%	0.78	0	0	-100.0%
Bosnia and Herzegovina	0.075	0.024	0.001	-98.7%	-8.3%	2675	2986	3382	26.4%	0.5%	3.94	1.765	0	-100.0%
Albania	0.008	0.003	0	-100.0%		2930	3235	3524	20.3%	0.4%	8.27	0	0	-100.0%
Macedonia	0.076	0.026	0.001	-98.7%	-8.3%	2695	2966	3372	25.1%	0.4%	4.546	2.246	0	-100.0%
Slovenia	0.073	0.024	0.001	-98.6%	-8.2%	3177	3441	3800	19.6%	0.4%	0	0	0	
Malta	0.071	0.026	0.001	-98.6%	-8.2%	3495	3662	3800	8.7%	0.2%	0	0	0	
Europe-South	**0.316**	**0.096**	**0.005**	**-98.4%**	**-8.0%**	**3470**	**3609**	**3759**	**8.3%**	**0.2%**	**0.493**	**0.113**	**0**	**-100.0%**
Germany	0.073	0.024	0.001	-98.6%	-8.2%	3451	3659	3800	10.1%	0.2%	0	0	0	
France	0.282	0.099	0.005	-98.2%	-7.7%	3611	3766	3800	5.2%	0.1%	0	0	0	
Netherlands	0.144	0.05	0.002	-98.6%	-8.2%	3391	3602	3800	12.1%	0.2%	0	0	0	
Belgium	0.218	0.075	0.004	-98.2%	-7.7%	3605	3641	3800	5.4%	0.1%	0	0	0	
Austria	0.21	0.068	0.003	-98.6%	-8.1%	3765	3800	3800	0.9%	0.0%	0	0	0	
Switzerland	0.273	0.093	0.004	-98.5%	-8.1%	3470	3679	3800	9.5%	0.2%	0	0	0	
Luxembourg	0.148	0.051	0.002	-98.6%	-8.2%	3645	3795	3800	4.3%	0.1%	0	0	0	
Europe-West	**0.168**	**0.059**	**0.003**	**-98.2%**	**-7.7%**	**3521**	**3695**	**3800**	**7.9%**	**0.2%**	**0**	**0**	**0**	

Health

Base Case Source: International Futures Version 5.47 March 2008	Malnourished Population (Percent)					Total Fertility Rate (Births)					Crude Birth Rate (Per Thousand)				
	2005	2030	2055	% Chg	% An Chg	2005	2030	2055	% Chg	% An Chg	2005	2030	2055	% Chg	% An Chg
World	11.05	5.14	1.484	-86.6%	-3.9%	2.678	2.292	2.046	-23.6%	-0.5%	20.71	15.98	12.82	-38.1%	-1.0%
Africa	24.26	15.84	5.11	-78.9%	-3.1%	4.919	3.743	2.684	-45.4%	-1.2%	36.67	28.64	20.14	-45.1%	-1.2%
Americas	5.732	1.617	0.179	-96.9%	-6.7%	2.271	1.874	1.809	-20.3%	-0.5%	18.01	13.04	10.62	-41.0%	-1.1%
Asia incl Oceania	11.04	3.338	0.483	-95.6%	-6.1%	2.489	2.045	1.89	-24.1%	-0.5%	19.64	13.83	10.93	-44.3%	-1.2%
Europe	1.171	0.04	0	-100.0%		1.407	1.518	1.624	15.4%	0.3%	9.905	8.038	7.74	-21.9%	-0.5%
World	11.05	5.14	1.484	-86.6%	-3.9%	2.678	2.292	2.046	-23.6%	-0.5%	20.71	15.98	12.82	-38.1%	-1.0%
Africa-Eastern	38.94	22.71	5.176	-86.7%	-4.0%	5.421	3.998	2.498	-53.9%	-1.5%	39.74	30.31	19.07	-52.0%	-1.5%
Africa-Middle	54.81	36.22	14.21	-74.1%	-2.7%	6.013	4.628	3.334	-44.6%	-1.2%	44.13	36.34	26.33	-40.3%	-1.0%
Africa-Northern	5.924	1.607	0	-100.0%		3.136	2.196	1.862	-40.6%	-1.0%	25.5	16.44	11.82	-53.6%	-1.5%
Africa-Southern	6.24	1.194	0	-100.0%		2.796	1.912	1.806	-35.4%	-0.9%	23.19	15.39	11.58	-50.1%	-1.4%
Africa-Western	12.42	9.019	3.105	-75.0%	-2.7%	5.624	4.185	2.999	-46.7%	-1.2%	40.95	32	22.64	-44.7%	-1.2%
Africa	24.26	15.84	5.11	-78.9%	-3.1%	4.919	3.743	2.684	-45.4%	-1.2%	36.67	28.64	20.14	-45.1%	-1.2%
America-Caribbean	19.48	9.965	4.016	-79.4%	-3.1%	2.494	2.241	2.087	-16.3%	-0.4%	20.03	15.59	12.92	-35.5%	-0.9%
America-Central	19.34	9.672	0.195	-99.0%	-8.8%	3.552	2.593	1.826	-48.6%	-1.3%	29.16	20.44	12.91	-55.7%	-1.6%
America-North	1.108	0.249	0	-100.0%		1.995	1.784	1.79	-10.3%	-0.2%	14.72	11.59	10.3	-30.0%	-0.7%
America-South	8.228	1.241	0	-100.0%		2.43	1.842	1.8	-25.9%	-0.6%	20.41	13.39	10.39	-49.1%	-1.3%
Americas	5.732	1.617	0.179	-96.9%	-6.7%	2.271	1.874	1.809	-20.3%	-0.5%	18.01	13.04	10.62	-41.0%	-1.1%
Asia-East	1.909	0.267	0	-100.0%		1.756	1.771	1.783	1.5%	0.0%	13.14	9.877	8.601	-34.5%	-0.8%
Asia-South Central	20.53	6.179	1.014	-95.1%	-5.8%	3.092	2.247	1.99	-35.6%	-0.9%	24.82	16.41	12.4	-50.0%	-1.4%
Asia-South East	9.846	2.18	0	-100.0%		2.463	1.98	1.803	-26.8%	-0.6%	20.72	14.18	10.75	-48.1%	-1.3%
Asia-West	10.57	3.382	0.18	-98.3%	-7.8%	3.417	2.318	1.894	-44.6%	-1.2%	26.02	17.35	12.2	-53.1%	-1.5%
Oceania	5.577	3.458	0.03	-99.5%	-9.9%	2.325	2.115	1.851	-20.4%	-0.5%	16.85	14.17	11.6	-31.2%	-0.7%
Asia incl Oceania	11.04	3.338	0.483	-95.6%	-6.1%	2.489	2.045	1.89	-24.1%	-0.5%	19.64	13.83	10.93	-44.3%	-1.2%
Europe-East	2.255	0.04	0	-100.0%		1.254	1.4	1.543	23.0%	0.4%	9.697	7.113	6.59	-32.0%	-0.8%
Europe-North	0.04	0	0	-100.0%		1.643	1.687	1.729	5.2%	0.1%	10.79	9.567	9.247	-14.3%	-0.3%
Europe-South	1.177	0.125	0	-100.0%		1.348	1.463	1.586	17.7%	0.3%	9.77	7.574	7.196	-26.3%	-0.6%
Europe-West	0	0	0			1.579	1.642	1.702	7.8%	0.2%	9.887	8.919	8.852	-10.5%	-0.2%
Europe	1.171	0.04	0	-100.0%		1.407	1.518	1.624	15.4%	0.3%	9.905	8.038	7.74	-21.9%	-0.5%

Multination Regional Analysis

Measures of Poverty, Health, Education, Infrastructure and Governance

Health

Base Case: Countries in Year 2055 Descending Population Sequence	Malnourished Population (Percent)					Total Fertility Rate (Births)					Crude Birth Rate (Per Thousand)				
	2005	2030	2055	% Chg	% An Chg	2005	2030	2055	% Chg	% An Chg	2005	2030	2055	% Chg	% An Chg
AFRICA															
Ethiopia	37.36	25.31	7.36	-80.3%	-3.2%	5.441	4.287	2.877	-47.1%	-1.3%	38.95	31.73	21.54	-44.7%	-1.2%
Tanzania	43.62	19.62	0	-100.0%		5.252	3.682	2.003	-61.9%	-1.9%	39.34	28.75	15.61	-60.3%	-1.8%
Uganda	19.73	8.28	0	-100.0%		6.583	4.085	1.8	-72.7%	-2.6%	46.81	32.61	15.21	-67.5%	-2.2%
Kenya	39.73	19.14	0	-100.0%		4.763	3.275	1.8	-62.2%	-1.9%	37.31	25.51	13.89	-62.8%	-2.0%
Madagascar	37.88	24.76	8.228	-78.3%	-3.0%	5.353	4.197	2.955	-44.8%	-1.2%	39.45	31.84	22.42	-43.2%	-1.1%
Mozambique	44.64	17.17	0	-100.0%		5.305	3.58	2.174	-59.0%	-1.8%	38.56	26.64	16.15	-58.1%	-1.7%
Malawi	28.04	20.6	6.439	-77.0%	-2.9%	5.955	4.444	2.885	-51.6%	-1.4%	42.96	34.01	22.7	-47.2%	-1.3%
Zambia	46.55	29.17	6.217	-86.6%	-3.9%	5.568	4.218	2.618	-53.0%	-1.5%	40.75	32.34	20.8	-49.0%	-1.3%
Zimbabwe	33.8	19.91	0.034	-99.9%	-12.9%	3.62	2.801	1.8	-50.3%	-1.4%	31.14	22.97	13.91	-55.3%	-1.6%
Burundi	70.23	53.96	17.92	-74.5%	-2.7%	6.606	5.139	3.575	-45.9%	-1.2%	43.02	35.34	25.78	-40.1%	-1.0%
Rwanda	38.02	23.15	4.834	-87.3%	-4.0%	5.643	4.206	2.704	-52.1%	-1.5%	40.84	30.38	20.04	-50.9%	-1.4%
Somalia	68.66	43	24.17	-64.8%	-2.1%	6.415	5.07	4.122	-35.7%	-0.9%	45.1	35.94	29.25	-35.1%	-0.9%
Eritrea	54.33	62.53	32.69	-39.8%	-1.0%	5.552	4.823	3.992	-28.1%	-0.7%	41.24	34.54	28.91	-29.9%	-0.7%
Mauritius	2.833	0	0	-100.0%		1.867	1.8	1.8	-3.6%	-0.1%	15.14	11.37	9.683	-36.0%	-0.9%
Comoros	46.07	30.16	10.18	-77.9%	-3.0%	4.17	3.499	2.512	-39.8%	-1.0%	32.3	26.16	18.55	-42.6%	-1.1%
Djibouti	28.16	20.11	7.656	-72.8%	-2.6%	5.055	4.184	3.141	-37.9%	-0.9%	35.01	31.21	22.75	-35.0%	-0.9%
Africa-Eastern	**38.94**	**22.71**	**5.176**	**-86.7%**	**-4.0%**	**5.421**	**3.998**	**2.498**	**-53.9%**	**-1.5%**	**39.74**	**30.31**	**19.07**	**-52.0%**	**-1.5%**
Congo, Dem. Rep. of the	77.2	47.4	17.81	-76.9%	-2.9%	6.445	4.972	3.474	-46.1%	-1.2%	46.85	38.92	27.98	-40.3%	-1.0%
Angola	41.39	22.47	8.871	-78.6%	-3.0%	6.327	4.528	3.298	-47.9%	-1.3%	45.35	34.96	25	-44.9%	-1.2%
Cameroon	21.69	16.92	7.688	-64.6%	-2.1%	4.814	3.898	2.939	-38.9%	-1.0%	37.33	31.47	22.44	-39.9%	-1.0%
Chad	22.91	13.03	7.447	-67.5%	-2.2%	6.033	4.259	3.253	-46.1%	-1.2%	44.27	33.75	25.16	-43.2%	-1.1%
Central African Republic	41.33	59.73	16.98	-58.9%	-1.8%	5.018	4.381	3.432	-31.6%	-0.8%	38.38	35.04	25.62	-33.2%	-0.8%
Congo, Rep. of	27.92	15.5	4.007	-85.6%	-3.8%	5.208	3.719	2.559	-50.9%	-1.4%	38.05	28.73	19.08	-49.9%	-1.4%
Gabon	7.134	1.505	0	-100.0%		4	2.28	1.8	-55.0%	-1.6%	32.27	18.86	12.72	-60.6%	-1.8%
Equatorial Guinea	7.239	0	0	-100.0%		5.363	2.857	1.942	-63.8%	-2.0%	39.55	23.84	14.71	-62.8%	-2.0%
São Tomé and Príncipe	24	19.61	12.98	-45.9%	-1.2%	4.05	3.392	2.904	-28.3%	-0.7%	36.6	26.54	21.05	-42.5%	-1.1%
Africa-Middle	**54.81**	**36.22**	**14.21**	**-74.1%**	**-2.7%**	**6.013**	**4.628**	**3.334**	**-44.6%**	**-1.2%**	**44.13**	**36.34**	**26.33**	**-40.3%**	**-1.0%**
Egypt	3.139	0	0	-100.0%		3.236	2.047	1.8	-44.4%	-1.2%	26.66	15.9	11.26	-57.8%	-1.7%
Sudan	16.9	7.55	0	-100.0%		4.379	3.06	2.065	-52.8%	-1.5%	33.25	23.33	14.99	-54.9%	-1.6%
Algeria	3.928	0	0	-100.0%		2.482	1.8	1.8	-27.5%	-0.6%	20.88	12.73	10.18	-51.2%	-1.4%
Morocco	3.945	0	0	-100.0%		2.52	1.998	1.8	-28.6%	-0.7%	21.56	14.35	11.03	-48.8%	-1.3%
Tunisia	2.203	0	0	-100.0%		1.962	1.8	1.8	-8.3%	-0.2%	16.76	11.59	9.459	-43.6%	-1.1%
Libya	0	0	0			2.899	1.8	1.8	-37.9%	-0.9%	23.11	12.76	9.937	-57.0%	-1.7%
Africa-Northern	**5.924**	**1.607**	**0**	**-100.0%**		**3.136**	**2.196**	**1.862**	**-40.6%**	**-1.0%**	**25.5**	**16.44**	**11.82**	**-53.6%**	**-1.5%**

Health

Base Case: Countries in Year 2055 Descending Population Sequence	Malnourished Population (Percent)					Total Fertility Rate (Births)					Crude Birth Rate (Per Thousand)				
	2005	2030	2055	% Chg	% An Chg	2005	2030	2055	% Chg	% An Chg	2005	2030	2055	% Chg	% An Chg
AFRICA continued															
South Africa	4.588	0	0	-100.0%		2.654	1.8	1.8	-32.2%	-0.8%	22.23	14.54	11.25	-49.4%	-1.4%
Namibia	7.7	4.373	0	-100.0%		4.02	2.501	1.8	-55.2%	-1.6%	29.85	19.81	13.25	-55.6%	-1.6%
Lesotho	24.09	14.55	0	-100.0%		3.731	3.012	1.936	-48.1%	-1.3%	30.03	23.48	14.5	-51.7%	-1.4%
Botswana	23.61	5.903	0	-100.0%		3.116	1.8	1.8	-42.2%	-1.1%	26.64	15.23	11	-58.7%	-1.8%
Swaziland	12.46	6.116	0	-100.0%		4.267	2.806	1.8	-57.8%	-1.7%	32.99	21.79	13.54	-59.0%	-1.8%
Africa-Southern	**6.24**	**1.194**	**0**	**-100.0%**		**2.796**	**1.912**	**1.806**	**-35.4%**	**-0.9%**	**23.19**	**15.39**	**11.58**	**-50.1%**	**-1.4%**
Nigeria	5.083	1.815	0.929	-81.7%	-3.3%	5.582	3.932	2.841	-49.1%	-1.3%	40.52	30.49	21.42	-47.1%	-1.3%
Niger	33.35	25.23	11.43	-65.7%	-2.1%	7.682	5.986	4.2	-45.3%	-1.2%	53.83	44.35	32.22	-40.1%	-1.0%
Ghana	6.217	7.109	3.142	-49.5%	-1.4%	4.344	3.65	2.79	-35.8%	-0.9%	32.49	26.74	20.15	-38.0%	-1.0%
Côte d'Ivoire	14.33	6.943	0	-100.0%		5.116	3.738	2.474	-51.6%	-1.4%	38.86	28.96	18.91	-51.3%	-1.4%
Mali	18.05	13.29	4.896	-72.9%	-2.6%	6.682	4.97	3.395	-49.2%	-1.3%	48.48	37.78	25.97	-46.4%	-1.2%
Burkina Faso	21.62	14.4	2.263	-89.5%	-4.4%	6.017	4.647	3.105	-48.4%	-1.3%	43.35	35.01	23.79	-45.1%	-1.2%
Senegal	23.48	13.46	1.132	-95.2%	-5.9%	5.007	3.713	2.459	-50.9%	-1.4%	37.53	27.91	18.28	-51.3%	-1.4%
Guinea	27.93	16.14	4.195	-85.0%	-3.7%	5.416	4.144	2.937	-45.8%	-1.2%	38.46	31.72	22.18	-42.3%	-1.1%
Benin	11.26	8.872	0.958	-91.5%	-4.8%	5.735	4.337	2.785	-51.4%	-1.4%	41.81	33.03	21.34	-49.0%	-1.3%
Togo	21.48	24.83	12.48	-41.9%	-1.1%	5.361	4.344	3.433	-36.0%	-0.9%	39.71	32.4	25.21	-36.5%	-0.9%
Liberia	38.77	81.04	16.06	-58.6%	-1.7%	6.548	5.248	3.811	-41.8%	-1.1%	48.18	41.31	28.54	-40.8%	-1.0%
Sierra Leone	41.08	23.92	9.652	-76.5%	-2.9%	6.047	4.441	3.14	-48.1%	-1.3%	43.08	36.08	24.49	-43.2%	-1.1%
Mauritania	10.85	7.446	2.391	-78.0%	-3.0%	5.605	4.294	3.091	-44.9%	-1.2%	40.29	31.72	23.03	-42.8%	-1.1%
Guinea-Bissau	31.42	34.98	20.26	-35.5%	-0.9%	6.895	5.621	4.392	-36.3%	-0.9%	48.23	41.54	32.92	-31.7%	-0.8%
Gambia	19.91	13.26	2.805	-85.9%	-3.8%	4.713	3.585	2.516	-46.6%	-1.2%	35.69	27.64	18.99	-46.8%	-1.3%
Cape Verde	6.398	1.837	0	-100.0%		3.675	2.157	1.8	-51.0%	-1.4%	31.04	17.64	11.94	-61.5%	-1.9%
Africa-Western	**12.42**	**9.019**	**3.105**	**-75.0%**	**-2.7%**	**5.624**	**4.185**	**2.999**	**-46.7%**	**-1.2%**	**40.95**	**32**	**22.64**	**-44.7%**	**-1.2%**

Health

Base Case: Countries in Year 2055 Descending Population Sequence	Malnourished Population (Percent)					Total Fertility Rate (Births)					Crude Birth Rate (Per Thousand)				
	2005	2030	2055	% Chg	% An Chg	2005	2030	2055	% Chg	% An Chg	2005	2030	2055	% Chg	% An Chg
AMERICAS															
Haiti	44.43	30.35	11.96	-73.1%	-2.6%	4.093	3.533	2.722	-33.5%	-0.8%	32.05	26.15	19.91	-37.9%	-0.9%
Dominican Republic	22.21	5.695	0	-100.0%		2.589	1.8	1.8	-30.5%	-0.7%	23.24	14.01	10.26	-55.9%	-1.6%
Cuba	10.56	0	0	-100.0%		1.591	1.646	1.701	6.9%	0.1%	11.4	8.891	8.031	-29.6%	-0.7%
Puerto Rico	0	0	0			1.8	1.8	1.8	0.0%	0.0%	13.55	10.98	9.669	-28.6%	-0.7%
Jamaica	7.103	1.163	0	-100.0%		2.438	1.8	1.8	-26.2%	-0.6%	20.28	13.38	10.26	-49.4%	-1.4%
Trinidad and Tobago	7.684	0	0	-100.0%		1.635	1.678	1.722	5.3%	0.1%	14.68	9.612	8.086	-44.9%	-1.2%
Bahamas	8.842	0	0	-100.0%		2.181	1.8	1.8	-17.5%	-0.4%	18.15	12.95	10.47	-42.3%	-1.1%
Barbados	1.285	0	0	-100.0%		1.753	1.765	1.778	1.4%	0.0%	13.67	10.06	8.77	-35.8%	-0.9%
Grenada	7.282	0	0	-100.0%		3.06	1.844	1.8	-41.2%	-1.1%	25.25	14.35	10.95	-56.6%	-1.7%
St. Vincent & the Grenadines	17.65	5.917	0	-100.0%		2.05	1.8	1.8	-12.2%	-0.3%	19.32	12.84	10.02	-48.1%	-1.3%
St. Lucia	3.857	0	0	-100.0%		1.89	1.8	1.8	-4.8%	-0.1%	16.15	11.57	8.609	-46.7%	-1.3%
America-Caribbean	**19.48**	**9.965**	**4.016**	**-79.4%**	**-3.1%**	**2.494**	**2.241**	**2.087**	**-16.3%**	**-0.4%**	**20.03**	**15.59**	**12.92**	**-35.5%**	**-0.9%**
Guatemala	25.84	12.81	0	-100.0%		4.543	3.025	1.8	-60.4%	-1.8%	35.67	24.44	13.88	-61.1%	-1.9%
Honduras	19.02	10.84	0	-100.0%		3.783	2.852	1.857	-50.9%	-1.4%	30.58	22.34	13.69	-55.2%	-1.6%
Nicaragua	26.56	15.45	1.309	-95.1%	-5.8%	3.425	2.714	1.906	-44.4%	-1.2%	30.32	21.85	14.12	-53.4%	-1.5%
El Salvador	13.52	4.044	0	-100.0%		2.889	1.97	1.8	-37.7%	-0.9%	25.1	15.36	11.14	-55.6%	-1.6%
Costa Rica	3.813	0	0	-100.0%		2.227	1.8	1.8	-19.2%	-0.4%	18.71	12.31	9.588	-48.8%	-1.3%
Panama	16.07	3.28	0	-100.0%		2.532	1.8	1.8	-28.9%	-0.7%	20.89	13.16	9.634	-53.9%	-1.5%
Belize	5.984	0	0	-100.0%		3.139	1.8	1.8	-42.7%	-1.1%	27.08	14.46	10.15	-62.5%	-1.9%
America-Central	**19.34**	**9.672**	**0.195**	**-99.0%**	**-8.8%**	**3.552**	**2.593**	**1.826**	**-48.6%**	**-1.3%**	**29.16**	**20.44**	**12.91**	**-55.7%**	**-1.6%**
United States	0	0	0			1.938	1.8	1.8	-7.1%	-0.1%	13.12	11.32	10.61	-19.1%	-0.4%
Mexico	4.574	0.987	0	-100.0%		2.303	1.8	1.8	-21.8%	-0.5%	20.61	13.06	9.722	-52.8%	-1.5%
Canada	0	0	0			1.506	1.583	1.661	10.3%	0.2%	10.19	9.03	9.222	-9.5%	-0.2%
America-North	**1.108**	**0.249**	**0**	**-100.0%**		**1.995**	**1.784**	**1.79**	**-10.3%**	**-0.2%**	**14.72**	**11.59**	**10.3**	**-30.0%**	**-0.7%**
Brazil	6.879	0	0	-100.0%		2.288	1.8	1.8	-21.3%	-0.5%	19.97	13	10.23	-48.8%	-1.3%
Colombia	10.71	2.144	0	-100.0%		2.571	1.8	1.8	-30.0%	-0.7%	21.55	13.4	10.5	-51.3%	-1.4%
Argentina	7.913	2.247	0	-100.0%		2.179	1.8	1.8	-17.4%	-0.4%	16.87	12.32	9.957	-41.0%	-1.0%
Peru	3.972	1.393	0	-100.0%		2.802	1.8	1.8	-35.8%	-0.9%	23.24	13.69	10.62	-54.3%	-1.6%
Venezuela	19.63	2.599	0	-100.0%		2.58	1.8	1.8	-30.2%	-0.7%	21.58	13.41	9.962	-53.8%	-1.5%
Chile	2.408	0	0	-100.0%		1.912	1.8	1.8	-5.9%	-0.1%	14.78	11.28	9.493	-35.8%	-0.9%
Ecuador	3.921	1.704	0	-100.0%		2.768	2.115	1.8	-35.0%	-0.9%	23.12	15.87	11.67	-49.5%	-1.4%
Bolivia	20.81	8.808	0	-100.0%		3.779	2.231	1.8	-52.4%	-1.5%	29.14	17.76	12.12	-58.4%	-1.7%
Paraguay	12.32	5.984	0	-100.0%		3.813	2.677	1.8	-52.8%	-1.5%	29.43	20.64	13.04	-55.7%	-1.6%
Uruguay	1.73	0	0	-100.0%		1.982	1.8	1.8	-9.2%	-0.2%	14.38	11.54	9.549	-33.6%	-0.8%
Guyana	11.41	3.433	0	-100.0%		2.289	1.832	1.8	-21.4%	-0.5%	21.08	13.53	10.75	-49.0%	-1.3%
Suriname	8.804	1.122	0	-100.0%		2.472	1.8	1.8	-27.2%	-0.6%	20.2	13.03	9.412	-53.4%	-1.5%
America-South	**8.228**	**1.241**	**0**	**-100.0%**		**2.43**	**1.842**	**1.8**	**-25.9%**	**-0.6%**	**20.41**	**13.39**	**10.39**	**-49.1%**	**-1.3%**

Health

Base Case: Countries in Year 2055 Descending Population Sequence	Malnourished Population (Percent)					Total Fertility Rate (Births)					Crude Birth Rate (Per Thousand)				
	2005	2030	2055	% Chg	% An Chg	2005	2030	2055	% Chg	% An Chg	2005	2030	2055	% Chg	% An Chg
ASIA INCL OCEANIA															
China	0.971	0	0	-100.0%		1.8	1.8	1.8	0.0%	0.0%	13.52	10.07	8.675	-35.8%	-0.9%
Japan	6.37	0	0	-100.0%		1.381	1.491	1.602	16.0%	0.3%	9.34	7.36	7.18	-23.1%	-0.5%
Korea, Rep. of	0	0	0			1.487	1.569	1.651	11.0%	0.2%	11.89	8.49	7.661	-35.6%	-0.9%
Taiwan	0	0	0			1.78	1.785	1.79	0.6%	0.0%	14.03	10.21	8.999	-35.9%	-0.9%
Korea, Dem. Rep. of	33.49	16.44	0	-100.0%		2.027	1.968	1.8	-11.2%	-0.2%	15.1	13.31	11.27	-25.4%	-0.6%
Hong Kong	0	0	0			1.073	1.265	1.456	35.7%	0.6%	8.74	6.894	7.425	-15.0%	-0.3%
Mongolia	38.57	18.27	0	-100.0%		2.531	2.026	1.8	-28.9%	-0.7%	23.63	15.14	10.99	-53.5%	-1.5%
Asia-East	**1.909**	**0.267**	**0**	**-100.0%**		**1.756**	**1.771**	**1.783**	**1.5%**	**0.0%**	**13.14**	**9.877**	**8.601**	**-34.5%**	**-0.8%**
India	20.03	3.367	0	-100.0%		2.891	1.897	1.8	-37.7%	-0.9%	23.41	13.86	10.4	-55.6%	-1.6%
Pakistan	15.88	8.109	0	-100.0%		4.458	3.391	2.329	-47.8%	-1.3%	32.71	24.72	16.66	-49.1%	-1.3%
Bangladesh	31.66	14.08	0	-100.0%		3.098	2.381	1.8	-41.9%	-1.1%	26.75	18.35	12.09	-54.8%	-1.6%
Iran, Islamic Rep. of	0	0	0			2.135	1.8	1.8	-15.7%	-0.3%	19.77	12.29	9.551	-51.7%	-1.4%
Afghanistan	66.42	46.66	24.11	-63.7%	-2.0%	7.574	6.087	4.503	-40.5%	-1.0%	49.46	42.35	32.55	-34.2%	-0.8%
Nepal	18.55	13.24	6.119	-67.0%	-2.2%	3.894	3.309	2.713	-30.3%	-0.7%	31.27	25.5	19.96	-36.2%	-0.9%
Uzbekistan	19.99	8.194	0	-100.0%		2.522	2.098	1.8	-28.6%	-0.7%	22.55	15.42	11.24	-50.2%	-1.4%
Sri Lanka	18.96	6.039	0	-100.0%		1.833	1.8	1.8	-1.8%	-0.0%	15.33	11.42	9.726	-36.6%	-0.9%
Kazakhstan	17.41	0	0	-100.0%		1.8	1.8	1.8	0.0%	0.0%	14.84	10.44	8.773	-40.9%	-1.0%
Tajikistan	58.67	28.37	5.738	-90.2%	-4.5%	3.681	2.639	1.848	-49.8%	-1.4%	29.21	20.47	12.88	-55.9%	-1.6%
Turkmenistan	5.284	0	0	-100.0%		2.682	1.8	1.8	-32.9%	-0.8%	22.67	13.24	10.31	-54.5%	-1.6%
Kyrgyzstan	3.276	2.808	0.468	-85.7%	-3.8%	2.373	2.203	2.032	-14.4%	-0.3%	20.53	15.77	13.15	-35.9%	-0.9%
Bhutan	15.36	0.824	0	-100.0%		4.276	2.43	1.8	-57.9%	-1.7%	31.11	18.69	12.48	-59.9%	-1.8%
Maldives	15.38	1.393	0	-100.0%		4.264	2.144	1.8	-57.8%	-1.7%	31.97	17.04	11.78	-63.2%	-2.0%
Asia-South Central	**20.53**	**6.179**	**1.014**	**-95.1%**	**-5.8%**	**3.092**	**2.247**	**1.99**	**-35.6%**	**-0.9%**	**24.82**	**16.41**	**12.4**	**-50.0%**	**-1.4%**
Indonesia	3.932	0	0	-100.0%		2.315	1.8	1.8	-22.2%	-0.5%	20.33	12.97	10.13	-50.2%	-1.4%
Philippines	19.91	8.355	0	-100.0%		3.375	2.397	1.8	-46.7%	-1.2%	26.85	18.15	12.26	-54.3%	-1.6%
Vietnam	13.16	0	0	-100.0%		1.839	1.8	1.8	-2.1%	-0.0%	16.54	11.85	9.802	-40.7%	-1.0%
Thailand	13.37	2.18	0	-100.0%		1.815	1.8	1.8	-0.8%	-0.0%	15.08	11.49	9.711	-35.6%	-0.9%
Myanmar	4.165	0.783	0	-100.0%		2.593	2.193	1.8	-30.6%	-0.7%	21.89	15.78	11.72	-46.5%	-1.2%
Malaysia	7.266	0	0	-100.0%		2.799	1.8	1.8	-35.7%	-0.9%	21.43	13.69	10.08	-53.0%	-1.5%
Cambodia	29.81	10.05	0	-100.0%		3.988	2.475	1.8	-54.9%	-1.6%	31.02	19.1	12.65	-59.2%	-1.8%
Laos	20.94	6.463	0	-100.0%		4.736	2.893	1.8	-62.0%	-1.9%	35.27	22.54	13.29	-62.3%	-1.9%
Singapore	1.725	0	0	-100.0%		1.461	1.55	1.639	12.2%	0.2%	10.36	8.903	8.955	-13.6%	-0.3%
Timor-Leste	9.21	5.357	0	-100.0%		6.342	4.462	2.839	-55.2%	-1.6%	39.53	30.45	21.37	-45.9%	-1.2%
Brunei	5.856	0	0	-100.0%		2.367	1.8	1.8	-24.0%	-0.5%	20.56	13.07	10.16	-50.6%	-1.4%
Asia-South East	**9.846**	**2.18**	**0**	**-100.0%**		**2.463**	**1.98**	**1.803**	**-26.8%**	**-0.6%**	**20.72**	**14.18**	**10.75**	**-48.1%**	**-1.3%**

Health

Base Case: Countries in Year 2055 Descending Population Sequence	Malnourished Population (Percent)					Total Fertility Rate (Births)					Crude Birth Rate (Per Thousand)				
	2005	2030	2055	% Chg	% An Chg	2005	2030	2055	% Chg	% An Chg	2005	2030	2055	% Chg	% An Chg
ASIA INCL OCEANIA continued															
Turkey	3.657	0	0	-100.0%		2.373	1.8	1.8	-24.1%	-0.6%	20.35	12.96	9.695	-52.4%	-1.5%
Yemen	30.36	14.31	1.082	-96.4%	-6.5%	6.149	3.965	2.375	-61.4%	-1.9%	41.77	29.66	18.04	-56.8%	-1.7%
Iraq	28.39	5.776	0	-100.0%		5.027	2.891	1.8	-64.2%	-2.0%	36.87	22.58	13.57	-63.2%	-2.0%
Saudi Arabia	2.319	0	0	-100.0%		3.992	1.8	1.8	-54.9%	-1.6%	27.27	14.39	10.72	-60.7%	-1.9%
Syria	1.913	0	0	-100.0%		3.466	2.273	1.8	-48.1%	-1.3%	29.39	17.73	12.15	-58.7%	-1.8%
Israel	0	0	0			2.666	1.8	1.8	-32.5%	-0.8%	19.84	13.28	10.42	-47.5%	-1.3%
Azerbaijan	16.44	1.399	0	-100.0%		1.921	1.8	1.8	-6.3%	-0.1%	16.52	11.28	9.101	-44.9%	-1.2%
Jordan	5.71	0	0	-100.0%		3.494	1.8	1.8	-48.5%	-1.3%	27.64	14.37	10.49	-62.0%	-1.9%
Palestine	29.65	14.98	0	-100.0%		4.804	2.922	1.8	-62.5%	-1.9%	34.36	23.55	13.94	-59.4%	-1.8%
Oman	11.15	5.434	0	-100.0%		3.974	1.853	1.8	-54.7%	-1.6%	26.89	13.66	11.08	-58.8%	-1.8%
Lebanon	2.063	0	0	-100.0%		2.32	1.8	1.8	-22.4%	-0.5%	19.04	12.77	9.538	-49.9%	-1.4%
United Arab Emirates	0	0	0			2.392	1.8	1.8	-24.7%	-0.6%	14.77	10.71	9.486	-35.8%	-0.9%
Kuwait	0	0	0			2.234	1.8	1.8	-19.4%	-0.4%	16.1	12.1	10.68	-33.7%	-0.8%
Georgia	10.84	6.056	0	-100.0%		1.536	1.605	1.675	9.0%	0.2%	11.54	9.036	8.344	-27.7%	-0.6%
Armenia	32.3	8.709	0	-100.0%		1.705	1.73	1.755	2.9%	0.1%	14.76	10.65	8.694	-41.1%	-1.1%
Bahrain	6.287	0.816	0	-100.0%		2.271	1.8	1.8	-20.7%	-0.5%	17.05	12.14	10.23	-40.0%	-1.0%
Qatar	3.183	0	0	-100.0%		2.866	1.8	1.8	-37.2%	-0.9%	16.42	12.23	10.41	-36.6%	-0.9%
Cyprus	0	0	0			1.648	1.688	1.728	4.9%	0.1%	11.97	9.345	8.68	-27.5%	-0.6%
Asia-West	**10.57**	**3.382**	**0.18**	**-98.3%**	**-7.8%**	**3.417**	**2.318**	**1.894**	**-44.6%**	**-1.2%**	**26.02**	**17.35**	**12.2**	**-53.1%**	**-1.5%**
Australia	0	0	0			1.758	1.769	1.78	1.3%	0.0%	12.31	10.65	10.22	-17.0%	-0.4%
Papua New Guinea	26.34	13.74	0.07	-99.7%	-11.2%	4.205	3.067	2.022	-51.9%	-1.5%	31.95	23.72	15.04	-52.9%	-1.5%
New Zealand	0	0	0			1.8	1.8	1.8	0.0%	0.0%	12.28	10.7	9.863	-19.7%	-0.4%
Solomon Islands	27.25	15.24	0.523	-98.1%	-7.6%	4.302	3.135	1.995	-53.6%	-1.5%	33.37	24.37	15.06	-54.9%	-1.6%
Fiji	5.495	0	0	-100.0%		2.896	1.846	1.8	-37.8%	-0.9%	23.41	13.83	9.936	-57.6%	-1.7%
Vanuatu	15.69	5.917	0	-100.0%		4.137	2.841	1.8	-56.5%	-1.7%	31	21.88	13.15	-57.6%	-1.7%
Micronesia	6.811	1.738	0	-100.0%		4.23	2.767	1.8	-57.4%	-1.7%	31.94	21.06	13.16	-58.8%	-1.8%
Samoa	5.89	0	0	-100.0%		3.923	2.409	1.8	-54.1%	-1.5%	25.67	18.57	11.93	-53.5%	-1.5%
Tonga	6.071	2.114	0	-100.0%		3.569	2.677	1.855	-48.0%	-1.3%	26.54	19.41	13.04	-50.9%	-1.4%
Oceania	**5.577**	**3.458**	**0.03**	**-99.5%**	**-9.9%**	**2.325**	**2.115**	**1.851**	**-20.4%**	**-0.5%**	**16.85**	**14.17**	**11.6**	**-31.2%**	**-0.7%**

Health

Base Case: Countries in Year 2055 / Descending Population Sequence	Malnourished Population (Percent)					Total Fertility Rate (Births)					Crude Birth Rate (Per Thousand)				
	2005	2030	2055	% Chg	% An Chg	2005	2030	2055	% Chg	% An Chg	2005	2030	2055	% Chg	% An Chg
EUROPE															
Russia	2.581	0	0	-100.0%		1.24	1.387	1.535	23.8%	0.4%	9.79	7.091	6.589	-32.7%	-0.8%
Poland	0	0	0			1.36	1.476	1.592	17.1%	0.3%	10.55	7.571	6.942	-34.2%	-0.8%
Ukraine	3.078	0	0	-100.0%		1.135	1.31	1.485	30.8%	0.5%	8.432	6.246	5.767	-31.6%	-0.8%
Romania	1.631	0	0	-100.0%		1.334	1.457	1.579	18.4%	0.3%	10.31	7.613	6.886	-33.2%	-0.8%
Belarus	0.321	0	0	-100.0%		1.315	1.443	1.571	19.5%	0.4%	10.03	7.593	6.948	-30.7%	-0.7%
Czech Republic	0	0	0			1.173	1.338	1.503	28.1%	0.5%	8.744	6.464	6.288	-28.1%	-0.7%
Hungary	0	0	0			1.344	1.464	1.584	17.9%	0.3%	9.676	7.637	7.216	-25.4%	-0.6%
Bulgaria	6.128	0	0	-100.0%		1.325	1.45	1.575	18.9%	0.3%	9.066	6.969	6.46	-28.7%	-0.7%
Slovak Republic	4.26	0	0	-100.0%		1.325	1.45	1.575	18.9%	0.3%	10.56	7.591	6.934	-34.3%	-0.8%
Moldova	11.48	2.848	0	-100.0%		1.325	1.45	1.575	18.9%	0.3%	11.3	8.296	7.513	-33.5%	-0.8%
Europe-East	**2.255**	**0.04**	**0**	**-100.0%**		**1.254**	**1.4**	**1.543**	**23.0%**	**0.4%**	**9.697**	**7.113**	**6.59**	**-32.0%**	**-0.8%**
United Kingdom	0	0	0			1.648	1.688	1.728	4.9%	0.1%	10.78	9.62	9.276	-14.0%	-0.3%
Sweden	0	0	0			1.553	1.618	1.683	8.4%	0.2%	9.551	8.598	8.642	-9.5%	-0.2%
Denmark	0	0	0			1.772	1.78	1.787	0.8%	0.0%	11.4	10.61	10.13	-11.1%	-0.2%
Norway	0	0	0			1.8	1.8	1.8	0.0%	0.0%	11.66	10.79	10.26	-12.0%	-0.3%
Ireland	0	0	0			1.8	1.8	1.8	0.0%	0.0%	14.12	11.07	10.12	-28.3%	-0.7%
Finland	0.05	0	0	-100.0%		1.734	1.751	1.769	2.0%	0.0%	10.61	9.578	9.521	-10.3%	-0.2%
Lithuania	0	0	0			1.411	1.513	1.615	14.5%	0.3%	10.02	7.913	7.367	-26.5%	-0.6%
Latvia	1.521	0	0	-100.0%		1.268	1.408	1.548	22.1%	0.4%	9.035	6.84	6.563	-27.4%	-0.6%
Estonia	0	0	0			1.363	1.478	1.593	16.9%	0.3%	9.488	6.883	6.854	-27.8%	-0.6%
Iceland	0	0	0			1.8	1.8	1.8	0.0%	0.0%	12.84	10.91	9.809	-23.6%	-0.5%
Europe-North	**0.04**	**0**	**0**	**-100.0%**		**1.643**	**1.687**	**1.729**	**5.2%**	**0.1%**	**10.79**	**9.567**	**9.247**	**-14.3%**	**-0.3%**
Italy	0	0	0			1.268	1.408	1.548	22.1%	0.4%	8.647	7.024	6.911	-20.1%	-0.4%
Spain	0	0	0			1.268	1.408	1.548	22.1%	0.4%	9.996	7.028	6.58	-34.2%	-0.8%
Greece	0	0	0			1.315	1.443	1.571	19.5%	0.4%	9.433	7.302	7.08	-24.9%	-0.6%
Portugal	0	0	0			1.534	1.604	1.674	9.1%	0.2%	11.16	8.866	8.132	-27.1%	-0.6%
Serbia and Montenegro	9.936	0.805	0	-100.0%		1.667	1.702	1.737	4.2%	0.1%	11.84	9.987	8.975	-24.2%	-0.6%
Croatia	10.38	0	0	-100.0%		1.411	1.513	1.615	14.5%	0.3%	9.448	7.769	7.27	-23.1%	-0.5%
Bosnia and Herzegovina	5.722	1.993	0	-100.0%		1.306	1.436	1.566	19.9%	0.4%	9.711	7.607	7.34	-24.4%	-0.6%
Albania	4.676	0	0	-100.0%		2.198	1.8	1.8	-18.1%	-0.4%	16.73	11.89	9.49	-43.3%	-1.1%
Macedonia	1.844	1.497	0	-100.0%		1.759	1.77	1.781	1.3%	0.0%	13.5	10.69	9.503	-29.6%	-0.7%
Slovenia	0.051	0	0	-100.0%		1.287	1.422	1.557	21.0%	0.4%	9.157	6.839	6.695	-26.9%	-0.6%
Malta	0	0	0	-100.0%		1.724	1.744	1.764	2.3%	0.0%	11.72	9.351	8.848	-24.5%	-0.6%
Europe-South	**1.177**	**0.125**	**0**	**-100.0%**		**1.348**	**1.463**	**1.586**	**17.7%**	**0.3%**	**9.77**	**7.574**	**7.196**	**-26.3%**	**-0.6%**
Germany	0	0	0			1.401	1.506	1.611	15.0%	0.3%	8.397	7.722	8.05	-4.1%	-0.1%
France	0	0	0			1.8	1.8	1.8	0.0%	0.0%	11.64	10.25	9.649	-17.1%	-0.4%
Netherlands	0	0	0			1.727	1.746	1.765	2.2%	0.0%	11.29	10.11	9.735	-13.8%	-0.3%
Belgium	0	0	0			1.667	1.702	1.737	4.2%	0.1%	10.44	9.38	9.236	-11.5%	-0.2%
Austria	0	0	0			1.382	1.492	1.602	15.9%	0.3%	8.697	7.564	7.633	-12.2%	-0.3%
Switzerland	0	0	0			1.515	1.59	1.665	9.9%	0.2%	9.611	8.403	8.329	-13.3%	-0.3%
Luxembourg	0	0	0			1.762	1.772	1.782	1.1%	0.0%	11.92	11.44	11.21	-6.0%	-0.1%
Europe-West	**0**	**0**	**0**			**1.579**	**1.642**	**1.702**	**7.8%**	**0.2%**	**9.887**	**8.919**	**8.852**	**-10.5%**	**-0.2%**

Multination Regional Analysis

Measures of Poverty, Health, Education, Infrastructure and Governance

Health

Base Case
Source: International Futures
Version 5.47 March 2008

	Crude Death Rate (Per Thousand)					Contraception Use (Percent)					Youth Bulge (Ratio)				
	2005	2030	2055	% Chg	% An Chg	2005	2030	2055	% Chg	% An Chg	2005	2030	2055	% Chg	% An Chg
World	9.022	8.518	9.726	7.8%	0.2%	63.08	78.34	88.36	40.1%	0.7%	0.366	0.292	0.241	-34.2%	-0.8%
Africa	13.05	10.42	9.382	-28.1%	-0.7%	27.41	44.64	65.47	138.9%	1.8%	0.489	0.429	0.354	-27.6%	-0.6%
Americas	6.938	7.919	9.555	37.7%	0.6%	73.21	90.95	98.23	34.2%	0.6%	0.344	0.264	0.211	-38.7%	-1.0%
Asia incl Oceania	8.306	7.571	9.317	12.2%	0.2%	66.39	83.47	94.08	41.7%	0.7%	0.366	0.273	0.212	-42.1%	-1.1%
Europe	10.41	11.95	14.84	42.6%	0.7%	77.3	95.86	99.79	29.1%	0.5%	0.245	0.176	0.157	-35.9%	-0.9%
World	9.022	8.518	9.726	7.8%	0.2%	63.08	78.34	88.36	40.1%	0.7%	0.366	0.292	0.241	-34.2%	-0.8%
Africa-Eastern	13.87	10.26	8.897	-35.9%	-0.9%	22.37	42.96	71.91	221.5%	2.4%	0.511	0.448	0.365	-28.6%	-0.7%
Africa-Middle	15.16	11.56	9.641	-36.4%	-0.9%	13.24	29.43	49.49	273.8%	2.7%	0.509	0.5	0.426	-16.3%	-0.4%
Africa-Northern	7.584	6.948	7.408	-2.3%	-0.0%	48.92	69.03	88.04	80.0%	1.2%	0.447	0.328	0.235	-47.4%	-1.3%
Africa-Southern	12.82	10.96	11.1	-13.4%	-0.3%	55.55	69.51	92.51	66.5%	1.0%	0.427	0.345	0.246	-42.4%	-1.1%
Africa-Western	15.24	11.98	10.49	-31.2%	-0.7%	17.71	36.25	54.13	205.6%	2.3%	0.5	0.446	0.369	-26.2%	-0.6%
Africa	13.05	10.42	9.382	-28.1%	-0.7%	27.41	44.64	65.47	138.9%	1.8%	0.489	0.429	0.354	-27.6%	-0.6%
America-Caribbean	8.567	9.164	10.1	17.9%	0.3%	61.22	75.96	81.93	33.8%	0.6%	0.374	0.295	0.243	-35.0%	-0.9%
America-Central	6.612	6.384	6.954	5.2%	0.1%	54.24	70.61	87.83	61.9%	1.0%	0.463	0.373	0.282	-39.1%	-1.0%
America-North	7.118	8.724	10.68	50.0%	0.8%	76.28	94.08	100	31.1%	0.5%	0.295	0.231	0.201	-31.9%	-0.8%
America-South	6.601	7.13	8.711	32.0%	0.6%	72.91	91.68	99.48	36.4%	0.6%	0.384	0.282	0.208	-45.8%	-1.2%
Americas	6.938	7.919	9.555	37.7%	0.6%	73.21	90.95	98.23	34.2%	0.6%	0.344	0.264	0.211	-38.7%	-1.0%
Asia-East	7.332	7.252	11.74	60.1%	0.9%	87.45	98.72	100	14.4%	0.3%	0.295	0.204	0.167	-43.4%	-1.1%
Asia-South Central	9.612	7.925	7.854	-18.3%	-0.4%	50.41	73.91	91.04	80.6%	1.2%	0.416	0.316	0.236	-43.3%	-1.1%
Asia-South East	7.959	7.901	9.579	20.4%	0.4%	59.25	79.85	93.53	57.9%	0.9%	0.4	0.285	0.216	-46.0%	-1.2%
Asia-West	6.667	6.002	7.274	9.1%	0.2%	51.66	72.97	88.64	71.6%	1.1%	0.423	0.334	0.247	-41.6%	-1.1%
Oceania	7.361	8.677	10.08	36.9%	0.6%	61.5	78.95	90.33	46.9%	0.8%	0.305	0.258	0.231	-24.3%	-0.6%
Asia incl Oceania	8.306	7.571	9.317	12.2%	0.2%	66.39	83.47	94.08	41.7%	0.7%	0.366	0.273	0.212	-42.1%	-0.7%
Europe-East	12.01	12.04	15.28	27.2%	0.5%	72.43	96.45	99.75	37.7%	0.6%	0.281	0.172	0.139	-50.5%	-1.4%
Europe-North	9.209	11.15	13.07	41.9%	0.7%	79.21	95.86	100	26.2%	0.5%	0.231	0.191	0.181	-21.6%	-0.5%
Europe-South	9.263	12.18	15.89	71.5%	1.1%	80.3	93.94	99.4	23.8%	0.4%	0.223	0.17	0.15	-32.7%	-0.8%
Europe-West	9.327	12.1	14.51	55.6%	0.9%	81.85	96.41	100	22.2%	0.4%	0.213	0.18	0.175	-17.8%	-0.4%
Europe	10.41	11.95	14.84	42.6%	0.7%	77.3	95.86	99.79	29.1%	0.5%	0.245	0.176	0.157	-35.9%	-0.9%

Health

Base Case: Countries in Year 2055 Descending Population Sequence	Crude Death Rate (Per Thousand)					Contraception Use (Percent)					Youth Bulge (Ratio)				
	2005	2030	2055	% Chg	% An Chg	2005	2030	2055	% Chg	% An Chg	2005	2030	2055	% Chg	% An Chg
AFRICA															
Ethiopia	15.09	12.13	10.16	-32.7%	-0.8%	7.804	24.84	52.02	566.6%	3.9%	0.494	0.423	0.366	-25.9%	-0.6%
Tanzania	13.6	9.118	6.69	-50.8%	-1.4%	30.08	59.6	97.82	225.2%	2.4%	0.504	0.451	0.345	-31.5%	-0.8%
Uganda	11.69	7.931	6.949	-40.6%	-1.0%	17.34	43.4	79.46	358.2%	3.1%	0.552	0.508	0.383	-30.6%	-0.7%
Kenya	11.19	8.144	7.499	-33.0%	-0.8%	42.03	65.52	100	137.9%	1.7%	0.532	0.437	0.325	-38.9%	-1.0%
Madagascar	12.92	11.39	9.32	-27.9%	-0.7%	22.36	38	61.11	173.3%	2.0%	0.48	0.432	0.373	-22.3%	-0.5%
Mozambique	15.73	9.879	8.836	-43.8%	-1.1%	11.99	42.45	71.07	492.7%	3.6%	0.485	0.425	0.334	-31.1%	-0.7%
Malawi	15.83	11.27	10.12	-36.1%	-0.9%	24.44	41.14	69.79	185.6%	2.1%	0.505	0.481	0.412	-18.4%	-0.4%
Zambia	15.67	9.65	9.178	-41.4%	-1.1%	30.01	47.3	76.86	156.1%	1.9%	0.532	0.479	0.402	-24.4%	-0.6%
Zimbabwe	13.74	8.588	9.102	-33.8%	-0.8%	56.2	70.09	96.61	71.9%	1.1%	0.542	0.421	0.321	-40.8%	-1.0%
Burundi	14.36	11.18	10.31	-28.2%	-0.7%	8.732	23.95	48.61	456.7%	3.5%	0.538	0.466	0.406	-24.5%	-0.6%
Rwanda	13.99	10.9	10.3	-26.4%	-0.6%	24.56	42.65	68.78	180.0%	2.1%	0.55	0.451	0.364	-33.8%	-0.8%
Somalia	16.89	14.34	13.01	-23.0%	-0.5%	8.781	28.08	42.26	381.3%	3.2%	0.483	0.452	0.397	-17.8%	-0.4%
Eritrea	12.21	13.55	10.88	-10.9%	-0.2%	8.796	14.54	26.83	205.0%	2.3%	0.514	0.477	0.427	-16.9%	-0.4%
Mauritius	6.174	7.745	10.95	77.4%	1.2%	78.32	97.73	100	27.7%	0.5%	0.327	0.228	0.19	-41.9%	-1.1%
Comoros	9.418	9.126	8.379	-11.0%	-0.2%	29.47	41.27	61.33	108.1%	1.5%	0.501	0.387	0.337	-32.7%	-0.8%
Djibouti	16.14	14.05	9.936	-38.4%	-1.0%	32.44	42.19	58.94	81.7%	1.2%	0.479	0.466	0.383	-20.0%	-0.4%
Africa-Eastern	**13.87**	**10.26**	**8.897**	**-35.9%**	**-0.9%**	**22.37**	**42.96**	**71.91**	**221.5%**	**2.4%**	**0.511**	**0.448**	**0.365**	**-28.6%**	**-0.7%**
Congo, Dem. Rep. of the	14.05	10.72	9.035	-35.7%	-0.9%	10.08	27.23	51.37	409.6%	3.3%	0.518	0.525	0.455	-12.2%	-0.3%
Angola	17.52	13.07	10.9	-37.8%	-0.9%	12.06	30.05	42.64	253.6%	2.6%	0.51	0.474	0.388	-23.9%	-0.5%
Cameroon	17.52	13.41	10.41	-40.6%	-1.0%	21.75	30.66	45.99	111.4%	1.5%	0.495	0.475	0.375	-24.2%	-0.6%
Chad	15.27	11.59	10.99	-28.0%	-0.7%	9.777	33.09	45.81	368.5%	3.1%	0.498	0.466	0.387	-22.3%	-0.5%
Central African Republic	16	17.2	11.61	-27.4%	-0.6%	15.39	22.72	39.15	154.4%	1.9%	0.488	0.452	0.383	-21.5%	-0.5%
Congo, Rep. of	12.67	9.08	8.488	-33.0%	-0.8%	22.9	45.72	65.22	184.8%	2.1%	0.504	0.421	0.342	-32.1%	-0.8%
Gabon	11.26	8.454	9.653	-14.3%	-0.3%	32.26	52.03	64.49	99.9%	1.4%	0.475	0.388	0.26	-45.3%	-1.2%
Equatorial Guinea	14.73	10.82	10.43	-29.2%	-0.7%	54.43	77.76	84.66	55.5%	0.9%	0.465	0.44	0.304	-34.6%	-0.8%
São Tomé and Príncipe	14.17	12.52	14.72	3.9%	0.1%	31.26	38.01	47.28	51.2%	0.8%	0.547	0.392	0.325	-40.6%	-1.0%
Africa-Middle	**15.16**	**11.56**	**9.641**	**-36.4%**	**-0.9%**	**13.24**	**29.43**	**49.49**	**273.8%**	**2.7%**	**0.509**	**0.5**	**0.426**	**-16.3%**	**-0.4%**
Egypt	6.999	6.214	5.665	-19.1%	-0.4%	57.84	79.12	100	72.9%	1.1%	0.444	0.343	0.226	-49.1%	-1.3%
Sudan	12.13	9.318	8.463	-30.2%	-0.7%	14.4	38.57	58.84	308.6%	2.9%	0.464	0.388	0.302	-34.9%	-0.9%
Algeria	5.724	5.896	9.154	59.9%	0.9%	50.72	69.49	86.11	69.8%	1.1%	0.457	0.277	0.196	-57.1%	-1.7%
Morocco	6.843	7.653	8.765	28.1%	0.5%	62.24	78.32	100	60.7%	1.0%	0.431	0.291	0.215	-50.1%	-1.4%
Tunisia	5.7	5.662	8.445	48.2%	0.8%	63.42	87.17	100	57.7%	0.9%	0.406	0.238	0.18	-55.7%	-1.6%
Libya	3.939	4.284	6.414	62.8%	1.0%	49.48	73.96	91.67	85.3%	1.2%	0.46	0.302	0.196	-57.4%	-1.7%
Africa-Northern	**7.584**	**6.948**	**7.408**	**-2.3%**	**-0.0%**	**48.92**	**69.03**	**88.04**	**80.0%**	**1.2%**	**0.447**	**0.328**	**0.235**	**-47.4%**	**-1.3%**

Health

Base Case: Countries in Year 2055 Descending Population Sequence	Crude Death Rate (Per Thousand)					Contraception Use (Percent)					Youth Bulge (Ratio)				
	2005	2030	2055	% Chg	% An Chg	2005	2030	2055	% Chg	% An Chg	2005	2030	2055	% Chg	% An Chg
AFRICA															
South Africa	12.82	11.39	11.62	-9.4%	-0.2%	59.05	73.13	95.96	62.5%	1.0%	0.414	0.333	0.237	-42.8%	-1.1%
Namibia	12.59	8.367	7.026	-44.2%	-1.2%	31.79	50.18	82.72	160.2%	1.9%	0.477	0.389	0.269	-43.6%	-1.1%
Lesotho	14.41	9.786	9.387	-34.9%	-0.9%	24.45	35.42	58.21	138.1%	1.7%	0.54	0.44	0.337	-37.6%	-0.9%
Botswana	13	8.521	9.943	-23.5%	-0.5%	47.4	72.65	95.52	101.5%	1.4%	0.507	0.376	0.238	-53.1%	-1.5%
Swaziland	10.05	7.659	8.536	-15.1%	-0.3%	21.61	40.05	66.34	207.0%	2.3%	0.541	0.436	0.305	-43.6%	-1.1%
Africa-Southern	**12.82**	**10.96**	**11.1**	**-13.4%**	**-0.3%**	**55.55**	**69.51**	**92.51**	**66.5%**	**1.0%**	**0.427**	**0.345**	**0.246**	**-42.4%**	**-1.1%**
Nigeria	15.7	11.32	10.3	-34.4%	-0.8%	19.48	42.33	57.49	195.1%	2.2%	0.499	0.448	0.36	-27.9%	-0.7%
Niger	19.38	16.58	12.8	-34.0%	-0.8%	9.864	23.47	46.42	370.6%	3.1%	0.515	0.486	0.431	-16.3%	-0.4%
Ghana	11.13	10.92	10.81	-2.9%	-0.1%	25.09	33.3	50.37	100.8%	1.4%	0.48	0.396	0.343	-28.5%	-0.7%
Côte d'Ivoire	13.67	10.63	10.08	-26.3%	-0.6%	16.11	35.08	56.58	251.2%	2.5%	0.503	0.432	0.349	-30.6%	-0.7%
Mali	17.06	13.31	10.59	-37.9%	-0.9%	10.46	28.6	51.56	392.9%	3.2%	0.532	0.476	0.401	-24.6%	-0.6%
Burkina Faso	14.11	10.93	9.515	-32.6%	-0.8%	14.97	31.38	57.14	281.7%	2.7%	0.532	0.464	0.396	-25.6%	-0.6%
Senegal	12.32	10.12	8.604	-30.2%	-0.7%	16.3	34.38	57.03	249.9%	2.5%	0.506	0.416	0.339	-33.0%	-0.8%
Guinea	14.54	12.22	10.44	-28.2%	-0.7%	7.938	22.6	39.01	391.4%	3.2%	0.468	0.419	0.36	-23.1%	-0.5%
Benin	14.77	12.22	8.937	-39.5%	-1.0%	18.87	34.55	60.4	220.1%	2.4%	0.498	0.448	0.372	-25.3%	-0.6%
Togo	13.1	11.6	11.72	-10.5%	-0.2%	25.12	34	46	83.1%	1.2%	0.499	0.435	0.38	-23.8%	-0.5%
Liberia	18.24	20.5	12.13	-33.5%	-0.8%	16.66	25.74	43.64	161.9%	1.9%	0.514	0.498	0.394	-23.3%	-0.5%
Sierra Leone	23.88	19.96	11.28	-52.8%	-1.5%	10.76	33.33	55.01	411.2%	3.3%	0.453	0.52	0.383	-15.5%	-0.3%
Mauritania	14.46	12.6	11.23	-22.3%	-0.5%	5.273	17.42	32.43	515.0%	3.7%	0.472	0.433	0.367	-22.2%	-0.5%
Guinea-Bissau	17.43	15.14	13.24	-24.0%	-0.5%	8.516	15.56	27.85	227.0%	2.4%	0.486	0.485	0.434	-10.7%	-0.2%
Gambia	12.96	11.49	9.716	-25.0%	-0.6%	17.6	32.96	53.69	205.1%	2.3%	0.438	0.401	0.338	-22.8%	-0.5%
Cape Verde	5.882	4.203	4.952	-15.8%	-0.3%	50.22	72.85	97.47	94.1%	1.3%	0.519	0.38	0.239	-53.9%	-1.5%
Africa-Western	**15.24**	**11.98**	**10.49**	**-31.2%**	**-0.7%**	**17.71**	**36.25**	**54.13**	**205.6%**	**2.3%**	**0.5**	**0.446**	**0.369**	**-26.2%**	**-0.6%**

Health

Base Case: Countries in Year 2055 Descending Population Sequence	Crude Death Rate (Per Thousand)					Contraception Use (Percent)					Youth Bulge (Ratio)				
	2005	2030	2055	% Chg	% An Chg	2005	2030	2055	% Chg	% An Chg	2005	2030	2055	% Chg	% An Chg
AMERICAS															
Haiti	12.7	10.78	10.6	-16.5%	-0.4%	18.3	28.18	46.26	152.8%	1.9%	0.511	0.419	0.352	-31.1%	-0.7%
Dominican Republic	7.318	6.662	8.774	19.9%	0.4%	67.54	88.89	100	48.1%	0.8%	0.429	0.306	0.209	-51.3%	-1.4%
Cuba	7.32	11.49	11.35	55.1%	0.9%	78.23	100	100	27.8%	0.5%	0.253	0.189	0.161	-36.4%	-0.9%
Puerto Rico	7.5	7.144	10.39	38.5%	0.7%	82.32	100	100	21.5%	0.4%	0.298	0.217	0.187	-37.2%	-0.9%
Jamaica	7.495	7.761	7.375	-1.6%	-0.0%	68.92	88.97	100	45.1%	0.7%	0.38	0.297	0.207	-45.5%	-1.2%
Trinidad and Tobago	7.146	6.829	12.36	73.0%	1.1%	68.89	96.34	100	45.2%	0.7%	0.375	0.218	0.162	-56.8%	-1.7%
Bahamas	7.581	8.658	10.73	41.5%	0.7%	76.74	90.08	100	30.3%	0.5%	0.357	0.269	0.211	-40.9%	-1.0%
Barbados	8.072	8.072	13.66	69.1%	1.1%	74.44	92.29	100	34.3%	0.6%	0.28	0.211	0.175	-37.5%	-0.9%
Grenada	5.645	6.43	5.988	6.1%	0.1%	59.21	75.54	100	68.9%	1.1%	0.404	0.33	0.219	-45.8%	-1.2%
St. Vincent & the Grenadines	5.88	6.49	7.858	33.6%	0.6%	53.12	69.97	94.58	78.0%	1.2%	0.442	0.268	0.198	-55.2%	-1.6%
St. Lucia	6.859	6.601	9.438	37.6%	0.6%	56.61	80.81	100	76.6%	1.1%	0.393	0.237	0.171	-56.5%	-1.7%
America-Caribbean	**8.567**	**9.164**	**10.1**	**17.9%**	**0.3%**	**61.22**	**75.96**	**81.93**	**33.8%**	**0.6%**	**0.374**	**0.295**	**0.243**	**-35.0%**	**-0.9%**
Guatemala	7.639	6.289	5.786	-24.3%	-0.6%	39.37	56.33	77.35	96.5%	1.4%	0.494	0.427	0.317	-35.8%	-0.9%
Honduras	7.39	7.701	7.668	3.8%	0.1%	52.35	66.79	87.45	67.0%	1.0%	0.482	0.389	0.304	-36.9%	-0.9%
Nicaragua	5.8	6.669	7.745	33.5%	0.6%	61.77	74.25	92.84	50.3%	0.8%	0.503	0.38	0.301	-40.2%	-1.0%
El Salvador	6.661	6.516	7.097	6.5%	0.1%	61.7	81.4	100	62.1%	1.0%	0.438	0.332	0.224	-48.9%	-1.3%
Costa Rica	4.136	4.8	8.6	107.9%	1.5%	78.01	100	100	28.2%	0.5%	0.388	0.255	0.189	-51.3%	-1.4%
Panama	5.466	4.683	8.007	46.5%	0.8%	57.24	86.44	100	74.7%	1.1%	0.375	0.279	0.196	-47.7%	-1.3%
Belize	5.561	3.583	5.713	2.7%	0.1%	50.72	77.96	100	97.2%	1.4%	0.47	0.336	0.205	-56.4%	-1.6%
America-Central	**6.612**	**6.384**	**6.954**	**5.2%**	**0.1%**	**54.24**	**70.61**	**87.83**	**61.9%**	**1.0%**	**0.463**	**0.373**	**0.282**	**-39.1%**	**-1.0%**
United States	7.901	9.599	11.17	41.4%	0.7%	78.96	97.27	100	26.6%	0.5%	0.26	0.219	0.204	-21.5%	-0.5%
Mexico	4.977	6.006	8.762	76.0%	1.1%	66.82	83.82	100	49.7%	0.8%	0.411	0.277	0.197	-52.1%	-1.5%
Canada	6.892	10.02	12.55	82.1%	1.2%	82.5	100	100	21.2%	0.4%	0.243	0.183	0.179	-26.3%	-0.6%
America-North	**7.118**	**8.724**	**10.68**	**50.0%**	**0.8%**	**76.28**	**94.08**	**100**	**31.1%**	**0.5%**	**0.295**	**0.231**	**0.201**	**-31.9%**	**-0.8%**
Brazil	6.833	7.841	9.313	36.3%	0.6%	78.95	95.96	100	26.7%	0.5%	0.383	0.276	0.205	-46.5%	-1.2%
Colombia	5.96	6.73	7.56	26.8%	0.5%	74.57	93.01	100	34.1%	0.6%	0.387	0.293	0.209	-46.0%	-1.2%
Argentina	7.002	6.428	9.239	31.9%	0.6%	72.52	94.66	100	37.9%	0.6%	0.346	0.247	0.196	-43.4%	-1.1%
Peru	6.899	6.611	8.022	16.3%	0.3%	67.34	87.54	100	48.5%	0.8%	0.414	0.304	0.21	-49.3%	-1.3%
Venezuela	5.105	4.989	6.918	35.5%	0.6%	57.61	80.92	100	73.6%	1.1%	0.403	0.29	0.202	-49.9%	-1.4%
Chile	5.188	6.007	10.24	97.4%	1.4%	65.76	90.92	100	52.1%	0.8%	0.322	0.222	0.182	-43.5%	-1.1%
Ecuador	6.002	7.643	10.23	70.4%	1.1%	61	76.72	91	49.2%	0.8%	0.415	0.31	0.239	-42.4%	-1.1%
Bolivia	9.617	7.472	6.464	-32.8%	-0.8%	50.52	73.88	100	97.9%	1.4%	0.441	0.359	0.24	-45.6%	-1.2%
Paraguay	5.848	6.311	6.246	6.8%	0.1%	58.42	72.35	94.56	61.9%	1.0%	0.45	0.369	0.281	-37.6%	-0.9%
Uruguay	8.493	7.718	10.13	19.3%	0.4%	65.79	89.6	100	52.0%	0.8%	0.298	0.227	0.186	-37.6%	-0.9%
Guyana	10.5	11.06	13.61	29.6%	0.5%	47.03	61.95	78.97	67.9%	1.0%	0.413	0.301	0.219	-47.0%	-1.3%
Suriname	7.062	7.398	9.282	31.4%	0.5%	46.51	64.17	87.19	87.5%	1.3%	0.395	0.291	0.197	-50.1%	-1.4%
America-South	**6.601**	**7.13**	**8.711**	**32.0%**	**0.6%**	**72.91**	**91.68**	**99.48**	**36.4%**	**0.6%**	**0.384**	**0.282**	**0.208**	**-45.8%**	**-1.2%**

Health

Base Case: Countries in Year 2055 Descending Population Sequence	Crude Death Rate (Per Thousand)					Contraception Use (Percent)					Youth Bulge (Ratio)				
	2005	2030	2055	% Chg	% An Chg	2005	2030	2055	% Chg	% An Chg	2005	2030	2055	% Chg	% An Chg
ASIA INCL. OCEANIA															
China	7.337	6.555	11.33	54.4%	0.9%	90.16	100	100	10.9%	0.2%	0.305	0.207	0.168	-44.9%	-1.2%
Japan	7.951	13.76	15.78	98.5%	1.4%	67.19	84.52	100	48.8%	0.8%	0.205	0.163	0.15	-26.8%	-0.6%
Korea, Rep. of	5.446	8.721	15.08	176.9%	2.1%	80.84	100	100	23.7%	0.4%	0.278	0.182	0.155	-44.2%	-1.2%
Taiwan	4.651	8.401	13.57	191.8%	2.2%	82.38	98.36	100	21.4%	0.4%	0.277	0.21	0.181	-34.7%	-0.8%
Korea, Dem. Rep. of	11.12	12.57	11.55	3.9%	0.1%	67.05	89.76	100	49.1%	0.8%	0.307	0.25	0.221	-28.0%	-0.7%
Hong Kong	4.92	8.971	14.36	191.9%	2.2%	90.37	100	100	10.7%	0.2%	0.239	0.16	0.153	-36.0%	-0.9%
Mongolia	7.792	8.88	10.33	32.6%	0.6%	61.22	80.62	100	63.3%	1.0%	0.452	0.308	0.222	-50.9%	-1.4%
Asia-East	**7.332**	**7.252**	**11.74**	**60.1%**	**0.9%**	**87.45**	**98.72**	**100**	**14.4%**	**0.3%**	**0.295**	**0.204**	**0.167**	**-43.4%**	**-1.1%**
India	9.737	7.684	7.309	-24.9%	-0.6%	53.12	80.28	100	88.3%	1.3%	0.398	0.3	0.206	-48.2%	-1.3%
Pakistan	10.16	8.071	7.234	-28.8%	-0.7%	21.57	39.64	59.85	177.5%	2.1%	0.473	0.38	0.312	-34.0%	-0.8%
Bangladesh	9.35	8.341	8.969	-4.1%	-0.1%	52.99	75.65	98.11	85.1%	1.2%	0.443	0.337	0.258	-41.8%	-1.1%
Iran, Islamic Rep. of	5.661	4.401	7.138	26.1%	0.5%	76.95	100	100	30.0%	0.5%	0.49	0.26	0.186	-62.0%	-1.9%
Afghanistan	18.74	16.4	13.46	-28.2%	-0.7%	13.12	23.18	39.79	203.3%	2.2%	0.488	0.467	0.423	-13.3%	-0.3%
Nepal	10.45	10.07	9.866	-5.6%	-0.1%	30.71	44.73	61.26	99.5%	1.4%	0.458	0.386	0.336	-26.6%	-0.6%
Uzbekistan	6.899	7.845	9.827	42.4%	0.7%	60.78	84.11	100	64.5%	1.0%	0.447	0.306	0.233	-47.9%	-1.3%
Sri Lanka	6.404	9.152	11.22	75.2%	1.1%	69.64	91.19	100	43.6%	0.7%	0.35	0.234	0.192	-45.1%	-1.2%
Kazakhstan	8.918	7.082	12.47	39.8%	0.7%	73.98	100	100	35.2%	0.6%	0.356	0.219	0.173	-51.4%	-1.4%
Tajikistan	9.324	9.043	9.891	6.1%	0.1%	28.14	51.48	73.67	161.8%	1.9%	0.488	0.354	0.268	-45.1%	-1.2%
Turkmenistan	8.176	5.394	9.624	17.7%	0.3%	24.71	56.89	64.98	163.0%	2.0%	0.44	0.292	0.203	-53.9%	-1.5%
Kyrgyzstan	7.567	9.976	12.83	69.6%	1.1%	62.76	76.21	93.54	49.0%	0.8%	0.422	0.29	0.248	-41.2%	-1.1%
Bhutan	10.01	6.429	4.225	-57.8%	-1.7%	13.02	40.68	74.49	472.1%	3.5%	0.472	0.374	0.244	-48.3%	-1.3%
Maldives	7.19	4.817	4.723	-34.3%	-0.8%	53.86	76.89	100	85.7%	1.2%	0.499	0.38	0.23	-53.9%	-1.5%
Asia-South Central	**9.612**	**7.925**	**7.854**	**-18.3%**	**-0.4%**	**50.41**	**73.91**	**91.04**	**80.6%**	**1.2%**	**0.416**	**0.316**	**0.236**	**-43.3%**	**-1.1%**
Indonesia	8.432	8.418	10.8	28.1%	0.5%	60.72	83.29	100	64.7%	1.0%	0.392	0.276	0.205	-47.7%	-1.3%
Philippines	5.75	6.139	7.124	23.9%	0.4%	51.88	68.78	88.91	71.4%	1.1%	0.444	0.351	0.257	-42.1%	-1.1%
Vietnam	7.32	7.263	9.277	26.7%	0.5%	80.62	100	100	24.0%	0.4%	0.42	0.239	0.188	-55.2%	-1.6%
Thailand	7.631	8.161	10.07	32.0%	0.6%	75.97	98.35	100	31.6%	0.6%	0.332	0.232	0.191	-42.5%	-1.1%
Myanmar	11.32	11.09	11.31	-0.1%	-0.0%	21.47	40.63	62.01	188.8%	2.1%	0.408	0.291	0.233	-42.9%	-1.1%
Malaysia	4.388	4.658	8.104	84.7%	1.2%	58.12	84.64	100	72.1%	1.1%	0.386	0.281	0.206	-46.6%	-1.2%
Cambodia	12.17	8.584	7.842	-35.6%	-0.9%	27.66	57.21	80.34	190.5%	2.2%	0.467	0.362	0.252	-46.0%	-1.2%
Laos	13	9.284	7.879	-39.4%	-1.0%	28.57	58.26	84.25	194.9%	2.2%	0.472	0.393	0.284	-39.8%	-1.0%
Singapore	4.158	8.645	13.29	219.6%	2.4%	69.9	88.58	100	43.1%	0.7%	0.242	0.174	0.173	-28.5%	-0.7%
Timor-Leste	13.63	12.65	9.414	-30.9%	-0.7%	28.44	43.59	64.95	128.4%	1.7%	0.488	0.438	0.37	-24.2%	-0.6%
Brunei	2.566	4.323	9.156	256.8%	2.6%	76.75	94.56	100	30.3%	0.5%	0.361	0.261	0.205	-43.2%	-1.1%
Asia-South East	**7.959**	**7.901**	**9.579**	**20.4%**	**0.4%**	**59.25**	**79.85**	**93.53**	**57.9%**	**0.9%**	**0.4**	**0.285**	**0.216**	**-46.0%**	**-1.2%**

Health

Base Case: Countries in Year 2055 Descending Population Sequence	Crude Death Rate (Per Thousand)					Contraception Use (Percent)					Youth Bulge (Ratio)				
	2005	2030	2055	% Chg	% An Chg	2005	2030	2055	% Chg	% An Chg	2005	2030	2055	% Chg	% An Chg
ASIA INCL OCEANIA continued															
Turkey	5.976	5.731	8.142	36.2%	0.6%	68.7	91.7	100	45.6%	0.8%	0.386	0.273	0.195	-49.5%	-1.4%
Yemen	10.79	7.758	6.082	-43.6%	-1.1%	24.09	52.2	76.74	218.6%	2.3%	0.533	0.452	0.356	-33.2%	-0.8%
Iraq	11.19	6.96	6.504	-41.9%	-1.1%	39.97	65.4	87.4	118.7%	1.6%	0.479	0.404	0.288	-39.9%	-1.0%
Saudi Arabia	4.074	3.796	6.92	69.9%	1.1%	34.58	56.12	77.6	124.4%	1.6%	0.421	0.337	0.216	-48.7%	-1.3%
Syria	4.088	5.035	5.874	43.7%	0.7%	42.51	62.24	86.84	104.3%	1.4%	0.506	0.366	0.249	-50.8%	-1.4%
Israel	5.394	6.089	8.422	56.1%	0.9%	82.9	100	100	20.6%	0.4%	0.336	0.272	0.212	-36.9%	-0.9%
Azerbaijan	6.292	7.764	10.71	70.2%	1.1%	62.7	91.36	100	59.5%	0.9%	0.375	0.233	0.18	-52.0%	-1.5%
Jordan	4.427	3.874	5.005	13.1%	0.2%	57.2	84.29	100	74.8%	1.1%	0.46	0.345	0.209	-54.6%	-1.6%
Palestine	4.536	4.64	4.835	6.6%	0.1%	52.73	68.46	92.13	74.7%	1.1%	0.489	0.413	0.307	-37.2%	-0.9%
Oman	3.116	3.655	6.909	121.7%	1.6%	25.96	45.62	61.25	135.9%	1.7%	0.43	0.332	0.212	-50.7%	-1.4%
Lebanon	6.867	5.383	7.823	13.9%	0.3%	65.03	95.83	100	53.8%	0.9%	0.374	0.263	0.191	-48.9%	-1.3%
United Arab Emirates	1.532	5.433	13.61	788.4%	4.5%	33.82	56.43	70.06	107.2%	1.5%	0.29	0.204	0.185	-36.2%	-0.9%
Kuwait	1.897	5.097	10.56	456.7%	3.5%	56.55	77.13	94.09	66.4%	1.0%	0.288	0.223	0.205	-28.8%	-0.7%
Georgia	12.06	14.39	14.89	23.5%	0.4%	47.86	69.94	90.74	89.6%	1.3%	0.286	0.201	0.173	-39.5%	-1.0%
Armenia	8.289	9.408	11.64	40.4%	0.7%	30.54	58.88	79.19	159.3%	1.9%	0.344	0.232	0.178	-48.3%	-1.3%
Bahrain	3.131	5.244	11.07	253.6%	2.6%	77.24	100	100	29.5%	0.5%	0.321	0.228	0.199	-38.0%	-1.0%
Qatar	3.636	7.914	12.49	243.5%	2.5%	45.42	67.36	76.74	69.0%	1.1%	0.262	0.231	0.209	-20.2%	-0.5%
Cyprus	6.779	8.591	12.6	85.9%	1.2%	80.22	98.61	100	24.7%	0.4%	0.285	0.193	0.168	-41.1%	-1.1%
Asia-West	**6.667**	**6.002**	**7.274**	**9.1%**	**0.2%**	**51.66**	**72.97**	**88.64**	**71.6%**	**1.1%**	**0.423**	**0.334**	**0.247**	**-41.6%**	**-1.1%**
Australia	6.431	8.826	10.98	70.7%	1.1%	69.74	89.88	100	43.4%	0.7%	0.256	0.206	0.195	-23.8%	-0.5%
Papua New Guinea	11.12	8.903	8.225	-26.0%	-0.6%	26.96	46.05	66.85	148.0%	1.8%	0.458	0.394	0.318	-30.6%	-0.7%
New Zealand	6.78	8.457	11.67	72.1%	1.1%	78.14	96.31	100	28.0%	0.5%	0.26	0.204	0.189	-27.3%	-0.6%
Solomon Islands	8.49	7.687	6.681	-21.3%	-0.5%	32.75	49.7	72.29	120.7%	1.6%	0.496	0.406	0.324	-34.7%	-0.8%
Fiji	6.304	6.944	8.317	31.9%	0.6%	51.54	71.95	95.84	86.0%	1.2%	0.411	0.324	0.208	-49.4%	-1.4%
Vanuatu	6.717	6.232	5.863	-12.7%	-0.3%	41.95	59.89	83.06	98.0%	1.4%	0.458	0.386	0.294	-35.8%	-0.9%
Micronesia	7.133	7.533	7.637	7.1%	0.1%	55.26	66.33	82.79	49.8%	0.8%	0.488	0.391	0.291	-40.4%	-1.0%
Samoa	5.713	5.469	6.222	8.9%	0.2%	51.87	69.91	94.29	81.8%	1.2%	0.44	0.364	0.254	-42.3%	-1.1%
Tonga	5.765	6.008	7.476	29.7%	0.5%	56.61	65.6	79.22	39.9%	0.7%	0.459	0.355	0.28	-39.0%	-1.0%
Oceania	**7.361**	**8.677**	**10.08**	**36.9%**	**0.6%**	**61.5**	**78.95**	**90.33**	**46.9%**	**0.8%**	**0.305**	**0.258**	**0.231**	**-24.3%**	**-0.6%**

Health

Base Case: Countries in Year 2055 Descending Population Sequence	Crude Death Rate (Per Thousand)					Contraception Use (Percent)					Youth Bulge (Ratio)				
	2005	2030	2055	% Chg	% An Chg	2005	2030	2055	% Chg	% An Chg	2005	2030	2055	% Chg	% An Chg
EUROPE															
Russia	12.67	11.74	15.94	25.8%	0.5%	72.58	99.35	100	37.8%	0.6%	0.287	0.173	0.139	-51.6%	-1.4%
Poland	9.058	10.67	14.16	56.3%	0.9%	79.18	98.54	100	26.3%	0.5%	0.291	0.178	0.143	-50.9%	-1.4%
Ukraine	13.55	13.79	14.85	9.6%	0.2%	73.04	99.27	100	36.9%	0.6%	0.266	0.158	0.124	-53.4%	-1.5%
Romania	11.3	12.51	15.19	34.4%	0.6%	69.11	87.97	100	44.7%	0.7%	0.282	0.18	0.146	-48.2%	-1.3%
Belarus	12.51	10.87	13.6	8.7%	0.2%	56.42	84.06	100	77.2%	1.2%	0.281	0.182	0.143	-49.1%	-1.3%
Czech Republic	9.42	12.32	15.79	67.6%	1.0%	73.73	88.3	100	35.6%	0.6%	0.253	0.156	0.132	-47.8%	-1.3%
Hungary	11.58	12.95	15.42	33.2%	0.6%	77.11	94.33	100	29.7%	0.5%	0.249	0.174	0.149	-40.2%	-1.0%
Bulgaria	13.48	13.97	14.57	8.1%	0.2%	46.03	67.28	89.01	93.4%	1.3%	0.244	0.166	0.136	-44.3%	-1.2%
Slovak Republic	8.394	10.68	13.68	63.0%	1.0%	78.44	94.03	100	27.5%	0.5%	0.293	0.178	0.144	-50.9%	-1.4%
Moldova	10.87	14.62	14.25	31.1%	0.5%	80.6	100	100	24.1%	0.4%	0.332	0.2	0.162	-51.2%	-1.4%
Europe-East	**12.01**	**12.04**	**15.28**	**27.2%**	**0.5%**	**72.43**	**96.45**	**99.75**	**37.7%**	**0.6%**	**0.281**	**0.172**	**0.139**	**-50.5%**	**-1.4%**
United Kingdom	9.127	11.13	13.11	43.6%	0.7%	74.8	93.74	100	33.7%	0.6%	0.227	0.19	0.181	-20.3%	-0.5%
Sweden	9.36	11.79	13.65	45.8%	0.8%	86.75	100	100	15.3%	0.3%	0.216	0.174	0.167	-22.7%	-0.5%
Denmark	9.607	11.77	12.65	31.7%	0.6%	87.55	100	100	14.2%	0.3%	0.21	0.199	0.197	-6.2%	-0.1%
Norway	9.076	10.46	12.08	33.1%	0.6%	92.2	100	100	8.5%	0.2%	0.226	0.202	0.197	-12.8%	-0.3%
Ireland	7.38	8.864	11.09	50.3%	0.8%	90.81	100	100	10.1%	0.2%	0.305	0.228	0.198	-35.1%	-0.9%
Finland	8.919	12.21	13.23	48.3%	0.8%	87.02	100	100	14.9%	0.3%	0.226	0.189	0.185	-18.1%	-0.4%
Lithuania	10.31	10.8	14.05	36.3%	0.6%	72.43	94.87	100	38.1%	0.6%	0.262	0.177	0.148	-43.5%	-1.1%
Latvia	11.54	11.63	15.47	34.1%	0.6%	92.33	100	100	8.3%	0.2%	0.261	0.165	0.134	-48.7%	-1.3%
Estonia	11.01	12.24	16.41	49.0%	0.8%	77.31	100	100	29.3%	0.5%	0.259	0.167	0.141	-45.6%	-1.2%
Iceland	6.528	8.861	11.97	83.4%	1.2%	90.11	100	100	11.0%	0.2%	0.28	0.212	0.19	-32.1%	-0.8%
Europe-North	**9.209**	**11.15**	**13.07**	**41.9%**	**0.7%**	**79.21**	**95.86**	**100**	**26.2%**	**0.5%**	**0.231**	**0.191**	**0.181**	**-21.6%**	**-0.5%**
Italy	9.564	13.25	17.32	81.1%	1.2%	91.62	100	100	9.1%	0.2%	0.192	0.156	0.145	-24.5%	-0.6%
Spain	8.526	11.41	16.97	99.0%	1.4%	75.27	91.96	100	32.9%	0.6%	0.229	0.167	0.141	-38.4%	-1.0%
Greece	8.69	10.77	15.17	74.6%	1.1%	79	97.66	100	26.6%	0.5%	0.233	0.165	0.146	-37.3%	-0.9%
Portugal	10.39	10.87	14.1	35.7%	0.6%	77.69	93.38	100	28.7%	0.5%	0.238	0.191	0.167	-29.8%	-0.7%
Serbia and Montenegro	10.93	13.83	10.33	-5.5%	-0.1%	63.64	85.5	100	57.1%	0.9%	0.273	0.213	0.182	-33.3%	-0.8%
Croatia	10.99	12.11	14.41	31.1%	0.5%	66.74	85.92	100	49.8%	0.8%	0.237	0.171	0.147	-38.0%	-1.0%
Bosnia and Herzegovina	8.496	13.61	14.78	74.0%	1.1%	52	67.5	86.08	65.5%	1.0%	0.263	0.173	0.154	-41.4%	-1.1%
Albania	6.765	8.671	10.16	50.2%	0.8%	62.73	83.92	100	59.4%	0.9%	0.351	0.249	0.19	-45.9%	-1.2%
Macedonia	8.664	11.68	12	38.5%	0.7%	56.2	69.24	88.23	57.0%	0.9%	0.298	0.225	0.191	-35.9%	-0.9%
Slovenia	8.849	11.74	16.98	91.9%	1.3%	87.66	100	100	14.1%	0.3%	0.24	0.16	0.139	-42.1%	-1.1%
Malta	7.475	9.57	12.66	69.4%	1.1%	77.09	94.39	100	29.7%	0.5%	0.266	0.194	0.172	-35.3%	-0.9%
Europe-South	**9.263**	**12.18**	**15.89**	**71.5%**	**1.1%**	**80.3**	**93.94**	**99.4**	**23.8%**	**0.4%**	**0.223**	**0.17**	**0.15**	**-32.7%**	**-0.8%**
Germany	9.841	13.12	16.01	62.7%	1.0%	86.85	100	100	15.1%	0.3%	0.199	0.162	0.161	-19.1%	-0.4%
France	8.943	10.92	12.8	43.1%	0.7%	77.11	94.04	100	29.7%	0.5%	0.232	0.201	0.189	-18.5%	-0.4%
Netherlands	8.379	11.23	13.32	59.0%	0.9%	75.43	91.21	100	32.6%	0.6%	0.214	0.194	0.19	-11.2%	-0.2%
Belgium	9.825	12.03	14.02	42.7%	0.7%	86.27	96.2	100	15.9%	0.3%	0.216	0.188	0.181	-16.2%	-0.4%
Austria	9.088	12.86	17.05	87.6%	1.3%	70.33	86.48	100	42.2%	0.7%	0.206	0.159	0.153	-25.7%	-0.6%
Switzerland	8.413	12.48	15.69	86.5%	1.3%	84.32	100	100	18.6%	0.3%	0.207	0.17	0.166	-19.8%	-0.4%
Luxembourg	8.084	9.57	10.32	27.7%	0.5%	93.27	100	100	7.2%	0.1%	0.221	0.214	0.213	-3.6%	-0.1%
Europe-West	**9.327**	**12.1**	**14.51**	**55.6%**	**0.9%**	**81.85**	**96.41**	**100**	**22.2%**	**0.4%**	**0.213**	**0.18**	**0.175**	**-17.8%**	**-0.4%**

Education

Base Case
Source: International Futures
Version 5.47 March 2008

	Literacy (Percent)					Adult (25+) Years of Education (Years)					Primary Education Completion (Percent)				
	2005	2030	2055	% Chg	% An Chg	2005	2030	2055	% Chg	% An Chg	2005	2030	2055	% Chg	% An Chg
World	81.23	86.67	89.41	10.1%	0.2%	6.194	8.056	9.939	60.5%	1.0%	93.95	98.7	99.37	5.8%	0.1%
Africa	65.09	78.23	85.01	30.6%	0.5%	3.575	5.382	7.357	105.8%	1.5%	69.42	85.72	95.33	37.3%	0.6%
Americas	94.3	98.85	99.45	5.5%	0.1%	8.497	10.39	12.06	41.9%	0.7%	105.2	100.1	99.61	-5.3%	-0.1%
Asia incl Oceania	78.61	84.66	87.73	11.6%	0.2%	5.623	7.77	10	77.8%	1.2%	95.04	102.2	100.9	6.2%	0.1%
Europe	99.46	99.95	100	0.5%	0.0%	9.72	12.22	14.34	47.5%	0.8%	105	100.2	99.84	-4.9%	-0.1%
World	81.23	86.67	89.41	10.1%	0.2%	6.194	8.056	9.939	60.5%	1.0%	93.95	98.7	99.37	5.8%	0.1%
Africa-Eastern	66.79	80.94	87.47	31.0%	0.5%	2.811	4.693	6.97	148.0%	1.8%	66.5	82.42	94.4	42.0%	0.7%
Africa-Middle	67.45	76.11	84.81	25.7%	0.5%	3.349	4.448	5.899	76.1%	1.1%	48.11	68.57	87.11	81.1%	1.2%
Africa-Northern	68.57	82.4	90.05	31.3%	0.5%	4.865	7.691	9.971	105.0%	1.4%	89.61	99.2	101.7	13.5%	0.3%
Africa-Southern	86.47	95.66	99.61	15.2%	0.3%	8.068	8.736	13.68	69.6%	1.1%	101.5	102.5	100.6	-0.9%	-0.0%
Africa-Western	55.47	71.51	78.81	42.1%	0.7%	2.66	4.47	6.742	153.5%	1.9%	60.6	87.29	97.19	60.4%	0.9%
Africa	65.09	78.23	85.01	30.6%	0.5%	3.575	5.382	7.357	105.8%	1.5%	69.42	85.72	95.33	37.3%	0.6%
America-Caribbean	84.08	89.2	90.5	7.6%	0.1%	6.375	8.423	10.24	60.6%	1.0%	96.14	96.72	98.74	2.7%	0.1%
America-Central	79.29	90.98	97.59	23.1%	0.4%	4.865	7.188	9.29	91.0%	1.3%	84.31	93.56	96.35	14.3%	0.3%
America-North	98.04	99.69	100	2.0%	0.0%	11.11	12.47	13.75	23.8%	0.4%	102	101.8	100	-2.0%	-0.0%
America-South	92.62	99.9	100	8.0%	0.2%	6.075	8.736	10.86	78.8%	1.2%	111.9	99.46	99.77	-10.8%	-0.2%
Americas	94.3	98.85	99.45	5.5%	0.1%	8.497	10.39	12.06	41.9%	0.7%	105.2	100.1	99.61	-5.3%	-0.1%
Asia-East	93.63	99.68	99.87	6.7%	0.1%	6.63	8.867	10.9	64.4%	1.0%	116.2	101.7	99.97	-14.0%	-0.3%
Asia-South Central	58.65	66.94	74.59	27.2%	0.5%	4.569	6.569	9.111	99.4%	1.4%	72.37	103.2	102	40.9%	0.7%
Asia-South East	91.81	98.67	99.64	8.5%	0.2%	5.599	8.307	10.42	86.1%	1.3%	101.3	100	99.53	-1.7%	-0.0%
Asia-West	81.99	90.98	94.52	15.3%	0.3%	5.664	8.314	10.62	87.5%	1.3%	94.07	103.3	100.5	6.8%	0.1%
Oceania	92.17	94.85	97.89	6.2%	0.1%	9.281	11.15	12.89	38.9%	0.7%	93.99	98.57	98.22	4.5%	0.1%
Asia incl Oceania	78.61	84.66	87.73	11.6%	0.2%	5.623	7.77	10	77.8%	1.2%	95.04	102.2	100.9	6.2%	0.1%
Europe-East	99.13	99.88	100	0.9%	0.0%	10.56	12.42	14.12	33.7%	0.6%	105.2	100.2	100	-4.9%	-0.1%
Europe-North	100	100	100	0.0%	0.0%	10.28	13.25	15.49	50.7%	0.8%	103.6	100.4	99.13	-4.3%	-0.1%
Europe-South	99.1	100	100	0.9%	0.0%	7.536	10.23	12.58	66.9%	1.0%	103.8	100.4	99.9	-3.8%	-0.1%
Europe-West	100	100	100	0.0%	0.0%	9.766	12.82	15.23	55.9%	0.9%	106.2	100.1	99.99	-5.8%	-0.1%
Europe	99.46	99.95	100	0.5%	0.0%	9.72	12.22	14.34	47.5%	0.8%	105	100.2	99.84	-4.9%	-0.1%

Multination Regional Analysis

Measures of Poverty, Health, Education, Infrastructure and Governance

Education

Base Case: Countries in Year 2055 Descending Population Sequence	Literacy (Percent)					Adult (25+) Years of Education (Years)					Primary Education Completion (Percent)				
	2005	2030	2055	% Chg	% An Chg	2005	2030	2055	% Chg	% An Chg	2005	2030	2055	% Chg	% An Chg
AFRICA															
Ethiopia	40.22	48.36	58.95	46.6%	0.8%	2.24	3.228	5.198	132.1%	1.7%	53.67	70.29	109.3	103.7%	1.4%
Tanzania	91.36	100	100	9.5%	0.2%	1.538	3.689	6.454	319.6%	2.9%	56.32	81.32	70.12	24.5%	0.4%
Uganda	72.25	92.92	100	38.4%	0.7%	3.471	6.601	9.73	180.3%	2.1%	86.9	96.33	101.3	16.6%	0.3%
Kenya	86.34	100	100	15.8%	0.3%	4.466	7.281	10.33	131.3%	1.7%	87.38	106.2	100	14.4%	0.3%
Madagascar	75.62	95.97	100	32.2%	0.6%	2.502	4.194	6.189	147.4%	1.8%	80.81	91.06	106	31.2%	0.5%
Mozambique	50.34	81.12	100	98.6%	1.4%	1.388	3.133	5.608	304.0%	2.8%	50.7	76.44	76.23	50.4%	0.8%
Malawi	66.56	87.36	96.13	44.4%	0.7%	3.179	6.24	8.294	160.9%	1.9%	102.5	91.27	104.5	2.0%	0.0%
Zambia	79.38	84.39	90.38	13.9%	0.3%	5.67	6.739	8.284	46.1%	0.8%	72.83	80.58	76.99	5.7%	0.1%
Zimbabwe	90.55	100	100	10.4%	0.2%	5.134	7.189	9.646	87.9%	1.3%	80.29	97.71	100	24.5%	0.4%
Burundi	56.99	85.41	100	75.5%	1.1%	1.526	3.106	4.844	217.4%	2.3%	48.82	61.25	92.81	90.1%	1.3%
Rwanda	71.73	96.85	100	39.4%	0.7%	2.278	4.318	6.768	197.1%	2.2%	54.79	79.41	102.5	87.1%	1.3%
Somalia	55.14	62.26	81.11	47.1%	0.8%	1.24	1.451	2.2	77.4%	1.2%	20.08	34.83	46.65	132.3%	1.7%
Eritrea	47.65	53.83	57.63	20.9%	0.4%	2.72	3.528	4.139	52.2%	0.8%	49.98	60.36	80.29	60.6%	1.0%
Mauritius	86.43	95.53	100	15.7%	0.3%	5.942	7.968	10.13	70.5%	1.1%	102	100.5	100	-2.0%	-0.0%
Comoros	56.02	61.31	71.61	27.8%	0.5%	3.745	4.663	7.149	90.9%	1.3%	52.39	93.78	108.7	107.5%	1.5%
Djibouti	53	54.71	59.08	11.5%	0.2%	3.886	4.193	5.094	31.1%	0.5%	30.48	42.57	55.69	82.7%	1.2%
Africa-Eastern	**66.79**	**80.94**	**87.47**	**31.0%**	**0.5%**	**2.811**	**4.693**	**6.97**	**148.0%**	**1.8%**	**66.5**	**82.42**	**94.4**	**42.0%**	**0.7%**
Congo, Dem. Rep. of the	68.89	76.2	84.6	22.8%	0.4%	3.359	4.249	5.566	65.7%	1.0%	40.34	61.67	86.89	115.4%	1.5%
Angola	68.03	76.23	86.05	26.5%	0.5%	3.434	4.497	6.21	80.8%	1.2%	51	81.47	88.38	73.3%	1.1%
Cameroon	73.86	87.86	96.71	30.9%	0.5%	3.426	5.232	6.838	99.6%	1.4%	61.47	74.4	82.88	34.8%	0.6%
Chad	44.86	57.98	67.73	51.0%	0.8%	2.291	3.913	5.825	154.3%	1.9%	53.66	70.8	80.56	50.1%	0.8%
Central African Republic	48.79	58.38	71.5	46.5%	0.8%	2.122	2.996	4.804	126.4%	1.6%	33.02	78.97	101	205.9%	2.3%
Congo, Rep. of	80.77	86.46	96.06	18.9%	0.3%	4.697	5.62	7.611	62.0%	1.0%	65.18	87.65	101.7	56.0%	0.9%
Gabon	88	97.94	100	13.6%	0.3%	6.884	9.587	11.96	73.7%	1.1%	119.1	100.9	100	-16.0%	-0.3%
Equatorial Guinea	88.47	97.87	100	13.0%	0.2%	6.313	8.542	10.71	69.6%	1.1%	102.5	91.35	90.67	-11.5%	-0.2%
São Tomé and Príncipe	75.61	88.75	93.81	24.1%	0.4%	4.534	7.021	8.308	83.2%	1.2%	92.79	88.03	99.22	6.9%	0.1%
Africa-Middle	**67.45**	**76.11**	**84.81**	**25.7%**	**0.5%**	**3.349**	**4.448**	**5.899**	**76.1%**	**1.1%**	**48.11**	**68.57**	**87.11**	**81.1%**	**1.2%**
Egypt	74.92	86.84	92.62	23.6%	0.4%	5.707	8.832	10.91	91.2%	1.3%	100.8	103	100	-0.8%	-0.0%
Sudan	63.2	87.16	100	58.2%	0.9%	2.235	4.434	7.165	220.6%	2.4%	48.47	85.89	107.5	121.8%	1.6%
Algeria	70.89	84.51	90.48	27.6%	0.5%	5.527	9.306	11.69	111.5%	1.5%	108.2	100.1	100	-7.6%	-0.2%
Morocco	49.65	54.32	59.39	19.6%	0.4%	5.506	7.106	9.368	70.1%	1.1%	79.94	106.5	100	25.1%	0.4%
Tunisia	75.93	91.57	99.54	31.1%	0.5%	4.964	8.49	11.16	124.8%	1.6%	109.9	100.2	100	-9.0%	-0.2%
Libya	92.61	100	100	8.0%	0.2%	3.537	8.422	11.32	220.0%	2.4%	116.2	100	100	-13.9%	-0.3%
Africa-Northern	**68.57**	**82.4**	**90.05**	**31.3%**	**0.5%**	**4.865**	**7.691**	**9.971**	**105.0%**	**1.4%**	**89.61**	**99.2**	**101.7**	**13.5%**	**0.3%**

Education

Base Case: Countries in Year 2055 Descending Population Sequence	Literacy (Percent)					Adult (25+) Years of Education (Years)					Primary Education Completion (Percent)				
	2005	2030	2055	% Chg	% An Chg	2005	2030	2055	% Chg	% An Chg	2005	2030	2055	% Chg	% An Chg
AFRICA continued															
South Africa	87.15	96.48	100	14.7%	0.3%	8.422	11.78	14.4	71.0%	1.1%	103.7	103	100	-3.6%	-0.1%
Namibia	82.95	89.92	97.37	17.4%	0.3%	6.521	8.303	10.75	64.9%	1.0%	94.39	109	112.7	19.4%	0.4%
Lesotho	84.49	96	100	18.4%	0.3%	4.703	6.657	9.357	99.0%	1.4%	66.23	95.79	103.2	55.8%	0.9%
Botswana	79.08	89.29	96	21.4%	0.4%	5.701	8.124	10.26	80.0%	1.2%	100.1	92.14	93.51	-6.6%	-0.1%
Swaziland	80.81	89.03	97.22	20.3%	0.4%	5.978	7.941	10.54	76.3%	1.1%	83.54	100.9	100	19.7%	0.4%
Africa-Southern	**86.47**	**95.66**	**99.61**	**15.2%**	**0.3%**	**8.068**	**11.16**	**13.68**	**69.6%**	**1.1%**	**101.5**	**102.5**	**100.6**	**-0.9%**	**-0.0%**
Nigeria	68.08	91.55	100	46.9%	0.8%	2.507	4.861	7.878	214.2%	2.3%	64.19	104.5	106.7	66.2%	1.0%
Niger	19.54	31.03	39.38	101.5%	1.4%	1	1.802	2.766	176.6%	2.1%	28.97	42.19	55.59	91.9%	1.3%
Ghana	73.02	80.83	86.16	18.0%	0.3%	4.226	5.488	6.56	55.2%	0.9%	68.76	68.07	92.42	34.4%	0.6%
Côte d'Ivoire	50.35	57.04	64.52	28.1%	0.5%	3.867	5.289	7.504	94.1%	1.3%	68.16	87.21	104	52.6%	0.8%
Mali	26.29	51.98	66.33	152.3%	1.9%	0.994	2.63	4.531	355.8%	3.1%	51.41	64.43	95.12	85.0%	1.2%
Burkina Faso	22.16	24.83	28.81	30.0%	0.5%	2.611	3.305	4.704	80.2%	1.2%	39.07	50.78	74.21	89.9%	1.3%
Senegal	40.21	51.93	60.98	51.7%	0.8%	2.518	4.414	6.808	170.4%	2.0%	56.01	81.24	95.13	69.8%	1.1%
Guinea	29.5	31.11	35.11	19.0%	0.3%	4.035	4.599	6.367	57.8%	0.9%	58	78.17	95.53	64.7%	1.0%
Benin	41.02	54.43	63.91	55.8%	0.9%	2.489	4.652	7.242	191.0%	2.2%	64.92	87.37	101.1	55.7%	0.9%
Togo	60.24	73.62	81.5	35.3%	0.6%	3.154	5.085	6.739	113.7%	1.5%	77.08	86.73	99.7	29.3%	0.5%
Liberia	56.61	71.87	82.44	45.6%	0.8%	2.486	4.163	5.95	139.3%	1.8%	55.03	90.22	107.9	96.1%	1.4%
Sierra Leone	37.72	49.86	58.99	56.4%	0.9%	2.261	4.059	6.304	178.8%	2.1%	59.21	87.53	102.1	72.4%	1.1%
Mauritania	43.57	57.9	68.66	57.6%	0.9%	2.224	4.022	6.277	182.0%	2.1%	58.59	79.85	84.41	44.1%	0.7%
Guinea-Bissau	63.67	79.93	88.59	39.1%	0.7%	2.436	3.951	5.11	109.8%	1.5%	52.43	68.94	87.75	67.4%	1.0%
Gambia	28.61	39.81	45.47	58.9%	0.9%	2.255	4.589	6.569	191.3%	2.2%	64.16	69.74	77.67	21.1%	0.4%
Cape Verde	76.16	85.07	90.45	18.8%	0.3%	6.264	8.729	10.67	70.3%	1.1%	110.6	103.2	100	-9.6%	-0.2%
Africa-Western	**55.47**	**71.51**	**78.81**	**42.1%**	**0.7%**	**2.66**	**4.47**	**6.742**	**153.5%**	**1.9%**	**60.6**	**87.29**	**97.19**	**60.4%**	**0.9%**

Education

Base Case: Countries in Year 2055 Descending Population Sequence	Literacy (Percent)					Adult (25+) Years of Education (Years)					Primary Education Completion (Percent)				
	2005	2030	2055	% Chg	% An Chg	2005	2030	2055	% Chg	% An Chg	2005	2030	2055	% Chg	% An Chg
AMERICAS															
Haiti	51.68	61.33	71.73	38.8%	0.7%	2.872	4.218	6.381	122.2%	1.6%	66.38	89.08	100.9	52.0%	0.8%
Dominican Republic	87.65	100	100	14.1%	0.3%	5.867	9.537	12	104.5%	1.4%	98.15	95.44	93.43	-4.8%	-0.1%
Cuba	98.03	100	100	2.0%	0.0%	8.122	10.01	11.82	45.5%	0.8%	108.6	100.9	100	-7.9%	-0.2%
Puerto Rico	95.39	100	100	4.8%	0.1%	9.657	12.37	14.38	48.9%	0.8%	123.6	102.6	100	-19.1%	-0.4%
Jamaica	89.27	100	100	12.0%	0.2%	5.618	8.136	10.22	81.9%	1.2%	91.43	100.9	100	9.4%	0.2%
Trinidad and Tobago	100	100	100	0.0%	0.0%	8.151	10.99	13.51	65.7%	1.0%	98.95	107	100	1.1%	0.0%
Bahamas	95.52	100	100	4.7%	0.1%	8.892	10.81	12.92	45.3%	0.8%	82.81	106.9	103.3	24.7%	0.4%
Barbados	100	100	100	0.0%	0.0%	8.795	10.79	12.6	43.3%	0.7%	98.49	106.4	100	1.5%	0.0%
Grenada	90.52	100	100	10.5%	0.2%	7.361	10.29	12.4	68.5%	1.0%	102.5	102.7	100	-2.4%	-0.0%
St. Vincent & the Grenadines	86.64	97.13	100	15.4%	0.3%	6.678	9.489	11.79	76.5%	1.1%	91.8	101.3	100	8.9%	0.2%
St. Lucia	87.73	97.26	100	14.0%	0.3%	6.845	9.407	11.34	65.7%	1.0%	104.7	100.8	100	-4.5%	-0.1%
America-Caribbean	**84.08**	**89.2**	**90.5**	**7.6%**	**0.1%**	**6.375**	**8.423**	**10.24**	**60.6%**	**1.0%**	**96.14**	**96.72**	**98.74**	**2.7%**	**0.1%**
Guatemala	73.6	92.01	100	35.9%	0.6%	3.628	6.434	8.588	136.7%	1.7%	80.09	87.71	93.61	16.9%	0.3%
Honduras	77.6	89.76	99.4	28.1%	0.5%	4.439	6.559	8.94	101.4%	1.4%	76.2	98.54	100.8	32.3%	0.6%
Nicaragua	68.18	77.37	84.87	24.5%	0.4%	4.688	6.609	8.749	86.6%	1.3%	65.7	90.18	95.18	44.9%	0.7%
El Salvador	81.83	94.07	100	22.2%	0.4%	4.975	7.349	9.493	90.8%	1.3%	90.59	97.05	95.52	5.4%	0.1%
Costa Rica	98.88	100	100	1.1%	0.0%	6.622	9.737	12.04	81.8%	1.2%	105.5	100.2	100	-5.2%	-0.1%
Panama	93.44	100	100	7.0%	0.1%	8.326	10.37	12.1	45.3%	0.8%	107.6	101.2	100	-7.1%	-0.1%
Belize	78.77	87.34	92.98	18.0%	0.3%	6.712	9.21	11.34	69.0%	1.1%	108.3	104.2	100	-7.7%	-0.2%
America-Central	**79.29**	**90.98**	**97.59**	**23.1%**	**0.4%**	**4.865**	**7.188**	**9.29**	**91.0%**	**1.3%**	**84.31**	**93.56**	**96.35**	**14.3%**	**0.3%**
United States	100	100	100	0.0%	0.0%	12.5	13.77	14.91	19.3%	0.4%	101.5	102.3	100	-1.5%	-0.0%
Mexico	91.92	98.78	100	8.8%	0.2%	7.023	8.753	10.3	46.7%	0.8%	104.4	100.7	100	-4.2%	-0.1%
Canada	100	100	100	0.0%	0.0%	11.71	13.26	14.58	24.5%	0.4%	99.55	100.2	100	0.5%	0.0%
America-North	**98.04**	**99.69**	**100**	**2.0%**	**0.0%**	**11.11**	**12.47**	**13.75**	**23.8%**	**0.4%**	**102**	**101.8**	**100**	**-2.0%**	**-0.0%**
Brazil	90.35	100	100	10.7%	0.2%	5.12	8.236	10.65	108.0%	1.5%	121.8	98.73	100	-17.9%	-0.4%
Colombia	93.96	100	100	6.4%	0.1%	5.356	7.44	9.621	79.6%	1.2%	93.82	103.2	100	6.6%	0.1%
Argentina	97.8	100	100	2.2%	0.0%	8.761	10.31	11.76	34.2%	0.6%	113.6	100.2	100	-12.0%	-0.3%
Peru	91.57	98.82	100	9.2%	0.2%	7.764	9.885	11.33	45.9%	0.8%	106.5	96.19	98.19	-7.8%	-0.2%
Venezuela	95.7	100	100	4.5%	0.1%	6.157	8.964	10.82	75.7%	1.1%	100.1	95.81	98.41	-1.7%	-0.0%
Chile	97.56	100	100	2.5%	0.0%	8.36	10.92	13.14	57.2%	0.9%	98.86	104	100	1.2%	0.0%
Ecuador	92.68	99.74	100	7.9%	0.2%	6.754	8.431	10.11	49.7%	0.8%	92.94	96.24	101.4	9.1%	0.2%
Bolivia	89.93	100	100	11.2%	0.2%	6.394	10.61	13.17	106.0%	1.5%	104.2	104.1	100	-4.0%	-0.1%
Paraguay	96.04	100	100	4.1%	0.1%	6.225	8.687	10.52	69.0%	1.1%	106.8	106.5	100	-6.4%	-0.1%
Uruguay	99.72	100	100	0.3%	0.0%	7.748	10.32	12.36	59.5%	0.9%	104	97.07	98.26	-5.5%	-0.1%
Guyana	99.03	100	100	1.0%	0.0%	6.384	8.282	10.17	59.3%	0.9%	108.8	104.3	100	-8.1%	-0.2%
Suriname	91.81	100	100	8.9%	0.2%	6.643	9.342	11.5	73.1%	1.1%	104.7	104.7	100	-4.5%	-0.1%
America-South	**92.62**	**99.9**	**100**	**8.0%**	**0.2%**	**6.075**	**8.736**	**10.86**	**78.8%**	**1.2%**	**111.9**	**99.46**	**99.77**	**-10.8%**	**-0.2%**

Education

Base Case: Countries in Year 2055 Descending Population Sequence	Literacy (Percent)					Adult (25+) Years of Education (Years)					Primary Education Completion (Percent)				
	2005	2030	2055	% Chg	% An Chg	2005	2030	2055	% Chg	% An Chg	2005	2030	2055	% Chg	% An Chg
ASIA INCL OCEANIA															
China	93.15	100	100	7.4%	0.1%	6.135	8.46	10.58	72.5%	1.1%	119.8	102.1	100	-16.5%	-0.4%
Japan	100	100	100	0.0%	0.0%	10.23	12.69	14.85	45.2%	0.7%	102.5	100.1	100	-2.4%	-0.0%
Korea, Rep. of	98.91	100	100	1.1%	0.0%	10.72	12.05	13.35	24.5%	0.4%	99.28	103.7	100	0.7%	0.0%
Taiwan	100	100	100	0.0%	0.0%	9.046	11.5	13.42	48.4%	0.8%	103.6	100.2	100	-3.5%	-0.1%
Korea, Dem. Rep. of	64.74	77.57	90.32	39.5%	0.7%	2.75	4.099	6.096	121.7%	1.6%	45.44	83.68	97.92	115.5%	1.5%
Hong Kong	100	100	100	0.0%	0.0%	9.97	12.44	14.69	47.3%	0.8%	104.8	100.7	100	-4.6%	-0.1%
Mongolia	100	100	100	0.0%	0.0%	4.085	7.672	9.934	143.2%	1.8%	90.3	103.4	100	10.7%	0.2%
Asia-East	**93.63**	**99.68**	**99.87**	**6.7%**	**0.1%**	**6.63**	**8.867**	**10.9**	**64.4%**	**1.0%**	**116.2**	**101.7**	**99.97**	**-14.0%**	**-0.3%**
India	58.54	66.74	74.47	27.2%	0.5%	5.049	7.29	10.31	104.2%	1.4%	70.61	108.3	104.8	48.4%	0.8%
Pakistan	50.91	60.82	74.12	45.6%	0.8%	2.535	3.692	6.116	141.3%	1.8%	56.75	93.84	101.5	78.9%	1.2%
Bangladesh	43.3	55.99	63.54	46.7%	0.8%	2.863	5.23	7.48	161.3%	1.9%	80.64	95.56	101.4	25.7%	0.5%
Iran, Islamic Rep. of	80.49	95.08	100	24.2%	0.4%	5.404	8.8	11.24	108.0%	1.5%	98.71	105.1	100	1.3%	0.0%
Afghanistan	28.3	40	53.14	87.8%	1.3%	1.156	1.857	3.164	173.7%	2.0%	19.4	51.59	68.46	252.9%	2.6%
Nepal	44.47	57.74	67.58	52.0%	0.8%	2.099	3.531	5.194	147.5%	1.8%	83.98	94.02	97.79	16.4%	0.3%
Uzbekistan	100	100	100	0.0%	0.0%	3.604	4.938	6.423	78.2%	1.2%	102.6	100.1	100	-2.5%	-0.1%
Sri Lanka	94.25	100	100	6.1%	0.1%	6.619	9.244	11.7	76.8%	1.1%	105.6	100	100	-5.3%	-0.1%
Kazakhstan	100	100	100	0.0%	0.0%	9.478	12.19	14.37	51.6%	0.8%	99.55	94.26	84.86	-14.8%	-0.3%
Tajikistan	100	100	100	0.0%	0.0%	9.801	11.06	11.94	21.8%	0.4%	103.6	89.22	90.02	-13.1%	-0.3%
Turkmenistan	100	100	100	0.0%	0.0%	5.537	7.945	10.22	84.6%	1.2%	105.1	113.9	100	-4.9%	-0.1%
Kyrgyzstan	100	100	100	0.0%	0.0%	3.984	6.491	7.191	80.5%	1.2%	96.03	84.6	90.45	-5.8%	-0.1%
Bhutan	77.44	91.54	100	29.1%	0.5%	4.998	8.044	11.08	121.7%	1.6%	75.04	103.8	100	33.3%	0.6%
Maldives	100	100	100	0.0%	0.0%	6.8	10.34	12.59	85.1%	1.2%	122.3	103.6	100	-18.2%	-0.4%
Asia-South Central	**58.65**	**66.94**	**74.59**	**27.2%**	**0.5%**	**4.569**	**6.569**	**9.111**	**99.4%**	**1.4%**	**72.37**	**103.2**	**102**	**40.9%**	**0.7%**
Indonesia	90.97	100	100	9.9%	0.2%	5.327	8.261	10.26	92.6%	1.3%	108.8	98.93	100.3	-7.8%	-0.2%
Philippines	92.85	96.54	100	7.7%	0.1%	7.682	8.67	10.04	30.7%	0.5%	92.29	102.9	100	8.4%	0.2%
Vietnam	95.64	100	100	4.6%	0.1%	4.419	8.023	10.77	143.7%	1.8%	104.3	100.3	100	-4.1%	-0.1%
Thailand	95.52	100	100	4.7%	0.1%	6.649	9.785	12.45	87.2%	1.3%	103.7	103.5	100	-3.6%	-0.1%
Myanmar	92.28	100	100	8.4%	0.2%	2.893	5.31	7.515	159.8%	1.9%	88.94	99.72	100	12.4%	0.2%
Malaysia	90.77	100	100	10.2%	0.2%	8.475	11.73	14.16	67.1%	1.0%	94.61	100.4	100	5.7%	0.1%
Cambodia	70.14	84.28	93.47	33.3%	0.6%	3.96	6.394	8.733	120.5%	1.6%	75.32	88.56	87.43	16.1%	0.3%
Laos	68.36	83.82	92.33	35.1%	0.6%	3.88	6.612	8.87	128.6%	1.7%	92.43	87.86	88.09	-4.7%	-0.1%
Singapore	93.63	100	100	6.8%	0.1%	8.414	10.58	13.16	56.4%	0.9%	78.59	102.3	101.4	29.0%	0.5%
Timor-Leste	72.29	86.75	93.95	30.0%	0.5%	4.077	6.599	8.387	105.7%	1.5%	93.62	88.87	101.4	8.3%	0.2%
Brunei	94.55	100	100	5.8%	0.1%	9.191	11.64	13.42	46.0%	0.8%	109.1	98.89	101.1	-7.3%	-0.2%
Asia-South East	**91.81**	**98.67**	**99.64**	**8.5%**	**0.2%**	**5.599**	**8.307**	**10.42**	**86.1%**	**1.3%**	**101.3**	**100**	**99.53**	**-1.7%**	**-0.0%**

Education

Base Case: Countries in Year 2055 Descending Population Sequence	Literacy (Percent)					Adult (25+) Years of Education (Years)					Primary Education Completion (Percent)				
	2005	2030	2055	% Chg	% An Chg	2005	2030	2055	% Chg	% An Chg	2005	2030	2055	% Chg	% An Chg
ASIA INCL OCEANIA continued															
Turkey	89.22	100	100	12.1%	0.2%	5.182	7.626	9.621	85.7%	1.2%	97.3	103.4	100	2.8%	0.1%
Yemen	50.62	70.69	82.81	63.6%	1.0%	2.543	5.478	8.71	242.5%	2.5%	71.51	106.1	100.5	40.5%	0.7%
Iraq	78	92.51	100	28.2%	0.5%	4.943	8.021	10.8	118.5%	1.6%	83.45	106.6	102.1	22.3%	0.4%
Saudi Arabia	77.61	83.72	87.93	13.3%	0.3%	8.58	11	13.05	52.1%	0.8%	99.6	104.5	102	2.4%	0.0%
Syria	77.19	87.09	92.52	19.9%	0.4%	6.34	9.137	11.16	76.0%	1.1%	101.9	100.4	100	-1.9%	-0.0%
Israel	96.32	100	100	3.8%	0.1%	9.715	11.85	13.55	39.5%	0.7%	107	101	100	-6.5%	-0.1%
Azerbaijan	100	100	100	0.0%	0.0%	5.067	8.799	11.72	131.3%	1.7%	98.01	103	100	2.0%	0.0%
Jordan	92.63	100	100	8.0%	0.2%	8.144	11.56	13.79	69.3%	1.1%	95.72	100.2	100	4.5%	0.1%
Palestine	97.85	100	100	2.2%	0.0%	6.326	10.41	12.37	95.5%	1.4%	102.8	98.27	100	-2.7%	-0.1%
Oman	72.96	77.9	82.08	12.5%	0.2%	8.529	10.55	12.64	48.2%	0.8%	91.85	102.8	109.2	18.9%	0.3%
Lebanon	82.89	93.1	98.73	19.1%	0.4%	6.177	8.748	10.6	71.6%	1.1%	100.6	98.3	100.5	-0.1%	-0.0%
United Arab Emirates	93.8	100	100	6.6%	0.1%	1.84	4.528	7.15	288.6%	2.8%	91.42	86.5	76.93	-15.8%	-0.3%
Kuwait	83.19	89.72	96.14	15.6%	0.3%	7.425	9.402	11.86	59.7%	0.9%	97.14	100.4	100	2.9%	0.1%
Georgia	73.85	84.45	91.08	23.3%	0.4%	4.308	6.135	7.654	77.7%	1.2%	102	104	100	-2.0%	-0.0%
Armenia	100	100	100	0.0%	0.0%	4.747	6.84	8.606	81.3%	1.2%	96.83	98.96	97.52	0.7%	0.0%
Bahrain	88.47	93.53	97.79	10.5%	0.2%	8.781	10.53	12.27	39.7%	0.7%	107.2	100.4	100	-6.7%	-0.1%
Qatar	89.68	94.38	98.66	10.0%	0.2%	9.647	11.45	13.38	38.7%	0.7%	98.73	96.58	100	1.3%	0.0%
Cyprus	98.34	100	100	1.7%	0.0%	9.139	11.01	12.81	40.2%	0.7%	97.95	100.6	100	2.1%	0.0%
Asia-West	**81.99**	**90.98**	**94.52**	**15.3%**	**0.3%**	**5.664**	**8.314**	**10.62**	**87.5%**	**1.3%**	**94.07**	**103.3**	**100.5**	**6.8%**	**0.1%**
Australia	100	100	100	0.0%	0.0%	10.99	13.32	15.14	37.8%	0.6%	102.4	100.3	100	-2.3%	-0.0%
Papua New Guinea	61.16	78.76	92.43	51.1%	0.8%	2.702	4.8	7.502	177.6%	2.1%	59.84	92.36	93.2	55.7%	0.9%
New Zealand	100	100	100	0.0%	0.0%	11.95	14.13	15.73	31.6%	0.6%	101.4	103	100	-1.4%	-0.0%
Solomon Islands	74.73	87.48	96.47	29.1%	0.5%	4.485	6.874	9.288	107.1%	1.5%	72.24	95.01	100	38.4%	0.7%
Fiji	95.56	100	100	4.6%	0.1%	6.481	8.84	10.73	65.6%	1.0%	103.8	100.1	100	-3.7%	-0.1%
Vanuatu	76.22	85.66	92.76	21.7%	0.4%	5.414	7.556	9.708	79.3%	1.2%	98.42	99.65	100	1.6%	0.0%
Micronesia	89.57	100	100	11.6%	0.2%	7.222	10.37	11.87	64.4%	1.0%	105.3	93.92	99.14	-5.8%	-0.1%
Samoa	100	100	100	0.0%	0.0%	6.318	9.151	10.71	69.5%	1.1%	94.7	85.78	97.06	2.5%	0.0%
Tonga	100	100	100	0.0%	0.0%	6.853	8.636	10.02	46.2%	0.8%	110.2	100.1	100	-9.3%	-0.2%
Oceania	**92.17**	**94.85**	**97.89**	**6.2%**	**0.1%**	**9.281**	**11.15**	**12.89**	**38.9%**	**0.7%**	**93.99**	**98.57**	**98.22**	**4.5%**	**0.1%**

Education

Base Case: Countries in Year 2055 Descending Population Sequence	Literacy (Percent)					Adult (25+) Years of Education (Years)					Primary Education Completion (Percent)				
	2005	2030	2055	% Chg	% An Chg	2005	2030	2055	% Chg	% An Chg	2005	2030	2055	% Chg	% An Chg
EUROPE															
Russia	100	100	100	0.0%	0.0%	10.78	12.35	13.98	29.7%	0.5%	106	99.72	100	-5.7%	-0.1%
Poland	93.96	99.15	100	6.4%	0.1%	10.33	12.42	14.09	36.4%	0.6%	100.3	100.4	100	-0.3%	-0.0%
Ukraine	100	100	100	0.0%	0.0%	10.87	12.82	14.43	32.8%	0.6%	105.8	100.2	100	-5.5%	-0.1%
Romania	99.56	100	100	0.4%	0.0%	9.966	12.04	13.76	38.1%	0.6%	106.4	101.8	100	-6.0%	-0.1%
Belarus	100	100	100	0.0%	0.0%	10.91	13.02	14.58	33.6%	0.6%	110.7	100.5	100	-9.7%	-0.2%
Czech Republic	98.64	100	100	1.4%	0.0%	9.846	11.64	13.37	35.8%	0.6%	103.6	100.2	100	-3.5%	-0.1%
Hungary	100	100	100	0.0%	0.0%	9.569	13.04	15.81	65.2%	1.0%	104.2	100.1	100	-4.0%	-0.1%
Bulgaria	99.77	100	100	0.2%	0.0%	10.19	12.27	13.89	36.3%	0.6%	110.5	100.1	100	-9.5%	-0.2%
Slovak Republic	100	100	100	0.0%	0.0%	10.05	13.71	16.39	63.1%	1.0%	104.7	100.2	100	-4.5%	-0.1%
Moldova	99.33	100	100	0.7%	0.0%	9.212	10.51	12.01	30.4%	0.5%	97.38	107.6	100	2.7%	0.1%
Europe-East	**99.13**	**99.88**	**100**	**0.9%**	**0.0%**	**10.56**	**12.42**	**14.12**	**33.7%**	**0.6%**	**105.2**	**100.2**	**100**	**-4.9%**	**-0.1%**
United Kingdom	100	100	100	0.0%	0.0%	9.968	13.33	15.85	59.0%	0.9%	101.9	100.3	99.12	-2.7%	-0.1%
Sweden	100	100	100	0.0%	0.0%	11.61	13.07	14.4	24.0%	0.4%	109.5	100.2	100	-8.7%	-0.2%
Denmark	100	100	100	0.0%	0.0%	10.63	13.21	15.02	41.3%	0.7%	112.4	100.2	100	-11.0%	-0.2%
Norway	100	100	100	0.0%	0.0%	12.17	13.94	15.35	26.1%	0.5%	100.7	101.7	100	-0.7%	-0.0%
Ireland	100	100	100	0.0%	0.0%	9.55	12.04	13.9	45.5%	0.8%	103.7	97.89	94.12	-9.2%	-0.2%
Finland	100	100	100	0.0%	0.0%	10.6	13.01	14.82	39.8%	0.7%	102.3	100.2	100	-2.2%	-0.0%
Lithuania	100	100	100	0.0%	0.0%	9.932	13.48	15.9	60.1%	0.9%	108.4	100	100	-7.7%	-0.2%
Latvia	100	100	100	0.0%	0.0%	10.09	13.26	15.7	55.6%	0.9%	104.4	110.8	100	-4.2%	-0.1%
Estonia	100	100	100	0.0%	0.0%	9.694	12.59	15.2	56.8%	0.9%	104.5	100.6	100	-4.3%	-0.1%
Iceland	100	100	100	0.0%	0.0%	9.488	12.63	14.95	57.6%	0.9%	101	100.4	100	-1.0%	-0.0%
Europe-North	**100**	**100**	**100**	**0.0%**	**0.0%**	**10.28**	**13.25**	**15.49**	**50.7%**	**0.8%**	**103.6**	**100.4**	**99.13**	**-4.3%**	**-0.1%**
Italy	100	100	100	0.0%	0.0%	7.566	10.41	12.95	71.2%	1.1%	104.4	100.1	100	-4.2%	-0.1%
Spain	100	100	100	0.0%	0.0%	7.864	10.6	12.91	64.2%	1.0%	108.1	100.3	100	-7.5%	-0.2%
Greece	98.36	100	100	1.7%	0.0%	8.847	10.61	12.38	39.9%	0.7%	97.4	100.3	100	2.7%	0.1%
Portugal	96.06	100	100	4.1%	0.1%	5.48	8.638	11.32	106.6%	1.5%	111.2	99.8	100	-10.1%	-0.2%
Serbia and Montenegro	98.39	100	100	1.6%	0.0%	7.968	10.63	12.77	60.3%	0.9%	101	102.3	100	-1.0%	-0.0%
Croatia	100	100	100	0.0%	0.0%	6.909	9.251	11.47	66.0%	1.0%	95.08	100.6	100	5.2%	0.1%
Bosnia and Herzegovina	96.67	100	100	3.4%	0.1%	6.46	8.354	10.59	63.9%	1.0%	69.97	105.2	100	42.9%	0.7%
Albania	87.93	100	100	13.7%	0.3%	5.935	9.224	11.45	92.9%	1.3%	103.6	95.43	98.94	-4.5%	-0.1%
Macedonia	98.82	100	100	1.2%	0.0%	6.921	9.446	11.26	62.7%	1.0%	101.4	99.23	95.82	-5.5%	-0.1%
Slovenia	100	100	100	0.0%	0.0%	8.021	11.17	13.85	72.7%	1.1%	101	104	100	-1.0%	-0.0%
Malta	93.15	98.57	100	7.4%	0.1%	9.004	10.85	12.72	41.3%	0.7%	105	100.4	100	-4.8%	-0.1%
Europe-South	**99.1**	**100**	**100**	**0.9%**	**0.0%**	**7.536**	**10.23**	**12.58**	**66.9%**	**1.0%**	**103.8**	**100.4**	**99.9**	**-3.8%**	**-0.1%**
Germany	100	100	100	0.0%	0.0%	10.35	13.48	15.96	54.2%	0.9%	105.4	100.1	100	-5.1%	-0.1%
France	100	100	100	0.0%	0.0%	8.972	12.23	14.78	64.7%	1.0%	106.1	100.1	100	-5.7%	-0.1%
Netherlands	100	100	100	0.0%	0.0%	9.759	12.6	14.78	51.4%	0.8%	109.2	100.2	100	-8.4%	-0.2%
Belgium	100	100	100	0.0%	0.0%	9.321	12.53	14.75	58.2%	0.9%	113	100.1	100	-11.5%	-0.2%
Austria	100	100	100	0.0%	0.0%	9.271	11.67	13.85	49.4%	0.8%	104.7	100.1	100	-4.5%	-0.1%
Switzerland	100	100	100	0.0%	0.0%	10.76	12.82	14.74	37.0%	0.6%	103.1	99.92	100	-3.0%	-0.1%
Luxembourg	100	100	100	0.0%	0.0%	10.87	11.86	13.52	24.4%	0.4%	103.8	99.54	97.47	-6.1%	-0.1%
Europe-West	**100**	**100**	**100**	**0.0%**	**0.0%**	**9.766**	**12.82**	**15.23**	**55.9%**	**0.9%**	**106.2**	**100.1**	**99.99**	**-5.8%**	**-0.1%**

Education

Base Case

Source: International Futures
Version 5.47 March 2008

	Adults (15+) with Primary Education (Percent)					Net Primary Education Enrollment (Percent)					Net Secondary Education Enrollment (Percent)				
	2005	2030	2055	% Chg	% An Chg	2005	2030	2055	% Chg	% An Chg	2005	2030	2055	% Chg	% An Chg
World	56.55	71.21	82.38	45.7%	0.8%	88.39	95.22	97.62	10.4%	0.2%	55.18	66.92	71.81	30.1%	0.5%
Africa	32.41	52.75	69.55	114.6%	1.5%	65.02	80.51	91.71	41.0%	0.7%	28.15	39.16	52.23	85.5%	1.2%
Americas	67.94	81.46	90.36	33.0%	0.6%	93.72	99.55	99.93	6.6%	0.1%	72.24	76.46	80.17	11.0%	0.2%
Asia incl Oceania	55.11	72.31	84.5	53.3%	0.9%	91.02	98.15	99.22	9.0%	0.2%	51.87	69.91	75.28	45.1%	0.7%
Europe	80.51	87.54	93.47	16.1%	0.3%	96.77	99.83	100	3.3%	0.1%	85.87	91.38	94.16	9.7%	0.2%
World	56.55	71.21	82.38	45.7%	0.8%	88.39	95.22	97.62	10.4%	0.2%	55.18	66.92	71.81	30.1%	0.5%
Africa-Eastern	25.46	48.02	67.08	163.5%	2.0%	57.97	76.89	90.34	55.8%	0.9%	15.25	28.14	49.22	222.8%	2.4%
Africa-Middle	28.81	45.12	61.64	114.0%	1.5%	53.98	70.15	87.17	61.5%	1.0%	15.49	24.89	36.56	136.0%	1.7%
Africa-Northern	48.25	70.52	83.81	73.7%	1.1%	84.5	94.89	99.19	17.4%	0.3%	54.89	68	78.44	42.9%	0.7%
Africa-Southern	57.24	78.21	89.82	56.9%	0.9%	91.2	99.32	99.75	9.4%	0.2%	60.32	67.8	73.46	21.8%	0.4%
Africa-Western	25.03	47.89	67.92	171.4%	2.0%	58.01	78.49	91.38	57.5%	0.9%	21.71	37.53	49.77	129.2%	1.7%
Africa	32.41	52.75	69.55	114.6%	1.5%	65.02	80.51	91.71	41.0%	0.7%	28.15	39.16	52.23	85.5%	1.2%
America-Caribbean	54.29	69.84	82.28	51.6%	0.8%	87	95.07	99.52	14.4%	0.3%	56.12	61.72	65.65	17.0%	0.3%
America-Central	42.51	67.54	82.65	94.4%	1.3%	86.37	96.76	99.57	15.3%	0.3%	40.62	51.37	61.31	50.9%	0.8%
America-North	85.85	91.65	95.81	11.6%	0.2%	95.9	99.99	99.99	4.3%	0.1%	81.23	87.95	90.97	12.0%	0.2%
America-South	51.36	73.34	86.53	68.5%	1.0%	92.67	99.86	99.95	7.9%	0.2%	66.87	68.71	72.99	9.2%	0.2%
Americas	67.94	81.46	90.36	33.0%	0.6%	93.72	99.55	99.93	6.6%	0.1%	72.24	76.46	80.17	11.0%	0.2%
Asia-East	68.21	81.82	90.78	33.1%	0.6%	99.21	99.74	99.93	0.7%	0.0%	61.15	74.49	78.13	27.8%	0.5%
Asia-South Central	41.27	62.69	78.65	90.6%	1.3%	83.18	96.91	98.8	18.8%	0.3%	41.87	68.49	74.78	78.6%	1.2%
Asia-South East	55.61	76.23	88.23	58.7%	0.9%	92.66	99.21	99.81	7.7%	0.1%	52.73	63.04	70.19	33.1%	0.6%
Asia-West	58.84	75.7	86.35	46.8%	0.8%	85.63	95.47	97.57	13.9%	0.3%	53.2	68.03	74.31	39.7%	0.7%
Oceania	74.72	83	90.91	21.7%	0.4%	91.87	98.28	99.7	8.5%	0.2%	75.68	81.25	84.71	11.9%	0.2%
Asia incl Oceania	55.11	72.31	84.5	53.3%	0.9%	91.02	98.15	99.22	9.0%	0.2%	51.87	69.91	75.28	45.1%	0.7%
Europe-East	83.44	88.15	92.45	10.8%	0.2%	96.46	99.59	100	3.7%	0.1%	80.76	88.87	92.31	14.3%	0.3%
Europe-North	83.37	90.97	96.34	15.6%	0.3%	99.51	99.99	99.99	0.5%	0.0%	94.22	96.52	97.63	3.6%	0.1%
Europe-South	71.13	82.84	91.82	29.1%	0.5%	98.16	99.95	100	1.9%	0.0%	85.66	88.58	90.56	5.7%	0.1%
Europe-West	81.55	88.26	94.39	15.7%	0.3%	94.77	100	100	5.5%	0.1%	89.94	94.39	97.26	8.1%	0.2%
Europe	80.51	87.54	93.47	16.1%	0.3%	96.77	99.83	100	3.3%	0.1%	85.87	91.38	94.16	9.7%	0.2%

Education

Base Case: Countries in Year 2055 Descending Population Sequence	Adults (15+) with Primary Education (Percent)					Net Primary Education Enrollment (Percent)					Net Secondary Education Enrollment (Percent)				
	2005	2030	2055	% Chg	% An Chg	2005	2030	2055	% Chg	% An Chg	2005	2030	2055	% Chg	% An Chg
AFRICA															
Ethiopia	21.55	34.74	55.52	157.6%	1.9%	37.74	58.97	88.2	133.7%	1.7%	12.99	23.69	53.43	311.3%	2.9%
Tanzania	18.78	44.05	62.02	230.2%	2.4%	55.63	78.15	80.73	45.1%	0.7%	6.069	21.95	35.3	481.6%	3.6%
Uganda	29.61	64.02	84.12	184.1%	2.1%	81.47	94.88	98.98	21.5%	0.4%	14.69	34.06	64.08	336.2%	3.0%
Kenya	34.75	63.09	82.97	138.8%	1.8%	69.91	93.13	100	43.0%	0.7%	23.7	42.17	64.28	171.2%	2.0%
Madagascar	25.99	51.69	74.51	186.7%	2.1%	64.75	83.3	99.04	53.0%	0.9%	12.89	23.56	43.73	239.3%	2.5%
Mozambique	14.46	40.72	62.77	334.1%	3.0%	56.37	80.6	92.49	64.1%	1.0%	10.8	28.53	42.21	290.8%	2.8%
Malawi	25.53	61.9	82.64	223.7%	2.4%	85.88	93.33	99.19	15.5%	0.3%	27.52	29.83	47.82	73.8%	1.1%
Zambia	42.26	56.45	70.92	67.8%	1.0%	62.18	75.49	93.69	50.7%	0.8%	17.38	24.7	34.93	101.0%	1.4%
Zimbabwe	52.28	71.71	86.2	64.9%	1.0%	83.46	97.27	99.94	19.7%	0.4%	39.21	51.31	68.95	75.8%	1.1%
Burundi	14.62	33.72	52.05	256.0%	2.6%	44.48	60.05	84.02	88.9%	1.3%	5.125	13.45	35.38	590.3%	3.9%
Rwanda	19.25	49.24	72.66	277.5%	2.7%	72.45	90.43	99.94	37.9%	0.6%	9.254	25.02	48.87	428.1%	3.4%
Somalia	6.366	10.48	20.85	227.5%	2.4%	10.87	24.8	40.67	274.1%	2.7%	3.306	9.106	14.9	350.7%	3.1%
Eritrea	25.36	36.78	47.48	87.2%	1.3%	40.08	49.11	64.93	62.0%	1.0%	21.43	24.12	31.92	49.0%	0.8%
Mauritius	53.42	74.52	88.3	65.3%	1.0%	94.25	99.83	99.83	5.9%	0.1%	62.93	73.38	75.71	20.3%	0.4%
Comoros	28.74	48.71	72.96	153.9%	1.9%	58.82	86.51	99.16	68.6%	1.0%	23.4	42.78	59.48	154.2%	1.9%
Djibouti	21.73	26.32	35.19	61.9%	1.0%	27.6	39.24	57.01	106.6%	1.5%	13.5	17.87	25.24	87.0%	1.3%
Africa-Eastern	**25.46**	**48.02**	**67.08**	**163.5%**	**2.0%**	**57.97**	**76.89**	**90.34**	**55.8%**	**0.9%**	**15.25**	**28.14**	**49.22**	**222.8%**	**2.4%**
Congo, Dem. Rep. of the	29.66	43.68	60.41	103.7%	1.4%	50.58	66.01	86.44	70.9%	1.1%	14.85	21.73	35.93	142.0%	1.8%
Angola	23.11	37.26	55.05	138.2%	1.8%	40.15	62.08	81.36	102.6%	1.4%	18.07	34.68	40.99	126.8%	1.7%
Cameroon	31.26	56.14	71.44	128.5%	1.7%	73.26	87.14	93.65	27.8%	0.5%	14.94	23.15	31.64	111.8%	1.5%
Chad	22.49	43.45	59.76	165.7%	2.0%	51.32	71.95	85.04	65.7%	1.0%	9.448	22.77	31.1	229.2%	2.4%
Central African Republic	15.69	38.68	61.42	291.5%	2.8%	57.55	79.88	94.83	64.8%	1.0%	8.721	25.32	37.93	334.9%	3.0%
Congo, Rep. of	43.21	59.28	76.98	78.2%	1.2%	67.46	88.95	98.91	46.6%	0.8%	27.62	41.69	55.13	99.6%	1.4%
Gabon	58.75	79.81	90.41	53.9%	0.9%	80.42	99.57	99.57	23.8%	0.4%	39.84	48.58	59.43	49.2%	0.8%
Equatorial Guinea	54.31	77.42	87.22	60.6%	1.0%	87.24	98.99	99.05	13.5%	0.3%	29.8	45.42	49.81	67.1%	1.0%
São Tomé and Príncipe	42.3	66.22	82.02	93.9%	1.3%	83.56	92.73	98.2	17.5%	0.3%	32.77	31.62	40.4	23.3%	0.4%
Africa-Middle	**28.81**	**45.12**	**61.64**	**114.0%**	**1.5%**	**53.98**	**70.15**	**87.17**	**61.5%**	**1.0%**	**15.49**	**24.89**	**36.56**	**136.0%**	**1.7%**
Egypt	57.94	82.14	92.01	58.8%	0.9%	96.26	100	100	3.9%	0.1%	69.24	77.8	83.72	20.9%	0.4%
Sudan	22.11	44.75	66.6	201.2%	2.2%	48.27	76.25	96.55	100.0%	1.4%	27.57	49.73	71.98	161.1%	1.9%
Algeria	54.17	76.75	88.55	63.5%	1.0%	94.75	100	100	5.5%	0.1%	61.82	69.33	77.01	24.6%	0.4%
Morocco	49.9	68.17	82.63	65.6%	1.0%	81.91	99.64	100	22.1%	0.4%	33.24	56.31	86.36	105.7%	1.5%
Tunisia	51.3	73.57	85.94	67.5%	1.0%	96.1	100	100	4.1%	0.1%	70.6	81.28	86.63	22.7%	0.4%
Libya	42.77	71.1	85.06	98.9%	1.4%	98.87	100	100	1.1%	0.0%	89.07	94.98	97.58	9.6%	0.2%
Africa-Northern	**48.25**	**70.52**	**83.81**	**73.7%**	**1.1%**	**84.5**	**94.89**	**99.19**	**17.4%**	**0.3%**	**54.89**	**68**	**78.44**	**42.9%**	**0.7%**

Education

Base Case: Countries in Year 2055 Descending Population Sequence	Adults (15+) with Primary Education (Percent)					Net Primary Education Enrollment (Percent)					Net Secondary Education Enrollment (Percent)				
	2005	2030	2055	% Chg	% An Chg	2005	2030	2055	% Chg	% An Chg	2005	2030	2055	% Chg	% An Chg
AFRICA continued															
South Africa	58.23	79.58	90.97	56.2%	0.9%	93.39	99.91	99.91	7.0%	0.1%	63.63	70.44	74.93	17.8%	0.3%
Namibia	58.32	75.11	86.45	48.2%	0.8%	74.54	96.53	96.93	30.0%	0.5%	38.49	57.36	68.89	79.0%	1.2%
Lesotho	30.8	59.61	79.88	159.4%	1.9%	76.99	96.12	100	29.9%	0.5%	21.2	40.86	60.09	183.4%	2.1%
Botswana	62.92	78.44	86.29	37.1%	0.6%	80.81	94.95	99.93	23.7%	0.4%	56.31	61.59	68.38	21.4%	0.4%
Swaziland	49.76	69.02	84.58	70.0%	1.1%	73.26	97.11	99.99	36.5%	0.6%	37.53	54.02	68.73	83.1%	1.2%
Africa-Southern	**57.24**	**78.21**	**89.82**	**56.9%**	**0.9%**	**91.2**	**99.32**	**99.75**	**9.4%**	**0.2%**	**60.32**	**67.8**	**73.46**	**21.8%**	**0.4%**
Nigeria	24.48	55.07	79.41	224.4%	2.4%	65.38	92.68	98.88	51.2%	0.8%	26.37	51.12	60.7	130.2%	1.7%
Niger	10.27	20.27	30.66	198.5%	2.2%	26.39	35.57	51.9	96.7%	1.4%	5.395	10.03	18.64	245.5%	2.5%
Ghana	34.41	46.17	59.3	72.3%	1.1%	57.36	66.37	88.63	54.5%	0.9%	30.75	27.79	40.66	32.2%	0.6%
Côte d'Ivoire	35.61	51.52	68.78	93.1%	1.3%	53.22	72.62	93.41	75.5%	1.1%	19.15	34.42	57.27	199.1%	2.2%
Mali	11.89	33.07	53.57	350.5%	3.1%	42.53	60.19	85.39	100.8%	1.4%	6.523	15.95	38.71	493.4%	3.6%
Burkina Faso	24.83	33.74	47.5	91.3%	1.3%	37.48	51.81	75.93	102.6%	1.4%	8.369	14.53	30.76	267.5%	2.6%
Senegal	23.72	44.66	66.34	179.7%	2.1%	56.6	77.01	96.67	70.8%	1.1%	13.12	27.13	46.64	255.5%	2.6%
Guinea	37.29	44.83	61.84	65.8%	1.0%	48.44	63.46	91.95	89.8%	1.3%	12.75	25.26	42.3	231.8%	2.4%
Benin	22.09	43.81	70.41	218.7%	2.3%	55.01	74.8	98.14	78.4%	1.2%	18.57	30.64	50.64	172.7%	2.0%
Togo	30.45	55.25	74.2	143.7%	1.8%	74.92	87.86	97.44	30.1%	0.5%	26.58	31.64	37.89	42.6%	0.7%
Liberia	21.89	49.85	72.83	232.7%	2.4%	68.51	88.39	97.25	42.0%	0.7%	25.26	37.4	49.61	96.4%	1.4%
Sierra Leone	20.68	48.16	71.47	245.6%	2.5%	60.36	81.38	97.78	62.0%	1.0%	22.95	35.29	50.2	118.7%	1.6%
Mauritania	20.24	43.27	65.76	224.9%	2.4%	58.15	77.57	94.79	63.0%	1.0%	15.77	28.66	38.85	146.4%	1.8%
Guinea-Bissau	10.1	30.96	49.09	386.0%	3.2%	46.58	59.07	80.61	73.1%	1.1%	14.68	19.78	28.84	96.5%	1.4%
Gambia	24.79	46.94	66.21	167.1%	2.0%	66.18	78.99	94.37	42.6%	0.7%	27.43	29.03	38.59	40.7%	0.7%
Cape Verde	60.14	84.41	92.63	54.0%	0.9%	98.32	100	100	1.7%	0.0%	48.34	59.45	71.05	47.0%	0.8%
Africa-Western	**25.03**	**47.89**	**67.92**	**171.4%**	**2.0%**	**58.01**	**78.49**	**91.38**	**57.5%**	**0.9%**	**21.71**	**37.53**	**49.77**	**129.2%**	**1.7%**

Education

Base Case: Countries in Year 2055 Descending Population Sequence	Adults (15+) with Primary Education Percent					Net Primary Education Enrollment Percent					Net Secondary Education Enrollment Percent				
	2005	2030	2055	% Chg	% An Chg	2005	2030	2055	% Chg	% An Chg	2005	2030	2055	% Chg	% An Chg
AMERICAS															
Haiti	24.43	45.86	69.2	183.3%	2.1%	60.85	82.45	98.61	62.1%	1.0%	23.87	34.12	46.21	93.6%	1.3%
Dominican Republic	44.17	70	83.5	89.0%	1.3%	89.84	100	100	11.3%	0.2%	42.53	56.17	60.34	41.9%	0.7%
Cuba	74.3	85.31	92.97	25.1%	0.4%	99.21	100	100	0.8%	0.0%	82.14	86.62	89.83	9.4%	0.2%
Puerto Rico	70.86	84.26	92.95	31.2%	0.5%	95.86	99.97	99.97	4.3%	0.1%	59	60.22	69.15	17.2%	0.3%
Jamaica	63.46	80.61	89.92	41.7%	0.7%	90.46	99.93	99.93	10.5%	0.2%	74.18	84.21	86.68	16.9%	0.3%
Trinidad and Tobago	67.88	80.43	89.58	32.0%	0.6%	96.24	100	100	3.9%	0.1%	76.1	86.8	84.78	11.4%	0.2%
Bahamas	67.31	78.11	87.19	29.5%	0.5%	86.16	96.85	99.8	15.8%	0.3%	75.98	93.95	97.08	27.8%	0.5%
Barbados	76.84	86.25	93.18	21.3%	0.4%	99.64	100	100	0.4%	0.0%	85.22	94.2	97.2	14.1%	0.3%
Grenada	64.04	81.76	91	42.1%	0.7%	90.19	100	100	10.9%	0.2%	66.98	74.26	79.9	19.3%	0.4%
St. Vincent & the Grenadines	58.21	75.9	86.76	49.0%	0.8%	88.67	100	100	12.8%	0.2%	57.02	79.19	84.17	47.6%	0.8%
St. Lucia	62.31	80.23	89.03	42.9%	0.7%	96.47	99.95	99.95	3.6%	0.1%	70.57	82.63	89.28	26.5%	0.5%
America-Caribbean	**54.29**	**69.84**	**82.28**	**51.6%**	**0.8%**	**87**	**95.07**	**99.52**	**14.4%**	**0.3%**	**56.12**	**61.72**	**65.65**	**17.0%**	**0.3%**
Guatemala	34.29	65.77	81.41	137.4%	1.7%	84.04	95.12	99.36	18.2%	0.3%	27.15	36.74	52.09	91.9%	1.3%
Honduras	41.07	65.26	83.16	102.5%	1.4%	84.04	97.33	99.52	18.4%	0.3%	51.59	63.54	70.64	36.9%	0.6%
Nicaragua	38.68	60.88	78.49	102.9%	1.4%	79.42	94.64	99.64	25.5%	0.5%	35.92	48.7	56.47	57.2%	0.9%
El Salvador	39.64	67.28	82.63	108.5%	1.5%	88.15	98.6	99.69	13.1%	0.2%	40.52	51.12	61.24	51.1%	0.8%
Costa Rica	52.23	74.31	86.58	65.8%	1.0%	93.68	100	100	6.7%	0.1%	51.57	67.46	76.52	48.4%	0.8%
Panama	76.99	88.56	94.14	22.3%	0.4%	98.6	99.99	99.99	1.4%	0.0%	61.56	80.08	83.12	35.0%	0.6%
Belize	59.44	81.25	89.77	51.0%	0.8%	94.65	99.87	99.87	5.5%	0.1%	62.53	75.75	79.79	27.6%	0.5%
America-Central	**42.51**	**67.54**	**82.65**	**94.4%**	**1.3%**	**86.37**	**96.76**	**99.57**	**15.3%**	**0.3%**	**40.62**	**51.37**	**61.31**	**50.9%**	**0.8%**
United States	90.55	93.84	96.95	7.1%	0.1%	95.34	100	100	4.9%	0.1%	87.58	94.51	97.35	11.2%	0.2%
Mexico	69.55	84.12	91.78	32.0%	0.6%	96.41	99.97	99.97	3.7%	0.1%	58.4	67.3	70.78	21.2%	0.4%
Canada	95.77	97.42	98.84	3.2%	0.1%	99.36	100	100	0.6%	0.0%	97.32	98.73	99.4	2.1%	0.0%
America-North	**85.85**	**91.65**	**95.81**	**11.6%**	**0.2%**	**95.9**	**99.99**	**99.99**	**4.3%**	**0.1%**	**81.23**	**87.95**	**90.97**	**12.0%**	**0.2%**
Brazil	40.02	66.73	83.26	108.0%	1.5%	92.4	100	100	8.2%	0.2%	70.06	66.91	70.5	0.6%	0.0%
Colombia	50.08	71.72	85.32	70.4%	1.1%	89.67	99.8	99.8	11.3%	0.2%	57.5	72.35	76.53	33.1%	0.6%
Argentina	81.16	90.08	95.2	17.3%	0.3%	98.55	99.99	99.99	1.5%	0.0%	80.76	79.85	82.54	2.2%	0.0%
Peru	67.58	82.42	90.5	33.9%	0.6%	94.14	99.68	99.91	6.1%	0.1%	63.24	65.39	70.52	11.5%	0.2%
Venezuela	60.95	79.99	89.28	46.5%	0.8%	91.92	100	100	8.8%	0.2%	51.41	59.32	69.33	34.9%	0.6%
Chile	62.56	78.09	88.65	41.7%	0.7%	90.34	100	100	10.7%	0.2%	75.31	86.48	85.45	13.5%	0.3%
Ecuador	54.88	72.58	85.34	55.5%	0.9%	89.46	98.05	99.96	11.7%	0.2%	49.82	57.46	65.53	31.5%	0.5%
Bolivia	48.31	78.21	90.38	87.1%	1.3%	94.18	99.81	99.81	6.0%	0.1%	66.99	75.15	80.73	20.5%	0.4%
Paraguay	57.65	80.76	92.03	59.6%	0.9%	92.04	99.84	99.84	8.5%	0.2%	47.19	54.58	63.42	34.4%	0.6%
Uruguay	64.19	80.44	89.89	40.0%	0.7%	95.39	99.94	99.94	4.8%	0.1%	71.19	77.35	79.84	12.2%	0.2%
Guyana	60.81	76.58	87.94	44.6%	0.7%	91.15	99.78	99.85	9.5%	0.2%	70.79	72.72	74.19	4.8%	0.1%
Suriname	59.04	77.72	87.77	48.7%	0.8%	93.43	100	100	7.0%	0.1%	63.02	73.91	76.29	21.1%	0.4%
America-South	**51.36**	**73.34**	**86.53**	**68.5%**	**1.0%**	**92.67**	**99.86**	**99.95**	**7.9%**	**0.2%**	**66.87**	**68.71**	**72.99**	**9.2%**	**0.2%**

Education

Base Case: Countries in Year 2055 Descending Population Sequence	Adults (15+) with Primary Education — Percent					Net Primary Education Enrollment — Percent					Net Secondary Education Enrollment — Percent				
	2005	2030	2055	% Chg	% An Chg	2005	2030	2055	% Chg	% An Chg	2005	2030	2055	% Chg	% An Chg
ASIA INCL OCEANIA															
China	66.08	81.13	90.63	37.2%	0.6%	99.81	99.96	99.96	0.2%	0.0%	56.7	72.11	76.32	34.6%	0.6%
Japan	86.6	91.82	96.39	11.3%	0.2%	100	100	100	0.0%	0.0%	99.28	99.66	99.84	0.6%	0.0%
Korea, Rep. of	89.97	93.11	96	6.7%	0.1%	98.83	99.93	99.93	1.1%	0.0%	88.49	94.93	97.57	10.3%	0.2%
Taiwan	81.48	89	94.97	16.6%	0.3%	98.35	100	100	1.7%	0.0%	78.77	80.29	82.4	4.6%	0.1%
Korea, Dem. Rep. of	26.18	42.17	62.7	139.5%	1.8%	63.3	83.85	97.42	53.9%	0.9%	21.42	44.41	59.84	179.4%	2.1%
Hong Kong	78.51	86.23	93.35	18.9%	0.3%	95.17	100	100	5.1%	0.1%	68.94	75.46	76.95	11.6%	0.2%
Mongolia	39.93	68.8	85.15	113.2%	1.5%	94.77	100	100	5.5%	0.1%	66.75	75.74	80.29	20.3%	0.4%
Asia-East	**68.21**	**81.82**	**90.78**	**33.1%**	**0.6%**	**99.21**	**99.74**	**99.93**	**0.7%**	**0.0%**	**61.15**	**74.49**	**78.13**	**27.8%**	**0.5%**
India	41.13	64.13	80.04	94.6%	1.3%	86.19	99.88	99.88	15.9%	0.3%	41.57	76.28	82.48	98.4%	1.4%
Pakistan	35.68	54.03	76.5	114.4%	1.5%	63.74	90.3	99.84	56.6%	0.9%	21.96	43.04	60.63	176.1%	2.1%
Bangladesh	32.71	60.85	79.87	144.2%	1.8%	88.58	96.19	99.78	12.6%	0.2%	44.12	54.45	65.84	49.2%	0.8%
Iran, Islamic Rep. of	55.2	72.78	84.14	52.4%	0.8%	82.52	97.58	100	21.2%	0.4%	66.14	81.52	81.96	23.9%	0.4%
Afghanistan	6.097	23.75	42.48	596.7%	4.0%	34.51	56.09	71.28	106.5%	1.5%	6.639	16.49	24.06	262.4%	2.6%
Nepal	31.5	56.63	76.44	142.7%	1.8%	75.13	91.95	97.5	29.8%	0.5%	29.62	35.94	41.41	39.8%	0.7%
Uzbekistan	68.24	75.12	83.4	22.2%	0.4%	72.44	86.88	99.02	36.7%	0.6%	80.96	81.67	80.75	-0.3%	-0.0%
Sri Lanka	68.43	82.47	91.61	33.9%	0.6%	99.19	100	100	0.8%	0.0%	68.41	74.36	76.79	12.2%	0.2%
Kazakhstan	77.51	85.9	91.1	17.5%	0.3%	99.38	100	100	0.6%	0.0%	85.01	95.47	97.83	15.1%	0.3%
Tajikistan	85.69	93.11	95.07	10.9%	0.2%	94.16	99.99	99.99	6.2%	0.1%	76.34	72.25	68.04	-10.9%	-0.2%
Turkmenistan	64.78	78.84	87.04	34.4%	0.6%	85.82	100	100	16.5%	0.3%	53.83	79.24	77.94	44.8%	0.7%
Kyrgyzstan	79.95	88.62	92.93	16.2%	0.3%	92.66	100	100	7.9%	0.2%	70.38	59.83	58.91	-16.3%	-0.4%
Bhutan	45.87	71.65	85.73	86.9%	1.3%	79.52	99.79	99.85	25.6%	0.5%	46.37	76.53	82.9	78.8%	1.2%
Maldives	62.11	85.61	93.27	50.2%	0.8%	96.34	99.95	99.95	3.7%	0.1%	34.99	49.53	63.1	80.3%	1.2%
Asia-South Central	**41.27**	**62.69**	**78.65**	**90.6%**	**1.3%**	**83.18**	**96.91**	**98.8**	**18.8%**	**0.3%**	**41.87**	**68.49**	**74.78**	**78.6%**	**1.2%**
Indonesia	56.28	79.12	90.66	61.1%	1.0%	96.16	100	100	4.0%	0.1%	49.25	56.19	65.87	33.7%	0.6%
Philippines	68.05	80.74	90.16	32.5%	0.6%	89.94	99.8	99.82	11.0%	0.2%	53.85	65.82	71.15	32.1%	0.6%
Vietnam	50.08	73.96	86.96	73.6%	1.1%	97.4	100	100	2.7%	0.1%	57.39	70.99	75.84	32.1%	0.6%
Thailand	56.41	73.38	86.12	52.7%	0.8%	85.4	98.34	100	17.1%	0.3%	70.32	81.18	81.68	16.2%	0.3%
Myanmar	38.15	63.03	81.47	113.6%	1.5%	85.02	96.53	99.92	17.5%	0.3%	38.12	50.72	63.49	66.6%	1.0%
Malaysia	71.23	85.12	92.49	29.8%	0.5%	97.41	99.88	99.88	2.5%	0.1%	70.86	82.83	84.64	19.4%	0.4%
Cambodia	38.25	64.45	78.84	106.1%	1.5%	86.74	95.65	97.41	12.3%	0.2%	19.46	39.87	52.46	169.6%	2.0%
Laos	37.37	65.79	79.87	113.7%	1.5%	81.67	94.84	96.95	18.7%	0.3%	30.88	41.92	55.48	79.7%	1.2%
Singapore	68.83	76.63	86.43	25.6%	0.5%	84.81	96.39	99.29	17.1%	0.3%	62.9	86.76	86.04	36.8%	0.6%
Timor-Leste	39.29	63.1	81.09	106.4%	1.5%	74.61	87.71	99.8	33.8%	0.6%	35.08	38.3	54.19	54.5%	0.9%
Brunei	78.58	88.24	93.75	19.3%	0.4%	95.2	99.78	99.79	4.8%	0.1%	68.54	69.26	70.91	3.5%	0.1%
Asia-South East	**55.61**	**76.23**	**88.23**	**58.7%**	**0.9%**	**92.66**	**99.21**	**99.81**	**7.7%**	**0.1%**	**52.73**	**63.04**	**70.19**	**33.1%**	**0.6%**

Education

Base Case: Countries in Year 2055 Descending Population Sequence	Adults (15+) with Primary Education (Percent)					Net Primary Education Enrollment (Percent)					Net Secondary Education Enrollment (Percent)				
	2005	2030	2055	% Chg	% An Chg	2005	2030	2055	% Chg	% An Chg	2005	2030	2055	% Chg	% An Chg
ASIA INCL OCEANIA continued															
Turkey	74.13	85.4	91.83	23.9%	0.4%	91.86	99.95	99.95	8.8%	0.2%	54.23	70.27	75.27	38.8%	0.7%
Yemen	22.43	57.29	81.41	263.0%	2.6%	62.85	92.38	99.6	58.5%	0.9%	36.13	56.5	63.91	76.9%	1.1%
Iraq	42.29	73.58	88.34	108.9%	1.5%	86.05	99.74	99.74	15.9%	0.3%	34.01	59.97	71.28	109.6%	1.5%
Saudi Arabia	55.83	63.17	69.16	23.9%	0.4%	61.75	73.23	82.81	34.1%	0.6%	53.1	69.36	75.67	42.5%	0.7%
Syria	57.29	81.61	91.83	60.3%	0.9%	96.22	100	100	3.9%	0.1%	39.89	55.32	70.89	77.7%	1.2%
Israel	79.88	90.66	96.24	20.5%	0.4%	99.19	99.99	99.99	0.8%	0.0%	76.46	82.66	85.58	11.9%	0.2%
Azerbaijan	47.14	70.84	85.37	81.1%	1.2%	91.55	100	100	9.2%	0.2%	77.54	93.31	96.74	24.8%	0.4%
Jordan	64.67	83.74	91.15	40.9%	0.7%	95.75	99.85	99.85	4.3%	0.1%	79.45	90.66	95.4	20.1%	0.4%
Palestine	57.91	85.05	94.41	63.0%	1.0%	96.31	99.91	99.91	3.7%	0.1%	74.13	72.19	78.87	6.4%	0.1%
Oman	72.79	81.96	88	20.9%	0.4%	83.83	93.03	97.75	16.6%	0.3%	67.05	82.15	82.76	23.4%	0.4%
Lebanon	56.96	78.9	88.72	55.8%	0.9%	96.54	99.97	99.97	3.6%	0.1%	67.9	75.43	82.73	21.8%	0.4%
United Arab Emirates	19.1	44.85	63.64	233.2%	2.4%	80.06	88.81	84.17	5.1%	0.1%	73.09	74.8	64.54	-11.7%	-0.2%
Kuwait	58.61	73.3	86.62	47.8%	0.8%	85.66	99.85	99.85	16.6%	0.3%	79.63	87.48	86.48	8.6%	0.2%
Georgia	86.72	91.57	95.73	10.4%	0.2%	96.68	100	100	3.4%	0.1%	72.64	81.35	80.74	11.2%	0.2%
Armenia	72.49	82.93	90.24	24.5%	0.4%	99.68	100	100	0.3%	0.0%	77.56	87.99	85.59	10.4%	0.2%
Bahrain	77.52	87.05	93.83	21.0%	0.4%	97.42	99.91	99.91	2.6%	0.1%	82.9	84.08	84.95	2.5%	0.0%
Qatar	83.64	89.83	94.9	13.5%	0.3%	96.71	99.97	99.98	3.4%	0.1%	79.32	83.13	86.74	9.4%	0.2%
Cyprus	87.63	91.76	95.44	8.9%	0.2%	97.29	100	100	2.8%	0.1%	88.91	94.81	97.5	9.7%	0.2%
Asia-West	**58.84**	**75.7**	**86.35**	**46.8%**	**0.8%**	**85.63**	**95.47**	**97.57**	**13.9%**	**0.3%**	**53.2**	**68.03**	**74.31**	**39.7%**	**0.7%**
Australia	85.37	90.61	95.36	11.7%	0.2%	95.66	100	100	4.5%	0.1%	89.72	94.99	97.59	8.8%	0.2%
Papua New Guinea	34.89	59.33	79.11	126.7%	1.7%	73.42	92.95	98.85	34.6%	0.6%	23.16	44.24	55.28	138.7%	1.8%
New Zealand	89.36	93.95	97.39	9.0%	0.2%	99.94	100	100	0.1%	0.0%	92.31	96.25	98.21	6.4%	0.1%
Solomon Islands	41.44	65.99	84.58	104.1%	1.4%	80.4	95.34	99.83	24.2%	0.4%	16.85	35.72	56.59	235.8%	2.5%
Fiji	59.8	81.32	91.11	52.4%	0.8%	98.15	99.95	99.95	1.8%	0.0%	77.13	79.47	81.95	6.2%	0.1%
Vanuatu	51.65	76.6	89.75	73.8%	1.1%	92.61	98.92	99.89	7.9%	0.2%	27.08	41.32	63.71	135.3%	1.7%
Micronesia	62.82	81.39	91.06	45.0%	0.7%	87.79	97.59	99.99	13.9%	0.3%	63.69	57.46	67.03	5.2%	0.1%
Samoa	58.4	79.54	86.99	49.0%	0.8%	92.7	96.11	99.73	7.6%	0.1%	65.97	63.54	72.87	10.5%	0.2%
Tonga	64.15	85.27	94.35	47.1%	0.8%	93.09	99.84	99.84	7.3%	0.1%	71.88	64.26	65.18	-9.3%	-0.2%
Oceania	**74.72**	**83**	**90.91**	**21.7%**	**0.4%**	**91.87**	**98.28**	**99.7**	**8.5%**	**0.2%**	**75.68**	**81.25**	**84.71**	**11.9%**	**0.2%**

Multination Regional Analysis

Measures of Poverty, Health, Education, Infrastructure and Governance

Education

Base Case: Countries in Year 2055 Descending Population Sequence	Adults (15+) with Primary Education (Percent)					Net Primary Education Enrollment (Percent)					Net Secondary Education Enrollment (Percent)				
	2005	2030	2055	% Chg	% An Chg	2005	2030	2055	% Chg	% An Chg	2005	2030	2055	% Chg	% An Chg
EUROPE															
Russia	82.05	86.78	91.13	11.1%	0.2%	100	100	100	0.0%	0.0%	77.27	89.5	94.36	22.1%	0.4%
Poland	94.5	96.53	98.11	3.8%	0.1%	98.93	100	100	1.1%	0.0%	91.51	95.83	98.01	7.1%	0.1%
Ukraine	80.45	84.07	89.07	10.7%	0.2%	84.45	97.14	100	18.4%	0.3%	80.65	82.25	84.46	4.7%	0.1%
Romania	84.28	90.23	94.72	12.4%	0.2%	99.24	100	100	0.8%	0.0%	79.45	85.02	83.91	5.6%	0.1%
Belarus	86.24	90.82	94.59	9.7%	0.2%	93.48	100	100	7.0%	0.1%	79.93	83	87.49	9.5%	0.2%
Czech Republic	81.94	87.75	93.09	13.6%	0.3%	91.97	100	100	8.7%	0.2%	88.42	93.65	96.93	9.6%	0.2%
Hungary	74.97	84.09	91.63	22.2%	0.4%	93.1	100	100	7.4%	0.1%	88	95.03	97.61	10.9%	0.2%
Bulgaria	85.23	90.66	94.99	11.5%	0.2%	100	100	100	0.0%	0.0%	86.98	95.21	97.7	12.3%	0.2%
Slovak Republic	79.93	87.34	93.21	16.6%	0.3%	93.76	100	100	6.7%	0.1%	76.37	78.4	80.85	5.9%	0.1%
Moldova	77.6	85.28	91.58	18.0%	0.3%	96.81	100	100	3.3%	0.1%	69.23	77.63	80.63	16.5%	0.3%
Europe-East	**83.44**	**88.15**	**92.45**	**10.8%**	**0.2%**	**96.46**	**99.59**	**100**	**3.7%**	**0.1%**	**80.76**	**88.87**	**92.31**	**14.3%**	**0.3%**
United Kingdom	80.45	89.68	96.03	19.4%	0.4%	99.98	100	100	0.0%	0.0%	94.95	97.57	98.85	4.1%	0.1%
Sweden	91.31	94.85	97.72	7.0%	0.1%	99.24	99.99	99.99	0.8%	0.0%	96.35	98.25	99.17	2.9%	0.1%
Denmark	85.81	92.27	96.99	13.0%	0.2%	99.29	99.91	99.91	0.6%	0.0%	89.44	82.67	80.18	-10.4%	-0.2%
Norway	95.83	97.51	98.88	3.2%	0.1%	99.72	99.98	99.98	0.3%	0.0%	95.48	97.83	98.98	3.7%	0.1%
Ireland	87.02	92.34	96.15	10.5%	0.2%	95.12	100	100	5.1%	0.1%	87.57	94.65	97.43	11.3%	0.2%
Finland	88.15	93.32	97.41	10.5%	0.2%	99.3	99.99	99.99	0.7%	0.0%	95.04	97.61	98.87	4.0%	0.1%
Lithuania	83.64	89.88	94.61	13.1%	0.2%	100	100	100	0.0%	0.0%	92.49	96.34	98.25	6.2%	0.1%
Latvia	85.15	89.71	93.77	10.1%	0.2%	95.71	100	100	4.5%	0.1%	89.94	95.36	97.78	8.7%	0.2%
Estonia	76.77	85.51	93.15	21.3%	0.4%	99	100	100	1.0%	0.0%	92.58	96.36	98.26	6.1%	0.1%
Iceland	83.35	91.01	96.24	15.5%	0.3%	99.76	99.97	99.97	0.2%	0.0%	83.42	86.72	84.97	1.9%	0.0%
Europe-North	**83.37**	**90.97**	**96.34**	**15.6%**	**0.3%**	**99.51**	**99.99**	**99.99**	**0.5%**	**0.0%**	**94.22**	**96.52**	**97.63**	**3.6%**	**0.1%**
Italy	71.74	83.27	92.48	28.9%	0.5%	98.72	100	100	1.3%	0.0%	85.12	83.8	84.25	-1.0%	-0.0%
Spain	74.71	85.15	93.03	24.5%	0.4%	99.89	100	100	0.1%	0.0%	93.31	96.74	98.45	5.5%	0.1%
Greece	80.1	87.12	93.26	16.4%	0.3%	97.51	100	100	2.6%	0.1%	86.71	94.62	97.41	12.3%	0.2%
Portugal	64.25	77.62	88.46	37.7%	0.6%	99.24	100	100	0.8%	0.0%	86.73	94.9	97.54	12.5%	0.2%
Serbia and Montenegro	61.04	80.61	92.02	50.8%	0.8%	98.58	100	100	1.4%	0.0%	72.92	77.11	87.13	19.5%	0.4%
Croatia	67.15	79.17	88.68	32.1%	0.6%	90.92	100	100	10.0%	0.2%	86.41	94.33	97.27	12.6%	0.2%
Bosnia and Herzegovina	59.33	67.98	80.27	35.3%	0.6%	78.28	98.33	100	27.7%	0.5%	47.53	71.08	72.91	53.4%	0.9%
Albania	55.18	78.41	90.52	64.0%	1.0%	100	100	100	0.0%	0.0%	74.52	76.53	80.32	7.8%	0.2%
Macedonia	61.54	80.05	91.44	48.6%	0.8%	95.52	100	100	4.7%	0.1%	69.67	68.67	70.5	1.2%	0.0%
Slovenia	73.88	84	92.38	25.0%	0.4%	99.19	100	100	0.8%	0.0%	95.69	97.93	99.02	3.5%	0.1%
Malta	79.08	87.72	94.51	19.5%	0.4%	97.56	100	100	2.5%	0.0%	79.98	82.25	84.58	5.8%	0.1%
Europe-South	**71.13**	**82.84**	**91.82**	**29.1%**	**0.5%**	**98.16**	**99.95**	**100**	**1.9%**	**0.0%**	**85.66**	**88.58**	**90.56**	**5.7%**	**0.1%**
Germany	84.01	88	93.23	11.0%	0.2%	89.53	100	100	11.7%	0.2%	88.26	92.57	96.38	9.2%	0.2%
France	77.01	87.54	95.1	23.5%	0.4%	99.97	100	100	0.0%	0.0%	93.06	96.62	98.39	5.7%	0.1%
Netherlands	86.95	92.68	97.09	11.7%	0.2%	99.4	100	100	0.6%	0.0%	89.75	94.93	97.56	8.7%	0.2%
Belgium	77.91	87.45	94.77	21.6%	0.4%	99.55	100	100	0.5%	0.0%	88.26	94.52	97.36	10.3%	0.2%
Austria	84.41	89.17	94.13	11.5%	0.2%	92.73	100	100	7.8%	0.2%	88.48	94.15	97.18	9.8%	0.2%
Switzerland	80.76	86.81	93.06	15.2%	0.3%	96.3	99.98	99.98	3.8%	0.1%	88.36	94.98	97.59	10.4%	0.2%
Luxembourg	84.33	90.58	95.81	13.6%	0.3%	96.55	99.89	99.89	3.5%	0.1%	80.51	82.79	80.03	-0.6%	-0.0%
Europe-West	**81.55**	**88.26**	**94.39**	**15.7%**	**0.3%**	**94.77**	**100**	**100**	**5.5%**	**0.1%**	**89.94**	**94.39**	**97.26**	**8.1%**	**0.2%**

Base Case

Source: International Futures
Version 5.47 March 2008

Education

Infrastructure

	Adults (15+) with Tertiary Education (Percent)					Knowledge Society Index (Index)					Water Use per Capita (Thousand Cubic Meters)				
	2005	2030	2055	% Chg	% An Chg	2005	2030	2055	% Chg	% An Chg	2005	2030	2055	% Chg	% An Chg
World	5.884	13.9	23.4	297.7%	2.8%	56.36	67.02	79.01	40.2%	0.7%	0.64	0.658	0.659	3.0%	0.1%
Africa	1.682	4.989	11.11	560.5%	3.8%	13.48	25.77	45.78	239.6%	2.5%	0.262	0.23	0.209	-20.2%	-0.5%
Americas	13.66	24.32	35.47	159.7%	1.9%	67.94	76.11	82.96	22.1%	0.4%	0.954	0.935	0.929	-2.6%	-0.1%
Asia incl Oceania	4.165	12.88	23.95	475.0%	3.6%	46.71	59.79	77.94	66.9%	1.0%	0.664	0.73	0.772	16.3%	0.3%
Europe	10.88	23.96	38.22	251.3%	2.5%	54.04	72.69	85.36	58.0%	0.9%	0.596	0.651	0.739	24.0%	0.4%
World	5.884	13.9	23.4	297.7%	2.8%	56.36	67.02	79.01	40.2%	0.7%	0.64	0.658	0.659	3.0%	0.1%
Africa-Eastern	0.483	2.323	9.632	1894.2%	6.2%	3.431	13.6	34.77	913.4%	4.7%	0.157	0.146	0.151	-3.8%	-0.1%
Africa-Middle	0.946	2.09	5.501	481.5%	3.6%	4.483	13.15	17.41	288.4%	2.8%	0.024	0.021	0.02	-16.7%	-0.4%
Africa-Northern	4.302	12.07	22.41	420.9%	3.4%	16.42	32.23	55.53	238.2%	2.5%	0.766	0.756	0.777	1.4%	0.0%
Africa-Southern	3.635	12.44	25.73	607.8%	4.0%	20.69	37.22	67.69	227.2%	2.4%	0.278	0.276	0.279	0.4%	0.0%
Africa-Western	1.012	4.207	9.129	802.1%	4.5%	4.167	11.62	19.22	361.2%	3.1%	0.112	0.112	0.109	-2.7%	-0.1%
Africa	1.682	4.989	11.11	560.5%	3.8%	13.48	25.77	45.78	239.6%	2.5%	0.262	0.23	0.209	-20.2%	-0.5%
America-Caribbean	5.269	12.02	20.45	288.1%	2.7%	27.23	53.36	75.47	177.2%	2.1%	0.449	0.412	0.387	-13.8%	-0.3%
America-Central	4.594	10.11	19.59	326.4%	2.9%	11.95	34.43	61.87	417.7%	3.3%	0.251	0.223	0.207	-17.5%	-0.4%
America-North	21.65	36.26	48.57	124.3%	1.6%	74.61	83.06	88.23	18.3%	0.3%	1.477	1.472	1.475	-0.1%	-0.0%
America-South	6.25	14.41	25.45	307.2%	2.8%	20.39	42.56	67.22	229.7%	2.4%	0.478	0.496	0.512	7.1%	0.1%
Americas	13.66	24.32	35.47	159.7%	1.9%	67.94	76.11	82.96	22.1%	0.4%	0.954	0.935	0.929	-2.6%	-0.1%
Asia-East	4.677	15.31	29.01	520.3%	3.7%	53.36	66.89	87.71	64.4%	1.0%	0.514	0.579	0.599	16.5%	0.3%
Asia-South Central	2.935	10.06	20.06	583.5%	3.9%	16.5	36.07	59.41	260.1%	2.6%	0.799	0.862	0.915	14.5%	0.3%
Asia-South East	4.982	13.66	23.11	363.9%	3.1%	23.46	38.99	54.85	133.8%	1.7%	0.613	0.622	0.631	2.9%	0.1%
Asia-West	5.931	15.18	26.31	343.6%	3.0%	33.95	57.62	80.69	137.7%	1.7%	0.849	0.847	0.85	0.1%	0.0%
Oceania	14.62	27.94	39.66	171.3%	2.0%	62.49	78.24	83.7	33.9%	0.6%	0.931	1.069	1.128	21.2%	0.4%
Asia incl Oceania	4.165	12.88	23.95	475.0%	3.6%	46.71	59.79	77.94	66.9%	1.0%	0.664	0.73	0.772	16.3%	0.3%
Europe-East	12	22.57	33.81	181.8%	2.1%	34.98	57.23	74.2	112.1%	1.5%	0.57	0.652	0.796	39.6%	0.7%
Europe-North	11.97	29.18	45.78	282.5%	2.7%	62.99	80.03	88.77	40.9%	0.7%	0.281	0.301	0.319	13.5%	0.3%
Europe-South	7.914	20.25	34.38	334.4%	3.0%	41.08	60.4	76.33	85.8%	1.2%	0.962	1.078	1.26	31.0%	0.5%
Europe-West	10.79	25.95	42.72	295.9%	2.8%	58.65	79.28	91.08	55.3%	0.9%	0.518	0.523	0.534	3.1%	0.1%
Europe	10.88	23.96	38.22	251.3%	2.5%	54.04	72.69	85.36	58.0%	0.9%	0.596	0.651	0.739	24.0%	0.4%

Education / Infrastructure

Base Case: Countries in Year 2055 Descending Population Sequence	Adults (15+) with Tertiary Education — Percent					Knowledge Society Index — Index					Water Use per Capita — Thousand Cubic Meters				
	2005	2030	2055	% Chg	% An Chg	2005	2030	2055	% Chg	% An Chg	2005	2030	2055	% Chg	% An Chg
AFRICA															
Ethiopia	0.287	1.115	7.026	2348.1%	6.6%	0.874	5.462	19.75	2159.7%	6.4%	0.087	0.089	0.105	20.7%	0.4%
Tanzania	0.482	1.5	10.67	2113.7%	6.4%	0.651	8.73	30.47	4580.5%	8.0%	0.147	0.13	0.124	-15.6%	-0.3%
Uganda	0.495	5.085	17.07	3348.5%	7.3%	8.879	21.41	46.69	425.8%	3.4%	0.012	0.012	0.015	25.0%	0.4%
Kenya	0.579	3.922	14.19	2350.8%	6.6%	2.332	12.74	37.52	1508.9%	5.7%	0.051	0.049	0.048	-5.9%	-0.1%
Madagascar	0.316	1.011	5.534	1651.3%	5.9%	1.33	5.054	15.69	1079.7%	5.1%	0.912	0.861	0.877	-3.8%	-0.1%
Mozambique	0.284	4.557	14	4829.6%	8.1%	6.3	19.96	35.45	462.7%	3.5%	0.035	0.034	0.032	-8.6%	-0.2%
Malawi	0.334	0.144	4.058	1115.0%	5.1%	0.622	0.926	14.29	2197.4%	6.5%	0.086	0.081	0.093	8.1%	0.2%
Zambia	0.647	1.321	7.665	1084.7%	5.1%	0.506	4.659	19.3	3714.2%	7.6%	0.161	0.151	0.14	-13.0%	-0.3%
Zimbabwe	1.838	5.291	14.93	712.3%	4.3%	4.893	14.48	35.49	625.3%	4.0%	0.332	0.309	0.298	-10.2%	-0.2%
Burundi	0.268	0.12	2.376	786.6%	4.5%	3.16	3.252	12.89	307.9%	2.9%	0.044	0.044	0.043	-2.3%	-0.0%
Rwanda	0.318	2.25	8.783	2661.9%	6.9%	0.736	7.289	21.07	2762.8%	6.9%	0.018	0.017	0.017	-5.6%	-0.1%
Somalia	0.292	0.123	0.865	196.2%	2.2%	0.541	0.847	3.6	565.4%	3.9%	0.456	0.431	0.4	-12.3%	-0.3%
Eritrea	0.525	0.232	0.262	-50.1%	-1.4%	0.955	0.889	2.413	152.7%	1.9%	0.083	0.073	0.068	-18.1%	-0.4%
Mauritius	1.716	10.15	23.34	1260.1%	5.4%	11.88	37.99	60.27	407.3%	3.3%	0.521	0.558	0.606	16.3%	0.3%
Comoros	1.643	2.891	8.368	409.3%	3.3%	2.218	8.077	19.85	795.0%	4.5%	0.018	0.018	0.018	0.0%	0.0%
Djibouti	1.894	3.26	8.006	322.7%	2.9%	3.362	8.005	16.98	405.1%	3.3%	0.028	0.028	0.027	-3.6%	-0.1%
Africa-Eastern	**0.483**	**2.323**	**9.632**	**1894.2%**	**6.2%**	**3.431**	**13.6**	**34.77**	**913.4%**	**4.7%**	**0.157**	**0.146**	**0.151**	**-3.8%**	**-0.1%**
Congo, Dem. Rep. of the	0.477	0.156	3.153	561.0%	3.8%	0.627	0.927	10.97	1649.6%	5.9%	0.01	0.009	0.01	0.0%	0.0%
Angola	1.5	5.734	11.01	634.0%	4.1%	4.203	13	18.33	336.1%	3.0%	0.025	0.025	0.025	0.0%	0.0%
Cameroon	1.741	4.546	8.159	368.6%	3.1%	5.907	8.712	15.71	166.0%	2.0%	0.066	0.063	0.059	-10.6%	-0.2%
Chad	0.285	3.415	8.063	2729.1%	6.9%	0.95	10.38	14.13	1387.4%	5.5%	0.028	0.028	0.027	-3.6%	-0.1%
Central African Republic	0.613	0.556	2.177	255.1%	2.6%	2.666	2.939	9.401	252.6%	2.6%	0.01	0.009	0.008	-20.0%	-0.4%
Congo, Rep. of	2.31	6.698	12.8	454.1%	3.5%	4.357	13.65	22.15	408.4%	3.3%	0.01	0.009	0.008	-20.0%	-0.4%
Gabon	5.155	11.42	22.86	343.5%	3.0%	5.903	26.36	39.98	577.3%	3.9%	0.092	0.083	0.082	-10.9%	-0.2%
Equatorial Guinea	4.256	10.52	21.8	412.2%	3.3%	9.431	33.03	39.55	319.4%	2.9%	0.245	0.254	0.277	13.1%	0.2%
São Tomé and Príncipe	3.249	5.95	7.103	118.6%	1.6%	8.555	8.067	9.575	11.9%	0.2%	0.284	0.276	0.253	-10.9%	-0.2%
Africa-Middle	**0.946**	**2.09**	**5.501**	**481.5%**	**3.6%**	**4.483**	**13.15**	**17.41**	**288.4%**	**2.8%**	**0.024**	**0.021**	**0.02**	**-16.7%**	**-0.4%**
Egypt	5.457	13.17	24.35	346.2%	3.0%	12.79	27.15	55.89	337.0%	3.0%	1.015	0.922	0.874	-13.9%	-0.3%
Sudan	1.419	7.978	16.78	1082.5%	5.1%	10.37	22.56	34.02	228.1%	2.4%	1.141	1.124	1.15	0.8%	0.0%
Algeria	4.614	15.21	25.69	456.8%	3.5%	21.5	35.48	49.38	129.7%	1.7%	0.2	0.207	0.222	11.0%	0.2%
Morocco	4.418	9.508	19.07	331.6%	3.0%	13.51	25.76	47.59	252.3%	2.6%	0.463	0.501	0.571	23.3%	0.4%
Tunisia	4.621	14.25	27.49	494.9%	3.6%	17.19	42.5	76.3	343.9%	3.0%	0.281	0.311	0.34	21.0%	0.4%
Libya	4.874	18.33	31.03	536.6%	3.8%	22.92	45.71	66.05	188.2%	2.1%	0.807	0.84	0.905	12.1%	0.2%
Africa-Northern	**4.302**	**12.07**	**22.41**	**420.9%**	**3.4%**	**16.42**	**32.23**	**55.53**	**238.2%**	**2.5%**	**0.766**	**0.756**	**0.777**	**1.4%**	**0.0%**

Education

Infrastructure

Base Case: Countries in Year 2055 Descending Population Sequence	Adults (15+) with Tertiary Education — Percent					Knowledge Society Index — Index					Water Use per Capita — Thousand Cubic Meters				
	2005	2030	2055	% Chg	% An Chg	2005	2030	2055	% Chg	% An Chg	2005	2030	2055	% Chg	% An Chg
AFRICA continued															
South Africa	3.923	13.18	26.59	577.8%	3.9%	21.59	37.1	66.48	207.9%	2.3%	0.283	0.282	0.287	1.4%	0.0%
Namibia	2.334	10.18	26.57	1038.4%	5.0%	11.34	30.19	76.74	576.7%	3.9%	0.157	0.148	0.144	-8.3%	-0.2%
Lesotho	0.869	3.881	12.23	1307.4%	5.4%	1.371	9.495	27.4	1898.5%	6.2%	0.028	0.027	0.025	-10.7%	-0.2%
Botswana	1.789	11.59	26.67	1390.8%	5.6%	12.58	45	78.92	527.3%	3.7%	0.107	0.104	0.102	-4.7%	-0.1%
Swaziland	1.951	7.543	20.55	953.3%	4.8%	6.415	22.61	51.14	697.2%	4.2%	0.974	0.885	0.873	-10.4%	-0.2%
Africa-Southern	**3.635**	**12.44**	**25.73**	**607.8%**	**4.0%**	**20.69**	**37.22**	**67.69**	**227.2%**	**2.4%**	**0.278**	**0.276**	**0.279**	**0.4%**	**0.0%**
Nigeria	1.035	5.661	10.76	939.6%	4.8%	4.729	12.5	16.76	254.4%	2.6%	0.069	0.071	0.065	-5.8%	-0.1%
Niger	0.289	0.099	2.288	691.7%	4.2%	0.678	0.852	9.198	1256.6%	5.4%	0.182	0.173	0.176	-3.3%	-0.1%
Ghana	0.742	3.312	8.375	1028.7%	5.0%	4.312	7.957	17.76	311.9%	2.9%	0.05	0.049	0.048	-4.0%	-0.1%
Côte d'Ivoire	2.011	5.417	12.81	537.0%	3.8%	4.442	13.41	24.96	461.9%	3.5%	0.055	0.048	0.045	-18.2%	-0.4%
Mali	0.357	1.343	6.494	1719.0%	6.0%	1.144	5.52	15.79	1280.2%	5.4%	0.566	0.54	0.514	-9.2%	-0.2%
Burkina Faso	0.521	2.233	7.927	1421.5%	5.6%	2.368	7.743	20.49	765.3%	4.4%	0.071	0.07	0.067	-5.6%	-0.1%
Senegal	1.179	4.303	11.36	863.5%	4.6%	2.728	11.13	23.83	773.5%	4.4%	0.213	0.199	0.191	-10.3%	-0.2%
Guinea	2.174	4.631	10.88	400.5%	3.3%	3.845	11.98	21.53	459.9%	3.5%	0.178	0.155	0.142	-20.2%	-0.5%
Benin	0.711	2.421	8.188	1051.6%	5.0%	2.212	6.766	19.15	765.7%	4.4%	0.018	0.018	0.017	-5.6%	-0.1%
Togo	1.109	2.068	3.777	240.6%	2.5%	6.188	7.874	11.51	86.0%	1.2%	0.031	0.029	0.027	-12.9%	-0.3%
Liberia	1.756	2.463	2.824	60.8%	1.0%	4.825	2.697	7.474	54.9%	0.9%	0.035	0.031	0.029	-17.1%	-0.4%
Sierra Leone	0.483	0.729	4.968	928.6%	4.8%	0.961	3.593	13.06	1259.0%	5.4%	0.083	0.079	0.074	-10.8%	-0.2%
Mauritania	0.738	3.52	9.333	1164.6%	5.2%	3.945	9.978	17.63	346.9%	3.0%	0.644	0.624	0.615	-4.5%	-0.1%
Guinea-Bissau	0.286	0.118	0.082	-71.3%	-2.5%	0.799	0.767	1.07	33.9%	0.6%	0.129	0.112	0.105	-18.6%	-0.4%
Gambia	0.536	3.212	9.985	1762.9%	6.0%	2.821	10.56	22.42	694.8%	4.2%	0.022	0.021	0.02	-9.1%	-0.2%
Cape Verde	3.648	9.102	22.73	523.1%	3.7%	6.533	29.27	60.33	823.5%	4.5%	0.045	0.044	0.043	-4.4%	-0.1%
Africa-Western	**1.012**	**4.207**	**9.129**	**802.1%**	**4.5%**	**4.167**	**11.62**	**19.22**	**361.2%**	**3.1%**	**0.112**	**0.112**	**0.109**	**-2.7%**	**-0.1%**

Education   Infrastructure

Base Case: Countries in Year 2055 / Descending Population Sequence	Adults (15+) with Tertiary Education (Percent)					Knowledge Society Index (Index)					Water Use per Capita (Thousand Cubic Meters)				
	2005	2030	2C55	% Chg	% An Chg	2005	2030	2055	% Chg	% An Chg	2005	2030	2055	% Chg	% An Chg
AMERICAS															
Haiti	0.403	1.342	5.392	1386.8%	5.5%	1.396	5.497	14.92	968.8%	4.9%	0.123	0.115	0.108	-12.2%	-0.3%
Dominican Republic	7.862	18.32	28.03	256.5%	2.6%	25.03	40	56.15	124.3%	1.6%	0.406	0.392	0.387	-4.7%	-0.1%
Cuba	5.978	12.76	23.34	290.4%	2.8%	18.16	33.84	66.8	267.8%	2.6%	0.742	0.763	0.827	11.5%	0.2%
Puerto Rico	9.398	23.1	30.88	324.3%	2.9%	36.62	70.45	91.72	150.5%	1.9%	0.738	0.697	0.667	-9.6%	-0.2%
Jamaica	3.208	11.7	22.68	607.0%	4.0%	12.78	25.57	56.31	340.6%	3.0%	0.16	0.155	0.152	-5.0%	-0.1%
Trinidad and Tobago	2.895	12.11	25.93	795.7%	4.5%	12.21	53.01	71.36	484.4%	3.6%	0.242	0.241	0.245	1.2%	0.0%
Bahamas	9.901	20.45	32.74	230.7%	2.4%	35.72	51.73	77.34	116.5%	1.6%	0.302	0.286	0.281	-7.0%	-0.1%
Barbados	9.496	19.56	33.05	248.0%	2.5%	34.29	57.05	85.01	147.9%	1.8%	0.345	0.363	0.383	11.0%	0.2%
Grenada	7.994	18.25	29.74	272.0%	2.7%	25.26	37.18	67.24	166.2%	2.0%	0.291	0.28	0.261	-10.3%	-0.2%
St. Vincent & the Grenadines	6.868	15.69	25.57	272.3%	2.7%	17.58	29.65	54.32	209.0%	2.3%	0.09	0.092	0.092	2.2%	0.0%
St. Lucia	5.239	11.49	23.9	356.2%	3.1%	11.2	37.62	81.58	628.4%	4.1%	0.068	0.081	0.093	36.8%	0.6%
America-Caribbean	**5.269**	**12.02**	**20.45**	**288.1%**	**2.7%**	**27.23**	**53.36**	**75.47**	**177.2%**	**2.1%**	**0.449**	**0.412**	**0.387**	**-13.8%**	**-0.3%**
Guatemala	2.661	8.49	18.77	605.4%	4.0%	6.901	20.18	37.93	449.6%	3.5%	0.176	0.154	0.146	-17.0%	-0.4%
Honduras	2.866	7.643	15.7	447.8%	3.5%	6.558	15.58	29.85	355.2%	3.1%	0.13	0.116	0.108	-16.9%	-0.4%
Nicaragua	4.637	8.167	15.04	224.3%	2.4%	6.637	14.44	26.56	300.2%	2.8%	0.262	0.241	0.225	-14.1%	-0.3%
El Salvador	4.09	9.596	19.65	380.4%	3.2%	6.726	23.01	45.59	577.8%	3.9%	0.201	0.189	0.186	-7.5%	-0.2%
Costa Rica	9.157	17.61	30.64	234.6%	2.4%	17.28	46.92	82.04	374.8%	3.2%	0.69	0.69	0.672	-4.0%	-0.1%
Panama	11.17	21.12	33.51	200.0%	2.2%	22.37	49.47	83.16	271.7%	2.7%	0.276	0.269	0.26	-5.8%	-0.1%
Belize	3.948	11.43	25.78	553.0%	3.8%	9.535	40.33	82.09	760.9%	4.4%	0.619	0.633	0.621	0.3%	0.0%
America-Central	**4.594**	**10.11**	**19.59**	**326.4%**	**2.9%**	**11.95**	**34.43**	**61.87**	**417.7%**	**3.3%**	**0.251**	**0.223**	**0.207**	**-17.5%**	**-0.4%**
United States	28.09	44.45	56.41	100.8%	1.4%	78.55	86.35	90.75	15.5%	0.3%	1.715	1.72	1.71	-0.3%	-0.0%
Mexico	5.866	15.37	26.33	348.9%	3.0%	17.99	36.16	56.74	215.4%	2.3%	0.804	0.815	0.852	6.0%	0.1%
Canada	13.89	32.57	50.15	261.1%	2.6%	65.2	81.99	89.24	36.9%	0.6%	1.472	1.45	1.368	-7.1%	-0.1%
America-North	**21.65**	**36.26**	**48.57**	**124.3%**	**1.6%**	**74.61**	**83.06**	**88.23**	**18.3%**	**0.3%**	**1.477**	**1.472**	**1.475**	**-0.1%**	**-0.0%**
Brazil	4.848	12.78	24.24	400.0%	3.3%	21.43	38.44	62.52	191.7%	2.2%	0.341	0.331	0.329	-3.5%	-0.1%
Colombia	5.294	12.97	24.17	356.6%	3.1%	12.36	29.69	57.36	364.1%	3.1%	0.251	0.243	0.247	-1.6%	-0.0%
Argentina	8.762	18.46	31.74	262.2%	2.6%	21.08	51.96	79.13	275.4%	2.7%	0.812	0.9	0.966	19.0%	0.3%
Peru	10.65	17.44	25.44	138.9%	1.8%	16.52	29.32	46.66	182.4%	2.1%	0.795	0.876	0.956	20.3%	0.4%
Venezuela	6.75	17.09	28.21	317.9%	2.9%	19.68	42.83	70.95	260.5%	2.6%	0.346	0.363	0.38	9.8%	0.2%
Chile	8.682	20.03	33.22	282.6%	2.7%	25.98	53.88	80.51	209.9%	2.3%	0.839	0.923	0.966	15.1%	0.3%
Ecuador	8.391	13.88	19.61	133.7%	1.7%	13.11	21.24	29.2	122.7%	1.6%	1.428	1.539	1.504	5.3%	0.1%
Bolivia	6.204	12.23	22.11	256.4%	2.6%	12.28	24.85	47.44	286.3%	2.7%	0.172	0.158	0.156	-9.3%	-0.2%
Paraguay	5.749	12.37	21.33	271.0%	2.7%	12.42	20.83	38.37	208.9%	2.3%	0.09	0.081	0.075	-16.7%	-0.4%
Uruguay	8.333	18.27	30.41	264.9%	2.6%	20.26	46.11	75.23	271.3%	2.7%	1.007	1.33	1.612	60.1%	0.9%
Guyana	2.719	8.592	16.83	519.0%	3.7%	9.632	20.78	34.36	256.7%	2.6%	2.362	3.327	4.839	104.9%	1.4%
Suriname	5.935	13.42	24.18	307.4%	2.8%	17.23	33.14	59.51	245.4%	2.5%	1.551	1.593	1.746	12.6%	0.2%
America-South	**6.25**	**14.41**	**25.45**	**307.2%**	**2.8%**	**20.39**	**42.56**	**67.22**	**229.7%**	**2.4%**	**0.478**	**0.496**	**0.512**	**7.1%**	**0.1%**

Education / Knowledge Society Index / Infrastructure

Base Case: Countries in Year 2055 Descending Population Sequence	Education — Adults (15+) with Tertiary Education (Percent)					Knowledge Society Index (Index)					Infrastructure — Water Use per Capita (Thousand Cubic Meters)				
	2005	2030	2055	% Chg	% An Chg	2005	2030	2055	% Chg	% An Chg	2005	2030	2055	% Chg	% An Chg
ASIA INCL OCEANIA															
China	3.329	14	27.92	738.7%	4.3%	25.1	56.28	85.57	240.9%	2.5%	0.459	0.535	0.556	21.1%	0.4%
Japan	13.78	25.2	39.88	189.4%	2.1%	63.87	84.45	96.83	51.6%	0.8%	0.7	0.711	0.744	6.3%	0.1%
Korea, Rep. of	15.15	27.96	41.84	176.2%	2.1%	59.93	89.07	97.1	62.0%	1.0%	0.396	0.383	0.391	-1.3%	-0.0%
Taiwan	10.79	26.3	41.51	284.7%	2.7%	57.41	73.79	86.66	50.9%	0.8%	2.947	3.042	3.199	8.6%	0.2%
Korea, Dem. Rep. of	0.896	5.005	11.62	1196.9%	5.3%	4.251	13.57	26.83	531.1%	3.8%	0.417	0.419	0.428	2.6%	0.1%
Hong Kong	8.662	22.66	39.94	361.1%	3.1%	37.9	61.48	72.98	92.6%	1.3%	0.599	0.582	0.577	-3.7%	-0.1%
Mongolia	4.552	13.7	20.06	340.7%	3.0%	21.13	22.24	30.68	45.2%	0.7%	0.182	0.197	0.202	11.0%	0.2%
Asia-East	**4.677**	**15.31**	**29.01**	**520.3%**	**3.7%**	**53.36**	**66.89**	**87.71**	**64.4%**	**1.0%**	**0.514**	**0.579**	**0.599**	**16.5%**	**0.3%**
India	3.088	11.18	22.96	643.5%	4.1%	17.79	34.97	60.92	242.4%	2.5%	0.646	0.705	0.762	18.0%	0.3%
Pakistan	1.75	6.326	14.46	726.3%	4.3%	5.109	15.13	27.73	442.8%	3.4%	1.239	1.214	1.194	-3.6%	-0.1%
Bangladesh	1.838	6.956	15.01	716.6%	4.3%	12.06	22.9	35.65	195.6%	2.2%	0.613	0.585	0.569	-7.2%	-0.1%
Iran, Islamic Rep. of	4.966	17.14	29.52	494.4%	3.6%	22.79	49.61	72.23	216.9%	2.3%	1.199	1.477	1.651	37.7%	0.6%
Afghanistan	1.343	0.351	0.869	-35.3%	-0.9%	0.751	0.818	4.525	502.5%	3.7%	1.065	0.971	0.923	-13.3%	-0.3%
Nepal	1.082	3.035	7.266	571.5%	3.9%	8.523	13.19	19.61	130.1%	1.7%	0.423	0.424	0.427	0.9%	0.0%
Uzbekistan	4.944	9.967	17.26	249.1%	2.5%	9.056	20.18	31.92	252.5%	2.6%	2.435	2.75	3.063	25.8%	0.5%
Sri Lanka	1.337	7.579	18.56	1288.2%	5.4%	6.979	25.3	45.88	557.4%	3.8%	0.651	0.654	0.669	2.8%	0.1%
Kazakhstan	6.104	17.94	30.23	395.2%	3.3%	20.15	56.87	71.19	253.3%	2.6%	2.417	2.747	3.408	41.0%	0.7%
Tajikistan	4.949	8.683	13.48	172.4%	2.0%	7.354	13.95	21.86	197.3%	2.2%	1.986	2.011	2.04	2.7%	0.1%
Turkmenistan	6.079	16.53	27.63	354.5%	3.1%	16.77	43.8	46.24	175.7%	2.0%	5.708	6.354	6.435	12.7%	0.2%
Kyrgyzstan	7.956	16.72	18.26	129.5%	1.7%	25.76	18.48	17.59	-31.7%	-0.8%	2.101	2.129	2.227	6.0%	0.1%
Bhutan	2.855	9.323	23.23	713.7%	4.3%	6.533	27.21	65.68	905.4%	4.7%	0.717	0.686	0.633	-11.7%	-0.2%
Maldives	4.099	10.36	25.76	528.4%	3.7%	8.286	32.62	77.67	837.4%	4.6%	0.01	0.01	0.01	0.0%	0.0%
Asia-South Central	**2.935**	**10.06**	**20.06**	**583.5%**	**3.9%**	**16.5**	**36.07**	**59.41**	**260.1%**	**2.6%**	**0.799**	**0.862**	**0.915**	**14.5%**	**0.3%**
Indonesia	2.454	11.63	20.73	744.7%	4.4%	13.59	25.5	37.88	178.7%	2.1%	0.407	0.426	0.45	10.6%	0.2%
Philippines	12.96	18.43	25.31	95.3%	1.3%	17.75	25.84	39.97	125.2%	1.6%	0.372	0.343	0.334	-10.2%	-0.2%
Vietnam	2.47	11.11	22.39	806.5%	4.5%	11.16	31.54	51.64	362.7%	3.1%	0.946	1.063	1.096	15.9%	0.3%
Thailand	9.554	21.52	32.82	243.5%	2.5%	27.96	43.93	62.27	122.7%	1.6%	1.336	1.368	1.39	4.0%	0.1%
Myanmar	2.187	7.359	14.23	550.7%	3.8%	8.208	16.03	27.48	234.8%	2.4%	0.696	0.686	0.699	0.4%	0.0%
Malaysia	4.799	17.78	31.9	564.7%	3.9%	21.45	52.21	79.98	272.9%	2.7%	0.389	0.376	0.366	-5.9%	-0.1%
Cambodia	1.939	8.262	18.97	878.3%	4.7%	5.443	23.71	40.98	652.9%	4.1%	0.326	0.365	0.407	24.8%	0.4%
Laos	1.605	7.367	18.08	1026.5%	5.0%	3.796	21.01	38.69	919.2%	4.8%	0.573	0.583	0.603	5.2%	0.1%
Singapore	6.841	23.88	41.01	499.5%	3.6%	58.29	79.36	85.28	46.3%	0.8%	0.047	0.045	0.045	-4.3%	-0.1%
Timor-Leste	2.637	6.421	11.85	349.4%	3.1%	6.704	12.03	22.38	233.8%	2.4%	0.362	0.344	0.324	-10.5%	-0.2%
Brunei	8.536	16.32	27.18	218.4%	2.3%	12.28	39.72	57.24	366.1%	3.1%	0.269	0.269	0.276	2.6%	0.1%
Asia-South East	**4.982**	**13.66**	**23.11**	**363.9%**	**3.1%**	**23.46**	**38.99**	**54.85**	**133.8%**	**1.7%**	**0.613**	**0.622**	**0.631**	**2.9%**	**0.1%**

Education   Knowledge Society Index   Infrastructure

Base Case: Countries in Year 2055 Descending Population Sequence	Adults (15+) with Tertiary Education — Percent					Knowledge Society Index — Index					Water Use per Capita — Thousand Cubic Meters				
	2005	2030	2055	% Chg	% An Chg	2005	2030	2055	% Chg	% An Chg	2005	2030	2055	% Chg	% An Chg
ASIA INCL OCEANIA continued															
Turkey	5.503	17.7	30.55	455.2%	3.5%	26.89	47.41	82.16	205.5%	2.3%	0.597	0.664	0.708	18.6%	0.3%
Yemen	0.598	4.35	12.37	1968.6%	6.2%	2.003	12.93	25.15	1155.6%	5.2%	0.363	0.343	0.336	-7.4%	-0.2%
Iraq	4.014	11.89	23.23	478.7%	3.6%	10.94	27.82	44.98	311.2%	2.9%	1.8	1.667	1.664	-7.6%	-0.2%
Saudi Arabia	8.574	20.46	35.07	309.0%	2.9%	27.87	58.17	86.43	210.1%	2.3%	0.846	0.895	0.936	10.6%	0.2%
Syria	6.098	12.91	22.87	275.0%	2.7%	13.29	25.4	46.75	251.8%	2.5%	1.144	0.996	0.957	-16.3%	-0.4%
Israel	13.7	29.9	45.73	233.8%	2.4%	81.18	107.7	117.5	44.7%	0.7%	0.313	0.268	0.246	-21.4%	-0.5%
Azerbaijan	4.407	14.35	24.82	463.2%	3.5%	18.29	36.39	52.73	188.3%	2.1%	2.149	2.207	2.283	6.2%	0.1%
Jordan	8.625	17.46	31.04	259.9%	2.6%	17.39	38.99	82.94	376.9%	3.2%	0.21	0.208	0.204	-2.9%	-0.1%
Palestine	5.362	12.78	21.92	308.8%	2.9%	15.17	23.79	41.83	175.7%	2.0%	0.622	0.559	0.567	-8.8%	-0.2%
Oman	8.341	17.14	30.85	269.9%	2.7%	23.55	50.47	74.99	218.4%	2.3%	0.553	0.527	0.518	-6.3%	-0.1%
Lebanon	6.221	16.47	28.04	350.7%	3.1%	20.05	42.51	79.3	295.5%	2.8%	0.416	0.398	0.363	-12.7%	-0.3%
United Arab Emirates	10.09	19.11	32.6	223.1%	2.4%	39.37	70	83.25	111.5%	1.5%	0.71	0.678	0.688	-3.1%	-0.1%
Kuwait	9.544	20.35	36.93	286.9%	2.7%	22.08	59.33	76.44	246.2%	2.5%	0.199	0.189	0.185	-7.0%	-0.1%
Georgia	10.43	21.23	28.24	170.8%	2.0%	29.16	31.49	37.31	27.9%	0.5%	0.798	1.006	1.247	56.3%	0.9%
Armenia	9.889	19.83	28.43	187.5%	2.1%	23.74	36.75	48.86	105.8%	1.5%	0.958	1.006	1.075	12.2%	0.2%
Bahrain	10.01	23.41	38.37	283.3%	2.7%	39.07	73.4	86.95	122.5%	1.6%	0.44	0.418	0.411	-6.6%	-0.1%
Qatar	9.934	19.83	34.25	244.8%	2.5%	17.75	52.67	66.07	272.2%	2.7%	0.48	0.473	0.48	0.0%	0.0%
Cyprus	10.41	17.95	31.86	206.1%	2.3%	18.21	51.15	73.96	306.2%	2.8%	0.302	0.288	0.293	-3.0%	-0.1%
Asia-West	**5.931**	**15.18**	**26.31**	**343.6%**	**3.0%**	**33.95**	**57.62**	**80.69**	**137.7%**	**1.7%**	**0.849**	**0.847**	**0.85**	**0.1%**	**0.0%**
Australia	19.18	37.56	52.37	173.0%	2.0%	64.45	80.08	85.01	31.9%	0.6%	1.336	1.615	1.762	31.9%	0.6%
Papua New Guinea	0.491	4.835	13.62	2673.9%	6.9%	2.887	15.55	29.75	930.5%	4.8%	0.019	0.017	0.016	-15.8%	-0.3%
New Zealand	17.2	33.3	47.49	176.1%	2.1%	53.89	72.59	85.16	58.0%	0.9%	0.585	0.764	0.951	62.6%	1.0%
Solomon Islands	3.21	8.455	15.35	378.2%	3.2%	9.227	16.16	28.98	214.1%	2.3%	0.319	0.306	0.297	-6.9%	-0.1%
Fiji	5.88	13.48	24.42	315.3%	2.9%	15.3	31.7	56.74	270.8%	2.7%	0.088	0.095	0.111	26.1%	0.5%
Vanuatu	3.32	7.693	17.75	434.6%	3.4%	6.22	19.82	40.51	551.3%	3.8%	0.291	0.288	0.296	1.7%	0.0%
Micronesia	6.954	13.47	21.15	204.1%	2.2%	17.98	24.12	37.36	107.8%	1.5%	0.286	0.271	0.26	-9.1%	-0.2%
Samoa	4.476	10.11	20.64	361.1%	3.1%	9.604	25.95	51.25	433.6%	3.4%	0.296	0.315	0.355	19.9%	0.4%
Tonga	5.109	8.308	17.38	240.2%	2.5%	9.741	20.98	35.3	262.4%	2.6%	0.283	0.291	0.311	9.9%	0.2%
Oceania	**14.62**	**27.94**	**39.66**	**171.3%**	**2.0%**	**62.49**	**78.24**	**83.7**	**33.9%**	**0.6%**	**0.931**	**1.069**	**1.128**	**21.2%**	**0.4%**

Education | Infrastructure

Base Case: Countries in Year 2055 / Descending Population Sequence	Adults (15+) with Tertiary Education — Percent					Knowledge Society Index — Index					Water Use per Capita — Thousand Cubic Meters				
	2005	2030	2055	% Chg	% An Chg	2005	2030	2055	% Chg	% An Chg	2005	2030	2055	% Chg	% An Chg
EUROPE															
Russia	13.09	22.92	34.14	160.8%	1.9%	33.53	61.34	74.5	122.2%	1.6%	0.54	0.603	0.778	44.1%	0.7%
Poland	9.379	22.6	35.35	276.9%	2.7%	36.92	52.57	74.75	102.5%	1.4%	0.315	0.346	0.383	21.6%	0.4%
Ukraine	13.47	23.45	33.33	147.4%	1.8%	39.87	54.53	74.13	85.9%	1.2%	0.791	1	1.241	56.9%	0.9%
Romania	6.544	16.02	26.39	303.3%	2.8%	22.81	37.39	52.59	130.6%	1.7%	0.296	0.347	0.413	39.5%	0.7%
Belarus	15.31	30.99	42.91	180.3%	2.1%	46.25	60.26	87.44	89.1%	1.3%	0.288	0.354	0.385	33.7%	0.6%
Czech Republic	8.846	19.36	32	261.7%	2.6%	36.6	54.95	77.24	111.0%	1.5%	0.199	0.265	0.35	75.9%	1.1%
Hungary	12.93	26.09	38.46	197.4%	2.2%	40.36	55.87	74.52	84.6%	1.2%	2.144	2.424	2.699	25.9%	0.5%
Bulgaria	14.85	25.97	35.71	140.5%	1.8%	34.48	47.11	67.04	94.4%	1.3%	0.906	1.148	1.399	54.4%	0.9%
Slovak Republic	9.363	20.38	32.15	243.4%	2.5%	31.76	47.16	67.81	113.5%	1.5%	0.201	0.233	0.27	34.3%	0.6%
Moldova	6.847	12.25	18.74	173.7%	2.0%	22.09	27.65	41.92	89.8%	1.3%	0.562	0.666	0.764	35.9%	0.6%
Europe-East	**12**	**22.57**	**33.81**	**181.8%**	**2.1%**	**34.98**	**57.23**	**74.2**	**112.1%**	**1.5%**	**0.57**	**0.652**	**0.796**	**39.6%**	**0.7%**
United Kingdom	11.8	28.28	44.53	277.4%	2.7%	58.36	76.72	86.07	47.5%	0.8%	0.198	0.196	0.194	-2.0%	-0.0%
Sweden	13.36	30.57	48.48	262.9%	2.6%	79	100.1	107.5	36.1%	0.6%	0.306	0.305	0.3	-2.0%	-0.0%
Denmark	12.04	31.23	49.58	311.8%	2.9%	67.94	83.68	92.16	35.6%	0.6%	0.132	0.146	0.145	9.8%	0.2%
Norway	11.98	33.61	51.42	329.2%	3.0%	69.29	76.52	81.86	18.1%	0.3%	0.535	0.522	0.523	-2.2%	-0.0%
Ireland	11.38	26.94	42.49	273.4%	2.7%	47.81	66.11	75.05	57.0%	0.9%	0.308	0.281	0.277	-10.1%	-0.2%
Finland	13.37	33.73	51.75	287.1%	2.7%	88.19	98.58	101.8	15.4%	0.3%	0.455	0.464	0.464	2.0%	0.0%
Lithuania	10.22	28.35	43.55	326.1%	2.9%	49.72	64.08	85	71.0%	1.1%	1.062	1.73	2.48	133.5%	1.7%
Latvia	11.89	30.2	45.49	282.6%	2.7%	49.31	66.79	83.83	70.0%	1.1%	0.111	0.125	0.131	18.0%	0.3%
Estonia	11.44	27.56	44.72	290.9%	2.8%	47.13	72.62	88.43	87.6%	1.3%	1.072	1.247	1.289	20.2%	0.4%
Iceland	10.35	27.64	43.89	324.1%	2.9%	70.3	85.77	95.3	35.6%	0.6%	0.614	0.633	0.636	3.6%	0.1%
Europe-North	**11.97**	**29.18**	**45.78**	**282.5%**	**2.7%**	**62.99**	**80.03**	**88.77**	**40.9%**	**0.7%**	**0.281**	**0.301**	**0.319**	**13.5%**	**0.3%**
Italy	6.956	18.32	32.91	373.1%	3.2%	36.06	54.19	73.79	104.6%	1.4%	0.749	0.807	0.902	20.4%	0.4%
Spain	8.894	24.02	39.69	346.3%	3.0%	49.55	68.54	77.63	56.7%	0.9%	0.938	0.975	1.047	11.6%	0.2%
Greece	12.05	25.27	39.73	229.7%	2.4%	39.35	62.77	80.03	103.4%	1.4%	0.807	0.828	0.842	4.3%	0.1%
Portugal	7.75	23.06	38.28	393.9%	3.2%	44.11	57.99	78.08	77.0%	1.1%	1.101	1.128	1.136	3.2%	0.1%
Serbia and Montenegro	5.995	10.75	19.31	222.1%	2.4%	32.7	42.52	69.13	111.4%	1.5%	2.308	3.184	4.449	92.8%	1.3%
Croatia	8.044	19.91	33.62	318.0%	2.9%	38.96	56.54	88.75	127.8%	1.7%	2.006	2.709	3.389	68.9%	1.1%
Bosnia and Herzegovina	5.106	12.35	21.6	323.0%	2.9%	18.85	30.08	46.08	144.5%	1.8%	0.969	1.28	1.756	81.2%	1.2%
Albania	4.929	12.55	21.86	343.5%	3.0%	15.71	29.78	46.41	195.4%	2.2%	0.563	0.572	0.587	4.3%	0.1%
Macedonia	6.273	12.64	21.12	236.7%	2.5%	17.11	26.95	43.24	152.7%	1.9%	1.144	1.21	1.38	20.6%	0.4%
Slovenia	12.7	29.32	44.82	252.9%	2.6%	60	71.64	86.97	45.0%	0.7%	0.483	0.571	0.666	37.9%	0.6%
Malta	9.2	17.75	31.7	244.6%	2.5%	19.62	46.19	73.52	274.7%	2.7%	0.053	0.059	0.066	24.5%	0.4%
Europe-South	**7.914**	**20.25**	**34.38**	**334.4%**	**3.0%**	**41.08**	**60.4**	**76.33**	**85.8%**	**1.2%**	**0.962**	**1.078**	**1.26**	**31.0%**	**0.5%**
Germany	11.56	26.9	43.92	279.9%	2.7%	61.74	83.51	94.51	53.1%	0.9%	0.468	0.48	0.495	5.8%	0.1%
France	9.13	24.52	41.76	357.4%	3.1%	57.22	78.32	90.19	57.6%	0.9%	0.57	0.571	0.565	-0.9%	-0.0%
Netherlands	12.21	28.31	44.54	264.8%	2.6%	57.2	75.24	84.25	47.3%	0.8%	0.556	0.525	0.533	-4.1%	-0.1%
Belgium	16.53	32.86	46.23	179.7%	2.1%	65	69.67	82.33	26.7%	0.5%	0.73	0.723	0.755	3.4%	0.1%
Austria	6.626	17.92	34.49	420.5%	3.4%	42.86	69.52	85.33	99.1%	1.4%	0.466	0.491	0.536	15.0%	0.3%
Switzerland	9.011	21.31	37.23	313.2%	2.9%	54.62	75.87	90.34	65.4%	1.0%	0.353	0.362	0.379	7.4%	0.1%
Luxembourg	10.33	17.73	34.89	237.8%	2.5%	29.92	55.08	73.9	147.0%	1.8%	0.138	0.135	0.15	8.7%	0.2%
Europe-West	**10.79**	**25.95**	**42.72**	**295.9%**	**2.8%**	**58.65**	**79.28**	**91.08**	**55.3%**	**0.9%**	**0.518**	**0.523**	**0.534**	**3.1%**	**0.1%**

Infrastructure

Base Case
Source: International Futures
Version 5.47 March 2008

	Crop Yield (Tons/Hectar)					Internet Use (Percent Use)					Electricity Use (Kilowatt Hours/Capita)				
	2005	2030	2055	% Chg	% An Chg	2005	2030	2055	% Chg	% An Chg	2005	2030	2055	% Chg	% An Chg
World	2.986	3.725	4.282	43.4%	0.7%	16.61	38.79	50.01	201.1%	2.2%	2350	4390	7648	225.4%	2.4%
Africa	2.018	2.788	3.543	75.6%	1.1%	6.042	24.4	29.73	392.1%	3.2%	572.4	1036	2463	330.3%	3.0%
Americas	3.276	4.031	4.482	36.8%	0.6%	31.06	51.27	60.7	95.4%	1.3%	6129	7784	10503	71.4%	1.1%
Asia incl Oceania	3.489	4.352	4.977	42.6%	0.7%	13.11	37.25	53.5	308.1%	2.9%	1336	3865	8494	535.8%	3.8%
Europe	3.278	3.768	4.042	23.3%	0.4%	30.96	61.23	70.14	126.6%	1.6%	5408	10028	12953	139.5%	1.8%
World	2.986	3.725	4.282	43.4%	0.7%	16.61	38.79	50.01	201.1%	2.2%	2350	4390	7648	225.4%	2.4%
Africa-Eastern	2.272	3.28	4.492	97.7%	1.4%	3.467	22.46	28.96	735.3%	4.3%	245.1	599.2	2268	825.3%	4.6%
Africa-Middle	1.824	2.521	3.196	75.2%	1.1%	5.756	22.01	23.83	314.0%	2.9%	173.5	453.7	969.7	458.9%	3.5%
Africa-Northern	2.62	3.283	3.87	47.7%	0.8%	10.43	30.31	43.51	317.2%	2.9%	888.2	2274	5951	570.0%	3.9%
Africa-Southern	1.24	1.329	1.402	13.1%	0.2%	16.23	37.39	58.15	258.3%	2.6%	3620	4744	9656	166.7%	2.0%
Africa-Western	1.891	2.717	3.336	76.4%	1.1%	3.732	22.49	24.68	561.3%	3.9%	247.6	574.5	1183	377.8%	3.2%
Africa	2.018	2.788	3.543	75.6%	1.1%	6.042	24.4	29.73	392.1%	3.2%	572.4	1036	2463	330.3%	3.0%
America-Caribbean	4.325	4.784	4.947	14.4%	0.3%	13.45	34.85	46.23	243.7%	2.5%	1544	3678	6642	330.2%	3.0%
America-Central	2.974	3.621	3.927	32.0%	0.6%	12.07	30.93	41.62	244.8%	2.5%	773.8	2251	5472	607.2%	4.0%
America-North	1.985	2.411	2.631	32.5%	0.6%	47.08	66.9	70.52	49.8%	0.8%	10706	12128	13226	23.5%	0.4%
America-South	2.814	3.983	4.843	72.1%	1.1%	16.38	38.56	54.58	233.2%	2.4%	1878	4194	8752	366.0%	3.1%
Americas	3.276	4.031	4.482	36.8%	0.6%	31.06	51.27	60.7	95.4%	1.3%	6129	7784	10503	71.4%	1.1%
Asia-East	5.023	5.482	5.543	10.4%	0.2%	17.14	48.6	73.7	330.0%	3.0%	2034	6411	13591	568.2%	3.9%
Asia-South Central	2.432	3.554	4.474	84.0%	1.2%	8.899	29.17	42.48	377.4%	3.2%	565.9	1982	5701	907.4%	4.7%
Asia-South East	2.935	3.847	4.577	55.9%	0.9%	11.83	31.58	41.77	253.1%	2.6%	809.7	2456	5510	580.5%	3.9%
Asia-West	5.097	6.034	5.641	30.3%	0.5%	15	39.36	56.12	274.1%	2.7%	2462	4956	9258	276.0%	2.7%
Oceania	1.4	1.966	2.476	76.9%	1.1%	37.13	60.68	61.8	66.4%	1.0%	7438	10482	10681	43.6%	0.7%
Asia incl Oceania	3.489	4.352	4.977	42.6%	0.7%	13.11	37.25	53.5	308.1%	2.9%	1336	3865	8494	535.8%	3.8%
Europe-East	2.492	2.953	3.217	29.1%	0.5%	18.34	46.47	62.73	242.0%	2.5%	3877	7766	10979	183.2%	2.1%
Europe-North	2.727	3.116	3.152	15.6%	0.3%	44.69	74.59	76	70.1%	1.1%	8427	13424	15474	83.6%	1.2%
Europe-South	3.355	4.188	4.761	41.9%	0.7%	32.85	61.81	71.6	118.0%	1.6%	4691	8974	13062	178.4%	2.1%
Europe-West	5.064	5.203	5.363	5.9%	0.1%	42.77	75.33	76	77.7%	1.2%	6867	12308	14174	106.4%	1.5%
Europe	3.278	3.768	4.042	23.3%	0.4%	30.96	61.23	70.14	126.6%	1.6%	5408	10028	12953	139.5%	1.8%

Infrastructure

Base Case: Countries in Year 2055 Descending Population Sequence	Crop Yield (Tons/Hectar)					Internet Use (Percent Use)					Electricity Use (Kilowatt Hours/Capita)				
	2005	2030	2055	% Chg	% An Chg	2005	2030	2055	% Chg	% An Chg	2005	2030	2055	% Chg	% An Chg
AFRICA															
Ethiopia	2.512	4.531	7.691	206.2%	2.3%	0.789	21.73	25.33	3110.4%	7.2%	60.43	334.1	1348	2130.7%	6.4%
Tanzania	2.99	3.311	3.646	21.9%	0.4%	3.534	22.33	32.11	808.6%	4.5%	90.65	502.7	3066	3282.2%	7.3%
Uganda	2.687	4.897	8.03	198.8%	2.2%	3.435	23.73	37.06	978.9%	4.9%	430.3	1067	4318	903.5%	4.7%
Kenya	2.225	2.987	3.625	62.9%	1.0%	7.627	23.05	33.8	343.2%	3.0%	147.8	629.4	3492	2262.7%	6.5%
Madagascar	2.196	2.863	3.852	75.4%	1.1%	2.986	21.62	24.13	708.1%	4.3%	327.5	487.5	1046	219.4%	2.3%
Mozambique	2.143	2.76	3.037	41.7%	0.7%	1.919	23.9	32.04	1569.6%	5.8%	104.8	755.3	3047	2807.4%	7.0%
Malawi	1.99	2.655	4.295	115.8%	1.6%	3.628	21.03	23.77	555.2%	3.8%	219.8	339.5	954.7	334.3%	3.0%
Zambia	0.796	1.031	1.123	41.1%	0.7%	6.106	21.67	25.9	324.2%	2.9%	602.9	708.7	1494	147.8%	1.8%
Zimbabwe	1.437	1.687	1.898	32.1%	0.6%	9.083	24.65	32.54	258.3%	2.6%	880	1230	3175	260.8%	2.6%
Burundi	3.13	6.152	9.744	211.3%	2.3%	1.567	20.95	22.95	1364.6%	5.5%	233.1	322.7	747	220.5%	2.4%
Rwanda	3.868	5.106	7.162	85.2%	1.2%	2.684	22.12	26.02	869.4%	4.6%	365	612.6	1524	317.5%	2.9%
Somalia	2.402	3.428	3.789	57.7%	0.9%	0.248	20.99	21.78	8682.3%	9.4%	189	325.2	451	138.6%	1.8%
Eritrea	2.736	3.328	3.634	32.8%	0.6%	2.76	21	21.6	682.6%	4.2%	376.6	376.6	405.8	7.8%	0.1%
Mauritius	1.44	2.579	3.816	165.0%	2.0%	20.89	46.2	59.25	183.6%	2.1%	3747	6711	9934	165.1%	2.0%
Comoros	1.681	2.648	3.59	113.6%	1.5%	6.01	22.71	25.5	324.3%	2.9%	621.7	753	1392	123.9%	1.6%
Djibouti	2.116	2.511	2.939	38.9%	0.7%	6.862	22.95	24.89	262.7%	2.6%	705.6	788	1238	75.5%	1.1%
Africa-Eastern	**2.272**	**3.28**	**4.492**	**97.7%**	**1.4%**	**3.467**	**22.46**	**28.96**	**735.3%**	**4.3%**	**245.1**	**599.2**	**2268**	**825.3%**	**4.6%**
Congo, Dem. Rep. of the	3.236	5.238	7.717	138.5%	1.8%	7.152	21.01	23.13	223.4%	2.4%	71.54	249	792.4	1007.6%	4.9%
Angola	1.703	3.126	4.367	156.4%	1.9%	4.174	23.72	25.22	504.2%	3.7%	172.5	709.8	1321	665.8%	4.2%
Cameroon	0.999	1.296	1.556	55.8%	0.9%	2.267	22.75	24.39	975.9%	4.9%	253.3	547.7	1111	338.6%	3.0%
Chad	0.967	1.709	2.52	160.6%	1.9%	1.791	22.65	23.87	1232.8%	5.3%	350.1	758.8	979.3	179.7%	2.1%
Central African Republic	0.814	0.884	1.116	37.1%	0.6%	9.346	21.36	22.46	140.3%	1.8%	428	428	622.7	45.5%	0.8%
Congo, Rep. of	5.191	5.425	5.345	3.0%	0.1%	9.023	23.37	26.65	195.4%	2.2%	131.2	651.5	1683	1182.8%	5.2%
Gabon	1.588	1.849	2.138	34.6%	0.6%	12.25	35.15	39.85	225.3%	2.4%	944	2982	5023	432.1%	3.4%
Equatorial Guinea	0.819	1.512	2.399	192.9%	2.2%	5.567	36.99	37.21	568.4%	3.9%	2068	4486	4676	126.1%	1.6%
São Tomé and Príncipe	1.097	1.654	1.608	46.6%	0.8%	13.06	22.35	22.76	74.3%	1.1%	665.9	665.9	699.8	5.1%	0.1%
Africa-Middle	**1.824**	**2.521**	**3.196**	**75.2%**	**1.1%**	**5.756**	**22.01**	**23.83**	**314.0%**	**2.9%**	**173.5**	**453.7**	**969.7**	**458.9%**	**3.5%**
Egypt	10.9	12.27	12.69	16.4%	0.3%	13.05	29.99	49.26	277.5%	2.7%	1077	2400	7405	587.6%	3.9%
Sudan	0.764	1.117	1.536	101.0%	1.4%	3.779	25.18	30.26	700.7%	4.2%	139.7	926.5	2596	1758.3%	6.0%
Algeria	0.883	1.285	1.811	105.1%	1.4%	10.73	34.12	42.54	296.5%	2.8%	852.7	2714	5704	568.9%	3.9%
Morocco	1.328	2.145	3.175	139.2%	1.8%	10.92	28.1	37.94	247.4%	2.5%	593.9	1583	4541	664.6%	4.2%
Tunisia	1.031	1.581	2.075	101.3%	1.4%	15.23	40.82	69.22	354.5%	3.1%	1201	4221	12457	937.2%	4.8%
Libya	0.809	1.305	1.93	138.6%	1.8%	6.511	44.47	61.31	841.6%	4.6%	4364	7929	10455	139.6%	1.8%
Africa-Northern	**2.62**	**3.283**	**3.87**	**47.7%**	**0.8%**	**10.43**	**30.31**	**43.51**	**317.2%**	**2.9%**	**888.2**	**2274**	**5951**	**570.0%**	**3.9%**

Infrastructure

Base Case: Countries in Year 2055 Descending Population Sequence	Crop Yield (Tons/Hectar)					Internet Use (Percent Use)					Electricity Use (Kilowatt Hours/Capita)				
	2005	2030	2055	% Chg	% An Chg	2005	2030	2055	% Chg	% An Chg	2005	2030	2055	% Chg	% An Chg
AFRICA continued															
South Africa	1.255	1.432	1.57	25.1%	0.4%	16.72	37.96	58.66	250.8%	2.5%	3861	4925	9786	153.5%	1.9%
Namibia	0.641	0.707	0.764	19.2%	0.4%	13.29	34.24	70.48	430.3%	3.4%	2203	3754	12777	480.0%	3.6%
Lesotho	1.411	1.485	1.414	0.2%	0.0%	6.371	24.1	29.06	356.1%	3.1%	941.3	1085	2293	143.6%	1.8%
Botswana	1.227	1.331	1.324	7.9%	0.2%	20.23	49.56	76	275.7%	2.7%	3247	7735	14174	336.5%	3.0%
Swaziland	1.667	1.689	1.939	16.3%	0.3%	11.64	29.12	43.91	277.2%	2.7%	1476	2413	6052	310.0%	2.9%
Africa-Southern	**1.24**	**1.329**	**1.402**	**13.1%**	**0.2%**	**16.23**	**37.39**	**58.15**	**258.3%**	**2.6%**	**3620**	**4744**	**9656**	**166.7%**	**2.0%**
Nigeria	3.382	6.154	7.887	133.2%	1.7%	2.868	22.62	24.26	745.9%	4.4%	111.2	523.3	1079	870.3%	4.6%
Niger	1.01	1.682	2.673	164.7%	2.0%	1.633	20.93	22.77	1294.4%	5.4%	251	329.4	701.6	179.5%	2.1%
Ghana	3.011	4.549	5.947	97.5%	1.4%	2.853	22.77	24.81	769.6%	4.4%	382.2	603.4	1216	218.2%	2.3%
Côte d'Ivoire	1.271	1.547	1.816	42.9%	0.7%	6.918	23.47	27.55	298.2%	2.8%	568.1	964.4	1912	236.6%	2.5%
Mali	1.008	1.645	2.168	115.1%	1.5%	3.732	21.69	24.33	551.9%	3.8%	308	514.9	1097	256.2%	2.6%
Burkina Faso	1.167	2.046	2.814	141.1%	1.8%	3.119	21.94	25.6	720.8%	4.3%	375.2	580.5	1418	277.9%	2.7%
Senegal	1.328	1.694	1.919	44.5%	0.7%	8.46	23.34	27.68	227.2%	2.4%	182.6	658.7	1945	965.2%	4.8%
Guinea	2.542	2.757	2.742	7.9%	0.2%	4.173	23.68	26.2	527.8%	3.7%	718.7	1014	1568	118.2%	1.6%
Benin	2.277	3.718	4.916	115.9%	1.6%	4.528	21.86	25.34	459.6%	3.5%	104.5	380.3	1351	1192.8%	5.3%
Togo	0.919	1.323	1.552	68.9%	1.1%	11.18	21.72	22.49	101.2%	1.4%	481	511.1	629.5	30.9%	0.5%
Liberia	1.706	1.835	1.713	0.4%	0.0%	0.592	21.13	22.31	3668.6%	7.5%	326.9	353.8	585.7	79.2%	1.2%
Sierra Leone	2.599	2.976	3.105	19.5%	0.4%	2.024	21.52	23.51	1061.6%	5.0%	212.1	443.3	887.2	318.3%	2.9%
Mauritania	1.016	1.476	1.96	92.9%	1.3%	5.351	23.12	24.99	367.0%	3.1%	696.9	874.6	1263	81.2%	1.2%
Guinea-Bissau	0.925	1.024	1.179	27.5%	0.5%	4.636	20.8	21.42	362.0%	3.1%	306	306	360.1	17.7%	0.3%
Gambia	1.433	1.524	1.571	9.6%	0.2%	10.02	23.24	26.76	167.1%	2.0%	610.1	895.8	1711	180.4%	2.1%
Cape Verde	4.661	7.517	9.41	101.9%	1.4%	13.05	33.41	52.21	300.1%	2.8%	1684	3528	8152	384.1%	3.2%
Africa-Western	**1.891**	**2.717**	**3.336**	**76.4%**	**1.1%**	**3.732**	**22.49**	**24.68**	**561.3%**	**3.9%**	**247.6**	**574.5**	**1183**	**377.8%**	**3.2%**

Infrastructure

Base Case: Countries in Year 2055 Descending Population Sequence	Crop Yield (Tons/Hectar)					Internet Use (Percent Use)					Electricity Use (Kilowatt Hours/Capita)				
	2005	2030	2055	% Chg	% An Chg	2005	2030	2055	% Chg	% An Chg	2005	2030	2055	% Chg	% An Chg
AMERICAS															
Haiti	2.286	2.389	2.267	-0.8%	-0.0%	7.019	22.2	24.03	242.4%	2.5%	95.63	391.7	1020	966.6%	4.8%
Dominican Republic	1.719	1.906	1.99	15.8%	0.3%	17.76	39.88	52.26	194.3%	2.2%	1081	3832	8166	655.4%	4.1%
Cuba	0.748	0.848	1.055	41.0%	0.7%	9.567	28.65	53.76	461.9%	3.5%	1203	2727	8544	610.2%	4.0%
Puerto Rico	10.25	9.947	8.987	-12.3%	-0.3%	23.85	64.97	76	218.7%	2.3%	4367	11768	14174	224.6%	2.4%
Jamaica	3.476	3.617	3.682	5.9%	0.1%	13.82	29.74	51.07	269.5%	2.6%	2355	3313	7863	233.9%	2.4%
Trinidad and Tobago	1.838	2.007	2.071	12.7%	0.2%	21.03	63.45	72.51	244.8%	2.5%	4781	11803	13399	180.3%	2.1%
Bahamas	10.33	10.3	10.15	-1.7%	-0.0%	31.38	52.11	72.6	131.4%	1.7%	6158	8195	13313	116.2%	1.6%
Barbados	6.392	8.028	8.761	37.1%	0.6%	20.67	55.58	76	267.7%	2.6%	5583	9130	14174	153.9%	1.9%
Grenada	3.656	4.14	4.112	12.5%	0.2%	15.71	35.49	59.97	281.7%	2.7%	2704	4024	10118	274.2%	2.7%
St. Vincent & the Grenadines	3.288	4.082	4.717	43.5%	0.7%	14.69	31.83	47.96	226.5%	2.4%	1956	3065	7077	261.8%	2.6%
St. Lucia	3.601	5.364	6.621	83.9%	1.2%	17.21	40.12	76	341.6%	3.0%	2301	5208	14174	516.0%	3.7%
America-Caribbean	**4.325**	**4.784**	**4.947**	**14.4%**	**0.3%**	**13.45**	**34.85**	**46.23**	**243.7%**	**2.5%**	**1544**	**3678**	**6642**	**330.2%**	**3.0%**
Guatemala	2.387	2.558	2.851	19.4%	0.4%	10.75	28.48	37.33	247.3%	2.5%	464	1604	4386	845.3%	4.6%
Honduras	1.894	1.885	1.758	-7.2%	-0.1%	10.7	25.59	31.2	191.6%	2.2%	582.3	1199	2836	387.0%	3.2%
Nicaragua	0.821	0.935	0.895	9.0%	0.2%	10.78	25.33	29.68	175.3%	2.0%	372	1014	2451	558.9%	3.8%
El Salvador	1.809	1.962	2.262	25.0%	0.4%	12.28	31.44	45.27	268.6%	2.6%	725.3	2266	6395	781.7%	4.4%
Costa Rica	8.136	10.29	11.07	36.1%	0.6%	18.26	48.19	76	316.2%	2.9%	1918	6133	14174	639.0%	4.1%
Panama	1.862	2.039	2.066	11.0%	0.2%	13.61	46.18	76	458.4%	3.5%	1583	5873	14174	795.4%	4.5%
Belize	3.91	5.676	6.588	68.5%	1.0%	16.5	42.45	76	360.6%	3.1%	2243	5892	14174	531.9%	3.8%
America-Central	**2.974**	**3.621**	**3.927**	**32.0%**	**0.6%**	**12.07**	**30.93**	**41.62**	**244.8%**	**2.5%**	**773.8**	**2251**	**5472**	**607.2%**	**4.0%**
United States	2.566	3.092	3.375	31.5%	0.5%	57.47	75.79	76	32.2%	0.6%	13297	14302	14302	7.6%	0.1%
Mexico	2.001	2.562	2.989	49.4%	0.8%	16.6	40.48	53.7	223.5%	2.4%	1877	4283	8528	354.3%	3.1%
Canada	1.388	1.579	1.529	10.2%	0.2%	50.88	75.86	76	49.4%	0.8%	15686	19174	19174	22.2%	0.4%
America-North	**1.985**	**2.411**	**2.631**	**32.5%**	**0.6%**	**47.08**	**66.9**	**70.52**	**49.8%**	**0.8%**	**10706**	**12128**	**13226**	**23.5%**	**0.4%**
Brazil	1.884	2.081	2.218	17.7%	0.3%	15.76	36.07	51.64	227.7%	2.4%	2002	3735	8008	300.0%	2.8%
Colombia	3.633	4.315	5.112	40.7%	0.7%	14.27	34.66	52.64	268.9%	2.6%	997.3	2889	8262	728.4%	4.3%
Argentina	1.632	2.313	2.793	71.1%	1.1%	22.45	59.78	76	238.5%	2.5%	2768	8272	14174	412.1%	3.3%
Peru	3.269	5.516	7.532	130.4%	1.7%	14.37	33.11	44.93	212.7%	2.3%	862.9	2629	6311	631.4%	4.1%
Venezuela	2.426	3.75	4.99	105.7%	1.5%	16.64	42.97	69.04	314.9%	2.9%	2930	6508	12411	323.6%	2.9%
Chile	4.812	7.07	8.238	71.2%	1.1%	25.56	52.9	76	197.3%	2.2%	2789	7709	14174	408.2%	3.3%
Ecuador	4.764	7.478	8.112	70.3%	1.1%	12.11	27.48	30.64	153.0%	1.9%	786.8	1606	2694	242.4%	2.5%
Bolivia	1.176	1.293	1.479	25.8%	0.5%	11.45	27.32	41.53	262.7%	2.6%	461	1530	5449	1082.0%	5.1%
Paraguay	1.932	2.44	2.68	38.7%	0.7%	10.92	27.49	36.06	230.2%	2.4%	939.6	1681	4064	332.5%	3.0%
Uruguay	2.585	4.476	6.139	137.5%	1.7%	19.99	50.89	76	280.2%	2.7%	2405	6853	14174	489.4%	3.6%
Guyana	1.479	2.371	3.514	137.6%	1.7%	16.01	28.18	33.03	106.3%	1.5%	1440	2070	3299	129.1%	1.7%
Suriname	4.179	4.699	5.307	27.0%	0.5%	12.81	34.51	51.49	302.0%	2.8%	2270	3732	7971	251.1%	2.5%
America-South	**2.814**	**3.983**	**4.843**	**72.1%**	**1.1%**	**16.38**	**38.56**	**54.58**	**233.2%**	**2.4%**	**1878**	**4194**	**8752**	**366.0%**	**3.1%**

Infrastructure

Base Case: Countries in Year 2055 Descending Population Sequence	Crop Yield (Tons/Hectar)					Internet Use (Percent Use)					Electricity Use (Kilowatt Hours/Capita)				
	2005	2030	2055	% Chg	% An Chg	2005	2030	2055	% Chg	% An Chg	2005	2030	2055	% Chg	% An Chg
ASIA INCL OCEANIA															
China	6.505	8.879	9.78	50.3%	0.8%	13.42	45.38	74.24	453.2%	3.5%	1181	5588	13728	1062.4%	5.0%
Japan	9.951	9.679	8.956	-10.0%	-0.2%	45.8	76	76	65.9%	1.0%	8283	13103	14174	71.1%	1.1%
Korea, Rep. of	10.4	10.37	9.944	-4.4%	-0.1%	31.53	75.91	76	141.0%	1.8%	5672	13464	14174	149.9%	1.8%
Taiwan	2.168	2.713	3.024	39.5%	0.7%	37.91	68.12	76	100.5%	1.4%	8118	12290	14174	74.6%	1.1%
Korea, Dem. Rep. of	3.358	3.584	3.805	13.3%	0.3%	9.263	23.51	28.88	211.8%	2.3%	428.3	900.9	2248	424.9%	3.4%
Hong Kong	2.071	2.036	1.988	-4.0%	-0.1%	44.32	75.83	76	71.5%	1.1%	6797	11948	14174	108.5%	1.5%
Mongolia	0.705	1.112	1.305	85.1%	1.2%	10.54	24.2	29.74	182.2%	2.1%	619.2	1108	2465	298.1%	2.8%
Asia-East	**5.023**	**5.482**	**5.543**	**10.4%**	**0.2%**	**17.14**	**48.6**	**73.7**	**330.0%**	**3.0%**	**2034**	**6411**	**13591**	**568.2%**	**3.9%**
India	2.504	4.104	5.784	131.0%	1.7%	9.736	29.96	47.84	391.4%	3.2%	495	2046	7046	1323.4%	5.5%
Pakistan	2.646	4.156	5.575	110.7%	1.5%	6.736	24.56	29.1	332.0%	3.0%	431.3	1015	2303	434.0%	3.4%
Bangladesh	5.7	6.721	7.255	27.3%	0.5%	2.696	24.88	30.65	1036.9%	5.0%	157.6	879.3	2694	1609.4%	5.8%
Iran, Islamic Rep. of	2.904	5.704	7.882	171.4%	2.0%	16.89	44.07	63.65	276.9%	2.7%	1748	5593	11048	532.0%	3.8%
Afghanistan	1.032	1.451	1.788	73.3%	1.1%	6.282	20.89	21.92	248.9%	2.5%	289.5	310.8	485.1	67.6%	1.0%
Nepal	3.531	5.326	6.926	96.1%	1.4%	4.084	22.34	24.01	487.9%	3.6%	106.7	434.1	1015	851.3%	4.6%
Uzbekistan	2.224	4.368	6.646	198.8%	2.2%	9.016	25.12	30.33	236.4%	2.5%	1746	2403	2614	49.7%	0.8%
Sri Lanka	3.022	3.16	3.39	12.2%	0.2%	9.706	30.48	40.25	314.7%	2.9%	448.9	1915	5125	1041.7%	5.0%
Kazakhstan	0.799	1.032	1.308	63.7%	1.0%	9.78	57.42	72.23	638.5%	4.1%	3421	12356	13911	306.6%	2.8%
Tajikistan	1.951	3.047	3.874	98.6%	1.4%	0.46	23.04	26.64	5691.3%	8.5%	2523	3003	3003	19.0%	0.3%
Turkmenistan	1.444	2.47	2.902	101.0%	1.4%	1.567	38.24	39.25	2404.8%	6.7%	1470	4817	5358	264.5%	2.6%
Kyrgyzstan	2.176	2.912	3.488	60.3%	0.9%	10.08	22.89	24.82	146.2%	1.8%	1658	1658	1658	0.0%	0.0%
Bhutan	1.96	2.335	2.33	18.9%	0.3%	8.389	30.45	59.83	613.2%	4.0%	1038	2784	10080	871.1%	4.7%
Maldives	2.162	2.965	3.485	61.2%	1.0%	13.85	36.35	71.17	413.9%	3.3%	2026	4300	12951	539.2%	3.8%
Asia-South Central	**2.432**	**3.554**	**4.474**	**84.0%**	**1.2%**	**8.899**	**29.17**	**42.48**	**377.4%**	**3.2%**	**565.9**	**1982**	**5701**	**907.4%**	**4.7%**
Indonesia	2.844	3.751	4.51	58.6%	0.9%	11.32	29.28	36.44	221.9%	2.4%	514.4	1826	4160	708.7%	4.3%
Philippines	3.377	3.617	3.883	15.0%	0.3%	12.97	29.27	37.74	191.0%	2.2%	632.4	1807	4489	609.8%	4.0%
Vietnam	6.417	8.562	9.979	55.5%	0.9%	11.07	30.4	44.28	300.0%	2.8%	412.7	2100	6146	1389.2%	5.6%
Thailand	3.129	3.56	3.808	21.7%	0.4%	16.34	40.28	58.14	255.8%	2.6%	1741	4528	9654	454.5%	3.5%
Myanmar	2.671	3.125	3.508	31.3%	0.5%	0.247	24.3	28.73	11531.6%	10.0%	146.2	748.5	2210	1411.6%	5.6%
Malaysia	0.582	0.622	0.598	2.7%	0.1%	26.63	52	76	185.4%	2.1%	2897	7907	14174	389.3%	3.2%
Cambodia	1.535	3.012	4.691	205.6%	2.3%	2.123	28.31	38.75	1725.2%	6.0%	751.5	2209	4746	531.5%	3.8%
Laos	3.176	4.457	5.713	79.9%	1.2%	9.915	26.47	37.05	273.7%	2.7%	590	1747	4316	631.5%	4.1%
Singapore	2.082	2.021	1.967	-5.5%	-0.1%	44.44	75.81	76	71.0%	1.1%	8404	13270	14174	68.7%	1.1%
Timor-Leste	4.252	6.426	7.602	78.8%	1.2%	9.74	23.05	26.56	172.7%	2.0%	620	843.4	1661	167.9%	2.0%
Brunei	2.216	3.167	4.09	84.6%	1.2%	30.76	60	66.25	115.4%	1.5%	7318	11192	11707	60.0%	0.9%
Asia-South East	**2.935**	**3.847**	**4.577**	**55.9%**	**0.9%**	**11.83**	**31.58**	**41.77**	**253.1%**	**2.6%**	**809.7**	**2456**	**5510**	**580.5%**	**3.9%**

Multination Regional Analysis

Infrastructure

Measures of Poverty, Health, Education, Infrastructure and Governance

Base Case: Countries in Year 2055 Descending Population Sequence	Crop Yield Tons/Hectar					Internet Use Percent Use					Electricity Use Kilowatt Hours/Capita				
	2005	2030	2055	% Chg	% An Chg	2005	2030	2055	% Chg	% An Chg	2005	2030	2055	% Chg	% An Chg
ASIA INCL OCEANIA															
Turkey	2.791	4.181	5.165	85.1%	1.2%	15.78	41.99	76	381.6%	3.2%	1785	4896	14174	694.1%	4.2%
Yemen	2.794	3.531	4.336	55.2%	0.9%	8.216	23.03	27.84	238.9%	2.5%	139.5	655	1984	1322.2%	5.5%
Iraq	1.161	1.351	1.799	55.0%	0.9%	10.21	29.22	39.68	288.6%	2.8%	1534	2933	4982	224.8%	2.4%
Saudi Arabia	1.859	3.484	4.975	167.6%	2.0%	18.5	57.89	76	310.8%	2.9%	5147	9965	14205	176.0%	2.1%
Syria	1.644	1.74	1.918	16.7%	0.3%	12.33	28.13	39.52	220.5%	2.4%	1005	2005	4941	391.6%	3.2%
Israel	9.218	8.949	8.132	-11.8%	-0.3%	35.84	75.57	76	112.1%	1.5%	6512	12841	14174	117.7%	1.6%
Azerbaijan	1.616	2.122	2.566	58.8%	0.9%	5.651	32.98	45.15	699.0%	4.2%	2350	4755	6367	170.9%	2.0%
Jordan	5.119	7.644	9.194	79.6%	1.2%	13.45	36.36	76	465.1%	3.5%	1440	4083	14174	884.3%	4.7%
Palestine	10.83	12	12.67	17.0%	0.3%	12.99	27.57	37.62	189.6%	2.1%	1365	2023	4460	226.7%	2.4%
Oman	7.372	8.905	9.882	34.0%	0.6%	19.34	51.7	68.69	255.2%	2.6%	3205	7212	12324	284.5%	2.7%
Lebanon	10.26	12.32	12.62	23.0%	0.4%	17.41	40.65	76	336.5%	3.0%	2042	5810	14174	594.1%	4.0%
United Arab Emirates	6.861	7.856	8.61	25.5%	0.5%	40.3	75.69	76	88.6%	1.3%	13187	18323	18323	38.9%	0.7%
Kuwait	10.89	11.72	12.16	11.7%	0.2%	26.5	75.27	76	186.8%	2.1%	11528	17083	17083	48.2%	0.8%
Georgia	2.498	3.481	4.387	75.6%	1.1%	9.537	27.42	34.21	258.7%	2.6%	1506	2394	3598	138.9%	1.8%
Armenia	2.665	3.362	4.084	53.2%	0.9%	10.57	32.92	44.76	323.5%	2.9%	1578	3792	6267	297.1%	2.8%
Bahrain	2.124	2.489	2.677	26.0%	0.5%	24.15	72.53	76	214.7%	2.3%	9061	16104	16501	82.1%	1.2%
Qatar	7.232	8.584	9.537	31.9%	0.6%	27.7	75.75	76	174.4%	2.0%	14991	21644	21644	44.4%	0.7%
Cyprus	4.814	4.905	4.828	0.3%	0.0%	33.78	68.66	76	125.0%	1.6%	4620	10468	14174	206.8%	2.3%
Asia-West	**5.097**	**6.034**	**6.641**	**30.3%**	**0.5%**	**15**	**39.36**	**56.12**	**274.1%**	**2.7%**	**2462**	**4956**	**9258**	**276.0%**	**2.7%**
Australia	0.962	1.456	1.844	91.7%	1.3%	46.16	75.76	76	64.6%	1.0%	9576	14131	14174	48.0%	0.8%
Papua New Guinea	2.712	2.853	3.016	11.2%	0.2%	9.643	25.36	30.8	219.4%	2.3%	830	1425	2732	229.2%	2.4%
New Zealand	1.188	2.132	2.993	151.9%	1.9%	44.84	69.92	76	69.5%	1.1%	9255	14012	15195	64.2%	1.0%
Solomon Islands	2.331	3.449	4.242	82.0%	1.2%	3.961	24.18	29.4	642.2%	4.1%	716.3	1137	2379	232.1%	2.4%
Fiji	1.138	1.635	2.23	96.0%	1.4%	13.26	33.14	49.73	275.0%	2.7%	1847	3377	7526	307.5%	2.8%
Vanuatu	0.668	1.063	1.553	129.5%	1.7%	12.12	27.05	35.91	196.3%	2.2%	1139	1872	4028	253.6%	2.6%
Micronesia	2.157	2.716	3.008	39.5%	0.7%	16.8	29.82	35.71	112.6%	1.5%	2290	2565	3976	73.6%	1.1%
Samoa	0.569	0.834	1.126	97.9%	1.4%	10.93	31.82	47.57	335.2%	3.0%	1825	3056	6977	282.3%	2.7%
Tonga	0.876	1.532	2.294	161.9%	1.9%	12.35	29.5	33.19	168.7%	2.0%	2330	2474	3339	43.3%	0.7%
Oceania	**1.4**	**1.966**	**2.476**	**76.9%**	**1.1%**	**37.13**	**60.68**	**61.8**	**66.4%**	**1.0%**	**7438**	**10482**	**10681**	**43.6%**	**0.7%**

Multination Regional Analysis

Measures of Poverty, Health, Education, Infrastructure and Governance

Infrastructure

Base Case: Countries in Year 2055 Descending Population Sequence	Crop Yield (Tons/Hectar)					Internet Use (Percent Use)					Electricity Use (Kilowatt Hours/Capita)				
	2005	2030	2055	% Chg	% An Chg	2005	2030	2055	% Chg	% An Chg	2005	2030	2055	% Chg	% An Chg
EUROPE															
Russia	0.938	1.045	1.361	45.1%	0.7%	19.55	50.32	62.51	219.7%	2.4%	4856	9803	11096	128.5%	1.7%
Poland	4.414	4.92	4.968	12.6%	0.2%	20.73	48.32	71.27	243.8%	2.5%	2885	6343	12978	349.8%	3.1%
Ukraine	1.731	2.026	2.267	31.0%	0.5%	11.83	37.45	58.64	395.7%	3.3%	2769	5486	9781	253.2%	2.6%
Romania	2.442	2.817	3.094	26.7%	0.5%	16.37	37.07	47.24	188.6%	2.1%	1888	3888	6896	265.3%	2.6%
Belarus	2.682	3.114	3.315	23.6%	0.4%	14.23	42.38	76	434.1%	3.4%	3258	7062	14174	335.1%	3.0%
Czech Republic	2.229	3.288	4.081	83.1%	1.2%	26.9	53.44	71.13	164.4%	2.0%	5440	8150	12941	137.9%	1.7%
Hungary	3.593	3.844	3.71	3.3%	0.1%	23.83	52.66	71.29	199.2%	2.2%	3556	7185	12982	265.1%	2.6%
Bulgaria	1.734	2.028	2.22	28.0%	0.5%	17.85	39.61	59.65	234.2%	2.4%	3410	5729	10035	194.3%	2.2%
Slovak Republic	2.886	3.757	4.264	47.7%	0.8%	23.88	46.56	63.22	164.7%	2.0%	4694	6854	10939	133.0%	1.7%
Moldova	2.267	2.69	2.893	27.6%	0.5%	8.703	24.76	32.89	277.9%	2.7%	884.6	1456	3263	268.9%	2.6%
Europe-East	**2.492**	**2.953**	**3.217**	**29.1%**	**0.5%**	**18.34**	**46.47**	**62.73**	**242.0%**	**2.5%**	**3877**	**7766**	**10979**	**183.2%**	**2.1%**
United Kingdom	5.629	5.788	5.402	-4.0%	-0.1%	44.23	76	76	71.8%	1.1%	6453	11991	14174	119.6%	1.6%
Sweden	2.803	2.791	2.452	-12.5%	-0.3%	53.1	76	76	43.1%	0.7%	14951	19041	19041	27.4%	0.5%
Denmark	5.512	6.631	6.459	17.2%	0.3%	50.62	76	76	50.1%	0.8%	6755	12010	14174	109.8%	1.5%
Norway	2.388	2.445	2.513	5.2%	0.1%	57.38	75.92	76	32.5%	0.6%	24765	25898	25898	4.6%	0.1%
Ireland	2.733	2.658	2.769	1.3%	0.0%	42.31	75.83	76	79.6%	1.2%	7058	11578	14174	100.8%	1.4%
Finland	2.175	2.29	2.117	-2.7%	-0.1%	48.99	76	76	55.1%	0.9%	15021	18184	18184	21.1%	0.4%
Lithuania	1.945	3.62	5.031	158.7%	1.9%	20.6	51.77	76	268.9%	2.6%	2452	6837	14174	478.1%	3.6%
Latvia	0.982	1.117	1.035	5.4%	0.1%	20.35	55.37	76	273.5%	2.7%	2659	7933	14174	433.1%	3.4%
Estonia	0.879	0.976	0.861	-2.0%	-0.0%	33.08	63.58	76	129.7%	1.7%	4771	11620	14507	204.1%	2.2%
Iceland	2.229	2.848	2.88	29.2%	0.5%	61.07	75.93	76	24.4%	0.4%	27107	29071	29071	7.2%	0.1%
Europe-North	**2.727**	**3.116**	**3.152**	**15.6%**	**0.3%**	**44.69**	**74.59**	**76**	**70.1%**	**1.1%**	**8427**	**13424**	**15474**	**83.6%**	**1.2%**
Italy	5.13	5.378	5.341	4.1%	0.1%	40.26	65	76	88.8%	1.3%	5272	9346	14174	168.9%	2.0%
Spain	2.774	2.862	2.735	-1.4%	-0.0%	33.54	73.04	76	126.6%	1.6%	5499	11399	14174	157.8%	1.9%
Greece	3.488	3.629	3.391	-2.8%	-0.1%	28.18	66.2	76	169.7%	2.0%	4919	10412	14174	188.1%	2.1%
Portugal	2.508	2.614	2.474	-1.4%	-0.0%	36.47	57.75	76	108.4%	1.5%	4119	8126	14174	244.1%	2.5%
Serbia and Montenegro	1.727	2.891	4.42	155.9%	1.9%	11.26	26.88	44.88	298.6%	2.8%	869.2	1755	6297	624.5%	4.0%
Croatia	3.306	4.813	5.762	74.3%	1.1%	20.95	46.17	76	262.8%	2.6%	3186	6234	14174	344.9%	3.0%
Bosnia and Herzegovina	2.824	4.845	6.985	147.3%	1.8%	12.82	32.29	41.13	220.8%	2.4%	1717	2863	5347	211.4%	2.3%
Albania	2.19	2.33	2.42	10.5%	0.2%	3.916	31.71	42.43	983.5%	4.9%	1387	2881	5677	309.3%	2.9%
Macedonia	2.977	3.449	4.147	39.3%	0.7%	17.23	31.6	40.49	135.0%	1.7%	2256	2957	5187	129.9%	1.7%
Slovenia	7.725	9.998	10.77	39.4%	0.7%	31.35	60.82	76	142.4%	1.8%	5969	9944	14174	137.5%	1.7%
Malta	2.257	3.263	3.928	74.0%	1.1%	29.77	59.53	76	155.3%	1.9%	4403	8746	14174	221.9%	2.4%
Europe-South	**3.355**	**4.188**	**4.761**	**41.9%**	**0.7%**	**32.85**	**61.81**	**71.6**	**118.0%**	**1.6%**	**4691**	**8974**	**13062**	**178.4%**	**2.1%**
Germany	5.814	5.886	5.418	-6.8%	-0.1%	44.59	76	76	70.4%	1.1%	6435	12364	14174	120.3%	1.6%
France	4.89	5.101	4.813	-1.6%	-0.0%	36.49	75.92	76	108.3%	1.5%	7067	12619	14174	100.6%	1.4%
Netherlands	10.36	10.03	9.939	-4.1%	-0.1%	52.29	75.98	76	45.3%	0.8%	6607	12060	14174	114.5%	1.5%
Belgium	2.066	2.011	2.123	2.8%	0.1%	43.21	64.47	76	75.9%	1.1%	8112	10340	14174	74.7%	1.1%
Austria	4.67	4.858	4.715	1.0%	0.0%	48.37	76	76	57.1%	0.9%	7293	12280	14174	94.4%	1.3%
Switzerland	5.461	5.807	5.736	5.0%	0.1%	45.13	76	76	68.4%	1.0%	8062	12339	14174	75.8%	1.1%
Luxembourg	2.182	2.731	4.797	119.8%	1.6%	49.71	75.6	76	52.9%	0.9%	13185	13747	14174	7.5%	0.1%
Europe-West	**5.064**	**5.203**	**5.363**	**5.9%**	**0.1%**	**42.77**	**75.33**	**76**	**77.7%**	**1.2%**	**6867**	**12308**	**14174**	**106.4%**	**1.5%**

Multination Regional Analysis

Measures of Poverty, Health, Education, Infrastructure and Governance

Infrastructure

Base Case
Source: International Futures
Version 5.47 March 2008

	Telephone Density (Lines per Thousand)					Road Density (Thousand Km/Million Hectares)					Economic Integration Index (Index)				
	2005	2030	2055	% Chg	% An Chg	2005	2030	2055	% Chg	% An Chg	2005	2030	2055	% Chg	% An Chg
World	176.5	299.3	474.1	168.6%	2.0%	5.767	8.582	13.51	134.3%	1.7%	18.12	25.59	28.38	56.6%	0.9%
Africa	29.8	66.33	162.1	444.0%	3.4%	1.335	2.62	5.021	276.1%	2.7%	13.64	16.64	15.04	10.3%	0.2%
Americas	367.8	479.1	638.8	73.7%	1.1%	4.452	10.46	20.7	365.0%	3.1%	14.1	26.46	34	141.1%	1.8%
Asia incl Oceania	118.3	277.1	527	345.5%	3.0%	6.15	9.04	14.05	128.5%	1.7%	10.38	18.72	22.8	119.7%	1.6%
Europe	438.9	679	790.4	80.1%	1.2%	10.84	15.41	24.66	127.5%	1.7%	32.99	39.8	41.31	25.2%	0.5%
World	176.5	299.3	474.1	168.6%	2.0%	5.767	8.582	13.51	134.3%	1.7%	18.12	25.59	28.38	56.6%	0.9%
Africa-Eastern	10.44	38.77	150.4	1340.6%	5.5%	1.328	2.501	5.121	285.6%	2.7%	9.612	13.47	11.51	19.7%	0.4%
Africa-Middle	7.277	32.18	71.89	887.9%	4.7%	0.695	1.402	2.496	259.1%	2.6%	30.37	33.01	24.08	-20.7%	-0.5%
Africa-Northern	71.42	154.9	372.8	422.0%	3.4%	0.898	3.025	7.987	789.4%	4.5%	11.31	13.29	15.4	36.2%	0.6%
Africa-Southern	124.1	235.4	596.7	380.8%	3.2%	3.261	5.327	11.84	263.1%	2.6%	9.858	13.65	18.49	87.6%	1.3%
Africa-Western	11.21	38.96	84.84	656.8%	4.1%	1.533	2.712	4.234	176.2%	2.1%	23.13	26.75	15.6	-32.6%	-0.8%
Africa	29.8	66.33	162.1	444.0%	3.4%	1.335	2.62	5.021	276.1%	2.7%	13.64	16.64	15.04	10.3%	0.2%
America-Caribbean	120.2	248.3	424.7	253.3%	2.6%	5.929	8.543	14.13	138.3%	1.8%	18.55	23.95	33.74	81.9%	1.2%
America-Central	90.16	174.6	344.6	282.2%	2.7%	2.782	5.01	9.717	249.3%	2.5%	18.35	22.47	26.78	45.9%	0.8%
America-North	581.6	700.4	791.5	36.1%	0.6%	6.172	16.04	31.54	411.0%	3.3%	14.1	28.13	38.1	170.2%	2.0%
America-South	175.4	301.3	542.2	209.1%	2.3%	2.495	5.304	11.53	362.1%	3.1%	13.37	17.67	20.34	52.1%	0.8%
Americas	367.8	479.1	638.8	73.7%	1.1%	4.452	10.46	20.7	365.0%	3.1%	14.1	26.46	34	141.1%	1.8%
Asia-East	199.6	484.5	838.4	320.0%	2.9%	4.83	9.705	19.26	298.8%	2.8%	7.982	18.66	25.68	221.7%	2.4%
Asia-South Central	43.38	132.4	357.2	723.4%	4.3%	8.887	9.77	11.36	27.8%	0.5%	3.964	8.306	10.57	166.6%	2.0%
Asia-South East	59	161.5	346.2	486.8%	3.6%	3.123	5.618	9.314	198.2%	2.2%	31.97	33	30	-6.2%	-0.1%
Asia-West	195	332.6	565.9	190.2%	2.2%	3.75	7.778	15.97	325.9%	2.9%	12.14	18.61	25.02	106.1%	1.5%
Oceania	426.4	622.6	655.2	53.7%	0.9%	2.216	9.805	24.82	1020.0%	5.0%	22.01	32.7	41.48	88.5%	1.3%
Asia incl Oceania	118.3	277.1	527	345.5%	3.0%	6.15	9.04	14.05	128.5%	1.7%	10.38	18.72	22.8	119.7%	1.6%
Europe-East	270.3	490.5	667.1	146.8%	1.8%	4.461	7.993	13.09	193.4%	2.2%	17.23	23.13	22.32	29.5%	0.5%
Europe-North	631.5	873.7	894.9	41.7%	0.7%	14.6	22.86	37.15	154.5%	1.9%	50.69	58.66	55.29	9.1%	0.2%
Europe-South	446.9	650.8	809.6	81.2%	1.2%	12.47	14.94	21.06	68.9%	1.1%	15.26	23.73	28.5	86.8%	1.3%
Europe-West	605.2	872.7	887.8	46.7%	0.8%	17.92	22.67	36.05	101.2%	1.4%	34.38	41.17	45.03	31.0%	0.5%
Europe	438.9	679	790.4	80.1%	1.2%	10.84	15.41	24.66	127.5%	1.7%	32.99	39.8	41.31	25.2%	0.5%

Infrastructure

Base Case: Countries in Year 2055 Descending Population Sequence	Telephone Density (Lines per Thousand)					Road Density (Thousand Km/Million Hectares)					Economic Integration Index (Index)				
	2005	2030	2055	% Chg	% An Chg	2005	2030	2055	% Chg	% An Chg	2005	2030	2055	% Chg	% An Chg
AFRICA															
Ethiopia	7.374	29.56	94.79	1185.5%	5.2%	0.448	1.667	3.893	769.0%	4.4%	8.836	15.87	9.628	9.0%	0.2%
Tanzania	8.134	38	198.6	2341.6%	6.6%	1.06	2.014	5.159	386.7%	3.2%	8.474	11.1	11.34	33.8%	0.6%
Uganda	7.233	50.41	274.2	3691.0%	7.5%	2.026	4.029	8.907	339.6%	3.0%	6.961	11.32	10.64	52.9%	0.9%
Kenya	14.13	47.92	224.3	1487.4%	5.7%	1.247	2.396	5.956	377.6%	3.2%	6.493	9.174	10.08	55.2%	0.9%
Madagascar	7.176	28.31	76.52	966.3%	4.8%	0.954	1.585	2.728	186.0%	2.1%	7.163	12.56	10.64	48.5%	0.8%
Mozambique	8.521	53.18	197.4	2216.6%	6.5%	0.513	1.678	4.575	791.8%	4.5%	15.1	18.16	17.23	14.1%	0.3%
Malawi	7.088	23.15	71.02	902.0%	4.7%	1.7	2.858	4.711	177.1%	2.1%	10.65	16.78	10.47	-1.7%	-0.0%
Zambia	11.34	31.67	103.6	813.6%	4.5%	0.962	1.399	2.73	183.8%	2.1%	20.58	28.75	17.21	-16.4%	-0.4%
Zimbabwe	24.88	64.49	205.1	724.4%	4.3%	2.473	2.844	4.851	96.2%	1.4%	7.606	10.42	9.095	19.6%	0.4%
Burundi	5.781	21.73	58.47	911.4%	4.7%	5.383	6.769	8.069	49.9%	0.8%	2.05	10.7	12.5	509.8%	3.7%
Rwanda	6.372	32.52	105.4	1554.1%	5.8%	4.888	6.889	9.17	87.6%	1.3%	5.541	12.32	10.01	80.7%	1.2%
Somalia	5.974	22.24	40.59	579.4%	3.9%	0.409	0.886	1.455	255.7%	2.6%	10.16	20.84	16.81	65.5%	1.0%
Eritrea	11.33	23.25	37.86	234.2%	2.4%	0.482	1.262	2.353	388.2%	3.2%	27.99	35.84	28.99	3.6%	0.1%
Mauritius	254	429.5	613.5	141.5%	1.8%	9.894	13.76	17.36	75.5%	1.1%	17.51	22.75	26.6	51.9%	0.8%
Comoros	14.86	40.95	97.41	555.5%	3.8%	4.163	5.61	7.409	78.0%	1.2%	4.698	10.53	11.12	136.7%	1.7%
Djibouti	20.83	44.39	88.13	323.1%	2.9%	1.361	1.754	2.581	89.6%	1.3%	9.503	13.22	12.28	29.2%	0.5%
Africa-Eastern	**10.44**	**38.77**	**150.4**	**1340.6%**	**5.5%**	**1.328**	**2.501**	**5.121**	**285.6%**	**2.7%**	**9.612**	**13.47**	**11.51**	**19.7%**	**0.4%**
Congo, Dem. Rep. of the	3.534	21.62	61.21	1632.0%	5.9%	0.754	1.383	2.545	237.5%	2.5%	6.488	15.26	22.74	250.5%	2.5%
Angola	11.36	50.28	93.17	720.2%	4.3%	0.56	1.442	2.418	331.8%	3.0%	55.71	47.42	34.09	-38.8%	-1.0%
Cameroon	12.53	39.3	80.47	542.2%	3.8%	0.879	1.585	2.705	207.7%	2.3%	6.768	10.84	12.1	78.8%	1.2%
Chad	5.472	37.68	72.5	1224.9%	5.3%	0.361	1.082	1.825	405.5%	3.3%	29.43	27.15	19.33	-34.3%	-0.8%
Central African Republic	6.766	24.29	50.96	653.2%	4.1%	0.442	0.774	1.339	202.9%	2.2%	5.816	14.49	16.25	179.4%	2.1%
Congo, Rep. of	12.15	48.85	115	846.5%	4.6%	0.49	1.347	2.719	454.9%	3.5%	49.09	41.38	26.1	-46.8%	-1.3%
Gabon	44.96	176.8	316.8	604.6%	4.0%	0.611	3.207	6.075	894.3%	4.7%	24.12	26.68	19	-21.2%	-0.5%
Equatorial Guinea	29.97	188.2	283.6	846.3%	4.6%	1.371	4.465	5.888	329.5%	3.0%	74.05	71.14	42.1	-43.1%	-1.1%
São Tomé and Príncipe	34.58	44.14	55.62	60.8%	1.0%	3.491	4.106	4.541	30.1%	0.5%	22.94	20.4	21.33	-7.0%	-0.1%
Africa-Middle	**7.277**	**32.18**	**71.89**	**887.9%**	**4.7%**	**0.695**	**1.402**	**2.496**	**259.1%**	**2.6%**	**30.37**	**33.01**	**24.08**	**-20.7%**	**-0.5%**
Egypt	91.65	169.7	460.7	402.7%	3.3%	0.946	3.309	10.17	975.1%	4.9%	11.98	14.98	16.12	34.6%	0.6%
Sudan	18.18	70.45	170.2	836.2%	4.6%	0.201	1.45	3.716	1748.8%	6.0%	4.929	6.803	7.455	51.2%	0.8%
Algeria	73.09	185.5	357.9	389.7%	3.2%	0.772	3.212	7.005	807.4%	4.5%	11.56	10.32	8.943	-22.6%	-0.5%
Morocco	58.59	116.3	287.7	391.0%	3.2%	1.546	3.116	6.671	331.5%	3.0%	11.66	13.89	13.65	17.1%	0.3%
Tunisia	114.9	298	765.9	566.6%	3.9%	1.577	5.487	15.28	868.9%	4.6%	19.66	22.79	26.86	36.6%	0.6%
Libya	130.3	349.1	645	395.0%	3.3%	0.886	5.043	11.98	1252.1%	5.3%	6.591	9.275	15.68	137.9%	1.7%
Africa-Northern	**71.42**	**154.9**	**372.8**	**422.0%**	**3.4%**	**0.898**	**3.025**	**7.987**	**789.4%**	**4.5%**	**11.31**	**13.29**	**15.4**	**36.2%**	**0.6%**

Infrastructure

Base Case: Countries in Year 2055 Descending Population Sequence	Telephone Density (Lines per Thousand)					Road Density (Thousand Km/Million Hectares)					Economic Integration Index (Index)				
	2005	2030	2055	% Chg	% An Chg	2005	2030	2055	% Chg	% An Chg	2005	2030	2055	% Chg	% An Chg
AFRICA continued															
South Africa	133.2	244.2	604.6	353.9%	3.1%	3.352	5.403	11.89	254.7%	2.6%	8.983	12.19	16.91	88.2%	1.3%
Namibia	76	190.2	785.2	933.2%	4.8%	1.082	3.336	14.52	1242.0%	5.3%	7.269	8.737	17.15	135.9%	1.7%
Lesotho	17.3	53.43	151.9	778.0%	4.4%	2.038	2.598	4.262	109.1%	1.5%	65.39	63.31	43.37	-33.7%	-0.8%
Botswana	112.9	385	869.7	670.3%	4.2%	5.512	10.45	18.52	236.0%	2.5%	13.32	20.43	28.86	116.7%	1.6%
Swaziland	38.92	117.5	378.9	873.5%	4.7%	1.852	3.74	8.688	369.1%	3.1%	56.78	56.88	43.59	-23.2%	-0.5%
Africa-Southern	**124.1**	**235.4**	**596.7**	**380.8%**	**3.2%**	**3.261**	**5.327**	**11.84**	**263.1%**	**2.6%**	**9.858**	**13.65**	**18.49**	**87.6%**	**1.3%**
Nigeria	8.328	39.11	78.51	842.7%	4.6%	1.893	3.464	5.168	173.0%	2.0%	30.52	32.54	17.87	-41.4%	-1.1%
Niger	5.028	21.46	55.72	1008.2%	4.9%	0.172	0.746	1.817	956.4%	4.8%	8.635	18.49	12.25	41.9%	0.7%
Ghana	17.89	41.65	86.82	385.3%	3.2%	1.851	2.716	4.032	117.8%	1.6%	17.17	22.74	18.94	10.3%	0.2%
Côte d'Ivoire	21.07	54.66	128.8	511.3%	3.7%	1.656	2.679	4.29	159.1%	1.9%	16.22	17.91	15.35	-5.4%	-0.1%
Mali	7.064	29.52	79.6	1026.8%	5.0%	0.221	0.873	2.119	858.8%	4.6%	10.14	15.53	13.57	33.8%	0.6%
Burkina Faso	8.626	32.52	99.04	1048.2%	5.0%	0.615	1.688	3.754	510.4%	3.7%	2.427	7.86	5.45	124.6%	1.6%
Senegal	25.85	55.95	130.8	406.0%	3.3%	0.926	2.153	4.274	361.6%	3.1%	12.37	13.9	12.23	-1.1%	-0.0%
Guinea	9.533	47.83	108.1	1034.0%	5.0%	1.339	2.188	3.4	153.9%	1.9%	5.393	13.66	12.06	123.6%	1.6%
Benin	12.05	33.29	94.97	688.1%	4.2%	1.84	2.652	4.148	125.4%	1.6%	9.705	13.39	10.47	7.9%	0.2%
Togo	13.05	30.83	51.37	293.6%	2.8%	1.513	2.716	4.209	178.2%	2.1%	16.63	22.76	20.91	25.7%	0.5%
Liberia	5.833	22.31	48.72	735.2%	4.3%	1.036	1.537	2.352	127.0%	1.7%	55.09	60.34	41.82	-24.1%	-0.5%
Sierra Leone	7.009	27.44	66.94	855.1%	4.6%	1.725	2.247	3.167	83.6%	1.2%	4.67	9.802	12.38	165.1%	2.0%
Mauritania	13.13	44.37	89.63	582.6%	3.9%	0.204	0.897	1.873	818.1%	4.5%	13.62	15.09	13.57	-0.4%	-0.0%
Guinea-Bissau	11.64	22.32	35.09	201.5%	2.2%	1.695	2.085	2.647	56.2%	0.9%	15.82	22.95	20.38	28.8%	0.5%
Gambia	29.42	55.4	116.7	296.8%	2.8%	2.593	3.769	5.482	111.4%	1.5%	26.28	29.61	23.48	-10.7%	-0.2%
Cape Verde	128.8	238	505.9	292.8%	2.8%	3.005	5.929	12.03	300.3%	2.8%	17.26	20.22	22.76	31.9%	0.6%
Africa-Western	**11.21**	**38.96**	**84.84**	**656.8%**	**4.1%**	**1.533**	**2.712**	**4.234**	**176.2%**	**2.1%**	**23.13**	**26.75**	**15.6**	**-32.6%**	**-0.8%**

Multination Regional Analysis

Measures of Poverty, Health, Education, Infrastructure and Governance

Infrastructure

Base Case: Countries in Year 2055 Descending Population Sequence	Telephone Density (Lines per Thousand)					Road Density (Thousand Km/Million Hectares)					Economic Integration Index (Index)				
	2005	2030	2055	% Chg	% An Chg	2005	2030	2055	% Chg	% An Chg	2005	2030	2055	% Chg	% An Chg
AMERICAS															
Haiti	13.04	34.56	74.93	474.6%	3.6%	1.875	4.072	6.779	261.5%	2.6%	7.32	12.28	10.69	46.0%	0.8%
Dominican Republic	121.3	282.7	506.7	317.7%	2.9%	3.105	7.021	12.12	290.3%	2.8%	20.77	23.58	23.91	15.1%	0.3%
Cuba	51.52	137.9	529.5	927.8%	4.8%	5.489	6.193	11.06	101.5%	1.4%	3.831	7.116	14.49	278.2%	2.7%
Puerto Rico	374.6	834.2	973.8	160.0%	1.9%	7.246	16.25	43.65	502.4%	3.7%	15.89	23.45	48.73	206.7%	2.3%
Jamaica	198.6	241.4	488.4	145.9%	1.8%	17.02	17.02	17.02	0.0%	0.0%	33.83	33.37	29.31	-13.4%	-0.3%
Trinidad and Tobago	293.2	715.2	819.3	179.4%	2.1%	17.63	24.38	24.38	38.3%	0.7%	55.13	53.9	41.54	-24.7%	-0.6%
Bahamas	382.4	506.7	817.7	113.8%	1.5%	2.649	7.103	15.55	487.0%	3.6%	15.77	21.78	27.4	73.7%	1.1%
Barbados	468	641.4	894.4	91.1%	1.3%	37.21	37.21	37.21	0.0%	0.0%	30.8	36.7	42.33	37.4%	0.6%
Grenada	332	349.4	624.6	88.1%	1.3%	33.15	33.15	33.15	0.0%	0.0%	42.19	43.06	39.16	-7.2%	-0.1%
St. Vincent & the Grenadines	220.4	255.1	440.9	100.0%	1.4%	21.26	21.26	21.26	0.0%	0.0%	64.84	61.39	45.9	-29.2%	-0.7%
St. Lucia	320.9	483.4	869.7	171.0%	2.0%	19.52	19.52	19.85	1.7%	0.0%	53.97	54.7	49.64	-8.0%	-0.2%
America-Caribbean	**120.2**	**248.3**	**424.7**	**253.3%**	**2.6%**	**5.929**	**8.543**	**14.13**	**138.3%**	**1.8%**	**18.55**	**23.95**	**33.74**	**81.9%**	**1.2%**
Guatemala	64.08	127	278.3	334.3%	3.0%	1.604	4.014	8.209	411.8%	3.3%	10.37	13.61	12.86	24.0%	0.4%
Honduras	51.24	88.24	184.6	260.3%	2.6%	1.426	2.762	5.173	262.8%	2.6%	17.51	19.28	16.6	-5.2%	-0.1%
Nicaragua	37.49	76.41	161.4	330.5%	3.0%	1.602	2.577	4.326	170.0%	2.0%	20.02	21.76	17.17	-14.2%	-0.3%
El Salvador	94.15	180	399.7	324.5%	2.9%	5.049	7.599	12.11	139.8%	1.8%	11.26	13.34	14.76	31.1%	0.5%
Costa Rica	234.8	490.1	877.2	273.6%	2.7%	7.205	11.84	23.33	223.8%	2.4%	22.09	25.49	33.23	50.4%	0.8%
Panama	164.8	437.2	871.7	428.9%	3.4%	1.886	6.931	23.56	1149.2%	5.2%	32.29	35.06	44.26	37.1%	0.6%
Belize	162.4	383.7	869.7	435.5%	3.4%	1.576	5.674	17.1	985.0%	4.9%	22.61	24.98	31.24	38.2%	0.6%
America-Central	**90.16**	**174.6**	**344.6**	**282.2%**	**2.7%**	**2.782**	**5.01**	**9.717**	**249.3%**	**2.5%**	**18.35**	**22.47**	**26.78**	**45.9%**	**0.8%**
United States	724.2	830.4	869.7	20.1%	0.4%	8.044	20.34	38.53	379.0%	3.2%	12.6	27.66	38.73	207.4%	2.3%
Mexico	137	280.4	528.6	285.8%	2.7%	2.094	5.404	10.8	415.8%	3.3%	14.06	17.16	17.9	27.3%	0.5%
Canada	720.7	950.5	950.5	31.9%	0.6%	2.236	12.94	36.06	1512.7%	5.7%	34.59	43.51	49.21	42.3%	0.7%
America-North	**581.6**	**700.4**	**791.5**	**36.1%**	**0.6%**	**6.172**	**16.04**	**31.54**	**411.0%**	**3.3%**	**14.1**	**28.13**	**38.1**	**170.2%**	**2.0%**
Brazil	184.6	272.9	497.1	169.3%	2.0%	2.255	4.522	9.691	329.8%	3.0%	10.32	13.06	14.16	37.2%	0.6%
Colombia	174.6	261.6	512.5	193.5%	2.2%	1.333	3.938	10.38	678.7%	4.2%	14.22	16.29	16.94	19.1%	0.4%
Argentina	263	586.9	869.7	230.7%	2.4%	7.898	13.47	24.31	207.8%	2.3%	12.98	19.65	28.4	118.8%	1.6%
Peru	78.66	184.6	394.6	401.7%	3.3%	0.909	3.278	7.878	766.7%	4.4%	10.77	12.25	12.87	19.5%	0.4%
Venezuela	126.8	340.5	763.2	501.9%	3.7%	1.487	5.683	14.78	893.9%	4.7%	16.74	19.18	21.17	26.5%	0.5%
Chile	244.4	542.7	872	256.8%	2.6%	1.579	7.296	20.05	1169.8%	5.2%	30.97	33.04	32.51	5.0%	0.1%
Ecuador	108.6	141.1	176.1	62.2%	1.0%	1.77	3.008	4.388	147.9%	1.8%	20.94	19.39	18.21	-13.0%	-0.3%
Bolivia	64.3	127.7	342.6	432.8%	3.4%	0.626	2.032	6.636	960.1%	4.8%	24.93	27.46	21.14	-15.2%	-0.3%
Paraguay	59.9	109.7	258.8	332.1%	3.0%	0.911	2.205	5.361	488.5%	3.6%	17.16	19.98	18.19	6.0%	0.1%
Uruguay	309.2	569.4	876.3	183.4%	2.1%	6.018	10.75	19.22	219.4%	2.3%	6.117	12.06	21.16	245.9%	2.5%
Guyana	84.14	128.8	212.6	152.7%	1.9%	0.573	1.846	4.009	599.7%	4.0%	49.94	47.89	38.66	-22.6%	-0.5%
Suriname	192.5	267.6	494.9	157.1%	1.9%	0.622	2.971	9.165	1373.5%	5.5%	4.364	6.923	11.59	165.6%	2.0%
America-South	**175.4**	**301.3**	**542.2**	**209.1%**	**2.3%**	**2.495**	**5.304**	**11.53**	**362.1%**	**3.1%**	**13.37**	**17.67**	**20.34**	**52.1%**	**0.8%**

Infrastructure

Base Case: Countries in Year 2055 Descending Population Sequence	Telephone Density (Lines per Thousand)					Road Density (Thousand Km/Million Hectares)					Economic Integration Index (Index)				
	2005	2030	2055	% Chg	% An Chg	2005	2030	2055	% Chg	% An Chg	2005	2030	2055	% Chg	% An Chg
ASIA INCL OCEANIA															
China	140.4	435.5	842.7	500.2%	3.6%	1.919	7.361	17.46	809.8%	4.5%	13.45	18.92	23.62	75.6%	1.1%
Japan	633.2	879.8	879.8	38.9%	0.7%	30.75	31.41	36.38	18.3%	0.3%	3.901	15.44	30.45	680.6%	4.2%
Korea, Rep. of	516.8	989.6	989.6	91.5%	1.3%	9.763	20.28	35.02	258.7%	2.6%	11.92	22.44	35.35	196.6%	2.2%
Taiwan	503.8	755.8	869.7	72.6%	1.1%	12.56	18.69	32.24	156.7%	1.9%	8.407	17.37	31.42	273.7%	2.7%
Korea, Dem. Rep. of	26.87	58.55	149.2	455.3%	3.5%	2.739	3.522	5.152	88.1%	1.3%	8.495	13.53	13.95	64.2%	1.0%
Hong Kong	673.6	883.5	883.5	31.2%	0.5%	21.25	41.8	59.72	181.0%	2.1%	43.15	48.26	49.39	14.5%	0.3%
Mongolia	54.07	82.57	162.3	200.2%	2.2%	0.424	1.176	3.073	624.8%	4.0%	18.39	18.58	16.65	-9.5%	-0.2%
Asia-East	**199.6**	**484.5**	**838.4**	**320.0%**	**2.9%**	**4.83**	**9.705**	**19.26**	**298.8%**	**2.8%**	**7.982**	**18.66**	**25.68**	**221.7%**	**2.4%**
India	41.37	138.9	439	961.2%	4.8%	10.09	10.79	12.61	25.0%	0.4%	1.363	4.864	9.94	629.3%	4.1%
Pakistan	27.49	68.06	152.4	454.4%	3.5%	3.093	4.788	7.043	127.7%	1.7%	3.498	5.934	6.265	79.1%	1.2%
Bangladesh	9.575	59.55	176.1	1739.2%	6.0%	14.57	15.11	15.11	3.7%	0.1%	1.056	5.297	6.406	506.6%	3.7%
Iran, Islamic Rep. of	164.6	403.7	680.8	313.6%	2.9%	4.323	8.828	13.48	211.8%	2.3%	7.675	12.81	13.78	79.5%	1.2%
Afghanistan	4.735	20.44	42.65	800.7%	4.5%	0.458	1.304	2.606	469.0%	3.5%	8.726	18.68	20.45	134.4%	1.7%
Nepal	15.65	38.47	74.64	376.9%	3.2%	1.201	3.034	5.286	340.1%	3.0%	3.648	8.905	9.147	150.7%	1.9%
Uzbekistan	72.44	112.2	171.3	136.5%	1.7%	1.976	3.013	4.479	126.7%	1.7%	14.11	9.935	10.16	-28.0%	-0.7%
Sri Lanka	51.3	141	323	529.6%	3.7%	3.284	5.771	9.421	186.9%	2.1%	11.62	14.47	15.56	33.9%	0.6%
Kazakhstan	148.9	616.8	822.3	452.2%	3.5%	4.129	13.59	15.58	277.3%	2.7%	34.47	41.86	31.27	-9.3%	-0.2%
Tajikistan	41.35	66.76	114.9	177.9%	2.1%	2.022	2.598	3.34	65.2%	1.0%	18.9	21.08	22.66	19.9%	0.4%
Turkmenistan	96.45	296.8	333.4	245.7%	2.5%	0.74	4.196	6.004	711.4%	4.3%	31.21	42.97	50.64	62.3%	1.0%
Kyrgyzstan	79.45	79.45	87.05	9.6%	0.2%	1.027	1.529	2.288	122.8%	1.6%	16.71	18.19	14.67	-12.2%	-0.3%
Bhutan	29.05	133.1	622.3	2042.0%	6.3%	2.629	4.64	11.97	355.1%	3.1%	5.241	8.199	15.67	199.0%	2.2%
Maldives	104.5	246.5	795.8	661.5%	4.1%	4.844	12.8	28.57	489.8%	3.6%	18.6	22.86	32.8	76.3%	1.1%
Asia-South Central	**43.38**	**132.4**	**357.2**	**723.4%**	**4.3%**	**8.887**	**9.77**	**11.36**	**27.8%**	**0.5%**	**3.964**	**8.306**	**10.57**	**166.6%**	**2.0%**
Indonesia	41.03	123.8	264.7	545.1%	3.8%	2.067	4.039	6.73	225.6%	2.4%	8.723	11.53	13.74	57.5%	0.9%
Philippines	50.02	123.3	284.6	469.0%	3.5%	6.874	8.076	9.739	41.7%	0.7%	17.65	20.41	18.6	5.4%	0.1%
Vietnam	40.75	148.2	384.7	844.0%	4.6%	2.566	5.478	10.46	307.6%	2.9%	35.9	35.75	30.1	-16.2%	-0.4%
Thailand	110.6	281.9	596.6	439.4%	3.4%	1.772	5.776	12.86	625.7%	4.0%	23.09	25.85	27.31	18.3%	0.3%
Myanmar	11.75	54.02	146.8	1149.4%	5.2%	0.645	1.99	4.115	538.0%	3.8%	3.519	8.588	12.49	254.9%	2.6%
Malaysia	214.1	519.2	869.7	306.2%	2.8%	2.499	8.537	19.48	679.5%	4.2%	43.76	48.62	50.96	16.5%	0.3%
Cambodia	9.468	93.64	300.1	3069.6%	7.2%	2.301	4.303	7.324	218.3%	2.3%	22.19	27.76	25.18	13.5%	0.3%
Laos	13.24	81.41	274.1	1970.2%	6.2%	1.042	2.576	5.887	465.0%	3.5%	10.53	17.85	19.29	83.2%	1.2%
Singapore	574.6	848.4	869.7	51.4%	0.8%	52.43	61.43	62.44	19.1%	0.4%	104.3	105.6	87.47	-16.1%	-0.4%
Timor-Leste	50.8	64.3	113.7	123.8%	1.6%	2.165	2.997	4.347	100.8%	1.4%	5.965	12.87	12.4	107.9%	1.5%
Brunei	265.6	545.2	720.6	171.3%	2.0%	2.772	9.217	14.7	430.3%	3.4%	17.95	19.68	24.2	34.8%	0.6%
Asia-South East	**59**	**161.5**	**346.2**	**486.8%**	**3.6%**	**3.123**	**5.618**	**9.314**	**198.2%**	**2.2%**	**31.97**	**33**	**30**	**-6.2%**	**-0.1%**

Infrastructure

Base Case: Countries in Year 2055 Descending Population Sequence	Telephone Density (Lines per Thousand)					Road Density (Thousand Km/Million Hectares)					Economic Integration Index (Index)				
	2005	2030	2055	% Chg	% An Chg	2005	2030	2055	% Chg	% An Chg	2005	2030	2055	% Chg	% An Chg
ASIA INCL OCEANIA continued															
Turkey	307.3	475.7	869.7	183.0%	2.1%	5.473	8.891	17.7	223.4%	2.4%	6.102	11.13	20.4	234.3%	2.4%
Yemen	21.28	55.76	133.2	525.9%	3.7%	1.338	2.411	4.094	206.0%	2.3%	13.57	8.365	7.141	-47.4%	-1.3%
Iraq	36.27	125.4	314.3	766.6%	4.4%	1.268	3.534	7.54	494.6%	3.6%	15.34	22.65	13.23	-13.8%	-0.3%
Saudi Arabia	164.2	480.7	869.7	429.7%	3.4%	1.37	7.632	22.09	1512.4%	5.7%	11.13	14.34	23.68	112.8%	1.5%
Syria	105	157.7	311.9	197.0%	2.2%	2.956	4.661	8.183	176.8%	2.1%	9.184	11.38	13.02	41.8%	0.7%
Israel	494.8	854	869.7	75.8%	1.1%	8.531	21.33	44.48	421.4%	3.4%	17.25	28.91	46.22	167.9%	2.0%
Azerbaijan	127.2	261.3	398	212.9%	2.3%	3.561	6.017	8.93	150.8%	1.9%	40.62	36.6	34.06	-16.1%	-0.4%
Jordan	135.2	297.5	869.7	543.3%	3.8%	1.163	4.675	20.2	1636.9%	5.9%	21.94	22.21	30.8	40.4%	0.7%
Palestine	81.79	127.4	282.8	245.8%	2.5%	7.859	41.95	84.64	977.0%	4.9%	5.231	8.208	10.25	95.9%	1.4%
Oman	114.6	379.5	757.9	561.3%	3.9%	1.622	6.766	14.27	779.8%	4.4%	20.05	16.26	18.96	-5.4%	-0.1%
Lebanon	209.4	450.4	869.7	315.3%	2.9%	7.355	11.66	23.31	216.9%	2.3%	4.792	9.795	23.32	386.6%	3.2%
United Arab Emirates	445.2	781.7	869.7	95.4%	1.3%	1.51	14.35	30.59	1925.8%	6.2%	15.31	34.13	42.14	175.2%	2.0%
Kuwait	308.2	725.4	869.7	182.2%	2.1%	3.837	14.07	29.91	679.5%	4.2%	13.23	27.34	34.99	164.5%	2.0%
Georgia	158.1	197.6	230.7	45.9%	0.8%	3.092	3.722	5.073	64.1%	1.0%	12.62	13.61	13.63	8.0%	0.2%
Armenia	187.3	324.6	391.9	109.2%	1.5%	2.813	5.305	8.71	209.6%	2.3%	15.07	16.23	18.3	21.4%	0.4%
Bahrain	298	744.1	869.7	191.8%	2.2%	46	50.68	50.68	10.2%	0.2%	17.96	26.68	39.11	117.8%	1.6%
Qatar	310.1	712.6	869.7	180.5%	2.1%	2.321	13.68	22.57	872.4%	4.7%	19.43	48.78	60.28	210.2%	2.3%
Cyprus	664.5	917.6	988.5	48.8%	0.8%	12.31	17.22	25.5	107.1%	1.5%	29.09	36.01	41.78	43.6%	0.7%
Asia-West	**195**	**332.6**	**565.9**	**190.2%**	**2.2%**	**3.75**	**7.778**	**15.97**	**325.9%**	**2.9%**	**12.14**	**18.61**	**25.02**	**106.1%**	**1.5%**
Australia	561.2	847.8	869.7	55.0%	0.9%	2.3	13.26	35.11	1426.5%	5.6%	19.16	30.64	40.69	112.4%	1.5%
Papua New Guinea	18.36	69.19	178.4	871.7%	4.7%	0.55	1.664	3.825	595.5%	4.0%	35.22	38.15	24.19	-31.3%	-0.7%
New Zealand	518.5	821	897.5	73.1%	1.1%	4.314	11.49	32.2	646.4%	4.1%	42.14	48.37	49.89	18.4%	0.3%
Solomon Islands	23.61	61.38	157.1	565.4%	3.9%	0.621	1.57	3.6	479.7%	3.6%	29.24	28.8	21.8	-25.4%	-0.6%
Fiji	112.3	208.1	468	316.7%	2.9%	2.071	4.2	9.444	356.0%	3.1%	29.45	33.22	32.38	9.9%	0.2%
Vanuatu	39.77	98.59	256.7	545.5%	3.8%	1.023	2.329	5.42	429.8%	3.4%	52.94	50.26	34.94	-34.0%	-0.8%
Micronesia	87.32	138.7	253.5	190.3%	2.2%	0.717	2.5	5.42	655.9%	4.1%	8.189	9.479	12.9	57.5%	0.9%
Samoa	61.41	155	434.9	608.2%	4.0%	3.677	5.069	9.176	149.6%	1.8%	15.91	17.81	20.88	31.2%	0.5%
Tonga	103.9	140.5	215.1	107.0%	1.5%	9.067	9.067	9.067	0.0%	0.0%	5.86	7.225	8.247	40.7%	0.7%
Oceania	**426.4**	**622.6**	**655.2**	**53.7%**	**0.9%**	**2.216**	**9.805**	**24.82**	**1020.0%**	**5.0%**	**22.01**	**32.7**	**41.48**	**88.5%**	**1.3%**

Infrastructure

Base Case: Countries in Year 2055 Descending Population Sequence	Telephone Density (Lines per Thousand)					Road Density (Thousand Km/Million Hectares)					Economic Integration Index (Index)				
	2005	2030	2055	% Chg	% An Chg	2005	2030	2055	% Chg	% An Chg	2005	2030	2055	% Chg	% An Chg
EUROPE															
Russia	254.6	545.2	664.1	160.8%	1.9%	0.782	5.954	12.34	1478.0%	5.7%	16.69	24.91	19.18	14.9%	0.3%
Poland	300.4	482.8	797.4	165.4%	2.0%	12.19	13.72	16.11	32.2%	0.6%	12.33	17.12	21.55	74.8%	1.1%
Ukraine	239	398	604.2	152.8%	1.9%	3.134	5.987	11.97	281.9%	2.7%	16.05	19.61	26.24	63.5%	1.0%
Romania	199.4	301.5	429.9	115.6%	1.5%	8.494	8.901	9.029	6.3%	0.1%	12.88	14.63	15.56	20.8%	0.4%
Belarus	310.9	545.3	869.7	179.7%	2.1%	4.07	8.005	20.32	399.3%	3.3%	16.36	19.08	29.79	82.1%	1.2%
Czech Republic	412.9	548.8	795.1	92.6%	1.3%	10.58	12.23	15.6	47.4%	0.8%	25.85	29.37	30.94	19.7%	0.4%
Hungary	416.5	577.3	797.6	91.5%	1.3%	17.4	17.65	17.65	1.4%	0.0%	29.35	33.85	33.68	14.8%	0.3%
Bulgaria	384.4	492	619.6	61.2%	1.0%	4.569	7.008	12.19	166.8%	2.0%	20.6	22.12	25.58	24.2%	0.4%
Slovak Republic	351.6	461.9	674.2	91.8%	1.3%	7.268	9.536	13.78	89.6%	1.3%	20.78	24.52	27.04	30.1%	0.5%
Moldova	145.7	158.7	210.5	44.5%	0.7%	3.79	3.79	5.259	38.8%	0.7%	20.82	21.16	18.51	-11.1%	-0.2%
Europe-East	**270.3**	**490.5**	**667.1**	**146.8%**	**1.8%**	**4.461**	**7.993**	**13.09**	**193.4%**	**2.2%**	**17.23**	**23.13**	**22.32**	**29.5%**	**0.5%**
United Kingdom	625.6	875.1	875.1	39.9%	0.7%	16.58	24.21	38.15	130.1%	1.7%	55.34	62.68	56.15	1.5%	0.0%
Sweden	779.4	1026	1026	31.6%	0.6%	14.54	26.07	41.4	184.7%	2.1%	55.92	64.79	62.88	12.4%	0.2%
Denmark	726.5	944.9	944.9	30.1%	0.5%	16.6	24.57	41.1	147.6%	1.8%	40.41	49.04	55.34	36.9%	0.6%
Norway	795.8	864.9	869.7	9.3%	0.2%	4.473	16.54	38.06	750.9%	4.4%	29.38	39.03	47.98	63.3%	1.0%
Ireland	531.7	759	869.7	63.6%	1.0%	15.94	25.82	30.46	91.1%	1.3%	50.97	62.64	60.54	18.8%	0.3%
Finland	594	859.3	869.7	46.4%	0.8%	3.562	12.72	34.34	864.1%	4.6%	37.63	44.99	47.7	26.8%	0.5%
Lithuania	385.2	623.7	901.4	134.0%	1.7%	12.62	15.82	22.57	78.8%	1.2%	17.81	22	31.34	76.0%	1.1%
Latvia	377.2	700	938.2	148.7%	1.8%	6.195	11.95	23.02	271.6%	2.7%	19.37	24.4	33.64	73.7%	1.1%
Estonia	451.9	874.9	1027	127.3%	1.7%	13.11	20.52	31.71	141.9%	1.8%	33	37.23	49.65	50.5%	0.8%
Iceland	793	930.8	930.8	17.4%	0.3%	2.884	15.26	38.89	1248.5%	5.3%	11.9	25.29	43.58	266.2%	2.6%
Europe-North	**631.5**	**873.7**	**894.9**	**41.7%**	**0.7%**	**14.6**	**22.86**	**37.15**	**154.5%**	**1.9%**	**50.69**	**58.66**	**55.29**	**9.1%**	**0.2%**
Italy	487	662.5	869.7	78.6%	1.2%	15.92	16.79	20.97	31.7%	0.6%	9.903	17.73	22.97	131.9%	1.7%
Spain	472.2	788.1	869.7	84.2%	1.2%	13.77	18.16	24.95	81.2%	1.2%	24.25	32.14	34.14	40.8%	0.7%
Greece	585.7	846	949.1	62.0%	1.0%	9.751	15.08	27.62	183.3%	2.1%	10.67	19.17	31.27	193.1%	2.2%
Portugal	437.7	611.2	872.1	99.2%	1.4%	7.738	11.69	21.73	180.8%	2.1%	21.66	26.56	29.85	37.8%	0.6%
Serbia and Montenegro	240.9	256.4	393.8	63.5%	1.0%	4.46	4.565	8.317	86.5%	1.3%	7.626	9.706	13.86	81.7%	1.2%
Croatia	421.3	551.5	869.7	106.4%	1.5%	5.556	8.731	20.53	269.5%	2.6%	18.05	22.01	31.02	71.9%	1.1%
Bosnia and Herzegovina	118	187.3	336.4	185.1%	2.1%	4.544	5.298	7.239	59.3%	0.9%	11.14	13.04	15.35	37.8%	0.6%
Albania	52.19	152.3	356.3	582.7%	3.9%	6.415	7.129	8.159	27.2%	0.5%	10.09	12.64	15.09	49.6%	0.8%
Macedonia	250.7	250.7	326.7	30.3%	0.5%	3.564	4.579	7.223	102.7%	1.4%	12.49	13.84	14.81	18.6%	0.3%
Slovenia	434.3	654.8	875.5	101.6%	1.4%	10.03	13.76	24.93	148.6%	1.8%	12.76	19.97	31.77	149.0%	1.8%
Malta	529.1	705.3	905.1	71.1%	1.1%	10.61	17.78	31.47	196.6%	2.2%	16.96	23.56	36.18	113.3%	1.5%
Europe-South	**446.9**	**650.8**	**809.6**	**81.2%**	**1.2%**	**12.47**	**14.94**	**21.06**	**68.9%**	**1.1%**	**15.26**	**23.73**	**28.5**	**86.8%**	**1.3%**
Germany	614.3	905.4	905.4	47.4%	0.8%	13.56	19.49	36.34	168.0%	2.0%	22.64	31.12	41.29	82.4%	1.2%
France	593.3	875	875	47.5%	0.8%	16.2	20.95	34.98	115.9%	1.6%	28.01	36.15	42.34	51.2%	0.8%
Netherlands	618.6	866.2	869.7	40.6%	0.7%	28.05	28.05	33.57	19.7%	0.4%	78.3	80.7	63.83	-18.5%	-0.4%
Belgium	545.8	658.7	869.7	59.3%	0.9%	48.22	48.22	48.22	0.0%	0.0%	91.46	89.67	67.13	-26.6%	-0.6%
Austria	510.3	788.3	869.7	70.4%	1.1%	16.06	21.14	30.64	90.8%	1.3%	18.76	29.3	38.71	106.3%	1.5%
Switzerland	750.1	906.4	906.4	20.8%	0.4%	17.52	23.96	36.38	107.6%	1.5%	48.81	57.13	53.68	10.0%	0.2%
Luxembourg	768.6	826	869.7	13.2%	0.2%	21.86	32.3	35.67	63.2%	1.0%	29.26	53.22	65.22	122.9%	1.6%
Europe-West	**605.2**	**872.7**	**887.8**	**46.7%**	**0.8%**	**17.92**	**22.67**	**36.05**	**101.2%**	**1.4%**	**34.38**	**41.17**	**45.03**	**31.0%**	**0.5%**

Infrastructure

Base Case
Source: International Futures
Version 5.47 March 2008

	R&D Expenditures (Percent of GDP)					Energy Demand Ratio to GDP (Barrels of Oil Equivalent/Thousand $)					Annual Carbon Emissions (Billion Tons)				
	2005	2030	2055	% Chg	% An Chg	2005	2030	2055	% Chg	% An Chg	2005	2030	2055	% Chg	% An Chg
World	2.169	2.534	2.943	35.7%	0.6%	2.07	1.444	0.796	-61.5%	-1.9%	7.513	12.05	9.154	21.8%	0.4%
Africa	0.41	0.643	1.326	223.4%	2.4%	4.357	2.961	1.391	-68.1%	-2.3%	0.348	0.71	0.935	168.7%	2.0%
Americas	2.501	2.733	2.855	14.2%	0.3%	1.801	1.222	0.709	-60.6%	-1.8%	2.467	3.462	2.71	9.9%	0.2%
Asia incl Oceania	2.067	2.37	3.09	49.5%	0.8%	2.541	1.649	0.83	-67.3%	-2.2%	3.152	6.196	4.397	39.5%	0.7%
Europe	1.94	2.795	3.067	58.1%	0.9%	1.749	1.178	0.659	-62.3%	-1.9%	1.546	1.683	1.113	-28.0%	-0.7%
World	2.169	2.534	2.943	35.7%	0.6%	2.07	1.444	0.796	-61.5%	-1.9%	7.513	12.05	9.154	21.8%	0.4%
Africa-Eastern	0.219	0.39	0.906	313.7%	2.9%	3.882	3.137	1.253	-67.7%	-2.2%	0.032	0.107	0.239	646.9%	4.1%
Africa-Middle	0.135	0.273	0.307	127.4%	1.7%	5.329	4.477	3.244	-39.1%	-1.0%	0.026	0.061	0.078	200.0%	2.2%
Africa-Northern	0.38	0.753	1.623	327.1%	2.9%	4.117	2.507	1.169	-71.6%	-2.5%	0.131	0.255	0.249	90.1%	1.3%
Africa-Southern	0.796	1.134	2.34	194.0%	2.2%	4.433	2.669	1.102	-75.1%	-2.7%	0.105	0.141	0.2	90.5%	1.3%
Africa-Western	0.119	0.195	0.334	180.7%	2.1%	4.923	3.871	2.376	-51.7%	-1.4%	0.054	0.145	0.169	213.0%	2.3%
Africa	0.41	0.643	1.326	223.4%	2.4%	4.357	2.961	1.391	-68.1%	-2.3%	0.348	0.71	0.935	168.7%	2.0%
America-Caribbean	0.746	1.83	2.563	243.6%	2.5%	2.184	1.273	0.615	-71.8%	-2.5%	0.036	0.059	0.061	69.4%	1.1%
America-Central	0.252	0.897	2.011	698.0%	4.2%	2.331	1.679	0.897	-61.5%	-1.9%	0.018	0.045	0.061	238.9%	2.5%
America-North	2.757	3.018	3.046	10.5%	0.2%	1.712	1.14	0.661	-61.4%	-1.9%	2.096	2.761	2.013	-4.0%	-0.1%
America-South	0.702	1.362	2.295	226.8%	2.4%	2.464	1.647	0.873	-64.6%	-2.1%	0.318	0.598	0.574	80.5%	1.2%
Americas	2.501	2.733	2.855	14.2%	0.3%	1.801	1.222	0.709	-60.6%	-1.8%	2.467	3.462	2.71	9.9%	0.2%
Asia-East	2.496	2.797	3.701	48.3%	0.8%	1.905	1.263	0.634	-66.7%	-2.2%	1.667	3.083	1.4	-16.0%	-0.3%
Asia-South Central	0.726	1.198	2.073	185.5%	2.1%	5.253	2.837	1.162	-77.9%	-3.0%	0.579	1.545	1.621	180.0%	2.1%
Asia-South East	0.525	1.008	1.645	213.3%	2.3%	3.693	2.306	1.209	-67.3%	-2.2%	0.316	0.593	0.394	24.7%	0.4%
Asia-West	1.442	2.228	3.105	115.3%	1.5%	3.866	2.001	0.93	-75.9%	-2.8%	0.4	0.733	0.759	89.8%	1.3%
Oceania	1.623	2.665	2.718	67.5%	1.0%	2.84	1.533	0.77	-72.9%	-2.6%	0.19	0.241	0.223	17.4%	0.3%
Asia incl Oceania	2.067	2.37	3.09	49.5%	0.8%	2.541	1.649	0.83	-67.3%	-2.2%	3.152	6.196	4.397	39.5%	0.7%
Europe-East	0.999	1.898	2.787	179.0%	2.1%	5.495	2.435	1.112	-79.8%	-3.1%	0.457	0.608	0.385	-15.8%	-0.3%
Europe-North	2.274	3.117	3.149	38.5%	0.7%	1.476	0.957	0.548	-62.9%	-2.0%	0.319	0.291	0.147	-53.9%	-1.5%
Europe-South	1.071	1.918	2.483	131.8%	1.7%	1.363	1.019	0.686	-49.7%	-1.4%	0.266	0.296	0.24	-9.8%	-0.2%
Europe-West	2.336	3.322	3.351	43.5%	0.7%	1.4	0.943	0.543	-61.2%	-1.9%	0.505	0.488	0.341	-32.5%	-0.8%
Europe	1.94	2.795	3.067	58.1%	0.9%	1.749	1.178	0.659	-62.3%	-1.9%	1.546	1.683	1.113	-28.0%	-0.7%

Multination Regional Analysis

Measures of Poverty, Health, Education, Infrastructure and Governance

Infrastructure

Base Case: Countries in Year 2055 Descending Population Sequence	R&D Expenditures (Percent of GDP)					Energy Demand Ratio to GDP (Barrels of Oil Equivalent/Thousand $)					Annual Carbon Emissions (Billion Tons)				
	2005	2030	2055	% Chg	% An Chg	2005	2030	2055	% Chg	% An Chg	2005	2030	2055	% Chg	% An Chg
AFRICA															
Ethiopia	0.091	0.134	0.321	252.7%	2.6%	6.225	5.676	2.209	-64.5%	-2.1%	0.006	0.018	0.032	433.3%	3.4%
Tanzania	0.071	0.171	0.704	891.5%	4.7%	2.222	2.037	0.914	-58.9%	-1.8%	0.003	0.014	0.047	1466.7%	5.7%
Uganda	0.732	0.835	1.522	107.9%	1.5%	4.751	3.339	1.185	-75.1%	-2.7%	0.004	0.019	0.047	1075.0%	5.1%
Kenya	0.107	0.212	0.8	647.7%	4.1%	2.941	2.472	1.026	-65.1%	-2.1%	0.004	0.017	0.047	1075.0%	5.1%
Madagascar	0.126	0.16	0.282	123.8%	1.6%	3.74	3.948	1.963	-47.5%	-1.3%	0.002	0.006	0.01	400.0%	3.3%
Mozambique	0.596	0.726	1.132	89.9%	1.3%	3.436	2.485	1.184	-65.5%	-2.1%	0.001	0.009	0.017	1600.0%	5.8%
Malawi	0.068	0.095	0.233	242.6%	2.5%	4.533	4.588	1.985	-56.2%	-1.6%	0.001	0.003	0.006	500.0%	3.6%
Zambia	0.019	0.067	0.292	1436.8%	5.6%	3.47	3.302	1.483	-57.3%	-1.7%	0.001	0.003	0.007	600.0%	4.0%
Zimbabwe	0.224	0.299	0.729	225.4%	2.4%	5.203	4.007	1.538	-70.4%	-2.4%	0.005	0.009	0.013	160.0%	1.9%
Burundi	0.304	0.312	0.392	28.9%	0.5%	6.923	6.433	2.685	-61.2%	-1.9%	0.001	0.002	0.003	200.0%	2.2%
Rwanda	0.049	0.107	0.314	540.8%	3.8%	4.169	3.947	1.775	-57.4%	-1.7%	0.001	0.003	0.006	500.0%	3.6%
Somalia	0.06	0.092	0.12	100.0%	1.4%	9.735	8.897	6.842	-29.7%	-0.7%	0	0.002	0.002		
Eritrea	0.098	0.091	0.11	12.2%	0.2%	6.626	7.705	3.942	-40.5%	-1.0%	0.001	0.001	0.001	0.0%	0.0%
Mauritius	0.386	1.078	1.828	373.6%	3.2%	1.809	1.404	0.899	-50.3%	-1.4%	0.001	0.002	0.002	100.0%	1.4%
Comoros	0.156	0.188	0.33	111.5%	1.5%	4.687	4.734	2.22	-52.6%	-1.5%	0	0	0		
Djibouti	0.177	0.195	0.296	67.2%	1.0%	4.345	3.668	1.863	-57.1%	-1.7%	0	0	0		
Africa-Eastern	**0.219**	**0.39**	**0.906**	**313.7%**	**2.9%**	**3.882**	**3.137**	**1.253**	**-67.7%**	**-2.2%**	**0.032**	**0.107**	**0.239**	**646.9%**	**4.1%**
Congo, Dem. Rep. of the	0.068	0.098	0.196	188.2%	2.1%	7.137	7.103	4.109	-42.4%	-1.1%	0.004	0.015	0.04	900.0%	4.7%
Angola	0.157	0.25	0.315	100.6%	1.4%	5.282	3.867	2.782	-47.3%	-1.3%	0.008	0.017	0.015	87.5%	1.3%
Cameroon	0.177	0.188	0.267	50.8%	0.8%	2.987	3.763	2.936	-1.7%	-0.0%	0.004	0.006	0.009	125.0%	1.6%
Chad	0.098	0.188	0.238	142.9%	1.8%	12.19	6.459	4.11	-66.3%	-2.2%	0.003	0.007	0.002	-33.3%	-0.8%
Central African Republic	0.243	0.233	0.274	12.8%	0.2%	5.108	6.075	3.088	-39.5%	-1.0%	0.001	0.001	0.001	0.0%	0.0%
Congo, Rep. of	0.027	0.143	0.316	1070.4%	5.0%	6.053	4.292	2.368	-60.9%	-1.9%	0.003	0.006	0.005	66.7%	1.0%
Gabon	0.012	0.44	0.713	5841.7%	8.5%	4.975	2.604	1.487	-70.1%	-2.4%	0.003	0.005	0.004	33.3%	0.6%
Equatorial Guinea	0.482	1.022	0.992	105.8%	1.5%	7.308	3.105	1.926	-73.6%	-2.6%	0.002	0.003	0.001	-50.0%	-1.4%
São Tomé and Príncipe	0.167	0.162	0.175	4.8%	0.1%	6.989	6.494	3.465	-50.4%	-1.4%	0	0	0		
Africa-Middle	**0.135**	**0.273**	**0.307**	**127.4%**	**1.7%**	**5.329**	**4.477**	**3.244**	**-39.1%**	**-1.0%**	**0.026**	**0.061**	**0.078**	**200.0%**	**2.2%**
Egypt	0.214	0.507	1.584	640.2%	4.1%	3.244	2.178	1.029	-68.3%	-2.3%	0.036	0.079	0.103	186.1%	2.1%
Sudan	0.488	0.64	0.888	82.0%	1.2%	4.16	3.037	1.928	-53.7%	-1.5%	0.008	0.027	0.039	387.5%	3.2%
Algeria	0.49	0.835	1.294	164.1%	2.0%	6.212	3.211	1.56	-74.9%	-2.7%	0.042	0.062	0.019	-54.8%	-1.6%
Morocco	0.635	0.777	1.303	105.2%	1.4%	2.718	2.47	1.17	-57.0%	-1.7%	0.012	0.025	0.033	175.0%	2.0%
Tunisia	0.507	1.173	2.752	442.8%	3.4%	2.885	1.729	0.862	-70.1%	-2.4%	0.007	0.019	0.025	257.1%	2.6%
Libya	0.309	1.13	2.07	569.9%	3.9%	5.136	2.711	1.218	-76.3%	-2.8%	0.025	0.044	0.03	20.0%	0.4%
Africa-Northern	**0.38**	**0.753**	**1.623**	**327.1%**	**2.9%**	**4.117**	**2.507**	**1.169**	**-71.6%**	**-2.5%**	**0.131**	**0.255**	**0.249**	**90.1%**	**1.3%**

Infrastructure

Base Case: Countries in Year 2055 Descending Population Sequence	R&D Expenditures (Percent of GDP)					Energy Demand Ratio to GDP (Barrels of Oil Equivalent/Thousand $)					Annual Carbon Emissions (Billion Tons)				
	2005	2030	2055	% Chg	% An Chg	2005	2030	2055	% Chg	% An Chg	2005	2030	2055	% Chg	% An Chg
AFRICA continued															
South Africa	0.815	1.096	2.248	175.8%	2.0%	4.636	2.856	1.144	-75.3%	-2.8%	0.102	0.133	0.185	81.4%	1.2%
Namibia	0.511	0.858	2.875	462.6%	3.5%	2.888	2.139	0.906	-68.6%	-2.3%	0.001	0.003	0.008	700.0%	4.2%
Lesotho	0.013	0.064	0.347	2569.2%	6.8%	4.75	4.922	2.611	-45.0%	-1.2%	0.001	0.001	0.001	0.0%	0.0%
Botswana	0.745	1.748	3.188	327.9%	3.0%	1.446	1.084	0.713	-50.7%	-1.4%	0.001	0.003	0.004	300.0%	2.8%
Swaziland	0.335	0.559	1.372	309.6%	2.9%	2.586	2.274	1.158	-55.2%	-1.6%	0	0.001	0.003		
Africa-Southern	**0.796**	**1.134**	**2.34**	**194.0%**	**2.2%**	**4.433**	**2.669**	**1.102**	**-75.1%**	**-2.7%**	**0.105**	**0.141**	**0.2**	**90.5%**	**1.3%**
Nigeria	0.101	0.188	0.263	160.4%	1.9%	5.434	3.843	2.879	-47.0%	-1.3%	0.035	0.093	0.091	160.0%	1.9%
Niger	0.074	0.093	0.176	137.8%	1.7%	5.063	5.345	2.497	-50.7%	-1.4%	0.001	0.004	0.007	600.0%	4.0%
Ghana	0.184	0.189	0.291	58.2%	0.9%	6.195	6.871	3.196	-48.4%	-1.3%	0.004	0.008	0.01	150.0%	1.8%
Côte d'Ivoire	0.142	0.234	0.446	214.1%	2.3%	2.999	2.697	1.472	-50.9%	-1.4%	0.003	0.01	0.015	400.0%	3.3%
Mali	0.087	0.134	0.264	203.4%	2.2%	3.96	3.889	1.963	-50.4%	-1.4%	0.001	0.004	0.007	600.0%	4.0%
Burkina Faso	0.175	0.216	0.398	127.4%	1.7%	4.439	4.254	1.891	-57.4%	-1.7%	0.002	0.005	0.009	350.0%	3.1%
Senegal	0.032	0.123	0.357	1015.6%	4.9%	3.68	3.198	1.582	-57.0%	-1.7%	0.002	0.006	0.01	400.0%	3.3%
Guinea	0.179	0.246	0.369	106.1%	1.5%	4.93	4.543	2.353	-52.3%	-1.5%	0.002	0.005	0.005	150.0%	1.8%
Benin	0.102	0.142	0.321	214.7%	2.3%	3.547	3.611	1.701	-52.0%	-1.5%	0.001	0.003	0.005	400.0%	3.3%
Togo	0.473	0.458	0.464	-1.9%	-0.0%	5.767	6.232	3.398	-41.1%	-1.1%	0.001	0.002	0.002	100.0%	1.4%
Liberia	0.092	0.098	0.15	63.0%	1.0%	5.537	6.317	3.031	-45.3%	-1.2%	0	0.001	0.001		
Sierra Leone	0.067	0.118	0.217	223.9%	2.4%	2.371	3.107	1.913	-19.3%	-0.4%	0	0.001	0.002		
Mauritania	0.175	0.214	0.301	72.0%	1.1%	4.817	4.526	2.425	-49.7%	-1.4%	0.001	0.002	0.002	100.0%	1.4%
Guinea-Bissau	0.084	0.083	0.1	19.0%	0.3%	6.432	7.361	3.985	-38.0%	-1.0%	0	0	0		
Gambia	0.155	0.219	0.401	158.7%	1.9%	4.838	4.423	2.087	-56.9%	-1.7%	0	0.001	0.001		
Cape Verde	0.395	0.807	1.841	366.1%	3.1%	2.942	2.164	1.023	-65.2%	-2.1%	0	0.001	0.001		
Africa-Western	**0.119**	**0.195**	**0.334**	**180.7%**	**2.1%**	**4.923**	**3.871**	**2.376**	**-51.7%**	**-1.4%**	**0.054**	**0.145**	**0.169**	**213.0%**	**2.3%**

Infrastructure

Base Case: Countries in Year 2055 Descending Population Sequence	R&D Expenditures (Percent of GDP)					Energy Demand Ratio to GDP (Barrels of Oil Equivalent/Thousand $)					Annual Carbon Emissions (Billion Tons)				
	2005	2030	2055	% Chg	% An Chg	2005	2030	2055	% Chg	% An Chg	2005	2030	2055	% Chg	% An Chg
AMERICAS continued															
Haiti	0.14	0.155	0.247	76.4%	1.1%	3.594	4.173	2.262	-37.1%	-0.9%	0.001	0.003	0.003	200.0%	2.2%
Dominican Republic	0.601	1.164	1.842	206.5%	2.3%	3.133	1.901	0.984	-68.6%	-2.3%	0.008	0.018	0.017	112.5%	1.5%
Cuba	0.543	0.843	2.231	310.9%	2.9%	3.068	1.403	0.535	-82.6%	-3.4%	0.01	0.012	0.016	60.0%	0.9%
Puerto Rico	0.995	2.649	3.187	220.3%	2.4%	0.916	0.66	0.411	-55.1%	-1.6%	0.006	0.014	0.018	200.0%	2.2%
Jamaica	0.094	0.367	1.575	1575.5%	5.8%	3.597	1.803	0.801	-77.7%	-3.0%	0.003	0.003	0.005	66.7%	1.0%
Trinidad and Tobago	0.336	1.926	2.448	628.6%	4.1%	5.408	2.388	1.146	-78.8%	-3.1%	0.006	0.008	0.002	-66.7%	-2.2%
Bahamas	1.395	1.85	2.993	114.6%	1.5%	0.592	0.715	0.59	-0.3%	-0.0%	0.001	0.001	0.001		
Barbados	1.249	2.06	3.188	155.2%	1.9%	0.951	0.874	0.618	-35.0%	-0.9%	0	0.001	0.001		
Grenada	0.603	0.918	2.281	278.3%	2.7%	1.371	1.356	0.795	-42.0%	-1.1%	0	0	0		
St. Vincent & the Grenadines	0.177	0.446	1.361	668.9%	4.2%	1.457	1.48	0.847	-41.9%	-1.1%	0	0	0		
St. Lucia	0.426	1.083	3.094	626.3%	4.0%	1.017	0.93	0.659	-35.2%	-0.9%	0	0	0		
America-Caribbean	**0.746**	**1.83**	**2.563**	**243.6%**	**2.5%**	**2.184**	**1.273**	**0.615**	**-71.8%**	**-2.5%**	**0.036**	**0.059**	**0.061**	**69.4%**	**1.1%**
Guatemala	0.161	0.359	0.844	424.2%	3.4%	2.119	2.01	1.105	-47.9%	-1.3%	0.005	0.014	0.021	320.0%	2.9%
Honduras	0.067	0.174	0.487	626.9%	4.0%	3.497	3.016	1.463	-58.2%	-1.7%	0.002	0.005	0.007	250.0%	2.5%
Nicaragua	0.052	0.135	0.378	626.9%	4.0%	4.021	3.646	1.787	-55.6%	-1.6%	0.002	0.004	0.005	150.0%	1.8%
El Salvador	0.088	0.407	1.187	1248.9%	5.3%	2.445	1.847	0.916	-62.5%	-1.9%	0.003	0.007	0.007	133.3%	1.7%
Costa Rica	0.441	1.405	2.947	568.3%	3.9%	1.666	1.113	0.669	-59.8%	-1.8%	0.002	0.005	0.007	250.0%	2.5%
Panama	0.437	1.447	3.089	606.9%	4.0%	2.378	1.285	0.703	-70.4%	-2.4%	0.003	0.008	0.013	333.3%	3.0%
Belize	0.52	1.336	3.187	512.9%	3.7%	1.628	1.116	0.716	-56.0%	-1.6%	0.001	0.001	0.001		
America-Central	**0.252**	**0.897**	**2.011**	**698.0%**	**4.2%**	**2.331**	**1.679**	**0.897**	**-61.5%**	**-1.9%**	**0.018**	**0.045**	**0.061**	**238.9%**	**2.5%**
United States	2.945	3.171	3.173	7.7%	0.1%	1.6	1.078	0.631	-60.6%	-1.8%	1.757	2.318	1.73	-1.5%	-0.0%
Mexico	0.39	0.85	1.602	310.8%	2.9%	1.987	1.446	0.897	-54.9%	-1.6%	0.13	0.217	0.176	35.4%	0.6%
Canada	2.06	2.956	2.972	44.3%	0.7%	3.032	1.653	0.771	-74.6%	-2.7%	0.209	0.225	0.108	-48.3%	-1.3%
America-North	**2.757**	**3.018**	**3.046**	**10.5%**	**0.2%**	**1.712**	**1.14**	**0.661**	**-61.4%**	**-1.9%**	**2.096**	**2.761**	**2.013**	**-4.0%**	**-0.1%**
Brazil	0.996	1.316	2.153	116.2%	1.6%	2.32	1.747	0.887	-61.8%	-1.9%	0.11	0.223	0.264	140.0%	1.8%
Colombia	0.205	0.576	1.595	678.0%	4.2%	3.93	2.473	1.136	-71.1%	-2.5%	0.045	0.077	0.042	-6.7%	-0.1%
Argentina	0.609	1.815	2.725	347.5%	3.0%	1.609	1.067	0.66	-59.0%	-1.8%	0.05	0.082	0.07	40.0%	0.7%
Peru	0.149	0.519	1.186	696.0%	4.2%	2.112	1.686	0.936	-55.7%	-1.6%	0.011	0.025	0.028	154.5%	1.9%
Venezuela	0.449	1.248	2.697	500.7%	3.7%	4.231	2.234	1.017	-76.0%	-2.8%	0.067	0.124	0.093	38.8%	0.7%
Chile	0.612	1.73	3.002	390.5%	3.2%	1.815	1.115	0.707	-61.0%	-1.9%	0.014	0.033	0.044	214.3%	2.3%
Ecuador	0.104	0.26	0.443	326.0%	2.9%	7.022	4.291	2.278	-67.6%	-2.2%	0.015	0.016	0.004	-73.3%	-2.6%
Bolivia	0.296	0.524	1.305	340.9%	3.0%	2.865	2.113	1.069	-62.7%	-2.0%	0.002	0.007	0.018	800.0%	4.5%
Paraguay	0.098	0.233	0.715	629.6%	4.1%	3.904	3.162	1.607	-58.8%	-1.8%	0.003	0.003	0.003		
Uruguay	0.356	1.369	2.777	680.1%	4.2%	1.217	0.95	0.671	-44.9%	-1.2%	0.003	0.006	0.008	166.7%	2.0%
Guyana	0.243	0.39	0.67	175.7%	2.0%	4.473	3.443	1.685	-62.3%	-1.9%	0	0	0		
Suriname	0.527	0.853	1.801	241.7%	2.5%	3.817	2.251	0.964	-74.7%	-2.7%	0.001	0.001	0.001		
America-South	**0.702**	**1.362**	**2.295**	**226.9%**	**2.4%**	**2.464**	**1.647**	**0.873**	**-64.6%**	**-2.1%**	**0.318**	**0.598**	**0.574**	**80.5%**	**1.2%**

Infrastructure

Base Case: Countries in Year 2055 Descending Population Sequence	R&D Expenditures (Percent of GDP)					Energy Demand Ratio to GDP (Barrels of Oil Equivalent/Thousand $)					Annual Carbon Emissions (Billion Tons)				
	2005	2030	2055	% Chg	% An Chg	2005	2030	2055	% Chg	% An Chg	2005	2030	2055	% Chg	% An Chg
ASIA INCL OCEANIA															
China	1.091	2.115	3.663	235.7%	2.5%	4.458	1.509	0.658	-85.2%	-3.8%	1.033	2.317	0.863	-16.5%	-0.4%
Japan	3.156	4.023	3.966	25.7%	0.5%	0.834	0.683	0.448	-46.3%	-1.2%	0.351	0.369	0.256	-27.1%	-0.6%
Korea, Rep. of	2.532	4.196	4.127	63.0%	1.0%	2.307	1.204	0.682	-70.4%	-2.4%	0.129	0.214	0.166	28.7%	0.5%
Taiwan	1.834	2.766	3.187	73.8%	1.1%	2.02	1.237	0.717	-64.5%	-2.1%	0.072	0.092	0.073	1.4%	0.0%
Korea, Dem. Rep. of	0.115	0.22	0.521	353.0%	3.1%	18.6	11.4	3.658	-80.3%	-3.2%	0.063	0.063	0.018	-71.4%	-2.5%
Hong Kong	0.82	1.7	1.801	119.6%	1.6%	0.897	0.711	0.489	-45.5%	-1.2%	0.018	0.026	0.019	5.6%	0.1%
Mongolia	0.241	0.345	0.643	166.8%	2.0%	7.087	4.533	2.15	-69.7%	-2.4%	0.001	0.002	0.004	300.0%	2.8%
Asia-East	**2.496**	**2.797**	**3.701**	**48.3%**	**0.8%**	**1.905**	**1.263**	**0.634**	**-66.7%**	**-2.2%**	**1.667**	**3.083**	**1.4**	**-16.0%**	**-0.3%**
India	0.872	1.193	2.144	145.9%	1.8%	5.008	2.847	1.117	-77.7%	-3.0%	0.372	1.018	1.042	180.1%	2.1%
Pakistan	0.146	0.26	0.5	242.5%	2.5%	4.296	3.238	1.58	-63.2%	-2.0%	0.036	0.101	0.143	297.2%	2.8%
Bangladesh	0.729	0.844	1.119	53.5%	0.9%	3.868	3.068	1.513	-60.9%	-1.9%	0.022	0.074	0.08	263.6%	2.6%
Iran, Islamic Rep. of	0.726	1.596	2.656	265.8%	2.6%	5.941	2.325	1.045	-82.4%	-3.4%	0.082	0.181	0.221	169.5%	2.0%
Afghanistan	0.08	0.089	0.127	58.8%	0.9%	6.416	6.979	3.484	-45.7%	-1.2%	0.002	0.005	0.008	300.0%	2.8%
Nepal	0.657	0.663	0.709	7.9%	0.2%	5.34	5.362	2.752	-48.5%	-1.3%	0.004	0.009	0.009	125.0%	1.6%
Uzbekistan	0.158	0.321	0.603	281.6%	2.7%	15.31	6.904	2.632	-82.8%	-3.5%	0.023	0.051	0.032	39.1%	0.7%
Sri Lanka	0.176	0.485	1.038	489.8%	3.6%	3.29	2.505	1.275	-61.2%	-1.9%	0.007	0.017	0.019	171.4%	2.0%
Kazakhstan	0.312	2.03	2.816	802.6%	4.5%	7.973	2.279	1.045	-86.9%	-4.0%	0.028	0.077	0.054	92.9%	1.3%
Tajikistan	0.104	0.202	0.395	279.8%	2.7%	8.253	4.364	1.845	-77.6%	-3.0%	0	0.002	0		
Turkmenistan	0.336	1.079	1.11	230.4%	2.4%	8.522	3.155	1.97	-76.9%	-2.9%	0.003	0.009	0.009	200.0%	2.2%
Kyrgyzstan	0.163	0.205	0.308	89.0%	1.3%	6.985	5.958	3.675	-47.4%	-1.3%	0	0.001	0.002		
Bhutan	0.251	0.641	2.272	805.2%	4.5%	2.981	1.92	0.874	-70.7%	-2.4%	0	0.001	0.001		
Maldives	0.469	0.98	2.914	521.3%	3.7%	1.723	1.368	0.768	-55.4%	-1.6%	0	0.001	0.001		
Asia-South Central	**0.726**	**1.198**	**2.073**	**185.5%**	**2.1%**	**5.253**	**2.837**	**1.162**	**-77.9%**	**-3.0%**	**0.579**	**1.545**	**1.621**	**180.0%**	**2.1%**
Indonesia	0.103	0.393	0.798	674.8%	4.2%	5.489	3.121	1.678	-69.4%	-2.3%	0.128	0.193	0.06	-53.1%	-1.5%
Philippines	0.138	0.351	0.828	500.0%	3.6%	3.567	2.93	1.414	-60.4%	-1.8%	0.028	0.082	0.106	278.6%	2.7%
Vietnam	0.228	0.64	1.404	515.8%	3.7%	4.614	2.519	1.28	-72.3%	-2.5%	0.023	0.05	0.018	-21.7%	-0.5%
Thailand	0.32	0.941	1.947	508.4%	3.7%	3.647	2.021	0.945	-74.1%	-2.7%	0.057	0.119	0.126	121.1%	1.6%
Myanmar	0.133	0.243	0.489	267.7%	2.6%	0.99	1.412	1.034	4.4%	0.1%	0.008	0.02	0.026	225.0%	2.4%
Malaysia	0.546	1.687	3.004	450.2%	3.5%	4.533	1.83	0.879	-80.6%	-3.2%	0.047	0.086	0.024	-48.9%	-1.3%
Cambodia	0.187	0.512	1.079	477.0%	3.6%	4.857	2.952	1.379	-71.6%	-2.5%	0.003	0.011	0.01	233.3%	2.4%
Laos	0.151	0.409	0.983	551.0%	3.8%	4.177	2.645	1.219	-70.8%	-2.4%	0.001	0.004	0.005	400.0%	3.3%
Singapore	2.245	3.207	3.205	42.8%	0.7%	1.286	0.954	0.636	-50.5%	-1.4%	0.016	0.024	0.016	0.0%	0.0%
Timor-Leste	0.149	0.207	0.39	161.7%	1.9%	3.926	3.937	1.884	-52.0%	-1.5%	0	0	0.001		
Brunei	0.069	1.057	1.477	2040.6%	6.3%	8.178	3.688	1.502	-81.6%	-3.3%	0.004	0.005	0.002	-50.0%	-1.4%
Asia-South East	**0.525**	**1.008**	**1.645**	**213.3%**	**2.3%**	**3.693**	**2.306**	**1.209**	**-67.3%**	**-2.2%**	**0.316**	**0.593**	**0.394**	**24.7%**	**0.4%**

Infrastructure

Base Case: Countries in Year 2055 Descending Population Sequence	R&D Expenditures (Percent of GDP)					Energy Demand Ratio to GDP (Barrels of Oil Equivalent/Thousand $)					Annual Carbon Emissions (Billion Tons)				
	2005	2030	2055	% Chg	% An Chg	2005	2030	2055	% Chg	% An Chg	2005	2030	2055	% Chg	% An Chg
ASIA INCL OCEANIA continued															
Turkey	0.726	1.399	3.282	352.1%	3.1%	2.456	1.464	0.775	-68.4%	-2.3%	0.067	0.152	0.21	213.4%	2.3%
Yemen	0.09	0.212	0.463	414.4%	3.3%	5.377	3.366	1.838	-65.8%	-2.1%	0.007	0.019	0.01	42.9%	0.7%
Iraq	0.248	0.568	1.133	356.9%	3.1%	8.144	3.561	1.49	-81.7%	-3.3%	0.03	0.073	0.098	226.7%	2.4%
Saudi Arabia	1.118	2.203	3.19	185.3%	2.1%	5.622	2.539	1.013	-82.0%	-3.4%	0.144	0.242	0.236	63.9%	1.0%
Syria	0.282	0.498	1.124	298.6%	2.8%	5.789	3.383	1.434	-75.2%	-2.8%	0.013	0.02	0.003	-76.9%	-2.9%
Israel	4.661	5.793	5.619	20.6%	0.4%	1.168	0.819	0.547	-53.2%	-1.5%	0.015	0.036	0.045	200.0%	2.2%
Azerbaijan	0.404	0.878	1.546	282.7%	2.7%	8.278	3.283	1.397	-83.1%	-3.5%	0.008	0.018	0.015	87.5%	1.3%
Jordan	0.307	0.91	3.115	914.7%	4.7%	4.076	1.831	0.793	-80.5%	-3.2%	0.005	0.012	0.027	440.0%	3.4%
Palestine	0.321	0.471	1.015	216.2%	2.3%	2.208	2.286	1.311	-40.6%	-1.0%	0.001	0.004	0.007	600.0%	4.0%
Oman	1.041	1.87	2.775	166.6%	2.0%	4.79	2.239	1.058	-77.9%	-3.0%	0.012	0.015	0.004	-66.7%	-2.2%
Lebanon	0.408	1.234	3.188	681.4%	4.2%	2.543	1.024	0.575	-77.4%	-2.9%	0.005	0.009	0.013	160.0%	1.9%
United Arab Emirates	2.122	3.189	3.188	50.2%	0.8%	3.713	2.011	0.937	-74.8%	-2.7%	0.041	0.059	0.037	-9.8%	-0.2%
Kuwait	0.399	1.856	1.946	387.7%	3.2%	5.658	2.788	1.127	-80.1%	-3.2%	0.032	0.048	0.036	12.5%	0.2%
Georgia	0.246	0.458	0.841	241.9%	2.5%	4.63	2.64	1.241	-73.2%	-2.6%	0.002	0.002	0.002	0.0%	0.0%
Armenia	0.264	0.744	1.397	429.2%	3.4%	4.078	2.134	1.063	-73.9%	-2.7%	0.001	0.003	0.003	200.0%	2.2%
Bahrain	1.43	3.049	3.188	122.9%	1.6%	1.951	1.179	0.695	-64.4%	-2.0%	0.002	0.004	0.002	0.0%	0.0%
Qatar	0.152	1.512	1.625	969.1%	4.9%	7.796	3.691	1.53	-80.4%	-3.2%	0.013	0.015	0.006	-53.8%	-1.5%
Cyprus	0.389	1.618	2.085	436.0%	3.4%	2.336	1.294	0.744	-68.2%	-2.3%	0.002	0.003	0.002	0.0%	0.0%
Asia-West	**1.442**	**2.228**	**3.105**	**115.3%**	**1.5%**	**3.866**	**2.001**	**0.93**	**-75.9%**	**-2.8%**	**0.4**	**0.733**	**0.759**	**89.8%**	**1.3%**
Australia	1.686	2.73	2.761	63.8%	1.0%	2.855	1.528	0.75	-73.7%	-2.6%	0.175	0.221	0.204	16.6%	0.3%
Papua New Guinea	0.2	0.338	0.63	215.0%	2.3%	5.137	3.634	2.003	-61.0%	-1.9%	0.002	0.004	0.004	100.0%	1.4%
New Zealand	1.299	2.493	2.819	117.0%	1.6%	2.623	1.347	0.708	-73.0%	-2.6%	0.012	0.014	0.013	8.3%	0.2%
Solomon Islands	0.179	0.273	0.551	207.8%	2.3%	2.525	2.607	1.37	-45.7%	-1.2%	0	0	0		
Fiji	0.42	0.774	1.701	305.0%	2.8%	1.923	1.635	0.952	-50.5%	-1.4%	0.001	0.001	0.001		
Vanuatu	0.27	0.437	0.919	240.4%	2.5%	2.404	2.204	1.109	-53.9%	-1.5%	0	0	0		
Micronesia	0.5	0.591	0.906	81.2%	1.2%	2.579	2.685	1.496	-42.0%	-1.1%	0	0	0		
Samoa	0.427	0.702	1.578	269.6%	2.6%	2.788	2.323	1.079	-61.3%	-1.9%	0	0	0		
Tonga	0.533	0.572	0.765	43.5%	0.7%	3.38	3.569	1.98	-41.4%	-1.1%	0	0	0		
Oceania	**1.623**	**2.665**	**2.718**	**67.5%**	**1.0%**	**2.84**	**1.533**	**0.77**	**-72.9%**	**-2.6%**	**0.19**	**0.241**	**0.223**	**17.4%**	**0.3%**

Infrastructure

Base Case: Countries in Year 2055 Descending Population Sequence	R&D Expenditures (Percent of GDP)					Energy Demand Ratio to GDP (Barrels of Oil Equivalent/Thousand $)					Annual Carbon Emissions (Billion Tons)				
	2005	2030	2055	% Chg	% An Chg	2005	2030	2055	% Chg	% An Chg	2005	2030	2055	% Chg	% An Chg
EUROPE															
Russia	1.167	2.2	2.836	143.0%	1.8%	7.173	2.593	1.245	-82.6%	-3.4%	0.238	0.336	0.181	-23.9%	-0.5%
Poland	0.737	1.462	2.755	273.8%	2.7%	3.349	1.776	0.847	-74.7%	-2.7%	0.085	0.102	0.075	-11.8%	-0.3%
Ukraine	1.27	1.815	2.951	132.4%	1.7%	9.121	3.693	1.364	-85.0%	-3.7%	0.038	0.06	0.054	42.1%	0.7%
Romania	0.461	0.882	1.459	216.5%	2.3%	5.069	2.668	1.211	-76.1%	-2.8%	0.023	0.026	0.012	-47.8%	-1.3%
Belarus	0.821	1.612	3.464	321.9%	2.9%	3.083	1.676	0.785	-74.5%	-2.7%	0.007	0.013	0.012	71.4%	1.1%
Czech Republic	1.371	1.926	2.918	112.8%	1.5%	3.825	2.154	0.965	-74.8%	-2.7%	0.031	0.032	0.023	-25.8%	-0.6%
Hungary	0.942	1.656	2.716	188.3%	2.1%	3.709	1.991	0.922	-75.1%	-2.7%	0.02	0.023	0.017	-15.0%	-0.3%
Bulgaria	0.611	1.158	2.281	273.3%	2.7%	5.072	2.546	1.029	-79.7%	-3.1%	0.006	0.004	0.002	-66.7%	-2.2%
Slovak Republic	0.792	1.301	2.25	184.1%	2.1%	4.161	2.298	1	-76.0%	-2.8%	0.008	0.011	0.008	0.0%	0.0%
Moldova	0.826	0.919	1.336	61.7%	1.0%	4.177	3.194	1.331	-68.1%	-2.3%	0.001	0.001	0.001	0.0%	0.0%
Europe-East	**0.999**	**1.898**	**2.787**	**179.0%**	**2.1%**	**5.495**	**2.435**	**1.112**	**-79.8%**	**-3.1%**	**0.457**	**0.608**	**0.385**	**-15.8%**	**-0.3%**
United Kingdom	2.005	2.948	2.965	47.9%	0.8%	1.223	0.83	0.496	-59.4%	-1.8%	0.182	0.159	0.087	-52.2%	-1.5%
Sweden	3.874	4.694	4.592	18.5%	0.3%	1.639	1.043	0.596	-63.6%	-2.0%	0.019	0.017	0	-100.0%	
Denmark	2.333	3.167	3.169	35.8%	0.6%	1.385	0.98	0.574	-58.6%	-1.7%	0.023	0.021	0.013	-43.5%	-1.1%
Norway	1.98	2.277	2.339	18.1%	0.3%	3.321	1.905	0.838	-74.8%	-2.7%	0.055	0.044	0.015	-72.7%	-2.6%
Ireland	1.614	2.115	2.187	35.5%	0.6%	0.98	0.697	0.48	-51.0%	-1.4%	0.012	0.018	0.013	8.3%	0.2%
Finland	3.536	4.41	4.328	22.4%	0.4%	1.72	1.138	0.639	-62.8%	-2.0%	0.017	0.018	0.011	-35.3%	-0.9%
Lithuania	0.783	1.736	3.087	294.3%	2.8%	2.249	1.35	0.718	-68.1%	-2.3%	0.002	0.003	0	-100.0%	
Latvia	0.659	1.861	3.013	357.2%	3.1%	3.286	1.521	0.766	-76.7%	-2.9%	0.004	0.006	0.005	25.0%	0.4%
Estonia	0.871	2.403	3.069	252.4%	2.6%	3.895	1.561	0.729	-81.3%	-3.3%	0.004	0.005	0.001	-75.0%	-2.7%
Iceland	3.149	3.639	3.61	14.6%	0.3%	2.478	1.336	0.707	-71.5%	-2.5%	0	0	0		
Europe-North	**2.274**	**3.117**	**3.149**	**38.5%**	**0.7%**	**1.476**	**0.957**	**0.548**	**-62.9%**	**-2.0%**	**0.319**	**0.291**	**0.147**	**-53.9%**	**-1.5%**
Italy	1.094	1.684	2.366	116.3%	1.6%	1.299	1.021	0.716	-44.9%	-1.2%	0.136	0.138	0.1	-26.5%	-0.6%
Spain	1.11	2.256	2.457	121.4%	1.6%	1.085	0.829	0.582	-46.4%	-1.2%	0.057	0.064	0.039	-31.6%	-0.8%
Greece	0.779	1.945	2.509	222.1%	2.4%	1.914	1.172	0.682	-64.4%	-2.0%	0.03	0.041	0.043	43.3%	0.7%
Portugal	0.817	1.568	2.625	221.3%	2.4%	1.791	1.221	0.72	-59.8%	-1.8%	0.018	0.021	0.018	0.0%	0.0%
Serbia and Montenegro	2.138	2.213	3.105	45.2%	0.7%	5.99	3.394	1.217	-79.7%	-3.1%	0.008	0.01	0.018	125.0%	1.6%
Croatia	1.349	1.969	3.612	167.8%	2.0%	2.723	1.604	0.772	-71.6%	-2.5%	0.006	0.008	0.01	66.7%	1.0%
Bosnia and Herzegovina	0.489	0.714	1.214	148.3%	1.8%	2.93	2.617	1.371	-53.2%	-1.5%	0.002	0.003	0.002	0.0%	0.0%
Albania	0.364	0.692	1.287	253.6%	2.6%	3.052	2.158	1.087	-64.4%	-2.0%	0.001	0.003	0.002	100.0%	1.4%
Macedonia	0.467	0.627	1.128	141.5%	1.8%	5.003	3.212	1.357	-72.9%	-2.6%	0.002	0.003	0.002	0.0%	0.0%
Slovenia	1.592	2.427	3.267	105.2%	1.4%	1.881	1.22	0.701	-62.7%	-2.0%	0.004	0.005	0.004	0.0%	0.0%
Malta	0.311	1.242	2.219	613.5%	4.0%	2.32	1.352	0.745	-67.9%	-2.2%	0.001	0.001	0.001	0.0%	0.0%
Europe-South	**1.071**	**1.918**	**2.483**	**131.8%**	**1.7%**	**1.363**	**1.019**	**0.686**	**-49.7%**	**-1.4%**	**0.266**	**0.296**	**0.24**	**-9.8%**	**-0.2%**
Germany	2.522	3.618	3.589	42.3%	0.7%	1.313	0.905	0.516	-60.7%	-1.9%	0.24	0.24	0.187	-22.7%	-0.5%
France	2.241	3.285	3.279	46.3%	0.8%	1.356	0.912	0.526	-61.2%	-1.9%	0.112	0.109	0.062	-44.6%	-1.2%
Netherlands	1.894	2.83	2.855	50.7%	0.8%	2.052	1.251	0.714	-65.2%	-2.1%	0.076	0.075	0.055	-27.6%	-0.6%
Belgium	2.088	2.38	3.043	45.7%	0.8%	1.944	1.294	0.754	-61.2%	-1.9%	0.041	0.035	0.026	-36.6%	-0.9%
Austria	2.048	2.876	2.897	41.5%	0.7%	1.213	0.849	0.523	-56.9%	-1.7%	0.018	0.014	0.005	-72.2%	-2.5%
Switzerland	2.667	3.256	3.252	21.9%	0.4%	0.903	0.696	0.443	-50.9%	-1.4%	0.012	0.011	0.003	-75.0%	-2.7%
Luxembourg	1.732	1.824	1.916	10.6%	0.2%	1.577	1.097	0.688	-56.4%	-1.6%	0.004	0.005	0.003	-25.0%	-0.6%
Europe-West	**2.336**	**3.322**	**3.351**	**43.5%**	**0.7%**	**1.4**	**0.943**	**0.543**	**-61.2%**	**-1.9%**	**0.505**	**0.488**	**0.341**	**-32.5%**	**-0.8%**

Governance

Base Case
Source: International Futures
Version 5.47 March 2008

	Freedom House Index Inverted (Index)					Polity Democracy Index (Index)					Economic Freedom (Index)				
	2005	2030	2055	% Chg	% An Chg	2005	2030	2055	% Chg	% An Chg	2005	2030	2055	% Chg	% An Chg
World	8.212	9.253	9.77	19.0%	0.3%	13.19	14.65	15.81	19.9%	0.4%	7.542	7.604	7.756	2.8%	0.1%
Africa	6.785	7.792	8.918	31.4%	0.5%	10.38	12.08	14.19	36.7%	0.6%	6.081	6.411	7.154	17.6%	0.3%
Americas	11.58	12.11	12.72	9.8%	0.2%	18.45	19.26	19.73	6.9%	0.1%	8.238	8.486	8.621	4.6%	0.1%
Asia incl Oceania	7.222	8.652	9.141	26.6%	0.5%	11.6	13.69	15.14	30.5%	0.5%	6.895	7.012	7.321	6.2%	0.1%
Europe	11.2	12.15	12.49	11.5%	0.2%	18.8	19.69	19.78	5.2%	0.1%	7.402	7.565	7.892	6.6%	0.1%
World	8.212	9.253	9.77	19.0%	0.3%	13.19	14.65	15.81	19.9%	0.4%	7.542	7.604	7.756	2.8%	0.1%
Africa-Eastern	6.737	8.138	9.921	47.3%	0.8%	10.86	12.65	15.51	42.8%	0.7%	5.906	6.53	7.531	27.5%	0.5%
Africa-Middle	3.793	4.265	4.895	29.1%	0.5%	6.856	8.327	10.37	51.3%	0.8%	5.202	5.39	5.125	-1.5%	-0.0%
Africa-Northern	4.73	5.267	5.986	26.6%	0.5%	4.927	7.347	10.44	111.9%	1.5%	6.008	6.436	7.166	19.3%	0.4%
Africa-Southern	12.7	13.39	13.56	6.8%	0.1%	18.66	19.34	19.6	5.0%	0.1%	6.84	7.081	7.526	10.0%	0.2%
Africa-Western	8.356	9.708	10.8	29.2%	0.5%	13.54	14.9	15.92	17.6%	0.3%	5.536	5.9	6.265	13.2%	0.2%
Africa	6.785	7.792	8.918	31.4%	0.5%	10.38	12.08	14.19	36.7%	0.6%	6.081	6.411	7.154	17.6%	0.3%
America-Caribbean	6.862	7.85	8.402	22.4%	0.4%	11.35	13.31	14.79	30.3%	0.5%	6.637	7.194	7.72	16.3%	0.3%
America-Central	10.5	11.2	12.25	16.7%	0.3%	17.86	18.61	19.73	10.5%	0.2%	6.914	7.436	8.002	15.7%	0.3%
America-North	13.28	13.48	13.73	3.4%	0.1%	19.5	19.81	20	2.6%	0.1%	8.496	8.828	9.089	7.0%	0.1%
America-South	10.21	11.15	12.13	18.8%	0.3%	18.02	19.31	19.91	10.5%	0.2%	6.349	6.786	7.139	12.4%	0.2%
Americas	11.58	12.11	12.72	9.8%	0.2%	18.45	19.26	19.73	6.9%	0.1%	8.238	8.486	8.621	4.6%	0.1%
Asia-East	4.446	5.146	5.413	21.7%	0.4%	5.787	8.638	11.03	90.6%	1.3%	6.998	7.023	7.27	3.9%	0.1%
Asia-South Central	9.843	11.65	11.73	19.2%	0.4%	16.57	17.2	17.55	5.9%	0.1%	6.099	6.711	7.321	20.0%	0.4%
Asia-South East	7.828	9.034	10.03	28.1%	0.5%	13.82	15.96	17.09	23.7%	0.4%	6.519	6.982	7.318	12.3%	0.2%
Asia-West	5.365	5.963	6.697	24.8%	0.4%	9.778	11.69	13.49	38.0%	0.6%	6.54	6.912	7.234	10.6%	0.2%
Oceania	13.11	13.37	13.81	5.3%	0.1%	19.62	19.81	19.92	1.5%	0.0%	8.061	8.447	8.822	9.4%	0.2%
Asia incl Oceania	7.222	8.652	9.141	26.6%	0.5%	11.6	13.69	15.14	30.5%	0.5%	6.895	7.012	7.321	6.2%	0.1%
Europe-East	8.663	9.79	10.24	18.2%	0.3%	17.58	19.54	19.63	11.7%	0.2%	5.653	5.837	6.156	8.9%	0.2%
Europe-North	13.42	14	14	4.3%	0.1%	19.93	19.99	19.99	0.3%	0.0%	7.998	8.361	8.729	9.1%	0.2%
Europe-South	12.42	13.07	13.55	9.1%	0.2%	19.46	19.7	19.88	2.2%	0.0%	7.176	7.396	7.659	6.7%	0.1%
Europe-West	13.21	13.94	14	6.0%	0.1%	19.69	19.73	19.78	0.5%	0.0%	7.497	7.752	8.136	8.5%	0.2%
Europe	11.2	12.15	12.49	11.5%	0.2%	18.8	19.69	19.78	5.2%	0.1%	7.402	7.565	7.892	6.6%	0.1%

Governance

Base Case: Countries in Year 2055 Descending Population Sequence	Freedom House Index Inverted					Polity Democracy Index					Economic Freedom				
	Index					Index					Index				
	2005	2030	2055	% Chg	% An Chg	2005	2030	2055	% Chg	% An Chg	2005	2030	2055	% Chg	% An Chg
AFRICA															
Ethiopia	6.217	7.116	8.973	44.3%	0.7%	11.34	12.63	15.52	36.9%	0.6%	5.354	5.633	6.208	16.0%	0.3%
Tanzania	8.671	11.9	14	61.5%	1.0%	12.85	16.4	20	55.6%	0.9%	5.954	6.697	7.733	29.9%	0.5%
Uganda	5.059	6.367	8.379	65.6%	1.0%	6.248	8.695	12.63	102.1%	1.4%	6.629	7.28	8.28	24.9%	0.4%
Kenya	5.112	6.28	8.368	63.7%	1.0%	8.267	10.53	14.62	76.8%	1.1%	6.554	7.113	8.113	23.8%	0.4%
Madagascar	10.29	11.55	13.98	35.9%	0.6%	17.11	17.28	18.79	9.8%	0.2%	5.859	6.119	6.617	12.9%	0.2%
Mozambique	9.64	12.91	14	45.2%	0.7%	16.76	20	20	19.3%	0.4%	5.545	6.232	6.865	23.8%	0.4%
Malawi	10.17	11.78	14	37.7%	0.6%	16.87	17.21	20	18.6%	0.3%	4.725	4.973	5.544	17.3%	0.3%
Zambia	7.28	8.369	10.83	48.8%	0.8%	11.38	12.72	16.06	41.1%	0.7%	6.793	7.157	7.977	17.4%	0.3%
Zimbabwe	5.04	5.41	6.509	29.1%	0.5%	5.365	7.205	10.43	94.4%	1.3%	4.315	4.45	4.851	12.4%	0.2%
Burundi	3.945	4.469	5.632	42.8%	0.7%	8.866	9.872	12.3	38.7%	0.7%	5.077	5.3	5.796	14.2%	0.3%
Rwanda	3.093	3.572	4.415	42.7%	0.7%	6.267	7.836	10.62	69.5%	1.1%	5.157	5.451	5.968	15.7%	0.3%
Somalia	2.961	3.605	3.969	34.0%	0.6%	3.168	4.884	6.406	102.2%	1.4%	5.014	5.359	5.554	10.8%	0.2%
Eritrea	3.959	3.856	4.136	4.5%	0.1%	4.201	5.017	6.328	50.6%	0.8%	5.402	5.351	5.491	1.6%	0.0%
Mauritius	13.21	14	14	6.0%	0.1%	20	20	20	0.0%	0.0%	7.357	7.733	7.986	8.5%	0.2%
Comoros	9.004	9.495	10.93	21.4%	0.4%	9.119	10.1	12.19	33.7%	0.6%	5.734	5.86	6.226	8.6%	0.2%
Djibouti	7.124	7.32	8.124	14.0%	0.3%	12.23	12.58	13.98	14.3%	0.3%	5.821	5.886	6.157	5.8%	0.1%
Africa-Eastern	**6.737**	**8.138**	**9.921**	**47.3%**	**0.8%**	**10.86**	**12.65**	**15.51**	**42.8%**	**0.7%**	**5.906**	**6.53**	**7.531**	**27.5%**	**0.5%**
Congo, Dem. Rep. of the	3.03	3.535	4.404	45.3%	0.8%	6.16	7.646	10.13	64.4%	1.0%	3.411	3.599	3.923	15.0%	0.3%
Angola	4.188	4.743	5.013	19.7%	0.4%	7.519	9.405	10.81	43.8%	0.7%	5.741	6.047	6.196	7.9%	0.2%
Cameroon	3.047	3.099	3.39	11.3%	0.2%	6.343	7.454	9.215	45.3%	0.7%	5.535	5.574	5.791	4.6%	0.1%
Chad	5.338	6.588	7	31.1%	0.5%	8.6	10.88	11.79	37.1%	0.6%	5.528	6	6.156	11.4%	0.2%
Central African Republic	8.861	8.839	9.961	12.4%	0.2%	14.6	13.88	14.89	2.0%	0.0%	4.871	4.867	5.098	4.7%	0.1%
Congo, Rep. of	6.3	7.633	8.678	37.7%	0.6%	4.471	6.694	8.998	101.3%	1.4%	4.481	4.843	5.126	14.4%	0.3%
Gabon	6.984	7.802	8.132	16.4%	0.3%	6.373	8.947	11.24	76.4%	1.1%	4.995	5.27	5.382	7.7%	0.1%
Equatorial Guinea	3.082	3.551	3.533	14.6%	0.3%	5.549	8.424	10.42	87.8%	1.3%	6.463	6.925	6.908	6.9%	0.1%
São Tomé and Príncipe	12.13	12.02	12.28	1.2%	0.0%	11.16	11.06	11.36	1.8%	0.0%	5.786	5.764	5.816	0.5%	0.0%
Africa-Middle	**3.793**	**4.265**	**4.895**	**29.1%**	**0.5%**	**6.856**	**8.327**	**10.37**	**51.3%**	**0.8%**	**5.202**	**5.39**	**5.125**	**-1.5%**	**-0.0%**
Egypt	5.071	5.808	6.944	36.9%	0.6%	4.471	7.058	10.73	140.0%	1.8%	6.742	7.18	7.855	16.5%	0.3%
Sudan	2.076	2.514	2.849	37.2%	0.6%	3.448	5.877	8.614	149.8%	1.8%	5.739	6.226	6.599	15.0%	0.3%
Algeria	5.109	5.661	6.108	19.6%	0.4%	7.488	9.872	12.38	65.3%	1.0%	4.343	4.564	4.743	9.2%	0.2%
Morocco	7.129	7.769	8.945	25.5%	0.5%	4.457	6.64	9.777	119.4%	1.6%	6.049	6.293	6.741	11.4%	0.2%
Tunisia	5.091	5.862	6.672	31.1%	0.5%	7.487	10.35	13.39	78.8%	1.2%	6.153	6.597	7.065	14.8%	0.3%
Libya	2.056	2.374	2.565	24.8%	0.4%	3.615	6.742	9.853	172.6%	2.0%	6.636	7.132	7.431	12.0%	0.2%
Africa-Northern	**4.73**	**5.267**	**5.986**	**26.6%**	**0.5%**	**4.927**	**7.347**	**10.44**	**111.9%**	**1.5%**	**6.008**	**6.436**	**7.166**	**19.3%**	**0.4%**

Governance

Base Case: Countries in Year 2055 Descending Population Sequence	Freedom House Index Inverted (Index)					Polity Democracy Index (Index)					Economic Freedom (Index)				
	2005	2030	2055	% Chg	% An Chg	2005	2030	2055	% Chg	% An Chg	2005	2030	2055	% Chg	% An Chg
AFRICA continued															
South Africa	13.18	13.94	14	6.2%	0.1%	19.21	20	20	4.1%	0.1%	6.846	7.041	7.495	9.5%	0.2%
Namibia	11.14	12.29	14	25.7%	0.5%	16.13	17.73	20	24.0%	0.4%	6.236	6.541	7.243	16.1%	0.3%
Lesotho	7.995	8.313	9.715	21.5%	0.4%	17.83	17.83	20	12.2%	0.2%	5.977	6.078	6.525	9.2%	0.2%
Botswana	12.2	14	14	14.8%	0.3%	19.24	20	20	4.0%	0.1%	7.26	7.819	8.303	14.4%	0.3%
Swaziland	4.954	5.518	6.487	30.9%	0.5%	1.513	4.12	7.75	412.2%	3.3%	6.236	6.555	7.104	13.9%	0.3%
Africa-Southern	**12.7**	**13.39**	**13.56**	**6.8%**	**0.1%**	**18.66**	**19.34**	**19.6**	**5.0%**	**0.1%**	**6.84**	**7.081**	**7.526**	**10.0%**	**0.2%**
Nigeria	8.369	10.27	11.22	34.1%	0.6%	14.3	16.22	16.6	16.1%	0.3%	5.387	5.834	6.057	12.4%	0.2%
Niger	8.049	8.864	10.93	35.8%	0.6%	13.87	13.96	15.74	13.5%	0.3%	5.812	6.012	6.517	12.1%	0.2%
Ghana	11.22	11.31	12.61	12.4%	0.2%	12.26	12.42	13.91	13.5%	0.3%	5.947	5.968	6.253	5.1%	0.1%
Côte d'Ivoire	4.975	5.718	6.624	33.1%	0.6%	13.83	15.22	16.94	22.5%	0.4%	5.689	6.025	6.435	13.1%	0.2%
Mali	11.34	13.21	14	23.5%	0.4%	16.08	16.86	18.51	15.1%	0.3%	6.065	6.419	6.934	14.3%	0.3%
Burkina Faso	8.175	9.23	11.39	39.3%	0.7%	7.281	8.766	11.51	58.1%	0.9%	5.444	5.705	6.238	14.6%	0.3%
Senegal	9.216	10.48	12.3	33.5%	0.6%	18.29	19.63	20	9.3%	0.2%	5.955	6.279	6.744	13.2%	0.2%
Guinea	5.027	5.465	6.01	19.6%	0.4%	9.181	10.6	12.33	34.3%	0.6%	5.829	6.038	6.298	8.0%	0.2%
Benin	12.24	13.7	14	14.4%	0.3%	16.11	16.93	19.63	21.8%	0.4%	5.44	5.679	6.216	14.3%	0.3%
Togo	5.969	6.081	6.445	8.0%	0.2%	8.02	8.551	9.578	19.4%	0.4%	4.99	5.026	5.144	3.1%	0.1%
Liberia	4.999	5.118	5.904	18.1%	0.3%	9.992	10.08	11.46	14.7%	0.3%	5.36	5.406	5.71	6.5%	0.1%
Sierra Leone	7.707	9.733	11.64	51.0%	0.8%	16.18	18.58	20	23.6%	0.4%	5.258	5.712	6.139	16.8%	0.3%
Mauritania	5.048	5.335	5.799	14.9%	0.3%	4.402	6.096	8.01	82.0%	1.2%	5.814	5.949	6.169	6.1%	0.1%
Guinea-Bissau	6.894	6.844	7.361	6.8%	0.1%	14.56	13.49	13.47	-7.5%	-0.2%	4.376	4.365	4.481	2.4%	0.0%
Gambia	4.057	4.461	5.141	26.7%	0.5%	5.342	7.055	9.479	77.4%	1.2%	5.734	5.963	6.35	10.7%	0.2%
Cape Verde	14	14	14	0.0%	0.0%	13.64	16.1	18.85	38.2%	0.6%	6.34	6.782	7.282	14.9%	0.3%
Africa-Western	**8.356**	**9.708**	**10.8**	**29.2%**	**0.5%**	**13.54**	**14.9**	**15.92**	**17.6%**	**0.3%**	**5.536**	**5.9**	**6.265**	**13.2%**	**0.2%**

Governance

Base Case: Countries in Year 2055 / Descending Population Sequence	Freedom House Index Inverted					Polity Democracy Index					Economic Freedom				
	Index 2005	2030	2055	% Chg	% An Chg	Index 2005	2030	2055	% Chg	% An Chg	Index 2005	2030	2055	% Chg	% An Chg
AMERICAS															
Haiti	4.923	5.076	5.757	16.9%	0.3%	8.022	8.825	10.64	32.6%	0.6%	6.361	6.439	6.786	6.7%	0.1%
Dominican Republic	12.23	13.79	14	14.5%	0.3%	18.29	20	20	9.3%	0.2%	6.559	6.961	7.238	10.4%	0.2%
Cuba	2.092	2.616	3.296	57.6%	0.9%	3.514	6.344	10.46	197.7%	2.2%	5.893	6.509	7.31	24.0%	0.4%
Puerto Rico	5.379	6.294	7.294	35.6%	0.6%	16.07	18.79	19.04	18.5%	0.3%	6.909	7.501	8.149	17.9%	0.3%
Jamaica	12.18	13.78	14	14.9%	0.3%	19.1	20	20	4.7%	0.1%	7.047	7.463	8.232	16.8%	0.3%
Trinidad and Tobago	12.58	14	14	11.3%	0.2%	20	20	20	0.0%	0.0%	7.165	7.771	7.882	10.0%	0.2%
Bahamas	14	14	14	0.0%	0.0%	16.93	18.15	18.85	11.3%	0.2%	6.511	6.667	6.932	6.5%	0.1%
Barbados	14	14	14	0.0%	0.0%	16.62	18.42	19.12	15.0%	0.3%	5.606	5.847	6.22	11.0%	0.2%
Grenada	13.02	14	14	7.5%	0.1%	14.73	16.2	18.65	26.6%	0.5%	6.603	6.861	7.411	12.2%	0.2%
St. Vincent & the Grenadines	13.12	14	14	6.7%	0.1%	13.87	15.27	17.99	29.7%	0.5%	6.425	6.698	7.198	12.0%	0.2%
St. Lucia	14	14	14	0.0%	0.0%	14.41	17.06	19.41	34.7%	0.6%	6.527	7.015	7.651	17.2%	0.3%
America-Caribbean	**6.862**	**7.85**	**8.402**	**22.4%**	**0.4%**	**11.35**	**13.31**	**14.79**	**30.3%**	**0.5%**	**6.637**	**7.194**	**7.72**	**16.3%**	**0.3%**
Guatemala	8.988	9.871	11.13	23.8%	0.4%	17.85	18.85	20	12.0%	0.2%	6.396	6.679	7.084	10.8%	0.2%
Honduras	10.1	10.87	12.34	22.2%	0.4%	17.04	17.76	19.47	14.3%	0.3%	6.426	6.641	7.048	9.7%	0.2%
Nicaragua	10.03	10.58	11.8	17.6%	0.3%	17.79	17.78	18.93	6.4%	0.1%	6.408	6.561	6.902	7.7%	0.1%
El Salvador	11.02	12.38	14	27.0%	0.5%	16.96	18.54	20	17.9%	0.3%	7.307	7.718	8.243	12.8%	0.2%
Costa Rica	13.18	14	14	6.2%	0.1%	20	20	20	0.0%	0.0%	7.348	7.91	8.543	16.3%	0.3%
Panama	13.26	14	14	5.6%	0.1%	19.29	20	20	3.7%	0.1%	7.167	7.861	8.566	19.5%	0.4%
Belize	14	14	14	0.0%	0.0%	14.36	17.39	18.84	31.2%	0.5%	6.262	6.817	7.347	17.3%	0.3%
America-Central	**10.5**	**11.2**	**12.25**	**16.7%**	**0.3%**	**17.86**	**18.61**	**19.73**	**10.5%**	**0.2%**	**6.914**	**7.436**	**8.002**	**15.7%**	**0.3%**
United States	14	14	14	0.0%	0.0%	20	20	20	0.0%	0.0%	8.649	9.01	9.296	7.5%	0.1%
Mexico	11.03	11.95	12.91	17.0%	0.3%	17.94	19.26	20	11.5%	0.2%	6.309	6.568	6.837	8.4%	0.2%
Canada	14	14	14	0.0%	0.0%	20	20	20	0.0%	0.0%	8.132	8.489	8.884	9.2%	0.2%
America-North	**13.28**	**13.48**	**13.73**	**3.4%**	**0.1%**	**19.5**	**19.81**	**20**	**2.6%**	**0.1%**	**8.496**	**8.828**	**9.089**	**7.0%**	**0.1%**
Brazil	10.04	10.92	12.16	21.1%	0.4%	18.02	19.23	20	11.0%	0.2%	5.912	6.161	6.512	10.1%	0.2%
Colombia	8.082	8.921	10.14	25.5%	0.5%	17.13	18.7	20	16.8%	0.3%	5.426	5.693	6.081	12.1%	0.2%
Argentina	13.35	14	14	4.9%	0.1%	18.5	20	20	8.1%	0.2%	7.298	7.744	8.202	12.4%	0.2%
Peru	10.18	11.46	12.73	25.0%	0.4%	19.14	20	20	4.5%	0.1%	6.959	7.362	7.763	11.6%	0.2%
Venezuela	8.267	9.693	10.85	31.2%	0.5%	17.51	20	20	14.2%	0.3%	5.586	6.046	6.419	14.9%	0.3%
Chile	12.23	14	14	14.5%	0.3%	19.32	20	20	3.5%	0.1%	7.571	8.146	8.62	13.9%	0.3%
Ecuador	10.27	11.17	11.91	16.0%	0.3%	16.34	17.28	17.86	9.3%	0.2%	5.667	5.887	6.069	7.1%	0.1%
Bolivia	12.14	14	14	15.3%	0.3%	19.01	20	20	5.2%	0.1%	6.734	7.257	7.957	18.2%	0.3%
Paraguay	8.993	9.592	10.96	21.9%	0.4%	17.03	17.94	19.88	16.7%	0.3%	6.398	6.59	7.03	9.9%	0.2%
Uruguay	14	14	14	0.0%	0.0%	20	20	20	0.0%	0.0%	6.687	7.155	7.589	13.5%	0.3%
Guyana	12.09	13.02	14	15.8%	0.3%	16.07	17.05	18.3	13.9%	0.3%	6.823	7.06	7.364	7.9%	0.2%
Suriname	13.38	14	14	4.6%	0.1%	14.39	16.06	18.51	28.6%	0.5%	6.519	6.815	7.269	11.5%	0.2%
America-South	**10.21**	**11.15**	**12.13**	**18.8%**	**0.3%**	**18.02**	**19.31**	**19.91**	**10.5%**	**0.2%**	**6.349**	**6.786**	**7.139**	**12.4%**	**0.2%**

Governance

Base Case: Countries in Year 2055 Descending Population Sequence	Freedom House Index Inverted					Polity Democracy Index					Economic Freedom				
	Index					Index					Index				
	2005	2030	2055	% Chg	% An Chg	2005	2030	2055	% Chg	% An Chg	2005	2030	2055	% Chg	% An Chg
ASIA INCL OCEANIA															
China	3.177	3.995	4.463	40.5%	0.7%	3.665	7.116	10.02	173.4%	2.0%	5.954	6.665	7.071	18.8%	0.3%
Japan	13.16	14	14	6.4%	0.1%	20	20	20	0.0%	0.0%	7.349	7.634	7.998	8.8%	0.2%
Korea, Rep. of	12.23	13.93	14	14.5%	0.3%	18.36	20	20	8.9%	0.2%	6.664	7.147	7.472	12.1%	0.2%
Taiwan	13.11	13.95	14	6.8%	0.1%	19.15	20	20	4.4%	0.1%	7.232	7.478	7.862	8.7%	0.2%
Korea, Dem. Rep. of	2.104	2.551	3.1	47.3%	0.8%	1.422	3.603	6.665	368.7%	3.1%	5.522	5.967	6.513	17.9%	0.3%
Hong Kong	3.642	3.88	4.017	10.3%	0.2%	18.32	18.98	19.19	4.7%	0.1%	8.9	9.214	9.394	5.6%	0.1%
Mongolia	11.39	13.1	14	22.9%	0.4%	20	20	20	0.0%	0.0%	6.287	6.667	7.19	14.4%	0.3%
Asia-East	**4.446**	**5.146**	**5.413**	**21.7%**	**0.4%**	**5.787**	**8.638**	**11.03**	**90.6%**	**1.3%**	**6.998**	**7.023**	**7.27**	**3.9%**	**0.1%**
India	11.47	14	14	22.1%	0.4%	19.52	20	20	2.5%	0.0%	6.311	6.912	7.531	19.3%	0.4%
Pakistan	5.128	5.783	6.57	28.1%	0.5%	4.419	6.515	9.191	108.0%	1.5%	5.456	5.744	6.091	11.6%	0.2%
Bangladesh	9.293	11.07	12.83	38.1%	0.6%	16.34	18.48	20	22.4%	0.4%	5.773	6.218	6.658	15.3%	0.3%
Iran, Islamic Rep. of	4.094	4.877	5.325	30.1%	0.5%	13.44	16.67	18.57	38.2%	0.6%	5.662	6.176	6.47	14.3%	0.3%
Afghanistan	2.025	2.107	2.402	18.6%	0.3%	3.291	4.463	6.23	89.3%	1.3%	5.257	5.331	5.597	6.5%	0.1%
Nepal	9.026	9.823	10.93	21.1%	0.4%	15.82	16.23	17.03	7.6%	0.1%	5.806	6.004	6.279	8.1%	0.2%
Uzbekistan	3.129	3.754	4.286	37.0%	0.6%	1.46	3.823	6.703	359.1%	3.1%	5.746	6.209	6.603	14.9%	0.3%
Sri Lanka	9.207	10.57	11.84	28.6%	0.5%	15.36	17.54	19.41	26.4%	0.5%	6.162	6.569	6.951	12.8%	0.2%
Kazakhstan	5.331	6.929	7.247	35.9%	0.6%	6.762	10.65	12.61	86.5%	1.3%	6.476	7.389	7.571	16.9%	0.3%
Tajikistan	4.355	5.353	6.279	44.2%	0.7%	9.574	11.54	13.8	44.1%	0.7%	5.448	5.91	6.34	16.4%	0.3%
Turkmenistan	2.069	2.6	2.613	26.3%	0.5%	1.542	4.644	7.477	384.9%	3.2%	6.237	6.958	6.975	11.8%	0.2%
Kyrgyzstan	5.083	5.474	6.12	20.4%	0.4%	7.294	8.655	10.58	45.1%	0.7%	5.687	5.861	6.148	8.1%	0.2%
Bhutan	3.122	3.823	4.738	51.8%	0.8%	2.545	5.453	9.426	270.4%	2.7%	6.052	6.641	7.409	22.4%	0.4%
Maldives	5.113	5.881	6.997	36.8%	0.6%	14.08	16.45	18.66	32.5%	0.6%	6.447	6.9	7.558	17.2%	0.3%
Asia-South Central	**9.843**	**11.65**	**11.73**	**19.2%**	**0.4%**	**16.57**	**17.2**	**17.55**	**5.9%**	**0.1%**	**6.099**	**6.711**	**7.321**	**20.0%**	**0.4%**
Indonesia	9.223	10.74	11.87	28.7%	0.5%	17.3	19.54	20	15.6%	0.3%	5.963	6.393	6.714	12.6%	0.2%
Philippines	11.16	12.23	13.67	22.5%	0.4%	18.23	19.66	20	9.7%	0.2%	7.146	7.458	7.878	10.2%	0.2%
Vietnam	3.15	3.998	4.607	46.3%	0.8%	3.521	6.433	9.661	174.4%	2.0%	5.991	6.674	7.164	19.6%	0.4%
Thailand	11.26	12.81	14	24.3%	0.4%	19.24	20	20	4.0%	0.1%	6.774	7.221	7.598	12.2%	0.2%
Myanmar	2.077	2.382	2.743	32.1%	0.6%	3.466	5.628	8.36	141.2%	1.8%	3.655	3.871	4.129	13.0%	0.2%
Malaysia	6.087	7.108	7.82	28.5%	0.5%	13.34	16.43	17.61	32.0%	0.6%	6.848	7.412	7.806	14.0%	0.3%
Cambodia	4.211	5.327	6.118	45.3%	0.7%	12.64	15.97	18.31	44.9%	0.7%	5.859	6.503	6.959	18.8%	0.3%
Laos	3.082	3.956	4.684	52.0%	0.8%	3.419	6.241	9.607	181.0%	2.1%	5.714	6.362	6.902	20.8%	0.4%
Singapore	6.154	6.661	6.891	12.0%	0.2%	8.48	10.48	12.48	47.2%	0.8%	8.616	8.996	9.169	6.4%	0.1%
Timor-Leste	9	9.884	11.49	27.7%	0.5%	16.17	17.15	18.56	14.8%	0.3%	5.704	5.928	6.332	11.0%	0.2%
Brunei	5.014	5.423	5.535	10.4%	0.2%	16.91	18.79	19.09	12.9%	0.2%	7.115	7.416	7.498	5.4%	0.1%
Asia-South East	**7.828**	**9.034**	**10.03**	**28.1%**	**0.5%**	**13.82**	**15.96**	**17.09**	**23.7%**	**0.4%**	**6.519**	**6.982**	**7.318**	**12.3%**	**0.2%**

Multination Regional Analysis   Measures of Poverty, Health, Education, Infrastructure and Governance

Governance

Base Case: Countries in Year 2055 Descending Population Sequence	Freedom House Index Inverted					Polity Democracy Index					Economic Freedom				
	Index					Index					Index				
	2005	2030	2055	% Chg	% An Chg	2005	2030	2055	% Chg	% An Chg	2005	2030	2055	% Chg	% An Chg
ASIA INCL OCEANIA continued															
Turkey	7.211	8.235	9.46	31.2%	0.5%	17.48	19.92	20	14.4%	0.3%	5.883	6.285	6.767	15.0%	0.3%
Yemen	5.125	6.74	8.075	57.6%	0.9%	8.274	11.34	14.11	70.5%	1.1%	5.339	5.941	6.438	20.6%	0.4%
Iraq	2.03	2.436	2.766	36.3%	0.6%	1.481	4.203	7.62	414.5%	3.3%	6.041	6.564	6.988	15.7%	0.3%
Saudi Arabia	2.018	2.251	2.483	23.0%	0.4%	0.708	4.118	7.467	954.7%	4.8%	6.98	7.39	7.798	11.7%	0.2%
Syria	2.022	2.29	2.664	31.8%	0.6%	3.49	6.005	9.269	165.6%	2.0%	4.823	5.104	5.498	14.0%	0.3%
Israel	12.04	13.53	14	16.3%	0.3%	20	20	20	0.0%	0.0%	6.511	6.937	7.286	11.9%	0.2%
Azerbaijan	5.359	6.584	7.347	37.1%	0.6%	3.629	6.611	9.815	170.5%	2.0%	6.214	6.84	7.23	16.4%	0.3%
Jordan	8.223	9.844	12.12	47.4%	0.8%	8.494	11.49	14.37	69.2%	1.1%	7.088	7.729	8.627	21.7%	0.4%
Palestine	7.244	7.87	9.1	25.6%	0.5%	12.92	14.17	16.85	30.4%	0.5%	6.209	6.45	6.922	11.5%	0.2%
Oman	5.019	5.527	5.867	16.9%	0.3%	1.651	4.86	8.209	397.2%	3.3%	7.114	7.478	7.722	8.5%	0.2%
Lebanon	5.129	6.321	7.498	46.2%	0.8%	15.39	19.07	20	30.0%	0.5%	6.359	7.04	7.713	21.3%	0.4%
United Arab Emirates	5.166	5.744	5.979	15.7%	0.3%	2.757	5.75	8.744	217.2%	2.3%	7.529	7.98	8.163	8.4%	0.2%
Kuwait	7.166	7.878	8.393	17.1%	0.3%	3.72	6.676	9.475	154.7%	1.9%	6.783	7.139	7.397	9.1%	0.2%
Georgia	8.524	9.947	11.24	31.9%	0.6%	15.85	17.9	19.52	23.2%	0.4%	6.86	7.348	7.794	13.6%	0.3%
Armenia	8.656	10.6	11.79	36.2%	0.6%	16.08	19.06	20	24.4%	0.4%	6.943	7.63	8.053	16.0%	0.3%
Bahrain	6.135	6.892	7.443	21.3%	0.4%	1.724	5.011	8.16	373.3%	3.2%	7.283	7.749	8.089	11.1%	0.2%
Qatar	4.028	4.465	4.522	12.3%	0.2%	0.762	4.133	7.467	879.9%	4.7%	7.314	7.736	7.791	6.5%	0.1%
Cyprus	14	14	14	0.0%	0.0%	20	20	20	0.0%	0.0%	6.237	6.512	6.8	9.0%	0.2%
Asia-West	**5.365**	**5.963**	**6.697**	**24.8%**	**0.4%**	**9.778**	**11.69**	**13.49**	**38.0%**	**0.6%**	**6.54**	**6.912**	**7.234**	**10.6%**	**0.2%**
Australia	14	14	14	0.0%	0.0%	20	20	20	0.0%	0.0%	8.039	8.441	8.808	9.6%	0.2%
Papua New Guinea	10.93	12.43	14	28.1%	0.5%	19.37	20	20	3.3%	0.1%	5.785	6.116	6.497	12.3%	0.2%
New Zealand	14	14	14	0.0%	0.0%	20	20	20	0.0%	0.0%	8.456	8.82	9.377	10.9%	0.2%
Solomon Islands	9.132	10.18	11.86	29.9%	0.5%	18.01	18.95	20	11.0%	0.2%	5.83	6.106	6.547	12.3%	0.2%
Fiji	6.018	6.788	7.764	29.0%	0.5%	16.03	17.81	20	24.8%	0.4%	6.109	6.47	6.928	13.4%	0.3%
Vanuatu	12.04	13.41	14	16.3%	0.3%	12.62	14.5	17.14	35.8%	0.6%	6.099	6.404	6.861	12.5%	0.2%
Micronesia	13.83	14	14	1.2%	0.0%	14.03	14.52	16.12	14.9%	0.3%	6.487	6.592	6.853	5.6%	0.1%
Samoa	12.26	13.54	14	14.2%	0.3%	13.86	15.64	18.27	31.8%	0.6%	6.388	6.696	7.189	12.5%	0.2%
Tonga	8.98	9.106	9.625	7.2%	0.1%	14.33	14.71	15.88	10.8%	0.2%	6.527	6.57	6.749	3.4%	0.1%
Oceania	**13.11**	**13.37**	**13.81**	**5.3%**	**0.1%**	**19.62**	**19.81**	**19.92**	**1.5%**	**0.0%**	**8.061**	**8.447**	**8.822**	**9.4%**	**0.2%**

Multination Regional Analysis

Measures of Poverty, Health, Education, Infrastructure and Governance

Governance

Base Case: Countries in Year 2055 Descending Population Sequence	Freedom House Index Inverted					Polity Democracy Index					Economic Freedom				
	Index					Index					Index				
	2005	2030	2055	% Chg	% An Chg	2005	2030	2055	% Chg	% An Chg	2005	2030	2055	% Chg	% An Chg
EUROPE															
Russia	6.227	7.302	7.672	23.2%	0.4%	17.48	20	20	14.4%	0.3%	4.989	5.409	5.553	11.3%	0.2%
Poland	13.19	14	14	6.1%	0.1%	19.05	20	20	5.0%	0.1%	6.345	6.665	6.987	10.1%	0.2%
Ukraine	8.377	9.932	11.26	34.4%	0.6%	17.71	20	20	12.9%	0.2%	4.8	5.212	5.564	15.9%	0.3%
Romania	12.42	13.73	14	12.7%	0.2%	18.57	20	20	7.7%	0.1%	4.98	5.231	5.44	9.2%	0.2%
Belarus	4.197	5.004	5.906	40.7%	0.7%	3.623	6.717	10.15	180.2%	2.1%	6.49	7.078	7.737	19.2%	0.4%
Czech Republic	13.23	13.98	14	5.8%	0.1%	20	20	20	0.0%	0.0%	6.762	6.959	7.198	6.4%	0.1%
Hungary	13.28	14	14	5.4%	0.1%	20	20	20	0.0%	0.0%	6.774	7.048	7.306	7.9%	0.2%
Bulgaria	11.37	12.82	14	23.1%	0.4%	18.51	20	20	8.0%	0.2%	5.181	5.497	5.824	12.4%	0.2%
Slovak Republic	13.33	14	14	5.0%	0.1%	19.42	20	20	3.0%	0.1%	6.379	6.596	6.861	7.6%	0.1%
Moldova	10.7	12.66	14	30.8%	0.5%	17.91	19.77	20	11.7%	0.2%	5.72	6.14	6.735	17.7%	0.3%
Europe-East	**8.663**	**9.79**	**10.24**	**18.2%**	**0.3%**	**17.58**	**19.54**	**19.63**	**11.7%**	**0.2%**	**5.653**	**5.837**	**6.156**	**8.9%**	**0.2%**
United Kingdom	13.13	13.48	14	6.6%	0.1%	20	20	20	0.0%	0.0%	8.242	8.614	9.008	9.3%	0.2%
Sweden	14	14	14	0.0%	0.0%	20	20	20	0.0%	0.0%	7.444	7.881	8.224	10.5%	0.2%
Denmark	14	14	14	0.0%	0.0%	20	20	20	0.0%	0.0%	7.717	8.069	8.474	9.8%	0.2%
Norway	14	14	14	0.0%	0.0%	20	20	20	0.0%	0.0%	7.244	7.512	7.787	7.5%	0.1%
Ireland	14	14	14	0.0%	0.0%	20	20	20	0.0%	0.0%	8.218	8.581	8.716	6.1%	0.1%
Finland	14	14	14	0.0%	0.0%	20	20	20	0.0%	0.0%	7.747	8.041	8.451	9.1%	0.2%
Lithuania	13.57	14	14	3.2%	0.1%	20	20	20	0.0%	0.0%	6.435	6.846	7.333	14.0%	0.3%
Latvia	13.69	14	14	2.3%	0.0%	18.89	20	20	5.9%	0.1%	6.769	7.292	7.763	14.7%	0.3%
Estonia	13.66	14	14	2.5%	0.0%	16.86	19.29	19.44	15.3%	0.3%	7.279	7.865	8.44	15.9%	0.3%
Iceland	14	14	14	0.0%	0.0%	20	20	20	0.0%	0.0%	7.802	8.144	8.472	8.6%	0.2%
Europe-North	**13.42**	**14**	**14**	**4.3%**	**0.1%**	**19.93**	**19.99**	**19.99**	**0.3%**	**0.0%**	**7.998**	**8.361**	**8.729**	**9.1%**	**0.2%**
Italy	13.01	13.48	14	7.6%	0.1%	20	20	20	0.0%	0.0%	7.104	7.238	7.47	5.2%	0.1%
Spain	13.18	14	14	6.2%	0.1%	20	20	20	0.0%	0.0%	7.453	7.726	8.005	7.4%	0.1%
Greece	12.25	13.32	14	14.3%	0.3%	20	20	20	0.0%	0.0%	6.975	7.292	7.692	10.3%	0.2%
Portugal	14	14	14	0.0%	0.0%	19.98	20	20	0.1%	0.0%	7.302	7.547	7.931	8.6%	0.2%
Serbia and Montenegro	8.403	9.805	12.35	47.0%	0.8%	17.58	19.31	20	13.8%	0.3%	5.945	6.365	7.128	19.9%	0.4%
Croatia	11.31	12.45	14	23.8%	0.4%	17.48	19.21	20	14.4%	0.3%	5.881	6.175	6.667	13.4%	0.3%
Bosnia and Herzegovina	7.172	7.722	8.485	18.3%	0.3%	14.19	15.55	17.34	22.2%	0.4%	6.473	6.707	7.03	8.6%	0.2%
Albania	7.239	8.251	9.209	27.2%	0.5%	15.5	17.65	19.61	26.5%	0.5%	5.787	6.155	6.503	12.4%	0.2%
Macedonia	9.089	9.565	10.55	16.1%	0.3%	16.14	16.91	18.59	15.2%	0.3%	5.636	5.776	6.066	7.6%	0.1%
Slovenia	13.22	14	14	5.9%	0.1%	20	20	20	0.0%	0.0%	5.952	6.176	6.531	9.7%	0.2%
Malta	14	14	14	0.0%	0.0%	16.93	18.38	18.72	10.6%	0.2%	6.502	6.763	7.134	9.7%	0.2%
Europe-South	**12.42**	**13.07**	**13.55**	**9.1%**	**0.2%**	**19.46**	**19.7**	**19.88**	**2.2%**	**0.0%**	**7.176**	**7.396**	**7.659**	**6.7%**	**0.1%**
Germany	13.03	13.98	14	7.4%	0.1%	20	20	20	0.0%	0.0%	7.611	7.906	8.356	9.8%	0.2%
France	13.06	13.97	14	7.2%	0.1%	19.04	19.21	19.37	1.7%	0.0%	7.017	7.279	7.673	9.3%	0.2%
Netherlands	13.99	14	14	0.1%	0.0%	19.99	20	20	0.1%	0.0%	7.998	8.259	8.62	7.8%	0.1%
Belgium	13.07	13.31	14	7.1%	0.1%	20	20	20	0.0%	0.0%	7.523	7.595	7.867	4.6%	0.1%
Austria	14	14	14	0.0%	0.0%	20	20	20	0.0%	0.0%	7.525	7.78	8.079	7.4%	0.1%
Switzerland	14	14	14	0.0%	0.0%	20	20	20	0.0%	0.0%	8.427	8.733	9.091	7.9%	0.2%
Luxembourg	14	14	14	0.0%	0.0%	20	20	20	0.0%	0.0%	7.852	8.075	8.133	3.6%	0.1%
Europe-West	**13.21**	**13.94**	**14**	**6.0%**	**0.1%**	**19.69**	**19.73**	**19.78**	**0.5%**	**0.0%**	**7.497**	**7.752**	**8.136**	**8.5%**	**0.2%**

Multinational Regional Analysis

Measures of Poverty, Health, Education, Infrastructure and Governance

Governance

Base Case
Source: International Futures
Version 5.47 March 2008

	Government Corruption Perception (Index 1-10)					Government Effectiveness (Index 0-5)					Globalization (Index)				
	2005	2030	2055	% Chg	% An Chg	2005	2030	2055	% Chg	% An Chg	2005	2030	2055	% Chg	% An Chg
World	3.674	4.896	6.461	75.9%	1.1%	2.659	3.165	3.749	41.0%	0.7%	39.7	53.43	61.99	56.1%	0.9%
Africa	2.71	2.926	3.641	34.4%	0.6%	1.892	2.086	2.491	31.7%	0.6%	43.27	51.16	51.53	19.1%	0.4%
Americas	5.462	6.67	7.989	46.3%	0.8%	3.265	3.757	4.332	32.7%	0.6%	45.78	60.44	70.5	54.0%	0.9%
Asia incl Oceania	3.177	4.741	6.98	119.7%	1.6%	2.569	3.213	4.008	56.0%	0.9%	33.68	48.36	61.14	81.5%	1.2%
Europe	5.368	7.474	8.886	65.5%	1.0%	3.357	4.236	4.779	42.4%	0.7%	60.25	82.91	89.61	48.7%	0.8%
World	3.674	4.896	6.461	75.9%	1.1%	2.659	3.165	3.749	41.0%	0.7%	39.7	53.43	61.99	56.1%	0.9%
Africa-Eastern	2.784	2.986	3.935	41.3%	0.7%	1.941	2.092	2.545	31.1%	0.5%	39.17	50.52	54.18	38.3%	0.7%
Africa-Middle	2.012	2.138	2.367	17.6%	0.3%	1.044	1.316	1.687	61.6%	1.0%	39.83	50.39	52.63	32.1%	0.6%
Africa-Northern	3.315	4.03	5.888	77.6%	1.2%	2.229	2.673	3.518	57.8%	0.9%	48.03	55.93	54.25	13.0%	0.2%
Africa-Southern	5.069	5.853	8.74	72.4%	1.1%	2.937	3.403	4.672	59.1%	0.9%	47.11	50.62	69.78	48.1%	0.8%
Africa-Western	2.012	2.198	2.486	23.6%	0.4%	1.744	1.922	2.178	24.9%	0.4%	44.95	49.59	45.13	0.4%	0.0%
Africa	2.71	2.926	3.641	34.4%	0.6%	1.892	2.086	2.491	31.7%	0.6%	43.27	51.16	51.53	19.1%	0.4%
America-Caribbean	3.207	4.352	5.859	82.7%	1.2%	2.218	2.732	3.444	55.3%	0.9%	35.46	50.75	64.36	81.5%	1.2%
America-Central	3.216	3.911	5.229	62.6%	1.0%	2.236	2.653	3.275	46.5%	0.8%	51.02	61.56	63.11	23.7%	0.4%
America-North	7.212	8.614	9.128	26.6%	0.5%	4.178	4.582	4.796	14.8%	0.3%	58.44	77.32	85.51	46.3%	0.8%
America-South	3.909	5.146	7.404	89.4%	1.3%	2.426	3.106	4.087	68.5%	1.0%	31.63	42.93	56.33	78.1%	1.2%
Americas	5.462	6.67	7.989	46.3%	0.8%	3.265	3.757	4.332	32.7%	0.6%	45.78	60.44	70.5	54.0%	0.9%
Asia-East	3.737	6.584	9.897	164.8%	2.0%	2.941	4.043	4.955	68.5%	1.0%	28.59	51.91	77.76	172.0%	2.0%
Asia-South Central	2.738	3.583	5.534	102.1%	1.4%	2.317	2.684	3.524	52.1%	0.8%	33.1	42.9	49.26	48.8%	0.8%
Asia-South East	2.497	3.44	4.881	95.5%	1.3%	2.287	2.8	3.443	50.5%	0.8%	45.15	51.16	56.39	24.9%	0.4%
Asia-West	3.512	4.944	7.202	105.1%	1.4%	2.272	3.03	3.956	74.1%	1.1%	40.23	54.69	69.43	72.6%	1.1%
Oceania	7.309	7.965	8.006	9.5%	0.2%	3.845	4.185	4.256	10.7%	0.2%	66.8	89	91.45	36.9%	0.6%
Asia incl Oceania	3.177	4.741	6.98	119.7%	1.6%	2.569	3.213	4.008	56.0%	0.9%	33.68	48.36	61.14	81.5%	1.2%
Europe-East	2.919	5.158	7.515	157.5%	1.9%	2.239	3.404	4.521	101.9%	1.4%	50.06	62.87	69.44	38.7%	0.7%
Europe-North	8.925	9.842	10	12.0%	0.2%	4.552	4.968	5	9.8%	0.2%	81.84	108.8	109.2	33.4%	0.6%
Europe-South	5.32	7.168	9.095	71.0%	1.1%	3.576	4.343	4.791	34.0%	0.6%	51.45	78.34	91.88	78.6%	1.2%
Europe-West	7.516	9.837	10	33.0%	0.6%	4.375	4.987	5	14.3%	0.3%	72.3	101.9	104.7	44.8%	0.7%
Europe	5.368	7.474	8.886	65.5%	1.0%	3.357	4.236	4.779	42.4%	0.7%	60.25	82.91	89.61	48.7%	0.8%

Governance

Base Case: Countries in Year 2055 Descending Population Sequence	Government Corruption Perception (Index 1-10)					Government Effectiveness (Index 0-5)					Globalization (Index)				
	2005	2030	2055	% Chg	% An Chg	2005	2030	2055	% Chg	% An Chg	2005	2030	2055	% Chg	% An Chg
AFRICA															
Ethiopia	3.221	3.335	3.834	19.0%	0.3%	2.029	2.037	2.263	11.5%	0.2%	41.01	51.36	51.41	25.4%	0.5%
Tanzania	2.528	2.797	4.223	67.0%	1.0%	2.143	2.245	2.84	32.5%	0.6%	35.52	47.53	58.45	64.6%	1.0%
Uganda	2.31	2.691	4.636	100.7%	1.4%	2.308	2.529	3.356	45.4%	0.8%	46.13	59.98	67.86	47.1%	0.8%
Kenya	2.117	2.397	3.97	87.5%	1.3%	1.813	2.122	2.948	62.6%	1.0%	37.29	47.65	54.85	47.1%	0.8%
Madagascar	3.117	3.213	3.547	13.8%	0.3%	1.954	2.032	2.223	13.8%	0.3%	37.4	48.47	50.02	33.7%	0.6%
Mozambique	2.242	2.679	3.854	71.9%	1.1%	1.973	2.159	2.686	36.1%	0.6%	44.62	52.68	60.66	35.9%	0.6%
Malawi	4.106	4.179	4.548	10.8%	0.2%	1.948	2.127	2.343	20.3%	0.4%	36.83	48.55	49.39	34.1%	0.6%
Zambia	3.422	3.537	4.127	20.6%	0.4%	1.891	2.009	2.343	23.9%	0.4%	40.92	52.65	53.7	31.2%	0.5%
Zimbabwe	3.018	3.22	4.37	44.8%	0.7%	1.456	1.819	2.578	77.1%	1.1%	45.33	54.15	41.65	-8.1%	-0.2%
Burundi	2.395	2.455	2.709	13.1%	0.2%	1.254	1.473	1.774	41.5%	0.7%	32.3	46.1	49.03	51.8%	0.8%
Rwanda	2.521	2.669	3.214	27.5%	0.5%	2.282	2.314	2.532	11.0%	0.2%	34.05	47.63	51.51	51.3%	0.8%
Somalia	2.096	2.181	2.257	7.7%	0.1%	0.241	0.631	1.055	337.8%	3.0%	13.15	28.34	28.11	113.8%	1.5%
Eritrea	2.893	2.875	2.926	1.1%	0.0%	2.107	2.043	1.992	-5.5%	-0.1%	42.74	54.32	52.92	23.8%	0.4%
Mauritius	4.891	6.664	8.593	75.7%	1.1%	3.279	3.952	4.695	43.2%	0.7%	49.3	62.53	73.27	48.6%	0.8%
Comoros	2.532	2.618	3	18.5%	0.3%	1.173	1.436	1.931	64.6%	1.0%	47.05	58.84	62.03	31.8%	0.6%
Djibouti	2.589	2.638	2.908	12.3%	0.2%	1.399	1.556	1.842	31.7%	0.6%	38.08	48.77	51.03	34.0%	0.6%
Africa-Eastern	**2.784**	**2.986**	**3.935**	**41.3%**	**0.7%**	**1.941**	**2.092**	**2.545**	**31.1%**	**0.5%**	**39.17**	**50.52**	**54.18**	**38.3%**	**0.7%**
Congo, Dem. Rep. of the	2.004	2.083	2.347	17.1%	0.3%	0.667	1.034	1.5	124.9%	1.6%	36.67	47.6	52.52	43.2%	0.7%
Angola	1.759	2.006	2.18	23.9%	0.4%	0.734	1.183	1.655	125.5%	1.6%	51.93	60.72	57.14	10.0%	0.2%
Cameroon	2.025	2.055	2.267	12.0%	0.2%	2.011	2.097	2.242	11.5%	0.2%	34.44	47.72	50.44	46.5%	0.8%
Chad	2.04	2.284	2.416	18.4%	0.3%	2.069	2.164	2.241	8.3%	0.2%	41.88	53.02	52.29	24.9%	0.4%
Central African Republic	2.386	2.384	2.516	5.4%	0.1%	1.401	1.524	1.77	26.3%	0.5%	37.75	47.63	49.72	31.7%	0.6%
Congo, Rep. of	2.241	2.536	2.983	33.1%	0.6%	0.784	1.24	1.837	134.3%	1.7%	51.71	58.24	44.97	-13.0%	-0.3%
Gabon	2.985	4.049	4.696	57.3%	0.9%	1.836	2.587	3.16	72.1%	1.1%	49.26	53.33	51.95	5.5%	0.1%
Equatorial Guinea	2.256	3.702	3.625	60.7%	1.0%	0.447	1.663	2.295	413.4%	3.3%	64.45	81.56	72.05	11.8%	0.2%
São Tomé and Príncipe	2.566	2.551	2.586	0.8%	0.0%	1.784	1.988	2.118	18.7%	0.3%	46.24	50.76	51.68	11.8%	0.2%
Africa-Middle	**2.012**	**2.138**	**2.367**	**17.6%**	**0.3%**	**1.044**	**1.316**	**1.687**	**61.6%**	**1.0%**	**39.83**	**50.39**	**52.63**	**32.1%**	**0.6%**
Egypt	3.15	3.919	6.783	115.3%	1.5%	2.776	3.124	4.205	51.5%	0.8%	55.85	62.44	60.9	9.0%	0.2%
Sudan	2.049	2.513	3.234	57.8%	0.9%	1.021	1.536	2.191	114.6%	1.5%	34.85	48.81	41.78	19.9%	0.4%
Algeria	3.229	4.156	5.383	66.7%	1.0%	1.891	2.628	3.378	78.6%	1.2%	42.89	41.87	44.52	3.8%	0.1%
Morocco	4.767	5.198	6.658	39.7%	0.7%	2.429	2.624	3.267	34.5%	0.6%	53.46	60.56	54.81	2.5%	0.0%
Tunisia	5.331	7.105	10	87.6%	1.3%	3.584	4.188	5	39.5%	0.7%	60.31	78.06	87.71	45.4%	0.8%
Libya	2.924	5.066	7.525	157.4%	1.9%	1.404	2.822	4.217	200.4%	2.2%	11.27	38.67	59.4	427.1%	3.4%
Africa-Northern	**3.315**	**4.03**	**5.888**	**77.6%**	**1.2%**	**2.229**	**2.673**	**3.518**	**57.8%**	**0.9%**	**48.03**	**55.93**	**54.25**	**13.0%**	**0.2%**

Governance

Base Case: Countries in Year 2055 Descending Population Sequence	Government Corruption Perception (Index 1-10)					Government Effectiveness (Index 0-5)					Globalization (Index)				
	2005	2030	2055	% Chg	% An Chg	2005	2030	2055	% Chg	% An Chg	2005	2030	2055	% Chg	% An Chg
AFRICA															
South Africa	5.147	5.907	8.997	74.8%	1.1%	2.976	3.457	4.789	60.9%	1.0%	45.95	47.6	66.59	44.9%	0.7%
Namibia	5.48	6.408	10	82.5%	1.2%	2.815	3.182	5	77.6%	1.2%	44.78	58.94	99.86	123.0%	1.6%
Lesotho	3.199	3.3	4.023	25.8%	0.5%	2.343	2.412	2.783	18.8%	0.3%	66.9	77.04	76.7	14.6%	0.3%
Botswana	6.172	8.858	10	62.0%	1.0%	3.374	4.365	5	48.2%	0.8%	45.69	57.06	83.54	82.8%	1.2%
Swaziland	2.462	3.061	5.237	112.7%	1.5%	1.886	2.327	3.426	81.7%	1.2%	67.71	79.9	73.2	8.1%	0.2%
Africa-Southern	**5.069**	**5.853**	**8.74**	**72.4%**	**1.1%**	**2.937**	**3.403**	**4.672**	**59.1%**	**0.9%**	**47.11**	**50.62**	**69.78**	**48.1%**	**0.8%**
Nigeria	1.228	1.463	1.664	35.5%	0.6%	1.534	1.823	2.153	40.4%	0.7%	46.26	44.27	35.18	-24.0%	-0.5%
Niger	2.303	2.353	2.576	11.9%	0.2%	1.493	1.579	1.741	16.6%	0.3%	42.03	51.81	49.49	17.7%	0.3%
Ghana	3.533	3.548	3.821	8.2%	0.2%	2.513	2.439	2.45	-2.5%	-0.1%	44.4	55.75	54.77	23.4%	0.4%
Côte d'Ivoire	2.694	2.941	3.508	30.2%	0.5%	1.663	1.897	2.311	39.0%	0.7%	40.29	50.92	54.87	36.2%	0.6%
Mali	2.817	2.942	3.29	16.8%	0.3%	1.784	1.884	2.088	17.0%	0.3%	47.31	59.51	59.03	24.8%	0.4%
Burkina Faso	3.016	3.138	3.64	20.7%	0.4%	2.103	2.084	2.262	7.6%	0.1%	44.54	56.95	52.74	18.4%	0.3%
Senegal	3.528	3.752	4.361	23.6%	0.4%	2.592	2.578	2.749	6.1%	0.1%	40.04	49.6	54	34.9%	0.6%
Guinea	1.909	2.088	2.42	26.8%	0.5%	2.145	2.175	2.35	9.6%	0.2%	35.53	49.72	52.47	47.7%	0.8%
Benin	2.514	2.623	3.102	23.4%	0.4%	2.447	2.435	2.595	6.0%	0.1%	47.77	59.04	56.47	18.2%	0.3%
Togo	2.395	2.414	2.489	3.9%	0.1%	1.05	1.378	1.709	62.8%	1.0%	53.62	61.9	56.08	4.6%	0.1%
Liberia	2.2	2.215	2.355	7.0%	0.1%	0.883	1.212	1.6	81.2%	1.2%	48.88	62.22	57.8	18.2%	0.3%
Sierra Leone	2.229	2.367	2.633	18.1%	0.3%	1.136	1.443	1.833	61.4%	1.0%	42.17	49.62	50.72	20.3%	0.4%
Mauritania	3.115	3.222	3.454	10.9%	0.2%	2.164	2.214	2.347	8.5%	0.2%	42.42	51.48	52.43	23.6%	0.4%
Guinea-Bissau	2.341	2.338	2.383	1.8%	0.0%	1.186	1.414	1.636	37.9%	0.6%	49.79	61.17	61.12	22.8%	0.4%
Gambia	2.519	2.69	3.178	26.2%	0.5%	2.386	2.437	2.586	8.4%	0.2%	45.49	54.6	56.64	24.5%	0.4%
Cape Verde	3.174	4.278	7.044	121.9%	1.6%	2.744	3.214	4.287	56.2%	0.9%	58.84	74.56	94.79	61.1%	1.0%
Africa-Western	**2.012**	**2.198**	**2.486**	**23.6%**	**0.4%**	**1.744**	**1.922**	**2.178**	**24.9%**	**0.4%**	**44.95**	**49.59**	**45.13**	**0.4%**	**0.0%**

Governance

Base Case: Countries in Year 2055 Descending Population Sequence	Government Corruption Perception Index 1-10					Government Effectiveness Index 0-5					Globalization Index				
	2005	2030	2055	% Chg	% An Chg	2005	2030	2055	% Chg	% An Chg	2005	2030	2055	% Chg	% An Chg
AMERICAS															
Haiti	1.78	1.82	2.067	16.1%	0.3%	0.822	1.173	1.665	102.6%	1.4%	48.38	58.91	60.78	25.6%	0.5%
Dominican Republic	2.948	4.457	6.276	112.9%	1.5%	2.37	3.23	4.127	74.1%	1.1%	54.85	58.36	66.76	21.7%	0.4%
Cuba	3.579	4.439	8.215	129.5%	1.7%	2.255	2.699	4.263	89.0%	1.3%	6.529	20.88	50.35	671.2%	4.2%
Puerto Rico	4.78	9.207	10	109.2%	1.5%	4.18	5	5	19.6%	0.4%	29.31	69.84	88.78	202.9%	2.2%
Jamaica	3.755	4.448	7.642	103.5%	1.4%	2.273	2.68	4.023	77.0%	1.1%	48.92	50.68	65.71	34.3%	0.6%
Trinidad and Tobago	3.786	7.936	9.227	143.7%	1.8%	3.341	5	5	49.7%	0.8%	41.7	76.54	81.49	95.4%	1.3%
Bahamas	5.851	7.07	10	70.9%	1.1%	3.286	3.939	5	52.2%	0.8%	48.24	58.4	78.8	63.3%	1.0%
Barbados	6.744	8.914	10	48.3%	0.8%	3.641	4.533	5	37.3%	0.6%	57.06	77.91	96.81	69.7%	1.1%
Grenada	3.513	4.357	8.003	127.8%	1.7%	2.518	3.058	4.623	83.6%	1.2%	64.17	75.72	89.73	39.8%	0.7%
St. Vincent & the Grenadines	3.328	4.001	6.401	92.3%	1.3%	2.483	2.905	3.956	59.3%	0.9%	67.06	76.4	68.66	2.4%	0.0%
St. Lucia	3.544	5.283	10	182.2%	2.1%	2.672	3.463	5	87.1%	1.3%	73.21	89.63	109.5	49.6%	0.8%
America-Caribbean	**3.207**	**4.352**	**5.859**	**82.7%**	**1.2%**	**2.218**	**2.732**	**3.444**	**55.3%**	**0.9%**	**35.46**	**50.75**	**64.36**	**81.5%**	**1.2%**
Guatemala	2.595	3.096	4.366	68.2%	1.0%	2.026	2.411	3.048	50.4%	0.8%	53.14	56.6	47.71	-10.2%	-0.2%
Honduras	2.526	2.782	3.588	42.0%	0.7%	2.083	2.301	2.752	32.1%	0.6%	54.97	64.86	70.36	28.0%	0.5%
Nicaragua	2.609	2.793	3.407	30.6%	0.5%	1.802	2.06	2.504	39.0%	0.7%	55.35	65.1	68.92	24.5%	0.4%
El Salvador	4.11	4.913	6.952	69.1%	1.1%	2.404	2.813	3.684	53.2%	0.9%	55.29	67.87	64.23	16.2%	0.3%
Costa Rica	5.533	8.068	10	80.7%	1.2%	3.179	4.227	5	57.3%	0.9%	38.12	62.16	89.64	135.2%	1.7%
Panama	3.238	5.922	10	208.8%	2.3%	2.548	3.73	5	96.2%	1.4%	33.14	54.41	85.68	158.5%	1.9%
Belize	3.638	5.82	10	174.9%	2.0%	2.229	3.296	5	124.3%	1.6%	63.59	82.68	99.28	56.1%	0.9%
America-Central	**3.216**	**3.911**	**5.229**	**62.6%**	**1.0%**	**2.236**	**2.653**	**3.275**	**46.5%**	**0.8%**	**51.02**	**61.56**	**63.11**	**23.7%**	**0.4%**
United States	8.342	10	10	19.9%	0.4%	4.624	5	5	8.1%	0.2%	66.64	85.56	91.21	36.9%	0.6%
Mexico	3.331	4.502	6.453	93.7%	1.3%	2.801	3.342	4.171	48.9%	0.8%	28.23	46.8	62.65	121.9%	1.6%
Canada	9.491	10	10	5.4%	0.1%	4.571	5	5	9.4%	0.2%	81.66	106.8	110	34.7%	0.6%
America-North	**7.212**	**8.614**	**9.128**	**26.6%**	**0.5%**	**4.178**	**4.582**	**4.796**	**14.8%**	**0.3%**	**58.44**	**77.32**	**85.51**	**46.3%**	**0.8%**
Brazil	3.934	4.858	7.166	82.2%	1.2%	2.412	2.981	4.035	67.3%	1.0%	18.64	32.34	48.31	159.2%	1.9%
Colombia	3.268	4.207	6.882	110.6%	1.5%	2.324	2.827	4.011	72.6%	1.1%	56.25	50.82	56.85	1.1%	0.0%
Argentina	3.935	7.072	10	154.1%	1.9%	3.052	4.409	5	63.8%	1.0%	30.48	60.95	81.13	166.2%	2.0%
Peru	4.494	5.437	7.175	59.7%	0.9%	2.174	2.746	3.578	64.6%	1.0%	55.73	49.46	50	-10.3%	-0.2%
Venezuela	2.925	5.045	8.905	204.4%	2.3%	1.825	2.998	4.776	161.7%	1.9%	31.06	46.02	72.43	133.2%	1.7%
Chile	7.619	10	10	31.3%	0.5%	3.856	4.908	5	29.7%	0.5%	33.85	57.68	80.53	137.9%	1.7%
Ecuador	2.689	3.072	3.527	31.2%	0.5%	1.548	1.984	2.451	58.3%	0.9%	47.64	41.5	33.39	-29.9%	-0.7%
Bolivia	2.726	3.349	5.454	100.1%	1.4%	2.237	2.737	3.69	65.0%	1.0%	58.22	63.53	72.84	25.1%	0.4%
Paraguay	2.597	2.916	4.163	60.3%	0.9%	1.349	1.872	2.707	100.7%	1.4%	55.28	56.6	46.82	-15.3%	-0.3%
Uruguay	6.696	9.328	10	49.3%	0.8%	3.188	4.282	5	56.8%	0.9%	31.89	53.84	78.7	146.8%	1.8%
Guyana	2.53	2.907	3.642	44.0%	0.7%	2.36	2.596	2.971	25.9%	0.5%	69.43	76.88	79.43	14.4%	0.3%
Suriname	3.186	4.06	6.596	107.0%	1.5%	2.491	2.998	4.11	65.0%	1.0%	48.56	62.92	66.6	37.1%	0.6%
America-South	**3.909**	**5.146**	**7.404**	**89.4%**	**1.3%**	**2.426**	**3.106**	**4.087**	**68.5%**	**1.0%**	**31.63**	**42.93**	**56.33**	**78.1%**	**1.2%**

Governance

Base Case: Countries in Year 2055 Descending Population Sequence	Government Corruption Perception (Index 1-10)					Government Effectiveness (Index 0-5)					Globalization (Index)				
	2005	2030	2055	% Chg	% An Chg	2005	2030	2055	% Chg	% An Chg	2005	2030	2055	% Chg	% An Chg
ASIA INCL OCEANIA															
China	3.366	6.22	10	197.1%	2.2%	2.839	3.955	5	76.1%	1.1%	25.04	47.95	77.24	208.5%	2.3%
Japan	6.876	10	10	45.4%	0.8%	3.899	5	5	28.2%	0.5%	59.96	88.35	93.53	56.0%	0.9%
Korea, Rep. of	4.415	9.712	10	126.5%	1.6%	3.42	5	5	46.2%	0.8%	38.53	81.5	85.55	122.0%	1.6%
Taiwan	5.754	8.251	10	73.8%	1.1%	3.845	5	5	30.0%	0.5%	38.95	66.87	79.59	104.3%	1.4%
Korea, Dem. Rep. of	2.423	2.706	3.512	44.9%	0.7%	1.168	1.511	2.106	80.3%	1.2%	7.015	17.42	23.59	236.3%	2.5%
Hong Kong	8.537	10	10	17.1%	0.3%	4.02	5	5	24.4%	0.4%	70.8	96.64	97.06	37.1%	0.6%
Mongolia	2.846	3.139	3.951	38.8%	0.7%	2.302	2.55	2.904	26.2%	0.5%	55.27	59.51	59.96	8.5%	0.2%
Asia-East	**3.737**	**6.584**	**9.897**	**164.8%**	**2.0%**	**2.941**	**4.043**	**4.955**	**68.5%**	**1.0%**	**28.59**	**51.91**	**77.76**	**172.0%**	**2.0%**
India	2.897	3.864	6.514	124.9%	1.6%	2.464	2.869	3.985	61.7%	1.0%	30.44	37.69	49.95	64.1%	1.0%
Pakistan	2.243	2.541	3.179	41.7%	0.7%	1.978	2.112	2.471	24.9%	0.4%	36.31	48.12	36.91	1.7%	0.0%
Bangladesh	2.042	2.448	3.285	60.9%	1.0%	2.032	2.282	2.691	32.4%	0.6%	43.91	58.97	51.14	16.5%	0.3%
Iran, Islamic Rep. of	2.856	5.213	8.08	182.9%	2.1%	2.5	3.61	4.844	93.8%	1.3%	20.63	42.36	61.51	198.2%	2.2%
Afghanistan	2.506	2.528	2.632	5.0%	0.1%	1.185	1.337	1.567	32.2%	0.6%	36.96	48.6	50.49	36.6%	0.6%
Nepal	2.503	2.61	2.826	12.9%	0.2%	1.87	1.956	2.104	12.5%	0.2%	45.7	58.03	60.26	31.9%	0.6%
Uzbekistan	2.455	2.891	3.647	48.6%	0.8%	1.567	1.892	2.353	50.2%	0.8%	42.52	51.23	36.61	-13.9%	-0.3%
Sri Lanka	3.181	3.981	5.437	70.9%	1.1%	2.218	2.708	3.439	55.0%	0.9%	52.54	67.77	65.82	25.3%	0.5%
Kazakhstan	3.343	7.912	9.988	198.8%	2.2%	2.07	4.161	5	141.5%	1.8%	58.85	83.69	84.45	43.5%	0.7%
Tajikistan	2.254	2.519	3.035	34.6%	0.6%	1.326	1.749	2.244	69.2%	1.1%	49.55	63.31	67.44	36.1%	0.6%
Turkmenistan	2.323	4.309	4.391	89.0%	1.3%	1.207	2.388	2.83	134.5%	1.7%	44.85	66.86	56.39	25.7%	0.5%
Kyrgyzstan	2.22	2.334	2.613	17.7%	0.3%	1.886	2.095	2.236	18.6%	0.3%	51.01	58.95	57.84	13.4%	0.3%
Bhutan	6.098	7.143	10	64.0%	1.0%	3.199	3.5	5	56.3%	0.9%	37.82	54.28	89.47	136.6%	1.7%
Maldives	3.371	4.739	9.916	194.2%	2.2%	2.681	3.379	5	86.5%	1.3%	48.15	66.32	103.8	115.6%	1.5%
Asia-South Central	**2.738**	**3.583**	**5.534**	**102.1%**	**1.4%**	**2.317**	**2.684**	**3.524**	**52.1%**	**0.8%**	**33.1**	**42.9**	**49.26**	**48.8%**	**0.8%**
Indonesia	1.771	2.518	3.573	101.8%	1.4%	2.164	2.634	3.155	45.8%	0.8%	50.52	49.64	48.11	-4.8%	-0.1%
Philippines	2.86	3.393	4.631	61.9%	1.0%	2.626	2.815	3.308	26.0%	0.5%	56.2	50.88	51.36	-8.6%	-0.2%
Vietnam	2.595	3.699	5.75	121.6%	1.6%	2.192	2.804	3.721	69.8%	1.1%	60.74	74.83	83.47	37.4%	0.6%
Thailand	3.372	4.99	7.636	126.5%	1.6%	2.768	3.536	4.668	68.6%	1.1%	22.93	40.05	59.9	161.2%	1.9%
Myanmar	1.951	2.243	2.894	48.3%	0.8%	1.201	1.634	2.191	82.4%	1.2%	0.024	16.1	22.96	956.7%	14.7%
Malaysia	4.949	7.969	10	102.1%	1.4%	3.269	4.535	5	53.0%	0.9%	48.89	64.43	87.72	79.4%	1.2%
Cambodia	2.183	3.055	4.573	109.5%	1.5%	2.036	2.497	3.206	57.5%	0.9%	50.41	62.2	71.17	41.2%	0.7%
Laos	2.634	3.326	4.863	84.6%	1.2%	1.809	2.272	3.032	67.6%	1.0%	40.31	53.54	66.32	64.5%	1.0%
Singapore	10	10	10	0.0%	0.0%	5	5	5	0.0%	0.0%	87.26	113.5	108.6	24.5%	0.4%
Timor-Leste	2.6	2.758	3.247	24.9%	0.4%	1.814	2.06	2.381	31.3%	0.5%	39.53	49.41	52.86	33.7%	0.6%
Brunei	5.854	8.273	9.171	56.7%	0.9%	3.299	4.458	4.984	51.1%	0.8%	41.11	67.12	77.66	88.9%	1.3%
Asia-South East	**2.497**	**3.44**	**4.881**	**95.5%**	**1.3%**	**2.287**	**2.8**	**3.443**	**50.5%**	**0.8%**	**45.15**	**51.16**	**56.39**	**24.9%**	**0.4%**

Multination Regional Analysis

Measures of Poverty, Health, Education, Infrastructure and Governance

Governance

Base Case: Countries in Year 2055 Descending Population Sequence	Government Corruption Perception (Index 1-10)					Government Effectiveness (Index 0-5)					Globalization (Index)				
	2005	2030	2055	% Chg	% An Chg	2005	2030	2055	% Chg	% An Chg	2005	2030	2055	% Chg	% An Chg
ASIA INCL OCEANIA continued															
Turkey	4.033	5.852	10	148.0%	1.8%	2.702	3.496	5	85.0%	1.2%	37.76	54.54	82.66	118.9%	1.6%
Yemen	2.614	2.942	3.613	38.2%	0.6%	1.769	2.073	2.536	43.4%	0.7%	51.32	58.83	61.91	20.6%	0.4%
Iraq	1.938	2.794	4.308	122.3%	1.6%	0.965	1.788	2.847	195.0%	2.2%	10.06	25.76	34.91	247.0%	2.5%
Saudi Arabia	3.452	6.354	10	189.7%	2.2%	2.582	4.026	5	93.6%	1.3%	29.2	62.2	87.66	200.2%	2.2%
Syria	2.934	3.51	5.186	76.8%	1.1%	1.573	2.146	3.087	96.2%	1.4%	52.94	39.16	40.66	-23.2%	-0.5%
Israel	6.704	10	10	49.2%	0.8%	3.764	5	5	32.8%	0.6%	76.42	99.28	97.22	27.2%	0.5%
Azerbaijan	1.686	2.975	4.785	183.8%	2.1%	1.678	2.54	3.545	111.3%	1.5%	59.67	71.47	80.95	35.7%	0.6%
Jordan	4.723	6.321	10	111.7%	1.5%	2.886	3.613	5	73.3%	1.1%	49.61	67.67	111.6	125.0%	1.6%
Palestine	2.609	3.01	4.468	71.3%	1.1%	2.947	3.193	3.69	25.2%	0.5%	53.31	63.71	73.57	38.0%	0.6%
Oman	5.461	7.681	10	83.1%	1.2%	3.38	4.298	5	47.9%	0.8%	37.74	58.05	75.51	100.1%	1.4%
Lebanon	3.721	5.933	10	168.7%	2.0%	2.34	3.354	5	113.7%	1.5%	59.97	81.6	100	66.8%	1.0%
United Arab Emirates	7.272	10	10	37.5%	0.6%	3.588	5	5	39.4%	0.7%	51.85	88.52	94.27	81.8%	1.2%
Kuwait	5.468	9.79	10	82.9%	1.2%	2.904	4.948	5	72.2%	1.1%	39.19	84.24	91.99	134.7%	1.7%
Georgia	2.927	3.5	4.529	54.7%	0.9%	1.832	2.208	2.739	49.5%	0.8%	56.47	67.8	72.62	28.6%	0.5%
Armenia	2.711	3.992	5.737	111.6%	1.5%	1.824	2.52	3.373	84.9%	1.2%	47.64	64.83	74.21	55.8%	0.9%
Bahrain	6.181	10	10	61.8%	1.0%	3.304	5	5	51.3%	0.8%	70.06	96.07	98.19	40.2%	0.7%
Qatar	6.228	10	10	60.6%	1.0%	3.424	5	5	46.0%	0.8%	41.48	90.8	100.1	141.3%	1.8%
Cyprus	5.905	8.979	10	69.3%	1.1%	3.805	5	5	31.4%	0.5%	75.13	90.35	92.32	22.9%	0.4%
Asia-West	**3.512**	**4.944**	**7.202**	**105.1%**	**1.4%**	**2.272**	**3.03**	**3.956**	**74.1%**	**1.1%**	**40.23**	**54.69**	**69.43**	**72.6%**	**1.1%**
Australia	8.638	10	10	15.8%	0.3%	4.537	5	5	10.2%	0.2%	72.75	101.4	105.6	45.2%	0.7%
Papua New Guinea	2.387	2.756	3.538	48.2%	0.8%	1.868	2.134	2.608	39.6%	0.7%	48.39	59.18	61.26	26.6%	0.5%
New Zealand	9.751	10	10	2.6%	0.1%	4.152	5	5	20.4%	0.4%	68.72	95.46	102.6	49.3%	0.8%
Solomon Islands	2.596	2.847	3.591	38.3%	0.7%	1.701	2.02	2.529	48.7%	0.8%	49.56	57.82	59.78	20.6%	0.4%
Fiji	4.016	4.962	7.444	85.4%	1.2%	2.077	2.666	3.815	83.7%	1.2%	62.32	77.57	75.79	21.6%	0.4%
Vanuatu	2.839	3.287	4.577	61.2%	1.0%	2.019	2.353	3.013	49.2%	0.8%	66.77	75.99	81.31	21.8%	0.4%
Micronesia	3.456	3.702	4.546	31.5%	0.5%	1.994	2.431	2.979	49.4%	0.8%	45.32	54.54	62.8	38.6%	0.7%
Samoa	3.259	3.996	6.341	94.6%	1.3%	2.646	3.036	3.956	49.5%	0.8%	54.93	70.06	89.23	62.4%	1.0%
Tonga	3.544	3.648	4.165	17.5%	0.3%	2.007	2.286	2.697	34.4%	0.6%	42.75	53.7	58.61	37.1%	0.6%
Oceania	**7.309**	**7.965**	**8.006**	**9.5%**	**0.2%**	**3.845**	**4.185**	**4.256**	**10.7%**	**0.2%**	**66.8**	**89**	**91.45**	**36.9%**	**0.6%**

Governance

Base Case: Countries in Year 2055 Descending Population Sequence	Government Corruption Perception Index 1-10					Government Effectiveness Index 0-5					Globalization Index				
	2005	2030	2055	% Chg	% An Chg	2005	2030	2055	% Chg	% An Chg	2005	2030	2055	% Chg	% An Chg
EUROPE															
Russia	2.428	5.27	7.052	190.4%	2.2%	1.999	3.441	4.48	124.1%	1.6%	43.39	60.78	64.42	48.5%	0.8%
Poland	4.291	6.2	9.628	124.4%	1.6%	3.116	3.994	5	60.5%	1.0%	63.07	66.98	81.74	29.6%	0.5%
Ukraine	1.713	3.314	6.496	279.2%	2.7%	1.888	2.835	4.367	131.3%	1.7%	50.43	63.71	68.85	36.5%	0.6%
Romania	3.141	4.249	5.777	83.9%	1.2%	1.994	2.757	3.657	83.4%	1.2%	52.88	58.83	53.72	1.6%	0.0%
Belarus	4.377	6.55	10	128.5%	1.7%	1.703	2.956	5	193.6%	2.2%	43.7	58.17	92.45	111.6%	1.5%
Czech Republic	4.672	6.159	8.815	88.7%	1.3%	3.44	4.159	5	45.3%	0.8%	61.35	70.81	86.63	41.2%	0.7%
Hungary	5.571	7.449	10	79.5%	1.2%	3.502	4.419	5	42.8%	0.7%	65.22	71.13	81.3	24.7%	0.4%
Bulgaria	3.742	5.208	8.218	119.6%	1.6%	2.513	3.285	4.62	83.8%	1.2%	65.1	79.65	79.28	21.8%	0.4%
Slovak Republic	3.864	5.187	7.686	98.9%	1.4%	3.019	3.837	5	65.6%	1.0%	61.86	60.03	69.23	11.9%	0.2%
Moldova	2.679	3.043	4.274	59.5%	0.9%	1.446	1.88	2.664	84.2%	1.2%	47.05	56.27	61.59	30.9%	0.5%
Europe-East	**2.919**	**5.158**	**7.515**	**157.5%**	**1.9%**	**2.239**	**3.404**	**4.521**	**101.9%**	**1.4%**	**50.06**	**62.87**	**69.44**	**38.7%**	**0.7%**
United Kingdom	9.071	10	10	10.2%	0.2%	4.701	5	5	6.4%	0.1%	77.6	107	105.8	36.3%	0.6%
Sweden	9.826	10	10	1.8%	0.0%	4.455	5	5	12.2%	0.2%	107.1	130.8	130.4	21.8%	0.4%
Denmark	9.972	10	10	0.3%	0.0%	4.446	5	5	12.5%	0.2%	97.66	122.4	125.1	28.1%	0.5%
Norway	9.685	10	10	3.3%	0.1%	4.485	5	5	11.5%	0.2%	99.89	116	119.7	19.8%	0.4%
Ireland	8.414	10	10	18.8%	0.3%	5	5	5	0.0%	0.0%	71.67	100.2	105.2	46.8%	0.8%
Finland	10	10	10	0.0%	0.0%	4.572	5	5	9.4%	0.2%	75.39	100.1	105.1	39.4%	0.7%
Lithuania	4.604	7.136	10	117.2%	1.6%	3.18	4.372	5	57.2%	0.9%	71.97	90.13	97.83	35.9%	0.6%
Latvia	3.958	7.141	10	152.7%	1.9%	3.034	4.48	5	64.8%	1.0%	72.06	92.75	101.8	41.3%	0.7%
Estonia	6.354	8.148	10	57.4%	0.9%	3.78	4.585	5	32.3%	0.6%	79.68	101.8	101.7	27.6%	0.5%
Iceland	10	10	10	0.0%	0.0%	5	5	5	0.0%	0.0%	70.1	84.64	89.11	27.1%	0.5%
Europe-North	**8.925**	**9.842**	**10**	**12.0%**	**0.2%**	**4.552**	**4.968**	**5**	**9.8%**	**0.2%**	**81.84**	**108.8**	**109.2**	**33.4%**	**0.6%**
Italy	4.633	6.05	9.419	103.3%	1.4%	3.48	4.376	5	43.7%	0.7%	46.57	69.6	85.47	83.5%	1.2%
Spain	7.427	10	10	34.6%	0.6%	4.486	5	5	11.5%	0.2%	52.38	93.21	102.1	94.9%	1.3%
Greece	5.4	8.388	10	85.2%	1.2%	3.603	4.888	5	38.8%	0.7%	50.96	85.63	100.8	97.8%	1.4%
Portugal	6.413	8.314	10	55.9%	0.9%	3.653	4.515	5	36.9%	0.6%	63.52	82.75	96.31	51.6%	0.8%
Serbia and Montenegro	1.395	1.925	4.643	232.8%	2.4%	1.788	2.287	3.593	101.0%	1.4%	58.65	68.29	84.09	43.4%	0.7%
Croatia	4.028	5.768	10	148.3%	1.8%	2.864	3.679	5	74.6%	1.1%	54.3	59.45	83.38	53.6%	0.9%
Bosnia and Herzegovina	3.045	3.647	4.986	63.7%	1.0%	2.057	2.503	3.258	58.4%	0.9%	56.37	69.89	80.56	42.9%	0.7%
Albania	2.735	3.614	5.208	90.4%	1.3%	1.883	2.54	3.396	80.4%	1.2%	48.95	68.23	81.87	67.3%	1.0%
Macedonia	2.766	3.186	4.52	63.4%	1.0%	2.021	2.472	3.223	59.5%	0.9%	63.78	71.96	76.82	20.4%	0.4%
Slovenia	5.897	8.148	10	69.6%	1.1%	3.482	4.585	5	43.6%	0.7%	57.7	72.74	88.27	53.0%	0.9%
Malta	6.411	8.716	10	56.0%	0.9%	3.269	4.351	5	53.0%	0.9%	54.1	70.02	85.58	58.2%	0.9%
Europe-South	**5.32**	**7.168**	**9.095**	**71.0%**	**1.1%**	**3.576**	**4.343**	**4.791**	**34.0%**	**0.6%**	**51.45**	**78.34**	**91.88**	**78.6%**	**1.2%**
Germany	7.694	10	10	30.0%	0.5%	4.477	5	5	11.7%	0.2%	68.33	98.67	103.1	50.9%	0.8%
France	6.868	10	10	45.6%	0.8%	4.144	5	5	20.7%	0.4%	64.78	98.12	100	54.4%	0.9%
Netherlands	8.88	10	10	12.6%	0.2%	4.601	5	5	8.7%	0.2%	108.3	130.9	126.3	16.6%	0.3%
Belgium	6.322	7.075	10	58.2%	0.9%	4.191	4.763	5	19.3%	0.4%	89.21	104	111.1	24.5%	0.4%
Austria	7.951	10	10	25.8%	0.5%	4.41	5	5	13.4%	0.3%	62.06	89.75	95.71	54.2%	0.9%
Switzerland	8.87	10	10	12.7%	0.2%	4.808	5	5	4.0%	0.1%	83.92	108	106.7	27.1%	0.5%
Luxembourg	9.508	10	10	5.2%	0.1%	5	5	5	0.0%	0.0%	99.03	123.2	129.2	30.5%	0.5%
Europe-West	**7.516**	**9.837**	**10**	**33.0%**	**0.6%**	**4.375**	**4.987**	**5**	**14.3%**	**0.3%**	**72.3**	**101.9**	**104.7**	**44.8%**	**0.7%**

Index

Page numbers followed by the letter n indicate entries in notes.

absolute poverty 11, 11–14, 80
Acemoglu, Daron 31
Adams, Richard H. 110n
Afghanistan: in category of failed state 141; considered to be in critical condition 113; devastation by conflict 126; "Development Profile" 168–9; landlocked and resource-poor status 126; as not included in World Bank database 113; patterns of extreme poverty 112, 130–1
Africa 14, 84, 113–14; combined intervention scenario for 123–4; continuing relevance of $1 per day measure 68; Dikhanov's scenario for pro-poor growth 46; domestic inequality forecasts 62–3; geographical/regional perspective 114–16; health spending and burden of disease 92; IFs forecast of worsening income distributions 75; IFs population forecasts 58; importance of fertility reduction 104, 118; inadequate foreign aid for 99–100; need for governance to be addressed 141; percentage living on below $1 per day 134; percentage living on below $5 per day 67; performance on mortality rates 47; poverty factors in biggest regional populations 116–20; problems of conflict and corruption 41–2; regions and subregions 171; slippage in primary education completion rates 84; UN continental and regional/subregional grouping 87; UN ECAF review of progress toward MDGs 121–3; as unlikely to meet most of MDGs 141; World Bank economic growth forecasts for 61
Agarwal, Bina 3, 148
age, relevance to poverty rates 3, 138
agriculture: fall in share of GDP with average income increases 67; IFs module 52; marketing of surplus crops in China 128; population and demand for land 73; products embedded in environmental goods and services 147
Ahluwalia, Montek S. 13, 27–8, 34, 44, 74
AIDS see HIV/AIDS
air pollution 146, 148
Aitchison, J. 166
Akramov, Kamiljon 158
Albania 140
Alesina, Alberto 157–8, 158
Algeria 121, 122
Ali, Abdel Gadir 14

Alonso-Terme, Rosa 33–4, 156
Americas: geographical/regional perspective 132–6; percentage of people living on below $1 per day 134; social stratifications affecting poverty 137–8, 141; as unlikely to meet poverty reduction MDG 141
Arab Human Development Report 2002 90
Archimedes 101
Argentina 83, 135, 136
Armenia 126
Aschauer, David A. 31
Asia: combined intervention scenario for 131–2; geographical/regional perspective 124–6; IFs forecast of poverty reduction 67; IFs population forecasts 58; low female-male ratio 3; overall success of fight against poverty 130; percentage of people living on below $1 per day 134; regions and subregions 171; tiger economies 90, 98, 107; UN continental and regional/subregional grouping 87
Asia and the Pacific (IFs regional representation) 126, 130
Asian Development Bank 38, 100, 144
Australia 87, 126, 158
Australia-New Zealand (UN region) 172
avian flu 76

Baldacci, Emanuele 92
Balkans 140–1
Baltic republics 88, 138
Banerjee, Abhijit 21n
Bangladesh: considered to be in critical condition 113; feasible goal of income poverty reduction 128; high poverty headcount 126; numbers of people living below $1 per day 112; trade openness 128
Barbados 63
Barney, Gerald O. 175
Barro, Robert J. 33, 68, 92
Bates, Robert H. 152
Becker, Gary S. 30, 32–3
Benhabib, Jess 30
Berthélemy, Jean-Claude 124
Bhalla, Surjit S. 19, 21n, 71n
Bils, Mark 30
Bloomberg, S. Brock 151
Bolivia 132, 135
Bolsa Escola (Brazil) 96
Bonfiglioli, Alessandra 37
Bosnia-Herzegovina 140, 142n
Bosworth, Barry 92

Botswana 116, 142n; good management of diamonds 114; improved governance after national plan 154–5; possibility of meeting first and second MDGs 121
Bourguignon, Franois 23, 24, 25, 26, 32, 175
"brain circulation" 42, 107
Brazil 64, 83; growth in labor force share 58; numbers of people living below $1 per day 112; progress toward reaching MDGs 135; targeted conditional transfer programs 96
BRICS (Brazil, Russia, India, China) 58, 59, 61–2
Brown, James Allen C. 166
Burkina Faso 121, 124
Burma see Myanmar
Burnside , Craig 157, 158
Burundi 112, 113, 124
business cycles 59
Bussolo, Maurizio 62
Butler, Colin 148

Cambodia 112, 126
Cameroon 121
Canada 87, 132
capabilities: approach to poverty 1, 4, 5, 11, 14–17, 34, 47, 82–4; HDI measurement 123, 160; IFs approach to poverty levels 68–70; IFs goals for development of 50
Cape Verde 122
capital: different types 22, 29, 90–1; as domestic driver for economic growth 88; flight resulting from civil conflict 154
capital accumulation, effect of diminishing returns 28–30
carbon dioxide levels 147, 149, 150, *see also* greenhouse gases
Caribbean 132; danger of stagnation in poverty reduction 80; developing countries' GDP per capita levels 82; domestic transfers 96; female share of official labor force 90; indigenous populations 136; interventions needed 109; outlook for poverty reduction 135–6, 136–7, 138; relationship between GDP and health spending 92; UN region 173; worker remittances 99
Carter, Michael R. 144
Carter, Nicholas 13, 27–8, 34, 44, 74
Caucasus 126
Caucutt, Elizabeth M. 32, 33
Central Africa see Middle Africa

Central African Republic 112, 113
Central America 132; countries 173; domestic transfers 96; high poverty rates in indigenous populations 136; increase in education spending 91; outlook for progress in poverty reduction 135–6, 136–7, 138; relationship between GDP and health spending 92; rise in female share of labor force 90; rise in savings and investment rates 90; worker remittances 99
Central Asia 124; developing countries' GDP per capita levels 82; developing countries' progress in reducing poverty 81; interventions needed 110; Islamist cause 153; oil and natural gas resources 126
Chen, Derek 92
Chen, Shaohua 19, 26
Chenery, Hollis 13, 27–8, 34, 44, 67, 74, 87
Chetwynd, Eric 156
children: environmental risks 146, 148, *see also* infant mortality
Chile 132, 135, 137
China: approaches to global inequality in 63; different poverty forecasts of World Bank and IFs 66; female share of official labor force 89; Goldman Sachs economic growth forecasts 61; high savings and investment rates 90; interventions in economic growth forecasts for 74; investment in human capital 91; labor force 58; numbers of people living below $1 per day 112; ongoing rapid economic growth 59, 60, 64, 124; poverty headcount 34, 126; push for access to raw materials in Africa 120; rapid reduction in poverty 2, 3, 121, 126; scenario of reversal of economic growth 131–2; significance in influencing global poverty reduction 76, 77, 84, 161; success in governance aiding poverty reduction 126–8, 141; sudden rise in economy in 1980s and 1990s 6; suggested overreporting of growth rates 19; in UN regional grouping of Eastern Asia 87; World Bank poverty headcounts 48
chronic poverty 16, 111, 153, 161
civil conflicts 120, 151, 153
class/caste, as factor in poverty rates 161, 165
Clemens, Michael A. 122–3
climate change 146, 147

"Dutch disease" 100, 105; economic effects 156; increasing 22, 42, 102, 105; influence on governance and corruption 157–8; Millennium Project's emphasis on 106; need for timing to help recovery from conflict 155; rebels'appropriation of 152; World Bank's policies regarding 36

foreign assistance 107–8, 155

foreign direct investment 97, 106, 169; China's taxes on 128; encouragement for 42, 107; enhancing technology flows 101; global increase needed 108

Foreign Policy magazine 113

forest areas 149, 150

fossil fuel resources 149

Foster, James *see* FGT family of poverty measures

France 138

Fraser Institute 108, 128

Fuhrmann, Bettina 158

Fukuda-Parr, Sakiko 15

functionings: distinction with capabilities 15; in forecasting 47, 160; link with poverty made by HPI 69, 160

The Fund for Peace 113

Gabon 122

Gallup, John Luke 146

Galor, Oded 33

Gambia 13

Gatune, Julius 114

GDP (gross domestic product): IFs forecasts for per capita growth 59; IFs forecasts on poverty rates 74; increase leading to fall in corruption 157; LINKAGE model forecasts 48; per capita rate growth in China and India 131; poverty in regions as function of 87–8; rankings in HPI 15–16; in regional income poverty calculations 82–4; relationship with fertility 88; relationship with health and education spending 92, 106; representation in IFs economic model 168; and risk of experiencing civil conflict 151; World Bank's analysis of effect of remittances on 48

gender equity: low level in Middle India 129; progress in education in Africa 121

gender inequality/discrimination 3, 17, 33; Latin America 138

geographical factors, in economic model for poverty trends 49–50

Germany 99, 138

Ghana 17–18, 18, 142n; patterns of extreme poverty 112; possibility of meeting first MDG 121; potential to become emerging country 124; risk of conflict 151

Gini coefficient 23, 62, 169–70

Glaeser, Edward L. 31

Global Environment Outlook (GEO) 78–9, 79–80

Global Insights, economic growth forecasts 59–60, 60, 61

global middle class 64–5, 67

Global Ministerial Forum (2000) 144

global perspectives 4, 162

global poverty 1, 2–3, 9, 102; IFs forecasts 70, 77, 160, 161

Global Scenario Group (GSG) 78

Global Trade Analysis Project (GTAP) 51, 53, 62, 110n, 169–70

Glover, Jonathan 3

Goldman Sachs 59, 61–2, 110n

Goodhand, Jonathan 153

governance: in Asian Development Bank's recommended policies 38; China's effectiveness 127–8, 141; corruption and increase in inequalities 33–4; corruption in Nigeria 117; country-specific characteristics 111; domestic self-help and improvement of 107, 108; as driver for productivity 92–4; human action leading to improvement in 72, 120; "improved" 42, 102; improvements with income rises 157; improving to reduce risk of conflict 154–5; influence of foreign aid on corruption 157–8; institutional capital 29, 31, 49, 90–1; interactions with foreign aid 156; and issue of land ownership in Ethiopia 119; issues facing Latin American countries 141; as key factor in South Africa's growth 119; problems in Afghanistan and Pakistan 131; relationship with poverty 9, 143, 155–8; World Bank's policies 36, 36–7, 38

government spending 168; adverse effects of corruption 107, 157; on education 22, 73, 88, 91–2, 106, 108; foreign aid as tied to 100; on health 22, 91, 92, 106, 108, 169; and inequality 33, 37–8

governments: initiation of diversionary conflict 151; involvement in poverty reduction efforts 143

Graff, Corinne 151, 153

green GDP 94–5

greenhouse gases 61, 147, *see also* carbon dioxide levels

Greer, Joel *see* FGT (Foster, Greer, and Thorbecke) family of poverty measures

Groot, Rudolf S. de 145

Grossman, Herschel 152

Group of 6 58

Guatemala 132, 136, 137

Guinea-Bissau 112, 113

Gupta, Sanjeev 33–4, 156

Gurr, Ted Robert 154

Gylfason, Thorvaldur 31

Haiti: considered to be in critical condition 113; high rate of population growth 136; indebtedness 132; patterns of extreme poverty 112, 136; poverty among indigenous peoples 132; trade deficit 137

health: in capabilities approach to poverty 11, 16, 17; challenges faced by Africa 141; effects of conflict 153–4; effects of extreme poverty 76; emphasis of UN Millennium Project 39; environmental goods and services as determinants of 146, 146–7; forecasting 47; in HDI aggregation of capabilities 82, 123; human capital 91; IFs module 50, 52; improvements in Americas 138; improvements increasing earning potential 23; public expenditure 22, 92, 106, 108, 169

Health and Environment Linkages Initiative (HELI) 146

Heaps, Charles 175

Heritage Foundation 128

Hess, Gregory D. 151

Heston, Alan W. 13

Hezbollah 153

Hillebrand, Evan E. 53

HIV/AIDS: impact on economies 119; impact on life expectancy in Africa 69, 84, 119, 123; mortality forecasts 58; scenario of South Africa's failure to control 124

Hoeffler, Anke 151, 153–4

Honduras 132, 135, 136

Hong Kong 87, 124, 128

Horn of Africa 120

household survey data 6, 17–18; reconciliation with national accounts 167

households: based on skilled and unskilled labor 53, 170; domestic transfers 96; use of social accounting matrix to analyse 169–70

Huang, Stewart C. 153

Hughes, Barry B. 7, 53, 85n

human action to reduce poverty 77–8, 85, 86–8, 102

human capital: challenges faced by Africa in developing 141; China's development of 127, 128, 141; country-specific stocks 111; as deep driver of economic growth 22, 23, 29, 30, 49; development through domestic self-help 107; as driver for productivity 90–2; improvements as leverage 88; input of health 146–7; issues facing Latin American countries 141; multiple effects of investments in 86; relationship with environment 147, 149

human development: IFs goals 56; positive feedback from variables 106; scenarios devised by Global Scenario Group 78; strategy of UN Millennium Project 39; sustainability 4, 50; World Bank's engagement with 23, 35, 36

human development index (HDI) 15, 17, 47, 68, 69, 70, 123; capabilities tapped by 82–4, 160; low value of Middle India 129; low values in landlocked African states 116; rising values in Americas 138

Human Development Reports 12, 45–6, 138

human poverty index (HPI) 15–16, 17, 147, 160; declining values in Americas 137, 138; differences with HDI 69–70, 123

human rights 158

Humphries, Jane 3

illiteracy 69, 123, 137

immigration 99

import duties 22

income: decreases caused by war 153; domestic interventions 96; emerging global middle class 64–5; future measures 67–8; HDI measurement 69, 123; HPI scaling of 70; low levels causing increased risk of conflict 150, 151; measures of poverty based on 5, 11, 14, 17; potential effects of environmental factors 148; shares accruing to skilled and unskilled households 170; World Bank's policies for raising 35

income distribution: changes affecting poverty numbers 26–7; inequality as increasing on risk of conflict 151; inequality represented by Lorenz curve 23–6; lognormal representations 14, 24, 27, 166

income inequality: caused by high corruption levels 156; Nigeria 118

income poverty 68, 70; in combined framing scenarios 80–2, 85; country-specific patterns 112–14; decline in Europe in recent years 140; forecasts for global reductions 107–8; IFs forecasting mechanisms 53–4;

proximate drivers 22; relationship with capability poverty 16; relative 14; and social exclusion 3; standard measure of $1 per day 2–3, 10, 80, 160

indebtedness 107; Latin America and Caribbean countries 132, 141; Nigeria's settlement using export revenues 117

India: absolute international poverty measure based on 13; absolute poverty rates in 2000 80; caste system 3; continuing rapid economic growth 59, 63, 64, 76, 80, 124, 127; discrepancy between surveys and national accounts 19; female share of official labor force 90; Goldman Sachs economic growth forecasts 61; growth in labor force share 58; high investment rates 90; large numbers in extreme income poverty 126; little poverty reduction in recent years 3; numbers of people living below $1 per day 112; outlook for poverty reduction 46, 128–32, 141; poverty headcount 126; reduction of extreme poverty in near future 80, 84; scenario of reversal of economic growth 131–2; subregion of Middle India 129, 141; sudden rise in economy in 1980s and 1990s 6; teacher absenteeism 33; trade openness 128; World Bank poverty headcounts 48

indigence, ECLAC threshold 134–5, 137

indigenous populations, Latin America and Caribbean 132, 136, 137, 141

Indonesia 126

industrial accidents 146

inequalities: connections with growth and poverty 23–6, 32, 146; deep drivers 33–4; in economic distribution 62–5; high levels in Latin America 141; high and low forecasts 75; redressed by transfers 37–8, 161; relationship with environment 146, 148; role of education subsidy 22–3

infant mortality: correlation with state failure 152; fall in African countries 121; increase in times of conflict 154; and poor families' "insurance" against expected loss 33

infrastructure: development in China 141; development through domestic self-help 107; improvements needed 109; issues facing Latin American countries 141; problems for flow of goods from Middle India 130; underdevelopment in Africa 141

infrastructure capital 29, 31, 91, 94, 147

institutional capital 29, 90–1, 147

intellectual property 100

intergovernmental organizations 143

Intergovernmental Panel on Climate Change 61, 85n

International Comparison Project (ICP) 13, 71n

international drivers and levers 96–101, 101, 104–5

International Energy Agency (IEA) 117

International Energy Outlook 80

international financial institutions (IFIs) 36, 100, 108

International Futures (IFs) Modeling System 5, 50–3; base case forecasts 56–8, 70, 77, 80, 88–9, 102, 161; exploration of deep drivers of economic growth 168–9; forecasts for poverty levels 65–70, 77; formulations used in forecasting model 164–5; foundations for poverty analysis 53–4; levers

spending 91; interventions needed 10; relationship between GDP and health spending 92; replacement fertility 88

South-Eastern Asia (UN region) 171

Southern Africa 114; domestic transfers 96; high poverty rate 88; infrastructure 94; interventions needed 109; life expectancy rate 123; need for increased female share of labor force 90; UN region 171

Southern African Development Community 124

Southern Europe: formerly communist countries 140, 142; UN region 138, 172; weakness of infrastructure 94

Soviet Union, former republics 124, 138

Spain 138

Special Report on Emissions Scenarois (SRES) (IPCC) 61

Spiegel, Mark M. 30

Squire, Lyn 23, 35

Sri Lanka 126

standard of living 82

state failure see failed states/state failure

Stewart, Frances 11, 154

Stockholm International Institute 78

Stokey, Nancy L. 31

structural adjustment 136–7

sub-Saharan Africa: absolute poverty rates 80; as area of greatest concern 7, 34, 75, 77, 85, 102, 108; as certain not to meet poverty reduction MDG 4, 48, 161, 162; comparison of poverty gap with headcount measure 82; completion rates for primary education 84; differences between World Bank and IFs forecasts 65–6, 66; domestic interventions as impacting on poverty reduction 106; exports 98; fall in GDP per capita 82, 114; female share of official labor force 90; and future of global distribution 64; interventions in economic growth forecasts for 74; low investment rates 90; percentage of population below $5 per day 67; poverty line 70; recent signs of economic growth 46, 76; relationship between conflict and poverty 151, 152, 154; rise in those living in extreme poverty 121; similarities of Middle India with landlocked countries of 130; World Bank data and forecasts 2, 3; World Bank estimate and GEO scenarios compared 79; World Bank's forecasts of net primary school enrollment 47

subpopulations: indigenous municipalities in Latin America 132; local conditions affecting interventions 161; social nature of poverty 3–4, 111

Subramarian, Arvind 124, 157

Sudan 112

Summers, Robert 13

sustainable development 4, 50, 144

sustainable economic growth 38

Svensson, Jacob 158

Syrquin, Moises 67, 87

Taiwan 87, 124

Tajikistan 126

Tamura, Robert 33

Tanzania 15, 112, 124

Tanzi, Vito 159n

targeted conditional transfer (TCT) programs 96

technology: access for developing countries 36; GEO scenarios addressing 78; greater availability 105; IFs module

52; relevance to economic forecasts 59; transfers 100–1; underdeveloped capabilities in Africa 141

terrorism 150, 151, 152–3

Thacker, Siddarth 151

Thailand 3, 26

Thorbecke, Erik see FGT family of poverty measures

Togo 112, 122

trade: greater openness to 23, 42, 95–6, 98, 128; and knowledge capital 95–6; multiple effects of increase 86; structural problems in Central America and Caribbean 137; World Bank's call for more liberalization 36, 38

transfers 35, 36, 38

transient poverty 16, 111; and conflict-inducing grievance 153

transition economies 64, 140, 142

Transparency International (TI) 93, 109, 127, 157

Treisman, Daniel 157, 159n

Tunisia 121, 122

Turkey 126

Uganda 124; patterns of extreme poverty 112; possibility of meeting first MDG 121; potential to become emerging country 124; reduction of HIV infection rates 119; risk of conflict 151

UN Development Programme (UNDP) 45–6, 160; Poverty and Environment Initiative (PEI) 144

UN Environment Programme (UNEP) 78–80, 144, 146

UNAIDS (UN Program on AIDS) 119, 142n

United Kingdom 138

United Nations (UN): Conference on Planning and Development 14; Department of Economic and Social Affairs 119; Economic Commission for Africa (UN ECAF) review of progress toward MDGs 121–3; Economic Commission for Latin America and the Caribbean (ECLAC) 132, 134–5135, 137; Educational, Scientific, and Cultural Organization (UNESCO) 47; Food and Agriculture Organization (UN FAO) 103; *Human Development Reports* and HDI 15; median variant population forecasts 57–8, 73, 102; Millennium Development Plan 38–9; Millennium Project (2005) 28, 39, 49, 99, 106, 108, 144, 169; monitoring of MDGs 162; population forecasts (1975) used in ACC model 44; regions and subregions 87, 114, 132, 138; six continental groupings 87; *World Population Prospects* 71n, see also Millennium Development Goals (MDGs); UN Development Programme (UNDP); UN Environment Programme (UNEP); UNAIDS

United States: African Americans 16; Census Bureau 57, 59; Department of Energy 60, 80, 117; economic growth forecasts in Goldman Sachs analysis 61; economic rise during and after World War II 63; female-male ratio 3; IFs grouping of Mexico in same region as 87, 88, 132; low rate of foreign aid 99; relative poverty levels 68; statement on CAFTA 142n

Uppsala Conflict Database 151–2

urbanization 20

urban-rural factors: Americas 137; Ghana 18; human development strategy of UN Millennium Project 39; in poverty

analysis 161, 169–70; poverty shares 3, 11

Uruguay 135

vaccines 36

Venezuela 132, 135, 136

Vietnam 3, 141

Villanueva, Delano 153

Vuuren, Detlef P. van 71n

Walle, Dominique van der 13, 14

Wang, M. 153

Warner, Andrew M. 31

water: effect of income rise on access to safe supplies 67; environmental factors influencing economic activity 148, 150; health risks from unsafe supplies 146; HP measurement of lack of access to safe supplies 69, 123, 137; increase in access to safe supplies in Africa 121; poor access to safe supplies in Middle India 129; use as indicator on pressure on environment 149

Weder, Beatrice 157–8, 158

Weil, David N. 30, 33

Weiss, John 26, 33, 38

welfare dependency 100

well-being: environmental contributions to 146; measures for forecasting 47

Western Africa 114; domestic transfers 96; failure to reduce fertility rate 88; increased savings and investment rates 90; interventions needed 109; low education spending rate 91; reduction in corruption perception index 157; relationship between GDP and health spending 92; UN region 171; weakness of infrastructure 94

Western Asia: domestic transfers 96; increased savings and investment rates 90; regions 126; UN region 171

Western Europe (UN region) 138, 172

Wolfensohn, James 35

women: effect of education level and employment on 32, 33; "missing" in less developed world 3; as more vulnerable to environmental factors 148; participation in labor force 32, 89–90, 169; supportive policies needed to reduce fertility rates 89, see also gender equity ; gender inequality/discrimination

Woodruff, Rosalie E. 148

worker remittances 42, 48, 169; international flows 96, 99; returning migrants' acquired skills 105, 107

World Bank 1, 10, 11, 108, 132, 140; aid flows from 100; analysis of Central America and Caribbea 137; analysis of poverty in conflict-affected countries 150, 155; on association of economic growth with decrease in poverty 23, 26; *Attacking Poverty* 47; data and forecasts of poverty 2–3, 44, 46–8, 65–6, 77; data on poverty in Latin America 135, 136; database of countries surveyed 113; definition of extreme poverty 5; economic growth forecasts 59–60, 60–1; estimate of benefits of Doha round proposals 101; on fertility changes in developing countries 33; figures on three high-poverty Asian countries 127; forecasts for domestic inequality 62, 62–3; *Global Economic Prospects 2007* 65, 154; *Global Economic Prospects 2008* 46, 47, 48; guidance on role of environment in poverty reduction 144;

headcount measure of poverty 13–14; policies on global poverty reduction 35–8; possible overestimation of global poverty 19, 20; poverty estimates compared with GEO scenarios 79–80; Poverty Reduction Strategy Papers (PRSP) 37; project on governance 92–3, 127, 156; reviews monitoring MDGs 162; study of role of infrastructure in economic growth 31; surveys on effects of policies on growth and inequality 37–8; use of country-based surveys 18–19; weaknesses in forecasting 48–9; *World Development Indicators* (WDI) 47, 53, 91; *World Development Report 1980* 23, 35; *World Development Report 1990* 35–6, 77; *World Development Report 2000–2001* 36–7

World Commission on Environment and Development (WCED) 143, 144

World Economic Forum (WEF) 94

World Economic Outlook (IMF) 59

World Energy Council 85n

World Food Program 103

World Health Organization (WHO) 52, 146

World Summit on Sustainable Development (2002) 10, 144, 146

World War II 63

Yemen 15

Yohe, Gary W. 146

Yugoslavia, former, conflicts 140

Zambia 112

Zimbabwe 112, 113, 122, 142n

Author Notes

Dr. Barry B. Hughes is a professor at the Josef Korbel School of International Studies, University of Denver, and is director of the Frederick S. Pardee Center for International Futures. He is the creator of the International Futures modeling system and leads the team that continues development of it.

Mohammod T. Irfan is a Ph.D. candidate in International Studies at the Joseph Korbel School of International Studies. His research focus is on long-term computer simulation of education systems around the world.

Dr. Haider Khan is a professor at the Josef Korbel School of International Studies and author of more than ten books and monographs on economy wide modeling. He is currently working on computable general equilibrium models for food and energy crises and global financial architecture.

Dr. Krishna B. Kumar is a senior economist at RAND, and a professor at the Pardee Rand Graduate School where he leads the Rosenfeld Program on Asian Development. His research interests lie in the areas of economic growth and development, human capital accumulation, and technological change.

Dr. Dale S. Rothman is a research associate and adjunct faculty with the Josef Korbel School of International Studies. He has extensive experience in the exploration of long-term scenarios on environment and development, most recently coordinating the development of scenarios for the United Nations Environment Programme's fourth Global Environmental Outlook.

José R. Solórzano, MSCS/MSF, is a Senior Consultant for the Frederick S. Pardee Center for International Futures. His main focus is on the technical side of the International Futures modeling system, design and implementation. He is currently helping develop the health module within IFs.